Ninth Edition

Research Methods in Psychology

John J. Shaughnessy

Hope College

Eugene B. Zechmeister

Loyola University of Chicago

Jeanne S. Zechmeister

Mc Graw Hill

Connect Learn Succeed™

The McGraw·Hill Companies

Connect
Learn
Succeed™

RESEARCH METHODS IN PSYCHOLOGY, NINTH EDITION
International Edition 2012

10 09 08 07 06 05 04 03 02 01
20 15 14 13 12 11
CTP SLP

When ordering this title, use ISBN 978-007-108681-3 or MHID 007-108681-1

Printed in Singapore

www.mhhe.com

Brief Contents

Contents

PART IV
Applied Research   279

About the Authors

JOHN J. SHAUGHNESSY is Professor of Psychology at Hope College, a relatively small, select, undergraduate liberal arts college in Holland, Michigan. After completing the B.S. degree at Loyola University of Chicago in 1969, he received the Ph.D. in 1972 from Northwestern University. He is a Fellow of the Association for Psychological Science and the Midwestern Psychological Association. His recent research has focused on practical aspects of memory. He is coauthor, with Benton J. Underwood, of *Experimentation in Psychology* (Wiley, 1975). Students selected him as the Hope Outstanding Professor Educator in 1992 and he received the Janet L. Andersen Excellence in Teaching Award from the college in 2008.

EUGENE B. ZECHMEISTER is Professor Emeritus of Psychology at Loyola University of Chicago, a large metropolitan university where he taught both undergraduate and graduate courses since 1970. Professor Zechmeister completed his B.A. degree in 1966 at the University of New Mexico. He later received both the M.S. (1968) and Ph.D. (1970) from Northwestern University. A specialist in the field of human cognition and experimental methodology, Professor Zechmeister has co-authored books on human memory, critical thinking, statistics and research methods. He has been a Fellow both of the American Psychological Association (Divisions 1, 2, and 3) and the Association for Psychological Science. In 1994 he was awarded the Loyola University Sujack Award for Teaching Excellence in the College of Arts and Sciences.

JEANNE S. ZECHMEISTER was a member of the Psychology faculty at Loyola University of Chicago from 1990 to 2002. Professor Zechmeister completed her B.A. at University of Wisconsin-Madison (1983) and her M.S. (1988) and Ph.D. (1990) in Clinical Psychology at Northwestern University. She taught undergraduate and graduate courses in research methodology, and her research focused on psychological processes associated with forgiveness. Her effectiveness as a teacher is evidenced by her many years of high teacher ratings and by her being identified consistently each year by graduating seniors as one of their best teachers at Loyola. Dr. Zechmeister now writes in Charlottesville, Virginia.

To Paula
(J.J.S.)

To the Memory of Ruth O'Keane,
James O'Keane,
Kathleen O'Keane Zechmeister,
and My Mother
(E.B.Z.)

To the Memory of
My Father, Harold W. Sumi
(J.S.Z.)

Preface

With this 9th edition we mark more than twenty-five years of introducing research methods to students through this textbook. We have benefited across the previous eight editions from numerous helpful comments made by both instructors and students so that sometimes it is hard to know what remain of our "original" ideas. Changes in this edition, too, reflect suggestions made by users of our textbook and we are, as always, greatly appreciative. We continue to strive to provide an introduction to research methods in psychology that both excites students about the research process and helps them to become competent practitioners of research methods.

Users of the previous editions have witnessed stylistic changes as well as the addition of pedagogical aids (for example, margin icons to identify key concepts and boxed "Stat Tips" to better link the method and analysis). These changes were well received and we continue them in the present edition. For those who are new to this textbook, let us first review our basic organization and approach. Those who have used the previous edition may want to go directly to "Changes in This Edition" to see what is new.

ORGANIZATION AND APPROACH

Our approach is based on our years of teaching experience. As instructors of research methods, we recognize that most students in our classes will be consumers of research and not producers of research. Students who choose to take on either role will benefit from developing critical thinking skills. We believe that we can best help our students think critically by taking a problem-solving approach to the study of research methods. As Sharon Begley, writer for *Newsweek*, commented in a recent essay critiquing science education: "Science is not a collection of facts but a way of interrogating the world." Moreover, "The most useful skill we could teach is the habit of asking oneself and others, *how do you know?*" (*Newsweek*, November 8, 2010, p. 26).

Researchers begin with a good question and then select a research method that can best help them answer their question. The sometimes painstaking task of gathering evidence is only the beginning of the research process. Analyzing and interpreting the evidence are equally important in making claims about psychological processes. Researchers (and students) must analyze the strengths and weaknesses of the method they have chosen in order to be able to evaluate critically the nature of the evidence they have obtained.

Another feature that we continue from our last edition is the website designed for our book. There are interactive exercises and quizzes for students to test their knowledge of text material, as well as links to other important psychology websites. Instructors will find the instructor's manual and lecture/discussion aids helpful. Both students and instructors may easily contact the authors via this site. Please come see us at *www.mhhe.com/shaughnessy9e.*

As has been our approach for each edition, students learn that a *multimethod approach* to answering questions will best advance the science of psychology and that one goal of this book is to "fill their toolbox" with strategies for conducting research. Thus, our organization following the introductory chapters is in terms of "methods," moving from the simplest of observational techniques to complex experimental designs.

We remain sensitive to ethical issues in psychological research and to the dilemmas researchers face when they study animal or human behavior. To emphasize our concern we give "ethics" its own chapter (Chapter 3) but also discuss specific ethical issues in other chapters as they relate to particular methodologies. The increase in Internet-based research, for example, raises new ethical questions and we identify some of them for our readers.

Finally, we believe that research methods are best taught in the context of published psychological research. Thus, we continue to use the rich psychology literature to provide examples of ways in which researchers actually use the methods we discuss. It is always fun for us to update the research examples, while continuing to include important "classic" findings and studies that have proved effective in helping students learn research methods. We believe that one way to motivate students to join us on this exciting path of pursuing knowledge is to show the "payoff" that psychological research provides.

CHANGES IN THIS EDITION

We continue to use bullet points within the chapters and Review Questions at the end of chapters to help students see clearly the points we think are most important for them to learn. And we continue to rely on the Challenge Questions at the end of chapters to help students learn to apply the principles they have learned. Building on the model of the Challenge Questions, we have embedded Stretching Exercises in most chapters to allow students to apply research principles while they are learning about the principles. An extensive review of statistics remains at the end of the book (Chapters 11 and 12), and we continue to introduce these issues briefly in the appropriate places in the text. One way this is done is through a pedagogical aid we call "Stat Tips," which draws students' attention to questions of statistical analysis. In some cases we answer those questions for students; in other instances we refer them to material in Chapters 11 and 12. We believe our approach provides important flexibility that allows instructors to decide when and how they will cover statistics in a research methods course.

Changes in this edition have been aimed at economizing, simplifying, and updating. For example, we continue to reduce in Chapter 3 the amount of material taken directly from the published APA ethics code (American Psychological Association, 2002) and material from the APA *Publication Manual* (2010), now in its sixth edition, in Chapter 13. Less reliance on direct quotations from these sources makes for a simpler introduction to these issues while safeguarding the integrity of the original sources, which students are urged to consult for more information. Moreover, the APA-sponsored website (www.apa.org) contains much information that need not be repeated herein. In addition, previous users will also notice the following:

- Minor changes have been made in sentence wording and paragraph structure in an effort to make it easier for students to understand concepts.
- Several major new research examples have been added (and older ones replaced). We have attempted to show students the "latest" in psychological research findings and, most importantly, to introduce studies that are relevant to today's students and also help teach clearly the methodology illustrated in the examples. For example, in Chapter 1 we discuss the recent criticism leveled against practitioners of clinical psychology by Baker, McFall, and Shoham (2009). These psychologists, clinicians themselves, argue that clinical psychologists fall short in their application of scientific findings when treating clients. What better way to begin a research methods textbook than challenging students to apply what they learn should they enter the field of clinical psychology or make use of mental health professionals? New research examples also are found in other chapters.
- We have kept some older examples because they not only remain relevant but have become "classics" as well. For example, we continue to include the well-known Rosenhan (1973) study using participant observation, as well as critiques of this research by others in the field. We also have kept the Langer and Rodin (1976) study of care in nursing homes (Chapter 10), which Zimbardo (2004) labeled a "classic" in the field of social psychology. This study, too, is a wonderful example of a particular research methodology, in this case, the nonequivalent control group design.
- Following the suggestion of users of our textbook, and as part of our economizing in this edition, we joined two chapters from earlier editions, Observation (Chapter 4) and Unobtrusive Measures of Behavior (previously Chapter 6), in a new Chapter 4. This required us to reduce the amount of space given to unobtrusive measures, but we continue to discuss this topic to show students creative applications of the multimethod approach.
- Changes, too, have been made in some of the "Stretching Exercises" and Boxes that appear across chapters in order to bring attention to timely psychological research. A favorite of ours is a study employing urine-sniffing dogs to detect cancer in individuals (see Chapter 2). As readers will see, the Clever Hans effect is alive and still with us!
- The American Psychological Association has placed strict limitations on the use of material from the most recent edition (6th) of the APA *Publication Manual* (2010). Therefore, previous users of our textbook will find substantially less specific information regarding the preparation of research manuscripts "according to APA style." The new *Publication Manual* is more compact than its predecessor and some instructors may wish to require students to purchase it. An introduction to APA style, including a free tutorial as well as a sample manuscript, can be found at www.apastyle.org. The information found there may be sufficient for students to complete a class assignment. Although we continue to provide an

overview of scientific communication, as well as what we hope are helpful tips when preparing a research manuscript (see Chapter 13), in this edition of our textbook we more frequently refer students to the *Publication Manual* and APA website.

- Finally, if there is anything that brings out the gray hair in authors of a methods textbook, it is the perennial questions regarding the melding of statistical analysis with methodology: How much "stat"? Where does it go? These questions have taken on a new flavor given the recent debate over null hypothesis significance testing (NHST) (see Chapter 11 for a brief review of the issues) and the recommended use of effect size measures and confidence intervals by, among others, the APA Task Force on Statistical Inference (see Wilkinson & The Task Force on Statistical Inference, 1999). Use of these statistical tools to supplement or even replace NHST is growing, but slowly (Cumming et al., 2007; Fidler, Thomason, Cumming, Finch, & Leeman, 2004; Gigerenzer, Krauss, & Vitouch, 2004). Moreover, new statistical measures are being presented, as is illustrated by the recent flurry of interest in "probability of replication," or p_{rep} (see Killeen, 2005). We mention this latest statistical innovation in Chapter 12 but await further discussion in the psychological literature before enlarging our presentation.

In this edition we have reduced the presentation of statistical analyses by removing many formulas and sample calculations, and have eliminated some of the statistical tables in the appendices. Most statistical analyses are done using computer software programs that deliver exact probabilities for test outcomes and various statistical tables, including those for conducting power analyses, are found on various sites on the Web. The table of *t* values is important for construction of confidence intervals and we kept this table, along with the *F* table and the random numbers table; the latter is useful for class exercises and random groups experiments.

We continue to try to meet three goals in our presentation of statistical analysis: (1) to provide an independent introduction to statistical analysis in Chapters 11 and 12 that will give students the means (no pun intended) to analyze a research study (and serve as a review for those who might already have had this introduction); (2) to show how method and analysis are related (see also our discussion of various methods and associated "Stat Tips"); and (3) to help students appreciate that there are many statistical tools available to them and they should not rely on only one as they seek to confirm what their data tell them (see our discussion of statistical issues throughout the text).

Online Learning Center

The ninth edition of Research Methods in Psychology is accompanied by student and instructor supplements available at www.mhhe.com/shaughnessy9e. These resources, created by Shaughnessy, Zechmeister, and Zechmeister to augment the text material, have been updated for the ninth edition by coauthor Jeanne Zechmeister.

For Students

Multiple choice, true or false, and matching quizzes, along with problems and exercises can be used as study aids or submitted to instructors as homework exercises. Students also have access to learning objectives, a glossary, and online resources for each chapter.

For Instructors

The following resources are available to instructors using Research Methods in Psychology. Contact your local McGraw-Hill sales representative to obtain a password to access the online instructor materials.

Instructor's Manual to Accompany Research Methods in Psychology   The updated manual includes chapter outlines and objectives, chapter review questions and answers, challenge questions and answers, issues and problems for class discussion, activities regarding how to read research critically, worksheets for students, classroom and homework projects, lecture and discussion aids for instructors, and pages which can be used in PowerPoint slides or study guides.

PowerPoint Presentations   PowerPoint slides for each chapter outline the key points of the chapter.

Test Banks   Test banks for each chapter includes short answer and multiple choice questions and answers to test students' knowledge. Each question is keyed according to whether the question assesses factual or conceptual understanding, or application of methodological concepts. The test bank is also available with EZ Test computerized testing software. EZ test provides a powerful, easy-to-use test maker to create printed quizzes and exams. For secure online testing, exams created in EZ Test can be exported to WebCT, Blackboard, and EZ Test Online. EZ Test comes with a Quick Start Guide; once the program is installed users have access to a User's Manual and Flash tutorials. Additional help is available at www.mhhe.com/eztest

WORDS OF THANKS

The cumulative contributions of many people to the 9th edition of our textbook are impossible to acknowledge adequately. Most recently we wish to thank the following reviewers, as well as offer our regrets if we were not able to incorporate all of their suggested changes: Susan Lima (University of Wisconsin-Milwaukee), Chris R. Logan (Southern Methodist University), and Joanne Walsh (Kean University).

John J. Shaughnessy
Eugene B. Zechmeister
Jeanne S. Zechmeister

PART ONE

General Issues

CHAPTER ONE

Introduction

CHAPTER OUTLINE

THE SCIENCE OF PSYCHOLOGY

- Psychologists develop theories and conduct psychological research to answer questions about behavior and mental processes; these answers can impact individuals and society.
- The scientific method, a means to gain knowledge, refers to the ways in which questions are asked and the logic and methods used to gain answers.
- Two important characteristics of the scientific method are an empirical approach and a skeptical attitude.

It seems safe to assume that you've been exposed to many research findings in psychology, both in media presentations and in your psychology course work. If you are like the authors of your textbook, you are very curious about the mind and behavior. You like to think about people's (and animals') behavior. You wonder about people—why they act the way they do, how they became the people they are, and how they will continue to grow and change. And you may wonder about your own behavior and how your mind works. These thoughts and reflections set you apart from other people—not everyone is curious about the mind, and not everyone considers the reasons for behavior. But if you are curious, if you do wonder why people and animals behave the way they do, you have already taken the first step in the intriguing, exciting, and, yes, sometimes challenging journey into research methods in psychology.

Many students enter the field of psychology because of their interest in improving people's lives. But what methods and interventions are helpful to people? For example, students with a career goal that involves conducting psychotherapy must learn to identify patterns of behavior that are maladaptive and to distinguish psychological interventions that are helpful from those that are not. Psychologists gain understanding and insight into the means for improving people's lives by developing theories and conducting psychological research to answer their questions about behavior.

Let us consider one very important research question among the many investigated by psychologists: What is the effect of violence in the media? Researchers have investigated aspects of this question for more than five decades in hundreds of research studies. A review of research on this topic appeared in *Psychological Science in the Public Interest* (Anderson et al., 2003), a psychology journal dedicated to publishing reports of behavioral research on important issues of public interest. Other recent topics in this journal include investigations suggesting that matching mode of instruction to students' learning style (e.g., visual, auditory) does *not* improve learning (Pashler, McDaniel, Rohrer, & Bjork, 2008), that maintaining an intellectually and physically active lifestyle promotes successful cognitive aging (Hertzog, Kramer, Wilson, & Lindenberger, 2008), and that different metaphors when describing the fight against terrorism produce different social and political decisions (Kruglanski, Crenshaw, Post, & Victoroff, 2007). Although these topics differ, the critical and common feature of research reported in this and other high-caliber psychology journals is the reliance on sound research design and methods to answer questions about behavior.

After decades of research, what do psychologists say about the behavioral, emotional, and social effects of media violence? Anderson et al. (2003) reported several key findings in their review of research that investigated violence in television, films, video games, the Internet, and music:

—Exposure to media violence causes an increase in the likelihood of aggressive and violent thoughts, emotions, and behavior in short- and long-term contexts.

—The effects of violence in the media are consistent across a variety of research studies and methods, types of media, and samples of people.

—Recent long-term studies link frequent childhood exposure to media violence with adult aggression, including physical assaults and spouse abuse.

—Research evidence supports psychologists' theories that media violence "activates" (primes) people's aggressive cognitions and physiological arousal, facilitates people's learning of aggressive behaviors through observation, and desensitizes people to violence.

—Factors that influence the likelihood of aggression in response to media violence include characteristics of viewers (e.g., age and extent to which they identify with aggressive characters), social environments (e.g., parental monitoring of media violence), and media content (e.g., realism of violent depictions and consequences of violence).

—*No one* is immune to the effects of media violence.

A number of studies reveal that children and youth spend an inordinate amount of time as media consumers, possibly second only to sleeping. Thus, an implication of the research findings listed is that one way to lessen the devastating impact of aggression and violence in our society is to decrease exposure to media violence. Indeed, psychological research played an important role in the development of the V-chip (the "V" stands for "Violence") on televisions so that parents can block violent content (Anderson et al., 2003).

More research questions remain. One important question concerns the distinction between *passive* observation of violence (e.g., television depictions) and the *active* engagement with violent media that occurs with video and Internet games (Figure 1.1). Is it possible that the effects of media violence are even stronger when viewers are actively engaged with violence while playing video games? This might be the case if active involvement reinforces aggressive tendencies to a greater degree than does passive observation. Other research questions concern the steps needed to decrease the impact of violence in our society and the role that limiting violence in the media should play in a free society. Perhaps these questions will some day be *your* research questions, or perhaps you are interested in exploring the causes of drug addiction or the roots of prejudice. Literally thousands of important research questions remain. As you continue your study of research in psychology, one day you may contribute to psychologists' efforts to improve our human condition!

Key Concept } Psychologists seek to answer questions about behavior, thoughts, and feelings by using the scientific method. The **scientific method** is an abstract concept that refers to the ways in which questions are asked and the logic and methods

FIGURE 1.1 Does the effect of violent media differ for (a) passive television viewing versus (b) active video game performance?

(a)

(b)

used to gain answers. Two important characteristics of the scientific method are the reliance on an empirical approach and the skeptical attitude scientists adopt toward explanations of behavior and mental processes. We will discuss these two characteristics as part of our introduction to psychological research in this chapter, and in Chapter 2 we will describe additional characteristics of the scientific method.

SCIENCE IN CONTEXT

- Science occurs in at least three contexts: historical, social-cultural, and moral contexts.

Although the concept of the scientific method may be abstract, the practice of psychological science is very much a concrete human activity that affects us on several levels. Psychologists can have an impact at the level of the individual (e.g., therapeutic intervention for aggression), the family (e.g., parental control over their children's media use), and society (e.g., efforts to decrease violent programming on television networks). *To be effective, however, psychologists must build upon a foundation of carefully designed and executed research.*

Human activities are influenced heavily by the context in which they occur, and scientific activity is no exception. We can suggest that at least three contexts play a critical role in influencing science: historical context, social-cultural context, and moral context. We will briefly describe each of these in turn.

Historical Context

- An empirical approach, which relies on direct observation and experimentation for answering questions, was critical for developing the science of psychology.
- The computer revolution has been a key factor in the shift from behaviorism to cognitive psychology as the dominant theme in psychological inquiry.

We don't really know exactly when psychology first became an independent discipline. Psychology emerged gradually, with roots in the thinking of Aristotle (Keller, 1937), in the writings of later philosophers such as Descartes and Locke and, later, in the work of early 19th-century physiologists and physicists. The official beginning of psychology is often marked as occurring in 1879 when Wilhelm Wundt established a formal psychology laboratory in Leipzig, Germany.

One of the decisions that faced early psychologists at the end of the 19th century concerned whether psychology should more closely affiliate with the physical sciences or remain a subdiscipline of philosophy (Sokal, 1992). With the development of psychophysical methods (especially Gustav Theodor Fechner) and reaction-time methods for understanding nervous system transmission (in particular, Hermann von Helmholtz), psychologists believed they could eventually measure thought itself (Coon, 1992). With these powerful methods of observation, psychology was on the way to becoming a quantifiable, laboratory-based science. Scientific psychologists hoped that their study of the mind would achieve equal prominence with the more established sciences of physics, chemistry, and astronomy (Coon, 1992).

One of the roadblocks to the emerging science of psychology was the public's strong interest in spiritualism and psychic phenomena at the turn of the 20th century (Coon, 1992). The general public viewed these topics of "the mind" to be within the province of psychology and sought scientific answers to their questions about clairvoyance, telepathy, and communication with the dead.

However, many psychologists wished to divorce the young science from these pseudoscientific topics. To establish psychology as a science, psychologists embraced empiricism as the means to advance understanding about human behavior. The **empirical approach** emphasizes direct observation and experimentation as a way of answering questions. It is perhaps the most important characteristic of the scientific method. Using this approach, psychologists focused on behaviors and experiences that could be *observed directly*.

Although psychology continues to emphasize the empirical approach, psychology has changed significantly since its beginnings. Early psychologists were primarily interested in questions of sensation and perception—for instance, visual illusions and imagery. In the early 20th century, psychology in the United States was heavily influenced by a behaviorist approach introduced by John B. Watson. Psychological theories focused on learning, and psychologists relied mostly on experiments with animals to test their theories. For behaviorism, the "mind" was a "black box" representing activity between an external stimulus and a behavioral response. Behaviorism was the dominant perspective in psychology well into the middle of the 20th century. Nevertheless, by the time Ulric Neisser's *Cognitive Psychology* was published in 1967, psychology had turned again to an interest in mental processes. Cognitive psychologists also returned to the reaction-time experiments that were used in the early psychology laboratories to investigate the nature of cognitive processes. The cognitive perspective is still dominant in psychology, and cognition recently has been a major topic within the field of neuroscience as investigators study the biology of the mind. There is great potential for the development of scientific psychology in the early 21st century.

A significant factor in the rise to prominence of cognitive psychology was the computer revolution (Robins, Gosling, & Craik, 1999). With the advent of computers, behaviorism's "black box" was represented using a computer metaphor. Psychologists spoke of information processing, storage, and retrieval between input (stimulus) and output (response). Just as the computer provided a useful metaphor for understanding cognitive processes, the continued development of readily available, powerful computers has proved to be exceptionally useful in broadening the scope and precision of measuring cognitive processes. Today in psychology laboratories throughout the United States and the world, computer technology is replacing paper-and-pencil measures of people's thoughts, feelings, and behaviors. Similarly, continued improvements in the technology of brain imaging (e.g., fMRI, functional magnetic resonance imaging) will advance neuroscience as an important discipline within the fields of psychology, biology, and chemistry.

These broad trends in the historical development of psychology, from behaviorism to cognitive neuroscience, represent the "bigger picture" of what happened in psychology in the 20th century. A closer look, however, reveals the myriad topics investigated in the science of psychology. Psychologists today do research in such general areas as clinical, social, organizational, counseling, physiological, cognitive, educational, developmental, and health psychology. Investigations in all of these areas help us to understand the complexity of behavior and mental processes.

Science in general—and psychology in particular—has changed because of the brilliant ideas of exceptional individuals. The ideas of Galileo, Darwin,

BOX 1.1

PSYCHOLOGY AND THE NOBEL PRIZE

Each year, the Royal Swedish Academy of Sciences awards the distinguished Nobel Prize for researchers' work in a variety of fields. In October 2002, Daniel Kahneman, Ph.D., became the first psychologist to win this award. He was recognized for his research on intuitive judgment, human reasoning, and decision making in conditions of uncertainty. His research, conducted with his long-term collaborator, Amos Tversky (1937–1996), was honored because of its influential role in economic theories (Kahneman, 2003). Kahneman shared the Nobel Economics Prize with economist Vernon Smith, who was cited for his work in developing laboratory experiments (an important topic in this text) in economics.

Although trained in fields other than psychology, several scientists have been awarded the Nobel Prize for research directly related to the behavioral sciences (Chernoff, 2002; Pickren, 2003), for example:

- **1904,** Physiology or Medicine: Ivan Pavlov won the Nobel Prize for his research on digestion, which subsequently influenced his work on classical conditioning.
- **1961,** Physiology or Medicine: A physicist, Georg von Békésy, won the Nobel Prize for his work on psychoacoustics—the perception of sound.
- **1973,** Physiology or Medicine: Three ethologists, Karl von Frisch, Konrad Lorenz, and Nikolaas Tinbergen, were honored with the first Nobel Prize awarded for purely behavioral research (Pickren, 2003). Ethology is a branch of biology in which researchers observe behavior of organisms in relation to their natural environment (see Chapter 4).
- **1978,** Economics: Herbert A. Simon was awarded the Nobel Prize for his groundbreaking research on organizational decision making (MacCoun, 2002; Pickren, 2003). Kahneman, referring to his 2002 Nobel Prize, cited Simon's research as instrumental for his own research.

- **1981,** Physiology or Medicine: The Nobel Prize was awarded to Roger W. Sperry, a zoologist who demonstrated the distinct roles of the two brain hemispheres using the "split-brain" procedure.

The achievements of these scientists and many others testify to the breadth and importance of behavioral research in the sciences. Although there is not a "Nobel Prize for Psychology" (a distinction shared by the field of Mathematics), the work of scientists in a variety of areas is recognized as contributing to our understanding of behavior.

and Einstein not only changed the way scientists viewed their disciplines, but their ideas also changed the way people understand themselves and their world. Similarly, many exceptional individuals have influenced the progress of psychology (Haggbloom et al., 2002), including Nobel Prize winners (see Box 1.1). Early in American psychology, William James (1842–1910) wrote

FIGURE 1.2   Many influential people helped to develop the field of psychology, including (a) William James, (b) B. F. Skinner, and (c) Sigmund Freud.

(a)   (b)   (c)

the first introductory textbook, *The Principles of Psychology*, and gained insight into mental processes using his technique of introspection (see Figure 1.2). As the prominence of behaviorism grew, B. F. Skinner (1904–1990) expanded our understanding of responses to reinforcement through the experimental analysis of behavior. Along with Skinner, Sigmund Freud (1856–1939) is often one of the most recognized figures in psychology, but the ideas and methods of the two could not be more different! Freud's theories on personality, mental disorders, and the unconscious dramatically shifted attention from behavior to mental processes through his method of free association. Many other individuals greatly influenced thinking within specific areas of psychology, such as developmental, clinical, social, and cognitive psychology. We hope you will be able to learn more about these influential psychologists, from both the past and the present, in the areas of most interest to you.

Science also changes less dramatically, in ways that result from the cumulative efforts of many individuals. One way to describe these more gradual changes is by describing the growth of the profession of psychology. The American Psychological Association (APA) was formed in 1892. The APA had only a few dozen members in that first year; in 1992, when the APA celebrated its 100th birthday, there were approximately 70,000 members. Fifteen years later, in 2007, APA membership doubled to over 148,000 members. Promotion of psychological research is a concern of the APA as well as the Association for Psychological Science (APS). APS was formed in 1988 to emphasize scientific issues in psychology. APA and APS both sponsor annual conventions, which psychologists attend to learn about the most recent developments in their fields. Each organization also publishes scientific journals in order to communicate the latest research findings to its members and to society in general.

You can become part of psychology's history in the making. Both APA and APS encourage student affiliation, which provides educational and research opportunities for both undergraduate and graduate psychology students.

Information about joining APA and APS as a regular member or as a student affiliate can be obtained by consulting their Internet websites:

(APA) www.apa.org
(APS) www.psychologicalscience.org

Both the APA and APS websites provide news about important recent psychological research findings, information about psychology publications (including relatively low-cost student subscription rates for major psychology journals), and links to many psychology organizations. Take a look!

Social and Cultural Context

- The social and cultural context influences researchers' choice of topics, society's acceptance of findings, and the locations in which research takes place.
- Ethnocentrism occurs when people's views of another culture are biased by the framework or lens of their own culture.

Science is influenced not only by its historical context but also by the prevailing social and cultural context. This prevailing context is sometimes referred to as the *zeitgeist*—the spirit of the times. Psychological research and its application exist in a reciprocal relationship with society: research has an effect on and is affected by society. The social and cultural context can influence what researchers choose to study, the resources available to support their research, and society's acceptance of their findings. For example, researchers have developed new research programs because of an increasing emphasis on women's issues (and because of increasing numbers of women doing research). Topics in this emerging area include the "glass ceiling" that impedes women's advancement in organizations, the interplay between work and family for dual-career couples, and the effects of the availability of quality child care on productivity in the workforce and on children's development. Social and cultural attitudes can affect not only what researchers study but how they choose to do their research. Society's attitude toward bilingualism, for instance, can affect whether researchers emphasize *problems* that arise for children in bilingual education or the *benefits* that children gain from bilingual education.

Social and cultural values can affect how people react to reported findings from psychological research. For example, reports of research on controversial topics such as sexual orientation, recovered memories of childhood sexual abuse, and televised violence receive more media attention because of the public's interest in these issues. At times, this greater interest engenders public debate about the interpretation of the findings and the implications of the findings for social policy. Public reaction can be extreme, as illustrated by the response to an article on child sexual abuse published in *Psychological Bulletin* (Rind, Tromovitch, & Bauserman, 1998). In their review and analysis of 59 studies of the effects of child sexual abuse (CSA), Rind et al. concluded that "CSA does not cause intense harm on a pervasive basis regardless of gender in the college population" (p. 46). After their research was promoted by pedophilia advocacy sites on the Web, "Dr. Laura" (talk show host Laura Schlessinger) characterized the article as endorsing adult sex with children (*not* the investigators' intention) and criticized the American Psychological Association for publishing the study in its prestigious journal, *Psychological Bulletin* (Ondersma et al., 2001). In 1999 the U.S. House of Representatives responded to negative media attention by passing unanimously a resolution of censure of the research reported in this article. Also, scientific debate over the controversial findings continues, with criticisms and rebuttals appearing in *Psychological Bulletin* (Dallam et al., 2001; Ondersma et al., 2001; Rind & Tromovitch, 2007; Rind, Tromovitch, & Bauserman, 2001), other journals, and books. An entire issue of *American Psychologist* was devoted to the political storm that resulted from this research (March 2002, Vol. 57, Issue 3). Such public criticisms of research findings, even findings based on solid, empirical science, appear to be a growing trend. Legal, administrative, and political attacks arise from those who oppose research findings because of strongly held personal beliefs or financial interests (Loftus, 2003). These attacks can have the unfortunate consequence of impeding legitimate scientific inquiry and debate.

Psychologists' sensitivity to societal concerns, such as child sexual abuse, is one reason why psychology has not developed strictly as a laboratory science. Although laboratory investigation remains at the heart of psychological inquiry, psychologists and other behavioral scientists do research in schools, clinics, businesses, hospitals, and other nonlaboratory settings, including the Internet. In fact, the Internet is becoming a useful and popular research tool for psychological scientists (e.g., Birnbaum, 2000). According to U.S. Census data, by the year 2000, 54 million U.S. households (51%) had one or more computers. In 44 million households (42%) there was at least one person who used the Internet at home (Newburger, 2001). These data obviously underestimate the number of U.S. Internet users since numbers refer to households and not individual users, and they do not consider online access through business or educational settings. Importantly, these figures also do not take into account the use of the Internet in countries other than the United States. By the end of 2009, the estimated number of Internet users in the world approached two billion (www.internetworldstats.com). Suffice it to say, it did not take behavioral scientists very long to recognize the potential of an amazingly large and diverse "participant pool" for their research (see, for example, Birnbaum, 2000; Gosling, Vazire, Srivastava, & John, 2004; Skitka & Sargis, 2005). Aided by the development of the Internet in the 1990s and associated hypertext markup languages (HTML), psychologists soon began to carry out online research (e.g., Musch & Reips, 2000). The Web allows practically any type of psychological research that uses computers as equipment and humans as participants (Krantz & Dalal, 2000). One way that researchers recruit participants for their studies is to post research opportunities on various research-based websites. For example, APS maintains a Web page that allows Internet users to participate in psychological research. Check out Internet research opportunities at http://psych.hanover.edu/research/exponnet.html. We will have much more to say about research on the Internet as we introduce you to particular research methods in psychology. Of particular importance are ethical issues raised by this form of research (see Chapter 3).

If we acknowledge that science is affected by social and cultural values, a question still remains as to whose culture is having—and whose culture should have—an influence. A recent analysis of a sample of psychological research revealed that the contributors, samples, and editors of six premier journals published by the American Psychological Association were predominantly American (Arnett, 2008). In contrast, Americans represent less than 5% of the world's population, and people throughout the world live in conditions very different from those of Americans. One may question, then, whether a psychological science that focuses heavily on Americans is complete.

Key Concept

A potential problem occurs when we attempt to understand the behavior of individuals in a *different* culture through the framework or views of our *own* culture (Figure 1.3). This potential source of bias is called **ethnocentrism.** As

FIGURE 1.3   By removing our cultural lenses, we gain new ideas for research topics that investigate (a) strengths in aging, (b) abilities rather than disabilities, and (c) stay-at-home fathers.

(a)

(b)

(c)

an example of ethnocentrism, let's consider the controversy concerning theories of moral development. In his six-stage theory of moral development, Kohlberg (1981, 1984) identified the highest stage of moral development (postconventional development) as one in which individuals make moral decisions based on their self-defined ethical principles and their recognition of individual rights. Research evidence suggests that Kohlberg's theory provides a good description of moral development for American and European males—cultures emphasizing individualism. In contrast, people who live in cultures that emphasize collectivism, such as communal societies in China or Papua New Guinea, do not fit Kohlberg's description. Collectivist cultures value the well-being of the community over that of the individual. We would be demonstrating ethnocentrism if we were to use Kohlberg's theory to declare that individuals from such collectivist cultures were less morally developed. We would be interpreting their behavior through an inappropriate cultural lens, namely, individualism. Cross-cultural research is one way to help us avoid studying only one dominant culture and to remind us that we need to be careful to use cultural lenses beyond our own in our research.

Moral Context

- The moral context of research demands that researchers maintain the highest standards of ethical behavior.
- The APA's code of ethics guides research and helps researchers to evaluate ethical dilemmas such as the risks and benefits associated with deception and the use of animals in research.

Science is a search for truth. Individual scientists and the collective enterprise of science need to ensure that the moral context in which scientific activity takes place meets the highest of standards. Fraud, lies, and misrepresentations should play no part in a scientific investigation. But science is also a human endeavor, and frequently much more is at stake than truth. Both scientists and the institutions that hire them compete for rewards in a game with jobs, money, and reputations on the line. The number of scientific publications authored by a university faculty member, for instance, is usually a major factor influencing decisions regarding professional advancement through promotion and tenure. Under these circumstances, there are unfortunate, but seemingly inevitable, cases of scientific misconduct.

A variety of activities constitute violations of scientific integrity. They include fabrication of data, plagiarism, selective reporting of research findings, failure to acknowledge individuals who made significant contributions to the research, misuse of research funds, and unethical treatment of humans or animals (see Adler, 1991). Some transgressions are easier to detect than others. Out-and-out fabrication of data, for instance, can be revealed when, in the normal course of science, independent researchers are not able to reproduce (replicate) results, or when logical inconsistencies appear in published reports. However, subtle transgressions, such as reporting only data that meet expectations or misleading reports of results, are difficult to detect. The dividing line between intentional misconduct and simply bad science is not always clear.

To educate researchers about the proper conduct of science, and to help guide them around the many ethical pitfalls that are present, most scientific organizations have adopted formal codes of ethics. In Chapter 3 we will introduce you to the APA ethical principles governing research with humans and animals. As you will see, ethical dilemmas often arise. Consider research by Klinesmith, Kasser, and McAndrew (2006), who tested whether male participants who handled a gun in a laboratory setting were subsequently more aggressive. Researchers told participants the experiment investigated whether paying attention to details influences sensitivity to tastes. Participants were randomly assigned to one of two attention conditions. In one group each participant handled a gun and wrote a set of instructions for assembling and disassembling the gun. In a second condition participants wrote similar instructions while interacting with the game Mouse Trap™. Afterward, each participant was asked to taste and rate a sample of water (85 g) with a drop of hot sauce in it, ostensibly prepared by the previous research participant. This was the "taste sensitivity" portion of the experiment. Next, participants were given water and hot sauce and asked to prepare the sample for the next participant. How much hot sauce they added served as the measure of aggression. Consistent with their predictions, the researchers found that participants who had handled the gun added significantly more hot sauce to the water ($M = 13.61$ g) than participants who interacted with the game ($M = 4.23$ g).

This research raises several important questions: Under what conditions should researchers be allowed to deceive research participants about the true nature of the experiment? Does the benefit of the information gained about guns and aggression outweigh the risk associated with deception? Would participants who handled the gun have added less hot sauce if they had known the experiment actually investigated the relationship between guns and aggression?[1]

Deception is just one of the many ethical issues that researchers must confront. As yet another illustration of ethical concerns, consider that animal subjects sometimes are used to help understand human psychopathology. This may mean exposing animal subjects to stressful and even painful conditions, and sometimes killing the animals for postmortem examinations. Under what conditions should psychological research with animal subjects be permitted? The list of ethical questions raised by psychological research is a lengthy one. Thus, it is of the utmost importance that you become familiar with the APA ethical principles and their application at an early stage in your research career, and that you participate (as research participant, assistant, or principal investigator) only in research that meets the highest standards of scientific integrity. Our hope is that your study of research methods will allow you to do good research and to discern what research is good to do.

---

[1]A critical component of any research that uses deception is the *debriefing* procedure at the end of the experiment during which the true nature of the experiment is explained to participants (see Chapter 3). Participants in the Klinesmith et al. (2006) study were told the experiment investigated aggression, not taste sensitivity, and that they should not feel badly about any aggressive behavior they exhibited. None of the participants reported suspicion about the true nature of the experiment during the debriefing. Interestingly, Klinesmith et al. noted that some participants were disappointed their hot-sauce sample would not be given to the next participant!

Thinking Like a Researcher

- To "think like a researcher" is to be skeptical regarding claims about the causes of behavior and mental processes, even those that are made on the basis of "published" scientific findings.
- The strongest evidence for a claim about behavior comes from converging evidence across many studies, although scientists recognize that claims are always probabilistic.

One important step a student of psychology must make is to learn to think like a researcher. More than anything else, scientists are skeptical. A skeptical attitude regarding claims about the causes of behavior and mental processes is another important characteristic of the scientific method in psychology. Not only do scientists want to "see it before believing it," but they are likely to want to see it again and again, perhaps under conditions of their own choosing. Researchers strive to draw conclusions based on empirical evidence rather than their subjective judgment (see Box 1.2). The strongest scientific evidence is converging evidence obtained across different studies examining the same research question. Behavioral scientists are skeptical because they recognize that behavior is complex and often many factors interact to cause a psychological phenomenon. Discovering these factors is often a difficult task. The explanations proposed are sometimes premature because not all factors that may account for a phenomenon have been considered or even noticed. Behavioral scientists also recognize that science is a human endeavor. People make mistakes. Human inference is not always to be trusted. Therefore, scientists tend to be skeptical about "new discoveries," treatments, and extraordinary claims, even those that are from "published" research studies.

The skepticism of scientists leads them to be more cautious than many people without scientific training. Many people are apparently all too ready to accept explanations that are based on insufficient or inadequate evidence. This is illustrated by the widespread belief in the occult. Rather than approaching the claims about paranormal events cautiously, many people accept these claims uncritically. According to public opinion surveys, a large majority of Americans believe in ESP (extrasensory perception), and some people are convinced that beings from outer space have visited Earth. About two in five Americans believe horoscopes are credible, and as many as 12 million adults report changing their behavior after reading astrology reports (Miller, 1986). Such beliefs are held despite minimal and often negative evidence for the validity of horoscopes.

Scientists do not, of course, automatically assume that unconventional interpretations of unexplained phenomena could not be true. They simply insist on being allowed to test all claims and to reject those that are inherently untestable. Scientific skepticism is a gullible public's defense against frauds and scams selling ineffective medicines and cures, impossible schemes to get rich, and supernatural explanations for natural phenomena. At the same time, however, it is important to remember that trust plays as large a role as skepticism in the life of a scientist. Scientists need to trust their instruments, their participants, their colleagues' reports of research, and their own professional judgment in carrying out their research.

BOX 1.2

CLINICAL PSYCHOLOGY AND SCIENCE

Do clinical psychologists apply the latest scientific findings from psychological research in the treatment of their patients?

In a recent critique of the practice of clinical psychology, Drs. Timothy Baker, Richard McFall, and Varda Shoham, themselves esteemed clinical psychologists, argue a resounding *"no"* to this question. Their extensive analysis of the practice of clinical psychologists, which appeared in the November 2009 issue of the APS journal, *Psychological Science in the Public Interest,* was picked up by various media sources, including coverage in *Newsweek* magazine (October 12, 2009).

Over the past several decades, clinical researchers have demonstrated the effectiveness—including cost-effectiveness—of psychological treatments (e.g., cognitive behavioral therapy) for many mental disorders. Yet, according to the authors, relatively few psychologists learn or practice these effective treatments. Baker et al. contend that present-day clinical psychology resembles the prescientific medical practice that took place in the 1800s and early 1900s, in which medical doctors rejected scientific practices in favor of their personal experience. Research indicates that today's clinical psychologist is more likely to rely on his or her own personal opinions

regarding "what works" rather than scientific evidence for empirically supported treatments (ESTs). In fact, Baker et al. report that the average clinical psychologist is unaware of research findings regarding ESTs and likely does not have the scientific training to understand the research methodology or findings.

Baker, McFall, and Shoham (2009) argue that urgent changes must be made to training programs for clinical psychologists, much like medical training was completely reformed in the early 1900s to make medicine scientifically based. Without scientific grounding, clinical psychologists will continue to lose their role in present-day mental and behavioral health care. Baker et al. believe that high-quality, science-centered education and training must be a central feature of clinical psychology training, and that the practice of clinical psychology without a strong basis in science should be stigmatized.

For students using this textbook who are interested in clinical psychology, we hope that as you learn about the various research methods in psychology, you will see this introduction to research methods as only the first step needed in your successful and ethical practice of clinical psychology.

We've indicated that to think like a researcher you need to be skeptical about evidence and claims. You already know something about evidence and claims if you've read any book detailing a crime and trial, or watched any number of popular movie or television legal dramas. Detectives, lawyers, and others in the legal profession collect evidence from a variety of sources and seek converging evidence in order to make claims about people's behavior. A small amount of evidence may be enough to *suspect* someone of a crime, but converging evidence from many sources is needed to *convict* the person. Psychological scientists work in much the same way—they collect evidence in order to make claims about behavior and psychological processes.

The main emphasis of this text will be to detail the different research methods that result in different types of evidence and conclusions. As you proceed in your study of research methods, you will find that there are important—and different—scientific principles that apply to reporting a survey statistic or behavioral observation, identifying a relationship between factors (or "variables"), and stating there is a causal link between variables. The strongest scientific evidence is akin to the converging evidence needed in a trial to obtain a conviction. Even when researchers have strong evidence for their conclusions from replications (repetitions) of an experiment, they are in a similar situation as juries that have found a person guilty beyond a reasonable doubt. Researchers and juries both seek the truth, but their conclusions are ultimately probabilistic. Certainty is often beyond the grasp of both jurors and scientists.

By learning to think like a researcher, you can develop two important sets of skills. The first skill will enable you to be a more effective consumer of scientific findings so that you can make more informed personal and professional decisions. The second skill will enable you to learn how to do research so that you can contribute to the science of psychology. We will be fleshing out these two aspects of the scientific method throughout the text, but we briefly outline them in this chapter. We first describe an illustration of why it is important to think like a researcher when evaluating research claims made in the media. We then describe how researchers get started when they want to gather evidence using the scientific method.

Evaluating Research Findings Reported in the Media

- Not all science reported in the media is "good science." We must question what we read and hear.
- Media reports summarizing original research reports may omit critical aspects of the method, results, or interpretation of the research.

Researchers in psychology report their findings in professional journals that are available in printed and electronic form. Most people who encounter psychological research findings, however, do so by learning about research findings in the media—on the Internet, in newspapers and magazines, and on radio and TV. Much of this research is worthwhile. Psychological research can help people in a variety of areas, such as helping people to learn ways to communicate with a relative with Alzheimer's, to avoid arguments, or to learn how to forgive. Two serious problems can arise, however, when research is reported in the media. The first problem is that the research reported in the media is not always good research. A critical reader needs to sort out the good research from the bad—what are solid findings and which have not yet been confirmed. We must also decide which findings are worth applying in our lives and which require a wait-and-see attitude. It is fair to say that much of the research is not very good given all the different media in which psychological research is reported. So we have good reason to question the research we read or hear about in the media.

A second problem that can arise when scientific research is reported in the media is that "something can be lost in the translation." Media reports are typically summaries of the original research, and critical aspects of the method, results, or interpretation of the research may be missing in the media summary. The more you learn about the scientific method, the better your questions will be for discerning the quality of research reported in the media and for determining the critical information that is lacking in the media report. For now, we can give you a taste of the types of questions you will want to ask by looking at an example of research reported in the media.

Not too long ago there was a widely publicized phenomenon called the "Mozart effect." Headlines such as "Classical Music Good for Babies' Brains" were common at the time. These headlines caught people's attention, especially the attention of new parents. Media reports indicated that parents were playing classical music to infants in the hope of raising their children's intelligence. One million new mothers were given a free CD called "Smart Symphonies" along with free infant formula. Clearly the distributors and many new parents were persuaded that the Mozart effect was real.

The idea that listening to music might raise the intelligence scores of newborns is an intriguing idea. When you encounter intriguing ideas in the media such as this one, a good first step is to *go to the original source in which the research was reported.* In this case the original article was reported in a respectable journal, *Nature.* Rauscher, Shaw, and Ky (1993) described an experiment in which a single group of college students listened to a 10-minute Mozart piece, sat in silence for 10 minutes, or listened to relaxation instructions for 10 minutes before taking a spatial reasoning test. Performance on the test was better after listening to Mozart than in the other two conditions, but the effect disappeared after an additional 10- to 15-minute period.

The findings reported in the original source may be judged as solid, but the extrapolations of these findings are very shaky. A million women were being encouraged to play "smart symphonies" for their infants on the basis of an effect demonstrated on a very specific type of reasoning test with college students and the effect lasted 15 minutes at the most! Although some studies with children were done, the ambiguous results of all the research studies indicate that something had been lost in the "translation" (by the media) from the original research reports to the widespread application of the Mozart effect. People who are skeptical enough to ask questions when they hear or read reports of research in the media and knowledgeable enough to read research in the original sources are less likely to be misinformed. Your job is to be skeptical; our job is to provide the knowledge in this text to allow you to read critically the original sources that report research findings.

Getting Started Doing Research

- When beginning a research study, students can answer the first question of "what to study?" by reviewing psychological topics in psychology journals, textbooks, and courses.
- A research hypothesis is a tentative explanation for a phenomenon; it is often stated in the form of a prediction together with an explanation for the predicted outcome.
- Researchers generate hypotheses in many ways, but they always review published psychological studies before beginning their research.
- To decide if their research question is a good one, researchers consider the scientific importance, scope, and likely outcomes of the research, and whether psychological science will be advanced.

- A multimethod approach, one that searches for answers using various research methodologies and measures, is psychology's best hope for understanding behavior and the mind.

As you begin learning about how researchers in psychology gather evidence, we will pass along advice from several expert researchers about one of the most fundamental aspects of research—getting started. We will organize this section around three questions that researchers ask themselves as they begin a research project:

—What should I study?
—How do I develop a hypothesis to test in my research?
—Is my research question a good one?

There are many decisions that must be made before beginning to do research in psychology. The first one, of course, is what topic to study. Many students approach the field of psychology with interests in psychopathology and issues associated with mental health. Others are intrigued with the puzzles surrounding human cognition, such as memory, problem solving, and decision making. Still others are interested in problems of developmental and social psychology. Psychology provides a smorgasbord of research possibilities to explore, as is illustrated by the literally hundreds of scientific journals that publish the results of psychological research. You can quickly find information about the many research areas within psychology by reviewing the contents of a standard introductory psychology textbook. More specific information can be found, of course, in the many classes offered by the psychology department of your college or university, such as abnormal psychology, cognitive psychology, and social psychology.

It's not just students who are concerned about research questions in psychology. In July 2009, an entire issue of the journal *Perspectives in Psychological Science* was devoted to discussions of research questions and directions for the future of psychology (Diener, 2009). Top researchers from various areas within psychology identified important questions in their fields—for example, questions addressing mind-brain connections, evolutionary psychology, and even human-android interactions. When searching for a research question, reading these articles may be a good place to start!

Students often develop their initial research topics through interactions with their psychology instructors. Many professors conduct research and are eager to involve students on research teams. You may only need to ask. Psychology departments also offer many other resources to help students develop research ideas. One opportunity is in the form of "colloquia" (singular: colloquium). A colloquium is a formal research presentation in which researchers, sometimes from other universities, present their theories and research findings to faculty and students in the department. Watch for announcements of upcoming colloquia in your psychology department.

No matter how or where you begin to develop a topic, an important initial step when getting started is to explore the published literature of psychological research. There are several reasons why you must search the psychology literature before beginning to do research. One obvious reason is that the answer to your research question may already be there. Someone else may have entertained the same question and provided an answer, or at least a partial one. It is very likely that you will discover research findings that are related to your research question. Although you may be disappointed to find your research question has been explored, consider that finding other people who have done research on the same or similar idea affirms the importance of your idea. Doing research without a careful examination of what is already known may be interesting or fun (it certainly may be easy); perhaps you could call it a "hobby," but we can't call it science. *Science is a cumulative enterprise—current research builds on previous research.*

Once you have identified a body of literature related to your research idea, your reading may lead you to discover inconsistencies or contradictions in the published research. You may also find that the research findings are limited in terms of the nature of the participants studied or the circumstances under which the research was done, or that there is a psychological theory in need of testing. Having made such a discovery, you have found a solid research lead, a path to follow.

When reading the psychological literature and thinking about possible research questions, you might also consider how the results of psychological studies are applied to societal problems. As you learn how to do research in psychology, you may consider ways this knowledge can be used to generate research investigations that will make humankind just a little better off.

Searching the psychological literature is not the tedious task that it once was; computer-aided literature searches, including use of the Internet, have made identifying psychological research a relatively easy, even exciting task. In Chapter 13 of this book, we outline how to search the psychology literature, including ways to use computer databases for your search.

Finally, as Sternberg (1997) points out, choosing a question to investigate should not be taken lightly. Some questions are simply not worth asking because their answers offer no hope of advancing the science of psychology. The questions are, in a word, meaningless, or at best, trivial. Sternberg (1997) suggests that students new to the field of psychological research consider several questions before deciding they have a good research question:

—Why might this question be scientifically important?
—What is the scope of this question?
—What are the likely outcomes if I carry out this research project?
—To what extent will psychological science be advanced by knowing the answer to this question?
—Why would anyone be interested in the results obtained by asking this question?

As you begin the research process, finding answers to these questions may require guidance from research advisors and others who have successfully conducted their own research. We also hope that your ability to answer these questions will be enhanced as you learn more about theory and research in psychology, and as you read about the many examples of interesting and meaningful psychological research that we describe in this book.

STRETCHING EXERCISE

In this exercise, form hypotheses using an item from each column. Link together an event or behavior from the first column with an outcome from the second column, and then a possible explanation from the third column. A sample hypothesis is illustrated.

Event or Behavior	Outcome	Explanation
1 exposure to thin body images	1 increased helping	1 reinterpretation of events
2 terrorism attack on 9/11/2001	2 health benefits	2 increased empathy
3 writing about emotional events	3 increased traffic fatalities	3 comparison of self to ideal
4 mimicking behavior and posture	4 body dissatisfaction	4 fear of air travel

Sample Hypothesis: Writing about emotional events causes health benefits, possibly due to a reinterpretation of events that occurs with writing. [Pennebaker & Francis, 1996]

Key Concept }

The next decision is a bit harder. As researchers get started, they seek to identify their research hypothesis. A **hypothesis** (plural: hypotheses) is a tentative explanation for a phenomenon. Often a hypothesis is stated in the form of a prediction for some outcome, along with an explanation for the prediction. We proposed a research hypothesis earlier when we suggested that the effects (e.g., increased aggression) of violent media may be stronger for video games than for passive television viewing because players are actively engaged in the aggressive actions, thus increasing their aggressive tendencies. (An alternative hypothesis might suggest that the effects of video games might be *less* because game players have the opportunity to release the aggressive impulses that passive television viewers do not.)

McGuire (1997) identified 49 simple rules ("heuristics") for generating a hypothesis to be tested scientifically. We cannot review all 49 suggestions here, but we can give you some insight into McGuire's thinking by listing some of these heuristics. He suggests, for example, that we might generate a hypothesis for a research study by

—thinking about deviations (oddities, exceptions) from a general trend or principle;
—imagining how we would behave in a task or if faced with a specific problem;
—considering similar problems whose solution is known;
—making sustained, deliberate observations of a person or phenomenon (e.g., performing a "case study");
—generating counterexamples for an obvious conclusion about behavior;
—borrowing ideas or theories from other disciplines.

Of course, identifying a research question and hypothesis doesn't necessarily tell you how to do the research. What is it exactly that you want to know? Answering this question will mean that you must make other decisions that we will address throughout this text. As a researcher, you will ask yourself questions such as "Should I do a qualitative or quantitative research study? What is the nature of

TABLE 1.1   STEPS OF THE RESEARCH PROCESS

Step	How?	Chapter
Develop a research question.	• Be aware of ethnocentrism.	1
	• Gain personal experiences doing research.	1
	• Read psychological literature.	1, 13
Generate a research hypothesis.	• Read psychological theories on your topic.	1, 2
	• Consider personal experience, think of exceptions, and notice inconsistencies in previous research.	1
Form operational definitions.	• Look to previous research to see how others have defined the same or similar constructs.	2
	• Identify the variables you will examine.	2
Choose a research design.	• Identify a sample of participants.	4, 5
	• Decide whether your research question seeks to describe, allow prediction, or identify causal relationships.	2
	➤ Choose observational and correlational designs for description and prediction.	4, 5
	➤ Choose an experimental design for a causal research question.	6, 7, 8
	➤ Choose a single-case design when seeking to understand and treat a small group or one individual.	9
	➤ Choose a quasi-experimental design for a causal research question in settings where experimental control is less feasible.	10
Evaluate the ethics of your research.	• Identify the potential risks and benefits of the research and the ways in which participants' welfare will be protected.	3
	• Submit a proposal to an ethics review committee.	3
	• Seek permission from those in authority.	3, 10
Collect and analyze data; form conclusions.	• Get to know the data.	11
	• Summarize the data.	11
	• Confirm what the data reveal.	12
Report research results.	• Present the findings at a psychology conference.	13
	• Submit a written report of the study to a psychology journal.	13

the variables I wish to investigate? How do I find reliable and valid measures of behavior? What is the research method best suited to my research question? What kinds of statistical analyses will be needed? Do the methods I choose meet accepted moral and ethical standards?" These and other steps associated with the scientific process are illustrated in Table 1.1. Don't be concerned if the terms in these questions and in Table 1.1 are unfamiliar. As you proceed through this text on research methods in psychology, you will learn about these steps of the research process. Table 1.1 will be a useful guide when you begin conducting your own research.

This text introduces you to the ways in which psychologists use the scientific method. As you know, psychology is a discipline with many areas of study

Key Concept

and many questions. No single research methodology can answer all the questions psychologists have about behavior and mental processes. Thus, the best approach to answering our questions is the **multimethod approach**—that is, searching for an answer using various research methodologies and measures of behavior. The goal of this book is to help you to fill a "toolbox" with strategies for conducting research. As you will learn throughout this text, any one method or measure of behavior may be flawed or incomplete in its ability to answer research questions fully. When researchers use multiple methods, the flaws associated with any particular method are surmounted by other methods that "fill in the gaps." Thus, an important advantage of the multimethod approach is that researchers obtain a more complete understanding of behavior and mental processes. It is our hope that with these tools—the research methods described in this text—you will be on the path toward answering your own questions in the field of psychology.

SUMMARY

Psychologists seek to understand behavior and mental processes by developing theories and conducting psychological research. Psychological studies can have an important impact on individuals and society; one example is research demonstrating the negative impact of violence in the media. Researchers use the scientific method, which emphasizes an empirical approach to understanding behavior; this approach relies on direct observation and experimentation to answer questions. Scientific practice occurs in historical, social-cultural, and moral contexts. Historically, the computer revolution was instrumental in the shift in emphasis from behaviorism to cognitive psychology. Many psychologists, past and present, have helped to develop the diverse field of psychology.

The social-cultural context influences psychological research in terms of what researchers choose to study and society's acceptance of their findings. Culture also influences research when ethnocentrism occurs. In this bias people attempt to understand the behavior of individuals who live in a different culture through the framework or views of their own culture. The moral context demands that researchers maintain the highest standards of ethical behavior. Clear violations of scientific integrity include fabrication of data, plagiarism, selective reporting of research findings, failure to acknowledge individuals who made significant contributions to the research, misuse of research funds, and unethical treatment of humans or animals. The APA's code of ethics guides research and helps researchers to evaluate ethical dilemmas such as the risks and benefits associated with deception and the use of animals in research.

Researchers must be skeptical regarding claims about behavior and mental processes. The strongest evidence for a claim comes from converging evidence across many studies, although scientists recognize that all research findings are probabilistic rather than definitive. Two problems arise with media reports of research: The research may not meet high standards, and media reports are typically summaries of the original research. An important first step in evaluating media reports is to go to the original publication to learn more about the methods and procedures of the research.

The first step in beginning research is to generate a research question. Students gain research ideas from their textbooks and courses, and through interactions with instructors. The next step is to develop a research hypothesis. A research hypothesis is a tentative explanation for the phenomenon to be tested, and it is often stated in the form of a prediction together with an explanation for the predicted outcome. Although research hypotheses are developed in many ways, an essential part of this step is to review psychological research literature related to the topic. Finally, it is important to evaluate whether answers to a research question will meaningfully contribute to psychologists' understanding of behavior and mental processes.

A multimethod approach employs various research methodologies and measures to answer research questions and to gain a more complete understanding of behavior. Scientists recognize that any one method or measure of behavior is flawed or incomplete; multiple methods allow researchers to "fill in the gaps" left by any particular method. The aim of this textbook is to introduce you to the variety of research methods used by psychologists to answer their questions.

Key Concepts

scientific method   4   hypothesis   21
empirical approach   7   multimethod approach   23
ethnocentrism   12

Review Questions

1 Describe two important characteristics of the scientific method.
2 Why did early psychologists choose the empirical approach as the favored method for psychological investigations?
3 Identify two ways in which the computer was critical to the development of psychology in the 20th century.
4 Provide an example of (1) how social and cultural factors may influence psychologists' choice of research topics and (2) how social-cultural factors may influence society's acceptance of research findings.
5 Describe how ethnocentrism can be a problem in research and suggest one way in which researchers can prevent this bias.
6 What does it mean that research is conducted in a "moral context"?
7 Describe two ethical dilemmas that psychologists may face when conducting research.
8 Explain why researchers are skeptical about research findings, and explain how their attitude likely differs from that of the general public.
9 Identify two reasons you would give another person as to why he or she should critically evaluate the results of the research reported in the news media (e.g., television, magazines).
10 What are the three initial steps researchers take as they begin a research project?
11 Identify two reasons it is important to search the psychological literature when beginning research.
12 Describe the multimethod approach to research and identify its main advantage.

CHALLENGE QUESTIONS

1 Consider the hypothesis that playing violent video games causes people to be more aggressive compared to watching violence passively on television.

   A How might you test this hypothesis? That is, what might you do to compare the two different experiences of exposure to violence?

   B How would you determine whether people acted in an aggressive manner after exposure to violence?

   C What additional factors would you have to consider to make sure that *exposure* to *violence*, not some other factor, was the important factor?

2 In your courses you have learned a variety of approaches to gaining knowledge about people. For example, in reading literature, we learn about people through the eyes of the author and the characters he or she has developed. How is this approach to gaining knowledge different from that used by researchers in psychology? What are the advantages and disadvantages of each approach?

3 Across the history of research in psychology, we have witnessed a change in emphases from sensation-perception to behaviorism and then to cognitive psychology. Within the different areas or subdisciplines of psychology (e.g., clinical, developmental, neuroscience, social), the number of research topics has increased tremendously.

   A What area(s) within psychology is of most interest to you, and why?

   B At your library, page through three or four current issues of journals within your area of interest (e.g., *Developmental Psychology, Journal of Consulting and Clinical Psychology, Journal of Personality and Social Psychology*). (Ask your instructor or librarian for names of additional journals.) What topics did the researchers investigate? Can you observe any trends in the topics or in the kind of research that is being conducted? Describe your findings.

4 Identify how ethnocentrism might play a role in the type of research the following groups choose to pursue by providing a sample research question that would likely be of interest for each group.

   A men vs. women

   B ethnic majority vs. ethnic minority

   C political conservative vs. political liberal

   D ages 18–25 vs. 35–45 vs. 55–65 vs. 75–85

Answer to Stretching Exercise

1 Exposure to thin body images causes body dissatisfaction, possibly due to a comparison of one's self to an ideal body image. [Dittmar, Halliwell, & Ive, 2006]

2 Following the terrorism attack on 9/11/2001, traffic fatalities increased, possibly due to an increased fear of air travel. [Gigerenzer, 2004]

3 Mimicking the behavior and posture of individuals causes them to help more, possibly due to increased feelings of empathy. [van Baaren, Holland, Kawakami, & van Knippenberg, 2004]

Answer to Challenge Question 1

A One way to test this hypothesis would be to have two groups of participants. One group would play violent video games, and a second group would watch violence on television. A second way to test the hypothesis would be to use the same group of participants and expose them to both types of violence at different points in time.

B To determine whether people behaved more aggressively following exposure to video games or television, you would need some measure of aggressive behavior. A potentially limitless number of measures exists, perhaps limited only by the ingenuity of the researcher. A good first step is to use measures that other investigators have used; that way, you can compare the results of your study with previous results. Measures of aggression include asking people to indicate how they would respond to hypothetical situations involving anger, or observing how they respond to experimenters (or others) following exposure to violence. In the latter case, the researcher would need a checklist or some other method for recording participants' violent (or nonviolent) behavior. Keep in mind that aggression can be defined in a number of ways, including physical behaviors, verbal behaviors, and even thoughts (but note the difficulty in measuring the latter).

C   It would be important to make sure that the two groups—television *vs.* video game—are similar in every way *except* for television or video game exposure. For example, suppose your research had two groups of participants: One group watched television and the other group played video games. Suppose, also, that your results indicated that participants who played video games were more aggressive than participants who watched television on your aggression measure.

One problem would occur if the video game participants were naturally more aggressive to begin with compared to the television participants. It would be impossible to know whether exposure to violence in your research or their natural differences in aggressiveness accounted for the observed difference in aggressiveness in your experiment. You would want to make sure, therefore, that the participants in each group are similar before the exposure to violence. Later in this text you will learn how to make the groups similar.

You would also want to make sure that other aspects of the participants' experiences are similar. For example, you would ensure that the length of time exposed to violence in each group is similar. In addition, you would try to make sure that the degree of violence in the television program is similar to the degree of violence in the video game. It would also be important that participants' experiences do not differ for a number of additional factors, such as whether other people are present and the time of day. In order to demonstrate that video game playing causes more (or less) aggression than television viewing, the most important point is that the only factor that should differ between the groups is the type of exposure.

CHAPTER TWO

The Scientific Method

CHAPTER OUTLINE

Scientific and Everyday Approaches to Knowledge

- The scientific method is empirical and requires systematic, controlled observation.
- Scientists gain the greatest control when they conduct an experiment; in an experiment, researchers manipulate independent variables to determine their effect on behavior.
- Dependent variables are measures of behavior used to assess the effects of independent variables.
- Scientific reporting is unbiased and objective; clear communication of constructs occurs when operational definitions are used.
- Scientific instruments are accurate and precise; physical and psychological measurement should be valid and reliable.
- A hypothesis is a tentative explanation for a phenomenon; testable hypotheses have clearly defined concepts (operational definitions), are not circular, and refer to concepts that can be observed.

For over 100 years the scientific method has been the basis for investigation in the discipline of psychology. The scientific method does not require a particular type of equipment, nor is it associated with a particular procedure or technique. As first described in Chapter 1, the scientific method refers to the ways in which scientists ask questions and the logic and methods used to gain answers. There are many fruitful approaches to gaining knowledge about ourselves and our world, such as philosophy, theology, literature, art, and other disciplines. The scientific method is distinguishable from the other approaches, but all of them share the same goal—seeking the truth. One of the best ways to understand the scientific method as a means of seeking truth is to distinguish it from our "everyday" ways of knowing. Just as a telescope and a microscope extend our everyday abilities to see, the scientific method extends our everyday ways of knowing.

Several major differences between scientific and our everyday ways of knowing are outlined in Table 2.1. Collectively, the characteristics listed under

TABLE 2.1   CHARACTERISTICS OF SCIENTIFIC AND NONSCIENTIFIC (EVERYDAY) APPROACHES TO KNOWLEDGE*

	Nonscientific (everyday)	Scientific
General approach:	Intuitive	Empirical
Attitude:	Uncritical, accepting	Critical, skeptical
Observation:	Casual, uncontrolled	Systematic, controlled
Reporting:	Biased, subjective	Unbiased, objective
Concepts:	Ambiguous, with surplus meanings	Clear definitions, operational specificity
Instruments:	Inaccurate, imprecise	Accurate, precise
Measurement:	Not valid or reliable	Valid and reliable
Hypotheses:	Untestable	Testable

*Based in part on distinctions suggested by Marx (1963).

"Scientific" define the scientific method. The distinctions made in Table 2.1 highlight differences between the ways of thinking that characterize a scientist's approach to knowledge and the informal and casual approach that often characterizes our everyday thinking. These distinctions are summarized in the following pages.

General Approach and Attitude

We described in Chapter 1 that in order to think like a researcher you must be skeptical. Psychological scientists are cautious about accepting claims about behavior and mental processes, and they critically evaluate the evidence before accepting any claims. In our everyday ways of thinking, however, we often accept evidence and claims with little or no evaluation of the evidence. In general, we make many of our everyday judgments using intuition. This usually means that we act on the basis of what "feels right" or what "seems reasonable." Although intuition can be valuable when we have little other information, intuition is not always correct. Consider, for example, what intuition might suggest regarding ratings of video games, movies, and television programs for violent and sexual content. Parents use ratings to judge appropriateness of media content for their children, and intuition might suggest that ratings are effective tools for preventing exposure to violent content. In fact, just the opposite may take place! Research indicates that these ratings can entice adolescent viewers to watch the violent and sexy programs—what Bushman and Cantor (2003) called a "forbidden-fruit effect." Thus, rather than limiting exposure to violent and sexual content, ratings may *increase* exposure because "ratings may serve as a convenient way to find such content" (p. 138).

When we rely on intuition to make judgments we often fail to recognize that our perceptions may be distorted by cognitive biases, or that we may not have considered all available evidence (Kahneman & Tversky, 1973; Tversky & Kahneman, 1974). Daniel Kahneman won the Nobel Prize in 2002 for his research on how cognitive biases influence people's economic choices. One type of cognitive bias, called illusory correlation, is our tendency to perceive a relationship between events when none exists. Susskind (2003) showed that children are susceptible to this bias when they make judgments about men's and women's behaviors. Children were shown many pictures of men and women performing stereotypical (e.g., a woman knitting), counterstereotypical (e.g., a man knitting), and neutral behaviors (e.g., a woman or a man reading a book), and then were asked to estimate how frequently they saw each picture. The results indicated that children overestimated the number of times they saw pictures displaying stereotypical behavior, showing an illusory correlation. Their expectations that men and women behave in stereotypical ways led the children to believe that these types of pictures were displayed more often than they were. One possible basis for the illusory correlation bias is that we are more likely to notice events that are consistent with our beliefs than events that contradict our beliefs.

The scientific approach to knowledge is empirical rather than intuitive. An empirical approach emphasizes *direct observation* and *experimentation* as a way of answering questions. This does not mean that intuition plays no role in science. Research at first may be guided by the scientist's intuition. Eventually, however, the scientist strives to be guided by the empirical evidence that direct observation and experimentation provide.

Observation

We can learn a great deal about behavior by simply observing the actions of others. However, everyday observations are not always made carefully or systematically. Most people do not attempt to control or eliminate factors that might influence the events they are observing. As a result, we often make incorrect conclusions based on our casual observations. Consider, for instance, the classic case of Clever Hans. Hans was a horse who was said by his owner, a German mathematics teacher, to have amazing talents. Hans could count, do simple addition and subtraction (even involving fractions), read German, answer simple questions ("What is the lady holding in her hands?"), give the date, and tell time (Watson, 1914/1967). Hans answered questions by tapping with his forefoot or by pointing with his nose at different alternatives shown to him. His owner considered Hans to be truly intelligent and denied using any tricks to guide his horse's behavior. And, in fact, Clever Hans was clever even when the questioner was someone other than his owner.

Newspapers carried accounts of Hans' performances, and hundreds of people came to view this amazing horse (Figure 2.1). In 1904 a scientific commission was established with the goal of discovering the basis for Hans' abilities. Much to his owner's dismay, the scientists observed that Hans was not clever in two situations. First, Hans did not know the answers to questions if the questioner also did not know the answers. Second, Hans was not very clever if he could not see his questioner. What did the scientists observe? They discovered that Hans was responding to the questioner's subtle movements. A slight bending forward by the questioner would start Hans tapping, and any movement upward or backward would cause Hans to stop tapping. The commission demonstrated that questioners were unintentionally cuing Hans as he tapped his forefoot or pointed. Thus, it seems that Hans was a better observer than many of the people who observed him!

This famous account of Clever Hans illustrates the fact that scientific observation (unlike casual observation) is systematic and controlled. Indeed, it has been suggested that **control** is the essential ingredient of science, distinguishing it from nonscientific procedures (Boring, 1954; Marx, 1963). In the case of Clever Hans, investigators exercised control by manipulating, one at a time, conditions such as whether the questioner knew the answer to the questions asked and whether Hans could see the questioner (see Figure 2.1). By using controlled observation, scientists gain a clearer picture of the factors that produce a phenomenon. The careful and systematic observation of Clever Hans

Key Concept

FIGURE 2.1   Top: Clever Hans performing before onlookers. Bottom: Hans being tested under more controlled conditions when Hans could not see the questioner.

Key Concept

is one example of the control used by scientists to gain understanding about behavior. Box 2.1 describes an example of how the story of Clever Hans from over 100 years ago informs scientists even today.

Scientists gain the greatest control when they conduct an experiment. In an **experiment,** scientists manipulate one or more factors and observe the effects of this manipulation on behavior. The factors that the researcher controls or

BOX 2.1

CAN DOGS DETECT CANCER? ONLY THE NOSE KNOWS

Research on methods to detect cancer took an interesting turn in 2004 when investigators reported the results of a study in the *British Medical Journal* demonstrating that dogs trained to smell urine samples successfully detected patients' bladder cancer at rates greater than chance (Willis et al., 2004). This research followed up many anecdotal reports in which dog owners described their pets as suddenly overprotective or obsessed with skin lesions prior to the owners' being diagnosed with cancer. Interest in the story was so great that similar demonstrations were conducted on television programs such as *60 Minutes*.

Skeptics, however, cited the example of Clever Hans to challenge the findings, arguing that the dogs relied on researchers' subtle cues in order to discriminate samples taken from cancer *vs.* control patients. Proponents of the study insisted that the researchers and observers were blind to the true status of the samples so could not be cuing the dogs. More recent studies suggest mixed results (e.g., Gordon et al., 2008; McCulloch et al., 2006). Researchers in this new area of cancer detection have applied for research funding to conduct more experiments. We now await the results of these rigorous studies to tell us whether dogs can, in fact, detect cancer.

Key Concept

manipulates in order to determine their effect on behavior are called the **independent variables.**[1] In the simplest of studies, the independent variable has two levels. These two levels often represent the presence and the absence of some treatment, respectively. The condition in which the treatment is present is commonly called the experimental condition; the condition in which the treatment is absent is called the control condition. For example, if we wanted to study the effect of drinking alcohol on the ability to process complex information quickly and accurately, the independent variable would be the presence or absence of alcohol in a drink. Participants in the experimental condition would

[1]Sometimes the levels of the independent variable are *selected* by a researcher rather than manipulated. An *individual differences variable* is a characteristic or trait that varies across individuals; for example, sex of the participants (male, female) is an individual differences variable. When researchers investigate whether behavior differs according to participants' sex, they select men and women and examine this factor as an individual differences variable. As we will see in Chapter 6, there are important differences between manipulated and selected independent variables.

receive alcohol, while participants in the control condition would receive the same drink without alcohol. After manipulating this independent variable, the researcher might ask participants to play a complicated video game to see whether they are able to process complex information.

The measures of behavior that are used to assess the effect (if any) of the independent variables are called **dependent variables.** In our example of a study that investigates the effects of alcohol on processing complex information, the researcher might measure the number of errors made by control and experimental participants when playing the difficult video game. The number of errors, then, would be the dependent variable.

Scientists seek to determine whether any differences in their observations of the dependent variable are caused by the different conditions of the independent variable. In our example, this would mean that a difference in errors when playing the video game is caused by the different independent variable conditions—whether alcohol is present or absent. To form this clear conclusion, however, scientists must use proper control techniques. Each chapter of this book will emphasize how researchers use control techniques to study behavior and the mind.

Reporting

Suppose you ask someone to tell you about a class you missed. You probably want an accurate report of what happened in class. Or perhaps you missed a party at which two of your friends had a heated argument, and you want to hear from someone what happened. As you might imagine, personal biases and subjective impressions often enter into everyday reports that we receive. When you ask others to describe an event, you are likely to receive details of the event (not always correct) along with their personal impressions.

When scientists report their findings, they seek to separate what they have observed from what they conclude or infer on the basis of these observations. For example, consider the photograph in Figure 2.2. How would you describe to someone what you see there? One way to describe this scene is to say that three people are running along a path. You might also describe this scene as three people racing each other. If you use this second description, you are reporting an inference drawn from what you have seen and not just reporting what you have observed. The description of three people running would be preferred in a scientific report.

This distinction between description and inference in reporting can be carried to extremes. For example, describing what is shown in Figure 2.2 as running could be considered an inference, the actual observation being that three people are moving their legs up and down and forward in rapid, long strides. Such a literal description also would not be appropriate. The point is that, in scientific reporting, observers must guard against a tendency to draw inferences too quickly. Further, events should be described in sufficient detail without including trivial and unnecessary minutiae. Proper methods for making observations and reporting them will be discussed in Chapter 4.

FIGURE 2.2   How would you describe this scene?

Scientific reporting seeks to be *unbiased* and *objective.* One way to determine whether a report is unbiased is to see if it can be verified by an independent observer. This is called "interobserver agreement" (see Chapter 4). Unfortunately, many biases are subtle and not always detected even in scientific reporting. Consider the fact that there is a species of fish in which the eggs are incubated in the mouth of the male parent until they hatch. The first scientist to observe the eggs disappear into their father's mouth could certainly be forgiven for assuming, momentarily, that he was eating them. That's simply what we expect organisms to do with their mouths! But the careful observer waits, watches for unexpected results, and takes nothing for granted.

Concepts

We use the term *concepts* to refer to things (both living and inanimate), to events (things in action), and to relationships among things or events, as well as to their characteristics (Marx, 1963). "Dog" is a concept, as is "barking," and so is "obedience." Concepts are the symbols by which we ordinarily communicate. Clear, unambiguous communication of ideas requires that we clearly define our concepts.

In everyday conversation we often get by without worrying too much about how we define a concept. Many words, for instance, are commonly used and

STRETCHING EXERCISE

In this exercise we ask you to respond to the questions that follow this brief description of a research report.

A relatively new area of psychology called "positive psychology" focuses on positive emotion, positive character traits, and positive institutions; the goal of research in positive psychology is to identify ways to foster well-being and happiness (Seligman, Steen, Park, & Peterson, 2005). One area of research focuses on *gratitude,* the positive emotion people feel when they are given something of value by another person (Bartlett & DeSteno, 2006). Some research suggests that people who feel gratitude are more likely to act prosocially— that is, to behave in ways that benefit others.

Bartlett and DeSteno (2006) tested the relationship between gratitude and participants' likelihood of helping another person in an experiment involving *confederates* (people working with the experimenter to create an experimental situation; see Chapter 4). Each participant first teamed up with a confederate to complete a long, boring task involving hand-eye coordination. Afterward, for one third of the participants their computer screen was designed to go blank and they were instructed they would need to complete the task again. The confederate, however, induced an emotion of gratitude by fixing the problem, saving the participant from having to redo the task. The situation differed for the other participants. After finishing the task, another one third of the participants watched an amusing video with the confederate (positive emotion) and the final one third of the participants had a brief verbal exchange with the confederate (neutral emotion). After completing some questionnaires, the confederate asked each participant to fill out a lengthy survey for one of her classes as a favor. Bartlett and DeSteno found that participants in the gratitude condition spent more time working on the survey ($M = 20.94$ minutes) than participants in the positive emotion ($M = 12.11$ min) and neutral emotion ($M = 14.49$ min) conditions.

1 Identify the independent variable (including its levels) and the dependent variable in this study.
2 How could the researchers determine that it was *gratitude*, not simply feeling positive emotions, that increased participants' willingness to help the confederate?

apparently understood even though neither party in the conversation knows exactly what the words mean. That is, people frequently communicate with one another without being fully aware of what they are talking about! This may sound ridiculous but, to illustrate our point, try the following.

Ask a few people whether they believe that intelligence is mostly inherited or mostly learned. You might try arguing a point of view opposite to theirs just for the fun of it. After discussing the roots of intelligence, ask them what they mean by "intelligence." You will probably find that most people have a difficult time defining this concept, even after debating its origins, and people will provide different definitions. That is, "intelligence" means one thing to one person and something else to another. Clearly, in order to attempt to answer the question of whether intelligence is mostly inherited or mostly learned, we need to have an exact definition that all parties involved can accept.

The study of "concepts" is so important in psychological science that researchers refer to concepts by a special name: constructs. A **construct** is a concept or idea; examples of psychological constructs include intelligence, depression, aggression, and memory. One way in which a scientist gives meaning to a construct is by defining it operationally. An **operational definition** explains a concept solely in terms of the observable procedures used to produce

Key Concepts

and measure it. Intelligence, for instance, can be defined operationally by using a paper-and-pencil test emphasizing understanding of logical relationships, short-term memory, and familiarity with the meaning of words. Some may not like this operational definition of intelligence, but once a particular test has been identified, there can at least be no argument about what intelligence means *according to this definition.* Operational definitions facilitate communication, at least among those who know how and why they are used.

Although exact meaning is conveyed via operational definitions, this approach to communicating about constructs has not escaped criticism. One problem has been alluded to already. That is, if we don't like one operational definition of intelligence, there is nothing to prevent us from giving intelligence another operational definition. Does this mean that there are as many kinds of intelligence as there are operational definitions? The answer, unfortunately, is that we don't really know. To determine whether a different procedure or test yields a new definition of intelligence, we would have to seek additional evidence. For example, do people who score high on one test also score high on the second test? If they do, the new test may be measuring the same construct as the old one.

Another criticism of using operational definitions is that the definitions are not always meaningful. This is particularly relevant in cross-cultural research where, for example, a paper-and-pencil test of intelligence may tap into knowledge that is specific to a particular cultural context. How do we decide whether a construct has been meaningfully defined? Once again, the solution is to appeal to other forms of evidence. How does performance on one test compare to performance on other tasks that are commonly accepted as measures of intelligence? Scientists are generally aware of the limitations of operational definitions; however, a major strength of using operational definitions is that they help to clarify communication among scientists about their constructs. This strength is assumed to outweigh the limitations.

Instruments

You depend on instruments to measure events more than you probably realize. For example, you rely on the speedometer in a car and the clock in your bedroom, and you can appreciate the problems that arise when these instruments are inaccurate. *Accuracy* refers to the difference between what an instrument says is true and what is known to be true. A clock that is consistently 5 minutes slow is not very accurate. Inaccurate clocks can make us late, and inaccurate speedometers can earn us traffic tickets. The accuracy of an instrument is determined by *calibrating* it, or checking it with another instrument known to be true.

Measurements can be made at varying levels of *precision.* A measure of time in tenths of a second is not as precise as one that is in hundredths of a second. One instrument that yields imprecise measures is the gas gauge in most older cars. Although reasonably accurate, gas gauges do not give precise readings. Most of us have wished at one time or another that the gas gauge would permit us to determine whether we had that extra half gallon of gas that would get us to the next service station.

We also need instruments to measure behavior. You can be assured that the precision, and even the accuracy, of instruments used in psychology have

FIGURE 2.3 Scientific instruments used in psychology have improved dramatically in their precision and accuracy.

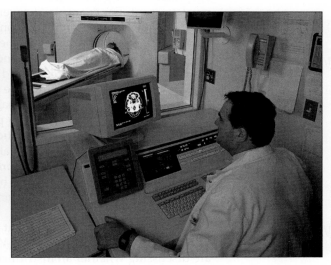

improved significantly since 1879, the founding of the first psychology laboratory. Today, many sophisticated instruments are used in contemporary psychology (Figure 2.3). To perform a psychophysiology experiment (e.g., when assessing a person's arousal level) requires instruments that give accurate measures of such internal states as heart rate and blood pressure. Tests of anxiety sometimes employ instruments to measure galvanic skin response (GSR). Other behavioral instruments are of the paper-and-pencil variety. Questionnaires and tests are popular instruments used by psychologists to measure behavior. So, too, are the rating scales used by human observers. For instance, rating aggression in children on a 7-point scale ranging from not at all aggressive (1) to very aggressive (7) can yield relatively accurate (although perhaps not precise) measures of aggression. It is the responsibility of the behavioral scientist to use instruments that are as accurate and as precise as possible.

Measurement

Scientists use two types of measurements to record the careful and controlled observations that characterize the scientific method. One type of scientific measurement, *physical measurement,* involves dimensions for which there is an agreed-upon standard and an instrument for doing the measuring. For example, length is a dimension that can be scaled with physical measurement, and there are agreed-upon standards for units of length (e.g., inches, meters). Similarly, units of weight and time represent physical measurement.

In most psychological research, however, the measurements do not involve physical dimensions. Rulers do not exist for measuring psychological constructs such as beauty, aggression, or intelligence. These dimensions require a second type of measurement—*psychological measurement*. In a sense, the human observer is the instrument for psychological measurement. More specifically, agreement among a number of observers provides the basis for psychological measurement. For example, if several independent observers agree that a certain action warrants a rating of 3 on a 7-point rating scale of aggression, that is a psychological measurement of the aggressiveness of the action.

Key Concept }

Measurements must be valid and reliable. In general, **validity** refers to the "truthfulness" of a measure. A valid measure of a construct is one that measures what it claims to measure. Suppose a researcher defines intelligence in terms of how long a person can balance a ball on his or her nose. According to the principle of "operationalism," this is a perfectly permissible operational definition. However, most of us would question whether such a balancing act is really a valid measure of intelligence. The validity of a measure is supported when people do as well on it as on other tasks presumed to measure the same construct. For example, if time spent balancing a ball is a valid measure of intelligence, then a person who does well on the balancing task should also do well on other accepted measures of intelligence.

Key Concept }

The **reliability** of a measurement is indicated by its consistency. Several kinds of reliability can be distinguished. When we speak of instrument reliability, we are discussing whether an instrument works consistently. A car that sometimes starts and sometimes doesn't is not very reliable. Observations made by two or more independent observers are said to be reliable if they show agreement—that is, if the observations are consistent from one observer to another. For example, when psychologists asked college students to rate the "happiness" of medal winners at the 1992 Summer Olympics in Barcelona, Spain, they found that rater agreement was very high (Medvec, Madey, & Gilovich, 1995). They also found, somewhat counterintuitively, that bronze (third place) medal winners were perceived as happier than silver (second place) medal winners, a finding that was explained by a theory of counterfactual thinking. Apparently, people are happier just making it (to the medal stand) than they are just missing it (i.e., missing a gold medal).

The validity and reliability of measurements are central issues in psychological research. You will encounter various ways in which researchers determine reliability and validity as we introduce you to different research methods.

Hypotheses

A hypothesis is a tentative explanation for something. Hypotheses frequently attempt to answer the questions "How?" and "Why?" At one level, a hypothesis may simply suggest how particular variables are related. For example, an emerging area of psychological research asks, Why do people purchase "green" products, especially when these products are often more expensive and may be less luxurious or effective than conventional, nongreen products? An example is the successful Toyota Prius, which is as expensive as cars that are more comfortable and perform better. One hypothesis for green purchases relates to altruism, the tendency toward selfless acts that benefit others (Griskevicius, Tybur, & Van den Bergh, 2010). Purchasing green products can be seen as altruistic because the environment and society benefit, with a greater cost to the selfless purchaser.

Recent theorists describe "competitive altruism," in which individuals are altruistic because being seen as prosocial and selfless enhances one's reputation and status in society (Griskevicius et al., 2010). Thus, altruistic acts may function as a "costly signal" of one's higher status—that one has the time, energy, wealth, and other resources to behave altruistically. Considered in this light, purchasing green products may signal the purchaser's higher social status. Griskevicius et al. hypothesized that activating (i.e., making prominent) people's desire for status should lead them to choose green products over more luxurious nongreen products.

Griskevicius et al. (2010) conducted three experiments to test their hypothesis. In each, they manipulated college student participants' motivation for status using two conditions: status and control. Status motives were activated by having participants in this condition read a short story about graduating from college, searching for a job, and then working for a desirable company with opportunities for promotion. In the control condition, participants read a story about searching for a lost concert ticket, finding it, and then attending the concert. After reading the story, participants believed they were completing a second, unrelated study about consumer preferences. They identified items they would likely purchase (e.g., car, dishwasher, backpack); in each case, a green product was paired with a nongreen, more luxurious item. Griskevicius et al. found that compared to the control condition, activating status motives increased the likelihood that participants would choose green products over the nongreen products (Experiment 1). Furthermore, the preference for green products occurred only when status-motivated participants imagined shopping in public, but not in private (online) situations (Experiment 2), and when green products cost more than nongreen products (Experiment 3).

At a theoretical level, a hypothesis may offer a reason (the "why") for the way particular variables are related. Griskevicius and his colleagues found a relationship between two variables: status motives and the likelihood of purchasing green products. Based on theories of competitive altruism, these variables are related because people gain social status when they are seen to behave altruistically, such as when purchasing green products. One practical implication for this finding is that sales of green products may be enhanced by linking these products with high status (e.g., celebrity endorsements), rather than by emphasizing the plight of the environment or by making green products less expensive.

Nearly everyone has proposed hypotheses to explain some human behavior at one time or another. Why do people commit apparently senseless acts of violence? What causes people to start smoking cigarettes? Why are some students academically more successful than others? One characteristic that distinguishes casual, everyday hypotheses from scientific hypotheses is *testability*. If a hypothesis cannot be tested, it is not useful to science (Marx, 1963). Three types of hypotheses fail to pass the "testability test." A hypothesis is not testable when its constructs are not adequately defined, when the hypothesis is circular, or when the hypothesis appeals to ideas not recognized by science.

Hypotheses are not testable if the concepts to which they refer are not adequately defined or measured. For example, to say that a would-be assassin shot a prominent figure or celebrity because the assassin is mentally disturbed is not a testable hypothesis unless we can agree on a definition of "mentally disturbed." Unfortunately, psychologists and psychiatrists cannot always agree on what terms such as "mentally disturbed" mean because an accepted operational definition is often not available for these concepts. You may have learned in a psychology course that many of Freud's hypotheses are not testable. This is because there are no clear operational definitions and measures for key constructs in Freud's theories, such as *id, ego,* and *superego.*

Hypotheses are also untestable if they are circular. A circular hypothesis occurs when an event itself is used as the explanation of the event (Kimble, 1989, p. 495). As an illustration, consider the statement that an "eight-year-old boy is distractable in school and having trouble reading because he has an attention deficit disorder." An attention deficit disorder is defined by the inability to pay attention. Thus, the statement simply says that the boy doesn't pay attention because he doesn't pay attention—that's a circular hypothesis.

A hypothesis also may be untestable if it appeals to ideas or forces that are not recognized by science. Science deals with the observable, the demonstrable, the empirical. To suggest that people who commit horrendous acts of violence are controlled by the Devil is not testable because it invokes a principle (the Devil) that is not in the province of science. Such hypotheses might be of value to philosophers or theologians, but not to the scientist.

GOALS OF THE SCIENTIFIC METHOD

- The scientific method is intended to meet four goals: description, prediction, explanation, and application.

In the first part of this chapter, we examined the ways in which our everyday ways of thinking differ from the scientific method. In general, the scientific method is characterized by an empirical approach, systematic and controlled observation, unbiased and objective reporting, clear operational definitions of constructs, accurate and precise instruments, valid and reliable measures, and testable hypotheses. In this next section, we examine goals of the scientific method. Psychologists use the scientific method to meet four research goals: description, prediction, explanation, and application (see Table 2.2).

Description

- Psychologists seek to describe events and relationships between variables; most often, researchers use the nomothetic approach and quantitative analysis.

Description refers to the procedures researchers use to define, classify, catalogue, or categorize events and their relationships. Clinical research, for instance, provides practitioners with criteria for classifying mental disorders. Many of these are found in the American Psychiatric Association's *Diagnostic and Statistical Manual of Mental Disorders* (4th ed., Text Revision, 2000), also known as DSM-IV-TR (see Figure 2.4). Consider, as one example, the criteria used to define the disorder labeled dissociative fugue (formerly psychogenic fugue).

TABLE 2.2   FOUR GOALS OF PSYCHOLOGICAL RESEARCH

Goal	What Is Accomplished	Example
Description	Researchers define, classify, catalogue, or categorize events and relationships to describe mental processes and behavior.	Psychologists describe symptoms of helplessness in depression, such as failure to initiate activities and pessimism regarding the future.
Prediction	When researchers identify correlations among variables they are able to predict mental processes and behavior.	As level of depression increases, individuals exhibit more symptoms of helplessness.
Explanation	Researchers understand a phenomenon when they can identify the cause(s).	Participants exposed to unsolvable problems become more pessimistic and less willing to do new tasks (i.e., become helpless) than participants who are asked to do solvable problems.
Application	Psychologists apply their knowledge and research methods to change people's lives for the better.	Treatment that encourages depressed individuals to attempt tasks that can be mastered or easily achieved decreases depressives' helplessness and pessimism.

Based on Table 1.2, Zechmeister, Zechmeister, & Shaughnessy, 2001, p. 12.

Diagnostic Criteria for Dissociative Fugue

A The predominant disturbance is sudden, unexpected travel away from home or one's customary place of work, with inability to recall one's past.

B Confusion about personal identity or assumption of a new identity (partial or complete).

C The disturbance does not occur exclusively during the course of Dissociative Identity Disorder and is not due to the direct physiological effects of a substance (e.g., a drug of abuse, medication) or a general medical condition (e.g., temporal lobe epilepsy).

D The symptoms cause clinically significant stress or impairment in social, occupational, or other important areas of functioning. (DSM-IV-TR, 2000, p. 526)

The diagnostic criteria used to define dissociative fugue provide an operational definition for this disorder. Dissociative fugues are relatively rare; thus, we typically learn about these kinds of disorders based on descriptions of individuals exhibiting them using "case studies." Researchers also seek to provide clinicians with descriptions of the prevalence of a mental disorder as well as the relationship between the presence of various symptoms and other variables such as gender and age. According to the DSM-IV-TR (2000), for instance, dissociative fugue is seen primarily in adults, and although it is relatively rare, it is more frequent "during times of extremely stressful events such as wartime or natural disaster" (p. 524).

Science in general and psychology in particular develop descriptions of phenomena using the *nomothetic approach*. Using the nomothetic approach,

FIGURE 2.4   Clinicians classify mental disorders according to the criteria found in the American Psychiatric Association's *Diagnostic and Statistical Manual of Mental Disorders.*

psychologists try to establish broad generalizations and general laws that apply to a diverse population. To accomplish this goal, psychological studies most often involve large numbers of participants. Researchers seek to describe the "average," or typical, performance of a group. This average may or may not describe the performance of any one individual in the group.

For example, Levine (1990) described the "pace of life" in various cultures and countries of the world by noting the accuracy of outdoor bank clocks and by timing the walking speed of pedestrians over a distance of 100 feet. The results of this study are shown in Figure 2.5. The citizens of Japan exhibited, overall, the fastest pace of life with U.S. citizens second. The citizens of Indonesia were the slowest. Not all citizens of Japan or the United States, however, are on the fast track. In fact, Levine (1990) and his colleagues found wide differences in the pace of life among various cities within the United States depending on the region of the country. Cities in the Northeast (e.g., Boston, New York) had a faster tempo than did cities on the West Coast (e.g., Sacramento, Los Angeles). Of course, there will be individual variations within cities as well. Not all citizens of Los Angeles are going to be slow-paced, nor are all New Yorkers going to be fast-paced. Nevertheless, the Japanese move *in general* at a faster pace than do Indonesians, and Americans on the West Coast exhibit, *on the average*, a slower pace of life than do residents of the Northeast.

Researchers who use the nomothetic approach appreciate that there are important differences among individuals; they seek, however, to emphasize the similarities rather than the differences. For example, a person's individuality

FIGURE 2.5   Measures of accuracy of a country's bank clocks, pedestrian walking speed, and the speed of postal clerks performing a routine task served to describe the pace of life in a country. In the graph a longer bar represents greater accuracy of clocks or greater speed of walking and performing a task. (From Levine, 1990.)

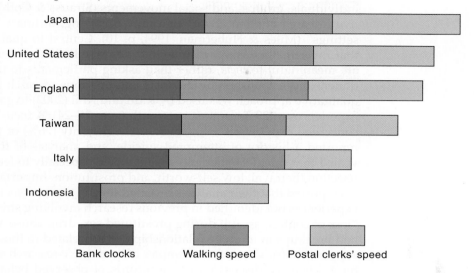

is not threatened by our knowledge that that person's heart, like the hearts of other human beings, is located in the upper left chest cavity. Similarly, we do not deny a person's individuality when we state that that person's behavior is influenced by patterns of reinforcement (e.g., rewards, punishments). Researchers merely seek to describe what organisms are like in general on the basis of the average performance of a group of different organisms.

Some psychologists, notably Gordon Allport (1961), argue that the nomothetic approach is inadequate—unique individuals cannot be described by an average value. Researchers who use the *idiographic approach* study the individual rather than groups. These researchers believe that although individuals behave in ways that conform to general laws or principles, the uniqueness of individuals must also be described. A major form of idiographic research is the case study method, which we will describe in Chapter 9.

Depending on their research question, researchers decide whether to describe groups of individuals or one individual's behavior. Although many researchers do mainly one or the other kind of research, others may do both. A clinical psychologist, for instance, may decide to pursue mainly idiographic investigations of a few clients in therapy but consider nomothetic issues when attempting to answer research questions with groups of college students. Another decision that the researcher must make is whether to do quantitative or qualitative research. *Quantitative research* refers to studies in which the findings are mainly the product of statistical summary and analysis. *Qualitative research* produces verbal summaries of research findings with few statistical summaries or analysis. Just as psychological research is more frequently nomothetic than idiographic, it is also more typically quantitative than qualitative.

Qualitative research is used extensively by sociologists and anthropologists (see, for example, Seale, 1999). The data of qualitative research are most commonly obtained from interviews and observations and can be used to describe individuals, groups, and social movements (Strauss & Corbin, 1990). Qualitative research is often about "naturally occurring, ordinary events in natural settings" (Miles & Huberman, 1994, p. 10). Central to qualitative research is that investigators ask participants to describe their experiences in ways that are meaningful to *them,* rather than asking participants to use categories and dimensions established by theorists and previous research (Kidd, 2002). This qualitative approach was used by Kidd and Kral (2002) to gain insight into the experiences of 29 Toronto street youth (ages 17–24). A focus of the interviews concerned experiences with suicide. The majority (76%) of those interviewed reported a history of attempted suicide, and analysis of their narratives revealed that suicidal experiences were linked especially to feelings of isolation, rejection/betrayal, low self-worth, and prostitution. Importantly, the researchers reported that their analyses revealed several topics associated with suicidal experiences not identified in previous research involving street youth. Namely, "loss of control, assault during prostituted sex, drug abuse as a 'slow suicide,' and breakups in intimate relationships" were related to these youths' suicidal experiences (p. 411). Other examples of qualitative research are found in Chapter 4 when we discuss narrative records of observed behavior; case studies described in Chapter 9 also are a form of qualitative research.

Prediction

- Correlational relationships allow psychologists to predict behavior or events, but do not allow psychologists to infer what causes these relationships.

Description of events and their relationships often provides a basis for *prediction,* the second goal of the scientific method. Many important questions in psychology call for predictions. For example: Does the early loss of a parent make a child especially vulnerable to depression? Are children who are overly aggressive likely to have emotional problems as adults? Do stressful life events lead to increased physical illness? Research findings suggest an affirmative answer to all of these questions. This information not only adds valuable knowledge to the discipline of psychology but also is helpful in both the treatment and prevention of emotional disorders.

An important occupation of many psychologists is the prediction of later performance (e.g., on the job, in school, or in specific vocations) on the basis of earlier performance on various standardized tests. For instance, scores on the Graduate Record Examination (GRE), as well as undergraduate grade point average (GPA), can be used to predict how well a student will do in graduate school. Sternberg and Williams (1997) did find that GRE scores predicted fairly well the first-year grades of graduate students at their institution. They also found, however, that the GRE did not predict other, important performance criteria such as advisors' ratings of a student's creativity, ability to teach, and ability to do research. Not surprisingly, these researchers have sparked a debate by questioning the predictive validity (i.e., accuracy of prediction) of the GRE, which is widely regarded as a predictor of students' later professional development (see, for example, "Comment" section of *American Psychologist*, 1998, 53, 566–577).

When scores on one variable can be used to predict scores on a second variable, we say that the two variables are correlated. A **correlation** exists when two different measures of the same people, events, or things vary together—that is, when particular scores on one variable tend to be associated with particular scores on another variable. When this occurs, the scores are said to "covary." For example, stress and illness are known to be correlated; the more stressful life events people experience, the more likely they are to experience physical illnesses.

Consider a measure with which you likely have had some experience, namely, teacher/course evaluations in classes you have taken. College students are commonly asked to evaluate their instructors and the course material toward the end of a course. By the time a course is over, you probably have formed many impressions of a teacher (e.g., whether the instructor is supportive, enthusiastic, likable). After all, you have just spent as many as 12 or 14 weeks (perhaps more than 30 hours) in this instructor's classroom. Ambady and Rosenthal (1993) asked how well teacher evaluations by students *not* enrolled in the class would correlate with end-of-the-semester evaluations made by students *in* the class. They showed video clips (without sound) of teachers to a group of female undergraduates. But, and here is the interesting part, they showed the video clips for only 30 seconds, 10 seconds, or just 6 seconds (across several studies). The researchers found that teacher evaluations based on these "thin slices of nonverbal behavior" correlated well with end-of-the-semester teacher evaluations made by students who were enrolled in the class. That is, more positive course evaluations of teachers were associated with higher ratings for their videotaped behavior; similarly, more negative course evaluations were associated with lower ratings of videotaped behavior. Thus, we can predict course evaluations of teachers' affective behavior (e.g., likableness) based on ratings of briefly depicted videotaped behavior. These results indicate that people (in this case, teachers) reveal much about themselves when their nonverbal behavior is seen only briefly, and also that we (as observers) can make relatively accurate judgments of affective behavior quite quickly. Ambady and Rosenthal's findings, of course, do not mean that all the information in teaching evaluations can be captured by this method as they focused only on judgments of affective behavior (e.g., likableness).

It is important to point out that successful prediction doesn't always depend on knowing *why* a relationship exists between two variables. Consider the report that some people rely on observing animal behavior to help them predict earthquakes. Certain animals apparently behave in an unusual manner just before an earthquake. The dog that barks and runs in circles and the snake seen fleeing its hole, therefore, may be reliable predictors of earthquakes. If so, they could be used to warn people of forthcoming disasters. We might even imagine that in areas where earthquakes are likely, residents would be asked to keep certain animals under observation (as miners once kept canaries) to warn them of conditions of which they are as yet unaware. This would not require that we understand *why* certain animals behave strangely before an earthquake, or even why earthquakes occur. Furthermore, we would never argue that an animal's strange behavior caused an earthquake.

Interestingly, Levine (1990) showed that measures of the pace of a city can be used to predict death rates from heart disease. However, we can only speculate about why these measures are related. One possible explanation for this correlation suggested by the researchers is that people living in time-urgent environments engage in unhealthy behaviors, for example, cigarette smoking and poor eating habits, which increase their risk of heart disease (Levine, 1990). Ambady and Rosenthal (1993) proposed an explanation for their correlation between teacher evaluations by students not enrolled in the class and by students enrolled in the class. They suggested that people are "attuned" to picking up information about a person's affect quickly because this information is important (adaptive) in real-life decision making. Without additional information, however, the proposed explanations for these two phenomena are speculative.

Explanation

- Psychologists understand the cause of a phenomenon when the three conditions for causal inference are met: covariation, time-order relationship, and elimination of plausible alternative causes.
- The experimental method, in which researchers manipulate independent variables to determine their effect on dependent variables, establishes time order and allows a clearer determination of covariation.
- Plausible alternative causes for a relationship are eliminated if there are no confoundings in a study.
- Researchers seek to generalize a study's findings to describe different populations, settings, and conditions.

Although description and prediction are important goals in science, they are only the first steps in our ability to explain and understand a phenomenon. Explanation is the third goal of the scientific method. We understand and can explain a phenomenon when we can identify its causes. Researchers typically conduct *experiments* to identify the causes of a phenomenon. Experimental research differs from descriptive and predictive (correlational) research because of the high degree of control scientists seek in experiments. Recall that when researchers control a situation, they manipulate independent variables one at a time to determine their effect on the dependent variable—the phenomenon of interest. By conducting controlled experiments, psychologists infer what causes a phenomenon; they make a causal inference. Because experiments are very important to psychologists' efforts to form causal inferences, we have dedicated Chapters 6, 7, and 8 to a detailed discussion of the experimental method.

Key Concept }

Scientists set three important conditions for making a **causal inference:** *covariation of events, a time-order relationship,* and *the elimination of plausible alternative causes.* A simple illustration will help you to understand these three conditions. Suppose you hit your head on a door and experience a headache; presumably you would *infer* that hitting your head *caused* the headache. The first condition for causal inference is covariation of events. If one event is the cause of another, the two events must vary together; that is, when one changes, the other must also change. In our illustration, the event of changing your head position from upright to hitting against the door must covary with experience of no headache to the experience of a headache.

The second condition for a causal inference is a *time-order relationship* (also known as contingency). The presumed cause (hitting your head) must occur before the presumed effect (headache). If the headache began before you hit your head, you wouldn't infer that hitting your head caused the headache. In other words, the headache was contingent on you hitting your head first. Finally, causal explanations are accepted only when other possible causes of the effect have been ruled out—when *plausible alternative causes have been eliminated*. In our illustration, this means that to make the causal inference that hitting your head caused the headache, you would have to consider and rule out other possible causes of your headache (such as reading a difficult textbook).

Unfortunately, people have a tendency to conclude that all three conditions for a causal inference have been met when really only the first condition is satisfied. For example, it has been suggested that parents who use stern discipline and physical punishment are more likely to have aggressive children than are parents who are less stern and use other forms of discipline. Parental discipline and children's aggressiveness obviously covary. Moreover, the fact that we assume parents influence how their children behave might lead us to think that the time-order condition has been met—parents use physical discipline and children's aggressiveness results. It is also the case, however, that infants vary in how active and aggressive they are and that the infant's behavior has a strong influence on the parents' responses in trying to exercise control. In other words, some children may be naturally aggressive and require stern discipline rather than stern discipline producing aggressive children. Therefore, the direction of the causal relationship may be opposite to what we thought at first.

It is important to recognize, however, that the causes of events cannot be identified unless covariation has been demonstrated. The first objective of the scientific method, description, can be met by describing events under a single set of circumstances. The goal of understanding, however, requires more than this. For example, suppose a teacher wished to demonstrate that so-called "active learning strategies" (e.g., debates, group presentations) help students learn. She could teach students using this approach and then describe the performance of the students who received instruction in this particular way. But, at this point, what would she know? Perhaps another group of students taught using a different approach might learn the same amount. Before the teacher could claim that active learning stategies *caused* the performance she observed, she would have to compare this method with some other reasonable approach. That is, she would look for a difference in learning between the group using active learning strategies and a group not using this method. Such a finding would show that teaching strategy and performance covary. When a controlled experiment is done, a bonus comes along when the independent and dependent variables covary. The time-order condition for a causal inference is met because the researcher manipulates the independent variable (e.g., teaching method) and *subsequently* measures the differences between conditions on the dependent variable (e.g., a measure of student learning).

By far the most challenging condition researchers must meet in order to make a causal inference is eliminating other plausible alternative causes. Consider a study in which the effect of two different teaching approaches (active and passive) is assessed. Suppose the researcher assigns students to teaching conditions by having all men in one group and all women in the other. If this were done, any difference between the two groups could be due either to the teaching method *or* to the gender of the students. Thus, the researcher would not be able to determine whether the difference in performance between the two groups was due to the independent variable she tested (active or passive learning) or to the alternative explanation of students' gender. Said more formally, the independent variable of teaching method would be "confounded" with the independent variable of gender. **Confounding** occurs when two potentially effective independent variables are allowed to covary simultaneously. When research is confounded, it is impossible to determine what variable is responsible for any obtained difference in performance.

Key Concept

Researchers seek to explain the causes of phenomena by conducting experiments. However, even when a carefully controlled experiment allows the researcher to form a causal inference, additional questions remain. One important question concerns the extent to which the findings of the experiment apply only to the people who participated in the experiment. Researchers often seek to generalize their findings to describe people who did not participate in the experiment.

Many of the participants in psychology research are introductory psychology students in colleges and universities. Are psychologists developing principles that apply only to college freshmen and sophomores? Similarly, laboratory research is often conducted under more controlled conditions than are found in natural settings. Thus, an important task of the scientist is to determine whether laboratory findings generalize to the "real world." Some people automatically assume that laboratory research is useless or irrelevant to real-world concerns. However, as we explore research methods throughout this text, we will see that these views about the relationship between laboratory science and the real world are not helpful or satisfying. Instead, psychologists recognize the importance of both: Findings from laboratory experiments help to explain phenomena, and this knowledge is applied to real-world problems in research and interventions.

Application

- In applied research, psychologists apply their knowledge and research methods to improve people's lives.
- Psychologists conduct basic research to gain knowledge about behavior and mental processes and to test theories.

The fourth goal of research in psychology is application. Although psychologists are interested in describing, predicting, and explaining behavior and mental processes, this knowledge doesn't exist in a vacuum. Instead, this knowledge exists in a world in which people suffer from mental disorders and are victims of violence and aggression, and in which stereotypes and prejudices impact how people live and function in society (to name but a few problems we face). The list of problems in our world may at times seem endless, but this shouldn't discourage us. The breadth of psychologists' research questions and findings provides many ways for researchers to help address important aspects of our lives and to create change in individuals' lives.

Key Concept }

Research on creating change is often called "applied research." In **applied research,** psychologists conduct research in order to change people's lives for the better. For people suffering from mental disorders, this change may occur through research on therapeutic techniques. However, applied psychologists are involved with many different types of interventions, including those aimed at improving the lives of students in schools, employees at work, and individuals in the community. On the other hand, researchers who conduct **basic research** seek primarily to understand behavior and mental processes. People often describe basic research as "seeking knowledge for its own sake." Basic research is typically carried out in a laboratory setting with the goal of testing a theory about a phenomenon.

Key Concept }

Throughout the history of psychology, tension has existed between basic research and applied research. Within the past several decades, however, researchers have increased their focus on important, creative applications of psychological principles for improving human life (Zimbardo, 2004). In fact, the application of well-known principles of psychology—discovered through basic research—is now so pervasive that people tend to forget the years of basic research in laboratories that preceded what we now understand to be commonplace. For example, the use of positive reinforcement techniques, psychological testing and therapies, and self-help practices has become part of everyday life. In addition, the application of psychological principles is becoming increasingly important in education, health, and criminal justice settings. To see some of the many applications of psychology in our everyday life, check out this website: www.psychologymatters.org.

One important factor ties together basic and applied research: the use of theories to guide research and application in the real world. In the next section we describe how psychological theories are developed.

SCIENTIFIC THEORY CONSTRUCTION AND TESTING

- Theories are proposed explanations for the causes of phenomena, and they vary in scope and level of explanation.
- A scientific theory is a logically organized set of propositions that defines events, describes relationships among events, and explains the occurrence of events.
- Intervening variables are concepts used in theories to explain why independent and dependent variables are related.
- Successful scientific theories organize empirical knowledge, guide research by offering testable hypotheses, and survive rigorous testing.
- Researchers evaluate theories by judging the theory's internal consistency, observing whether hypothesized outcomes occur when the theory is tested, and noting whether the theory makes precise predictions based on parsimonious explanations.

Theories are "ideas" about how nature works. Psychologists propose theories about the nature of behavior and mental processes, as well as about the reasons people and animals behave and think the way they do. A psychological theory can be developed using different levels of explanation; for example, the theory can be developed on either a physiological or a conceptual level (see Anderson, 1990; Simon, 1992). A physiologically based theory of schizophrenia would propose biological causes such as specific genetic carriers. A theory developed on a conceptual level would more likely propose psychological causes such as patterns of emotional conflict or stress. It would also be possible for a theory of schizophrenia to include both biological and psychological causes.

Theories often differ in their scope—the range of phenomena they seek to explain. Some theories attempt to explain specific phenomena. For example, Brown and Kulik's (1977) theory attempted to explain the phenomenon of "flashbulb memory," in which people remember very specific personal circumstances surrounding particularly surprising and emotional events, such as the horrific events of September 11, 2001. Other theories have much broader scope as they try to describe and explain more complex phenomena such as love (Sternberg, 1986) or human cognition (Anderson, 1990, 1993; Anderson & Milson, 1989). In general, the greater the scope of a theory, the more complex it is likely to be. Most theories in contemporary psychology tend to be relatively modest in scope, attempting to account only for a limited range of phenomena.

Scientists develop theories from a mixture of intuition, personal observation, and known facts and ideas. The famous philosopher of science Karl Popper (1976) suggested that truly creative theories spring from a combination of intense interest in a problem and critical imagination—the ability to think critically and "outside the box." Researchers begin constructing a theory by considering what is known about a problem or research question and also looking for errors or what is missing. The approach is similar to the one we described in Chapter 1 for getting started in research and forming hypotheses.

Key Concept }   Although theories differ in their level of explanation and scope, amid these differences there are commonalities that define all theories (see Table 2.3). We can offer the following formal definition of a scientific **theory:** *a logically organized*

TABLE 2.3   CHARACTERISTICS OF THEORIES

Definition	A theory is a logically organized set of propositions that serves to define events, describe relationships among these events, and explain the occurrence of these events.
Scope	Theories differ in the breadth of events they seek to explain, from very specific phenomena (e.g., flashbulb memory) to complex phenomena (e.g., love).
Functions	A theory organizes empirical knowledge from previous studies and guides future research by suggesting testable hypotheses.
Important Features	Intervening variables provide an explanatory link between variables. Good theories are: • *Logical.* They make sense and predictions can be logically deduced. • *Precise.* Predictions about behavior are specific rather than general. • *Parsimonious.* The simplest explanation for a phenomenon is best.

Based on Table 2.3, Zechmeister, Zechmeister, & Shaughnessy, 2001, p. 29.

set of propositions (claims, statements, assertions) that serves to define events (concepts),
describe relationships among these events, and explain the occurrence of these events.
For example, a theory of flashbulb memory must state exactly what a flashbulb
memory is and how a flashbulb memory differs from typical memories. The
theory would include descriptions of relationships, such as the relationship
between degree of emotional involvement and amount remembered. Finally,
the theory would also have to explain why in some cases a person's so-called
flashbulb memory is clearly wrong, even though the individual is very confident
about the (inaccurate) memory (see Neisser & Harsch, 1992). Such was the case
in Talarico and Rubin's (2003) findings for students' memories of the September
11, 2001, terrorist attacks; despite a decrease in the accuracy of their memories
over time, participants maintained confidence in their very vivid memories.

The major functions of a theory are to *organize* empirical knowledge and to
guide research (Marx, 1963). Even in relatively specific areas of research such as
flashbulb memories, many studies have been done. As the scope of a research area
increases, so does the number of relevant studies. Scientific theories are important because they provide a logical organization of many research findings and
identify relationships among findings. This logical organization of findings guides
researchers as they identify testable hypotheses for their future research.

Theories frequently require that we propose intervening processes to account
for observed behavior (Underwood & Shaughnessy, 1975). These intervening
processes provide a link between the independent variables researchers manipulate and the dependent variables they subsequently measure. Because these processes "go between" the independent and dependent variables, they are called
intervening variables. You probably are familiar with what we mean by an intervening variable if you think about your computer use. As you press keys on the
keyboard or click the mouse, you see (and hear) various outcomes on the monitor, printer, and from the speakers. Yet it isn't your keystrokes and mouse clicks
that *directly* cause these outcomes; the intervening variable is the "invisible" software that serves as a connection between your keystrokes and the outcome on
your monitor.

Intervening variables are like computer software. Corresponding to the connection between keystrokes and what you see on your monitor, intervening variables connect independent and dependent variables. Another familiar example
from psychology is the construct of "thirst." For example, a researcher might manipulate the number of hours participants are deprived of liquid and, after the
specified time, measure the amount of liquid consumed. Between the deprivation
time and the time participants are allowed to drink liquid, we may say that the
participants are "thirsty"—the psychological experience of needing to replenish
body fluids. Thirst is a construct that allows theorists to connect variables such
as the number of hours deprived of liquid (the independent variable) and the
amount of liquid consumed (the dependent variable). *Intervening variables such*
as thirst not only link independent and dependent variables; intervening variables also
are used to explain why the variables are connected. Thus, intervening variables play
an important role when researchers use theories to explain their findings.

Intervening variables and theories are useful because they allow researchers to identify relationships among seemingly dissimilar variables. Other

independent variables likely influence "thirst." Consider, for example, a different independent variable: amount of salt consumed. On the surface, these two independent variables—number of hours deprived of liquid and amount of salt consumed—are very dissimilar. However, both influence subsequent consumption of liquid and can be explained by the intervening variable of thirst. Other independent variables related to liquid consumption include amount of exercise and temperature; the more exercise or the higher the temperature, the more people are "thirsty" and the more liquid they consume. Although these examples emphasize independent variables, it's important to note that dependent variables also play a role in theory development. Thus, rather than measuring "liquid consumption" as the dependent variable, inventive researchers may measure other effects related to the psychological experience of thirst. For example, when deprived of liquid, individuals may go to greater efforts to obtain liquid or may even drink liquids that taste bitter. Thus, effort to obtain liquids or the amount of bitterness in the liquid could be measured as dependent variables.

Intervening variables are critical to theory development in psychology. In our example, the apparently dissimilar variables of liquid deprivation, salt consumption, exercise, temperature, liquid consumption, effort to obtain liquid, and taste of liquids can be united in one theory that relies on the intervening variable "thirst." Other examples of intervening variables—and theories— abound in psychology. The intervening variable "depression," for example, connects the factors theorized to cause depression (e.g., neurological factors, exposure to trauma) and the various symptoms (e.g., sadness, hopelessness, sleep and appetite disturbance). Similarly, "memory" as an intervening variable is used to explain the relationship between the amount (or quality) of time spent studying and later performance on a test. As you will learn in your study of psychology, intervening variables provide the key that unlocks the complex relationships among variables.

How we evaluate and test scientific theories is one of the most difficult issues in psychology and philosophy (e.g., Meehl, 1978, 1990a, 1990b; Popper, 1959). Kimble (1989) has suggested a simple and straightforward approach. He says, "The best theory is the one that survives the fires of logical and empirical testing" (p. 498). Scientists first evaluate a theory by considering whether it is logical. That is, they determine whether the theory makes sense and whether its propositions are free of contradictions. The logical consistency of theories is tested through the lens of the critical eye of the scientific community.

The second "fire" that Kimble (1989) recommends for evaluating theories is to subject hypotheses derived from a theory to empirical tests. Successful tests of a hypothesis serve to increase the acceptability of a theory; unsuccessful tests serve to decrease the theory's acceptability. The best theory, in this view, is the one that passes these tests successfully. But there are serious obstacles to testing hypotheses and, as a consequence, to confirming or disconfirming scientific theories. For example, a theory, especially a complex one, may produce many specific testable hypotheses. A theory is not likely to fail on the basis of a single test (e.g., Lakatos, 1978). Moreover, theories may include concepts that are not adequately defined or suggest complex relationships among intervening variables and behavior. Such theories may have a long life, but their value to science is questionable (Meehl, 1978). Ultimately, the scientific community determines whether any test of a theory is definitive.

In general, theories that provide *precision of prediction* are likely to be much more useful (Meehl, 1990a). For example, a theory that predicts that children will typically demonstrate abstract reasoning by age 12 is more precise (and testable) in its predictions than a theory that predicts the development of abstract reasoning by ages 12 to 20. When constructing and evaluating a theory, scientists also place a premium on parsimony (Marx, 1963). The *rule of parsimony* is followed when the simplest of alternative explanations is accepted. Scientists prefer theories that provide the simplest explanations for phenomena.

In summary, a good scientific theory is one that is able to pass the most rigorous tests. Somewhat counterintuitively, rigorous testing will be more informative when researchers do tests that seek to *falsify* a theory's propositions than when they do tests that seek to confirm them (Shadish, Cook, & Campbell, 2002). Although tests that confirm a particular theory's propositions do provide support for the specific theory that is being tested, confirmation logically does not rule out other, alternative theories of the same phenomenon. Tests of falsification are the best way to prune a theory of its dead branches. Constructing and evaluating scientific theories is at the core of the scientific enterprise and is absolutely essential for the healthy growth of the science of psychology.

SUMMARY

As an approach to knowledge, the scientific method is characterized by a reliance on empirical procedures, rather than relying only on intuition, and by an attempt to control the investigation of those factors believed responsible for a phenomenon. Scientists gain the greatest control when they conduct an experiment. In an experiment, those factors that are systematically manipulated in an attempt to determine their effect on behavior are called independent variables. The measures of behavior used to assess the effect (if any) of the independent variables are called dependent variables.

Scientists seek to report results in an unbiased and objective manner. This goal is enhanced by giving operational definitions to concepts. Psychological researchers refer to concepts as "constructs." Scientists also use instruments that are as accurate and precise as possible. Phenomena are quantified with both physical and psychological measurement. Scientists seek measures that have both validity and reliability. Hypotheses are tentative explanations of events. To be useful to the scientist, however, hypotheses must be testable. Hypotheses that lack adequate definition, that are circular, or that appeal to ideas or forces outside the province of science are not testable. Hypotheses are often derived from theories.

The goals of the scientific method are description, prediction, explanation, and application. Both quantitative and qualitative research are used to describe behavior. Observation is the principal basis of scientific description. When two measures correlate, we can predict the value of one measure by knowing the value of the other. Understanding and explanation are achieved when the causes of a phenomenon are discovered. This requires that evidence be provided for covariation of events, that a time-order relationship exists, and that alternative causes be eliminated. When two potentially effective variables covary such that the independent effect of each variable on behavior cannot be determined, we say that our research is confounded. Even when a carefully controlled experiment allows the researcher to form a causal inference, additional questions remain concerning the extent to which the findings may generalize to describe other people and settings. In applied research, psychologists strive to apply their knowledge and research methods to improve people's lives. Basic research is conducted to gain knowledge about behavior and mental processes and to test theories.

Scientific theory construction and testing are at the core of the scientific approach to psychology. A theory is defined as a logically organized set of propositions that serves to define events, describe relationships among these events, and explain the occurrence of the events. Theories have the important functions of organizing empirical knowledge and guiding research by offering testable hypotheses. Intervening variables are critical to theory development in psychology because these constructs allow researchers to explain the relationships between independent and dependent variables.

KEY CONCEPTS

control 30	reliability 38
experiment 31	correlation 45
independent variable 32	causal inference 46
dependent variable 33	confounding 48
construct 35	applied research 49
operational definition 35	basic research 49
validity 38	theory 50

REVIEW QUESTIONS

1 For each of the following characteristics, distinguish between the scientific approach and everyday approaches to knowledge: general approach and attitude, observation, reporting, concepts, instruments, measurement, and hypotheses.

2 Differentiate between an independent variable and a dependent variable, and provide an example of each that could be used in an experiment.

3 What is the major advantage of using operational definitions in psychology? In what two ways has the use of operational definitions been criticized?

4 Distinguish between the accuracy and the precision of a measuring instrument.

5 What is the difference between the validity of a measure and the reliability of a measure?

6 Which three types of hypotheses lack the critical characteristic of being testable?

7 Identify the four goals of the scientific method and briefly describe what each goal is intended to accomplish.

8 Distinguish between the nomothetic approach and the idiographic approach in terms of who is studied and the nature of the generalizations that are sought.

9 Identify two differences between quantitative and qualitative research.

10 What are researchers able to do when they know that two variables are correlated?

11 Give an example from a research study described in the text that illustrates each of the three conditions for a causal inference. [You may use the same example for more than one condition.]

12 What is the difference between basic and applied research?

13 What is an intervening variable? Propose a psychological construct that could serve as an intervening variable between "insult" (present/absent) and "aggressive responses." Explain how these variables might be related by proposing a hypothesis that includes your intervening variable.

14 Describe the roles of logical consistency and empirical testing in evaluating a scientific theory.

15 Explain why rigorous tests of a theory that seek to falsify a theory's propositions can be more informative than tests that seek to confirm a theory's propositions.

CHALLENGE QUESTIONS

1 In each of the following descriptions of research studies, you are to identify the independent variable(s). You should also be able to identify at least one dependent variable in each study.

   A A psychologist was interested in the effect of food deprivation on motor activity. She assigned each of 60 rats to one of four conditions differing in the length of time for which the animals were deprived of food: 0 hours, 8 hours, 16 hours, 24 hours. She then measured the amount of time the animals spent in the activity wheel in their cages.

   B A physical education instructor was interested in specifying the changes in motor coordination that occur as children gain experience with large playground equipment (e.g., slides, swings, climbing walls). For a span of 8 weeks, preschool children were assigned to 4, 6, or 8 hours per week for time allowed on the equipment. She then tested their motor coordination by asking them to skip, jump, and stand on one foot.

   C A developmental psychologist was interested in the amount of verbal behavior very young children displayed depending on who else was present. The children in the study were 3 years old. These children were observed in a laboratory setting for a 30-minute period. Half of the children were assigned to a condition in which an adult was present with the child during the session. The other half of the children were assigned to a condition in which another young child was present during the session with the child being observed. The psychologist measured the number, duration, and complexity of the verbal utterances of each observed child.

2 A physiological psychologist developed a drug that she thought would revolutionize the world of horse racing. She named the drug Speedo, and it was her contention that this drug would lead horses to

run much faster than they do now. (For the sake of this hypothetical problem, we are ignoring the fact that it is illegal to give drugs to racehorses.) She selected two groups of horses and gave one of the groups injections of Speedo once a week for 4 weeks. Because Speedo was known to have some negative effects on the horses' digestive systems, those horses given the Speedo had to be placed on a special high-protein diet. Those horses not given the Speedo were maintained on their regular diet. After the 4-week period, all the horses were timed in a 2-mile race and the mean (average) times for the horses given Speedo were significantly faster than the mean times for those not given Speedo. The psychologist concluded that her drug was effective.

   A Identify the independent variable of interest (and its levels) and a potentially relevant independent variable with which the primary independent variable is confounded. Explain clearly how the confounding occurred.

   B State exactly what conclusion about the effect of the drug Speedo can be supported by the evidence presented.

   C Finally, suggest ways in which the study could be done so that you could make a clear conclusion about the effectiveness of the drug Speedo.

3 The *New York Times* reported the results of a 2-year, $1.5 million study by researchers at Carnegie Mellon University funded by the National Science Foundation and major technology companies. There were 169 participants in the study drawn from the Pittsburgh area. The researchers examined the relationship between Internet use and psychological well-being. A director of the study stated that the study did not involve testing extreme amounts of Internet use. The participants were normal adults and their families. On average, for those who used the

(continued)

Internet the most, psychological well-being was the worst. For example, 1 hour a week of Internet use led to slight increases on a depression scale and on a loneliness scale and a reported decline in personal interaction with family members. The researchers concluded that Internet use appears to cause a decline in psychological well-being. They suggested that users of the Internet were building shallow relationships that led to an overall decline in feelings of connection to other people.

A   The researchers claim that use of the Internet leads to a decline in people's well-being. What evidence is present in this summary of the report to meet the conditions necessary for drawing this causal inference and what evidence is lacking?

B   What sources beyond this question would you want to check before reaching a conclusion about the findings reported here? [You might begin with the *New York Times* piece "The Lonely Net," August 30, 1998, and the *Washington Post* piece "Net Depression Study Criticized," September 7, 1998.]

4   A study was done to determine whether taking notes in a developmental psychology course affected students' test performance. Students recorded their notes over the entire semester in a 125-page study guide. The study guide included questions on course content covered both in the textbook and in class lectures. Students' notes were measured using three dimensions: completeness, length, and accuracy. Results of the study indicated that students with more accurate notes performed better on essay and multiple-choice tests in the course than did students with less accurate notes. Based on these findings, the researchers suggested that instructors should use instructional techniques such as pausing for brief periods during the lecture and asking questions to clarify information. The researchers argued that these techniques could facilitate the accuracy of the notes students take in class, and that accurate note taking could contribute significantly to students' overall success in college courses.

A   What evidence is present in this report to meet the conditions for a causal inference between accuracy of students' notes and their test performance? What evidence is lacking? (Be sure to identify clearly the three conditions for a causal inference.)

B   Identify a goal of the scientific method that could be met on the basis of findings of this study.

Answer to Stretching Exercise

1   The independent variable in this study is the emotion condition participants experienced after completing the hand-eye coordination task. There were three levels: gratitude, positive emotion, and neutral. The dependent variable was the number of minutes participants helped by completing the confederate's survey.

2   An alternative explanation for the study's finding is that participants simply felt good when the confederate fixed the computer problem and therefore helped more at the end of the experiment. To show that the specific emotion of gratitude was important, the researchers used one experimental condition, the amusing video condition, to control for positive emotions in general. That is, if simply positive emotions cause greater helping, then these participants should show greater helping also. Because only participants in the gratitude condition showed the greatest helping, the researchers can argue that gratitude specifically caused increased helping.

Answer to Challenge Question 1

A   Independent variable (IV): hours of food deprivation with four levels (0, 8, 16, 24); dependent variable (DV): time (e.g., in minutes) animals spent in activity wheel

B   IV: time on playground equipment with three levels: 4, 6, or 8 hours per week; DV: scores on test of motor coordination

C   IV: additional person present with two levels (adult, child); DV: number, duration, and complexity of child's verbal utterances

CHAPTER THREE

Ethical Issues in the Conduct of Psychological Research

CHAPTER OUTLINE

INTRODUCTION

Good science requires good scientists. Scientists' professional competence and integrity are essential for ensuring high-quality science. Maintaining the integrity of the scientific process is a shared responsibility of individual scientists and the community of scientists (as represented by professional organizations such as APA and APS). Each individual scientist has an ethical responsibility to seek knowledge and to strive to improve the quality of life. Diener and Crandall (1978) identify several specific responsibilities that follow from this general mandate. Scientists should

— carry out research in a competent manner;
— report results accurately;
— manage research resources honestly;
— fairly acknowledge, in scientific communications, the individuals who have contributed their ideas or their time and effort;
— consider the consequences to society of any research endeavor;
— speak out publicly on societal concerns related to a scientist's knowledge and expertise.

In striving to meet these obligations, individual scientists face challenging and, at times, ambiguous ethical issues and questions. To guide individual psychologists in making ethical decisions, the American Psychological Association (APA) has formulated an Ethics Code. The APA Ethics Code sets standards of ethical behavior for psychologists who do research or therapy or who teach or serve as administrators (see American Psychological Association, 2002). The Ethics Code deals with such diverse issues as sexual harassment, fees for psychological services, providing advice to the public in the media, test construction, and classroom teaching. It is also important for all students of psychology to make every effort to live up to these stated ideals and standards of behavior. You can familiarize yourself with the Ethics Code by going to the APA website: www.apa.org/ethics.

Many of the standards in the APA Ethics Code deal directly with psychological research (see especially Standards 8.01 to 8.15 of the Code), including the treatment of both humans and animals in psychological research. As with most ethics codes, the standards tend to be general in nature and require specific definition in particular contexts. More than one ethical standard can apply to a specific research situation, and at times the standards may even appear to contradict one another. For instance, ethical research requires that human participants be protected from physical injury. Research that involves drugs or other invasive treatments, however, may place participants at risk of physical harm. The welfare of animal subjects should be protected, but certain kinds of research may involve inflicting pain or other suffering on an animal. Solving these ethical dilemmas is not always easy and requires a deliberate, conscientious, problem-solving approach to ethical decision making.

The Internet has changed the way many scientists do research, and psychologists are no exception. Researchers from around the world, for example, often collaborate on scientific projects and can now quickly and easily exchange ideas and findings with one another via the Internet. Vast quantities of archival information are accessible through government-sponsored Internet sites (e.g., U.S. Census Bureau). Because researchers can collect data from human participants via the World Wide Web, there is the potential to include *millions* of people in one study! Types of psychological research on the Internet include simple observation (e.g., recording "behavior" in chat rooms), surveys (questionnaires, including personality tests), and experiments involving manipulated variables.

Although the Internet offers many opportunities for the behavioral scientist, it also raises many ethical concerns. Major issues arise due to the absence of the researcher in an online research setting, the difficulty of obtaining adequate informed consent and providing debriefing, and concerns about protecting participant confidentiality (see especially Kraut et al., 2004, and Nosek, Banaji, & Greenwald, 2002, for reviews of these problems and some suggested solutions). We discuss some of these ethical issues in the present chapter and also continue this discussion in later chapters when we describe specific studies using the Internet.

Ethical decisions are best made after consultation with others, including one's peers but especially those who are more experienced or knowledgeable in a particular area. In fact, review of a research plan by people not involved in the research is legally required in most situations. In the remaining sections of this chapter, we comment on those standards from the Ethics Code that deal specifically with psychological research. We also present several hypothetical research scenarios that raise ethical questions. By putting yourself in the position of having to make judgments about the ethical issues raised in these research proposals, you will begin to learn to grapple with the challenges that arise in applying particular ethical standards and with the difficulties of ethical decision making in general (see Figure 3.1). We urge you to discuss these proposals with peers, professors, and others who have had prior experience doing psychological research.

ETHICAL ISSUES TO CONSIDER BEFORE BEGINNING RESEARCH

- Prior to conducting any study, the proposed research must be reviewed to determine if it meets ethical standards.
- Institutional Review Boards (IRBs) review psychological research to protect the rights and welfare of human participants.
- Institutional Animal Care and Use Committees (IACUCs) review research conducted with animals to ensure that animals are treated humanely.

Researchers must consider ethical issues before they begin a research project. Ethical problems can be avoided only by planning carefully and consulting with appropriate individuals and groups *prior to doing the research*. The failure to conduct research in an ethical manner undermines the entire scientific process, impedes the advancement of knowledge, and erodes the public's respect for scientific and academic communities (see Figure 3.2). It can also lead to significant legal and financial penalties for individuals and institutions. An important step that researchers must take as they begin to do psychological research is to gain institutional approval.

FIGURE 3.1   Many ethical questions are raised when research is performed with humans.

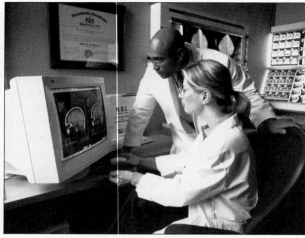
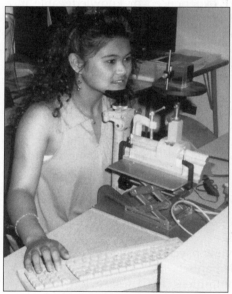
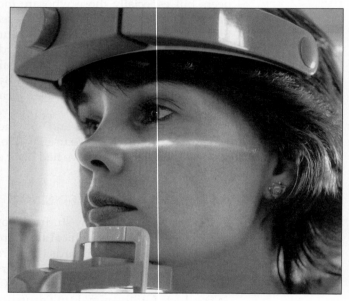

The 1974 National Research Act resulted in the creation of the National Commission for the Protection of Human Subjects of Biomedical and Behavioral Research. This act requires that institutions seeking research funds from specific federal agencies must establish committees to review research sponsored by the institution. Colleges and universities have established these committees, referred to as *Institutional Review Boards (IRBs)*. You can review the federal regulations for IRBs at the website: www.hhs.gov/ohrp. An institution's IRB review can ensure that researchers protect participants from harm

FIGURE 3.2   Following World War II, the Nuremberg War Crimes Court charged German doctors with crimes against humanity, which included performing medical experiments on human beings without their consent. The Court's verdict in these cases led to the development of the Nuremberg Code, which set rules for permissible experimentation with human beings.

and safeguard participants' rights. Federal regulations impose very specific requirements on the membership and duties of IRBs (see *Federal Register*, June 23, 2005). For example, an IRB must be composed of at least five members with varying backgrounds and fields of expertise. Both scientists and nonscientists must be represented, and there must be at least one IRB member who is not affiliated with the institution. Responsible members of the community, such as members of the clergy, lawyers, and nurses, are often asked to serve on these committees.

The IRB has the authority to approve, disapprove, or require modifications of the research plan prior to its approval of the research. The IRB also has the ethical responsibility to make sure its review of research proposals is fair by considering the perspectives of the institution, the researcher, and the research participants (Chastain & Landrum, 1999).

In 1985 the U.S. Department of Agriculture, as well as the U.S. Public Health Service, formulated new guidelines for the care of laboratory animals (Holden, 1987). As a result, institutions doing research with animal subjects are now required to have an Institutional Animal Care and Use Committee (IACUC). These committees must include, minimally, a scientist, a veterinarian, and at least one person not affiliated with the institution. Review of animal research by IACUCs extends to more than simply overseeing the research procedures. Federal regulations governing the conduct of animal research extend to specifications of animal living quarters and the proper training of personnel who work directly with the animals (Holden, 1987).

Nearly every college and university require that all research conducted at the institution be reviewed prior to data collection by an independent committee.

Violation of federal regulations regarding the review of research involving humans or animals can bring a halt to all research at an institution, spell the loss of federal funds, and result in substantial fines (Holden, 1987). *Any individual who wants to do research should inquire of the proper authorities, prior to starting research, about the appropriate procedure for institutional review.* Helpful advice is available for students planning to submit a research proposal to an IRB (McCallum, 2001) or to an IACUC (LeBlanc, 2001).

THE RISK/BENEFIT RATIO

- A subjective evaluation of the risks and benefits of a research project is used to determine whether the research should be conducted.

In addition to checking if appropriate ethical principles are being followed, an IRB considers the *risk/benefit ratio* for a study. Society and individuals benefit from research when new knowledge is gained and when treatments are identified that improve people's lives. There are also potential costs when research is *not* done. We miss the opportunity to gain knowledge and, ultimately, we lose the opportunity to improve the human condition. Research can also be costly to individual participants if they are harmed during a research study. The principal investigator must, of course, be the first one to consider these potential costs and benefits. An IRB is made up of knowledgeable individuals who do not have a personal interest in the research. As such, an IRB is in a better position to determine the risk/benefit ratio and, ultimately, to decide whether to approve the proposed research.

Key Concept

The **risk/benefit ratio** asks the question "Is it worth it?" There are no mathematical answers to the risk/benefit ratio. Instead, members of an IRB rely on a *subjective* evaluation of the risks and benefits both to individual participants and to society, and ask, *are the benefits greater than the risks?* When the risks outweigh the potential benefits, then the IRB does not approve the research; when the benefits outweigh the risks, the IRB approves the research.

Many factors affect the decision regarding the proper balance of risks and benefits of a research activity. The most basic are the nature of the risk and the magnitude of the probable benefit to the participant as well as the potential scientific and social value of the research (Fisher & Fryberg, 1994). Greater risk can be tolerated when clear and immediate benefits to individuals are foreseen or when the research has obvious scientific and social value. For instance, a research project investigating a new treatment for psychotic behavior may entail risk for the participants. If the proposed treatment has a good chance of having a beneficial effect, however, then the possible benefits to both the individuals and society could outweigh the risk involved in the study.

In determining the risk/benefit ratio, researchers also consider the quality of the research, that is, whether valid and interpretable results will be produced. More specifically, "If because of the poor quality of the science no good can come of a research study, how are we to justify the use of participants' time, attention, and effort and the money, space, supplies, and other resources that have been expended on the research project?" (Rosenthal, 1994b, p. 128). Thus, *an investigator is obliged to seek to do research that meets the highest standards of scientific excellence.*

When there is potential risk, a researcher must make sure there are no alternative, low-risk procedures that could be substituted. The researcher must also be sure that previous research has not already successfully addressed the research question being asked. Without careful prior review of the psychological literature, a researcher might carry out research that has already been done, thus exposing individuals to needless risk.

Determining Risk

- Potential risks in psychological research include risk of physical injury, social injury, and mental or emotional stress.
- Risks must be evaluated in terms of potential participants' everyday activities, their physical and mental health, and capabilities.

Determining whether research participants are "at risk" illustrates the difficulties involved in ethical decision making. Life itself is risky. Commuting to work or school, crossing streets, and riding elevators have an element of risk. Simply showing up for a psychology experiment has some degree of risk. To say that human participants in psychological research can never face any risks would bring all research to a halt. Decisions about what constitutes risk must take into consideration those risks that are part of everyday life.

Researchers must also consider the characteristics of the participants when they determine risk. Certain activities might pose a serious risk for some individuals but not for others. Running up a flight of stairs may increase the risk of a heart attack for an elderly person, but the same task would probably not be risky for most young adults. Similarly, individuals who are exceptionally depressed or anxious might show more severe reactions to certain psychological tasks than would other people. Thus, when considering risk, researchers must consider the specific populations or individuals who are likely to participate in the study.

We often think of risk in terms of the possibility of physical injury. Frequently, however, participants in social science research risk social or psychological injury. For example, if participants' personal information were revealed to others, a potential for social risk such as embarrassment exists. Personal information collected during psychological research may include facts about intelligence; personality traits; political, social, or religious beliefs; and particular behaviors. A research participant probably does not want this information revealed to teachers, employers, or peers. Failure to protect the confidentiality of participants' responses may increase the possibility of social injury.

The greatest risk to participants in Internet-based research is the possible disclosure of identifiable personal information outside the research situation (Kraut et al., 2004). Other researchers suggest that although the Internet affords a "perception of anonymity" (Nosek et al., 2002, p. 165), in some circumstances that perception is false, and investigators must consider ways to protect confidentiality in data transmission, data storage, and poststudy interactions with participants.

Some psychological research may pose psychological risk if participants in the study experience serious mental or emotional stress. Imagine the stress a participant may experience when smoke enters the room in which she is waiting. The smoke may be entering the room so that the researcher can simulate an emergency. Until the true nature of the smoke is revealed, participants may experience considerable distress. Anticipating when emotional or psychological stress may occur is not always easy.

Consider the dilemma posed when researchers seek to gather information about child abuse and interpersonal violence (see Becker-Blease & Freyd, 2006). Asking individuals to describe instances of child abuse or family violence from their past can be emotionally stressful. Yet, most researchers agree that knowledge of such experiences can help provide behavioral scientists with important insights into some of society's ills (e.g., divorce, poor school performance, criminality) as well as guide clinical research studies. But how and when to do it? Becker-Blease and Freyd (2006) discuss the ethics of asking and not asking about abuse. They point out that *not* asking has its costs, too, in the form of impeding science and preventing participants from getting help or learning about normal reactions to abuse and about community resources that may help. Studies of child abuse may also help break the taboo against speaking about abuse and let victims know that these discussions can be important. In Becker-Blease and Freyd's view, not asking "helps abusers, hurts victims" (p. 225). Thus, the cost of not asking must be importantly weighed in any risk/benefit analysis.

Simply participating in a psychology experiment is anxiety-provoking for some individuals. After learning a list of nonsense syllables (e.g., *HAP, BEK*), a student participant once said that he was sure the researcher now knew a great deal about him! The student assumed the psychologist was interested in learning about his personality by examining the word associations he had used when learning the list. In reality, this person was participating in a simple memory experiment designed to measure forgetting. *A researcher is obligated to protect participants from emotional or mental stress, including, when possible, stress that might arise due to participants' misconceptions about the psychological task.*

Minimal Risk

- A study is described as involving "minimal risk" when the procedures or activities in the study are similar to those experienced by participants in their everyday life.

Key Concept

A distinction is sometimes made between a participant "at risk" and one who is "at minimal risk." **Minimal risk** means that the harm or discomfort participants may experience in the research *is not greater than* what they might experience in their daily lives or during routine physical or psychological tests. As an example of minimal risk, consider the fact that many psychology laboratory studies involve lengthy paper-and-pencil tests intended to assess various mental abilities. Participants may be asked to complete the tests quickly and may receive specific feedback about their performance. Although there is likely to be stress in this situation, the risk of psychological injury is likely no greater than that typically experienced by students. Therefore, such studies would involve only minimal risk for college students. When the possibility of injury is judged to be more than minimal, individuals are considered to be *at risk*. When a study places participants at risk, the researcher has more serious obligations to protect their welfare.

Dealing with Risk

- Whether "at risk" or "at minimal risk," research participants must be protected. More safeguards are needed as risks become greater.
- To protect participants from social risks, information they provide should be anonymous, or if that is not possible, the confidentiality of their information should be maintained.

Even if the potential risk is small, researchers should try to minimize risk and protect participants. For instance, simply by stating at the beginning of a memory experiment that the tasks do not measure intelligence or personality reduces the stress that some participants experience. In situations where the possibility of harm is judged to be significantly greater than that occurring in daily life, the researcher's obligation to protect participants increases correspondingly. For example, when participants are exposed to the possibility of serious emotional stress in a psychology experiment, an IRB could require that a clinical psychologist be available to counsel individuals about their experience in the study. As you can imagine, online research poses difficult ethical dilemmas in this regard. Participants can experience emotional distress in the context of an Internet study just as they do in a laboratory-based study. However, because they are absent from the research situation, researchers may be less able to monitor distress and reduce harm during online studies (Kraut et al., 2004). One approach might be to obtain preliminary data with the goal of identifying those who might be at risk and to exclude them from the actual study. It may be the case, however, that studies with high risk may not be ethically performed on the Internet (Kraut et al., 2004).

Research activity involving more than minimal risk to participants should not be carried out unless alternative methods of data collection with lower risk have been explored. In some cases, descriptive approaches involving observation or questionnaires should be used instead of experimental treatments. Researchers can also take advantage of naturally occurring "treatments" that do not involve experimentally inducing stress. For example, Anderson (1976) interviewed owner-managers of small businesses that had been damaged by hurricane floods. He found that there was an optimum level of stress that led to effective problem solving and coping behaviors by the participants. Above or below this optimum stress level, problem-solving performance decreased. A similar relationship has been demonstrated in a number of experimental laboratory tasks using experimenter-induced stress.

In order to protect research participants from social injury, data collection should keep participants' responses anonymous by asking participants not to use their names or any other identifying information. When this is not possible, researchers should keep participants' responses confidential by removing any identifying information from their records during the research. When the

STRETCHING EXERCISE I

For each of the following research situations, you are to decide whether "minimal risk" is present (i.e., risk not greater than that of everyday life) or if participants are "at risk." If you decide that participants are "at risk," think of recommendations you could make to the researcher that reduce risk to participants. As you do so, you will undoubtedly begin to anticipate some of the ethical issues yet to be discussed in this chapter.

1 College students are asked to complete an adjective checklist describing their current mood. The researcher is seeking to identify students who are depressed so that they can be included in a study examining cognitive deficits associated with depression.

2 Elderly adults in a nursing home are given a battery of achievement tests in the dayroom at their home. A psychologist seeks to determine if there is a decline in mental functioning with advancing age.

3 Students in a psychology research methods class see another student enter their classroom in the middle of the class period, speak loudly and angrily with the instructor, and then leave. As part of a study of eyewitness testimony, the students are then asked to describe the intruder.

4 A researcher recruits students from introductory psychology classes to participate in a study of the effects of alcohol on cognitive functioning. The experiment requires that some students drink 2 ounces of alcohol (mixed with orange juice) before performing a computer game.

researcher must test people on more than one occasion or otherwise track specific individuals, or when information supplied by participants is particularly sensitive, code numbers can be randomly assigned to participants at the beginning of a study. Only these numbers need appear on participants' response sheets. Names are linked with the code numbers on a master list, and access to this list is restricted by keeping it under lock and key. Online researchers need to be particularly sensitive to the possibility of electronic eavesdropping or hacking of stored data and must take appropriate precautions to minimize social risk (see Kraut et al., 2004).

Making sure participants' responses are anonymous or confidential can also benefit the researcher if this leads participants to be more honest and open when responding (Blanck, Bellack, Rosnow, Rotheram-Borus, & Schooler, 1992). Participants may be less likely to lie or withhold information if they do not worry about who may have access to their responses.

INFORMED CONSENT

- Researchers and participants enter into a social contract, often using an informed consent procedure.
- Researchers are ethically obligated to describe the research procedures clearly, identify any aspects of the study that might influence individuals' willingness to participate, and answer any questions participants have about the research.
- Research participants must be allowed to withdraw their consent at any time without penalties.
- Individuals must not be pressured to participate in research.
- Research participants are ethically obligated to behave appropriately during the research by not lying, cheating, or engaging in other fraudulent behavior.

- Informed consent must be obtained from legal guardians for individuals unable to provide consent (e.g., young children, mentally impaired individuals); assent to participate should be obtained from individuals unable to provide informed consent.
- Researchers should consult with knowledgeable others, including an IRB, when deciding whether to dispense with informed consent, such as when research is conducted in public settings. These settings require special attention to protecting individuals' privacy.
- Privacy refers to the rights of individuals to decide how information about them is to be communicated to others.

Key Concept }

A substantial portion of the Ethics Code dealing with research is devoted to issues related to informed consent. This is appropriate because informed consent is an essential component of the social contract between the researcher and the participant. **Informed consent** is a person's explicitly expressed willingness to participate in a research project based on a clear understanding of the nature of the research, of the consequences for not participating, and of all factors that might be expected to influence that person's willingness to participate (see Figure 3.3).

FIGURE 3.3   The U.S. Public Health Service between 1932 and 1972 examined the course of untreated syphilis in poor African American men from Macon County, Alabama, who had not given informed consent. They were unaware they had syphilis and their disease was left untreated. Survivors were recognized by the Clinton administration.

Researchers must make reasonable efforts to respond to any questions the participants have about the research and to respect the dignity and rights of the individual during the research experience. In this way individuals can make an informed decision about their participation. Participants' consent must be given freely, without undue inducement or pressure. Participants should also know they are free to withdraw their consent at any time without penalty or prejudice. Researchers should always obtain informed consent. *Written informed consent is absolutely essential when participants are exposed to more than minimal risk.*

Research participants who consent to participate in research also have ethical responsibilities to behave in an appropriate manner. For example, participants should pay attention to instructions and perform tasks in the manner requested by the researcher. Taylor and Shepperd (1996) describe a study that illustrates the possible consequences when participants do not behave responsibly. In the study, participants were briefly left alone by an experimenter who admonished them not to discuss the experiment among themselves. Once they were alone, however, the participants talked about the experiment and obtained information from each other that in effect negated the value of the research. Moreover, when the experimenter later asked the participants about what they knew of the procedures and goals of the study, none revealed that they had gained important knowledge about the study during their illicit conversation. This example illustrates the broader principle that *lying, cheating, or other fraudulent behavior by research participants violates the scientific integrity of the research situation.*

True informed consent cannot be obtained from certain individuals, such as the mentally impaired or emotionally disturbed, young children, and those

FIGURE 3.4   The issue of informed consent is especially important when children participate in research.

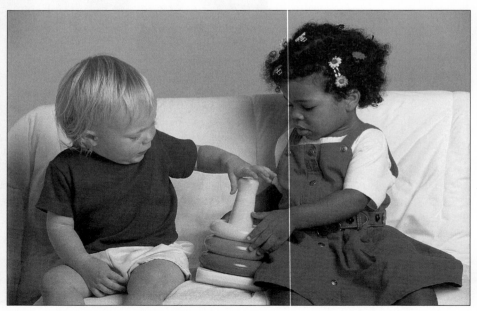

who have limited ability to understand the nature of research and the possible risks (see Figure 3.4). In these cases formal informed consent must be obtained from the participants' parents or legal guardians. Whenever possible, however, "assent," that is, an expressed willingness to participate, should always be obtained from the participants themselves.

Online research poses particular ethical problems for obtaining informed consent. Consider that in most cases online participants typically click on their computer mouse to indicate that they have read and understood the consent statement. But does this constitute a legally binding "signature" of the research participant? How does a researcher know if participants are the required age or that they fully understood the informed consent statement? One suggestion for determining whether participants have understood the informed consent statement is to administer short quizzes about its content; procedures to distinguish children from adults might include requiring information that is generally available only to adults (Kraut et al., 2004). Whenever such ethical dilemmas arise, it is wise to seek advice from knowledgeable professionals, but the *final responsibility for conducting ethical research always rests with the investigator.*

It is not always easy to decide what constitutes undue inducement or pressure to participate. Paying college students $9 an hour to take part in a psychology experiment would not generally be considered improper coercion. Recruiting very poor or disadvantaged persons from the streets with a $9 offer may be more coercive and less acceptable (Kelman, 1972). Prisoners may believe that any refusal on their part to participate in a psychology experiment will be viewed by the authorities as evidence of uncooperativeness and will therefore make it more difficult for them to be paroled.

When college students are asked to fulfill a class requirement by serving as participants in psychology experiments (an experience that presumably has some educational value), an alternative method of fulfilling the class requirement must be made available to those who do not wish to participate in psychological research. The time and effort required for these alternative options should be equivalent to that required for research participation. Alternative assignments that are used frequently include reading and summarizing journal articles describing research, making informal field observations of behavior, attending presentations of research findings by graduate students or faculty, and doing volunteer community service (see Kimmel, 1996).

IRBs require investigators to document that the proper informed consent procedure has been followed for any research involving human participants. However, it is important to recognize that, as guidelines from the federal Office for Human Research Protections state, "informed consent is a process, not just a form." One IRB chairperson told us that she tells investigators to imagine they are sitting down with the person and explaining the project. In Box 3.1 we provide some tips on the process of obtaining proper informed consent rather than providing a sample form that may imply "one form fits all." Proper consent procedures and written documentation will vary somewhat across situations and populations. Members of an IRB are a good source for advice on how to obtain and document informed consent in a way that meets ethical guidelines and protects the rights of participants.

BOX 3.1

TIPS ON OBTAINING INFORMED CONSENT

A proper informed consent should clearly indicate the purpose or research question, the identity and affiliation of the researcher, and procedures to be followed during the research experience. After participants read the consent form and their questions are answered, the form must be signed and dated by the researcher and participant. The federal Office for Human Research Protections (OHRP) has published tips to aid researchers in the Informed Consent process. Our adaptation of the OHRP tips follows and includes additional requirements of the consent form. An IRB may require additional information. The complete text of the OHRP tips, as well as links to important related federal documents, can be obtained from www.hhs.gov/ohrp/humansubjects/guidance/ictips.htm.

- Avoid scientific jargon or technical terms; the informed consent document should be written in language clearly understandable to the participant.
- Avoid use of the first person (e.g., "I understand that . . ." or "I agree to . . ."), as this can be interpreted as suggestive and incorrectly used as a substitute for sufficient factual information. Phrasing such as "If you agree to participate, you will be asked to do the following" would be preferred. Think of the document primarily as a teaching tool and not as a legal instrument.
- Describe the overall experience that will be encountered in a way that identifies the nature of the experience (e.g., how it is experimental), as well as

reasonably foreseeable harms, discomfort, inconveniences, and risks.
- Describe the benefits to the participants for their participation. If the benefits simply are helping society or science in general, that should be stated.
- Describe any alternatives to participation. If a college student "participant pool" is being tapped, then alternative ways to learn about psychological research must be explained.
- Participants must be told how personally identifiable information will be held in confidence. In situations where highly sensitive information is collected, an IRB may require additional safeguards such as a Certificate of Confidentiality.
- If research-related injury is possible in research that is more than minimal risk, then an explanation must be given regarding voluntary compensation and treatment.
- Legal rights of participants must not be waived.
- A "contact person" who is knowledgeable about the research must be identified so that participants who have postresearch questions may have them answered. Questions may arise in any of the following three areas, *and these areas must be explicitly stated and addressed in the consent process and documentations:* the research experience, rights of the participants, and research-related injuries. At times this may involve more than one contact person, for example, referring the participant to the IRB or an institutional representative.
- A statement of voluntary participation must be included, which emphasizes the participant's right to withdraw from the research at any time without penalty.

Key Concept }

In some situations researchers are not required to obtain informed consent. The clearest example is when researchers are observing individuals' behavior in public places without any intervention. For instance, an investigator might want to gather evidence about race relations on a college campus by observing the frequency of mixed-race versus non-mixed-race groups walking across campus. The investigator would not need to obtain students' permission before making the observations. Informed consent would be required, however, if the identity of specific individuals was going to be recorded.

Deciding when behavior is public or private is not always clear-cut. **Privacy** refers to the rights of individuals to decide how information about them is to be communicated to others. Diener and Crandall (1978) identify three major dimensions that researchers can consider to help them decide what information is private: the sensitivity of the information, the setting, and the method of dissemination of the information. Clearly, some kinds of information are more sensitive than others. Individuals interviewed about their sexual practices, religious beliefs, or criminal activities are likely to be very concerned about how their information will be used.

The setting also plays a role in deciding whether behavior is public or private. Some behaviors, such as attending a concert, can reasonably be considered public. In public settings, people give up a certain degree of privacy. Some behaviors that occur in public settings, however, are not easily classified as public or private (see Figure 3.5). When you drive in your car, use a public bathroom, or enjoy a family picnic in the park, are these behaviors public or private? Is communication in an Internet "chat room" public or private? Decisions about ethical practice in these situations depend on the sensitivity of the data being gathered and the ways in which the information will be used.

When information is disseminated in terms of group averages or proportions, it is unlikely to reveal much about specific individuals. In other situations, code systems can be used to protect participants' confidentiality. *Disseminating sensitive information about individuals or groups without their permission is a serious breach of ethics.* When potentially sensitive information about individuals has been collected without their knowledge (e.g., by a concealed observer), the researcher can contact the individuals after the observations have been made and ask whether he or she can use the information. The researcher would not be able to use the information from participants who decline to give their permission. The most difficult decisions regarding privacy involve situations in which there is an obvious ethical problem on one dimension but not on the other two, or situations in which there is a slight

FIGURE 3.5   Deciding what is public or what is private behavior is not always easy.

STRETCHING EXERCISE II

The APA Ethics Code states that psychologists may dispense with informed consent when research involves naturalistic observation (see Standard 8.05). As we have just seen, however, deciding when naturalistic observation is being done in a "public" setting is not always easy. Consider the following research scenarios and decide whether you think informed consent of participants should be required before the researcher begins the research. It may be that you will want more information from the researcher. If so, what additional information would you want before deciding whether informed consent is needed in the situation? You will see that requiring informed consent can have a dramatic effect on a research situation. Requiring informed consent, for example, can make it difficult for a researcher to record behavior under "natural" conditions. Such are the dilemmas of ethical decision making.

1 In a study of drinking behavior of college students, an undergraduate working for a faculty member attends a fraternity party and records the amount drunk by other students at the party.

2 As part of a study of the gay community, a gay researcher joins a gay baseball team with the goal of recording behaviors of participants in the context of team competition during the season. All the games are played in a city recreation league with the general public as spectators.

3 Public bathroom behavior (e.g., flushing, hand washing, littering, writing graffiti) of men and women is observed by male and female researchers concealed in the stalls of the respective restrooms.

4 A graduate student wants to investigate cheating behaviors of college students. He conceals himself in a projection booth in an auditorium where exams are administered to students in very large classes. From his vantage point he can see the movements of most students with the aid of binoculars. He records head movements, switching papers, passing notes, use of cell phones, texting, and other suspicious exam-taking behaviors.

problem on all three dimensions. For instance, the behavior of individuals in the darkened setting of a movie theater would appear to have the potential of yielding sensitive information about the individual, but the setting could be reasonably classified as public.

Whenever possible, the manner in which participants' information will be kept confidential should be explained to participants so that they may judge for themselves whether the safeguards taken to ensure their confidentiality are reasonable. Implementing the principle of informed consent requires that the investigator seeks to balance the need to investigate human behavior on the one hand with the rights of human participants on the other.

DECEPTION IN PSYCHOLOGICAL RESEARCH

- Deception in psychological research occurs when researchers withhold information or intentionally misinform participants about the research. By its nature, deception violates the ethical principle of informed consent.
- Deception is considered a necessary research strategy in some psychological research.
- Deceiving individuals in order to get them to participate in the research is always unethical.
- Researchers must carefully weigh the costs of deception against the potential benefits of the research when considering the use of deception.

FIGURE 3.6   In the 1960s, participants in Stanley Milgram's experiments were not told that the purpose of the research was to observe people's obedience to authority, and many followed the researcher's instructions to give severe electric shock to another human being. For an update on this research, see Burger (2009).

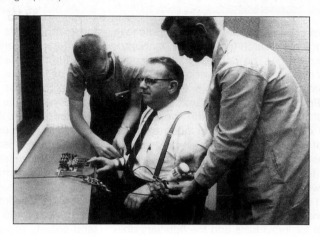

Key Concept }

One of the most controversial ethical issues related to research is the use of deception. **Deception** can occur either through *omission,* the withholding of information, or *commission,* intentionally misinforming participants about an aspect of the research. Some people argue that research participants should *never* be deceived because ethical practice requires that the relationship between experimenter and participant be open and honest (e.g., Baumrind, 1995). To some, deception is morally repugnant; it is no different from lying. Deception contradicts the principle of informed consent. Despite the increased attention given to deception in research over the last several decades, the use of deception in psychological research has not declined and remains a popular research strategy (Sharpe, Adair, & Roese, 1992). For example, Skitka and Sargis (2005) surveyed social psychologists who used the Internet as a data collection tool and found that 27 percent of the reported studies involved deception of Internet participants.

How is it that deception is still widely used, despite ethical controversies? One reason is that it is impossible to carry out certain kinds of research without withholding information from participants about some aspects of the research (see Figure 3.6). In other situations, it is necessary to misinform participants in order to have them adopt certain attitudes or behaviors. For example, Kassin and Kiechel (1996) investigated factors affecting whether people will falsely confess to having done something they did not do. Their goal was to understand factors that lead criminal suspects to falsely confess to a crime. In their experiment, the participants' task was to type letters that were being read aloud. They were told not to hit the Alt key while typing because this would crash the computer. The computer was rigged to crash after a brief time and the experimenter accused the participant of hitting the Alt key. Even though none of the participants had hit the Alt key, nearly 70% of the participants signed a written confession that they had done so. If the participants had known in advance that the procedures were designed to elicit

BOX 3.2

TO DECEIVE OR NOT TO DECEIVE: THAT'S A TOUGH QUESTION

Researchers continue to use deceptive practices in psychological research (e.g., Sieber, Iannuzzo, & Rodriguez, 1995). The debate in the scientific community concerning the use of deception also has not abated (see, for example, Bröder, 1998; Fisher & Fryberg, 1994; Ortmann & Hertwig, 1997). It is a complex issue, with those taking part in the debate sometimes at odds over the definition of deception (see Ortmann & Hertwig, 1998). Fisher and Fryberg (1994) summarized the debate as follows: "Ethical arguments have focused on whether deceptive research practices are justified on the basis of their potential societal benefit or violate moral principles of beneficence and respect for individuals and the fiduciary obligations of psychologists to research participants" (p. 417). This is quite a mouthful; so let's break it down.

A moral principle of "beneficence" refers to the idea that research activities should be beneficent (bring benefits) for individuals and society. If deception is shown to harm individuals or society, then the beneficence of the research can be questioned. The moral principle of "respect for individuals" is just that: People should be treated as persons and not "objects" for study, for example. This principle would suggest that people have a right to make their own judgments about the procedures and purpose of the research in which they are participating (Fisher & Fryberg, 1994). "Fiduciary obligations of psychologists" refer to the responsibilities of individuals who are given trust over others, even if only temporarily. In the case of psychological research, the researcher is considered to have responsibility for the welfare of participants during the study and for the consequences of their participation.

These ideas and principles can perhaps be illustrated through the arguments of Baumrind (1985), who argues persuasively that "the use of intentional deception in the research setting is unethical, imprudent, and unwarranted scientifically" (p. 165). Specifically, she argues that the costs to the participants, to the profession, and to society of the use of deception are too great to warrant its continued use. Although these arguments are lengthy and complex, let us attempt a brief summary. First, according to Baumrind, deception exacts a cost to participants because it undermines the participants' trust in their own judgment and in a "fiduciary" (someone who is holding something in trust for another person). When research participants find they have been duped or tricked, Baumrind believes this may lead the participants to question what they have learned about themselves and to lead them to distrust individuals (e.g., social scientists) whom they might have previously trusted to provide valid information and advice. A cost to the profession is exacted because participants (and society at large) soon come to realize that psychologists are "tricksters" and not to be believed when giving instructions about research participation. If participants tend to suspect psychologists of lying, then one may question whether deception will work as it is intended by the researcher, a point raised earlier by Kelman (1972). Baumrind also argues that the use of deception reveals psychologists are willing to lie, which seemingly contradicts their supposed dedication to seeking truth. Finally, there is harm done to society because deception undermines people's trust in experts and makes them suspicious in general about all contrived events.

Of course, these are not the views of all psychologists (see Christensen, 1988; Kimmel, 1998). Milgram (1977), for instance, suggested that deceptive practices of psychologists are really a kind of "technical illusion" and should be permitted in the interests of scientific inquiry. After all, illusions are sometimes created in real-life situations in order to make people believe something. When listening to a radio program, people are not generally bothered by the fact that the thunder they hear or the sound of a horse galloping is merely a technical illusion created by a sound effects specialist. Milgram argues that technical illusions should be permitted in the case of scientific inquiry. We deceive children into believing in Santa Claus. Why cannot scientists create illusions in order to help them understand human behavior?

Just as illusions are often created in real-life situations, in other situations, Milgram points out, there can be a suspension of a general moral principle. If we learn of a crime, we are ethically bound to report it to the authorities. On the other hand, a lawyer who is given information by a client must consider this information privileged even if it reveals that the client is guilty. Physicians perform very personal examinations of our bodies. Although it is morally permissible in a physician's office, the same type of behavior would not be condoned outside the office. Milgram argues that, in the interest of science, psychologists should occasionally be allowed to suspend the moral principle of truthfulness and honesty.

Those who defend deception point to studies showing that participants typically do not appear to react negatively to being deceived (e.g., Christensen, 1988; Epley & Huff, 1998; Kimmel, 1996). Although people's "suspiciousness" about psychological research may increase, the overall effects seem to be small (see Kimmel, 1998). Nevertheless, the bottom line according to those who argue for the continued use of deception is well summarized by Kimmel (1998): "An absolute rule prohibiting the use of deception in all psychological research would have the egregious consequence of preventing researchers from carrying out a wide range of important studies" (p. 805). No one in the scientific community suggests that deceptive practices be taken lightly; however, for many scientists the use of deception is less noxious (to use Kelman's term) than doing without the knowledge gained by such studies.

Do you think deception should be used in psychological research?

their false confessions, they probably would not have confessed. The disclosure required for informed consent would have made it impossible to study the likelihood that people would make a false confession.

Although deception is sometimes justified to make it possible to investigate important research questions, deceiving participants for the purpose of getting them to participate in research that involves more than minimal risk is always unethical. As stated in the Ethics Code, *"Psychologists do not deceive prospective participants about research that is reasonably expected to cause physical pain or severe emotional distress"* (Standard 8.07b).

A goal of research is to observe individuals' normal behavior. A basic assumption underlying the use of deception is that sometimes it's necessary to conceal the true nature of an experiment so that participants will behave as they normally would, or act according to the instructions provided by the experimenter. Problems may arise, however, with frequent and casual use of deception (Kelman, 1967). If people believe that researchers often mislead participants, they may expect to be deceived when participating in a psychology experiment. Participants' suspicions about the research may prevent them from behaving as they normally would (see Box 3.2). This is exactly the opposite of what the researchers hope to achieve. Interestingly, Epley and Huff (1998) directly compared reactions of participants who were told or not told in a debriefing following the experiment that they had been deceived. Those who were told of the deception were subsequently more suspicious about future psychological research than were participants who were unaware of the deception. As the frequency of online research increases, it is important that researchers give particular attention to the use of deception, not only because of the potential for increasing the distrust of researchers by society's members, but also because deception has the potential to "poison" a system (i.e., the Internet) that people use for social support and connecting with others (Skitka & Sargis, 2005).

Kelman (1972) suggests that, *before using deception, a researcher must give very serious consideration to (1) the importance of the study to our scientific knowledge, (2) the availability of alternative, deception-free methods, and (3) the "noxiousness" of the deception.* This last consideration refers to the degree of deception involved and to the possibility of injury to the participants. In Kelman's view: "Only if a study is very important and no alternative methods are available can anything more than the mildest form of deception be justified" (p. 997).

DEBRIEFING

- Researchers are ethically obligated to seek ways to benefit participants even after the research is completed. One of the best ways to accomplish this goal is by providing participants with a thorough debriefing.
- Debriefing benefits both participants and researchers.
- Researchers are ethically obligated to explain to participants their use of deception as soon as is feasible.
- Debriefing informs participants about the nature of the research and their role in the study and educates them about the research process. The overriding goal of debriefing is to have individuals feel good about their participation.
- Debriefing allows researchers to learn how participants viewed the procedures, allows potential insights into the nature of the research findings, and provides ideas for future research.

Over the years, many researchers have fallen into the trap of viewing human participants in their research as "objects" from which to obtain data in order to meet their own research goals. Researchers sometimes have considered that their responsibility to participants ends when the final data are collected. A handshake or "thank you" was frequently all that marked the end of the research session. Participants likely left with unanswered questions about the research situation and with only the vaguest idea of their role in the study. It is important when planning and conducting research to consider how the experience may affect the research participants *after* the research is completed and to seek ways in which the participants can benefit from participation. These concerns follow directly from two of the moral principles identified in the APA Ethics Code, those of beneficence (acting for the good of the person) and respect for people's rights and dignity.

Key Concept

Earlier we discussed that protecting the confidentiality of participants' responses benefits both the participants (safeguarding them from social injury) and the researcher (e.g., by increasing the likelihood that participants will respond honestly). Similarly, **debriefing** participants at the end of a research session benefits both participants and the researcher (Blanck et al., 1992). When deception has been used in research, *debriefing is necessary to explain to participants the need for deception, to address any misconceptions participants may have about their participation, and to remove any harmful effects resulting from the deception. Debriefing also has the important goals of educating participants about the research (rationale, method, results) and of leaving them with positive feelings about*

FIGURE 3.7   An informative debriefing is critical in ensuring that research participants have a good experience.

their participation. Researchers should provide opportunities for participants to learn more about their particular contribution to the research study and to feel more personally involved in the scientific process (see Figure 3.7). Following a debriefing, participants in the Kassin and Kiechel (1996) experiment on false confessions reported they found the study meaningful and thought their own contribution to the research was valuable.

Debriefing provides an opportunity for participants to learn more about their specific performance in the study and about research in general. For instance, participants can learn that their individual performance in a study may reflect their abilities, but also situational factors such as what the researcher asked them to do and the conditions of testing. Because the educational value of participation in psychological research is used to justify the use of large numbers of volunteers from introductory psychology classes, researchers who test college students have an important obligation to ensure that research participation is an educational experience. Classroom instructors have sometimes built on the educational foundation of the debriefing and asked their students to reflect on their research experience by writing brief reports describing details about the study's purpose, the techniques used, and the significance of the research for understanding behavior. An evaluation of one such procedure showed that students who wrote reports were more satisfied with their research experience and they gained a greater overall educational benefit from it than did students who did not write reports (Richardson, Pegalis, & Britton, 1992).

Debriefing helps researchers learn how participants viewed the procedures in the study. A researcher may want to find out whether participants perceived a particular experimental procedure in the way the investigator intended (Blanck et al., 1992). For example, a study of how people respond to failure may include tasks that are impossible to complete. If participants don't judge their performance as a failure, however, the researcher's hypothesis cannot be tested. Debriefing allows the investigator to find out whether participants judged their performance to be a failure or whether they recognized it was impossible for them to succeed.

When trying to learn participants' perceptions of the study, researchers shouldn't press them too hard. Research participants generally want to help with the scientific process. The participants may know that information may be withheld from them in psychological research. They may even fear they will "ruin" the research if they reveal they really did know important details about the study (e.g., the tasks really were impossible). To avoid this possible problem, debriefing should be informal and indirect. This is often best accomplished by using general questions in an open-ended format (e.g., "What do you think this study was about?" or "What did you think about your experience in this research?"). The researcher can then follow up with specific questions about the research procedures. As much as possible, these specific questions should not cue the participant about what responses are expected (Orne, 1962).

Debriefing also benefits researchers because it can provide "leads for future research and help identify problems in their current protocols" (Blanck et al., 1992, p. 962). Debriefing, in other words, can provide clues to the reasons for participants' performance, which may help researchers to interpret the results of the study. Researchers also can discover ideas for future research during debriefings. Finally, participants sometimes detect errors in experimental materials—for instance, missing information or ambiguous instructions—and they can report these to the researcher during the debriefing. As we said, *debriefing is good for both the participant and the researcher.*

Because the researcher is absent in an online research setting, an appropriate debriefing process may be difficult. This aspect of Internet research adds to the list of ethical dilemmas posed by this kind of research (Kraut et al., 2004). The fact that online participants can easily withdraw from the study at any time is particularly troublesome in this regard. One suggestion is to program the experiment in such a way that a debriefing page is presented automatically if a participant prematurely closes the window (Nosek et al., 2002). When a study is finally completed, researchers can e-mail a report summarizing the study's findings to the participants so that they can better understand how the study's goals were related to the experimental outcome. Following an Internet study, a researcher may post debriefing material at a website and even update these materials as new results come in (see Kraut et al., 2004).

RESEARCH WITH ANIMALS

- Animals are used in research to gain knowledge that will benefit humans, for example, by helping to cure diseases.
- Researchers are ethically obligated to acquire, care for, use, and dispose of animals in compliance with current federal, state, and local laws and regulations, and with professional standards.

• The use of animals in research involves complex issues and is the subject of much debate.

Each year millions of animals are tested in laboratory investigations aimed at answering a wide range of important questions. New drugs are tested on animals before they are used with humans. Substances introduced into the environment are first given to animals to test their effects. Animals are exposed to diseases so that investigators may observe symptoms and test various possible cures. New surgical procedures—especially those involving the brain—are often first tried on animals. Many animals are also studied in behavioral research, for example, by ethologists and experimental psychologists. For instance, animal models of the relationship between stress and diabetes have helped researchers to understand psychosomatic factors involved in diabetes (Surwit & Williams, 1996). These investigations yield much information that contributes to human welfare (Miller, 1985). In the process, however, many animals are subjected to pain and discomfort, stress and sickness, and death. Although rodents, particularly rats and mice, are the largest group of laboratory animals, researchers use a wide variety of species in their investigations, including monkeys, fish, dogs, and cats. Specific animals are frequently chosen because they provide good models for human responses. For example, psychologists interested in hearing sometimes use chinchillas as subjects because their auditory processes are very similar to those of humans.

The use of animals as laboratory subjects has often been taken for granted. In fact, the biblical reference to humans' "dominion" over all lesser creatures is sometimes invoked to justify the use of animals as laboratory subjects (Johnson, 1990). More often, however, research with animal subjects is justified by the need to gain knowledge *without putting humans in jeopardy*. Most cures, drugs, vaccines, or therapies have been developed through experimentation on animals (Rosenfeld, 1981). Maestripieri and Carroll (1998) also point out that investigation of naturally occurring infant maltreatment in monkeys can inform scientists about child abuse and neglect.

Many questions, however, have been raised about the role of animal subjects in laboratory research (Novak, 1991; Shapiro, 1998; Ulrich, 1991). These questions include the most basic one, whether animals should ever be used in scientific investigations, as well as important questions about the care and protection of animal subjects (see Figure 3.8). Clearly, according to the APA Ethics Code, *the researcher who uses animal subjects in an investigation has an ethical obligation to acquire, care for, use, and dispose of animals in compliance with federal, state, and local laws and regulations, and with professional standards.* Partly in response to concerns expressed by members of animal rights groups during the 1980s, investigators must satisfy many federal, state, and local requirements, including inspection of animal facilities by veterinarians from the U.S. Department of Agriculture (see National Research Council, 1996). These regulations are often welcomed by members of the scientific community, and many animal researchers belong to groups that seek to protect laboratory animals. The APA has developed a list of specific guidelines to be followed when animal subjects are used in psychological research. These guidelines can be found on the website

FIGURE 3.8   Ethical guidelines for the use of animals in research address how animals may be treated before, during, and after they are tested.

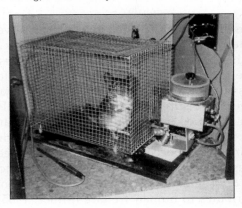 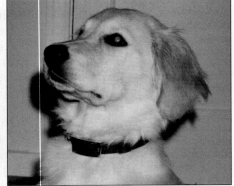

sponsored by the APA Committee on Animal Research and Ethics (CARE) at http://www.apa.org/science/leadership/care/index.aspx.

Research with animals is a highly regulated enterprise with the overriding goal of protecting the welfare of research animals. Only individuals qualified to do research and to manage and care for the particular species should be allowed to work with the animals. Animals may be subjected to pain or discomfort only when alternative procedures are not available and when the scientific, educational, or applied goals justify the procedures. As we noted earlier, animal review boards (IACUCs) are now in place at research facilities that receive funds from the U.S. Public Health Service. These committees determine the adequacy of the procedures for controlling pain, carrying out euthanasia, housing animals, and training personnel. IACUCs also determine whether experimental designs are sufficient to gain important new information and whether the use of an animal model is appropriate or whether nonanimal models (e.g., computer simulations) could be used (Holden, 1987).

As with any ethically sensitive issue, however, compromises must be made with regard to the use of animals in research. For example, until alternatives to animal research can be found, the need to conduct research using animal subjects in order to battle human disease and suffering must be balanced against the need to protect the welfare of animals in laboratory research (Goodall, 1987). As APA's former chief executive officer, Raymond Fowler, pointed out, it is also important that the use of animal subjects not be restricted when the application of the research is not immediately apparent (Fowler, 1992). "The charge that animal research is of no value because it cannot always be linked to potential applications is a charge that can be made against all basic research." Such an indictment "threatens the intellectual and scientific foundation" of all psychology, including both "scientists and practitioners" (p. 2).

Although few scientists disagree that restrictions are necessary to prevent needless suffering in animals, most want to avoid a quagmire of bureaucratic restrictions and high costs that will undermine research. Feeney (1987) suggests that severe restrictions and high costs, as well as the negative publicity

---

BOX 3.3

MORAL STATUS OF HUMANS AND NONHUMAN ANIMALS

Ethical decision making often pits opposing philosophical positions against each other. This is clearly seen in the debate over the use of animals in research. At the center of this debate is the question of the "moral status" of humans and nonhuman animals. As the Australian philosopher Peter Singer (1990, p. 9) points out, two generally accepted moral principles are

1 All humans are equal in moral status.
2 All humans are of superior moral status to nonhuman animals.

Thus, Singer continues, "On the basis of these principles, it is commonly held that we should put human welfare ahead of the suffering of nonhuman animals; this assumption is reflected in our treatment of animals in many areas, including farming, hunting, experimentation, and entertainment" (p. 9).

Singer, however, does not agree with these commonly held views. He argues that "there is no rational ethical justification for always putting human suffering ahead of that of nonhuman animals" (p. 9). Unless we appeal to religious viewpoints (which Singer rejects as a basis for making decisions in a pluralistic society), there is, according to Singer, no special moral status to "being human." This position has roots in the philosophical tradition known as utilitarianism, which began with the writings of David Hume (1711–1776) and Jeremy Bentham (1748–1832), as well as John Stuart Mill (1806–1873) (Rachels, 1986). Basically, this viewpoint holds that whenever we have choices between alternative actions we should choose the one that has the best overall consequences (produces the most "happiness") for everyone involved. What matters in this view is whether the individual in question is capable of experiencing happiness/unhappiness, pleasure/pain; whether the individual is human or nonhuman is not relevant (Rachels, 1986).

What do you think about the moral status of humans and animals and its relation to psychological research?

(and occasional emotional demonstrations) directed toward individuals and institutions by extremists within the animal activist groups, may deter young scientists from entering the field of animal research. If this were to occur, the (presently) incurably ill or permanently paralyzed could possibly be deprived of the hope that can come through scientific research. Clearly, the many issues surrounding the debate over the relevance of animal research to the human condition are complex (see Box 3.3). Ulrich (1992) said it well—the discussion of these issues must be approached with "wisdom and balance" (p. 386).

REPORTING OF PSYCHOLOGICAL RESEARCH

- Investigators attempt to communicate their research findings in peer-reviewed scientific journals, and the APA Code of Ethics provides guidelines for this process.
- Decisions about who should receive publication credit are based on the scholarly importance of the contribution.
- Ethical reporting of research requires recognizing the work of others by using proper citations and references; failure to do so may result in plagiarism.

- Proper citation includes using quotation marks when material is taken directly from a source and citing secondary sources when an original source is not consulted.

A completed research study begins its journey toward becoming part of the scientific literature when the principal investigator writes a manuscript for submission to one of the dozens of psychology-related scientific journals (see Chapter 13 for information about this publication process). The primary goal of publishing research in a psychology journal is to communicate the results of the study to members of the scientific community and to society in general. Publishing research in journals is also a way to enhance the researcher's reputation and even the reputation of the institution that sponsored the research. But getting the results of a scientific investigation published is not always an easy process, especially if the researcher wants to publish in one of the prestigious scientific journals. Because of the importance of publications for the science of psychology, the APA Code of Ethics provides guidelines for this process.

The ethical standards covering the reporting of the results of a scientific investigation seem more straightforward than in the other areas of the Ethics Code we have discussed. Even here, however, ethical decisions regarding such issues as assigning credit for publication and plagiarism are not always clear-cut. Conducting a research study often involves many people. Colleagues offer suggestions about a study's design, graduate or undergraduate students assist an investigator by testing participants and organizing data, technicians construct specialized equipment, and expert consultants give advice about statistical analyses. When preparing a manuscript for publication, should all of these individuals be considered "authors" of the study? *Publication credit* refers to the process of identifying as authors those individuals who have made significant contributions to the research project. Because authorship of a published scientific study frequently is used to measure an individual's competence and motivation in a scientific field, *it is important to acknowledge fairly those who have contributed to a project.*

It's not always easy to decide whether the contribution an individual has made to a research project warrants being an "author" of a scientific paper or whether that individual's contribution should be acknowledged in a less visible way (such as in a footnote). Also, once authorship is granted, then the order of authors' names must be decided. "First author" of a multiple-authored article generally indicates a greater contribution than does "second author" (which is greater than third, etc.). Authorship decisions should be based mainly in terms of the scholarly importance of the contribution (e.g., aiding the conceptual aspects of a study), not by the time and energy invested in the study (see Fine & Kurdek, 1993).

Ethical concerns associated with assigning authorship can take many forms. For example, not only is it unethical for a faculty member to take credit for a student's work, it is also unethical for students to be given undeserved author credit. This latter situation may arise, for instance, in a misguided attempt by a faculty mentor to give a student an edge when competing for a position in a competitive graduate program. According to Fine and Kurdek (1993), awarding students undeserved author credit may falsely represent the student's expertise, give the student an unfair advantage over peers, and, perhaps, lead others to create impossible expectations for the student. These authors recommend that faculty and students collaborate in the process of determining authorship credit and discuss early in the project what level of participation warrants author credit. Due to differences in faculty–student power and position, the faculty member should initiate discussions regarding authorship credit for student contributors (see Behnke, 2003).

Key Concept }

A rather troublesome area of concern in the reporting of research, not only for some professionals but frequently for students, is **plagiarism.** Again, the ethical standard seems clear enough: Don't present substantial portions or elements of another's work as your own. But what constitutes "substantial portions or elements," and how does one avoid giving the impression that another's work is one's own? Making these decisions can be like walking a tightrope. On one side is the personal goal of being recognized for making a scholarly contribution; on the other side is the ethical obligation to recognize the previous contributions others have made. The fact that both professionals and students commit acts of plagiarism suggests that many people too often veer from the tightrope by seeking their own recognition instead of giving due credit to the work of others.

Sometimes acts of plagiarism result from sloppiness (failing to double-check a source to verify that an idea did not originate with someone else, for example). Errors of this kind are still plagiarism; *ignorance is not a legitimate excuse.* Mistakes can be made all too easily. For example, researchers (and students) occasionally ask "how much" of a passage can be used without putting it in quotation marks or otherwise identifying its source. A substantial element can be a single word or short phrase if that element serves to identify a key idea or concept that is the result of another's thinking. Because there is no clear guideline for how much material constitutes a substantial element of a work, students must be particularly careful when referring to the work of others. At times, especially among students, plagiarism can result from failure to use quotation marks around passages taken directly from a source. *Whenever material is taken directly from a source, it must be placed in quotation marks and the source must be properly identified.* It is also important to cite the source of material you include in your paper when you paraphrase (i.e., reword) the material. *The ethical principle is that you must cite the sources of your ideas when you use the exact words and when you paraphrase.* See Table 3.1 for examples of correct and incorrect citations.

Plagiarism also occurs when individuals fail to acknowledge secondary sources. A *secondary source* is one that discusses other (original) work. Secondary sources include textbooks and published reviews of research such as those that appear in scientific journals like the *Psychological Bulletin.* When your only source for an idea or findings comes from a secondary source, it is always unethical to report that information in *a way that suggests you consulted the original work.* It is far better to try to locate and read the original source rather than citing a secondary source. If that is not possible, you must inform the reader that you did not read the original source by using a phrase like "as cited in . . ." when referring to the original work. By citing the secondary

TABLE 3.1   EXAMPLE OF PLAGIARISM AND CORRECT CITATION

Actual Text (Example of a Correctly Cited Direct Quote)

"Informed by developments in case law, the police use various methods of interrogation—including the presentation of false evidence (e.g., fake polygraph, fingerprints, or other forensic test results; staged eyewitness identifications), appeals to God and religion, feigned friendship, and the use of prison informants" (Kassin & Kiechel, 1996, p. 125).

Example of Plagiarism (No Citation Accompanying Paraphrased Material)

Research investigations of deceptive interrogation methods to extract confessions are important because police use false evidence (e.g., fake test results) and false witnesses when interrogating suspects. Interrogators also pressure suspects by pretending to be their friends.

Paraphrased Material with Correct Citation

Research investigations of deceptive interrogation methods to extract confessions are important because police use false evidence (e.g., fake test results) and false witnesses when interrogating suspects (Kassin & Kiechel, 1996). In addition, Kassin and Kiechel state that interrogators pressure suspects by pretending to be their friends.

Based on Table 3.4, Zechmeister, Zechmeister, & Shaughnessy, 2001, p. 71.

source, you are telling the reader that you are presenting another person's interpretation of the original material. Again, ignorance concerning the proper form of citation is not an acceptable excuse, and on unfortunate occasions researchers—professors as well as students—have seen their careers ruined by accusations of plagiarism.

STEPS FOR ETHICAL COMPLIANCE

- Ethical decision making involves reviewing the facts of the proposed research situation, identifying relevant ethical issues and guidelines, and considering multiple viewpoints and alternative methods or procedures.
- Authors who submit research manuscripts to an APA journal also must submit forms describing their compliance with ethical standards.

Should research participants be placed at risk for serious injury to gain information about human behavior? Should psychologists use deception? Is it acceptable to allow animals to suffer in the course of research? These questions, part of ethical decision making, are difficult to answer and require a thoughtful decision-making process that, in the end, may lead to answers that do not make everyone "happy." An ethically informed decision process should include the following steps:

—Review the facts of the proposed research situation (e.g., participants, procedure).
—Identify the relevant ethical issues, guidelines, and law.
—Consider multiple viewpoints (e.g., participants, researchers, institutions, society, moral values).
—Consider alternative methods or procedures and their consequences, including the consequences of not doing the proposed research.

With careful consideration of these factors, a "correct" decision to proceed with the proposed research is based on a diligent review of the research and ethical issues, and not simply on what might make the researcher or other individuals "happy."

Authors of manuscripts submitted to an APA journal must submit forms stating their compliance with ethical standards (see *Publication Manual of the American Psychological Association*, APA, 2010). These forms can be found in the *Publication Manual* (pp. 233–235), as well as on the APA journal Web page (http://www.apa.org/pubs/journals). Of course, a consideration of ethical issues should be made before initiating a research project, during the research process itself as problems arise (e.g., participants' unanticipated reactions), and in preparation for discussion with editors and reviewers of the journal selected for submission of the manuscript. To help ensure ethical compliance throughout the research process, APA has published an Ethical Compliance Checklist (see *Publication Manual*, p. 20). The Checklist covers many of the ethical issues discussed in this chapter, including institutional review, informed consent, treatment of animal subjects (if applicable), proper citation of other published work, and order of authorship. Remember: Careful review of these issues and others described in the APA compliance forms should be made *prior to* beginning your research.

SUMMARY

Psychological research raises many ethical questions. Thus, before beginning a research project, you must consider both the specific ethical issues from the APA Ethics Code and the laws and regulations that are relevant to your project. In most cases formal institutional approval—for example, from an IRB or IACUC—must be obtained before beginning to do research. One function of an IRB is to reach a consensus regarding the risk/benefit ratio of the proposed research. Risk can involve physical, psychological, or social injury. Informed consent must be obtained from human participants in most psychological research. Researchers must take special safeguards to protect human participants when more than minimal risk is present and to provide appropriate debriefing following their participation. Serious ethical questions arise when researchers withhold information from participants or misinform them about the nature of the research. When deception is used, debriefing should inform participants about the reasons for having used deception. Debriefing can also help participants feel more fully involved in the research situation as well as help the researcher learn how the participants perceived the treatment or task. Online research presents new ethical dilemmas for a researcher, and consultation with IRB members, as well as researchers experienced with Internet data collection, is urged prior to planning such a study.

Psychologists who test animal subjects must obey a variety of federal and state guidelines and, in general, must protect the welfare of the animals. Animals may be subjected to pain or discomfort only when alternative procedures are not available and when the goals of the research are judged to justify such procedures in terms of the scientific, educational, or applied value of the research. Until alternatives to animal research can be found, many people accept the compromise of conducting research using animal subjects to battle disease and suffering while protecting the welfare of animals in laboratory research.

Reporting of psychological findings should be done in a manner that gives appropriate credit to the individuals who contributed to the project. When previously published work contributes to an investigator's thinking about a research study, the investigator must acknowledge this contribution by properly citing the individuals who reported the previous work. Failure to do so represents a serious ethical problem: plagiarism. Ethical decision making involves reviewing the facts of the proposed research situation, identifying relevant ethical issues and guidelines, and considering multiple viewpoints and alternative methods or procedures. Authors who submit research manuscripts to an APA journal also must submit forms describing their compliance with ethical standards.

KEY CONCEPTS

risk/benefit ratio 62	deception 73
minimal risk 64	debriefing 76
informed consent 67	plagiarism 83
privacy 70	

REVIEW QUESTIONS

1 Explain why researchers submit research proposals to Institutional Review Boards (IRBs) or Institutional Animal Care and Use Committees (IACUCs) before beginning a research project, and briefly describe the functions of these committees in the research process.

2 Explain how the risk/benefit ratio is used in making ethical decisions. What factors contribute to judging the potential benefits of a research project?

3 Explain why research cannot be risk free and describe the standard that researchers use to determine whether research participants are "at risk." Describe briefly how characteristics of the participants in the research can affect the assessment of risk.

4 Differentiate among the three possible types of risk that can be present in psychological research: physical, psychological, social. How do researchers typically safeguard against the possibility of social risk?

5 What are three important ethical issues raised by online research?

6 What information does the researcher have an ethical obligation to make clear to the participant in order to ensure the participant's informed consent? Under what conditions does the APA Ethics Code indicate that informed consent may not be necessary?

7 What three dimensions do Diener and Crandall (1978) recommend that researchers consider when they attempt to decide whether information is public or private?

8 Explain why deception may sometimes be necessary in psychological research. Describe briefly the questions researchers should ask before using deception, and describe the conditions under which it is always unethical to deceive participants.

9 In what ways can debriefing benefit the participant? In what ways can debriefing benefit the researcher?

10 What ethical obligations are specified in the APA Ethics Code for researchers who use animals in their research?

11 What conditions are required by the APA Ethics Code before animals may be subjected to stress or pain?

12 Explain how researchers decide when an individual can be credited as an author of a published scientific report.

13 Describe the procedures an author must follow to avoid plagiarism when citing information from an original source or from a secondary source.

14 Identify the steps in an ethically informed decision process regarding whether a proposed research project should be conducted.

15 According to APA, what must authors include when submitting a research manuscript to an APA journal?

CHALLENGE QUESTIONS

Note: Unlike in other chapters, no answers to the Challenge Questions or Stretching Exercises are provided in this chapter. To resolve ethical dilemmas, you must be able to apply the appropriate ethical standards and to reach an agreement regarding the proposed research after discussion with others whose backgrounds and knowledge differ from your own. You will therefore have to consider points of view different from your own. We urge you to approach these problems as part of a group discussion of these important issues.

The first two challenge questions for this chapter include a hypothetical research proposal involving a rationale and method similar to that of actual published research. To answer these questions, you will need to be familiar with the APA ethical principles and other material on ethical decision making presented in this chapter, including the recommended steps for decision making that were outlined at the end of this chapter. As you will see, your task is to decide whether specific ethical standards have been violated and to make recommendations regarding the proposed research, including the most basic recommendation of whether the investigator should be allowed to proceed.

1. IRB Proposal

Instructions   Assume you are a member of an Institutional Review Board (IRB). Besides yourself, the committee includes a clinical psychologist, a social psychologist, a social worker, a philosopher, a Protestant minister, a history professor, and a

respected business executive in the community. The following is a summary of a research proposal that has been submitted to the IRB for review. You are asked to consider what questions you might want to ask the investigator and whether you would approve carrying out the study at your institution in its present form, whether modification should be made before approval, or whether the proposal should not be approved. (An actual research proposal submitted to an IRB would include more details than we present here.)

Rationale   Psychological conformity occurs when people accept the opinions or judgments of others in the absence of significant reasons to do so or in the face of evidence to the contrary. Previous research has investigated the conditions under which conformity is likely to occur and has shown, for example, that conformity increases when people anticipate unpleasant events (e.g., shock) and when the pressure to conform comes from individuals with whom the individuals identify. The proposed research examines psychological conformity in the context of discussions about alcohol consumption among underage students. The goal of the research is to identify factors that contribute to students' willingness to attend social events where alcohol is served to minors and to allow obviously intoxicated persons to drive an automobile. This research seeks to investigate conformity in a natural setting and in circumstances where unpleasant events (e.g., legal penalties, school suspension, injury, or even death) can be avoided by not conforming to peer pressure.

Method   The research will involve 36 students (ages 18–19) who volunteer to participate in a research project investigating "beliefs and

(continued)

attitudes of today's students." Participants will be assigned to four-person discussion groups. Each person in the group will be given the same 20 questions to answer; however, they will be asked to discuss each question with members of the group before writing down their answers. Four of the 20 questions deal with alcohol consumption by people under age 21 and with possible actions that might be taken to reduce teenage drinking and driving. One member of the group will be appointed discussion leader by the principal investigator. Unknown to the participants, they will be assigned randomly to three different groups. In each group, there will be 0, 1, or 2 students who are actually working for the principal investigator. Each of these "confederates" has received prior instructions from the investigator regarding what to say during the group discussion of the critical questions about underage drinking. (The use of confederates in psychological research is discussed in Chapter 4.) Specifically, confederates have been asked to follow a script which presents the argument that the majority of people who reach the legal driving age (16), and all individuals who are old enough (18) to vote in national elections and serve in the armed forces, are old enough to make their own decisions about drinking alcohol; moreover, because it is up to each individual to make this decision, other individuals do not have the right to intervene if someone under the legal age chooses to drink alcohol. Each of the confederates "admits" to drinking alcohol on at least two previous occasions. Thus, the experimental manipulation involves 0, 1, or 2 persons in the four-person groups suggesting they do not believe students have a responsibility to avoid situations where alcohol is served to minors or to intervene when someone chooses to drink and drive. The effect of this argument on the written answers given by the actual participants in this experiment will be evaluated. Moreover, audiotapes of the sessions will be made without participants' knowledge, and the contents of these audiotapes will be analyzed. Following the experiment, the nature of the deception and the reasons for making audiotapes of the discussions will be explained to the participants.

2. IACUC Proposal

Instructions   Assume you are a member of an Institutional Animal Care and Use Committee (IACUC). Besides yourself, the committee includes a veterinarian, a biologist, a philosopher, and a respected business executive in the community. The following is a summary of a research proposal that has been submitted to the IACUC for review.

You are asked to consider what questions you might want to ask the investigator and whether you would approve carrying out this study at your institution in its present form, whether modification should be made before approval, or whether the proposal should not be approved. (An actual research proposal submitted to an IACUC would include more details than we present here.)

Rationale   The researchers seek to investigate the role of subcortical structures in the limbic system in moderating emotion and aggression. This proposal is based on previous research from this laboratory which has shown a significant relationship between damage in various subcortical brain areas of monkey subjects and changes in eating, aggression, and other social behaviors (e.g., courtship). The areas under investigation are those that sometimes have been excised in psychosurgery with humans when attempting to control hyperaggressive and assaultive behaviors. Moreover, the particular subcortical area that is the focus of the present proposal has been hypothesized to be involved in controlling certain sexual activities that are sometimes the subject of psychological treatment (e.g., hypersexuality). Previous studies have been unable to pinpoint the exact areas thought to be involved in controlling these behaviors; the proposed research seeks to improve on this knowledge.

Method   Two groups of rhesus monkeys will be the subjects. One group ($N = 4$) will be a control group. These animals will undergo a sham operation, which involves anesthetizing them and drilling a hole in the skull. These animals then will be tested and evaluated in the same manner as the experimental animals. The experimental group ($N = 4$) will undergo an operation to lesion a small part of a subcortical structure known as the amygdala. Two of the animals will have lesions in one site; the remaining two will receive lesions in another site of this structure. After recovery, all animals will be tested on a variety of tasks measuring their food preferences, social behaviors with same-sex and opposite-sex monkeys, and emotional responsiveness (e.g., reactions to a novel fear stimulus: an experimenter in a clown face). The animals will be housed in a modern animal laboratory; the operations will be performed and recovery monitored by a licensed veterinarian. After testing, the experimental animals will be sacrificed and the brains prepared for histological examination. (Histology is necessary to confirm the locus and extent of lesions.) The control animals will not be killed; they will be returned to the colony for use in future experiments.

3. Research done by Stanley Milgram on compliance has led to a great deal of discussion about the ethical issues surrounding the use of deception in psychological research (see Box 3.2). Compliance involves the likelihood that a person will follow instructions given by an authority figure. For Part A of this question, you are to read a summary describing the basic procedure Milgram used in his experiments. Then you are to treat this summary as if it were a research proposal submitted to an IRB of which you are a member. For the second part of the question, you are to consider the additional information in Part B about Milgram's research on compliance using this paradigm. Then you are to explain why you would or would not change the decision you made based on your review in Part A.

A Two people come to a psychology laboratory supposedly to participate in a learning experiment. They were told that the study was concerned with the effects of punishment on learning. The individuals drew slips of paper to determine who would be the "teacher" and who would be the "learner." One person was actually an accomplice of the principal investigator, and the drawing was rigged so that the real participant in the experiment was always given the role of teacher. The participant watched as the learner was taken to an adjacent room and strapped into a chair and an electrode was attached to the wrist. The participant then heard the experimenter say that the learner would receive an electric shock for every error made while learning a list of word pairs. The teacher was then taken to the laboratory room, which housed an impressive-looking shock generator with 30 lever switches. Each switch was labeled with a voltage designation (ranging from 15 to 450 volts), and next to the switches were verbal labels describing the amount of shock, for example, "Slight Shock," "Strong Shock," "Danger, Severe Shock." Two switches after the last verbal description were simply marked XXX. The teacher was given a sample shock and told to administer the electric shock to the learner whenever the learner made a mistake. The learner's responses were communicated via a set of four switches that lit up a number on the top of the shock generator. The teacher was also told to move one lever higher on the shock generator after each wrong response. As the experiment progressed, the learner offered various protests to the shock. These complaints could be heard through the walls of the room and included shouts to the effect that the shocks were becoming painful and, later, that the learner wanted the experimenter to end the procedure. When the teacher moved the switch to 180 volts, the learner yelled, "I can't stand it any more" and at the 270 volts gave an agonizing scream. At 300 volts the learner yelled, "I will not give any more answers" but continued to scream. After the switch corresponding to 330 volts was pressed, the learner was not heard from any more. The learner was not actually shocked, and the major dependent variable was the maximum shock that the participant would give in response to the "orders" of the experimenter. All participants were debriefed after the experiment and, at times, the researcher talked with a participant for some length of time. All participants also received a follow-up questionnaire. Before conducting the experiment, Milgram described his planned procedure to 37 psychiatrists; none predicted that participants would administer the maximum shock.

B Milgram conducted more than a dozen experiments using this procedure (see Milgram, 1974). In an experiment when the teacher could hear the screams of the learner but not actually see the learner, approximately 60% of the participants gave the learner the maximum shock. The major justification for continuing this line of research after such an unexpected finding was that no participants were apparently seriously injured by the experiment and that an overwhelming majority (84%) said they were glad to have been in the experiment. Many participants (74%) responded to the follow-up questionnaire saying that they had gained something of personal value from the experience. In subsequent experiments Milgram found that the likelihood of participants complying was affected by situational factors. For example, participants were less likely to comply when the learner was in the room with the teacher and participants were least likely to administer the maximum shock when the teacher could choose the level of voltage. One interpretation of the original finding is that people will readily comply—they behave like proverbial sheep. A different view of people's willingness to comply is evidenced by the findings of the entire series of experiments. Milgram demonstrated that people are sensitive to many aspects of the situation in which they are asked to comply. A question remains: Does

(continued)

the benefit of what we have learned about people's tendencies to comply based on Milgrim's findings warrant the risks that his paradigm entails? More generally, how can IRBs best estimate the potential benefits of proposed research when it is impossible for them to use the outcome of the research in their assessment of its potential benefits?

4. Consider the following scenario presented by Fine and Kurdek (1993) as part of their discussion of the issue of determining authorship of a publication.

An undergraduate student asked a psychology faculty member to supervise an honors thesis. The student proposed a topic, the faculty member primarily developed the research methodology, the student collected and entered the data, the faculty member conducted the statistical analyses, and the student used part of the analyses for the thesis.

The student wrote the thesis under very close supervision by the faculty member. After the honors thesis was completed, the faculty member decided that data from the entire project were sufficiently interesting to warrant publication as a unit. Because the student did not have the skills necessary to write the entire study for a scientific journal, the faculty member did so. The student's thesis contained approximately one third of the material presented in the article.

A   Explain what factors of the situation you would consider to determine if the student should be an author of any publication resulting from this work or if the student's work should be acknowledged in a footnote to the article.

B   If you decide that the student should be an author, explain whether you think the student should be the first author or the second author of the article.

PART TWO

Descriptive Methods

CHAPTER FOUR

Observation

CHAPTER OUTLINE

OVERVIEW

We observe behavior every day. Admit it. Many of us are people watchers. And it isn't simply because we are dedicated voyeurs or even exceptionally curious, although human behavior is certainly often interesting. People's behaviors—gestures, expressions, postures, choice of apparel—contain a lot of information as popular books on "body language" seek to emphasize (e.g., Pease & Pease, 2004). Whether it is a simple smile or a subtle courtship ritual, another person's behavior frequently provides cues that are quickly recognized. Indeed, research reveals that many of our expressions are "universal" signals, that is, recognized in all cultures (e.g., Ekman, 1994). Scientists, too, rely on their observations to learn a lot about behavior (although see Baumeister, Vohs, & Funder, 2007, for an opinion that psychologists don't observe actual behavior enough).

Our everyday observations and those of scientists differ in many ways. When we observe casually, we may not be aware of factors that bias our observations. Moreover, we rarely keep formal records of our observations. Instead, we rely on our memory of the events even though our own experience (and psychological research) confirms that our memory is not perfect!

Scientific observation is made under precisely defined conditions, in a systematic and objective manner, and with careful record keeping. The primary goal of observational methods is to describe behavior. Scientists strive to describe behavior *fully* and as *accurately* as possible. Researchers face serious challenges in reaching this goal. Clearly, it is impossible for researchers to observe *all* of a person's behavior. Scientists rely on observing *samples* of people's behavior, but they must decide whether their samples represent people's *usual* behavior. In this chapter we describe how scientists select samples of behavior. Researchers face a second challenge in trying to describe behavior fully: Behavior frequently changes depending on the situation or context in which the behavior occurs. Consider your own behavior. Do you behave the same at home as in school, or at a party compared to in a classroom? Does your observation of others, such as your friends, lead you to conclude that context is important? Have you observed that children sometimes change their behavior when they are with one or the other of their parents? Complete descriptions of behavior require that observations be made across many different situations and at different times. Observation provides a rich source of hypotheses about behavior, and so observation can also be a first step in discovering why we behave the way we do.

In this chapter you will see that the scientist-observer is not always passively recording behavior as it occurs. We will take a look at reasons why scientists intervene to create special situations for their observations. We'll also look at ways to investigate behavior that do not require direct observation of people. By examining physical traces (e.g., graffiti, textbook underlining) and archival records (e.g., marriage licenses, high school yearbooks), scientists gain important insights into people's behavior. We also introduce you to methods for recording and for analyzing observational data. Finally, we describe important challenges that can make it difficult to interpret the results of observational studies.

SAMPLING BEHAVIOR

- When a complete record of behavior cannot be obtained, researchers seek to obtain a representative sample of behavior.
- The extent to which observations may be generalized (external validity) depends on how behavior is sampled.

Before conducting an observational study, researchers must make a number of important decisions about when and where observations will be made. Because the investigator typically cannot observe all behavior, only certain behaviors occurring at particular times, in specific settings, and under particular conditions can be observed. In other words, behavior must be *sampled*. This sample is used to *represent* the larger population of all possible behaviors. By choosing times, settings, and conditions for their observations that are representative of a population of behaviors, researchers can *generalize* their findings to that population. That is, results can be generalized only to participants, times, settings, and conditions *similar* to those in the study in which the observations were made. The key feature of *representative samples* is that they are "like" the larger population from which they are drawn. For example, observations made of classroom behavior at the beginning of a school year may be representative of behavior early in the school year, but may not yield results that are typical of behavior seen at the end of the school year.

Key Concept }

External validity refers to the extent to which the results of a research study can be generalized to different populations, settings, and conditions. Recall that validity concerns "truthfulness." When we seek to establish the external validity of a study, we examine the extent to which a study's findings may be used accurately to describe people, settings, and conditions beyond those used in the study. In this section we describe how time, event, and situation sampling are used to enhance the external validity of observational findings.

Time Sampling

- Time sampling refers to researchers choosing time intervals for making observations either systematically or randomly.
- When researchers are interested in events that happen infrequently, they rely on event sampling to sample behavior.

Key Concept }

Researchers typically use a combination of time sampling and situation sampling to identify representative samples of behavior. In **time sampling,** researchers seek representative samples by choosing various time intervals for their observations. Intervals may be selected systematically (e.g., observing the first day of each week), randomly, or both. Consider how time sampling could be used to observe children's classroom behavior. If the researchers restricted their observations to certain times of the day (say, mornings only), they would not be able to generalize their findings to the rest of the school day. One approach to obtaining a representative sample is to schedule observation periods *systematically* throughout the school day. Observations might be made during four 30-minute periods every 2 hours. A *random* time-sampling technique could be used in the same situation by distributing four 30-minute periods randomly over the course of the day. A different random schedule would be determined for each day observations are made. Times would vary from day to day, but, over the long run, behavior would be sampled equally from all times of the school day.

Electronic devices provide a major advantage in carrying out time sampling using randomization. Electronic pagers can be programmed to signal observers on a random time schedule (normal sleeping times are excluded). For example, in their study of middle-class youth, Larson and others (Larson, Richards, Moneta, Holmbeck, & Duckett, 1996) obtained self-reports on adolescents' experiences at "16,477 random moments" in their lives. Systematic and random time-sampling procedures are often combined, as when observation intervals are scheduled systematically but observations within an interval are made at random times. For example, electronic pagers might be programmed to signal every 3 hours (systematic), but at a randomly selected time during each 3-hour interval. Whatever time-sampling procedure is used, the goal of time sampling is to obtain a representative sample of behavior that will represent an organism's usual behavior.

Time sampling is not an effective method for sampling behavior when the event of interest occurs infrequently. Researchers who use time sampling for infrequent events may miss the event entirely. Or, if the event lasts a long time, time sampling may lead the researcher to miss an important portion of the event, such as its beginning or end. In *event sampling* the observer records each event that meets a predetermined definition. For example, researchers interested in observing children's reactions to special events in school, such as a holiday play, would use event sampling. The special event defines when the observations are to be made.

Event sampling also is useful for observing behavior during events that occur unpredictably, such as natural or technical disasters. Whenever possible, observers try to be present at those times when an event of interest occurs or is likely to occur. Although event sampling is an effective and efficient method for observing infrequent or unpredictable events, the use of event sampling can easily introduce biases into the record of behavior. For instance, event sampling could lead an observer to sample at the times that are most "convenient" or only when an event is certain to occur. The resulting sample of behavior at these times may not be representative of the same behavior at other times. There is yet another sampling procedure that also may be used to obtain a representative sample: situation sampling.

Situation Sampling

- Situation sampling involves studying behavior in different locations and under different circumstances and conditions.
- Situation sampling enhances the external validity of findings.
- Within situations, subject sampling may be used to observe some people in the setting.

Key Concept }

Researchers can significantly increase the external validity of observational findings by using situation sampling. **Situation sampling** involves observing behavior in as many different locations and under as many different circumstances and conditions as possible. By sampling various situations, researchers reduce the chance that their results will be unique to specific circumstances or conditions. For example, animals do not behave the same way in zoos as they do in the wild or, it seems, in different locales. This is seen in studies of mutual eye gaze between mother and infant chimpanzees. Mutual eye gaze occurs in chimps as it does in humans, but in one study of chimpanzees the frequency of this behavior differed between animals observed in the United States and in Japan (Bard et al., 2005). Similarly, we can expect human behavior to differ across different settings.

By sampling different situations, a researcher can also increase the diversity of the subject sample and, hence, achieve greater generality of findings than could be claimed if only particular types of individuals were observed. For example, LaFrance and Mayo (1976) investigated racial differences in eye contact and sampled many different situations. Pairs of individuals were observed in college cafeterias, business-district fast-food outlets, hospital and airport waiting rooms, and restaurants. By using situation sampling, the investigators were able to include in their sample people who differed in age, socioeconomic status, sex, and race. Their observations of cultural differences in eye contact have considerably greater external validity than if they had studied only certain types of participants in only a specific situation.

There are many situations where there may be more behavior going on than can be effectively observed. For example, if researchers observed students' food selections in the dining hall during peak hours, they would not be able to observe all the students. In this case, and in others like it, the researcher would use *subject sampling* to determine which students to observe. Similar to the procedures for time sampling, the researcher could either select students systematically (e.g., every 10th student) or select students randomly. In what is likely by now a familiar refrain, the goal of subject sampling is to obtain a representative sample, in this example, of all students eating in the dining hall.

OBSERVATIONAL METHODS

- Observational methods can be classified as direct observation or indirect observation.

Researchers often observe behavior while it occurs—that is, through *direct observation*. However, observations also can be made indirectly, as when researchers examine evidence of past behavior using physical traces or archival records. This is *indirect* (or unobtrusive) observation. Figure 4.1 illustrates the organization of observational methods. First we will discuss direct observational methods and then indirect (unobtrusive) methods.

FIGURE 4.1 Flow diagram of observational methods.

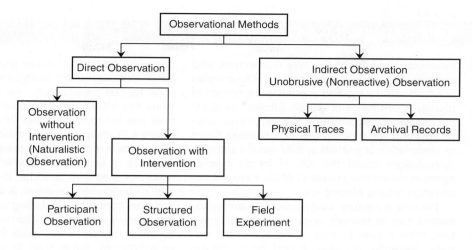

DIRECT OBSERVATIONAL METHODS

- Direct observational methods can be classified as "observation without intervention" or "observation with intervention."

When observing behavior directly, researchers make a decision regarding the extent to which they will intervene in the situation they observe. In this case, intervention refers to researchers' efforts to change or create the context for observation. The extent of intervention varies on a continuum from none (observation without intervention) to intervention that involves carrying out an experiment in a natural setting.

Observation without Intervention

- The goals of naturalistic observation are to describe behavior as it normally occurs and to examine relationships among variables.
- Naturalistic observation helps to establish the external validity of laboratory findings.
- When ethical and moral considerations prevent experimental control, naturalistic observation is an important research strategy.

Key Concept }

Direct observation of behavior in a natural setting *without* any attempt by the observer to intervene is frequently called **naturalistic observation.** An observer using this method of observation acts as a passive recorder of events as they occur naturally. Although it is not easy to define a natural setting precisely (see Bickman, 1976), we can consider a natural setting one in which behavior ordinarily occurs and that has not been arranged specifically for the purpose of observing behavior. For example, Matsumoto and Willingham (2006) observed athletes in the "natural" (for these athletes) setting of an Olympic judo competition. Box 4.1 describes recent findings based on naturalistic observation within the field of ethology.

BOX 4.1

OBSERVATION: TAKING ANOTHER LOOK

Psychologists are not the only researchers who observe behavior in natural settings. Observation is a fundamental method in *ethology,* a branch of biology (Eibl-Eibesfeldt, 1975). Ethologists study the behavior of organisms in relation to their natural environment, typically logging countless hours of observation of animals in their natural settings. Speculations about the role of innate mechanisms in determining human behavior are not uncommon among ethologists.

For over a century, many biologists simply assumed that all animals engaged in female-male sex, without even looking at the sex of the animals. Recently, however, based on increasing numbers of observations from a large, diverse array of species, biologists suggest that same-sex sexual behavior is a nearly universal phenomenon (Bagemihl, 2000; Zuk, 2003). Biologists are taking another look at sex.

Researchers who study mating and procreation among animals have been struggling to interpret evidence indicating sexual and parenting

behaviors among same-sex animals (Mooallem, 2010). Although most biologists avoid comparisons to human sexuality, the observations of same-sex behavior and co-parenting among animals has led to a great deal of controversy (see Figure 4.2). People on both sides of the sociopolitical debate regarding homosexuality have used evidence of same-sex behavior among animals to further their own agendas. A hallmark of scientific observation, however, is that it is objective and free from bias—including political agendas. Yet, many would wish to interpret animal sexuality using human terms, such as homosexuality or lesbianism, rather than to interpret the animal's behavior in its own context, with its own purpose.

The problem in understanding same-sex behaviors lies at the heart of evolutionary biology, namely, that all evolutionary-adaptive behavior is guided by a central goal: passing on genes. Nevertheless, biologists recently have developed theories suggesting that certain behaviors,

FIGURE 4.2   The children's book, *And Tango Makes Three* (Richardson & Parnell, 2005) is based on the story of two male penguins that were observed fostering a penguin chick at Central Park Zoo. The American Library Association reports that this was the most frequently banned book in 2009.

including sexual and parenting behaviors among same-sex animals, may be by-products of adaptation. This process of objective observation and theory construction forms the basis for all science. Yet, science, as we noted in Chapter 1, takes place in a cultural context that can lead some people to be less than objective when interpreting the results of this process.

Observing people in a psychological laboratory would not be considered naturalistic observation because a lab is created specifically to study behavior. Observation in natural settings often serves, among other functions, as a way to establish the external validity of laboratory findings—bringing the lab into the "real world." This is one goal of research conducted by researcher A.D.I. Kramer, who examines happiness using Facebook entries (*New York Times,* October 12, 2009). Observation of behavior in Internet discussion groups and chat rooms is yet another way that researchers have sought to describe behavior as it normally occurs (e.g., Whitlock, Powers, & Eckenrode, 2006). This recent form of "naturalistic" observation, however, raises the serious ethical issues that we discussed in Chapter 3 and will discuss later in this chapter (see also Kraut et al., 2004).

The major goals of observation in natural settings are to describe behavior as it ordinarily occurs and to investigate the relationship among variables that are present. Hartup (1974), for instance, chose naturalistic observation to investigate the frequency and types of aggression exhibited by preschoolers in a St. Paul, Minnesota, children's center. He distinguished hostile aggression (person-directed) from instrumental aggression (aimed at the retrieval of an object, territory, or privilege). Although he observed boys to be more aggressive overall than girls, his observations provided no evidence that the types of aggression differed between the sexes. Thus, Hartup was able to conclude that, with respect to hostile aggression, there was no evidence that boys and girls were "wired" differently.

Hartup's study of children's aggression illustrates why a researcher may choose to use naturalistic observation rather than to manipulate experimental conditions to study behavior. There are certain aspects of human behavior that moral or ethical considerations prevent us from controlling. For example, researchers are interested in the relationship between early childhood isolation and later emotional and psychological development. However, we would object strenuously if they tried to take children from their parents in order to raise them in isolation. Alternative methods of data collection must be considered if childhood isolation is to be investigated. For example, the effect of early isolation on later development has been studied through experimentation on animal subjects (Harlow & Harlow, 1966); observations of so-called feral children raised outside of human culture, presumably by animals (Candland, 1993); case studies of children subjected to unusual conditions of isolation by their parents (Curtiss, 1977); and systematic, direct observation of institutionalized children (Spitz, 1965). Moral and ethical sanctions also apply to investigating the nature of children's aggression. We would not want to see children intentionally harassed and picked on simply to record their reactions. However, as anyone who has observed children knows, there is plenty of naturally occurring aggression.

Hartup's study shows how naturalistic observation can be a useful method of gaining knowledge about children's aggression within moral and ethical constraints.

Observation with Intervention

- Most psychological research uses observation with intervention.
- The three methods of observation with intervention are participant observation, structured observation, and the field experiment.
- Whether "undisguised" or "disguised," participant observation allows researchers to observe behaviors and situations that are not usually open to scientific observation.
- If individuals change their behavior when they know they are being observed ("reactivity"), their behavior may no longer be representative of their normal behavior.
- Often used by clinical and developmental psychologists, structured observations are set up to record behaviors that may be difficult to observe using naturalistic observation.
- In a field experiment, researchers manipulate one or more independent variables in a natural setting to determine the effect on behavior.

It's not a secret. Scientists like to "tamper" with nature. They like to intervene in order to observe the effects and perhaps to test a theory. Intervention, rather than nonintervention, characterizes most psychological research. There are three important methods of observation that researchers use when they choose to intervene in natural settings: participant observation, structured observation, and the field experiment. The nature and degree of intervention varies across these three methods. We will consider each method in turn.

Key Concept

Participant Observation   In **participant observation,** observers play a dual role: They observe people's behavior and they participate actively in the situation they are observing. In *undisguised* participant observation, individuals who are being observed know that the observer is present for the purpose of collecting information about their behavior. This method is used frequently by anthropologists who seek to understand the culture and behavior of groups by living and working with members of the group.

Key Concept

In *disguised* participant observation, those who are being observed do not know that they are being observed. As you might imagine, people do not always behave in the way they ordinarily would when they know their behavior is being recorded. As we'll discuss later in this chapter, a major problem when observing behavior is **reactivity.** Reactivity occurs when people react to the fact they are being observed by changing their normal behavior. Remember, researchers want to describe people's *usual* behavior. Therefore, researchers may decide to disguise their role as observers if they believe that people being observed will change their behavior once they know their activities are being recorded. Disguised participant observation raises ethical issues (e.g., privacy and informed consent) that must be addressed prior to implementing the study. We have considered these ethical issues in Chapter 3 and will discuss them further later in this chapter.

Participant observation allows an observer to gain access to a situation that is not usually open to scientific observation. For example, a researcher analyzing hate crimes against African Americans entered various "White racist Internet chat rooms" while posing as a "curious neophyte" (Glaser, Dixit, & Green, 2002). Such venues, of course, where violence is sometimes advocated, would normally not be open to scientific investigation.

In a classic study of psychiatric diagnosis and hospitalization of the mentally ill, Rosenhan (1973) employed disguised participant observers who sought admission to mental hospitals. Each complained of the same general symptom: That he or she was hearing voices. Most of the pseudopatients were diagnosed with schizophrenia. Immediately after being hospitalized, the participant observers stopped complaining of any symptoms and waited to see how long it took for a "sane" person to be released from the hospital. Once hospitalized, they recorded their observations. The researchers were hospitalized from 7 to 52 days, and when discharged, their schizophrenia was said to be "in remission." Apparently, once the pseudopatients were labeled schizophrenic, they were stuck with that label. There are, however, reasons to challenge this specific conclusion and other aspects of Rosenhan's (1973) study (see Box 4.2).

Because disguised participant observers have similar experiences as the people under study, they gain important insights and understanding of individuals or groups. The pseudopatients in the Rosenhan study, for instance, felt what it was like to be labeled schizophrenic and not to know how long it would be before they could return to society. An important contribution of Rosenhan's (1973) study was its illustration of the dehumanization that can occur in institutional settings.

A participant observer's role in a situation can pose serious problems in carrying out a successful study. Observers may, for instance, lose their scientific objectivity if they identify too closely with the people and situation they are observing. For example, a criminologist, Kirkham (1975), went through police academy training as an undisguised participant observer and became a uniformed patrol officer assigned to a high-crime area. His experiences as an officer led to unexpected and dramatic changes in his attitudes, personality, mood, and behavior. As Kirkham himself noted, he displayed "punitiveness, pervasive cynicism and mistrust of others, chronic irritability and free-floating hostility, racism, [and] a diffuse personal anxiety over the menace of crime and criminals" (p. 19). In situations such as these, participant observers must be aware of the threat to objective reporting due to their involvement in the situation, particularly as their involvement increases.

Another potential problem with participant observation is that the observer can influence the behavior of people being studied. It is likely that the participant observer will have to interact with people, make decisions, initiate activities, assume responsibilities, and otherwise act like everyone else in that situation. By participating in the situation, do observers change the participants and events? If people do not act as they normally would because of the participant observer, it is difficult to generalize results to other situations.

The extent of a participant observer's influence on the behavior under observation is not easily assessed. Several factors must be considered, such as whether participation is disguised or undisguised, the size of the group entered,

BOX 4.2

THINKING CRITICALLY ABOUT "ON BEING SANE IN INSANE PLACES"

In his article "On Being Sane in Insane Places," Rosenhan (1973) questioned the nature of psychiatric diagnosis and hospitalization. How could normal people be labeled as schizophrenic, one of the most severe mental illnesses we know? Why didn't the hospital staff recognize the pseudopatients were faking their symptoms? After days or weeks of hospitalization, why didn't the staff recognize that the pseudopatients were "sane," not insane?

These are important questions. After Rosenhan's research article was published in *Science* magazine, many psychologists and psychiatrists discussed and wrote articles in response to Rosenhan's questions (e.g., Spitzer, 1976; Weiner, 1975). Presented below are just a few of the criticisms of Rosenhan's research.

—We cannot criticize the staff for making a wrong diagnosis: A diagnosis based on faked symptoms will, of course, be wrong.
—The pseudopatients had more than one symptom; they were anxious (about being "caught"), reported they were distressed, and sought hospitalization. Is it "normal" to seek admission into a mental hospital?
— Did the pseudopatients really behave normally once in the hospital? Perhaps normal behavior would be to say something like, "Hey, I only pretended to be insane to see if I could be hospitalized, but really, I lied, and now I want to go home."
—Schizophrenics' behavior is not always psychotic; "true" schizophrenics often behave "normally." Thus, it's not surprising that the staff took many days to determine that the pseudopatients no longer experienced symptoms.

—A diagnosis of "in remission" was quite rare and reflects staff members' recognition that a pseudopatient was no longer experiencing symptoms. However, research on schizophrenia demonstrates that once a person shows signs of schizophrenia, he or she is more likely than others to experience these symptoms again. Therefore, the diagnosis of "in remission" guides mental health professionals as they try to understand a person's subsequent behavior.
—"Sane" and "insane" are legal terms, not psychiatric. The legal decision of whether someone is insane requires a judgment about whether a person knows right from wrong, which is irrelevant to this study.

As you can see, Rosenhan's research was controversial. Most professionals now believe that this study does not help us to understand psychiatric diagnosis. However, several important long-term benefits of Rosenhan's research have emerged:

—Mental health professionals are more likely to postpone a diagnosis until more information is gathered about a patient's symptoms; this is called "diagnosis deferred."
—Mental health professionals are more aware of how their theoretical and personal biases may influence interpretations of patients' behaviors, and guard against biased judgments.
—Rosenhan's research illustrated the depersonalization and powerlessness experienced by many patients in mental health settings. His research influenced the mental health field to examine its practices and improve conditions for patients.

and the role of the observer in the group. When the group under observation is small or the activities of the participant observer are prominent, the observer is more likely to have a significant effect on people's behavior. This problem confronted several social psychologists who infiltrated a group of people who claimed to be in contact with beings from outer space (Festinger, Riecken, & Schachter, 1956). The group's leader said he had received a message from the aliens predicting a cataclysmic flood on a specific date. Because of the attitudes of members of the group toward "nonbelievers," the researchers were forced to make up bizarre stories in order to gain access to the group. This tactic worked too well. One of the participant observers was even thought to be a spaceman bringing a message. The researchers had inadvertently reinforced the group's beliefs and influenced in an undetermined way the course of events that followed. As you are no doubt aware, a flood covering the entire northern hemisphere never occurred, but at least some of the group members came to use this disconfirmation as a means of strengthening their initial belief because their faith had prevented the prophesied flood. Thus, although participant observation may permit an observer to gain access to situations not usually open to scientific investigation, the observer using this technique must seek ways to deal with the possible loss of objectivity and the potential effects an observer may have on the behavior under study.

Structured Observation   There are a variety of observational methods using intervention that are not easily categorized. These procedures differ from naturalistic observation because researchers intervene to exert some control over the events they are observing. The degree of intervention and control over events is less, however, than that seen in field experiments (which we describe briefly in the next section and in more detail in Chapter 6). We have labeled these procedures **structured observation.** Often the observer intervenes in order to cause an event to occur or to "set up" a situation so that events can be more easily recorded.

Key Concept

Researchers may create elaborate procedures to investigate a particular behavior fully. In a study of a phenomenon called inattentional blindness, researchers examined people's ability to notice unusual events while using a cell phone (Hyman, Boss, Wise, McKenzie, & Caggiano, 2009). Inattentional blindness occurs when people fail to notice new and distinctive stimuli in their environment, particularly when attention is focused elsewhere, such as a cell phone conversation. In their study the researchers used a *confederate*, that is, an individual in the research situation who is instructed to behave a certain way in order to create a situation for observing behavior. In Hyman et al.'s study, a confederate dressed as a clown rode a unicycle around a large sculpture in a central plaza area on a university campus (see Figure 4.3). Over a 1-hour period in which the clown was present, interviewers asked pedestrians who walked across the plaza whether they had seen anything unusual. If they answered yes, they were asked to specify what they had seen. If pedestrians did not mention the clown, they were asked specifically whether they had seen the unicycling clown.

This structured-observation procedure created the context for noting whether people are more likely to exhibit inattentional blindness while using a cell phone. The researchers classified pedestrians into one of four groups: cell phone user, single walker (with no electronics), walking singly while listening to music (e.g., using an MP3 player), or walking as a pair. Results indicated the cell phone users were least likely to notice the clown. Only 25% of cell phone users noticed the clown, compared to 51% of pedestrians walking alone, 61% of those listening to music, and 71% of individuals walking in pairs. Note that the individuals who might experience distractions due to music or walking with another person were more likely to notice the clown. This suggests that

FIGURE 4.3   A photo of the unicycling clown in Hyman et al.'s (2009) study of inattentional blindness.

something particular about the divided attention when using a cell phone may be related to inattentional blindness. Hyman et al. (2009) note that if such a high degree of inattentional blindness is present during the simple activity of walking, the "blindness" that occurs with cell phone use may be much greater while driving a car.

Structured observations may be arranged in a natural setting, as in the Hyman et al. (2009) study, or in a laboratory setting. Clinical psychologists often use structured observations when making behavioral assessments of parent-child interactions. For example, researchers have observed play between mothers and children from maltreating (e.g., abusing, neglecting) families and nonmaltreating families (Valentino, Cicchetti, Toth, & Rogosch, 2006). Mothers were videotaped in a laboratory setting through a one-way mirror while interacting with their children in different contexts arranged by the researchers. In these structured observations, children from abusing families engaged in less independent play than children from nonmaltreating families and mothers in these families differed in their attention-directing behaviors. Valentino et al. suggest their study sheds light on the effect of a maltreating environment on children's social cognitive development, and they discuss implications for intervention.

Developmental psychologists frequently use structured observations. Jean Piaget (1896–1980) is perhaps most notable for his use of these methods (see Figure 4.4). In many of Piaget's studies, a child is first given a problem to solve

FIGURE 4.4 Jean Piaget (1896–1980) used structured observation to investigate children's cognitive development.

and then given several variations of the problem to test the limits of the child's understanding. These structured observations have provided a wealth of information regarding children's cognition and are the basis for Piaget's "stage theory" of intellectual development (Piaget, 1965).

Structured observation is a middle ground between the passive nonintervention of naturalistic observation and the systematic control and manipulation of independent variables in laboratory experiments. This compromise allows researchers to make observations in more natural settings than the laboratory. Nevertheless, there may be a price to pay. If observers fail to follow similar procedures each time they make an observation, it is difficult for other observers to obtain the same results when investigating the same problem. Uncontrolled, and perhaps unknown, variables may play an important part in producing the behavior under observation. To prevent this problem, researchers must be consistent in their procedures and try to "structure" their observations as similarly as possible across observations.

Field Experiments   When a researcher manipulates one or more independent variables in a natural setting in order to determine the effect on behavior, the procedure is called a **field experiment.** The field experiment represents the most extreme form of intervention in observational methods. The essential difference

Key Concept

between field experiments and other observational methods is that researchers exert more control in field experiments when they manipulate an independent variable. Field experiments are frequently used in social psychology. For example, confederates have posed as robbers to investigate people's reaction to a crime, and researchers may manipulate the number of other bystanders (confederates) present to determine when people are most likely to help (Latané & Darley, 1970). Similarly, confederates have been used to cut into a waiting line in order to study those already in line (Milgram, Liberty, Toledo, & Wackenhut, 1986). In one field experiment, people's reactions to the intrusion were lessened when confederates also waited in line but did not object to the line cutting. Our discussion of experimental methods will continue in Chapter 6.

INDIRECT (UNOBTRUSIVE) OBSERVATIONAL METHODS

- An important advantage of indirect observational methods is that they are nonreactive.
- Indirect, or unobtrusive, observations can be obtained by examining physical traces and archival records.

STRETCHING EXERCISE

In this exercise we ask you to respond to the questions that follow this brief description of an observational study.

Students in a research methods class did an observational study to investigate whether students' ability to concentrate while studying was affected by where they studied. Specifically, students were observed in two locations on campus, the library and a lounge in the student union. The research methods students made their observations while appearing to be studying in the library or the lounge. They observed only students sitting alone in each location who had study materials such as a textbook or a notebook open in front of them. During a 5-minute observation period, the observers recorded the amount of time each student was studying, as indicated by either looking at the materials or writing. The student observers expected to find that students would be able to concentrate better in the library than in the student union.

Five student observers made observations for a total of 60 students in the library and 50 students in the student-union lounge from 9 to 11 P.M. on the same Monday evening. The mean time that students in the library spent studying was 4.4 of the 5.0 minutes. The corresponding mean time

for students in the student union was 4.5 of the 5.0 minutes. The research methods students were surprised by two aspects of their findings. First, they were surprised to find that students studied for nearly 90% of the 5-minute study interval. They were even more surprised that, contrary to their prediction, the study times did not differ for the two locations.

1 Identify what type of observational method the students used in their study, and explain what characteristics of their study you used to make your identification.

2 How might the decision to use 5-minute observation periods affect the observers' ability to study concentration?

3 Why would the time-sampling plan in a study of this type be especially important? How could the time-sampling plan used in this study be improved to increase external validity?

4 Consider for the sake of this question that students can concentrate better in the library than in the student-union lounge. How could the nature of the material that the students were studying in the two locations have led to the finding that there was no difference between the observed concentration by students in the library and in the student union?

TABLE 4.1   INDIRECT (UNOBTRUSIVE) MEASURES

Physical Traces	Archival Records
1. *Use traces:* physical evidence that results from the use (or nonuse) of an item *Examples:* cans in a recycling bin, pages highlighted in a textbook, wear and tear on video game controllers 2. *Products:* creations, constructions, or other artifacts of behavior *Examples:* petroglyphs (ancient rock paintings), MTV, *Harry Potter* action figures	1. *Running records:* public and private documents that are produced continuously *Examples:* records for sports teams, Facebook and Twitter entries 2. *Records for specific episodes:* documents that describe specific events *Examples:* birth certificates, marriage licenses, college degrees

Based on distinctions made by Webb et al. (1981).

Key Concept

We have been discussing observational methods in which an observer directly observes and records behavior in a setting. However, behavior can also be observed indirectly through records and other evidence of people's behavior. These methods are often called **unobtrusive measures** because the researcher does not intervene in the situation and individuals are not aware of the observations. An important advantage of these methods is that they are *nonreactive*. A behavioral measure is reactive when participants' awareness of an observer affects the measurement process. Because unobtrusive observations are made indirectly, it is impossible for people to react, or change their behavior, while researchers observe. Unobtrusive methods also yield important information that can confirm or challenge conclusions based on direct observation, making these methods an important tool in the multimethod approach to research.

In this section we will describe these indirect methods, which involve the investigation of physical traces and archival records (see Table 4.1).

Physical Traces

- Two categories of physical traces are "use traces" and "products."
- Use traces reflect the physical evidence of use (or nonuse) of items and can be measured in terms of natural or controlled use.
- By examining products people own or the products produced by a culture, researchers test hypotheses about attitudes, preferences, and behavior.
- The validity of physical trace measures is examined by considering possible sources of bias and by seeking converging evidence.

Key Concept

As everyone who has read a few detective stories knows, examining physical evidence of past behavior can provide important clues about the characteristics of individuals and events. For example, the size of footprints in the ground says something about the size and age of the person who stepped there. The distance between footprints can indicate whether the person was walking or running. **Physical traces** are the remnants, fragments, and products of past behavior. Two categories of physical traces are "use traces" and "products."

Use traces are what the label implies—the physical evidence that results from the use (or nonuse) of an item. Remains of cigarettes in ashtrays, aluminum cans in a recycling bin, and fingerprints on a murder weapon are examples of use traces. Clock settings are a use trace that may tell us about the degree to which people in different cultures are concerned with punctuality, and marks in textbooks may inform researchers which classes a students likes the best (or, at least, studies the most).

In addition, we can classify use traces according to whether the researcher intervenes while collecting data regarding the use of particular items. *Natural-use traces* are observed without any intervention by a researcher and reflect naturally occurring events. In contrast, *controlled-use traces* result from some intervention by a researcher. A study by Friedman and Wilson (1975) illustrates the distinction between these two types of use measures.

The investigators used both natural- and controlled-use traces to investigate college students' use of textbooks. Prior to the start of a course, they affixed tiny glue seals between pages of the textbooks. At the end of the course, they examined the textbooks to determine how many seals had been broken and where the broken seals were located. Because they controlled the presence of glue seals in the books, this would be an example of a controlled-use trace. These investigators also analyzed the frequency and nature of underlining in the textbooks, a natural-use measure because underlining is typically associated with textbook use. Analysis of both types of use traces indicated that students more often read the early chapters of the book than the later chapters.

Products are the creations, constructions, or other artifacts of behavior. Anthropologists often are interested in the surviving products of ancient cultures. By examining the types of vessels, paintings, tools, and other artifacts, anthropologists can describe patterns of behavior from thousands of years ago. Plenty of modern-day products provide insight into our culture and behavior, including television shows, music, fashion, and electronic devices. For instance, vehicle bumper stickers permit an acceptable outlet for the expression of public emotion and also allow individuals to reveal their identification with particular groups and beliefs (Endersby & Towle, 1996; Newhagen & Ancell, 1995). Tattoos and body piercings may function in a similar way in some cultures (see Figure 4.5).

The examination of products allows researchers to test important hypotheses about behavior. For example, psychologists examined food-related products in the United States and France to investigate the "French paradox" (Rozin, Kabnick, Pete, Fischler, & Shields, 2003). The term "French paradox" refers to the fact that obesity rates and the mortality rate from heart disease are much lower in France than the U.S., despite the fact that the French eat more fatty foods and fewer reduced-fat foods than Americans. Several hypotheses have been offered for these differences, ranging from metabolism differences, stress levels, and consumption of red wine. Rozin et al. hypothesized that the French simply eat less and they examined food products, specifically portion sizes, in both countries to test this hypothesis. They found that American restaurant portions were on average 25% greater than in comparable French restaurants, and that portion sizes on American supermarket shelves were generally larger. Their observation of products supported their hypothesis that the differences in obesity and mortality due to heart disease are because the French eat less than Americans.

FIGURE 4.5 Many cultures have used tattoos and body piercings as a means of self-expression and group identification.

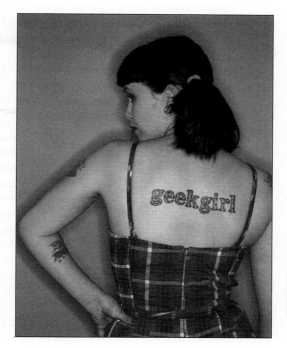

The indirect observation of physical traces offers researchers valuable and sometimes innovative means to study behavior, and the measures available are limited only by the ingenuity and resourcefulness of the investigator. However, the validity of physical-trace measures must be examined carefully and verified through independent sources of evidence. Validity refers to the truthfulness of a measure and we must ask, as with all measurement, whether physical traces truthfully inform us about people's behavior.

Bias can be introduced in the way use traces are laid down and the manner in which traces survive over time. For example, does a well-worn path to the right in a museum indicate people's interest in objects in that direction or simply a natural human tendency to turn right? Does the number of cans found in recycling containers at a university reflect students' preferences for certain brands or simply what is available in campus vending machines? Does highlighting in a textbook reflect a particular student's study of the material or the accumulated use of the book over time by many students as the book is sold and resold? Do product sizes on supermarket shelves in America and France reflect different family sizes in the two countries or preferences for portion sizes? Whenever possible, researchers need to obtain supplementary evidence for the validity of physical traces (see Webb et al., 1981). Alternative hypotheses for observations of physical traces must be considered and care must also be taken when comparing results across studies to make sure that measures are defined similarly.

Archival Records

- Archival records are the public and private documents describing the activities of individuals, groups, institutions, and governments, and comprise running records and records of specific, episodic events.
- Archival data are used to test hypotheses as part of the multimethod approach, to establish the external validity of laboratory findings, and to assess the effects of natural treatments.
- Potential problems associated with archival records include selective deposit, selective survival, and the possibility of spurious relationships.

Consider for a moment all of the data about you that exist in various records: birth certificate; school enrollment and grades; credit/debit card purchases; driver's license, employment and tax records; medical records; voting history; e-mail, texting, and cell phone accounts; and if you're active on sites such as Facebook and Twitter, countless entries describing your daily life. Now multiply this by the millions of other people for whom similar records exist and you will only touch upon the amount of data "out there." Add to this all of the data available for countries, governments, institutions, businesses, media, and you will begin to appreciate the wealth of data available to psychologists to describe people's behavior using archival records.

Key Concept }

Archival records are the public and private documents describing the activities of individuals, groups, institutions, and governments. Records that are continuously kept and updated are referred to as *running records*. The records of your academic life (e.g., grades, activities) are an example of running records, as are the continuous records of sports teams and the stock market. Other records, such as personal documents (e.g., birth certificates, marriage licenses), are more likely to describe specific events or episodes, and are referred to as *episodic records* (Webb et al., 1981).

As measures of behavior, archival data share some of the same advantages as physical traces. They are unobtrusive measures that are used to complement hypothesis testing based on other methods, such as direct observation, laboratory experiments, and surveys. When findings from these various approaches converge (or agree), the external validity of the findings increases. That is, we can say the findings *generalize* across the different research methods and enhance support for the hypothesis being tested. For example, recall the physical trace measures relating to portion size used to test the hypothesis concerning the "French paradox," namely, that the French eat less than Americans (Rozin et al., 2003). These researchers also examined archival records to test their hypothesis. They examined restaurant guides in two cities, Philadelphia and Paris, and recorded the number of references to "all-you-can-eat" buffets. Using an existing archival record (restaurant guides), they found converging evidence for their hypothesis: Philadelphia had 18 all-you-can-eat options and Paris had none.

Researchers may examine archives to assess the effect of a *natural treatment*. Natural treatments are naturally occurring events that significantly impact society or individuals. Because it is not always possible to anticipate these events, researchers who want to assess their impact must use a variety of behavioral

---

BOX 4.3

THE SCIENCE OF FREAKONOMICS

Do school teachers cheat on tests so that they and their students will look good?

Do police really lower crime rates?

Why does capital punishment not deter criminals?

Which is more dangerous to your child: the family owning a swimming pool or a gun?

Why are doctors so bad at washing their hands?

What's the best way to catch a terrorist?

Are people hard-wired for altruism or selfishness?

Why is chemotherapy prescribed so often if it's so ineffective?

These questions, and others, were asked by the maverick social scientist, Steven D. Levitt, in his best-selling books, *Freakonomics* and *Super-Freakonomics* (Levitt & Dubner, 2005; 2009). The answers he gives come from archival analyses of student test scores, sports records, crime statistics, birth and death statistics, and much more. We won't give away all the answers based on this clever researcher's mining of society's archives, but we will say that in this era of high-stakes testing, public school teachers sometimes cheat, and if you own both a gun and a swimming pool, your child is 100 times more likely to die by drowning than by gunplay.

---

measures, including archival data. Acts of terrorism such as 9/11, drastic economic events such as the worldwide economic collapse in 2008, and the enactment of new laws and reforms are examples of the kinds of events that may have important effects on behavior and can be investigated using archival data. Also, individuals experience naturally occurring events in their lives, such as death or divorce of parents, chronic illness, or relationship difficulties. The effects of these events can be explored using archival data. For example, a researcher may examine school records of absenteeism or grades to investigate children's responses to parental divorce. Similarly, Friedman et al. (1995) and Tucker et al. (1997) used archival data available from a longitudinal study begun in 1921 on a sample of 1,500 children. By also examining death records years later for individuals in the original sample, these investigators were able to determine that parental divorce was associated with earlier death for individuals in the study.

Researchers gain several practical advantages by using archival records. Archival data are plentiful and researchers can avoid an extensive data collection stage—data are simply waiting for researchers! Also, because archival information is often part of the public record and usually does not identify individuals, ethical concerns are less worrisome. As more and more archival sources become available through the Internet, researchers will find it even easier to examine behavior in this way (see Box 4.3).

Researchers, however, need to be aware of the problems and limitations of archival records. Two problems are *selective deposit* and *selective survival* (see Webb et al., 1981). These problems occur because there are biases in how archives are produced. **Selective deposit** occurs when some information is selected to be deposited in archives, but other information is not. For example, consider that great archive, the high school yearbook. Not all activities, events, and groups are selected to appear in the yearbook. Who decides what is prominently displayed

Key Concept

in the yearbook? When some events, activities, or groups have a better chance to be selected than others, bias exists. Or consider the fact that politicians and others who are constantly exposed to reporters know how to "use" the media by declaring that some statements are "off the record." This can be seen as a problem of selective deposit—only certain information is "for the record." You might also recognize this as a problem of reactivity, in that when deciding what is "for the record," individuals are reacting to the fact that their remarks are being recorded.

Interestingly, the *Congressional Record* is ostensibly a spontaneous record of speeches and remarks made before the Congress, but legislators actually have the opportunity to edit and alter the record before it is permanently recorded, and even to add documents into the record that were never read before Congress! No doubt remarks that are, in hindsight, less than politically expedient are changed prior to publication in the *Congressional Record*. This, too, is an example of selective deposit and can result in a biased account of the activities presented before Congress.

Key Concept

Selective survival arises when records are missing or incomplete (something an investigator may not even be aware of). Researchers must consider whether some records "survived," whereas others did not. Documents that are particularly damaging to certain individuals or groups may vanish, for example, during the change from one presidential administration to another. Family photo albums may "mysteriously" lose photos of individuals now divorced or photos from "fat years." In an archival study of letters printed in advice columns, Schoeneman and Rubanowitz (1985) cautioned that when analyzing the contents of the columns, they could not avoid the possibility of bias due to selective survival because advice columnists only print a fraction of the letters they receive; that is, only some of the letters "survived" to be printed in the newspaper column.

Another problem that can occur in the analysis of archival data is the possibility of identifying a *spurious relationship*. A spurious relationship exists when evidence falsely indicates that two or more variables are associated (see Chapter 5). False evidence can arise because of inadequate or improper statistical analyses, or more often, when variables are accidentally or coincidentally related. An association, or correlation, between two variables can occur when another, usually unidentified, third variable accounts for the relationship. For instance, archival records indicate that ice cream sales and crime rates are associated (as ice cream sales increase, so also do crime rates). Before we can conclude that eating ice cream causes people to commit crimes, it is important to consider that both variables, ice cream sales and crime rates, are likely affected by a third variable, seasonal temperatures. The spurious relationship between ice cream sales and crime rates can be accounted for by the third variable, temperature.

The possibility of biases due to selective deposit and selective survival, as well as spurious relationships, causes researchers to be appropriately cautious in reaching final conclusions based solely on the outcome of an archival study. Archival data are most useful when they provide complementary evidence in a multimethod approach to the investigation of a phenomenon.

RECORDING BEHAVIOR

- The goals of observational research determine whether researchers seek a comprehensive description of behavior or a description of only selected behaviors.
- How the results of a study are ultimately summarized, analyzed, and reported depends on how behavioral observations are initially recorded.

In addition to direct and indirect observation, observational methods also differ in the manner in which behavior is recorded. Sometimes researchers seek a *comprehensive* description of behavior and the situation in which it occurs. More often, they focus on only certain behaviors or events. Whether all behavior in a setting or only *selected* behaviors are observed depends on the researchers' goals. The important choice of how behavior is recorded ultimately determines how the results are measured, summarized, analyzed, and reported.

Comprehensive Records of Behavior

- Narrative records in the form of written descriptions of behavior, and audio and video recordings, are comprehensive records.
- Researchers classify and organize data from narrative records to test their hypotheses about behavior.
- Narrative records should be made during or soon after behavior is observed, and observers must be carefully trained to record behavior according to established criteria.

Key Concept

When researchers seek a comprehensive record of behavior, they often use narrative records. **Narrative records** provide a more or less faithful reproduction of behavior as it originally occurred. To create a narrative record, an observer can write descriptions of behavior, or use audio or video recordings. For example, videos were used to record the mother-child interactions among maltreating and nonmaltreating families (Valentino et al., 2006).

Once narrative records are created, researchers can study, classify, and organize the records to test their hypotheses or expectations about the behaviors under investigation. Narrative records differ from other forms of recording and measuring behavior because the classification of behaviors is done *after* the observations are made. Thus, researchers must make sure that the narrative records capture the information that will be needed to evaluate the hypotheses of the study.

Hartup (1974) obtained narrative records as part of his naturalistic study of children's aggression. Consider this sample narrative record from Hartup's study:

Marian [a 7-year old] . . . is complaining to all that David [who is also present] had squirted her on the pants she has to wear tonight. She says, "I'm gonna do it to him to see how he likes it." She fills a can with water and David runs to the teacher and tells of her threat. The teacher takes the can from Marian. Marian attacks David and pulls his hair very hard. He cries and swings at Marian as the teacher tries to restrain him; then she takes him upstairs. . . . Later, Marian and Elaine go upstairs and into the room where David is seated with a teacher. He throws a book at Marian. The teacher asks Marian to leave. Marian kicks David, then leaves. David cries and screams, "Get out of here, they're just gonna tease me." (p. 339)

Hartup instructed his observers to use precise language when describing behavior and to avoid making inferences about the intentions, motives, or feelings of the participants. Note that we are not told why David might want to throw a book at Marian or how Marian feels about being attacked. Hartup believed that certain antecedent behaviors were related to specific types of aggression. By strictly excluding any references or impressions of the observers, individuals who examined the narrative would not be influenced by the observer's inferences. Thus, the content of the narrative records could be classified and coded in an objective manner.

Not all narrative records are as focused as those obtained by Hartup, nor do narrative records always avoid inferences and impressions of the observer. Narrative records also are not always meant to be comprehensive descriptions of behavior. For example, *field notes* include only the observer's running descriptions of the participants, events, settings, and behaviors that are of particular interest to the observer, and may not contain an exact record of everything that occurred. Field notes are used by journalists, social workers, anthropologists, psychologists, and others, and are probably used more frequently than any other kind of narrative record. Events and behaviors are likely to be interpreted in terms of the observer's specialized knowledge and field notes tend to be highly personalized (Brandt, 1972). For example, a clinical psychologist may record specific behaviors of an individual with knowledge of that individual's diagnosis or particular clinical issues. The usefulness of field notes as scientific records depends on the accuracy and precision of their content which, in turn, depend critically on the training of the observer and the extent to which the recorded observations can be verified by independent observers and through other means of investigation.

Practical and methodological considerations dictate the manner in which narrative records are made. *As a general rule, records should be made during or as soon as possible after behavior is observed.* The passage of time blurs details and makes it harder to reproduce the original sequence of actions. In addition, decisions regarding what should be included in a narrative record, the degree of observer inference, and the completeness of the narrative record must be decided prior to beginning a study (see, for example, Brandt, 1972). Once the content of narrative records is decided, observers must be trained to record behavior according to the criteria that have been set up. Practice observations may have to be conducted and records critiqued by more than one investigator before "real" data are collected.

Selected Records of Behavior

- When researchers seek to describe specific behaviors or events, they often obtain quantitative measures of behavior, such as the frequency or duration of its occurrence.
- Quantitative measures of behavior use one of four levels of measurement scales: nominal, ordinal, interval, and ratio.

- Rating scales, often used to measure psychological dimensions, are frequently treated as if they are interval scales even though they usually represent ordinal measurement.
- Electronic recording devices may be used in natural settings to record behavior, and pagers sometimes are used to signal participants to report their behavior (e.g., on a questionnaire).

Often researchers are interested only in certain behaviors or specific aspects of individuals and settings. They may have specific hypotheses about the behavior they expect and clear definitions of the behaviors they are investigating. In this type of observational study, researchers typically measure the occurrence of the specific behavior while making their observations. For example, in their study of inattentional blindness, Hyman and his colleagues (2009) selected the behavior of whether people noticed the clown and quantified the number of people who noticed or did not notice the clown.

Suppose you wish to observe people's reactions to individuals with obvious physical disabilities using naturalistic observation. First you would need to define who is a "physically disabled person" and what constitutes a "reaction" to such a person. Are you interested in helping behaviors, approach/avoidance behaviors, eye contact, length of conversation, or in another physical reaction? Next you would need to decide how to measure these behaviors. Assume you choose to measure people's reactions by observing eye contact between individuals with and without physical disabilities. Exactly how should you measure eye contact? Should you simply measure whether an individual does or does not make eye contact, or do you want to measure the duration of any eye contact? Your decisions will depend on the hypotheses or goals of your study, and will be influenced by information gained by reading previous studies that used the same or similar behavioral measures. Unfortunately, previous research indicates that reactions to physically disabled individuals frequently can be classified as unfavorable (Thompson, 1982).

Key Concept }

Measurement Scales   When researchers decide to measure and quantify specific behaviors they must decide what scale of measurement to use. There are four levels of measurement, or **measurement scales,** that apply to both physical and psychological measurement: nominal, ordinal, interval, and ratio. The characteristics of each measurement scale are described in Table 4.2, and a detailed

TABLE 4.2   CHARACTERISTICS OF MEASUREMENT SCALES

Type of Scale	Operations	Objective
Nominal	Equal/not equal	Sort stimuli into discrete categories
Ordinal	Greater than/less than	Rank-order stimuli on a single dimension
Interval	Addition/multiplication/ subtraction/division	Specify the distance between stimuli on a given dimension
Ratio	Addition/multiplication subtraction/division/ formation of ratios of values	Specify the distance between stimuli on a given dimension and express ratios of scale values

BOX 4.4

MEASUREMENT "ON THE LEVEL"

The lowest level of measurement is called a *nominal scale;* it involves categorizing an event into one of a number of discrete categories. For instance, we could measure the color of people's eyes by classifying them as "brown-eyed" or "blue-eyed." When studying people's reactions to individuals with obvious physical disabilities, a researcher might use a nominal scale by measuring whether participants make eye contact or do not make eye contact with someone who has an obvious physical disability.

Summarizing and analyzing data measured on a nominal scale is limited. The only arithmetic operations that we can perform on nominal data involve the relationships "equal" and "not equal." A common way of summarizing nominal data is to report frequency in the form of proportion or percent of instances in each of the several categories.

The second level of measurement is called an ordinal scale. An *ordinal scale* involves ordering or ranking events to be measured. Ordinal scales add the arithmetic relationships "greater than" and "less than" to the measurement process. The outcome of a race is a familiar ordinal scale. When we know that an Olympic distance runner won a silver medal, we know the runner placed second but we do not know whether she finished second in a photo finish or trailed 200 meters behind the gold medal winner.

The third level of measurement is called an interval scale. An *interval scale* involves specifying how far apart two events are on a given dimension. On an ordinal scale, the difference between an event ranked first and an event ranked third does not necessarily equal the distance between those events ranked third and fifth. For example, the difference between the finishing times of the first- and third-place runners may not be the same as the difference in times between the third- and fifth-place runners. On an interval scale, however, differences of the same numerical size in scale values are equal. For example, the difference between 50 and 70 correct answers on an aptitude test is equal to the difference between 70 and 90 correct answers. What is missing from an interval scale is a meaningful zero point. For instance, if someone's score is zero on a verbal aptitude test, he or she would not necessarily have absolutely zero verbal ability (after all, the person presumably had enough verbal ability to take the test). Importantly, the standard arithmetic operations of addition, multiplication, subtraction, and division can be performed on data measured on an interval scale. Whenever possible, therefore, psychologists try to measure psychological dimensions using at least interval scales.

The fourth level of measurement is called a ratio scale. A *ratio scale* has all the properties of an interval scale, but a ratio scale also has an absolute zero point. In terms of arithmetic operations, a zero point makes the ratio of scale values meaningful. For example, temperature as expressed on the Celsius scale represents an interval scale of measurement. A reading of 0 degrees Celsius does not really mean absolutely no temperature. Therefore, it is not meaningful to say that 100 degrees Celsius is twice as hot as 50 degrees, or that 20 degrees is three times colder than 60 degrees. On the other hand, the Kelvin scale of temperature does have an absolute zero, and the ratio of scale values can be meaningfully calculated. Physical scales measuring time, weight, and distance can usually be treated as ratio scales. For example, someone who is 200 pounds weighs twice as much as someone who weighs 100 pounds.

description of measurement scales is provided in Box 4.4. You will need to keep these four measurement scales in mind as you select statistical procedures for analyzing the results of a research study. How data are analyzed depends on the measurement scale used. In this section we describe how the measurement scales can be used in observational research.

A *checklist* is often used to record nominal scale measures. To return to our example, an observer could record on a checklist whether individuals make eye contact or do not make eye contact with a physically disabled person, representing two discrete categories of behavior (a nominal measure). Checklists often include space to record observations regarding characteristics of participants, such as their race, sex, and age, as well as characteristics of the setting, such as time of day, location, and whether other people are present. Researchers typically are interested in observing behavior as a function of these participant and context variables. For example, Hyman et al. (2009) classified pedestrians in their study of inattentional blindness into four categories based on whether they were walking alone or in pairs and whether they were using a cell phone or music player (note that other categories, such as people walking in groups of three or more, were excluded).

The second level of measurement, an ordinal scale, involves ordering or ranking observations. Tassinary and Hansen (1998) used ordinal measurement to test a specific prediction of evolutionary psychology, namely, that female attractiveness is based on physical cues that simultaneously signal attractiveness *and* reproductive potential. The specific measure in this theory is the waist-to-hip ratio, with hips wider than waist indicating greater reproductive potential. In their study, undergraduates rank-ordered line drawings of female figures that varied in terms of height, weight, and hip size. That is, they ordered the drawings from least attractive to most attractive. Contrary to the prediction based on evolutionary psychology, physical attractiveness of the figures was directly and negatively related only to hip size, not the waist-to-hip ratio. Drawings with wider hips were more likely to be rank-ordered as lower in attractiveness.

In order to quantify behavior in an observational study, observers sometimes make *ratings* of behaviors and events based on their subjective judgments about the degree or quantity of some trait or condition (see Brandt, 1972). For example, Dickie (1987) asked trained observers to rate parent-infant interactions in a study designed to assess the effect of a parent training program. Observers visited the home and asked parents to "act as normal as possible—just as if we [the observers] weren't here." Observers made ratings using 7-point scales on 13 dimensions describing characteristics of verbal, physical, and emotional interaction. Ratings of 1 represented the absence or very little of the characteristic, and larger numbers represented increasing amounts of the trait. An example of one dimension, "parent's warmth and affection toward infant" is described in Table 4.3. Note that precise verbal descriptions are given for the four odd-numbered scale values to help the observers define different degrees of this trait. The even-numbered values (2, 4, 6) are used by observers to rate behaviors that they judge fall between the defined values. Based on observers' ratings, parents who took part in the program aimed at helping them to deal with their infant were rated higher on many of the 13 parent-child interaction variables than were parents who did not participate in the program.

At first glance, a rating scale such as the one in Table 4.3 appears to represent an interval scale of measurement—there is no true zero and the intervals between numbers appear to be equal. Closer examination, however, reveals that

TABLE 4.3 EXAMPLE OF RATING SCALE USED TO MEASURE A PARENT'S WARMTH AND AFFECTION TOWARD AN INFANT CHILD*

Scale Value	Description
1	There is an absence of warmth, affection, and pleasure. Excessive hostility, coldness, distance, and isolation from the child are predominant. Relationship is on an attacking level.
2	
3	There is occasional warmth and pleasure in interaction. Parent shows little evidence of pride in the child, or pride is shown in relation to deviant or bizarre behavior by the child. Parent's manner of relating is contrived, intellectual, not genuine.
4	
5	There is moderate pleasure and warmth in the interaction. Parent shows pleasure in some areas but not in others.
6	
7	Warmth and pleasure are characteristic of the interaction with the child. There is evidence of pleasure and pride in the child. Pleasure response is appropriate to the child's behavior.

*From materials provided by Jane Dickie.

most rating scales used by observers to evaluate people or events on a psychological dimension really yield only *ordinal* information. For a rating scale to be truly an interval level of measurement, a rating of 2, for instance, would have to be the same distance from a rating of 3 as a rating of 4 is from 5 or a rating of 6 is from 7. It is highly unlikely that human observers can make subjective judgments of traits such as warmth, pleasure, aggressiveness, or anxiety in a manner that yields precise interval distances between ratings. *However, most researchers assume an interval level of measurement when they use rating scales.* Deciding what measurement scale applies for any given measure of behavior is not always easy. If you are in doubt, you should seek advice from knowledgeable experts so that you can make appropriate decisions about the statistical description and analysis of your data.

Checklists also can be used to measure the *frequency* of particular behaviors in an individual or group over a period of time. The presence or absence of specific behaviors is noted at the time of each observation. After all the observations are made, researchers add up the number of times a particular behavior occurred. In these situations, frequency of responding can be assumed to represent a ratio level of measurement. That is, if "units" of some behavior (e.g., occasions when a child leaves a classroom seat) are counted, then zero represents the absence of that specific behavior. Ratios of scale values also would be meaningful. For example, a child who leaves her seat 20 times would have exhibited the target behavior twice as much as a child who leaves his seat 10 times.

Electronic Recording and Tracking Behavior also can be measured using electronic recording and tracking devices. For example, as part of a study investigating the relationship between cognitive coping strategies and blood pressure among college students, participants wore an ambulatory blood pressure monitor on two "typical" school days, including a day with an exam (Dolan, Sherwood, & Light, 1992). Participants also completed questionnaires about their coping strategies and daily activities. The researchers compared blood pressure readings for different times of the day and as a function of coping style. Students who exhibited "high self-focused coping" (e.g., "keep to themselves and/or blame themselves in stressful situations," p. 233) had higher blood pressure during and after an exam than did those who did not use self-focused coping strategies.

Another electronic method is the "Internet daily diary" in which participants log on daily to a secure Internet site (with e-mail reminders) to report on daily events. Park, Armeli, and Tennen (2004) used this method to examine college students' moods and coping. Each day, students reported their most stressful event and how they coped with it. Results of this study indicated that positive moods were linked more with problem-focused coping strategies than with avoidance strategies, especially when the stressful events were perceived as controllable. Other researchers have asked participants to carry hand-held computers and to make "electronic diary" notes when prompted (e.g., McCarthy, Piasecki, Fiore, & Baker, 2006; Shiffman & Paty, 2006). Undoubtedly, as Internet access with cell phones becomes commonplace, electronic methods for data collection increasingly will be used by researchers.

Electronic recording methods often rely on participants' self-reports of mood and activities, not on direct observation of their behavior. As such, it is important that researchers devise techniques to detect biases in data collection (e.g., possible misrepresentation or omission of activities; see Larson, 1989, for a discussion of possible biases). These problems can be weighed against the time and costs sometimes required to obtain a comprehensive description of behavior using direct observation (e.g., Barker, Wright, Schoggen, & Barker, 1978).

ANALYSIS OF OBSERVATIONAL DATA

- Researchers choose qualitative data analysis or quantitative data analysis to summarize observational data.

After recording their observations of behavior, researchers analyze observational data in order to summarize people's behavior and to determine the reliability of their observations. The type of data analysis that researchers choose depends on the data they've collected and the goals of their study. For example, when researchers record selected behaviors using a measurement scale, the preferred data analysis is quantitative (i.e., statistical summaries and analyses). When comprehensive narrative records are obtained, researchers may choose either quantitative or qualitative analyses. We will describe qualitative analyses first.

Qualitative Data Analysis

- Data reduction is an important step in the analysis of narrative records.
- Researchers code behaviors according to specific criteria, for example, by categorizing behaviors.

- Content analysis is used to examine archival records and includes three steps: identifying a relevant source, sampling sections from the source, and coding units of analysis.

Analysis of Narrative Records   Observational studies that use comprehensive narrative records or archival records provide a wealth of information–sometimes piles and piles of papers, video and audio recordings. Once the data are collected, how do researchers summarize all of this information? An important step in analyzing the content of narrative records is **data reduction,** the process of abstracting and summarizing behavioral data. In *qualitative* data analysis, researchers seek to provide a verbal summary of their observations and to develop a theory that explains behavior in the narrative records (see Miles & Huberman, 1994; Strauss & Corbin, 1990). In qualitative analysis, data reduction occurs when researchers verbally summarize information, identify themes, categorize and group pieces of information, and record their own observations about the narrative records.

Data reduction often involves the process of **coding,** which is the identification of units of behavior or particular events according to specific criteria that are related to the goals of the study. For example, in a study of preschool children, McGrew (1972) developed coding schemes to classify 115 different patterns of behavior according to the body part involved, ranging from facial expressions such as bared teeth, grin face, and pucker face, to locomotion behaviors such as gallop, crawl, run, skip, and step. Observers used the coding schemes to classify these behavioral patterns while they watched videos of children in preschool. Data reduction in this way (i.e., from videos to coded behaviors) allows researchers to determine relationships between specific types of behavior and the events that are antecedents of these behaviors. For example, McGrew found that children exhibit a "pout face" after losing a fight over a toy. McGrew also studied young chimpanzees and noted that these animals show a pout face when seeking reunion with their mother. Just after being frustrated (and often just prior to weeping), children exhibited a "pucker face." Interestingly, there was no record of a pucker face in the nonhuman primates.

Content Analysis of Archival Records   As with narrative records, the amount of data obtained from archival records can be daunting, and the researcher's first step involves data reduction. In the simplest cases, only data reduction may be necessary. For example, a simple tally of votes by legislators on a particular issue may quickly and effectively summarize data in a government record. In many cases, however, gleaning relevant data from an archival source can require careful procedures and relatively complex analysis of the source's content.

Content analysis can be generally defined as any objective coding technique that allows researchers to make inferences based on specific characteristics in archival records (Holsti, 1969). Although content analysis is associated primarily with written communications, it may be used with any form of communication, including television and radio programs, speeches, films, interviews, and Internet content (including text and e-mail messages, "tweets," etc.). When television or radio broadcasts are studied, time is often used as a unit of *quantitative*

Key Concept

Key Concept

Key Concept

measurement (e.g., the amount of time members of different ethnic groups appear on screen). When the communication is written, quantitative analysis may examine single words, characters, sentences, paragraphs, themes, or particular items (Holsti, 1969). For example, researchers studying the quality of a marital relationship may count the couple's use of pronouns (*we, you, I, he,* and *she*) found in transcripts of their interactions (e.g., Simmons, Gordon, & Chambless, 2005). When newspaper content is analyzed, a frequently used quantitative measure is space—for instance, the number of column inches devoted to particular topics. Qualitative data analysis of archival records using content analysis is similar to the methods described for narrative records.

The three basic steps of content analysis for archival records include identifying a relevant source, sampling selections from the source, and coding units of analysis. A relevant archival source is one that allows researchers to answer the research questions of the study. Although researchers can be quite ingenious when identifying their source, often the identification of the archival source is relatively straightforward, as, for example, when researchers investigated the relationship between the likelihood of being sentenced to death and the extent to which defendants had a stereotypical Black appearance (Eberhardt, Davies, Purdie-Vaughns, & Johnson, 2006). They used as their archival source an extensive database of death-eligible cases from the state of Pennsylvania that contained prisoners' photographs, crime data, and sentencing outcomes. Their results indicated a disturbing outcome: Defendants who appeared more stereotypically Black (based on independent ratings) were more likely to receive the death sentence than those with less stereotypical features.

The second step in content analysis involves sampling appropriately from the archival source. Many databases and archival sources are so extensive that it would be impossible for an investigator to analyze all of the information in the source; therefore, the investigator must select some of the data with the goal of obtaining a representative sample. Ideally, a researcher would use some technique for randomly selecting portions of the archive. The extent to which the results of an archival study can be generalized (external validity) depends on the representativeness of the sample. Earlier we mentioned the results of an archival study that examined the relationship between parental divorce and premature mortality (Friedman et al., 1995). The sample of data for this archival study was based on a sample of children initially studied in 1921; clearly, it was not a random sample of divorce and mortality statistics. We might question the external validity of findings for the impact of parental divorce on children's lives at the beginning of the 20th century when divorce was less frequent and less socially acceptable. Very different findings may be observed today.

The last step in performing a content analysis is *coding*. This step requires that relevant descriptive categories and appropriate units of measure be defined (see Holsti, 1969). As with the choice of the archival source itself, the descriptive categories depend on the goals of the study. In order for coders to make reliable judgments about the archival data, they must be carefully trained and precise operational definitions must be used. For example, in a study of adolescents' self-injury behaviors, researchers used a set of binary (present/absent) codes to analyze the content of Internet message boards related to adolescent self-injury

(Whitlock, Powers, & Eckenrode, 2006). They derived their codes from interviews with self-injurers and from observations of messages posted on the Internet. They then examined 3,219 Internet postings from 10 Internet message boards over a 2-month period and coded, or categorized, the content into different themes, such as motivation for self-injury and methods of concealing their behavior. Similar to analysis of narrative records, data reduction using coding allows researchers to determine relationships between specific types of behavior and the events that are antecedents of these behaviors. Whitlock and her colleagues, for instance, identified "triggers" of self-injury behaviors in their coding and were able to identify the proportion of messages that described each trigger. Based on their coding, they observed that "conflict with important others" was the most frequent trigger (34.8%) of self-injury. By counting the occurrence of these triggers, these investigators moved from qualitative coding of the data to quantitative data analysis.

Quantitative Data Analysis

- Data are summarized using descriptive statistics such as frequency counts, means, and standard deviations.
- Interobserver reliability refers to the extent to which independent observers agree in their observations.
- Interobserver reliability is increased by providing clear definitions about behaviors and events to be recorded, by training observers, and by providing feedback about the accuracy of observations.
- High interobserver reliability increases researchers' confidence that observations about behavior are accurate (valid).
- Interobserver reliability is assessed by calculating percentage agreement or correlations, depending on how the behaviors were measured and recorded.

The goal of *quantitative data analysis* is to provide a numerical, or quantitative, summary of observations in a study. An important step is to calculate descriptive statistics that summarize the observational data, such as relative frequency, means, and standard deviations. Another important aspect of analyzing observational data is assessing the reliability of the observations. Unless the observations are reliable, they are unlikely to tell us anything meaningful about behavior. We will describe each of these aspects of quantitative data analysis in turn.

Descriptive Statistics   The type of descriptive statistics used to summarize observational data depends on the scale of measurement used to record the data. As we saw, a nominal scale of measurement is used when behaviors and events are classified into mutually exclusive categories. Because a frequently used nominal measurement is whether a behavior is present or absent, the most common descriptive statistic for the nominal scale is *relative frequency*. To calculate a relative frequency the number of times a behavior or event occurs is tallied and then divided by the total number of observations. Relative frequency measures are expressed as either a proportion or a percentage (by multiplying the proportion by 100). We mentioned earlier that Whitlock and her colleagues coded triggers for self-injury behavior among adolescents, with the most frequent trigger being "conflict with important others." They counted 212 mentions of conflict among the 609 messages in which triggers were mentioned. The relative frequency, then, is .348 (212 ÷ 609), or 34.8% of the messages.

When describing ordinal data, researchers often report the item most frequently ranked first among a set of items. For example, in surveys addressing citizens' concerns about the country, researchers may ask people to rank order items such as the economy, wars, education, environment, national security, and so forth, in terms of the priority for government action. When reporting the results, researchers may describe an item according to the percentage of people who ranked it first, such as "35% of respondents ranked the economy as their top priority for government action" (hypothetical data). A more complete description would include the percentage of first-rankings for the remaining items, such as "28% of respondents indicated the environment is their top priority, 25% indicated that wars are their top priority," and so on. Another way to describe ordinal data focuses on describing the percentages of 1st, 2nd, and 3rd, etc. rankings for a particular item selected from among the set of items. Hypothetically, this might appear as "35% of respondents ranked the economy as 1st priority, 25% of respondents ranked the economy as their 2nd in priority, 12% ranked it 3rd," and so on.

Different—and more informative—descriptive statistics are reported when behavior is recorded on at least an interval scale of measurement. One or more measures of central tendency are used when observations are recorded using interval-scale ratings or when ratio-scale measures of time (duration, latency) are used. The most common measure of central tendency is the *arithmetic mean*, or *average*. The mean describes the "typical" score in a group of scores and provides a useful measure to summarize the performance of an individual or group. For a more complete description of performance, researchers also report a measure of variability or dispersion of scores around the mean. The *standard deviation* approximates the average distance of a score from the mean.

Now may be a good time to review measures of central tendency and variability, as well as general guidelines for systematically analyzing data sets. The first few pages of Chapter 11 are devoted to these issues.

LaFrance and Mayo (1976) reported means and standard deviations in their study of eye contact between same-race pairs of Black and White people in conversation. The number of seconds that each listener in a pair spent looking into the speaker's face was recorded. Table 4.4 gives the means and standard deviations summarizing the results of this study. The means indicate that on average, White listeners spent more time looking into the faces of speakers than did Black listeners. This finding was obtained for both same-sex pairs and male-female pairs. The standard deviations indicate that male pairs showed less variability than either female pairs or male-female pairs. Measures of central tendency and variability provide a remarkably efficient and effective summary of the large numbers of observations that were made in this study.

TABLE 4.4   MEANS AND STANDARD DEVIATIONS DESCRIBING THE TIME (IN SECONDS) THAT LISTENERS SPENT LOOKING INTO THE FACE OF A SAME-RACE SPEAKER PER 1-MINUTE OBSERVATION UNIT*

Group	Mean	Standard Deviation
Black conversants		
Male pairs	19.3	6.9
Female pairs	28.4	10.2
Male–female pairs	24.9	11.6
White conversants		
Male pairs	35.8	8.6
Female pairs	39.9	10.7
Male–female pairs	29.9	11.2

*From LaFrance and Mayo (1976).

Observer Reliability   In addition to descriptive statistics, researchers examine the extent to which the observations in their study are reliable. You may recall that reliability refers to consistency, and an analysis of reliability in an observational study asks if independent observers viewing the same events would obtain the same results. The degree to which two (or more) independent observers agree is referred to as **interobserver reliability.** When observers disagree, we become uncertain about what is being measured and the behaviors and events that actually occurred. Low interobserver reliability is likely to result when the event to be recorded is not clearly defined and observers are left to their own subjective judgments to make decisions about behavior. In addition to providing precise verbal definitions to improve reliability among observers, researchers can give concrete examples, including photographs and videos of specific behaviors to be observed. Interobserver reliability is also generally increased by training observers and giving them opportunities to practice making their observations. It is especially helpful during the training and practice to give observers specific feedback regarding any discrepancies between their observations and those of others (Judd, Smith, & Kidder, 1991).

Highly reliable observations do not necessarily mean the observations will be accurate. Consider two observers who reliably agree about what they saw but both are "in error" to the same degree. Neither observer would be providing an accurate record of behavior. For example, both might be influenced in a similar way by what they expect the results of their observation to be. Instances are occasionally reported in the media of several observers claiming to see the same thing (such as an unidentified flying object, or UFO), only to have the event turn out to be something else (a weather balloon). Nevertheless, when two independent observers agree, we are generally more inclined to believe that their observations are accurate and valid than when data are based on the observations of a single observer. In order for observers to be independent, each must be unaware of what the other has recorded. The chance of both observers being influenced to the same degree by expectancies, fatigue, or boredom is generally small enough that we can be confident that what they agree upon in their reports actually occurred. Of course, the more independent observers agree, the more confident we become.

Key Concept

The way in which interobserver reliability is assessed depends on how behavior is measured. When events are classified according to mutually exclusive categories (nominal scale), observer reliability is generally assessed using a percentage agreement measure. A formula for calculating percentage agreement between observers is

$$\frac{\text{Number of times two observers agree}}{\text{Number of opportunities to agree}} \times 100$$

In his study of childhood aggression, Hartup (1974) reported measures of reliability using percentage agreement that ranged from 83% to 94% for observers who coded type of aggression and the nature of antecedent events in narrative records. Although there is no hard-and-fast rule that defines low interobserver reliability, researchers generally report estimates of reliability that exceed 85% in the published literature, suggesting that percentage agreement much lower than that is unacceptable.

In many observational studies, data are collected by several observers who observe at different times. Under these circumstances, researchers select a sample of the observations to measure reliability. For example, two observers might record behavior according to time-sampling procedures and observe at the same time for only a subset of times. The percentage agreement for the times in which both observers are present can be used to estimate the degree of reliability for the study as a whole.

When data are measured using an ordinal scale, the Spearman rank-order correlation is used to assess interobserver reliability. When observational data are measured on an interval or ratio scale, such as when time is the measured variable, observer reliability can be assessed using a Pearson Product-Moment Correlation Coefficient, *r*. For example, LaFrance and Mayo (1976) obtained measures of reliability when observers recorded how much time a listener gazed into the speaker's face during a conversation. Observer reliability in their study was good; they found an average correlation of .92 between pairs of observers who recorded time spent in eye contact.

Key Concept

A *correlation* exists when two different measures of the same people, events, or things vary together—that is, when scores on one variable covary with scores on another variable. A **correlation coefficient** is a quantitative index of the degree of this covariation. When observation data are measured using interval or ratio scales, a Pearson correlation coefficient, *r*, may be used to obtain a measure of interobserver reliability. The correlation tells us how well the ratings of two observers agree.

The correlation coefficient indicates the *direction* and *strength* of the relationship. Direction can be either positive or negative. A positive correlation indicates that as the values for one measure increase, the values of the other measure also increase. For example, measures of smoking and lung cancer are positively correlated. A negative correlation indicates that as the values of one measure increase, the values of the second measure decrease. For instance, time spent watching television and scores on academic tests are negatively correlated. When assessing interobserver reliability, researchers seek positive correlations.

The strength of a correlation refers to the degree of covariation present. Correlations range in size from −1.00 (a perfect negative relationship) to 1.00 (a perfect positive relationship). A value of 0.0 indicates there is no relationship between the two variables. The closer a correlation coefficient is to 1.0 or −1.0, the stronger the relationship between the two variables. Note that the sign of a correlation signifies only its direction; a correlation coefficient of −.46 indicates a stronger relationship than one that is .20. We suggest that measures of interobserver reliability that exceed .85 indicate good agreement between observers (but the higher, the better!).

In Chapter 5 we discuss the use of correlations for making predictions. In addition, Chapter 11 provides a detailed discussion of correlations, including how relationships between two variables can be described graphically using scatterplots, how Pearson Product-Moment Correlation Coefficients are computed, and how these correlations are best interpreted. If you want to become more familiar with the topic of correlation, refer to Chapter 11.

Thinking Critically About Observational Research

A good observational study involves choosing how to sample behavior and events to observe, selecting the appropriate observational method, and deciding how to record and analyze observational data. Now that you know the basics of observational methods, you also need to know about potential problems that can occur. The first problem is associated with the influence of the observer on behavior; a second problem occurs when observers' biases influence what behavior they choose to record. We'll consider each of these problems in turn.

Influence of the Observer

- The problem of reactivity occurs when the observer influences the behavior being observed.
- Research participants may respond to demand characteristics in the research situation to guide their behavior.
- Methods to control reactivity include concealing the observer's presence, adaptation (habituation, desensitization), and indirect observation (physical traces, archival records).
- Researchers must consider ethical issues when attempting to control reactivity.

Reactivity   The presence of an observer can lead people to change their behavior because they know they are being observed. We first addressed this issue of *reactivity* in the section describing participant observation. When individuals "react" to the presence of an observer, their behavior may not represent their typical behavior—that is, their behavior when an observer is not present. Underwood and Shaughnessy (1975) relate how a student, as part of a class assignment, set out to observe whether drivers came to a complete stop at an intersection with a stop sign. The observer positioned himself on the street corner with clipboard in hand, and soon noticed that all of the drivers stopped at the stop sign. His presence influenced their behavior. When he concealed himself near the intersection, he found that drivers' behavior changed and he was able to gather data for his study.

Research participants can respond in very subtle ways when they are aware that their behavior is being observed. For instance, participants are sometimes apprehensive and anxious about participating in psychological research, and measures of arousal (e.g., heart rate) may change simply because an observer is present. Research participants who wear an electronic beeper that signals them to record their behavior and mood also can be expected to change their behavior (e.g., Larson, 1989).

Individuals often react to the presence of an observer by trying to behave in ways they think the researcher wants them to behave. Knowing they are part of a scientific investigation, individuals usually want to cooperate and be "good" participants. Research participants often try to guess what behaviors are expected, and they may use cues and other information to guide their behavior (Orne, 1962). These cues in the research situation are called **demand characteristics.** Orne suggests that individuals generally ask themselves the question, "What am I supposed to be doing here?" To answer this question, participants pay attention to the cues present in the setting, the research procedure, and implicit cues given by the researcher. To the extent that participants change their behavior as they pay attention to demand characteristics, the external validity of the research is threatened. The ability to generalize the research findings (external validity) is threatened when research participants behave in a manner that is not representative of their behavior outside the research setting. In addition, interpretation of the study's findings can be threatened because participants may unintentionally make a research variable more effective than it actually is, or even nullify the effect of an otherwise important variable. One way to reduce the problem of demand characteristics is to limit participants' knowledge about their role in the study or about the hypotheses of the study, that is, to provide as few "cues" as possible. You may remember, however, that withholding information from participants can raise ethical concerns, particularly concerning informed consent.

Key Concept

Controlling Reactivity   There are several approaches that researchers use to control the problem of reactivity. Several of the observational methods discussed earlier in this chapter are designed to limit reactivity. Reactivity can be eliminated if research participants do not know that an observer is present in the setting. Disguised participant observation achieves this goal because individuals are not aware of the presence of the observer. We can presume, then, that they behave as they normally would. Recall that this procedure was used in Rosenhan's (1973) study of hospitalization of the mentally ill and social psychologists' observations of individuals who claimed to be in contact with aliens

(Festinger et al., 1956). Observers can also conceal themselves while making observations in natural settings (naturalistic observation), as seen in the stop-sign study, or they can use hidden cameras or tape recorders to make their observations (but they must be aware of ethical concerns related to privacy).

An important advantage of indirect observation, or unobtrusive methods, is that these observations are nonreactive. Researchers observe physical traces and archival records to learn about people's past behavior. Because the individuals are no longer present in the situation and likely do not even know the physical traces or archival records are being observed by researchers, it is impossible for them to change their behavior. One researcher investigated the drinking behavior of people living in a town that was officially "dry" by counting empty liquor bottles in their trash cans (see Figure 4.6). Another researcher used the archival records kept by a library to assess the effect of the introduction of television in a community. Withdrawal of fiction titles dropped, but the demand for nonfiction was not affected (see Webb et al., 1981). It would be interesting to conduct a similar study today, considering the widespread availability of science, history, and biography cable programs. One might hypothesize that the advent of these programs is correlated with a decline in nonfiction rentals from libraries.

Another approach researchers use to deal with reactivity is to adapt participants to the presence of an observer. We can assume that as participants get used to an observer's presence, they will eventually behave normally in the observer's presence. Adaptation can be accomplished through either habituation or desensitization. In a *habituation* procedure, observers simply enter

FIGURE 4.6   Unobtrusive (nonreactive) measures of people's behavior can be obtained by searching their trash for physical traces, but ethical issues regarding privacy must be considered.

into the setting on many different occasions until the participants stop reacting to their presence (i.e., their presence becomes normal). Habituation was used to film a documentary titled *An American Family*, which was shown on public television in the 1970s. The camera crew literally moved into a California home and recorded the family for seven months. Although it's impossible to tell how much the family's behavior was influenced by the presence of these observers, the events that unfolded on camera provided evidence that family members had habituated to the cameras. Most notably, the family broke up and the wife asked the husband to move out of the house. When interviewed later about having the divorce announced to millions of viewers, the husband said that although they could have asked the camera crew to leave, by that time, he said, "we had gotten used to it" (*Newsweek*, 1973, p. 49). It's likely that similar processes of habituation take place during more contemporary "reality shows," but one must also wonder whether some of the behavior displayed on these shows occurs precisely *because* the individuals are on television!

Desensitization as a means of dealing with reactivity is similar to the procedures used by clinical psychologists in the behavioral treatment of phobias. In a therapy situation, an individual with a specific fear (e.g., spiders) is first exposed to the feared stimulus at a very low intensity. For example, the individual may be asked to think of things related to spiders, such as cobwebs. At the same time, the therapist helps the client to practice relaxation. Gradually the intensity of the stimulus is increased until the client can tolerate the actual feared object, for example, by holding a spider. Desensitization is often used by animal researchers to adapt animal subjects to the presence of an observer. Prior to her violent murder in Africa, Dian Fossey (1981, 1983) conducted fascinating observational studies of mountain gorillas in Rwanda. Over a period of time she moved closer and closer to the gorillas so they could adapt to her presence. She found that by imitating their movements—for instance, by munching the foliage they ate and by scratching herself—she could put the gorillas at ease. Eventually she was able to sit among the gorillas and observe them as they touched her and explored her research equipment.

Ethical Issues   Whenever researchers try to control reactivity by observing individuals without their knowledge, important ethical issues arise. For instance, observing people without their consent can represent a serious invasion of privacy. Deciding what constitutes an invasion of privacy is not always easy (see Chapter 3), and must include consideration of the sensitivity of the information, the setting where observation takes place, and the method for disseminating the information (e.g., Diener & Crandall, 1978).

Recent behavioral studies using the Internet introduce new ethical dilemmas. For example, when researchers enter Internet chat rooms as disguised participant observers to find out what makes racists advocate racial violence (Glaser et al., 2002), the information they obtained could be seen as incriminating evidence without the respondents' knowledge, much like a "sting" operation. The dilemma, of course, is that if informed consent were obtained it is very unlikely that respondents would cooperate. In this case, the IRB approved the research by agreeing with the researchers that a chat room is a "public forum," that these topics were common to that forum, and that the researchers had appropriately established safeguards to protect respondents' identities (e.g., by separating names or pseudonyms from comments). On the other hand, there are instances in which people have felt their privacy was violated when they learned that researchers observed their online discussions without their knowledge (see Skitka & Sargis, 2005). Although Internet message boards may be considered "public," researchers investigating adolescent messages about self-injurious behaviors were required by their university IRB to paraphrase participants' comments rather than use exact quotes (Whitlock et al., 2006). Behavioral research using the Internet is in its early stages, and both researchers and IRB members are still learning and applying creative problem solving for ethical dilemmas as they arise (see Kraut et al., 2004).

When individuals are involved in situations that are deliberately arranged by an investigator, as occurs in structured observation and field experiments, ethical problems associated with placing participants at risk may arise. Consider, for example, a field experiment in which students walking across campus were questioned about their attitudes toward racial harassment (Blanchard, Crandall, Brigham, & Vaughn, 1994). In one condition of the experiment, a confederate, posing as a student, condemned racist acts and in a second condition, the confederate condoned racist acts. Individual participants were then asked about their attitudes. The results of the study indicated that the views expressed by the confederate caused participants to be more likely to express similar statements compared to a third condition, in which the confederate didn't express any opinion. We can ask, were these participants "at risk"? Did the goals of the study, which were to show how outspoken people can influence interracial social settings, outweigh any risks involved in the study? Although participants were "debriefed immediately" in this study, is that sufficient to address any concerns about how they may have behaved when confronted with racist opinions? Did debriefing restore their confidence in a science that seeks knowledge through deception? Any attempt to answer these questions highlights the difficulty of ethical decision making.

Finally, we can turn to unobtrusive measures such as physical traces and archival data to address another ethical issue: scientists' ethical obligation to improve individual and societal conditions. There are many serious issues that confront us today, including violence, race relations, suicide, domestic conflict, and many other social issues, for which research involving direct observation may be difficult to justify when considering a risk/benefit ratio. That is, some research methods simply may involve too great a risk to research participants. However, psychologists' ethical obligation to improve the conditions of individuals, organizations, and society requires that they seek methods to gain knowledge in these important areas, for the cost of *not* doing research to solve these problems is high. Research involving the use of physical traces and archival data can be carried out on these important problems under conditions where ethical issues are often minimal relative to more intrusive methods. Thus, unobtrusive observational methods represent an important tool in the multimethod approach for investigating important social issues with less risk.

Observer Bias

- Observer bias occurs when researchers' biases determine which behaviors they choose to observe, and when observers' expectations about behavior lead to systematic errors in identifying and recording behavior.
- Expectancy effects can occur when observers are aware of hypotheses for the outcome of a study or the outcome of previous studies.
- The first step in controlling observer bias is to recognize that it may be present.
- Observer bias may be reduced by keeping observers unaware ("blind") of the goals and hypotheses of the study.

As an example of disguised participant observation, we described Rosenhan's (1973) classic study in which observers were admitted to psychiatric hospitals. Once in the hospital they observed and recorded behavior of hospital staff. Rosenhan's research identified a serious bias on the part of the staff. Once the observers (called "pseudopatients") were labeled schizophrenic, staff members interpreted their behavior solely according to this label. Behaviors that otherwise might be considered normal were interpreted by the staff as evidence of the pseudopatients' illness. For instance, the pseudopatients quickly learned they could record their observations openly—no one paid much attention to what they were doing. When Rosenhan later checked the medical records for the pseudopatients, he found that staff members had cited the note taking as a symptom of their illness. (Don't worry—taking notes is not a sign of mental illness!) Because staff members interpreted the pseudopatients' behavior in terms of the schizophrenic label, their "sanity" was not detected. This example clearly illustrates the danger of **observer bias,** the systematic errors in observation that result from an observer's expectations. In this case, the staff members demonstrated observer bias.

Key Concept }

Expectancy Effects   In many scientific studies the observer has some expectations about what behavior should be like in a particular situation or following a specific psychological treatment. When researchers design a study they review the previously published research literature to help them develop their hypotheses. This knowledge can lead researchers to form expectancies about what should occur in a research situation; in fact, hypotheses are predictions about what is expected to happen. However, expectancies can be a source of observer bias—*expectancy effects*—if they lead to systematic errors in observation (Rosenthal, 1966, 1976). A classic study documented expectancy effects (Cordaro & Ison, 1963). College student observers recorded the number of head turns and body contractions made by flatworms. Observers in one group were led to expect a high rate of movement, whereas observers in a second group expected a low rate. The two groups of flatworms were essentially identical; however, results showed that when observers expected to see lots of movement, they recorded twice as many head turns and three times as many body contractions compared to observers who expected a low rate of movement. Apparently, the students systematically interpreted the actions of the worms differently depending on what they expected to observe.

Other Biases   An observer's expectancies regarding the outcome of a study may not be the only source of observer bias. You might think that using automated equipment such as video cameras would eliminate observer bias. Although automation reduces the opportunity for bias, it does not necessarily eliminate it. Consider the fact that, in order to record behavior on film, the researcher must determine the angle, location, and time of filming. To the extent that these aspects of the study are influenced by the researcher's personal biases, such decisions can introduce systematic errors into the results. For example, Altmann (1974) described an observational study of animal behavior in which the observers biased the results by taking midday breaks, which coincided with a time of relative inactivity among the animals. Observations of the animals during these periods of inactivity were conspicuously absent for the observational records, which biased the results to make the animals appear more active than they were. In addition, the use of automated equipment generally only postpones the process of classification and interpretation, and it is perfectly possible for the effects of observer bias to be introduced when narrative records are coded and analyzed.

Controlling Observer Bias   Observer bias is difficult to eliminate, but it can be reduced in several ways. As we mentioned, the use of automatic recording equipment can help, although the potential for bias is still present. *Probably the most important factor in dealing with observer bias is the awareness that it might be present.* That is, an observer who knows about this bias will be more likely to take steps to reduce its effect. One important way researchers reduce observer bias is to limit the information provided to observers. When observers and coders do not know the hypotheses of a study they cannot form expectations about behavior. In a manner of speaking, observers can be kept "blind" regarding certain aspects of the study. Observers are blind when they do not know the reasons for the observations or the goals of the study. For example, when trained coders analyzed the videotapes of interactions between mothers and children from maltreating and nonmaltreating families, they were not aware of which type of family they were observing (Valentino et al., 2006). As you might imagine, observers' expectancies regarding maltreating families might influence their interpretation of behaviors, just as staff members in Rosenhan's (1973) study interpreted pseudopatients' behavior according to their diagnostic label. Using blind observers greatly reduces the possibility of introducing systematic errors due to observer expectancies.

SUMMARY

Researchers rarely observe all behavior that occurs. Consequently, researchers must use some form of behavior sampling such as time and situation sampling. An important goal of sampling is to achieve a representative sample of behavior. External validity refers to the extent to which observations from a study can be generalized to describe different populations, settings, and conditions; external validity is enhanced when a representative sample is obtained. Observational methods can be classified as direct observation or indirect observation. Direct observation in a natural setting without intervention is called naturalistic observation. Observation with intervention can take the form of participant observation, structured observation, and field experiments. An important advantage of indirect observational methods is that they are nonreactive. Reactivity occurs when people change their behavior because they know they are being observed. Indirect, or unobtrusive, observations can be obtained by examining physical traces and archival records. Physical traces include use traces (natural or controlled) and products. Archival data are the records of the activities of individuals, institutions, governments, and other groups. Problems associated with physical traces include potential biases in how traces accumulate or survive over time, and problems with archival data include selective deposit, selective survival, and the potential for spurious relationships in the data.

In observational studies, behavior can be recorded either with a comprehensive description of behavior or by recording only certain predefined units of behavior. Narrative records are used to provide comprehensive descriptions of behavior, and checklists typically are used when researchers are interested in whether a specific behavior has occurred (and under what conditions). Frequency, duration, and ratings of behavior are common variables examined in observational studies. The analysis of narrative records involves coding as one step in data reduction. Content analysis is used to examine archival records. How quantitative data are analyzed depends on the measurement scale used. The four measurement scales are nominal, ordinal, interval, and ratio. When a nominal scale is used to record behavior (e.g., present, absent), data are summarized using proportions or percentages to indicate relative frequency of behavior. When describing ordinal data, researchers often describe results according to the percentage of people who ranked items first among a set of items. When behavior is measured using interval and ratio scales, data are summarized using the mean and standard deviation. It is essential to provide measures of observer reliability when reporting the results of an observational study. Depending on the level of measurement used, either a percentage agreement measure or a correlation coefficient can be used to assess reliability.

Possible problems due to reactivity or observer bias must be controlled in any observational study. One form of reactivity is when participants pay attention to the demand characteristics of a research situation to guide their behavior. Observational methods in which the participants are not aware they are being observed (e.g., disguised participant observation, unobtrusive methods) limit reactivity; in other situations, participants may adapt to the presence of an observer. Observer bias occurs when researchers' biases determine which behaviors they choose to observe and when observers' expectations about behavior lead to systematic errors in identifying and recording behavior (expectancy effects). Important steps in reducing observer bias are to be aware of its presence and to keep observers blind regarding the goals and hypotheses of the study. Ethical issues must be considered prior to beginning any observational study. Depending on the nature of the observations, ethical issues might include deception, privacy, informed consent, and the risk/benefit ratio.

KEY CONCEPTS

REVIEW QUESTIONS

1 Describe the types of sampling researchers use in observational studies and what the proper use of sampling is intended to accomplish.
2 Explain the difference between direct and indirect observational methods and how the degree of intervention can be used to distinguish direct observational methods.
3 Describe a research situation in which naturalistic observation can be useful when ethical considerations prevent researchers from intervening to study behavior.
4 Explain why reactivity is a problem in observational studies.
5 Explain how structured observation represents a "middle ground" in psychological research and identify the primary advantage and potential cost of this compromise.
6 Explain why physical traces and archival data are attractive alternatives to direct observation.
7 Describe the different types of physical-trace measures available to psychologists and the ways in which these measures may be biased.
8 Explain how archival data may be used to test the effect of a natural treatment.
9 Explain how selective deposit, selective survival, and spurious relationships may bias the interpretation of archival records.
10 Describe how data reduction and coding are used in qualitative analyses of narrative records and archival data.
11 Give an example using each of the four measurement scales to describe how a researcher could measure eye contact between pairs of people in conversation with each other.
12 What are the most common descriptive measures (a) when events are measured on a nominal scale, (b) when items are ranked using an ordinal scale, and (c) when behavior is recorded on at least an interval scale.
13 Describe the procedures researchers can use to increase interobserver reliability.
14 Identify the measurement scales that require a correlation coefficient to assess interobserver reliability, and explain what a negative correlation would indicate in this situation.
15 Explain whether high interobserver reliability ensures that the observations are accurate and valid.
16 Describe two ways in which observer bias (expectancy effects) can occur in psychological research.
17 Explain how researchers may reduce observer bias.

CHALLENGE QUESTIONS

1 Students in a developmental psychology lab course conducted an observational study of parent–infant interactions in the home. When they first entered the home on each of the 4 days they observed a given family, they greeted both the parents and the infant (and any other children at home). They instructed the family to follow its daily routine, and they asked a series of questions about the activities of that day to determine whether it was a "normal" day or whether anything unusual had happened. The students tried to make the family feel comfortable, but they also tried to minimize their interactions with the family and with each other. For any given 2-hour observation period there were always two student observers present in the home, and the two observers recorded their notes independently of each other. Each of six pairs of students was randomly assigned to observe two of the 12 families who volunteered to serve in the study. The same pair of observers always observed a given family for the entire 8 hours of observation for that family. The observers used rating scales to record behaviors on a number of different dimensions, such as mutual warmth and affection of the parent–infant interaction.

   A Cite two specific procedures used by the students to ensure the reliability of their findings.

   B Cite one possible threat to the external validity of the findings of this study; once again, cite a specific example from the description provided.

   C Cite one specific aspect of their procedure that indicated that the students were sensitive to the possibility that their measurements might be reactive. What other methods might they have used to deal with this problem of reactivity?

2 An observational study was done to assess the effects of environmental influences on drinking by college students in a university-sponsored pub. Eighty-two students over the age of 21 were observed. The observers used a checklist to record whether the participant was male or female and whether the participant was with one other person or was in a group of two or more other people. Each observation session was always from 3 P.M. to 1 A.M., and observations were made Monday through Saturday. The observations were made over a 3-month period. Two observers were always present during any observation session. Each participant was observed for up to 1 hour from

the time he or she ordered the first beer. The data were summarized in terms of the number of beers drunk per hour. The results showed that men drank more and men drank faster than did women. Men drank faster when with other men, and women also drank faster with men present. Both men and women drank more in groups than when with one other person. These results indicate that the environment within which drinking occurs plays an important role in the nature and extent of that drinking.

   A Identify the observational method being used in this study, and explain why you decided on the observational method you chose.

   B Identify the independent and dependent variables in this study, and describe the operational definition of each level of the independent variable.

   C How could the researchers control for reactivity in this study? What ethical concerns might arise from their approach?

   D Identify one aspect of the procedures in this study that would likely *increase* the reliability of the observations.

   E Identify one aspect of the procedures in this study that would likely *limit* the external validity of the findings of this study.

3 A bright female graduate student in psychology has been offered a job with both *Newsweek* and *Time*. The salary offers of the two companies are basically the same, and it appears that both the working conditions and the job responsibilities are similar. To help her decide which job to accept, she resolves to determine whether one magazine has a better attitude toward women than the other. She appeals to you to help her with a content analysis of these two news magazines. What specific advice would you give her regarding each of the following steps of her content analysis?

   A Sampling

   B Coding

   C Reliability

   D Quantitative and qualitative measures

4 Four students were doing internships at the Social Science Research Institute of their university. The research institute had a contract to do a series of studies on traffic safety for the downtown development agency of a small city near the university. The internship students were assigned to carry out one of the studies. Specifically, they

(continued)

were to do a study to determine how likely it was that cars actually came to a stop at intersections with stop signs with pedestrian crosswalks in the downtown area. You are to respond to the following questions that the students are considering in planning their study.

A The students want to distinguish the extent to which the cars stop beyond a "yes" or "no" classification. How could the students develop an operational definition for the cars stopping that would include cars that came to a full stop, came to a rolling stop, and did not stop at all?

B What steps could the students take before beginning to collect data for the actual study to increase the interobserver reliability of their observations?

C The students are interested in determining the likelihood that cars will stop when pedestrian traffic downtown is light and when it is heavy. What time-sampling plan could the students use to make this determination?

D The students are especially interested in determining the likelihood of cars stopping at the stop sign independent of whether other cars have stopped. How would the students need to sample the cars they observed in order to study the independent stopping of cars? What information could the students record that would allow them to include all cars in their sample and still determine the likelihood of cars stopping independently?

Answer to Stretching Exercise

1 Because the students did not intervene in the situations (natural settings) they observed, this study is best described as naturalistic observation.

2 The students' choice of a 5-minute observation interval may have limited their ability to measure concentration effectively. The time interval may have been too short to show changes in concentration, making it difficult to detect differences between the two locations.

3 Time-sampling is important in this study because students' ability to concentrate may vary across days of the week and times of the day. By choosing only one time period (Monday, 9 to 11 P.M.), the external validity of the study is limited. Sampling different times of the day, days of the week, and weeks of the semester would improve the external validity of the study.

4 One possibility is that students choose different types of material to study in the two locations. If studying in a student union is more difficult, then students may choose easier material that requires less effort to maintain concentration while studying in the student union. This difference in study material might account for the observation that concentration times did not differ. One of the challenges of naturalistic observation is that researchers cannot control factors (e.g., type of material studied) that could influence the outcome of observations.

Answer to Challenge Question 1

A The students' procedures that enhanced reliability were as follows: observing each family for 8 hours, using two independent observers, and using checklists to provide operational definitions.

B One possible threat to the external validity of the findings was that the 12 families volunteered for the study and such families may differ from typical families.

C The students' efforts to minimize interactions with the family and with each other suggests that they were sensitive to the problem of reactivity. Two other methods they might have used are habituation and desensitization.

CHAPTER FIVE

Survey Research

CHAPTER OUTLINE

OVERVIEW

Are Americans romantic? Are they romantic compared to the French, who are renowned for their passion for passion? These were some of the questions asked in a 2009 survey of American romance—a survey conducted specifically to compare findings to a French survey regarding love and relationships (Schwartz, 2010).

Survey results indicated that Americans are just as "in love" as the French, even more so when considering older respondents. For individuals over age 65, 63% of Americans described themselves as "in love," compared to 46% of French in that age group. When do Americans and French respondents differ? When asked about sex. One question asked, "can true love exist without a radiant sex life?" A majority of Americans (77%) ages 18–65+ claimed this was true, whereas only 35% of French claimed true love can exist without such sex.

Based on these results, we can *describe* people's responses about being in love. Also, we can *predict* responses about being in love based on age and nationality (French or American). The findings also allow us to predict, knowing whether someone is American or French, what he or she may say about true love and sex. But does being French or American *cause* these attitudes? That is another matter entirely.

> *Key Concept*

Correlational research provides a basis for making predictions. Relationships among naturally occurring variables are assessed with the goal of identifying *predictive relationships*. As we discussed in Chapter 4, a *correlation coefficient* is a quantitative index of the direction and magnitude of a predictive relationship. We will discuss correlational research in the context of survey methodology later in this chapter.

Surveys typically are conducted with samples of people. In this chapter we first introduce the basic logic and techniques of sampling—the process of selecting a subset of a population to represent the population as a whole. You will then learn about the advantages and disadvantages of various survey-research methods and survey-research designs. The primary instrument of survey research is the questionnaire, and so we describe the basics of constructing a good questionnaire. We also discuss an important question that needs to be addressed in survey research, "Do people really do what they say they do?" We conclude the chapter by critically examining a broader question, "Just what can we conclude about causality when a correlation exists between two variables?"

USES OF SURVEYS

- Survey research is used to assess people's thoughts, opinions, and feelings.
- Surveys can be specific and limited in scope or more global in their goals.
- The best way to determine whether results of a survey are biased is to examine the survey procedures and analyses.

We discussed in Chapter 4 how psychologists use observational methods to infer what people must have been thinking or feeling to have behaved in a certain way. Survey research is designed to deal more directly with the nature of people's thoughts, opinions, and feelings. On the surface, survey research is deceptively simple. If you want to know what people are thinking, ask them! Similarly, if you want to know what people are doing, observe them! As we have seen, however, when we hope to infer general principles of behavior, our observations must be more sophisticated than our everyday, casual observations. So, too, survey research requires more than simply asking people questions.

Social scientists, such as political scientists, psychologists, and sociologists, use surveys in their research for a variety of reasons, both theoretical and applied. Surveys also are used to meet the more pragmatic needs of the media, political candidates, public health officials, professional organizations, and advertising and marketing directors. Surveys often are used to promote political or social agendas, as in the public health initiative to eliminate depictions of smoking in movies. Heatherton and Sargent (2009) analyzed survey data and found that as exposure to smoking in movies increases among adolescents, the likelihood of trying smoking or becoming smokers increases, especially among adolescents typically regarded as having low risk for smoking (e.g., nonsmoking parents).

In addition, the scope and purpose of surveys can be limited and specific, or they can be more global. An example of a survey with limited scope is an investigation of gratitude and communal strength in a relationship (Lambert, Clark, Durtschi, Fincham, & Graham, 2010). Communal strength refers to the degree to which individuals feel responsible for a relationship partner's welfare. Lambert and his colleagues surveyed participants to assess the extent to which individuals express gratitude in a close relationship and their feelings of communal strength in that relationship. The results of their survey supported their hypothesis that expressing gratitude is related to individuals' perception of communal strength.

Myers and Diener (1995), on the other hand, conducted a survey that addressed complex issues of global concern. They sampled people from 24 countries representing every continent but Antarctica. One of the research questions was whether people in wealthy countries have a greater sense of personal well-being than those in not-so-wealthy countries. The survey results showed that national wealth, as measured by gross national product per capita, is positively correlated with personal well-being (.67). But this relationship is not simple because national wealth is also correlated with other variables that are themselves highly correlated with well-being, such as number of continuous years of democracy (.85).

One of the ways that surveys can be used deserves mention because it raises ethical concerns. An ethical dilemma arises when sponsors of research have vested interests in the survey results. Crossen (1994) highlighted this by stating that "more and more of the information we use to buy, elect, advise, acquit, and heal has been created not to expand our knowledge but to sell a product or advance a cause" (p. 14). Crossen cites an example of a survey sponsored by a manufacturer of cellular phones showing that 70% of respondents (all of whom used cellular phones) agreed that people who use cellular telephones are more successful in business than those who do not use cell phones.

Is it reasonable to conclude that survey results are biased anytime the outcome of the survey is favorable for the sponsoring agency? Answers to ethical questions are rarely simple, and the answer to this one is not simple. High-quality and ethical research can be done when the sponsor has an interest in the outcome. Knowing the sponsor of the research is important when evaluating survey results but is not sufficient for judging whether the study is biased. It is much more important to know whether a biased sample has been used, or whether the wording of questions has been slanted, or whether the data have been selectively analyzed or reported. Any of these aspects of survey research can bias the results, and unethical researchers can use these techniques to make the results "turn out right." The best protection against unethical researchers and poor-quality research is to examine carefully the procedures and analyses used in the survey research.

Characteristics of Surveys

- Survey research involves selecting a sample (or samples) and using a predetermined set of questions.

All properly conducted surveys share common characteristics that make surveys an excellent method for describing people's attitudes and opinions. First, surveys generally involve sampling, which is a characteristic of nearly all behavioral research. This concept was introduced in our discussion of time and situation sampling in observational research in Chapter 4. We will discuss sampling as it is used in survey research in the next section. Surveys also are characterized by their use of a set of predetermined questions for all respondents. Oral, written, or computer-entered responses to these questions constitute the principal data obtained in a survey. By using the same phrasing and ordering of questions, it is possible to summarize the views of all respondents succinctly.

When a *representative sample* of people is asked the same set of questions, we can describe the attitudes of the population from which the sample was drawn. Furthermore, when the same questions are used, we can compare the attitudes of different populations or look for changes in attitudes over time. Surveys are a powerful tool in researchers' toolbox. In the remainder of this chapter, we highlight the methods that make surveys an effective strategy for examining people's thoughts, opinions, and feelings.

Sampling in Survey Research

- Careful selection of a survey sample allows researchers to generalize findings from the sample to the population.

Assume you've decided your research question is best answered using a survey, and you've determined the population of interest for your survey. The next step is to decide who should respond to your survey questions. This involves carefully selecting a sample of respondents to represent the population. Whether describing a national population or a much smaller one (e.g., the students of one university), the procedures for obtaining a representative sample are the same.

Basic Terms of Sampling

- The identification and selection of elements that will make up the sample is at the heart of all sampling techniques; the sample is chosen from the sampling frame, or list of all members of the population of interest.
- Researchers are not interested simply in the responses of those surveyed; instead, they seek to describe the larger population from which the sample was drawn.
- The ability to generalize from a sample to the population depends critically on the representativeness of the sample.
- A biased sample is one in which the characteristics of the sample are systematically different from the characteristics of the population.
- Selection bias occurs when the procedures used to select a sample result in the overrepresentation or underrepresentation of some segment(s) of the population.

Key Concept }

As we begin to talk about sampling techniques, we need to be clear about the definitions of four terms: *population, sampling frame, sample,* and *element.* The relationships among the four critical sampling terms are summarized in Figure 5.1. A **population** is the set of all cases of interest. For example, if you are interested in the attitudes of students on your campus toward computer services, your population is all students on your campus. Contacting everyone in a large

FIGURE 5.1   Illustration of relationships among four basic terms in sampling.

population is often practically impossible. Therefore, researchers usually select a subset of the population to represent the population as a whole.

We need to develop a specific list of the members of the population in order to select a subset of that population. This specific list is called a *sampling frame* and is, in a sense, an operational definition of the population of interest. In a survey of students' attitudes toward computer services, the sampling frame might be a list obtained from the registrar's office of all currently enrolled students. The extent to which the sampling frame truly reflects the population of interest determines the adequacy of the sample we ultimately select. The list provided by the registrar should provide a good sampling frame, but some students might be excluded, such as students who registered late.

Key Concept

The subset of the population actually drawn from the sampling frame is called the **sample.** We might select 100 students from the registrar's list to serve as the sample for our computer survey. How closely the attitudes of this sample of students will represent all students' attitudes depends critically on how the sample is selected. Each member of the population is called an *element*. The identification and selection of elements that will make up the sample are at the heart of all sampling techniques.

It is important to emphasize at this point that samples are of little or no interest in themselves. A new computer facility is not going to be built for the sole use of the 100 students surveyed. Similarly, the social psychologist is not

---

STRETCHING EXERCISE I

Identifying representative samples

Presented on the left side are descriptions of four populations. Find the sample on the right side that represents each population.

Populations	Samples
1 60% women, 40% men 90% ages 18–22, 10% age >22 70% freshman/sophomore, 30% junior/senior	**A** 132 women, 44 men 114 ages 18–22, 62 age >22 141 freshman/sophomore, 35 junior/senior
2 80% women, 20% men 60% ages 18–22, 40% age >22 70% freshman/sophomore, 30% junior/senior	**B** 244 women, 61 men 183 ages 18–22, 122 age >22 213 freshman/sophomore, 92 junior/senior
3 75% women, 25% men 65% ages 18–22, 35% age >22 80% freshman/sophomore, 20% junior/senior	**C** 48 women, 12 men 54 ages 18–22, 6 age >22 42 freshman/sophomore, 18 junior/senior
4 80% women, 20% men 90% ages 18–22, 10% age >22 70% freshman/sophomore, 30% junior/senior	**D** 150 women, 100 men 225 ages 18–22, 25 age >22 175 freshman/sophomore, 75 junior/senior

From Zechmeister, Zechmeister, & Shaughnessy, *Essentials of Research Methods in Psychology*, McGraw-Hill, 2001, p. 124.

interested solely in the racial attitudes of the 50 people he surveyed, nor is the marketing director interested only in the preferences of the 200 consumers she surveyed. *Populations, not samples, are of primary interest.* The "power" of samples to describe the larger population is based on the assumption that survey responses in a sample can be applied to the population from which the sample was drawn.

Key Concept ⎬

The ability to generalize from a sample to the population depends critically on the **representativeness** of the sample. Clearly, individuals in a population differ in many ways, and populations differ from each other. For example, one population might be 40% female and 60% male, whereas in another population the distribution might be 75% female and 25% male. *A sample is representative of the population to the extent that it exhibits the same distribution of characteristics as the population.* If a representative sample of 200 adults has 80 men and 120 women, which of the above-mentioned populations does it represent? You can use the illustrations in Stretching Exercise I to gain additional practice in identifying representative samples.

The major threat to representativeness is bias. A *biased sample* is one in which the distribution of characteristics in the sample is systematically different from the target population. A sample of 100 adults that included 80 women and 20 men would likely be biased if the population were 60% female and 40% male. In this case, women would be overrepresented and men would be underrepresented in the sample. There are two sources of bias in samples: selection bias and response rate bias. **Selection bias** occurs when the *procedures* used to select the sample result in the overrepresentation of some segment of the population or, conversely, in the exclusion or underrepresentation of a significant segment. We will describe problems associated with response rate bias in the next section, "Survey Methods."

Key Concept ⎬

Selection bias is likely, for example, when exit polls are used to survey people's attitudes. Research indicates that demographic characteristics such as age, race, education, and income of voters interviewed in exit polls differ from characteristics of the population based on U.S. Census data (Madigan, 1995). Note that U.S. Census data represents the entire population and includes voters and nonvoters, whereas only voters are selected for exit-poll samples. Thus, exit-poll samples may not represent the population due to a selection bias. Although a voter poll may accurately reflect the interests and attitudes of people *who vote*, their survey responses may not be used to characterize the attitudes of the population (which includes people who did not vote). Clearly, politicians cannot assume a "mandate" based on a biased sample of individuals who voted.

A more general lesson can be learned from the exit-poll example. Namely, what constitutes a representative sample depends on the population of interest. For example, if a university wants to know student drivers' opinions about on-campus parking, then the target population is college students who bring cars to campus (not college students in general). An unbiased sample would, in this case, be one that is representative of the population of students who have cars on campus.

Approaches to Sampling

- Two approaches to selecting a survey sample are nonprobability sampling and probability sampling.
- Nonprobability sampling (such as convenience sampling) does not guarantee that every element in the population has an equal chance of being included in the sample.
- Probability sampling is the method of choice for obtaining a representative sample.
- In simple random sampling, each element of the population has an equal chance of being included in the sample; in stratified random sampling, the population is divided into subpopulations (strata), and random samples are drawn from the strata.

Key Concept }

There are two basic approaches to sampling—nonprobability sampling and probability sampling. In **nonprobability sampling** we have no guarantee that each element has some chance of being included and no way to estimate the probability of each element's being included in the sample. In the computer-services survey we described earlier, if a researcher interviewed the first 30 students who entered the library, she would be using nonprobability sampling. Clearly, not all students would be equally likely to be at the library at that particular time, and some students would have essentially no chance of being included in the sample (e.g., if at work or in class).

Key Concept }

By contrast, if the researcher were to select 100 students randomly from the registrar's list of enrolled students, she would be using probability sampling. In **probability sampling,** all registered students (elements) have an equal chance of being included in the sample. We can describe this researcher's approach as probability sampling because her sampling procedure (i.e., random selection from a predetermined list) allows all students to have an equal chance of being selected for the survey. *Probability sampling is far superior to nonprobability sampling in ensuring that selected samples represent the population.* Thus, the researcher who selects 30 students randomly from the registrar's list of students is more likely to have a representative sample than the researcher who bases her survey results on the first 30 students who show up at the library.

Nonprobability Sampling   The most common form of nonprobability sampling is convenience sampling. *Convenience sampling* involves selecting respondents primarily on the basis of their availability and willingness to respond. For example, newspapers often publish the comments of "the person on the street." Their comments may make interesting reading, but their opinions likely do not represent those of the wider community. This lack of representativeness arises because convenience sampling is nonprobability sampling, and we can't be sure that every person in the community had a chance to be included in the sample. Convenience sampling also is involved when people respond to surveys in magazines because the magazine has to be available (and purchased), and people must be willing to send in their responses. The "participant pool" that is tapped by many psychologists at colleges and universities is a convenience sample typically comprised of students registered for the introductory psychology course.

Crossen (1994) describes the drawbacks of another variation of convenience sampling, call-in surveys. Call-in surveys are used by TV and radio shows to poll the views of their audience. Those who happen to be "tuned in" and who are willing to call (and sometimes to pay the charge for calling a 900 number) make up the sample for these call-in surveys. People who make calls in response to a call-in request differ from the general population not only because they are part of the particular show's audience, but because they are motivated enough to make a call. Similarly, online computer users who respond to a "pop up" survey question displayed on their home page will differ from those who choose not to respond (or are not regular computer users).

A prime-time TV news show once conducted a call-in survey with a question concerning whether the United Nations (UN) headquarters should remain in the United States (Crossen, 1994). It turns out that another survey research study involving about 500 randomly selected respondents also asked the same question. Of the 186,000 callers who responded, a solid majority (67%) wanted the UN *out of the United States.* Of the 500 respondents to the survey research study, a clear majority (72%) wanted the UN *to stay in the United States.* How could these two surveys yield such different—even opposite—results? Should we put more confidence in the results of the call-in survey because of the massive sample size? Absolutely not! A large convenience sample is just as likely to be an unrepresentative sample as is any other convenience sample. As a general rule, *you should consider that convenience sampling will result in a biased sample unless you have strong evidence confirming the representativeness of the sample.*

Probability Sampling   The distinguishing characteristic of probability sampling is that the researcher can specify, for each element of the population, the probability that it will be included in the sample. Two common types of probability sampling are simple random sampling and stratified random sampling. Simple random sampling is the basic technique of probability sampling. The most common definition of **simple random sampling** is that every element has an equal chance of being included in the sample. The procedures for simple random sampling are outlined in Box 5.1.

Key Concept

One critical decision that must be made in selecting a random sample is how large it should be. For now, we will simply note that the size of a random sample needed to represent a population depends on the degree of variability in the population. For example, college students in Ivy League schools represent a more homogeneous population than college students in *all* U.S. colleges in terms of their academic abilities. At one extreme, the most homogeneous population would be one in which all members of the population are identical. A sample of one element would be representative of this population regardless of the size of the population. At the other extreme, the most heterogeneous population would be one in which each member was completely different from all other members on all characteristics. No sample, regardless of its size, could be representative of this population. Every individual would have to be included

BOX 5.1

HOW TO DRAW RANDOM SAMPLES

The following names represent a scaled-down version of a sampling frame obtained from the registrar's office of a small college campus. Procedures for drawing both a simple random sample and a stratified random sample from this list are described.

Adamski	F	Jr
Alderink	F	Sr
Baxter	M	Sr
Bowen	F	Sr
Broder	M	So
Brown	M	Jr
Bufford	M	So
Campbell	F	Fr
Carnahan	F	So
Cowan	F	Fr
Cushman	M	Sr
Dawes	M	Jr
Dennis	M	Sr
Douglas	F	Fr
Dunne	M	So
Fahey	M	Fr
Fedder	M	Fr
Foley	F	So
Gonzales	F	Jr
Harris	F	Jr
Hedlund	F	So
Johnson	F	Fr
Klaaren	F	Jr
Ludwig	M	Fr
Martinez	F	Sr
Nowaczyk	M	Jr
O'Keane	F	Sr
Osgood	M	So
Owens	F	So
Penzien	M	Jr
Powers	M	Sr
Romero	M	Fr
Sawyer	M	Jr
Shaw	M	Sr
Sonders	F	Sr
Suffolk	F	So
Taylor	F	Fr
Thompson	M	Fr
Watterson	F	Jr
Zimmerman	M	So

Drawing a simple random sample:

Step 1. Number each element in the sampling frame: Adamski would be number 1, Harris number 20, and Zimmerman number 40.

Step 2. Decide on the sample size you want to use. This is just an illustration, so we will use a sample size of 5.

Step 3. Choose a starting point in the Table of Random Numbers in the Appendix (Table A.1) (a finger stab with your eyes closed works just fine—our stab came down at column 8, row 22 at the entry 26384). Because our sampling frame ranges only from 1 to 40, we had decided *prior* to entering the table to use the left two numbers in each set of five and to go across the table from left to right. We could just as easily have decided to go up, down, or from right to left. We could also have used the middle two or the last two digits of each set of five, but one should make these decisions before entering the table.

Step 4. Identify the numbers to be included in your sampling by moving across the table. We got the numbers 26, 06, 21, 15, and 32. Notice that numbers over 40 are ignored. The same would be true if we had come across a repetition of a number we had already selected.

Step 5. List the names corresponding to the selected numbers. In our case the sample will include Nowaczyk, Brown, Hedlund, Dunne, and Romero.

An even easier system, called *systematic sampling,* can be used to obtain a random sample. In this procedure you divide the sample size you want into the size of the sampling frame to obtain the value k. Then you select every kth element after choosing the first one randomly. In our example we want a sample size of 5 from a sampling frame of 40, so k would be 8. Thus, we would choose one of the first eight people randomly and then take every eighth person thereafter. If Alderink were chosen from among the first eight, the remaining members of the sample would be Cowan, Foley, Nowaczyk, and Shaw. *Note:* This system should *not* be used if the sampling frame has a periodic organization—if, for example, you had a list of dormitory residents arranged by room and every 10th pair listed occupied a corner room. You can readily see that, in such a list, if your sampling interval was 10 you could end up with all people from corner rooms or no people from corner rooms.

Freshmen
1 Campbell
2 Cowan
3 Douglas
4 Fahey
5 Fedder
6 Johnson
7 Ludwig
8 Romero
9 Taylor
10 Thompson

Sophomores
1 Broder
2 Bufford
3 Carnahan
4 Dunne
5 Foley
6 Hedlund
7 Osgood
8 Owens
9 Suffolk
10 Zimmerman

Juniors
1 Adamski
2 Brown
3 Dawes
4 Gonzales
5 Harris
6 Klaaren
7 Nowaczyk
8 Penzien
9 Sawyer
10 Watterson

Seniors
1 Alderink
2 Baxter
3 Bowen
4 Cushman
5 Dennis
6 Martinez
7 O'Keane
8 Powers
9 Shaw
10 Sonders

Drawing a stratified random sample:

Step 1. Arrange the sampling frame in strata. For our example we stratified by class standing. In the example the strata are equal in size, but this need not be the case.

Step 2. Number each element within each stratum, as has been done in the foregoing list.

Step 3. Decide on the overall sample size you want to use. For our example we will draw a sample of 8.

Step 4. Draw an equal-sized sample from each stratum such that you obtain the desired overall sample size. For our example this would mean drawing 2 from each stratum.

Step 5. Follow the steps for drawing a random sample and repeat for each stratum. We used a different starting point in the Table of Random Numbers (Table A.1), but this time we used the last two digits in each set of five. The numbers identified for each stratum were Freshmen (04 and 01), Sophomores (06 and 04), Juniors (07 and 09), and Seniors (02 and 09).

Step 6. List the names corresponding to the selected numbers. Our stratified random sample would include Fahey, Campbell, Hedlund, Dunne, Nowaczyk, Sawyer, Baxter, and Shaw.

to describe such a heterogeneous population. In practice, the populations with which survey researchers work typically fall somewhere between these two extremes.

Key Concept

The representativeness of a sample can often be improved by using stratified random sampling. In **stratified random sampling,** the population is divided into subpopulations called *strata* (singular: *stratum*) and random samples are drawn from each of these strata. There are two general ways to determine how many elements should be drawn from each stratum. One way (illustrated in the last example of Box 5.1) is to draw equal-sized samples from each stratum. The second way is to draw elements for the sample on a proportional basis. Consider a population of undergraduate students made up of 30% freshmen, 30% sophomores, 20% juniors, and 20% seniors (class years are the strata). A stratified random sample of 200 students drawn from this population would include 60 freshmen, 60 sophomores, 40 juniors, and 40 seniors. In contrast, drawing equal-sized samples from each stratum would result in 50 students for each class year. *Only the stratified sample on a proportional basis would be representative.*

In addition to its potential for increasing the representativeness of samples, stratified random sampling is useful when you want to describe specific portions of the population. For example, a simple random sample of 100 students would be sufficient to survey students' attitudes on a campus of 2,000 students. Suppose, however, your sample included only 2 of the

STRETCHING EXERCISE II

Two student researchers have been asked to do a survey to determine the attitudes of students toward fraternities and sororities on campus. There are 3,200 students in the school. About 25% of the students belong to the Greek organizations and 75% do not. The two student researchers disagree about what sampling plan is best for the study. One researcher thinks they should draw a stratified random sample of 200 students: 100 from among those students who belong to Greek organizations and 100 from among the independent students. The second researcher thinks they should draw one simple random sample of 100 students from the campus as a whole.

1 Comment critically on these two sampling plans in terms of their representativeness and the likelihood that they would measure reliably the views of students who belong to Greek organizations.
2 Develop your own sampling plan if you decide that neither of the ones proposed so far is optimal.

40 chemistry majors on campus, and you wish to describe the views of students according to different majors. Although this accurately reflects the proportion of chemistry majors in the campus population, it would be risky to use the views of only 2 chemistry students to represent all 40 chemistry majors (2 is too few). In this case (and more generally when a stratum is small in number), you could sample more chemistry majors to describe their views better. We can't say precisely how many to sample because, as we learned earlier, the sample size needed to represent a population depends on the degree of variability in the population.

SURVEY METHODS

- Four methods for obtaining survey data are mail surveys, personal interviews, telephone interviews, and Internet surveys.

Selecting the sample is only one of several important decisions to make when doing survey research. You also need to decide how you will obtain information from the respondents. There are four general methods: mail surveys, personal interviews, telephone interviews, and Internet surveys. As is often true when doing research, there is no one best survey method for all circumstances. Each survey method has its own advantages and disadvantages. The challenge you face is to select the method that best fits your research question.

Mail Surveys

- Although mail surveys are quick and convenient, there may be a problem with the response rate when individuals fail to complete and return the survey.
- Due to problems with the response rate, the final sample for a mail survey may not represent the population.

Mail surveys are used to distribute self-administered questionnaires that respondents fill out on their own. One advantage of mail surveys is that they usually can be completed relatively quickly. Because they are self-administered, mail surveys also avoid the problems due to interviewer bias (to be defined in the next section). Among the four survey methods, mail surveys are the best for dealing with highly personal or embarrassing topics, especially when anonymity of respondents is preserved.

Unfortunately, there are many disadvantages to mail surveys. Some of these disadvantages are less serious than others. For instance, because respondents will not be able to ask questions, the questionnaire used in the survey must be completely self-explanatory. A second, less serious disadvantage is that the researcher has little control over the order in which the respondent answers the questions. The order of questions may affect how respondents answer certain questions. A serious problem with mail surveys, however, is a low response rate that can result in response rate bias.

Key Concept

Response rate refers to the percentage of people who complete the survey. For example, if 30 of 100 people sampled complete the survey, the response rate is 30%. *A low response rate indicates there could be a* **response rate bias** *that threatens the representativeness of a sample.* There are many reasons why this occurs. For example, respondents with literacy problems, low educational background, or vision problems may not complete the survey; therefore, people with these characteristics may not be represented well in the final sample of respondents. Often, people randomly selected for a sample are too busy or not interested enough in the study to return a completed questionnaire. Low response rate (i.e., failure to complete and return the survey) is the major factor leading to samples that do not represent the population of interest, resulting in a response rate bias. Thus, a carefully selected probability sample may become a nonprobability sample—a convenience sample in which individuals' availability and willingness determine whether they complete the survey.

Unless the return rate is 100%, the potential for response rate bias exists regardless of how carefully the initial sample was selected. However, a low response rate does not automatically indicate the sample does not represent the population. The researcher must demonstrate the extent to which the final sample of respondents who returned the survey is representative of the population, and that no segment of the population is overrepresented or underrepresented. For example, Berdahl and Moore (2006) commented that their sample likely underrepresented the harassment experiences of recent immigrants with poor English skills who may have had difficulty with the questionnaire.

The typical return rate for mail surveys is only around 30%. There are things you can do, however, to increase the return rate. Return rates generally will be higher when

—the questionnaire has a "personal touch" (e.g., respondents are addressed by name and not simply "resident" or "student");
—responding requires minimal effort from the respondent;
—the topic of the survey is of intrinsic interest to the respondent;
—the respondent identifies in some way with the organization or researcher sponsoring the survey.

Personal Interviews

- Although costly, personal interviews allow researchers to gain more control over how the survey is administered.
- Interviewer bias occurs when survey responses are recorded inaccurately or when interviewers guide individuals' responses.

When personal interviews are used to collect survey data, respondents are usually contacted in their homes or in a shopping mall, and trained interviewers administer the questionnaire. The personal interview allows greater flexibility in asking questions than does the mail survey. During an interview the respondent can obtain clarification when questions are unclear, and the trained interviewer can follow up incomplete or ambiguous answers to open-ended questions. The interviewer controls the order of questions and can ensure that all respondents complete the questions in the same order. Traditionally, the response rate to personal interviews has been higher than that for mail surveys.

The advantages of using personal interviews are impressive, but there are also a few disadvantages. Increasing fear of urban crime and an increasing number of households with no one home during the day have reduced the attractiveness of using personal interviews in the home. A significant disadvantage of conducting personal interviews is the cost. The use of trained interviewers is expensive in terms of both money and time. Perhaps the most critical disadvantage of personal interviews involves the potential for interviewer bias. The interviewer should be a neutral medium through which questions and answers are transmitted. **Interviewer bias** occurs when the interviewer records only selected portions of the respondents' answers or tries to adjust the wording of a question to "fit" the respondent. For example, suppose a respondent in a survey about television states, "The biggest problem with TV shows is too much violence." Interviewer bias would occur if the interviewer writes down "TV violence" instead of the respondent's full response. In a follow-up question, interview bias also would occur if the interviewer asked, "By violence, do you mean murders and rapes?" A more neutral probe would allow the respondent to describe what he or she means by asking, "Could you elaborate on what you mean by violence?"

The best protection against interviewer bias is to employ highly motivated, well-paid interviewers who are trained to follow question wording exactly, to record responses accurately, and to use follow-up questions judiciously. Interviewers should also be given a detailed list of instructions about how difficult or confusing situations are to be handled. Finally, interviewers should be closely supervised by the director of the survey project.

Computer technology makes it possible to use a hybrid of a self-administered survey and a personal interview. A person can listen to computer-recorded questions read by an interviewer and then respond to the questions on the computer. With this technology each respondent literally hears the questions read by the same interviewer in the same way, thereby reducing the risk of interviewer bias. This technology also allows respondents to answer very personal questions in relative privacy (Rasinski, Willis, Baldwin, Yeh, & Lee, 1999).

Key Concept

Telephone Interviews

- Despite some disadvantages, telephone interviews are used frequently for brief surveys.

The prohibitive cost of personal interviews and difficulties supervising interviewers have led survey researchers to turn to telephone or Internet surveys. Phone interviewing met with considerable criticism when it was first used because of serious limitations on the sampling frame of potential respondents. Many people had unlisted numbers, and the poor and those in rural areas were less likely to have a phone. By 2000, however, more than 97% of all U.S. households had telephones (U.S. Census Bureau, 2000), and households with unlisted numbers could be reached using random-digit dialing. The random-digit dialing technique permits researchers to contact efficiently a generally representative sample of U.S. telephone owners. Telephone interviewing also provides better access to dangerous neighborhoods, locked buildings, and respondents available only during evening hours (have you ever been asked to complete a telephone survey during dinner?). Interviews can be completed more quickly when contacts are made by phone, and interviewers can be better supervised when all interviews are conducted from one location (Figure 5.2).

The telephone survey, like the other survey methods, is not without its drawbacks. A possible selection bias exists when respondents are limited to those who have telephones and the problem of interviewer bias remains. There is a limit to how long respondents are willing to stay on the phone, and individuals

FIGURE 5.2   Random-digit dialing allows researchers efficient access to a generally representative sample of telephone owners for brief surveys.

may respond differently when talking to a "faceless voice" than they would to a personal interviewer. The proliferation of cell phones also adds an unknown effect, given that cell phone users are frequently "on the go" or in business settings when they answer their phone. This cultural change may result in lower response rates from telephone surveys. In addition, one may assume that individuals from higher socioeconomic groups are more likely to have multiple phone numbers and hence might be overrepresented in a survey based on random-digit dialing. Hippler and Schwarz (1987) suggest that people take less time to form judgments during phone interviews and may have difficulty remembering the response options offered by the interviewer. Moreover, extensive use of phone solicitation for selling products and requesting contributions has led many people to be less willing to be interviewed. Options that allow for screening calls and voice mail have made it easier for people to avoid unwanted calls. And many people who are working two jobs are rarely at home to answer the phone. In spite of these limitations and perhaps others you can think of, telephone interviews are frequently used for brief surveys.

Internet Surveys

- The Internet offers several advantages for survey research because it is an efficient, low-cost method for obtaining survey responses from large, potentially diverse and underrepresented samples.
- Disadvantages associated with Internet survey research include the potential for response rate bias and selection bias, and lack of control over the research environment.

Surveys were among the earliest Internet-based behavioral studies. Participants complete a questionnaire online and click on a "submit" button to have their responses recorded. Depending on the sophistication of the software, there is the potential for literally millions of responses to be automatically recorded and summarized as they are processed by the receiving server. Programs also exist to permit manipulation of variables and the random assignment of participants to experimental conditions. (See, for example, Fraley, 2004, for a "beginner's guide" to HTML-based psychological research on the Internet, and Kraut et al., 2004, for useful Internet resources.)

Numerous advantages of using the Internet for survey research immediately come to mind. At the top of the list are efficiency and cost (e.g., see Buchanan, 2000; Skitka & Sargis, 2005). Thousands, if not millions, of participants who vary in age, ethnicity, and even nationality can be contacted through a few keystrokes on a computer. Time and labor are dramatically reduced relative to mail or telephone surveys, let alone personal interviews. Online questionnaires are paperless, thus saving natural resources and copying costs. Participants may respond when it is convenient and do so without leaving the comfort of their home, office, dorm room, or other Internet site.

In addition to reaching large and potentially diverse samples, Skitka and Sargis (2005) suggest that the Internet also has the potential for accessing groups that typically are underrepresented in psychological research. The prevalence on the Web of chat rooms, special interest groups, and support groups provides an "in" for a researcher seeking specific samples of participants, whether it be pet owners, members of hate groups, cancer survivors, victims of various crimes, or any of a multitude of respondent types that may not be as easily reached by traditional survey methods. Because the Internet is truly a worldwide source of participants, it also opens up new possibilities for cross-cultural research (e.g., Gosling et al., 2004).

Internet-based surveys are also not without their disadvantages. At the top of this list is the potential for sample biases (Birnbaum, 2000; Kraut et al., 2004; Schmidt, 1997). Both response rate bias and selection bias are likely to be present. Problems with low response rates can occur due to nonresponding just as it does for other survey methods. In fact, response rates typically are lower for online surveys than for comparable mail or telephone surveys (see Kraut et al., 2004; Skitka & Sargis, 2005). As we have seen, individuals who respond to a survey are going to differ on important characteristics from those who do not respond. Selection bias is present because respondents are a convenience sample comprised of individuals who have Internet access. Higher income households in the United States are more likely to have Internet access, and those households with children are more likely to have access than those without children. White and Asian householders are nearly twice as likely to have Internet access as those householders who are Black or Hispanic (Newburger, 2001).

Selection biases can be exaggerated due to the method of soliciting participants. Researchers can obtain samples of respondents by posting research notices on websites that promote research opportunities (e.g., the website associated with APS identified in Chapter 1) or by simply creating a Web page with the survey (e.g., *personality survey*) and wait for users to locate it ("hits") via Internet search engines (Krantz & Dalal, 2000). More active strategies include sending notices of the research project to individuals or groups likely to respond because of their interest in the survey topic. As Skitka and Sargis (2005) emphasize, however, not only are Internet users not representative of the general population, but also members of Internet special interest groups are not necessarily representative of their specific groups. At present there is no way to generate a random sample of Internet users (Kraut et al., 2004).

Lack of control over the research environment is also a major disadvantage of Internet surveys (Birnbaum, 2000; Kraut et al., 2004). As we mentioned in Chapter 3, this lack of control raises serious ethical issues related to informed consent and protecting individuals from harm as a consequence of their participation (e.g., emotional distress over survey questions). Because the researcher is not present, there is no easy way to determine if respondents have a clear understanding of the instructions, are answering conscientiously and not frivolously or even maliciously, or are creating multiple submissions (e.g., Kraut et al., 2004). Respondents may participate alone or in groups, under distracting conditions, without the knowledge of the researcher (Skitka & Sargis, 2005). One Internet researcher worried that respondents to survey questions about probability and risk were using calculators even though instructions requested them not to (Birnbaum, 2000). It seems safe to say that the advantages of Internet surveys outweigh many of the disadvantages. As technology improves and

IRB committees devise acceptable methods for protecting human participants, survey research on the Internet will continue to improve as a method for collecting survey data.

SURVEY-RESEARCH DESIGNS

- The three types of survey design are the cross-sectional design, the successive independent samples design, and the longitudinal design.

One of the most important decisions survey researchers must make is the choice of a research design. A survey-research design is the overall plan or structure used to conduct the entire study. There are three general types of survey-research designs: the cross-sectional design, the successive independent samples design, and the longitudinal design. There is no all-purpose survey-research design. Researchers choose a design based on the goals of the study.

Cross-Sectional Design

- In the cross-sectional design, one or more samples are drawn from the population(s) at one time.
- Cross-sectional designs allow researchers to describe the characteristics of a population or the differences between two or more populations, and correlational findings from cross-sectional designs allow researchers to make predictions.

Key Concept

The cross-sectional design is one of the most commonly used survey-research designs. In a **cross-sectional design,** one or more samples are drawn from the population *at one time*. The focus in a cross-sectional design is description—describing the characteristics of a population or the differences among two or more populations at a particular time. For example, a cross-sectional design was used in a nationwide study of Internet use among 1,100 teens aged 12–17 (Lenhart, Madden, & Hitlin, 2005). Using random-digit dialing, they conducted a telephone survey of parents and teens as part of the Pew Internet and American Life Project, which is designed to examine the impact of the Internet on children, families, communities, the workplace, schools, health care, and civic/political life.

Although their findings are too numerous to describe fully here, Lenhart and her colleagues presented data that give a detailed description of teens' use of the Internet and other technology. For example, close to 9 in 10 teens reported using the Internet (compared to 66% of adults), and half of the teens reported being online at least daily. In addition, 81% of teens play games online, 76% get news online, 42% have made purchases online, and 31% reported using the Internet to get health information. Although e-mail was popular, instant messaging (IM) was preferred. Approximately 75% of the online teens in their survey (compared to 42% of online adults) use instant messaging, with half of these teens using IM every day. In fact, teens commented that they view e-mail as something for talking to "old people," institutions, or large groups.

These researchers also examined relationships among demographic variables and Internet-use variables. For example, Lenhart et al. (2005) noted that teens who are online are more likely to live in families with higher income and greater access to technology, and are disproportionately likely to be White or English-speaking Hispanic teens.

Cross-sectional designs are ideally suited for the descriptive and predictive goals of survey research. Surveys are also used to assess changes in attitudes or behaviors over time and to determine the effect of some naturally occurring event, such as the effect of the economic collapse of 2008. For these purposes the cross-sectional design is not the method of choice. Rather, research designs are needed that systematically sample respondents over time. Two such designs are discussed in the next two sections.

Successive Independent Samples Design

- In the successive independent samples design, different samples of respondents from the population complete the survey over a time period.
- The successive independent samples design allows researchers to study changes in a population over time.
- The successive independent samples design does not allow researchers to infer how individual respondents have changed over time.
- A problem with the successive independent samples design occurs when the samples drawn from the population are not comparable—that is, not equally representative of the population.

Key Concept

In the **successive independent samples design,** a series of cross-sectional surveys are conducted over time (successively). The samples are independent because a *different* sample of respondents completes the survey at each point in time. There are two key ingredients: (1) The same set of questions should be asked of each sample of respondents, and (2) the different samples should be drawn from the same population. If these two conditions are met, researchers can legitimately compare survey responses over time. This design is most appropriate when the major goal of the study is to describe changes in the attitudes or behaviors within a population over time. For example, public opinion researchers frequently ask independent samples of Americans the extent to which they approve of the U.S. president (referred to as the president's "approval ratings"). Changes in approval ratings over time are used to characterize Americans' opinions of the president's actions.

As another example, consider a study that you may have been part of, one that has been conducted every year since 1966. Each year some 350,000 full-time freshmen from a nationally representative sample of approximately 700 colleges and universities are surveyed (Pryor, Hurtado, DeAngelo, Patuki Blake, & Tran, 2009; Sax et al., 2003). This research project represents the largest and longest empirical study of higher education in the United States, with over 1,500 universities and over 10 million students participating over the 40-plus years of the study. Students are asked approximately 40 questions covering a number of topics, and although some changes have

FIGURE 5.3   Contrasting trends in values for college freshmen from 1966 to 2003.
Source: Sax et al. (2003), Figure 7 (p. 7).

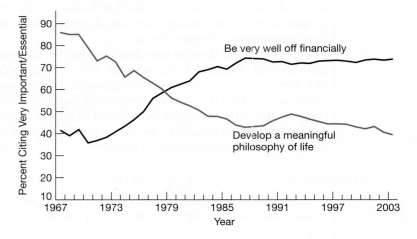

occurred in the questions over the decades, many questions have been asked each year, making this an excellent example of a successive independent samples design.

What can be said about changes in students' values and goals during this time period? Sax et al. (2003) reported the results for the portion of the survey in which students are asked to rate the importance of different values to assess students' need for meaning and purpose in their life. Two values were of particular interest: "the importance of developing a meaningful philosophy of life" and "the importance of being very well off financially" (pp. 6–7). Figure 5.3 displays the results for the percentage of students who endorsed these values as "very important" or "essential." In the late 1960s, over 80% of students indicated that developing a meaningful philosophy of life was very important or essential—in fact, this was the top value endorsed by students. In contrast, being well-off financially was very important or essential to less than 45% of the students, and ranked fifth or sixth among students' values during the late 1960s.

In 2003, the position of these values was reversed, with 73.8% of students endorsing being well-off financially as very important or essential. In 2003, developing a meaningful philosophy of life dropped to its lowest value in the survey history, with 39.3% of students endorsing this as very important or essential. As can be seen in Figure 5.3, these contrasting trends in values began to shift in the early 1970s, crossed in 1977, and were completely reversed by the late 1980s. Sax et al. (2003) emphasize that the contrasting trends in values since the late 1980s "reflect the continuing tension between extrinsic and intrinsic values within this generation of college students" (p. 7). Data from the 2009 sample may be used to illustrate the effect of a natural treatment—the dramatic collapse of the world economy near the end of 2008. In the 2009 sample, a record 78.1% of freshmen identified "being well-off financially" as a very important or essential objective, higher than any other item on the survey (Pryor et al., 2009). The researchers cited the economic downturn as an important factor in students' responses to the survey, including items reflecting the increasing financial difficulties associated with attending college.

The successive independent samples design has limitations. Consider hypothetical results from a successive independent samples design. Suppose you hear it reported that in 1977, 35% of college students surveyed said they don't trust the U.S. government, 25% reported they have mixed feelings, and 40% reported they do trust the U.S. government. Then you hear it reported that in 2007 results to the same survey question showed that 55% of students say they don't trust the government, 25% say they have mixed feelings, and 20% do have trust. How can we interpret these results? To account for the attitude change in the 2007 sample, can we conclude, for example, that 20% of the 1977 "do trust" group changed their minds and now don't trust the government? No! And perhaps you can see why.

What we must remember is that the students surveyed in 1977 (in our hypothetical survey) were not the same students surveyed in 2007. The extent to which specific individuals change their views over time can be determined only by testing the *same* individuals on both occasions. We cannot determine in the successive independent samples design who has changed their views or by how much. You may have considered a similar problem of interpretation when examining the results of the Sax et al. (2003) survey presented in Figure 5.3. What accounts for the changes in students' attitudes observed from 1966 to 2003? We can't say on the basis of these data. The purpose of the successive independent samples design is to describe changes over time in the distribution of *population* characteristics, not to describe changes in *individual* respondents. Accordingly, the successive independent samples design is not always helpful in ferreting out reasons for observed changes like those shown in Figure 5.3. (As you will soon see, another survey design, the longitudinal design, is more appropriate in these situations.)

A second potential limitation of the successive independent samples design arises when the successive samples are not representative of the same population. Imagine that in our hypothetical survey of students' attitude toward the U.S. government, the sample comprised students from small rural colleges in 1977 and students from large urban universities in 2007. The comparisons of students' attitudes toward the government over this time period would be meaningless. That is, we wouldn't be able to state that the student population had become less trusting over time because it's possible that the degree of trust differs for rural and urban students, which could also account for the difference between 1977 and 2007 results. The rural and urban samples illustrate the problem of *noncomparable successive samples*. *Changes in the population across time can be described accurately only when the successive independent samples represent the same population.* Although sophisticated statistical procedures exist to help unravel the problems associated with noncomparable successive samples, the best solution is to avoid the problem by carefully selecting successive samples that represent *the same* population.

Longitudinal Design

- In the longitudinal design, the same respondents are surveyed over time in order to examine changes in individual respondents.
- Because of the correlational nature of survey data, it is difficult to identify the causes of individuals' changes over time.
- As people drop out of the study over time (attrition), the final sample may no longer be comparable to the original sample or represent the population.

Key Concept

The distinguishing characteristic of the **longitudinal design** is that the same sample of respondents is surveyed more than once. The longitudinal design has two important advantages. First, the investigator can determine the direction and extent of change for individual respondents. Also, because changes in each individual's responses are assessed, it's easier to investigate reasons for attitude or behavior changes. Second, the longitudinal design is the best survey design when a researcher wishes to assess the effect of some naturally occurring event.

For example, Lucas (2005) examined changes in life satisfaction before and after divorce in an 18-year longitudinal study of German households that began in 1984. Many cross-sectional surveys have demonstrated that divorced people are less satisfied with life than are married people. Lucas sought to determine if divorce causes lower life satisfaction. Results indicated that these individuals' life satisfaction dropped before the divorce and gradually increased again following the divorce but did not return to their baseline state, indicating that the divorce likely decreased life satisfaction. However, Lucas also discovered that people who eventually divorced were less satisfied at the beginning of the study than those who stayed married—even before either group was married. Lucas concluded that the relationship between divorce and life satisfaction is due to preexisting differences in life satisfaction and to lasting changes due to divorce.

Heatherton, Keel, and their colleagues have used the longitudinal design to investigate changes in attitudes and behaviors related to eating during the transitions from college to early adulthood and from early adulthood to middle years (Heatherton, Mahamedi, Striepe, Field, & Keel, 1997; Keel, Baxter, Heatherton, & Joiner, 2007). Although much is known about eating disorders in adolescents and college students, less information is available about how disordered eating may progress as individuals settle down, marry, establish careers, raise children, and gain a stronger sense of identity. These researchers hypothesized that as individuals change their roles and life goals during adulthood, their emphasis on physical appearance may decrease, which would decrease the prevalence of eating disordered attitudes and behaviors (see Figure 5.4).

The first "panel" of the study took place in 1982, when a randomly selected sample of 800 women and 400 men from a private northeastern college was asked to complete a survey about eating and dieting. The response rate was 78% ($N = 625$) for women and 69% ($N = 276$) for men. In 1992 the researchers contacted these same individuals (with the help of the alumni office) and gave them the same survey again about their eating attitudes and behaviors. The third panel of data was collected in 2002, when the same individuals were in their early forties. The distinguishing characteristic of the longitudinal design is

FIGURE 5.4   Survey research such as that of Heatherton, Keel, and their colleagues (1997; 2007) investigates how individuals are affected by eating disorders as they grow older.

the fact that the *same* individuals were surveyed in each phase of the study. Although longitudinal designs involve a massive effort, the potential power of such an effort is that researchers can examine changes within individuals over time.

The researchers observed that eating attitudes and behaviors changed over time. In the decade after college, women's eating-disorder symptoms, chronic dieting, and body dissatisfaction decreased (Heatherton et al., 1997). However, despite these decreases, women's dissatisfaction with their body and their desire to lose weight remained high. Men, in contrast, rarely had problems with eating and weight during college. Ten years later, however, they had experienced weight gain (an average of almost 12 pounds, compared to women's average gain of 4 pounds). Men also reported increased dieting and symptoms of disordered eating in the 10 years after college, although this was still low relative to women.

Heatherton et al. (1997) made some interesting observations that are relevant to our understanding of longitudinal surveys. They proposed that decreases in women's eating problems reflect their maturation during their 20s, changes in their roles, and being away from the college campus (and the pressures to be thin that occur on college campuses). It's possible, however, that other processes may account for changes within the individuals in the sample. Using a successive independent samples design in which *separate* samples of college students were surveyed in 1982 and 1992, Heatherton, Nichols, Mahamedi, and Keel (1995) noted that eating-disorder symptoms and body dissatisfaction also were lower for the college students in the 1992 sample relative to the 1982 sample. These findings suggest that decreases in eating-disorder attitudes and behaviors may reflect changes at a societal level over the 10-year period (e.g., due to increasing information about eating disorders in the media). One potential problem with longitudinal survey designs is that it is difficult to pinpoint the exact causes for individuals' changes over time.[1]

What can be said about eating attitudes and behaviors 20 years following college? Overall, women demonstrated more weight dissatisfaction, dieting, and eating-disorder attitudes than men across the 20 years of the survey (Keel et al., 2007). In the 2002 survey, researchers observed that, on average, body weight increased significantly for both men (17 pounds since college) and women (14 pounds since college). Men's dieting and weight dissatisfaction was greatest in 2002, paralleling their weight gain. Interestingly, by the time the women in the study were in their early forties, despite their weight gain, they reported less dieting, less disordered eating, and less dissatisfaction with their body. In fact, women's greatest dissatisfaction with their body occurred while in college. Based on their statistical analyses, Keel et al. suggested that adult roles attained through marriage, parenthood, and careers were associated with decreases in women's disordered eating. That is, while physical appearance was important during college years (e.g., for attracting a potential mate), changes in priorities associated with marriage and becoming a mother made women's desire for thinness less important.

Another potential problem with longitudinal designs is that it can be difficult to obtain a sample of respondents who will agree to participate over time in a longitudinal study. In addition, you might think the longitudinal design solves the problem of noncomparable samples because the same people participate over and over (so of course the sample represents the same population each time). Unfortunately, the samples over time in a longitudinal design are identical *only if* all members of the original sample participate throughout the study. This is unlikely. For example, in the Heatherton et al. (1997) study, of the 901 participants in the original 1982 sample, only 724 (80%) returned a usable survey in 1992. In the third panel in 2002, 654 (73%) of the original 900 participants from 1982 responded to the survey and of these, 561 (86%) also responded to the 1992 survey. Thus, by the end of the 20 years, the researchers had survey responses for each of the three time periods (1982, 1992, 2002) for 62.3% of their original sample of 900 respondents.

Unless all the respondents in the original sample complete all phases of a longitudinal design, there is a possible problem due to *attrition*. Attrition is probably the most serious disadvantage of the longitudinal design because as samples decrease over time, they are less likely to represent the original population from which the sample was drawn. It is usually possible, however, to determine whether the final sample is comparable to the original sample in a longitudinal design. The characteristics of nonrespondents in the follow-up phase(s) are known because they participated in the original sample. Therefore, researchers

[1]Heatherton et al. (1997) noted that because the decreases in problem eating were larger among individuals in the longitudinal survey than in the successive independent samples survey, maturational processes within individuals, in addition to societal changes, likely were operating to decrease problem eating over time.

can look at characteristics of original participants to see how these nonresponding individuals may differ from those who continued their participation.

Keel et al. (2007) examined problems associated with attrition by comparing the responses of individuals who responded to the original 1982 survey but did not continue (nonrespondents) to responses of individuals who continued the study through the 2002 survey. They found that, compared to nonrespondents, individuals who continued to participate in the study described themselves as heavier, dieting more frequently, and had a greater desire for thinness. This represents a potential response rate bias because continued participation in 2002 may have been related to interest in the survey topic. Keel et al. suggested that weight and body concerns in the 2002 survey may have been inflated because of this potential response rate bias.

The advantages of the longitudinal design, such as determining changes for individual respondents, arise because the same individuals are surveyed more than once. Paradoxically, problems can also arise in longitudinal designs because of this same feature. One possible problem is that respondents may strive heroically to be consistent across surveys. This can be particularly troublesome if the study is designed to assess changes in respondents' attitudes! Although their attitudes have actually changed, people may report their original attitudes in an effort to appear consistent (perhaps they know researchers value reliability). Another potential problem is that the initial survey may sensitize respondents to the issue under investigation. For example, consider a longitudinal design used to assess students' concern about crime on campus. Once the study starts, participants may pay more attention to crime reports than they normally would. You might recognize this as an illustration of reactive measurement—people behaving differently because they know they are participating in a study.

Rather than trying to be heroically consistent in their eating attitudes and behaviors over time, Heatherton et al. (1997) noted that their participants may have been reluctant to report that they were having the same problems with eating as when they were in college. Thus, the decreases the researchers observed in problem eating during the 10-year period may be due to the fact that "women who are approaching their thirties may be embarrassed to admit they are experiencing problems typically associated with adolescence" (p. 124). When survey respondents are asked to report their attitudes and behaviors, researchers must be alert to reasons why their respondents' reports may not correspond to their actual behavior. We will return to this important issue later in this chapter.

QUESTIONNAIRES

Even if the sample of respondents was perfectly representative, the response rate was 100%, and the research design was elegantly planned and perfectly executed, the results of a survey will be useless if the questionnaire is poorly constructed. In this section we describe the most common survey research instrument, the questionnaire. To be useful, questionnaires should yield reliable and valid measures of demographic variables and of individual differences on self-report scales. Although there is no substitute for experience when it comes to preparing a good questionnaire, there are a few general principles of questionnaire construction with which you should be familiar. We describe six basic steps in preparing a questionnaire and then offer specific guidelines for writing and administering individual questions.

Questionnaires as Instruments

- Most survey research relies on the use of questionnaires to measure variables.
- Demographic variables describe the characteristics of people who are surveyed.
- The accuracy and precision of questionnaires requires expertise and care in their construction.
- Self-report scales are used to assess people's preferences or attitudes.

Key Concept

The value of survey research (and any research) ultimately depends on the quality of the measurements that researchers make. The quality of these measurements, in turn, depends on the quality of the instruments used to make the measurements. The primary research instrument in survey research is the **questionnaire.** On the surface, a questionnaire may not look like the high-tech instruments used in much modern scientific research; but, when constructed and used properly, a questionnaire is a powerful scientific instrument for measuring different variables.

Demographic Variables   Demographic variables are an important type of variable frequently measured in survey research. Demographic variables are used to describe the characteristics of the people who are surveyed. Measures such as race, ethnicity, age, and socioeconomic status are examples of demographic variables. Whether we decide to measure these variables depends on the goals of our study, as well as on other considerations. For example, Entwisle and Astone (1994) noted that "the ethnic and racial diversity of the U.S. population is now projected to increase through the middle of this 21st century, so that by then the majority of the U.S. population will be persons whose ethnicity would now be classified as 'nonwhite'" (p. 1522). By asking respondents to identify their race and ethnicity, we are able to document the mix of our sample and, if related to our research questions, compare groups according to race and ethnicity.

Measuring a demographic variable such as race may at first seem very easy. One straightforward method is simply to ask respondents to identify their race in an open-ended question: What is your race? _____ Such an approach may be straightforward, but the resulting measurement of race may not be satisfactory. For example, some respondents may mistakenly confuse "race" and "ethnicity." Important distinctions in identifying ethnic groups may go unrecognized by respondents and researchers. For instance, Hispanic does not identify a race; Hispanic designates all those whose country of origin is Spanish speaking. So, a person born in Spain would be classified as Hispanic. Latino is a term that is sometimes used interchangeably with Hispanic, but Latino designates people whose origin is from the countries of North and

FIGURE 5.5 Although ethnic background is an important demographic variable, accurately classifying people on this variable is not an easy task.

South America, excluding Canada and the United States. Distinctions like these can be confused (see Figure 5.5). For example, a person known to the authors is of European Spanish heritage and correctly considers himself a Caucasian, and not Latino. His ethnicity is Hispanic.

In general, "quick and dirty" approaches to measurement in survey research tend to yield messy data that are hard to analyze and interpret. For example, many individuals identify themselves as "multi-racial"; however, if researchers fail to include this as a possible response option, the information from participants may be incorrect—or they may skip the question entirely. Entwisle and Astone (1994) recommend a deliberate—and effective—approach when measuring race. They outline a series of nine questions to measure a person's race. One of these questions is "What race do you consider yourself to be?" Other questions seek information such as what countries the person's ancestors came from and whether Latino respondents are Mexican, Puerto Rican, Cuban, or something else. This more detailed series of questions allows researchers to measure race and ethnicity less ambiguously, more accurately, and more precisely. We use this example of measuring race and ethnicity to illustrate a more general principle: *The accuracy and precision of questionnaires as survey-research instruments depends upon the expertise and care that go into their construction.*

Preferences and Attitudes   Individuals' preferences and attitudes are frequently assessed in surveys. For example, a marketing researcher may be interested in consumers' preferences for different brands of coffee, or a political group may be interested in potential voters' attitudes regarding controversial public issues. Psychologists have long been interested in measuring people's thoughts and feelings on a vast array of topics, and often develop self-report scales for people to provide oral or written responses to items on the scale.

Self-report scales are commonly used to measure people's judgments about items presented on the scale (e.g., divorce, political candidates, life events) or to determine differences among people on some dimension presented on the scale (e.g., personality traits, amount of stress). For example, respondents may be asked to rate different life events according to how stressful they perceive the events to be. The researcher then may develop a list of life events that vary on the dimension of stressfulness. This type of scale focuses on differences among the items on the scale, not differences among individuals. To measure individual differences, respondents may be asked to report how often during the past year they experienced different stressful life events listed on a scale. A total stress score can be obtained for each individual by summing responses to the items on the scale. Individuals can then be compared according to the amount of stress experienced during the past year.[2]

Self-report measures, often in the form of a questionnaire, are among the most frequently used tools in psychology. Given their importance, it is critical that these measures be developed carefully. Two critical characteristics of the measurements made using self-report questionnaires are essential characteristics of all measurements—reliability and validity.

Reliability and Validity of Self-Report Measures

- Reliability refers to the consistency of measurement and is frequently assessed using the test–retest reliability method.
- Reliability is increased by including many similar items on a measure, by testing a diverse sample of individuals, and by using uniform testing procedures.
- Validity refers to the truthfulness of a measure: Does it measure what it intends to measure?
- Construct validity represents the extent to which a measure assesses the theoretical construct it is designed to assess; construct validity is determined by assessing convergent validity and discriminant validity.

Reliable self-report measures, like reliable observers or any other reliable measurements, are characterized by consistency. A reliable self-report measure is one that yields similar (consistent) results each time it is administered. Self-report measures must be reliable when making predictions about behavior. For example, in order to predict stress-related health problems, measures of individuals' life stress must be reliable. There are several ways to determine a test's reliability. One common method is to compute a *test–retest reliability*. Usually, test–retest reliability involves administering the same questionnaire to a large sample of people at two different times (hence, test and retest). For a questionnaire to yield reliable measurements, people need not obtain identical scores on

---

[2]The area of psychological measurement concerned with scaling items or stimuli is known as psychophysics, and the area of measurement concerned with individual differences is referred to as psychometrics.

the two administrations of the questionnaire, but a person's relative position in the distribution of scores should be similar at the two test times. The consistency of this relative positioning is determined by computing a correlation coefficient using the two scores on the questionnaire for each person in the sample. A desirable value for test–retest reliability coefficients is .80 or above, but the size of the coefficient will depend on factors such as the number and types of items.

A self-report measure with many items to measure a construct will be more reliable than a measure with few items. For example, we are likely to have unreliable measures if we try to measure a baseball player's hitting ability based on a single time at bat or a person's attitude toward the death penalty based on a single question on a survey. The reliability of our measures will increase greatly if we average the behavior in question across a large number of observations—many at-bats and many survey questions (Epstein, 1979). Of course, researchers must walk a fine line between too few items and too many items. Too many items on a survey can cause respondents to become tired or careless about their responses.

In general, measurements will also be more reliable when there is greater variability on the factor being measured among the individuals being tested. Often the goal of measurement is to determine the extent to which individuals differ. A sample of individuals who vary a great deal from one another is easier to differentiate reliably than are individuals who differ by only a small amount. Consider this example. Suppose we wish to assess soccer players' ability to pass the ball effectively to other players. We will be able to differentiate more reliably good players from poor players if we include in our sample a wider range of players—for example, professionals, high school players, and peewee players. It would be much harder to differentiate players reliably if we tested only professional players—they'd all be good! Thus, a test is often more reliable when administered to a diverse sample than when given to a restricted sample of individuals.

A third and final factor affecting reliability is related to the conditions under which the questionnaire is administered. Questionnaires will yield more reliable measurements when the testing situation is free of distractions and when clear instructions are provided for completing the questionnaire. You may remember times when your own test performance was hindered by noise or when you weren't sure what a question was asking.

The reliability of a survey measure is easier to determine and to achieve than the validity of a measure. The definition of validity is deceptively straightforward—a valid questionnaire measures what it is intended to measure. Have you ever heard students complain that questions on a test didn't seem to address the material covered in class? This is an issue of validity.

At this point, we will focus on construct validity, which is just one of the many ways in which the validity of a measurement is assessed. The *construct validity* of a measure represents the extent to which it measures the theoretical construct it is designed to measure. One approach to determining the construct validity of a test relies on two other kinds of validity: convergent validity and discriminant validity. These concepts can best be understood by considering an example.

TABLE 5.1   EXAMPLE OF CONSTRUCT VALIDITY*

	SWLS	LS-5	PA
SWLS	(.88)		
LS-5	.77	(.90)	
PA	.42	.47	(.81)

*Data from Lucas et al. (1996), Table 3.
Note: SWLS = Satisfaction with Life Scale; LS-5 = 5-item Life Satisfaction scale; PA = Positive Affect scale.

Table 5.1 presents data showing how we might assess the construct validity of a measure of "life satisfaction." Lucas, Diener, and Suh (1996) note that psychologists are increasingly examining factors such as happiness, life satisfaction, self-esteem, optimism, and other indicators of well-being. However, it's not clear whether these different indicators all measure the same construct (e.g., well-being) or whether each is a distinguishable construct. Lucas and his colleagues conducted several studies in which they asked individuals to complete questionnaire measures of these different indicators of well-being. For our purposes we will focus on a portion of their data from their third study, in which they asked participants to complete three scales: two life satisfaction measures, the Satisfaction with Life Scale (SWLS) and a 5-item Life Satisfaction measure (LS-5); and a measure of Positive Affect (PA). At issue in this example is whether the construct of life satisfaction—the quality of being happy with one's life—can be distinguished from being happy more generally (positive affect).

The data in Table 5.1 are presented in the form of a correlation matrix. A correlation matrix is an easy way to present a number of correlations. Look first at the values in parentheses that appear on the diagonal. These parenthesized correlation coefficients represent the values for the reliability of each of the three measures. As you can see, the three measures show good reliability (each is above .80). Our focus, however, is on measuring the construct validity of "life satisfaction," so let's look at what else is in Table 5.1.

It is reasonable to expect that scores on the Satisfaction with Life Scale (SWLS) should correlate with scores on the 5-item Life Satisfaction measure; after all, both measures were designed to assess the life satisfaction construct. In fact, Lucas et al. observed a correlation between these two measures of .77, which indicates that they correlate as expected. This finding provides evidence for *convergent validity* of the measures; the two measures converge (or "go together") as measures of life satisfaction.

The case for the construct validity of life satisfaction can be made even more strongly when the measures are shown to have discriminant validity. As can be seen in Table 5.1, the correlations between the Satisfaction with Life Scale (SWLS) and Positive Affect (.42) and between the 5-item Life Satisfaction measure (LS-5) and Positive Affect (.47) are lower. These findings show that life satisfaction measures do not correlate as well with a measure of another theoretical construct—namely, positive affect. The lower correlations between the life satisfaction tests and the positive affect test indicate that *different* constructs are being measured. Thus, there is evidence for *discriminant validity* of the life

---

BOX 5.2

COLLEGE STUDENTS' VALUES REVISITED: RELIABILITY AND VALIDITY

When describing the successive independent samples design, we presented data that suggest that first-year college students' values are oriented toward "being well-off financially" rather than "developing a meaningful philosophy of life." Now we can ask, "Do these two questions assess students' desire for meaning and purpose in their life in a reliable and valid manner?"

Reliable and valid measurement of a psychological construct such as "meaning and purpose in life" requires more than two questions and, in fact, data from the 2006 sample of students suggest that students are not concerned simply with financial goals (Bryant & Astin, 2006). Here are the percentages for other items endorsed by students as "essential" or "very important":

Attaining wisdom	77%
Becoming a more loving person	67%
Seeking beauty in my life	54%

Improving the human condition	54%
Attaining inner harmony	49%
Finding answers to mysteries of life	45%
Developing a meaningful philosophy of life	42%

Results for these additional items show that students clearly are interested in developing a meaningful life in ways other than pursuing purely financial goals. The item "developing a meaningful philosophy of life" seems to show weaker agreement or convergent validity with the other items, perhaps making it a poor item to represent the broader construct of meaning and purpose in life.

Could there be a problem with the wording "meaningful philosophy of life"? Students may have been less clear about the meaning of this item than the more concrete life goals indicated by the other items. Reliable and valid measurement requires clear, unambiguous questions—a topic addressed in the next section.

---

satisfaction measures because they seem to "discriminate" life satisfaction from positive affect—being satisfied with one's life is not the same as general happiness. The construct validity of life satisfaction gains support in our example because there is evidence for both convergent validity and discriminant validity. Box 5.2 provides another example of reliable and valid measurement.

Constructing a Questionnaire

- Constructing a questionnaire involves deciding what information should be sought and how to administer the questionnaire, writing a draft of the questionnaire, pretesting the questionnaire, and concluding with specifying the procedures for its use.
- The wording of questionnaires should be clear and specific using simple, direct, and familiar vocabulary.
- The order in which questions are asked on a questionnaire needs to be considered seriously because the order can affect respondents' answers.

Steps in Preparing a Questionnaire   Constructing a questionnaire that will yield reliable and valid measurements is a challenging task. In this section we suggest a series of steps that can help you meet this challenge, especially if you are constructing a questionnaire for the first time as part of a research project.

1 Decide what information should be sought.
2 Decide how to administer the questionnaire.

3 Write a first draft of the questionnaire.
4 Reexamine and revise the questionnaire.
5 Pretest the questionnaire.
6 Edit the questionnaire and specify the procedures for its use.

Step 1. The warning "Watch out for that first step!" is appropriate here. The first step in questionnaire construction—deciding what information is to be sought—should actually be the first step in planning the survey as a whole. This decision, of course, determines the nature of the questions to be included in the questionnaire. It is important to predict the likely results of a proposed questionnaire and decide whether these "findings" would answer the questions of the study. Surveys are frequently done under considerable time pressure, and inexperienced researchers are especially prone to impatience. A poorly conceived questionnaire, however, takes as much time and effort to administer and analyze as does a well-conceived questionnaire. The difference is that a well-constructed questionnaire leads to interpretable results. The best that can be said for a poorly designed one is that it is a good way to learn the importance of careful deliberation in the planning stages.

Step 2. The next step is to decide how to administer the questionnaire. For example, will it be self-administered, or will trained interviewers be using it? This decision is determined primarily by the survey method that has been selected. For instance, if a telephone survey is to be done, trained interviewers will be needed. In designing the questionnaire, one should also consider using items that have been prepared by other researchers. For example, there is no reason to develop your own instrument to assess racial prejudice if a reliable and valid one is already available. Besides, if you use items from a questionnaire that has already been used, you can compare your results directly with those of earlier studies.

Step 3. If you decide that no available instrument suits your needs, you will have to take the third step and write a first draft of your own questionnaire. Guidelines concerning the wording and ordering of questions are presented later in this section.

Step 4. The fourth step in questionnaire construction—reexamining and rewriting—is an essential one. Questions that appear objective and unambiguous to you may strike others as slanted or ambiguous. It is most helpful to have your questionnaire reviewed by experts, both those who have knowledge of survey research methods and those with expertise in the area on which your study is focused. For example, if you are doing a survey of students' attitudes toward the campus food service, it would be advisable to have your questionnaire reviewed by the campus food-service director. When you are dealing with a controversial topic, it is especially important to have representatives of both sides of the issue screen your questions for possible bias.

Step 5. By far the most critical step in the development of an effective questionnaire is to do a pretest. A pretest involves actually administering the questionnaire to a small sample of respondents under conditions similar to those anticipated in the final administration of the survey. Pretest respondents must also be typical of those to be included in the final sample; it makes little sense to pretest a survey of nursing home residents by administering the questionnaire to college students. There is one way, however, in which a pretest does differ from the final administration of the survey. Respondents should be interviewed at length regarding their reactions to individual questions and to the questionnaire as a whole. This provides information about potentially ambiguous or offensive items.

The pretest should also serve as a "dress rehearsal" for interviewers, who should be closely supervised during this stage to ensure that they understand and adhere to the proper procedures for administering the questionnaire. If major changes have to be made as a result of problems discovered during the pretest, a second pretest may be needed to determine whether these changes solved the problems.

Step 6. After pretesting is completed, the final step is to edit the questionnaire and to specify the procedures to be followed in its final administration. To reach this final step successfully, it is important to consider guidelines for the effective wording of questions and for the ordering of questions.

Guidelines for the Effective Wording of Questions   Lawyers have long known that how a question is phrased has great impact on how that question is answered. Survey researchers need to be equally conscious of this principle. This point is illustrated in a study that examined people's opinions about allocating scarce vaccines during a hypothetical flu epidemic (Li, Vietri, Galvani, & Chapman, 2010). These researchers found that respondents' decisions about vaccine allocation (in effect, who would live and who would die) were affected by whether vaccination policies were written in terms of "saving lives" *versus* "lives lost." Thus, the way the questions were worded influenced how respondents judged the value of people's lives. In a typical survey, only one wording is used for each question so, unfortunately, the influence of the wording of questions in a given survey can almost never be determined precisely.

Clark and Schober (1992) point out that respondents presume that the meaning of a question is obvious. This has important implications. For instance, when a question includes a vague word, respondents may interpret the word in various ways according to their individual biases and their own ideas of what is "obvious." Thus, words like "few" or "usually," or terms such as "global warming," may be interpreted differently by different individuals. Respondents also tend to assume that words in a survey are used in the same way as in their subculture or culture. A recent example in popular culture is figuring out whether "bad" means "good." Clark and Schober (1992) cite as an example a surveyor who wanted to ask Mexican residents in the Yucatán the question "How many children do you have?" When translated into Spanish, the surveyor used the word *niños* for children, but villagers in this area of Mexico treated *niños* as including living children and children who have died. Respondents also may reasonably assume that if the surveyor asks a question, then it is one that the respondent can answer. This assumption can lead respondents to give answers to questions that have no (valid) answers! For example, when asked to give opinions about nationalities that didn't actually exist, respondents nevertheless gave opinions.

Although it's clear that question wording in surveys can pose problems, the solution is less clear. *At a minimum, the exact wording of critical questions should always be reported along with the data describing respondents' answers.* The problem of the potential influence of the wording of questions is yet another illustration of why a multimethod approach is so essential in investigating behavior.

Survey researchers usually choose from two general types of questions when writing a questionnaire. The first type is a *free-response* (open-ended) question and the second type is a *closed* (multiple-choice) question. Free-response questions, like the essay questions on a classroom test, merely specify the area to be addressed in a response. For example, the question "What are your views on legal abortion?" is a free-response question. By contrast, closed questions provide specific response alternatives. "Is police protection very good, fairly good, neither good nor bad, not very good, or not good at all?" is a closed question about the quality of police protection in a community.

The primary advantage of free-response questions is that they offer the respondent greater flexibility than closed questions. However, this advantage is often more than offset by the difficulties that arise in recording and scoring responses to free-response questions. For example, extensive coding is frequently necessary to summarize rambling responses to free-response questions. Closed questions, on the other hand, can be answered more easily and quickly and fewer scoring problems arise. It is also much easier to summarize responses to closed questions because the answers are readily comparable across respondents. A major disadvantage of closed questions is that they reduce expressiveness and spontaneity. Further, respondents may have to choose a less-than-preferred response because no presented alternative really captures their views. Hence, the responses obtained may not accurately reflect the respondents' opinion.

Regardless of the type of question used, the *vocabulary should be simple, direct, and familiar to all respondents.* Questions *should be as clear and specific as possible. Double-barreled questions should be avoided.* An example of a double-barreled question is "Have you suffered from headaches and nausea recently?" A person may respond "no" if both symptoms have not occurred at exactly the same time or may respond "yes" if either symptom has occurred. The solution to the problem of double-barreled questions is a simple one—rewrite them as separate questions.

Survey questions should be as short as possible without sacrificing the clarity of the questions' meaning. Twenty or fewer words should suffice for most survey questions. *Each question should be carefully edited for readability and should be phrased in such a way that all conditional information precedes the key idea.* For example, it would be better to ask, "If you were forced to leave your present job, what type of work would you seek?" than to ask, "What type of work would you seek if you were forced to leave your present job?"

Leading or loaded questions should also be avoided in a questionnaire. *Leading* questions take the form "Most people favor the use of nuclear energy. What do you think?" To avoid bias, it is better to mention all possible perspectives or to mention none. A survey question about attitudes toward nuclear energy could read, "Some people favor the use of nuclear energy, some people oppose the use of nuclear energy, and some people have no opinion one way or the other. What do you think?" or "What do you think about the use of nuclear energy?" *Loaded* questions are questions that contain emotion-laden words. For example, terms such as "radical" and "racist" should be avoided. To guard against loaded questions, it is best to have your questionnaire reviewed by individuals representing a range of social and political perspectives.

Finally, when using multiple items to assess a construct, it's important to word some of the items in the opposite direction to avoid problems associated with *response bias.* The potential for response bias exists when respondents use only extreme points on rating scales, or only the midpoint, or when respondents agree (or disagree) with every item. For example, an assessment of emotional well-being might include the following items:

My mood is generally positive.

1 ------ 2 ------ 3 ------ 4 ------ 5

Strongly   Strongly
disagree   agree

I am often sad.

1 ------ 2 ------ 3 ------ 4 ------ 5

Strongly   Strongly
disagree   agree

Respondents with a response bias in which they always agree with statements might circle "5" on both scales, resulting in an unreliable assessment of emotional well-being. More consistent responding would require participants to use the opposite end of the self-rating scale. Responses to these reversed items are "reverse-scored" ($1 = 5, 2 = 4, 4 = 2, 5 = 1$) when participants' responses are summed to derive a total score for emotional well-being.

In summary, good questionnaire items should

—use vocabulary that is simple, direct, and familiar to all respondents;
—be clear and specific;
—not involve leading, loaded, or double-barreled questions;
—be as short as possible (20 or fewer words);
—present all conditional information prior to the key idea;
—avoid potential response bias; and
—be checked for readability.

Ordering of Questions   The order of the questions in a survey requires careful consideration. The first few questions set the tone for the rest of the questionnaire, and determine how willingly and conscientiously respondents will work on subsequent questions. For self-administered questionnaires, it is best to begin with the most interesting set of questions in order to capture the respondents' attention. Demographic data should be obtained at the end of a self-administered questionnaire. For personal or telephone interviews, on the other hand, demographic questions are frequently asked at the beginning because they are easy for the respondent to answer and thus bolster the respondent's confidence. They also allow time for the interviewer to establish rapport before asking questions about more sensitive matters.

The order in which particular questions are asked can have dramatic effects, as illustrated in a study by Schuman, Presser, and Ludwig (1981). They found differential responding depending on the order of two questions concerning abortion, one general and one specific. The general question was "Do you think it should be possible for a pregnant woman to obtain a legal abortion if she is married and does not want any more children?" The more specific question was "Do you think it should be possible for a pregnant woman to obtain a legal abortion if there is a strong chance of a serious defect in the baby?" When the general question was asked first, 60.7% of respondents said "yes," but when the general question followed the specific question, only 48.1% of respondents said "yes." The corresponding values for the specific question were 84% and 83% agreement in the first and second positions, respectively. The generally accepted method for dealing with this problem is to use *funnel questions*, which means starting with the most general question and moving to specific questions pertaining to a given topic.

The final aspect of the ordering of survey questions that we will consider is the use of *filter questions*—general questions asked of respondents to find out whether they need to be asked specific questions. For example, the question "Do you own a car?" might precede a series of questions about the costs of maintaining a car. In this instance, the respondents would answer the specific questions only if their response to the general question was "yes." If that answer was "no," the interviewer would not ask the specific questions (in a self-administered questionnaire, the respondent would be instructed to skip that section). When the filter questions involve objective information (e.g., "Are you over 65?"), their use is relatively straightforward. Caution must be exercised, however, in using behavioral or attitudinal questions as filter questions. Smith (1981) first asked respondents whether they approved of hitting another person in "any situations you can imagine." Logically, a negative response to this most general question should imply a negative response to any specific questions. Nonetheless, over 80% of the people who responded "no" to the general question then reported that they approved of hitting another person in specific situations, such as in self-defense. Although findings such as this suggest that filter questions should be used cautiously, the need to demand as little of the respondents' time as possible makes filter questions an essential tool in the design of effective questionnaires.

A well-conducted survey is an efficient way to accomplish the research goals of description and prediction. When distributed to dozens if not hundreds of individuals, even a modest-sized questionnaire can quickly generate many thousands of responses to individual items. And, as we have seen, by using the Internet, researchers can literally obtain millions of responses in a short period of time. But there is a catch! How does one deal with this multitude of responses? The answer is: By careful planning!

Data analysis of responses obtained from questionnaires must be considered prior to writing the survey items. Will open-ended questions be used? Is the goal mainly descriptive; for example, are proportions or percentages of events in a population of primary interest? Is the goal correlational, for example, relating responses on one question to those of another? Will respondents use a yes–no response format? A yes–maybe–no format? Self-report scales? These response formats provide different kinds of data. As you have learned, qualitative data in the form of open-ended responses will require rules for coding and methods for getting intercoder reliabilities. Categorical data obtained from a yes–no format yield nominal data, whereas scales are typically assumed to provide interval data (see Chapter 4 for comments on types of scales). These types of data require different approaches for statistical analysis.

It is important to anticipate the likely results of the proposed questionnaire and then to decide whether these "findings" will answer the research questions. When "predicting" your results, you will want to make sure that the results can be analyzed appropriately. In other words, *you should have an analysis plan prior to conducting the survey*. During the planning stage, we suggest that you consult with experienced survey researchers regarding the correct statistical analyses.

Once again we refer you to Chapters 11 and 12 of this textbook to gain (or regain) familiarity with statistical procedures. Should your interest in conducting a survey lead you to look for relationships (correlations) among categorical (nominal) variables, you will need to go beyond this textbook. *The appropriate statistical analysis for examining relationships between nominal variables is the chi-square test of contingency*. An introduction to this test is found in nearly all introductory statistics books (e.g., Zechmeister & Posavac, 2003). If you are going to correlate responses to interval scales, then a Pearson Product-Moment correlation (*r*) is appropriate. This type of analysis was introduced in Chapter 4 when we discussed interobserver reliability. We will have more to say about correlational analyses toward the end of this chapter. Procedures for calculating a Pearson *r* are found in Chapter 11.

THINKING CRITICALLY ABOUT SURVEY RESEARCH

Correspondence Between Reported and Actual Behavior

- Survey research involves reactive measurement because individuals are aware that their responses are being recorded.
- Social desirability refers to pressure that respondents sometimes feel to respond as they "should" believe rather than how they actually believe.
- Researchers can assess the accuracy of survey responses by comparing these results with archival data or behavioral observations.

Regardless of how carefully survey data are collected and analyzed, the value of these data depends on the truthfulness of respondents' answers to the survey questions. Should we believe that people's responses on surveys reflect their true thoughts, opinions, feelings, and behavior? The question of the truthfulness of verbal reports has been debated extensively, and no clear-cut conclusion has emerged. In everyday life, however, we regularly accept the verbal reports of others as valid. If a friend tells you she enjoyed reading a certain novel, you may ask why, but you do not usually question whether the statement accurately reflects your friend's feelings. There are some situations in everyday life, however, when we *do* have reason to suspect the truthfulness of someone's statements. When looking for a used car, for instance, we might not always want to trust the "sales pitch" we receive. Generally, however, we accept people's remarks at their face value unless we have reason to suspect otherwise. We apply the same standards to the information we obtain from survey respondents.

By its very nature, survey research involves reactive measurement. Respondents know their responses are being recorded, and they may also suspect their responses may prompt some social, political, or commercial action. Hence, pressures are strong for people to respond as they "should" believe, not as they actually believe. The term often used to describe these pressures is **social desirability** (the term "politically correct" refers to similar pressures). For example, if respondents are asked whether they favor giving help to the needy, they may say "yes" because they believe this is the most socially acceptable attitude to have. In survey research, as was true with observational research, the best protection against reactive measurement is to be aware of its existence.

Sometimes researchers can examine the accuracy of verbal reports directly. For example, Judd, Smith, and Kidder (1991) describe research by Parry and Crossley (1950) wherein responses obtained by experienced interviewers were subsequently compared with archival records for the same respondents kept by various agencies. Their comparisons revealed that 40% of respondents gave inaccurate reports to a question concerning contributions to United Fund (a charitable organization), 25% reported they had registered and voted in a recent election (but they did not), and 17% misrepresented their age. A pessimist might find these figures disturbingly high, but an optimist would note that a majority of respondents' reports were accurate even when social desirability pressures were high, as in the question pertaining to charitable contributions.

Another way researchers can assess the accuracy of verbal reports is by directly observing respondents' behavior. An experiment done by Latané and Darley (1970) illustrates this approach. They found that bystanders are more likely to help a victim when the bystander is alone than when other witnesses are present. Subsequently, a second group of participants was asked whether the presence of others would influence the likelihood they would help a victim. They uniformly said that it would not. Thus, individuals' verbal reports *may not* correspond well to behavior (see Figure 5.6). Research findings such as these should make us extremely cautious of reaching conclusions about people's behavior solely on the basis of verbal reports. Of course, we should

Key Concept

FIGURE 5.6 How people say they would respond to this type of situation does not always match what they actually do.

be equally cautious of reaching conclusions about what people think solely on the basis of direct observation of their behavior. The potential discrepancy between observed behavior and verbal reports illustrates again the wisdom of a multimethod approach in helping us identify and address potential problems in understanding behavior and mental processes.

Correlation and Causality

- When two variables are related (correlated), we can make predictions for the variables; however, we cannot, simply knowing a correlation, determine the cause of the relationship.
- When a relationship between two variables can be explained by a third variable, the relationship is said to be "spurious."
- Correlational evidence, in combination with a multimethod approach, can help researchers identify potential causes of behavior.

Surveys are often used in correlational research, and correlational research is an excellent method for meeting the scientific goals of description and prediction. For example, studies demonstrating correlations between physical health and psychological well-being allow researchers to make predictions regarding health-related problems.

Correlational evidence allows researchers to make predictions for the correlated variables. However, the familiar maxim, "Correlation does not imply causation," reminds us that our ability to make causal inferences based solely on a correlation between two variables is very limited. For instance, there is a reliable correlation between being outgoing (socially active) and being satisfied with one's life (Myers & Diener, 1995). Based on this correlation alone, however, we could not argue convincingly that being more outgoing and socially active *causes* people to be more satisfied with their lives. Although it is possible that being outgoing causes people to be more satisfied, the "reverse" causal relationship also may be true: Being satisfied with life may cause people to be more outgoing and socially active. The causal relationship could go either way—being more outgoing causes greater life satisfaction or being more satisfied with life causes people to be more outgoing. It is impossible to determine the correct causal direction simply by knowing the correlation between the two variables.

Not being able to determine the direction of the relationship in a correlation is only one challenge we face. It's possible there is another causal interpretation for the correlation between the two variables. For example, a third variable, number of friends, could cause people to be more outgoing *and* more satisfied with their lives. A correlation that can be explained by a third variable is called a **spurious relationship** (Kenny, 1979). In this particular example, "number of friends" is a possible third variable that could account for the relationship between being outgoing and being satisfied with one's life. Individuals with more friends may be more likely to be outgoing and satisfied with life than people with fewer friends. This isn't to say that the original positive correlation between being outgoing and life satisfaction doesn't exist (it certainly does); it just means that other variables that were not measured (e.g., number of friends) may explain *why* the relationship exists.

It is extremely important to understand why it is not possible to make a causal inference based only on a correlation between two variables. It is equally important to recognize that correlational evidence can be very useful in identifying *potential* causes of behavior. Sophisticated statistical techniques can be used to help with causal interpretations of correlational studies. *Path analysis* is one sophisticated statistical technique that can be used with correlational data (Baron & Kenny, 1986; Holmbeck, 1997). Path analysis involves the identification of mediator variables and moderator variables. A *mediator* variable is a variable that is used to explain the correlation between two variables. A *moderator* variable is a variable that affects the direction or strength of the correlation between two variables.

Figure 5.7 illustrates an example of a mediating variable in a study of the effects of poverty on children's psychological adjustment (Evans, Gonnella, Marcynyszyn, Gentile, & Salpekar, 2005). Consistent with previous research, these investigators observed a correlation between their measures of poverty and psychological distress: the greater the poverty, the greater the distress among children (path *a* in Figure 5.7). Evans and his colleagues also proposed a mediating variable, *chaos*, to account for this relationship. They theorized that

Key Concept

FIGURE 5.7   An example of a mediating variable.

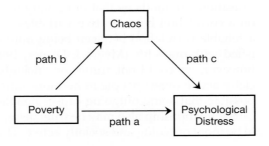

chaotic living conditions characterized by unpredictability, confusion, lack of structure, noise, overcrowding, and poor-quality housing can explain the relationship between poverty and children's psychological distress. This is shown in paths *b* and *c* in Figure 5.7.

Consistent with their predictions, the results of their study indicated that greater poverty was associated with greater chaos in the home (path *b*). Also, greater chaos was associated with greater psychological distress (path *c*). The final step in path analysis is to show that when the correlations between paths *b* and *c* are taken into account using a statistical procedure, the correlation observed initially for path *a* (between poverty and distress) becomes zero (i.e., no relationship). This is exactly what Evans and his colleagues found. Their path analysis allowed them to say that the relationship between poverty and children's distress can be explained by, or *is mediated by*, the degree of chaos in the home.

Although Evans and his colleagues did not describe potential moderating variables, we can offer a hypothetical illustration. Suppose the pattern of correlations observed in Figure 5.7 is different for boys compared to girls. We could hypothesize, for example, that the mediating effect of chaos exists only for boys and not for girls. In this case we would be arguing that the sex of the child, boy or girl, is a moderating variable—that is, it affects the direction or strength of the correlations among poverty, chaos, and psychological distress. Other potential moderating variables might include population density (e.g., urban *vs.* rural) and the extent of resilience in the children's personality (e.g., high *vs.* low resilient). Can you develop hypotheses for how the relationships among poverty, chaos, and psychological distress may differ based on these moderating variables?

Although correlational research is not an absolutely firm basis for making causal inferences, patterns of correlations observed in path analysis provide important clues for identifying causal relationships among variables. The next step for researchers who wish to make causal inferences is to conduct experiments, as described in Chapters 6–8. For example, a laboratory manipulation of chaos (e.g., unpredictable outcomes, noise) might cause different levels of distress among individuals from different economic backgrounds. This multimethod approach would help to provide converging evidence regarding the causal role of chaos in understanding the relationship between poverty and psychological adjustment.

SUMMARY

Survey research provides an accurate and efficient means for describing people's characteristics (e.g., demographic variables) and their thoughts, opinions, and feelings. In addition, predictive relationships can be identified by assessing the covariation (correlation) among naturally occurring variables. Surveys differ in purpose and scope, but they generally involve sampling. Results obtained for a carefully selected sample are used to describe the entire population of interest. Surveys also involve the use of a predetermined set of questions, generally in the form of a questionnaire.

Sampling is a procedure whereby a specified number of elements are drawn from a sampling frame that represents an actual list of the possible elements in the population. Our ability to generalize from the sample to the population depends critically on the representativeness of the sample, the extent to which the sample has the same characteristics as the population. Representativeness is best achieved by using probability sampling rather than nonprobability sampling. In simple random sampling, the most common type of probability sampling, every element is equally likely to be included in the sample. Stratified random sampling is used when analysis of subsamples is of interest.

There are four general survey methods: mail surveys, personal interviews, telephone interviews, and Internet surveys. Mail surveys avoid problems of interviewer bias and are especially well suited for examining personal or embarrassing topics. Potential problems due to response rate bias are a serious limitation of mail surveys. Personal interviews and phone surveys usually have higher response rates and provide greater flexibility. The phone survey is frequently used for brief surveys. Internet surveys are efficient and cost effective and open new opportunities for survey researchers; however, they are also prone to sample biases and raise both methodological and ethical issues primarily due to the lack of control over the research environment.

Survey research is carried out according to an overall plan called a research design. There are three survey-research designs: the cross-sectional design, the successive independent samples design, and the longitudinal design. Cross-sectional designs focus on describing the characteristics of a population or the differences between two or more populations at one point in time. Describing changes in attitudes or opinions over time requires the use of successive independent samples or longitudinal designs. The longitudinal design is generally preferred because it allows the researcher to assess changes for specific individuals and avoids the problem of noncomparable successive samples.

The primary instrument for survey research is the questionnaire. Questionnaires can be used to measure demographic variables and to assess people's preferences or attitudes. In order to construct questionnaires that will yield reliable and valid measurements, researchers must decide what information should be sought and how to administer the questionnaire, and what order of questions will be most effective. Most importantly, questions must be written so that they are clear, specific, and as unambiguous as possible.

Survey results, like those of other verbal reports, can be accepted at face value unless there is reason to do otherwise, such as pressures on respondents to give socially desirable responses. People's behavior does not always conform to what they say they would do, so survey research will never replace direct observation. However, survey research does provide an excellent way to begin to examine people's attitudes and opinions.

The greatest challenge in interpreting correlational evidence is understanding the relationship between correlation and causality. A correlation between two variables is not sufficient evidence to demonstrate a causal relationship between the two variables. Correlational evidence can contribute, however, to identifying causal relationships when used in combination with sophisticated statistical techniques (such as analyses of mediators and moderators in path analysis) and the multimethod approach.

Key Concepts

correlational research 138	response rate bias 149
population 141	interviewer bias 150
sample 142	cross-sectional design 154
representativeness 143	successive independent samples
selection bias 143	design 155
nonprobability sampling 144	longitudinal design 158
probability sampling 144	questionnaire 162
simple random sampling 145	social desirability 174
stratified random sampling 147	spurious relationship 176

Review Questions

1 Briefly identify the goal of survey research and how correlations are used within survey research.

2 Describe the information you would examine to determine whether survey results are biased because the sponsoring agency of the survey has a vested interest in how the results turn out.

3 What two characteristics do surveys have in common regardless of the purpose for which the survey has been done?

4 Explain why there is likely to be a serious threat to the interpretability of the results of a survey when a convenience sample is used.

5 Explain the relationship between the homogeneity of the population from which a sample is to be drawn and the size of a sample needed to ensure representativeness.

6 Explain why you would choose to use a mail survey, personal interviews, telephone interviews, or an Internet survey for your survey-research project.

7 Explain why it is not possible to conclude a sample does not represent a population simply by knowing that the response rate was 50%.

8 What are the major advantages and disadvantages of Internet surveys?

9 Describe the relationship that would need to exist among the samples in a successive independent samples design in order to be able to interpret population changes in attitudes over time.

10 You are interested in assessing the direction and extent of change over time in the opinions of individual respondents. Identify the survey-research design you would choose, and explain why you would make this choice.

11 Describe one method for determining the reliability and one method for determining the validity of a self-report measure.

12 Describe three factors that affect the reliability of self-report measures in survey research.

13 How would you respond if someone told you that survey results were useless because people do not respond truthfully to questions on surveys?

14 Explain why "correlation does not imply causation," and explain how correlational evidence can be useful in identifying potential causes of behavior.

15 Define *mediator* and *moderator* and provide an example of each.

CHALLENGE QUESTIONS

1 Survey research is difficult to do well, and this can be especially the case when the topic is people's sexual attitudes and practices. For a book focusing in part on women's sexuality, an author mailed 100,000 questionnaires to women who belonged to a variety of women's groups in 43 states. These groups ranged from feminist organizations to church groups to garden clubs. The author's questionnaire included 127 essay questions. The author received responses from 4,500 women.

Findings in this survey included that 70% of respondents married 5 years or more reported having extramarital affairs and that 95% of respondents felt emotionally harassed by the men they love.

A The final sample in this study is large (4,500). Is this sufficient to ensure the representativeness of the sample? If not, what potential survey-research problem could lessen the sample's representativeness?

B Is it possible on the basis of your response to Part A of this question to argue that any conclusions drawn by the author from her data are incorrect? What could you do to determine whether the results are correct?

2 Two different national organizations that conduct research on higher education did independent surveys asking faculty how well prepared they thought their students were. The results of these two surveys drew attention when they were reported in the *Chronicle of Higher Education* because the findings from the two surveys were very different. Researchers from Research Foundation A found that nearly 75% of professors said that their students were "seriously underprepared." Researchers from Research Foundation B found that only 18.8% of the faculty they surveyed said that their students were "not at all prepared." Survey-research findings can be expected to vary from one survey to another, but the large discrepancy found in these two surveys could make one wonder about the reliability and credibility of survey findings. Before reaching this conclusion, it is useful to consider several details of the two surveys. [*Note:* This question is based on a report from the *NCRIPTAL Update,* Spring 1990, Vol. 3, No. 1, pp. 2–3.]

A *Who was asked?* The original sample for Foundation A included 10,000 college professors who taught undergraduate and graduate students in all types of institutions. Of the original sample, 54.5% responded. Foundation B omitted research universities (25% of Foundation A's sample). Foundation B had a final sample of 2,311 (62% response rate). Approximately 90% of the final sample were teaching introductory-level students. *How might the characteristics of the samples surveyed by Foundations A and B affect the findings obtained in the two surveys?*

B *What was asked?* Foundation A asked its respondents: "The undergraduates with whom I have close contact are seriously underprepared in basic skills such as those required for written and oral communication." The responses for this statement were: strongly agree, agree with reservations, neutral, disagree with reservations, and disagree. Foundation B asked its respondents: "In their background preparation, students who enroll in this course are most typically. . . ." The response choices were: not at all prepared, somewhat prepared, very well prepared, and extremely well prepared. *How might the nature of these questions affect the findings obtained in the two surveys?*

C How were the results reported? The findings for the Foundation A survey (75% of students seriously underprepared) were reported in the Chronicle by combining the response categories "strongly agree" and "agree with reservations." The findings for the Foundation B survey (18.8% of students not at all prepared) represented only respondents who chose the "not at all prepared" response category. *How do you think the results might look if the Foundation A estimate included only the respondents who chose the "strongly agree" response?*

3 A task force has been established at a small liberal arts college under the direction of the dean of students to examine the quality of students' experiences on their campus. The task force decided to do a survey to determine students' knowledge of and their perceptions of the fairness of the judicial system used to enforce the rules in the living units on campus. The questionnaire for the survey included personal questions asking students to describe their own experiences when they had violated college policies or when they had known other students who had violated college policies. A stratified random sample was drawn from the registrar's list of full-time students living on and off campus. The sample size was 400 on a campus with 2,000 full-time students. Questionnaires were returned by 160 students for a response rate of 40%. One important finding from the survey was that over a third of the respondents rated the judicial system as unfair. The task force met to decide whether to include the survey findings such as this one in its final report to the dean of students.

A Was the initial sample of 400 students likely to be representative of the population of 2,000 full-time students? Why or why not?

B Identify a potential survey research problem that could be present in this study that would lead the task force to be concerned that the final sample was not representative of the population of 2,000 students.

C Using only the evidence that the response rate for the survey was 40%, the task force concluded that the final sample was not representative of the population of students. They further decided that the ratings of the judicial system as unfair by more than a third of the students was an incorrect overestimate. Do you agree that the finding represents an incorrect estimate? Why or why not?

D While the task force was meeting to discuss their final report, one member of the task force expressed the opinion that students' responses were unlikely to have been truthful and so the results of the survey were useless and should not be reported at all. The director of the task force calls on you to respond to this statement. What would you say?

4 As an intern with the alumni relations office at a small college, one of your assignments is to help develop a survey-research project. The college is interested in finding out about the alumni's attitudes toward their academic and extracurricular experiences while enrolled in college. The director also wants to include questions to assess the alumni's opinions about the different activities the college sponsors for them (e.g., reunions) and how they

prefer to be kept informed about issues and activities on campus (e.g., newsletters, e-mails, postings on the college website). One of the major goals of the survey-research project is to determine how the attitudes of alumni change 1, 5, or 10 years after graduation.

A The first step is to select the survey-research design for the project. Describe the two designs that can be used to measure changes in attitudes over time. Outline how each of these designs would be implemented for this project, and identify the advantages and possible limitations of each design.

B The second step is to select the survey-research method for the project. Members of the planning committee proposed three different approaches: (1) select a random sample of alumni from the alumni relations office list and use a phone survey to administer the questionnaire; (2) send an e-mail to a random sample of alumni that includes a link to an Internet site where alumni can complete the questionnaire; (3) post an announcement about the survey and a link to the questionnaire on the college's website with the request that all alumni visiting the website complete the questionnaire. Describe to the committee the advantages and limitations of each approach, and provide a recommendation and rationale for which approach you think would be best.

C The third step is to prepare the questionnaire. Describe the different formats that can be used to write the questionnaire items and prepare an example of a free-response (open-ended) and closed (multiple-choice) question. Use these examples to describe the advantages and disadvantages of each type of question.

Answer to Stretching Exercise I

1 D   2 B   3 A   4 C

Answer to Stretching Exercise II

1 The first student researcher is proposing a stratified random sample in which 100 "Greek" and 100 "independent" students are sampled. In this plan the equal-sized strata would have representative samples for each stratum. A potentially serious flaw of this plan is that the overall sample would not represent the proportions of Greeks and independents in the population (25% and 75%, respectively). This would result in a biased sample because Greeks would be systematically overrepresented in the survey. The second student researcher is proposing a simple random sample of 100 students from the campus population. While this is likely to lead to a more representative sample, it will probably result in too few respondents in the "Greek" category (we'd expect about 25 Greeks) to adequately represent their viewpoint.

2 A preferred sampling plan would use a stratified random sample in which the sample sizes for Greeks and independents are proportional to the population values. With 200 students in the sample, you would select 150 students from the sampling frame of independent students and 50 students from the sampling frame of Greek students.

Answer to Challenge Question 1

A In general, larger sample sizes do make it more likely that the sample will be representative. The problem in this study is that the final sample (though large) represents a low response rate from the original sample of 100,000 (4.5%). The low response rate and the topic of the survey make it likely that only women who were very motivated to complete the survey responded. It is unlikely the sample of 4,500 women represents the entire population of women.

B The low response rate does not make it possible to argue that the conclusions drawn by the author are incorrect. Neither can the author argue on the basis of this sample that the conclusions are correct. We simply cannot know based on this evidence whether the conclusions are correct or incorrect. There is at least one good way to determine if the results of this survey are correct. You would need to obtain from the literature the results of one or more surveys on women's sexual attitudes and practices. It would be essential that these other surveys had used representative samples of women. Then you would compare the results of this survey with those of the other surveys. Only if the results of the present survey corresponded to those of the surveys with the representative samples would we consider the results of the present survey correct. Of course, you could also carry out your own survey, one that avoids the problems that are present in this survey, and determine whether your results are similar to those of this author-researcher!

PART THREE

Experimental Methods

CHAPTER SIX

Independent Groups Designs

CHAPTER OUTLINE

OVERVIEW

In Chapter 2 we introduced you to the four goals of research in psychology: description, prediction, explanation, and application. Psychologists use observational methods to develop detailed descriptions of behavior, often in natural settings. Survey research methods allow psychologists to describe people's attitudes and opinions. Psychologists are able to make predictions about behavior and mental processes when they discover measures and observations that covary (correlations). Description and prediction are essential to the scientific study of behavior, but they are not sufficient for understanding the causes of behavior. Psychologists also seek explanation—the "why" of behavior. We achieve scientific explanation when we identify the causes of a phenomenon. Chapters 6, 7, and 8 focus on the best available research method for identifying causal relationships—*the experimental method*. We will explore how the experimental method is used to test psychological theories as well as to answer questions of practical importance.

As we have emphasized, the best overall approach to research is the *multi-method approach*. We can be more confident in our conclusions when we obtain comparable answers to a research question after using different methods. Our conclusions are then said to have *convergent validity*. Each method has different shortcomings, but the methods have complementary strengths that overcome these shortcomings. The special strength of the experimental method is that it is especially effective for establishing cause-and-effect relationships. In this chapter we discuss the reasons researchers conduct experiments and we examine the underlying logic of experimental research. Our focus is on a commonly used experimental design—the random groups design. We describe the procedures for forming random groups and the threats to interpretation that apply specifically to the random groups design. Then we describe the procedures researchers use to analyze and interpret the results they obtain in experiments, and also explore how researchers establish the external validity of experimental findings. We conclude the chapter with consideration of two additional designs involving independent groups: the matched groups design and the natural groups design.

WHY PSYCHOLOGISTS CONDUCT EXPERIMENTS

- Researchers conduct experiments to test hypotheses about the causes of behavior.
- Experiments allow researchers to decide whether a treatment or program effectively changes behavior.

One of the primary reasons that psychologists conduct experiments is to make empirical tests of hypotheses they derive from psychological theories. For example, Pennebaker (1989) developed a theory that keeping in thoughts and feelings about painful experiences might take a physical toll. According to this "inhibition theory," it's physically stressful to keep these experiences to oneself.

Pennebaker and his colleagues conducted many experiments in which they assigned one group of participants to write about personal emotional events and another group to write about superficial topics. Consistent with the hypotheses derived from the inhibition theory, participants who wrote about emotional topics had better health outcomes than participants who wrote about superficial topics. Not all the results, however, were consistent with the inhibition theory. For example, students asked to dance expressively about an emotional experience did not experience the same health benefits as students who danced and wrote about their experience. Pennebaker and Francis (1996) did a further test of the theory and demonstrated that cognitive changes that occur through writing about emotional experiences were critical in accounting for the positive health outcomes.

Our brief description of testing the inhibition theory illustrates the general process involved when psychologists do experiments to test a hypothesis derived from a theory. If the results of the experiment are consistent with what is predicted by the hypothesis, then the theory receives support. On the other hand, if the results differ from what was expected, then the theory may need to be modified and a new hypothesis developed and tested in another experiment. Testing hypotheses and revising theories based on the outcomes of experiments can sometimes be a long and painstaking process, much like combining the pieces to a puzzle to form a complete picture. The self-correcting interplay between experiments and proposed explanations is a fundamental tool psychologists use to understand the causes of the ways we think, feel, and behave.

Well-conducted experiments also help to solve society's problems by providing vital information about the effectiveness of treatments in a wide variety of areas. This role of experiments has a long history in the field of medicine (Thomas, 1992). For example, near the beginning of the 19th century, typhoid fever and delirium tremens were often fatal. The standard medical practice at that time was to treat these two conditions by bleeding, purging, and other similar "therapies." In an experiment to test the effectiveness of these treatments, researchers randomly assigned one group to receive the standard treatment (bleeding, purging, etc.) and a second group to receive nothing but bed rest, good nutrition, and close observation. Thomas (1992) describes the results of this experiment as "unequivocal and appalling" (p. 9): The group given the standard medical treatment of the time did worse than the group left untreated. Treating such conditions using early-19th-century practices was worse than not treating them at all! Experiments such as these contributed to the insight that many medical conditions are self-limited: The illness runs its course, and patients recover on their own.

LOGIC OF EXPERIMENTAL RESEARCH

- Researchers manipulate an independent variable in an experiment to observe the effect on behavior, as assessed by the dependent variable.
- Experimental control allows researchers to make the causal inference that the independent variable *caused* the observed changes in the dependent variable.

- Control is the essential ingredient of experiments; experimental control is gained through manipulation, holding conditions constant, and balancing.
- An experiment has internal validity when it fulfills the three conditions required for causal inference: covariation, time-order relationship, and elimination of plausible alternative causes.
- When confounding occurs, a plausible alternative explanation for the observed covariation exists, and therefore, the experiment lacks internal validity. Plausible alternative explanations are ruled out by holding conditions constant and balancing.

A true experiment involves the *manipulation* of one or more factors and the *measurement* (observation) of the effects of this manipulation on behavior. As you saw in Chapter 2, the factors the researcher controls or manipulates are called the *independent variables*. An independent variable must have at least two levels (also called conditions). One level may be considered the "treatment" condition and a second level the control (or comparison) condition. Often, more than two levels are used for additional comparisons between groups. The measures used to observe the effect (if any) of the independent variables are called *dependent variables*. One way to remember the distinction between these two types of variables is to understand that the outcome (dependent variable) *depends* on the independent variable.

Experiments are effective for testing hypotheses because they allow us to exercise a relatively high degree of control in a situation. Researchers use control in experiments to be able to state with confidence that the independent variable *caused* the observed changes in the dependent variable. The three conditions needed to make a causal inference are covariation, time-order relationship, and elimination of plausible alternative causes (see Chapter 2).

Covariation is met when we observe a relationship between the independent and dependent variables of an experiment. A time-order relationship is established when researchers manipulate an independent variable and *then* observe a subsequent difference in behavior (i.e., the difference in behavior is contingent on the manipulation). Finally, elimination of plausible alternative causes is accomplished through the use of control procedures, most importantly, through *holding conditions constant* and *balancing*. When the three conditions for a causal inference are met, the experiment is said to have **internal validity,** and we can say the independent variable *caused* the difference in behavior as measured by the dependent variable.

Key Concept

RANDOM GROUPS DESIGN

- In an independent groups design, each group of subjects participates in only one condition of the independent variable.
- Random assignment to conditions is used to form comparable groups by balancing or averaging subject characteristics (individual differences) across the conditions of the independent variable manipulation.
- When random assignment is used to form independent groups for the levels of the independent variable, the experiment is called a random groups design.

Key Concepts }

In an **independent groups design,** each group of subjects participates in a different condition of the independent variable.[1] The most effective independent groups design is one that uses **random assignment** of subjects to conditions in order to form comparable groups prior to implementing the independent variable. When random assignment to conditions is used, the independent groups design is called a **random groups design.** The logic of the design is straightforward. The groups are formed so as to be similar on all important characteristics at the start of the experiment. Next, in the experiment itself, the groups are treated the same except for the level of the independent variable. Thus, any difference between the groups on the dependent variable must be caused by the independent variable.

An Example of a Random Groups Design

The logic of the experimental method and the application of control techniques that produce internal validity can be illustrated in an experiment investigating girls' dissatisfaction with their body, conducted in the United Kingdom by Dittmar, Halliwell, and Ive (2006). Their goal was to determine whether exposure to very thin body images causes young girls to experience negative feelings about their own body. Many experiments conducted with adolescent and adult participants demonstrate that women report greater dissatisfaction about themselves after exposure to a thin female model compared to other types of images. Dittmar and her colleagues sought to determine whether similar effects are observed for girls as young as 5 years old. The very thin body image they tested was the Barbie doll. Anthropological studies that compare the body proportions of Barbie to actual women reveal that the Barbie doll has very unrealistic body proportions, yet Barbie has become a sociocultural ideal for female beauty (see Figure 6.1).

In the experiment small groups of young girls (5½–6½ years old) were read a story about "Mira" as she went shopping for clothes and prepared to go to a birthday party. As they heard the story, the girls looked at picture books with six scenes related to the story. In one condition of the experiment, the picture books had images of Barbie in the scenes of the story (e.g., shopping for a party outfit, getting ready for the party). In a second condition the picture books had similar scenes but the figure pictured was the "Emme" doll. The Emme fashion doll is an attractive doll with more realistic body proportions, representing a U.S. dress size 16 (see Figure 6.2). Finally, in the third condition of the experiment the picture books did not depict Barbie or Emme (or any body) but, instead, showed neutral images related to the story (e.g., windows of clothes shops, colorful balloons). These three versions of the picture books (Barbie, Emme, neutral) represent three levels of the independent variable that was manipulated in the experiment. Because different groups of girls participated in each level of the independent variable, the experiment is described as an independent groups design.

---

[1]Another term for independent groups design is *between-subjects design.* Both terms are used to describe studies in which groups of participants are compared and there is no overlap of participants in the groups of the study (i.e., each participant is in only one condition).

FIGURE 6.1 In the United States, 99% of young girls aged 3–10 have at least one Barbie, and the typical young girl has eight Barbie dolls (Rogers, 1999).

Manipulation   Dittmar et al. (2006) used the control technique of *manipulation* to test their hypotheses about girls' body dissatisfaction. The three conditions of the independent variable allowed these researchers to make comparisons relevant to their hypotheses. If they tested only the Barbie condition, it would be impossible to determine whether those images influenced girls' body dissatisfaction in any way. Thus, the neutral-image condition created a comparison—a way to see if the girls' body dissatisfaction differed depending on whether they looked at a thin ideal *vs.* neutral images. The Emme condition added an important comparison. It is possible that *any* images of bodies might influence girls' perceptions of themselves. Dittmar and her colleagues tested the hypothesis that only thin body ideals, as represented by Barbie, would cause body dissatisfaction.

   At the end of the story, the young girls turned in their picture books and completed a questionnaire designed for their age level. Although Dittmar and her colleagues used a number of measures designed to assess the girls' satisfaction with their body, we will focus on one measure, the Child Figure Rating Scale. This scale has two rows of seven line drawings of girls' body shapes ranging

FIGURE 6.2 The "Emme" doll was introduced in 2002 to promote a more realistic body image for young girls. The doll is based on the U.S. supermodel named Emme.

from very thin to very overweight. Each girl was asked first to color in the figure in the top row that most looks like her own body right now (a measure of perceived actual body shape). Then, on a second row of the same figures, the girls were asked to color in the figure that shows the way they most want to look (ideal body shape). Girls were told they could pick any of the figures and that they could choose the same figure in each row. A body shape dissatisfaction score, the dependent variable, was computed by counting the number of figures between each girl's actual shape and her ideal shape. A score of zero indicated no body shape dissatisfaction, a negative score indicated a desire to be thinner, and a positive score indicated a desire to be bigger.

The results of this experiment were clear: Young girls exposed to the images of Barbie were more dissatisfied with their body shape than were girls who were exposed to the Emme images or to the neutral images. The average body-dissatisfaction score for the 20 girls in the Emme condition and for the 20 girls in the neutral-image condition was zero. In contrast, the average dissatisfaction score for the 17 girls in the Barbie-image condition was −.76, indicating their desire to be thinner. Through the control technique of manipulation, the first two requirements for causal inference were met in this experiment: (1) Differences in the girls' body dissatisfaction covaried with the conditions of the experiment and (2) body dissatisfaction came *after* viewing the images (time-order relationship). The third requirement for causal inference, elimination of alternative explanations, was accomplished in this experiment through holding conditions constant and balancing.

Holding Conditions Constant   In Dittmar et al.'s experiment, several factors that could have affected the girls' attitudes toward their body were kept the same across the three conditions. All of the girls heard the same story about shopping and attending a birthday party, and they looked at their picture books for the same amount of time. They all received the same instructions throughout the experiment and received the exact same questionnaire at the conclusion. Researchers use *holding conditions constant* to make sure that the independent variable is the *only* factor that differs systematically across the groups.

If the three groups had differed on a factor other than the picture books, then the results of the experiment would have been uninterpretable. Suppose the participants in the Barbie condition had heard a different story, for example, a story about Barbie being thin and popular. We wouldn't know whether the observed difference in the girls' body dissatisfaction was due to viewing the images of Barbie or to the different story. When the independent variable of interest and a different, potential independent variable are allowed to covary, a *confounding* is present. When there are no confoundings, an experiment has *internal validity*.

Holding conditions constant is a control technique that researchers use to avoid confoundings. By holding constant the story the girls heard in the three conditions, Dittmar and her colleagues avoided confoundings by this factor. In general, a factor that is held constant cannot possibly covary with the manipulated independent variable. More importantly, a factor that is held constant does not change, so it cannot possibly covary with the dependent variable either. Thus, researchers can rule out factors that are held constant as potential causes for the observed results.

It is important to recognize, however, that we choose to control only those factors we think might influence the behavior we are studying—what we consider *plausible* alternative causes. For instance, Dittmar et al. held constant the story the girls heard in each condition. It is unlikely, however, that they controlled factors such as the room temperature to be constant across the conditions because room temperature probably would not likely affect body image (at least when varying only a few degrees). Nevertheless, we should constantly remain alert to the possibility that there may be confounding factors in our experiments whose influence we had not anticipated or considered.

Balancing   Clearly, one key to the logic of the experimental method is forming comparable (similar) groups at the start of the experiment. The participants in each group should be comparable in terms of various characteristics such as their personality, intelligence, and so forth (also known as *individual differences*). The control technique of *balancing* is required because these factors often cannot be held constant. The goal of random assignment is to establish equivalent groups of participants by balancing, or averaging, individual differences across the conditions. The random groups design used by Dittmar et al. (2006) may be described as follows:

Stage 1	Stage 2	Stage 3
R_1	X_1	O_1
R_2	X_2	O_1
R_3	X_3	O_1

where R_1, R_2, and R_3 refer to the random assignment of subjects to the three independent conditions of the experiment; X_1 is one level of an independent variable (e.g., Barbie), X_2 is a second level of the independent variable (e.g., Emme), and X_3 is a third level of the independent variable (e.g., neutral images). An observation of behavior (O_1) in each group is then made.

In the Dittmar et al. (2006) study of girls' body image, if participants viewing the Barbie images were shown to be more overweight or to own more Barbie dolls than participants viewing the Emme or neutral images, a plausible alternative explanation for the findings exists. It's possible that being overweight or having more Barbie dolls, not the version of the images, could explain why participants in the Barbie condition experienced greater body dissatisfaction. (In the language of the researcher, a confounding would be present.) Similarly, individual differences in the girls' body dissatisfaction *before* the experiment was conducted could be a reasonable alternative explanation for the study's findings. When random assignment is used to balance these individual differences across the groups, however, we can logically rule out the alternative explanation that any differences we obtain between the groups on the dependent variable are due to characteristics of the participants.

When we balance a factor such as body weight, we make the three groups equivalent in terms of their *average* body weight. Note that this differs from holding body weight constant, which would require that all of the girls in the study have the same body weight. Similarly, balancing the number of Barbie dolls owned by girls in the three groups would mean that the *average* number of dolls owned in the three groups is the same, not that the number of dolls owned by each girl is held constant at some number. The beauty of random assignment is that *all* individual differences are balanced, not just the ones we've mentioned. Therefore, we can rule out alternative explanations due to *any* individual differences among participants.

In summary, Dittmar and her colleagues concluded that exposure to thin body images, such as Barbie, *causes* young girls to be dissatisfied with their own bodies. They were able to make this conclusion because they

- manipulated an independent variable that varied the images girls viewed,
- eliminated other plausible explanations through holding relevant conditions constant, and
- balanced individual differences among the groups through random assignment to conditions.

Box 6.1 summarizes how Dittmar and her colleagues applied the experimental method, specifically, the random groups design, to their study of young girls' body image.

BOX 6.1

SUMMARY OF GIRLS' BODY IMAGE EXPERIMENT

Overview of experimental procedure. Young girls (ages 5½–6½) were assigned to look at one of three different picture books while listening to a story. After viewing the books, participants answered questions about their body image.

Independent variable. Version of picture book viewed by participants (Barbie, Emme, or neutral images).
Dependent variable. Body dissatisfaction measured by assessing the difference between girls' actual body image and their ideal body image.
Explanation of control procedures
  Holding conditions constant. Girls in the three conditions listened to the same story, were given the same instructions, and answered the same questions at the conclusion.

Balancing. Individual differences among the girls were balanced through random assignment to different experimental conditions.
Explanation of experimental logic providing evidence for causality
  Covariation. The girls' body dissatisfaction was found to vary with experimental condition.
  Time-order relationship. The version of the picture book was manipulated prior to measuring body dissatisfaction.
  Elimination of plausible alternative causes. Control procedures of holding conditions constant and balancing individual differences through random assignment protected against confoundings.
Conclusion. Exposure to very thin body images (the Barbie picture books) caused body dissatisfaction.

(Based on Dittmar, Halliwell, & Ive, 2006)

STRETCHING EXERCISE I

In this exercise you are to respond to the questions that appear after this brief description of an experiment.

Bushman (2005) examined whether people's memory for advertisements is affected by the type of television program they watch. Participants ($N = 336$, ages 18–54) were randomly assigned to watch one of four types of television programs: violent (e.g., *Cops*), sexually explicit (e.g., *Sex and the City*), violence and sex (e.g., *CSI Miami*), or neutral (e.g., *America's Funniest Animals*). Within each TV program were embedded the same 12 (30-second) ads. To make sure participants were likely to have equal exposure to the brands represented in the ads, the researchers selected relatively unfamiliar brands (e.g., "Dermoplast," "José Olé"). Three commercial breaks, each with four ads, were placed at approximately 12, 24, and 36 minutes into each program. Two random orders of ads were used. Participants were tested in small groups, and each session was conducted in a comfortable setting in which participants sat in padded chairs and were provided soft drinks and snacks. After they watched the program, participants received surprise memory tests for the content of the ads. The results indicated that memory for the advertised brands was poorer when the television program contained violence or sex. Memory impairment for ads was greatest for programs that contained sexually explicit material.

1 What aspect of the experiment did Bushman (2005) control by using manipulation?
2 What aspect of the experiment did Bushman control by holding conditions constant?
3 What aspect of the experiment did Bushman control by using balancing?

From Bushman, B. J. (2005). Violence and sex in television programs do not sell products in advertisements. *Psychological Science, 16,* 702–708.

Block Randomization

- Block randomization balances subject characteristics and potential confoundings that occur during the time in which the experiment is conducted, and it creates groups of equal size.

Key Concept

A common procedure for carrying out random assignment is **block random-ization.** First, let us describe exactly how block randomization is carried out, and then we will look at what it accomplishes. Suppose we have an experiment with five conditions (labeled, for convenience, as A, B, C, D, and E). One "block" is made up of a random order of all five conditions:

One block of conditions	→	Random order of conditions
A B C D E		C A E B D

In block randomization, we assign subjects to conditions one block at a time. In our example with five conditions, five subjects would be needed to complete the first block with one subject in each condition. The next five subjects would be assigned to one of each of the five conditions to complete a second block, and so on. If we want to have 10 subjects in each of five conditions, then there would be 10 blocks in the block-randomized schedule. Each block would consist of a random arrangement of the five conditions. This procedure is illustrated below for the first 11 participants.

10 Blocks	Participants		Condition	
1) C A E B D	1) Cara	→	C	⎫
2) E C D A B	2) Andy	→	A	
3) D B E A C	3) Jacob	→	E	⎬ First block
4) B A C E D	4) Molly	→	B	
5) A C E D B	5) Emily	→	D	⎭
6) A D E B C	6) Eric	→	E	⎫
7) B C A D E	7) Anna	→	C	
8) D C A E B	8) Laura	→	D	⎬ Second block
9) E D B C A	9) Sarah	→	A	
10) C E B D A	10) Lisa	→	B	⎭
	11) Tom	→	D	
	and so on for 50 participants			

There are several advantages when block randomization is used to randomly assign subjects to groups. First, block randomization produces groups that are of equal size. This is important because the number of observations in each group affects the reliability of the descriptive statistics for each group, and it is desirable to have the reliability of these measures comparable across groups. Block randomization accomplishes this. Second, block randomization controls for time-related variables. Because experiments often take a substantial amount of time to complete, some participants can be affected by events that occur during the time the experiment is conducted. In block randomization, every condition is tested in each block so these time-related variables are balanced across the conditions of the experiment. If, for example, a traumatic event occurs on a college campus in which an experiment is being conducted, the number of participants who experienced the event will be equivalent in each condition if block randomization is used. We assume, then, that the effects of the event on participants' performance will be equivalent, or averaged, across the conditions. Block randomization also works to balance other time-related variables, such as changes in experimenters or even changes in the populations from which subjects are drawn. For example, a perfectly acceptable experiment could be done drawing students from both fall and spring semester classes if a block randomization schedule is used. The beauty of block randomization is that it will balance (or average) any characteristics of participants (including the effects of time-related factors) across the conditions of an experiment.

If you want to practice the procedure of block randomization, you can do Challenge Question 1A at the end of this chapter.

Threats to Internal Validity

- Randomly assigning intact groups to different conditions of the independent variable creates a potential confounding due to preexisting differences among participants in the intact groups.
- Block randomization increases internal validity by balancing extraneous variables across conditions of the independent variable.
- Selective subject loss, but not mechanical subject loss, threatens the internal validity of an experiment.
- Placebo control groups are used to control for the problem of demand characteristics, and double-blind experiments control both demand characteristics and experimenter effects.

Key Concept }

We've seen that *internal validity* is the degree to which differences in performance on a dependent variable can be attributed clearly and unambiguously to an effect of an independent variable, as opposed to some other uncontrolled variable. These uncontrolled variables are often referred to as **threats to internal validity.** These threats are potential alternative explanations for a study's findings. In order to make a clear cause-and-effect inference about an independent variable, threats to internal validity must be controlled. We next describe several problems in experimental research that can result in threats to internal validity, and methods to control these threats.

Testing Intact Groups   Random assignment is used to form comparable groups in the random groups design. There are times, however, when *non*comparable groups are formed even when random assignment appears to have been used. This problem occurs when intact groups (not individuals) are randomly assigned to the conditions of an experiment. Intact groups are formed prior to the start of the experiment. For example, the different sections of an introductory psychology course are intact groups. Students are not randomly assigned to different sections of introductory psychology (although sometimes scheduling classes seems random!). Students often choose to be in a particular section because of the time the class meets, the instructor, friends who will be in the class, and any number of other factors. If a researcher were to randomly assign different sections to levels of an independent variable, a confounding due to testing intact groups could occur.

The source of the confounding due to noncomparable groups arises when individuals differ systematically across the intact groups. For example, students who choose to take an 8 A.M. section may differ from students who prefer a 2 P.M. section. Random assignment of these intact groups to experimental conditions is simply not sufficient to balance the systematic differences among the intact groups. These systematic differences between the two intact groups are almost guaranteed to threaten the internal validity of the experiment. The solution to this problem is simple—do not use intact groups in a random groups design.

Balancing Extraneous Variables   A number of factors in an experiment may vary as a result of practical considerations when carrying out the study. For example, to complete an experiment more quickly, a researcher might decide to have several different experimenters test small groups of participants. The sizes of the groups and the experimenters themselves become potentially relevant variables that could confound the experiment. For example, if all the individuals in the experimental group were tested by one experimenter and all of those in the control group were tested by another experimenter, the levels of the intended independent variable would become confounded with the two experimenters. We would not be able to determine whether an observed difference between the two groups was due to the independent variable or to the fact that different experimenters tested participants in the experimental and control groups.

Potential variables that are not directly of interest to the researcher but that could still be sources of confounding in the experiment are called *extraneous variables*. But don't let the term fool you! An experiment confounded by an extraneous variable is no less confounded than if the confounding variable were of considerable inherent interest. For example, Evans and Donnerstein (1974) found that students who volunteer for research participation early in an academic term are more academically oriented and are more likely to have an internal locus of control (i.e., they emphasize their own responsibility, rather than external factors, for their actions) than students who volunteer late in a term. Their findings suggest it would not be wise to test all of the participants in the experimental condition at the beginning of the term and participants in the control condition at the end of the term, as this would potentially confound the independent variable with characteristics of the participants (e.g., locus of control, academic focus).

Block randomization controls extraneous variables by balancing them across groups. All that is required is that entire blocks be tested at each level of the extraneous variable. For example, if there were four different experimenters, entire blocks of the block-randomized schedule would be assigned to each experimenter. Because each block contains all the conditions of the experiment, this strategy guarantees that each condition will be tested by each experimenter. Usually, we would assign the same number of blocks to each experimenter, but this is not essential. What is essential is that entire blocks be tested at each level of the extraneous variable, which, in this case, is the four experimenters. The balancing act can become a bit tricky when there are several extraneous variables, but careful advance planning can avoid confounding by such factors.

Subject Loss We have emphasized that the logic of the random groups design requires that the groups in an experiment differ only because of the levels of the independent variable. We have seen that forming comparable groups of subjects at the beginning of an experiment is another essential characteristic of the random groups design. It is equally important that the groups be comparable except for the independent variable at the end of the experiment. When subjects begin an experiment but fail to complete it successfully, the internal validity of the experiment can be threatened. It is important to distinguish between two ways in which subjects can fail to complete an experiment: mechanical subject loss and selective subject loss.

Key Concept }   **Mechanical subject loss** occurs when a subject fails to complete the experiment because of an equipment failure (in this case, the experimenter is considered part of the equipment). Mechanical subject loss can occur if a computer crashes, or if the experimenter reads the wrong set of instructions, or if someone inadvertently interrupts an experimental session. Mechanical loss is a less critical problem than selective subject loss because the loss is unlikely to be related to any characteristic of the subject. As such, mechanical loss should not lead to systematic differences between the characteristics of the subjects who successfully complete the experiment in the different conditions of the experiment. Mechanical loss can also reasonably be understood as the result of chance events that should occur equally across groups. Hence, internal validity is not typically threatened when subjects must be excluded from the experiment due to mechanical loss. When mechanical subject loss occurs, it should be documented. The name or subject number of the dropped subject and the reason for the loss should be recorded. The lost subject can then be replaced by the next subject tested.

Key Concept }   Selective subject loss is a far more serious matter. **Selective subject loss** occurs (1) when subjects are lost differentially across the conditions of the experiment; (2) when some characteristic of the subject is responsible for the loss; and (3) when this subject characteristic is related to the dependent variable used to assess the outcome of the study. Selective subject loss destroys the comparable groups that are essential to the logic of the random groups design and can thus render the experiment uninterpretable.

We can illustrate the problems associated with selective subject loss by considering a fictitious but realistic example. Assume the directors of a fitness center decide to test the effectiveness of a 1-month fitness program. Eighty people volunteer for the experiment, and they randomly assign 40 to each of two groups. Random assignment to conditions creates comparable groups at the start of the experiment by balancing individuals' characteristics such as weight, fitness level, motivation, and so on across the two groups. Members

STRETCHING EXERCISE II

In this exercise you will need a deck of cards. Set aside the face cards (Jack, Queen, King) and use the cards 1–10 (assign a value of one to the Aces). Shuffle the cards well.

In order to get a feel for how random assignment to conditions works to create equivalent groups, deal the shuffled (randomized) cards into two piles, each with 20 cards. One pile will represent "participants" randomly assigned to an experimental condition and the second pile will represent participants randomly assigned to a control condition. Assume the value on each card indicates participants' score (1–10) on an individual differences measure, such as memory ability.

1   Compute a mean score for participants in each condition (pile) by summing the value on each card and dividing by 20. Are the two groups equivalent in terms of their average memory ability?

To understand the problems associated with selective subject loss, assume that participants with low memory ability (values of 1 and 2) are unable to complete an experimental task and drop out of the experimental condition. To simulate this, remove cards with values of 1 and 2 from the pile that represents your experimental condition.

2   Compute a new mean score for the pile in the experimental condition. Following selective subject loss, how do the mean memory ability scores for the two groups compare? What does this indicate for the equivalence of the two groups initially formed using random assignment?

3   For each "participant" (card) dropped from the experimental group, remove a comparable card from the control group. Note that you may not have exact matches, and you may have to substitute a "1" for a "2" or vice versa. Compute a new mean for the control group. Did this procedure restore the initial equivalence of the two groups?

4   Shuffle the 40 cards again and deal the cards into four groups. Compute a mean for each pile of 10 cards. With fewer "participants" in each group, did randomization (shuffling) lead to equivalent groups?

of the control group are simply asked to take a fitness test at the end of the month. Those in the experimental group participate in a vigorous fitness program for 1 month prior to the test. Assume 38 control participants show up for the fitness test at the end of the month, but only 25 of the experimental participants stay with the rigorous fitness program for the full month. Also assume that the average fitness score for the 25 people remaining in the experimental group is significantly higher than the average score for the people in the control group. The directors of the fitness center then make the claim, "A scientifically based research study has shown that our program leads to better fitness."

Do you think the fitness center's claim is justified? It's not. This hypothetical study represents a classic example of selective subject loss, so the results of the study can't be used to support the fitness center's claim. The loss occurred differentially across conditions; participants were lost mainly from the experimental group. The problem with differential loss is not that the groups ended up different in size. The results would have been interpretable if 25 people had been randomly assigned to the experimental group and 38 to the control group and all the individuals had completed the experiment. Rather, selective subject loss is a problem because the 25 experimental participants who completed the fitness program are not likely to be comparable to the 38 control participants. The 15 experimental participants who could not complete the rigorous program are likely to have been less fit (even before the program began) than the

FIGURE 6.3 Many people who begin a rigorous exercise program fail to complete it. In a sense, only the "fittest" survive, a situation that could cause problems of interpretation if different types of fitness programs were being compared.

25 experimental participants who completed the program. The selective loss of participants in the experimental group likely destroyed the comparable groups that were formed by random assignment at the beginning of the experiment. In fact, the final fitness scores of the 25 experimental participants might have been higher than the average in the control group even if they had not participated in the fitness program because they were more fit when they began! Thus, the subject loss in this experiment meets the other two conditions for selective subject loss. Namely, the loss is likely due to a characteristic of the participants—their original level of fitness—and this characteristic is relevant to the outcome of the study (see Figure 6.3).

If selective subject loss is not identified until after the experiment is completed, little can be done except to chalk up the experience of having conducted an uninterpretable experiment. Preventive steps can be taken, however, when researchers realize in advance that selective loss may be a problem. One alternative is to administer a pretest and screen out subjects who are likely to be lost. For example, in the exercise study, an initial test of fitness could have been given, and only those participants who scored above some minimal level would have participated in the experiment. Screening participants in this way would involve a potential cost. The results of the study would likely apply only for people above the minimal fitness level. This cost may be well worth paying because an interpretable study of limited generality is still preferable to an uninterpretable study.

There is a second preventive approach that researchers can use when facing the possibility of selective subject loss. Researchers can give all subjects a pretest but then simply randomly assign participants to conditions. Then, if a subject is lost from the experimental group, a subject with a comparable pretest score can be dropped from the control group. In a sense, this approach tries to restore the initial comparability of the groups. Researchers must be able to anticipate possible factors that could lead to selective subject loss, and they must make sure their pretest measures these factors.

Placebo Control and Double-Blind Experiments   The final challenge to internal validity we will describe arises because of expectations held by both participants and experimenters. Demand characteristics represent one possible source of bias due to participants' expectations (Orne, 1962). *Demand characteristics* refer to the cues and other information that participants use to guide their behavior in a psychological study (see Chapter 4). For example, research participants who know they have been given alcohol in an experiment may expect to experience certain effects, such as relaxation or giddiness. They may then behave consistent with these expectations rather than in response to the effects of the alcohol per se. Potential biases can also arise due to the expectations of the experimenters. The general term used to describe these biases is **experimenter effects** (Rosenthal, 1963, 1994a). Experimenter effects may be a source of confounding if experimenters treat subjects differently in the different groups of the experiment in ways other than those required to implement the independent variable. In an experiment involving alcohol, for instance, experimenter effects could occur if the experimenters read the instructions more slowly to participants who had been given alcohol than to those who had not. Experimenter effects also can occur when experimenters make biased observations based on the treatment a subject has received. For example, biased observations might arise in the alcohol study if the experimenters were more likely to notice unusual motor movements or slurred speech among the "drinkers" (because they "expect" drinkers to behave this way). (See discussion of expectancy effects in Chapter 4.)

Researchers can never completely eliminate the problems of demand characteristics and experimenter effects, but there are special research designs that control these problems. Researchers use a **placebo control group** as one way to control demand characteristics. A *placebo* (from the Latin word meaning "I shall please") is a substance that looks like a drug or other active substance but is actually an inert, or inactive, substance. Some research even indicates that there can be therapeutic effects from the placebo itself, based on participants' expectations for an effect of a "drug" (e.g., Kirsch & Sapirstein, 1998). Researchers test the effectiveness of a proposed treatment by comparing it to a placebo. Both groups have the same "awareness" of taking a drug and, therefore, similar expectations for a therapeutic effect. That is, the demand characteristics are similar for the groups—participants in both groups expect to experience effects of a drug. Any differences between the experimental groups and the placebo control group could legitimately be attributed to the actual effect of the drug taken by the experimental participants, and not the participants' expectations about receiving a drug.

The use of placebo control groups in combination with a double-blind procedure can control for both demand characteristics and experimenter effects. In a **double-blind procedure,** both the participant and the observer are blind to (unaware of) what treatment is being administered. In an experiment testing the effectiveness of a drug treatment, two researchers would be needed to accomplish the double-blind procedure. The first researcher would prepare the drug capsules and code each capsule in some way; the second researcher would distribute the drugs to the participants, recording the code for each drug as it was given to an individual. This procedure ensures there is a record of which drug each person received, but neither the participant nor the experimenter who actually administers the drugs (and observes their effects) knows which treatment the participant received. Thus, experimenter expectancies about the effects of the treatment are controlled because the researcher who makes the observations is unaware of who received the treatment and who received the placebo. Similarly, demand characteristics are controlled because participants remain unaware of whether they received the drug or placebo.

Experiments that involve placebo control groups are a valuable research tool for assessing the effectiveness of a treatment while controlling for demand characteristics. The use of placebo control groups, however, does raise special ethical concerns. The benefits of the knowledge gained using placebo control groups must be evaluated in light of the risks involved when research participants who expect to receive a drug may instead receive a placebo. Typically, the ethics of this procedure are addressed in the informed consent procedure prior to the start of the experiment. Participants are told they may receive a drug or a placebo. Only individuals who consent to receiving either the placebo or the drug participate in the research. Should the experimental drug prove effective, then the researchers are ethically required to offer the treatment to participants in the placebo condition.

Key Concept }

ANALYSIS AND INTERPRETATION OF EXPERIMENTAL FINDINGS

The Role of Data Analysis in Experiments

- Data analysis and statistics play a critical role in researchers' ability to make the claim that an independent variable has had an effect on behavior.
- The best way to determine whether the findings of an experiment are reliable is to do a replication of the experiment.

A good experiment, as is true of all good research, begins with a good research question. We have described how researchers use control techniques to design and implement an experiment that will allow them to gather interpretable evidence to answer their research question. However, simply conducting a good experiment is not sufficient. Researchers must also present the evidence in a convincing way to demonstrate that their findings support their conclusions based on that evidence. Data analysis and statistics play a critical role in the analysis and interpretation of experimental findings.

Robert Abelson, in his book *Statistics as Principled Argument* (1995), suggests that the primary goal of data analysis is to determine whether observations support a claim about behavior. That is, can we "make the case" for a conclusion based on the evidence gathered in an experiment? We provide a more complete description of how researchers use data analysis and statistics in Chapters 11 and 12. Here we will introduce the central concepts of data analysis that apply to the interpretation of the results of experiments. But first let us mention one very important way that researchers can make their case concerning the results of their research.

Key Concept }

The best way to determine whether the findings obtained in an experiment are reliable (consistent) is to replicate the experiment and see if the same outcome is obtained. **Replication** means repeating the procedures used in a particular experiment in order to determine whether the same results will be obtained a second time. As you might imagine, an exact replication is almost impossible to carry out. The subjects tested in the replication will be different from those tested in the original study; the testing rooms and experimenters also may be different. Nevertheless, replication is still the best way to determine whether a research finding is reliable. If we required, however, that the reliability of every experiment be established by replication, the process would be cumbersome and inefficient. Participants for experiments are a scarce resource, and doing a replication means we won't be doing an experiment to ask new and different questions about behavior. Data analysis and statistics provide researchers with an alternative to replication for determining whether the results of a single experiment are reliable and can be used to make a claim about the effect of an independent variable on behavior.

Data analysis of an experiment involves three stages: (1) getting to know the data, (2) summarizing the data, and (3) confirming what the data reveal. In the first stage we try to find out what is going on in the data set, look for errors, and make sure the data make sense. In the second stage we use descriptive statistics and graphical displays to summarize what was found. In the third stage we seek evidence for what the data tell us about behavior. In this stage we make our conclusions about the data using various statistical techniques.

In the following sections we provide only a brief introduction to these stages of data analysis. A more complete introduction to data analysis is found in Chapters 11 and 12 (see especially Box 11.1). These later chapters will become particularly important if you need to read and interpret the results of a psychology experiment published in a scientific journal or if you carry out your own psychology experiment.

We will illustrate the process of data analysis by examining the results of an experiment that investigated the effects of rewards and punishments while participants played violent video games. Carnagey and Anderson (2005) noted that a large body of research evidence demonstrates that playing violent video games increases aggressive affect, cognitions, and behavior. They wondered, however, whether the effects of violent video games would differ when players are *punished* for violent game actions compared to when the same actions are *rewarded* (as in most video games). One hypothesis formed by Carnagey and Anderson was that when violent video-game actions are punished, players would be less aggressive. Another hypothesis, however, stated that when punished for their violent actions, players would become frustrated and therefore more aggressive.

In Carnagey and Anderson's studies, undergraduate participants played one of three versions of the same competitive race-car video game ("Carmageddon 2") in a laboratory setting. In the reward condition, participants were rewarded (gained points) for killing pedestrians and race opponents (this is the unaltered version of the game). In the punishment condition, the video game was altered so that participants lost points for killing or hitting opponents. In a third condition, the game was altered to be nonviolent and participants gained points for passing checkpoints as they raced around the track (all pedestrians were removed and race opponents were programmed to be passive).

Carnagey and Anderson (2005) reported the results of three experiments in which participants were randomly assigned to play one of the three versions of the video game. The primary dependent variables were measures of participants' hostile emotions (Experiment 1), aggressive thinking (Experiment 2), and aggressive behaviors (Experiment 3). Across the three studies, participants who were rewarded for violent actions in the video game were higher in aggressive emotions, cognitions, and behavior compared to the punishment and nonviolent game conditions. Punishing aggressive actions in the video game caused participants to experience greater hostile emotions (similar to the reward condition) relative to nonviolent play, but did not cause them to experience increased aggressive cognitions and behavior.

In order to illustrate the process of data analysis, we will examine more closely Carnagey and Anderson's results for aggressive cognitions (Experiment 2). After playing one of the three video-game versions, participants completed a word fragment task in which they were asked to complete as many words (out of 98) as they could in 5 minutes. Half of the word fragments had aggressive possibilities. For example, the word fragment "K I ___ ___" could be completed as "kiss" or "kill" (or other possibilities). Aggressive cognition was operationally defined as the proportion of word fragments a participant completed with aggressive words. For example, if a participant completed 60 of the word fragments in 5 minutes and 12 of those expressed aggressive content, the participant's aggressive cognition score would be .20 (i.e., $12/60 = .20$).

Describing the Results

- The two most common descriptive statistics that are used to summarize the results of experiments are the mean and standard deviation.
- Measures of effect size indicate the strength of the relationship between the independent and dependent variables, and they are not affected by sample size.

- One commonly used measure of effect size, *d*, examines the difference between two group means relative to the average variability in the experiment.
- Meta-analysis uses measures of effect size to summarize the results of many experiments investigating the same independent variable or dependent variable.

Data analysis should begin with a careful inspection of the data set with special attention given to possible errors or anomalous data points. Techniques for inspecting the data ("getting to know the data") are described in Chapter 11. The next step is to describe what was found. At this stage the researcher wants to know "What happened in the experiment?" To begin to answer this question, researchers use *descriptive statistics*. The two most commonly reported descriptive statistics are the mean (a measure of central tendency) and the standard deviation (a measure of variability). The means and standard deviations for aggressive cognition in the video-game experiment are presented in Table 6.1. The means show that aggressive cognition was highest in the reward condition (.210) and lowest in the nonviolent condition (.157). Aggressive cognition in the punishment condition (.175) fell between the nonviolent and reward conditions. We can note that for participants in the reward condition, approximately 1 in 5 words was completed with aggressive content (remember, though, that only half of the word fragments had aggressive possibilities).

In a properly conducted experiment, the standard deviation in each group should reflect only individual differences among the subjects who were randomly assigned to that group. Subjects in each group should be treated in the same way, and the level of the independent variable to which they've been assigned should be implemented in the same way for each subject in the group. The standard deviations shown in Table 6.1 indicate that there was variation around the mean in each group and that the variation was about the same in all three groups.

Key Concept

One important question researchers ask when describing the results of an experiment is how large an effect the independent variable had on the dependent variable. Measures of **effect size** can be used to answer this question because they indicate the strength of the relationship between the independent and dependent variables. One advantage of measures of effect size is that they are not influenced by the size of the samples tested in the experiment. Measures of effect size take into account more than the mean difference between two conditions

TABLE 6.1 MEAN AGGRESSIVE COGNITION, STANDARD DEVIATIONS, AND CONFIDENCE INTERVALS FOR THE THREE CONDITIONS OF THE VIDEO-GAME EXPERIMENT

Video-Game Version	Mean	*SD*	.95 Confidence Interval*
Reward	.210	.066	.186–.234
Punishment	.175	.046	.151–.199
Nonviolent	.157	.050	.133–.181

*Confidence intervals were estimated based on data reported in Carnagey and Anderson (2005).

Key Concept

in an experiment. The mean difference between two groups is always *relative* to the average variability in participants' scores. One frequently used measure of effect size is **Cohen's *d*.** Cohen (1992) developed procedures that are now widely accepted. He suggested that *d* values of .20, .50, and .80 represent small, medium, and large effects of the independent variable, respectively.

We can illustrate the use of Cohen's *d* as a measure of effect size by comparing two conditions in the video-game experiment, the reward condition and the nonviolent condition. The *d* value is .83 based on the difference between the mean aggressive cognition in the reward condition (.210) and the nonviolent condition (.157). This *d* value allows us to say that the video-game independent variable, reward *vs.* nonviolent, had a large effect on the aggressive cognition in these two conditions. Effect-size measures provide researchers with valuable information for describing the findings of an experiment.

Measures of central tendency and variability, as well as effect size, are described in Chapters 11 and 12. In those chapters we outline the computational steps for these measures and discuss their interpretation. Many different effect-size measures are found in the psychology literature. In addition to Cohen's *d*, for example, a popular measure of effect magnitude is eta squared, which is a measure of the strength of association between the independent and dependent variables (see Chapter 12). That is, eta squared estimates the proportion of total variance accounted for by the effect of the independent variable on the dependent variable. Measures of effect size are most helpful when comparing the numeric values of a measure from two or more studies or when averaging measures across studies, as is done when a meta-analysis is performed (see below).

Key Concept

Researchers also use measures of effect size in a procedure called meta-analysis. **Meta-analysis** is a statistical technique used to summarize the effect sizes from several independent experiments investigating the same independent or dependent variable. In general, the methodological quality of the experiments included in the meta-analysis will determine its ultimate value (see Judd, Smith, & Kidder, 1991). Meta-analyses are used to answer questions like: Are there gender differences in conformity? What are the effects of class size on academic achievement? Is cognitive therapy effective in the treatment of depression? Box 6.2 describes a meta-analysis of studies on effective psychotherapy for youth with psychological disorders. The results of individual experiments, no matter how well done, often are not sufficient to provide answers to questions about such important general issues. We need to consider a body of literature (i.e., many experiments) pertaining to each issue. (See Hunt, 1997, for a good and readable introduction to meta-analysis.) Meta-analysis allows us to draw stronger conclusions about the principles of psychology because these conclusions emerge only after looking at the results of many individual experiments. These analyses provide an efficient and effective way to summarize the results of large numbers of experiments using effect-size measures.

BOX 6.2

AN EXAMPLE OF META-ANALYSIS: "EVIDENCE-BASED YOUTH PSYCHOTHERAPIES VERSUS USUAL CLINICAL CARE"

Weisz, Jensen-Doss, and Hawley (2006) used meta-analysis to summarize the results of 32 psychotherapy studies with youth that compared the effects of "evidence-based treatments" and "usual care." An evidence-based treatment (EBT) is one that has received empirical support—that is, it has been shown in clinical research to help individuals. Although it seems obvious that EBTs should be widely used in clinical practice because of this empirical support, many therapists argue that these treatments would not be effective in usual clinical contexts. EBTs are structured and require therapists to follow a treatment manual. Some clinicians argue that EBTs are inflexible, rigid treatments that cannot be individualized according to clients' needs. Furthermore, opponents of EBTs argue that empirical studies that indicate effectiveness typically involve clients with less severe or less complicated problems than those seen in usual clinical practice. These arguments suggest that usual care (UC) in the form of psychotherapy, counseling, or case management as regularly conducted by mental health providers would better meet the needs of the clients typically seen in community settings.

Weisz and his colleagues used meta-analysis to compare directly the outcomes associated with EBTs and usual care. Across 32 studies that compared EBT and UC, the average effect size was 0.30. Thus, youth treated with an evidence-based treatment were better off, on average, than youth treated with usual care. The value of 0.30 falls between Cohen's (1988) criteria for small and medium effects. This effect size represents the difference between the two types of treatments, not the effect of psychotherapy per se. Weisz et al. note that when EBTs are contrasted with no-treatment control groups (e.g., waiting list), the effect sizes for EBT typically range from 0.50 to 0.80 (medium-to-large effects). In additional analyses the authors grouped studies according to factors such as the severity and complexity of treated problems, treatment settings, and characteristics of the therapists. These analyses were done to determine whether the concerns voiced by critics of evidence-based treatments warrant the continued use of usual care. Weisz and his colleagues found that grouping studies according to these various factors did not influence the overall outcome that EBTs outperformed UC.

This meta-analysis allows psychologists to make the claim with more confidence for a general psychological principle regarding psychotherapy: Evidence-based treatments provide better outcomes for youth than usual care.

Confirming What the Results Reveal

- Researchers use inferential statistics to determine whether an independent variable has a reliable effect on a dependent variable.
- Two methods to make inferences based on sample data are null hypothesis testing and confidence intervals.
- Researchers use null hypothesis testing to determine whether mean differences among groups in an experiment are greater than the differences that are expected simply because of error variation.
- A statistically significant outcome is one that has a small likelihood of occurring if the null hypothesis were true.
- Researchers determine whether an independent variable has had an effect on behavior by examining whether the confidence intervals for different

samples in an experiment overlap. The degree of overlap provides information as to whether the sample means estimate the same population mean or different population means.

Perhaps the most basic claim that researchers want to make when they do an experiment is that the independent variable did have an effect on the dependent variable. Another way to phrase this claim is to say that researchers want to confirm that the independent variable *produced a difference in behavior*. Descriptive statistics alone are not sufficient evidence to confirm this basic claim.

To confirm whether the independent variable has produced an effect in an experiment, researchers use *inferential statistics*. They need to use inferential statistics because of the nature of the control provided through random assignment in experiments. As we have previously described, random assignment does not *eliminate* the individual differences among subjects. Random assignment simply *balances,* or averages, the individual differences among subjects across the groups of the experiment. The nonsystematic (i.e., random) variation due to differences among subjects within each group is called *error variation*. The presence of error variation poses a potential problem because the means of the different groups in the experiment may differ simply because of error variation, not because the independent variable has an effect. Thus, by themselves, the mean results of the best-controlled experiment do not permit a definite conclusion about whether the independent variable has produced a difference in behavior. Inferential statistics allow researchers to test whether differences between group means are due to an effect of the independent variable, not just due to chance (error variation). Researchers use two types of inferential statistics to make decisions about whether an independent variable has had an effect: null hypothesis testing and confidence intervals.

We realize that it may be frustrating to learn that the results of the best-controlled experiment often do not permit a definite conclusion about whether the independent variable produced a difference in behavior. In other words, what you have learned so far about research methods is not enough! Unfortunately, even with the tools of data analysis we cannot give you a way to make *definite* conclusions about what produced a difference in behavior. But what we can give you is a way (actually, several ways) to make the best possible statement about what produced a difference. The conclusion will be based on a *probability*—namely, a probability that will help you to decide whether your effect is or is not simply due to chance. It is easy to get lost in the complexities of null hypothesis testing and confidence intervals, but keep in mind the following two critical points:

First and foremost, differences in behavior can arise simply due to chance (often referred to as *error variation*). What you want to know is, how likely it is that the difference you have observed is only due to chance (not to the effect of your independent variable)? Actually, what you would really like to know is, how likely it is that your independent variable had an effect? However, we can't answer these questions using statistical inference. As you will see, statistical inference is indirect (see, for example, Box 12.1 in Chapter 12).

Second, the data you have collected represent *samples* from a population; but in a sense, it is *populations*, not samples, that really matter. (If only sample means mattered, then you could simply look at the sample means to see if they were different.) The mean performance for the samples in the various conditions of your experiment provides estimates that are used to *infer* the mean of the population. When you make statements of statistical inference, you are using the sample means to make decisions (inferences) about differences between (or among) population means. Once again we refer you to Chapter 12 for a more complete discussion of these issues.

Key Concept }

Key Concept }

Null Hypothesis Significance Testing (NHST)　Researchers most frequently use **null hypothesis significance testing (NHST)** to decide whether an independent variable has produced an effect in an experiment. Null hypothesis significance testing begins with the assumption that the independent variable has had *no* effect. If we assume that the null hypothesis is true, we can use probability theory to determine the probability that the difference we did observe in our experiment would occur "by chance." *A **statistically significant** outcome is one that has only a small likelihood of occurring if the null hypothesis were true.* A statistically significant outcome means only that the difference we obtained in our experiment is larger than would be expected if error variation alone (i.e., chance) were responsible for the outcome.

The outcome of an experiment is usually expressed in terms of the differences between the means for the conditions in the experiment. How do we know the probability of the obtained outcome in an experiment? Most often, researchers use inferential statistics tests such as the *t*-test or *F*-test. The *t*-test is used when there are two levels of the independent variable, and the *F*-test is used when there are three or more levels of the independent variable. Each value of a *t*- or *F*-test has a probability value associated with it when the null hypothesis is assumed. This probability can be determined once the researcher has computed the value of the test statistic.

Assuming the null hypothesis is true, just how small does the probability of our outcome need to be in order to be statistically significant? Scientists tend to agree that outcomes with probabilities (p) of less than 5 times out of 100 (or $p < .05$) are judged to be statistically significant. The probability value researchers use to decide that an outcome is statistically significant is called the *level of significance*. The level of significance is indicated by the Greek letter alpha (α).

We can now illustrate the procedures of null hypothesis testing to analyze the video-game experiment we described earlier (see Table 6.1, p. 204). The first research question we would ask is whether there was any *overall* effect of the independent variable of video-game version. That is, did aggressive cognition differ as a function of the three versions of the video game? The null hypothesis for this overall test is that there is no difference among the population means represented by the means of the experimental conditions (remember that the null hypothesis assumes no effect of the independent variable). The p value for the F-test that was computed for the effect of the video-game version was less than the .05 level of significance; thus, the overall effect of the video-game variable was statistically significant. To interpret this outcome, we would need to refer to the descriptive statistics for this experiment in Table 6.1. There we see that the mean aggressive cognition for the three video-game conditions was different. For example, aggressive cognition was highest with the reward video game (.210) and lowest with the nonviolent video game (.157). The statistically significant outcome of the F-test allows us to make the claim that the video-game version did produce a difference in aggressive cognition.

Researchers want to make more specific claims about the effects of independent variables on behavior than that the independent variable did have an effect. F-tests of the overall differences among the means tell us that something happened in the experiment, but they don't tell us much about what did happen. One way to gain this more specific information about the effects of independent variables is to use confidence intervals.

Using Confidence Intervals to Examine Mean Differences   The confidence intervals for each of the three groups in the video-game experiment are shown in Table 6.1 on page 204. A confidence interval is associated with a probability (usually .95) that the interval contains the true population mean. The width of the interval tells us how precise our estimate is (the narrower the better).

Confidence intervals can also be used to compare differences between two population means. We can use the .95 confidence intervals presented in Table 6.1 to ask specific questions about the effects of the video-game version on aggressive cognition. We accomplish this by examining whether the confidence intervals for the different video-game groups overlap. *When the confidence intervals do not overlap, we can be confident that the population means for the two groups differ.* For example, notice that the confidence interval for the reward group is .186 to .234. This indicates there is a .95 probability that the interval .186 to .234 contains the population mean for aggressive cognition in the reward condition (remember the sample mean of .210 only *estimates* the population mean). The confidence interval for the nonviolent group is .133 to .181. This confidence interval does not overlap at all with the confidence interval for the reward group (i.e., the upper limit of .181 for the nonviolent group is less than the lower limit of .186 for the reward group). With this evidence we can make the claim that aggressive cognition in the reward condition was greater than aggressive cognition in the nonviolent video-game condition.

When we compare the confidence intervals for the reward group (.186–.234) and the punishment group (.151–.199), however, we come to a different conclusion. The confidence intervals for these groups do overlap. Even though the sample means of .210 and .175 differ, we cannot conclude that the population means differ because of the overlap of the confidence intervals. We can offer the following rule of thumb for interpreting this result: *If intervals overlap slightly, then we must acknowledge our uncertainty about the true mean difference and postpone judgment; if the intervals overlap such that the mean of one group lies within the interval of another group, we may conclude that the population* *means **do not** differ*. In the video-game experiment, the overlap is small and the sample means for each condition do not fall within the intervals for the other group. We want to decide whether the populations differ, but all we can really say is that we don't have sufficient evidence to decide one way or the other. In this situation we must postpone judgment until the next experiment is done.

> The logic and computational procedures for confidence intervals and for the *t*-test are found in Chapter 11. The *F*-test (in its various forms) is discussed in Chapter 12.

What Data Analysis Can't Tell Us

We've already alluded to one thing that our data analysis can't tell us. Even if our experiment is internally valid and the results are statistically significant, we cannot say *for sure* that our independent variable had an effect (or did not have an effect). We must learn to live with probability statements. The results of our data analysis also can't tell us whether the results of our study have practical value or even if they are meaningful. It is easy to do experiments that ask trivial research questions (see Sternberg, 1997, and Chapter 1). It is also easy (maybe too easy!) to do a bad experiment. Bad experiments—that is, ones that lack internal validity—can easily produce statistically significant outcomes and nonoverlapping confidence intervals; however, the outcome will be uninterpretable.

When an outcome is statistically significant, we conclude that the independent variable produced an effect on behavior. Yet, as we have seen, our analysis does not provide us with certainty regarding our conclusion, even though we reached the conclusion "beyond a reasonable doubt." Also, when an outcome is *not* statistically significant, we cannot conclude with certainty that the independent variable did *not* have an effect. All we can conclude is there is not sufficient evidence in the experiment to claim that the independent variable produces an effect. Determining that an independent variable has not had an effect can be even more crucial in applied research. For example, is a generic drug as effective as its brand-name counterpart? To answer this research question, researchers often seek to find no difference between the two drugs. The standards for experiments attempting to answer questions regarding no difference between conditions are higher than those for experiments seeking to confirm that an independent variable does have an effect. We describe these standards in Chapter 12.

Because researchers rely on probabilities to make decisions about the effects of independent variables, there is always some chance of making an error. There are two types of errors that can occur when researchers use inferential statistics. When we claim that an outcome is statistically significant and the null hypothesis (no difference) is really true, we are making a Type I error. A *Type I error* is like a false alarm—saying that there is a fire when there is not. When we conclude that we have insufficient evidence to reject the null hypothesis and it is, in fact, false, we are making a *Type II error* (Type I and Type II errors are described more fully in Chapter 12). We would never make either of these errors if we could know for sure whether the null hypothesis was true or false. While being mindful of the possibility that data analysis can lead to incorrect decisions, we must also remember that data analysis can and often does lead to correct decisions. The most important thing for researchers to remember is that inferential statistics can never replace replication as the ultimate test of the reliability of an experimental outcome.

ESTABLISHING THE EXTERNAL VALIDITY OF EXPERIMENTAL FINDINGS

- The findings of an experiment have external validity when they can be applied to other individuals, settings, and conditions beyond the scope of the specific experiment.
- In some investigations (e.g., theory-testing), researchers may choose to emphasize internal validity over external validity; other researchers may choose to increase external validity using sampling or replication.
- Conducting field experiments is one way that researchers can increase the external validity of their research in real-world settings.
- Partial replication is a useful method for establishing the external validity of research findings.
- Researchers often seek to generalize results about conceptual relationships among variables rather than specific conditions, manipulations, settings, and samples.

As you learned in Chapter 4, *external validity* refers to the extent to which findings from a research study can be generalized to individuals, settings, and conditions beyond the scope of the specific study. A frequent criticism of highly controlled experiments is that they lack external validity; that is, the findings observed in a controlled laboratory experiment may describe what happens only in that specific setting, with the specific conditions that were tested, and with the specific individuals who participated. Consider again the video-game experiment in which college students played a race-car video game in a laboratory setting. The laboratory setting is ideally suited for exercising control procedures that ensure the internal validity of an experiment. But do these findings help us understand violence and aggression in a natural setting? When a different type of exposure to violence is involved? When the people exposed to violence are senior citizens? These are questions of external validity, and they raise a more general question. If the findings of laboratory experiments are so specific, what good are they to society?

One answer to this question is a bit unsettling, at least initially. Mook (1983) argued that, when the purpose of an experiment is to test a specific hypothesis derived from a psychological theory, the question of external validity of the findings is irrelevant. An experiment is often done to determine whether subjects *can* be induced to behave in a certain way. The question whether subjects *do* behave that way in their natural environment is secondary to the question raised in the experiment. The issue of the external validity of experiments is not a new one, as reflected in the following statement by Riley (1962): "In general, laboratory experiments are not set up to imitate the most typical case found in nature. Instead, they are intended to answer some specific question of interest to the experimenter" (p. 413).

Of course, researchers often do want to obtain findings that they can generalize beyond the boundaries of the experiment itself. To achieve this goal, researchers can include the characteristics of the situations to which they wish to generalize in their experiments. For example, Ceci (1993) described a research program that he and his colleagues conducted on children's eyewitness testimony. He described how their research program was motivated in part because previous studies on this topic did not capture all the dimensions of an *actual* eyewitness situation. Ceci described how their research program included factors such as multiple suggestive interviews, very long retention intervals, and recollections of stressful experiences. Including these factors made the experiments more representative of situations that are actually involved when children testify (see Figure 6.4).

Ceci (1993) also pointed out, however, that important differences remained between the experiments and real-life situations:

> High levels of stress, assaults to a victim's body, and the loss of control are characteristics of events that motivate forensic investigations. Although these factors are at play in some of our other studies, we will never mimic experimentally the assaultive nature of acts perpetrated on child victims, because even those studies that come closest, such as the medical studies, are socially and parentally sanctioned, unlike sexual assaults against children. (pp. 41–42)

As Ceci's comments reveal, in some situations, such as those involving eyewitness testimony about despicable acts, there may be important ethical constraints on establishing the external validity of experiments.

The external validity of research findings is frequently questioned because of the nature of the "subjects." As you are aware, many studies in psychology involve college students who participate in experiments as part of their introductory psychology course. Dawes (1991), among others, argues that college students are a select group who may not always provide a good basis for building general conclusions about human behavior and mental processes. Similarly, Sue (1999) argues that researchers' greater emphasis on internal validity over external validity lessens the attention paid to the representativeness of the people who are studied. However, psychologists generally believe their findings will generalize to populations other than those specifically tested in their research, and there is little reason to cross-validate the findings by testing ethnic minority populations or other underrepresented populations. Questions about the external validity of research findings based on the populations being studied are especially important in applied research. In medical research, for example, effective treatments for men may not be effective for women, and effective treatments for adults may not be effective for children.

Field experiments, which we mentioned briefly in Chapter 4, are one way to increase the external validity of a research study. They can also yield practical knowledge. For example, to investigate people's perceptions of risks,

FIGURE 6.4   How similar can experiments be to real-life situations such as children testifying in court?

participants in two field experiments were asked to answer questions about risks during the 2009 H1N1 flu pandemic (Lee, Schwarz, Taubman, & Hou, 2010). The first experiment was conducted on a university campus and the second was conducted in shopping malls and near downtown businesses. Individuals who agreed to participate were randomly assigned to an experimental condition, in which the confederate sneezed and coughed prior to the administration of a brief questionnaire, or to a control condition (no sneezes, coughs). Results indicated that this simple manipulation influenced participants' perceptions of risk. Participants in the sneeze condition, compared to the no-sneeze condition, rated more highly their risk of contracting a serious disease, their risk of a heart attack before age 50, and their risk of dying from a crime or accident. Interestingly, compared to participants in the control condition, individuals in the sneeze condition also were more likely to favor federal spending for flu vaccines rather than the creation of "green" jobs. Because this experiment was carried out in a natural setting, it is more likely to be representative of "real-world" conditions. Thus, we can be more confident that the results will generalize to other real-world settings than if an artificial situation had been created in the laboratory.

The external validity of experimental findings also can be established through *partial replication*. Partial replications are commonly done as a routine part of the process of investigating the conditions under which a phenomenon reliably occurs. A partial replication can help to establish external validity by showing that a similar experimental result occurs when slightly different experimental procedures are used. Consider the same basic experiment done in both a large metropolitan private university and in a small rural community college; the participants and the settings in the experiments are very different. If the same results are obtained even with these different participants and settings, we can say the findings can be generalized across these two populations and settings. Notice that neither experiment alone has external validity; it is *the findings* that occur in *both* experiments that have external validity.

Researchers can also establish the external validity of their findings by doing *conceptual replications*. What we wish to generalize from any one study are conceptual relationships among variables, not the specific conditions, manipulations, settings, or samples (see Banaji & Crowder, 1989; Mook, 1983). Anderson and Bushman (1997) provide an example illustrating the logic of a conceptual replication. Consider a study with 5-year-old children to determine if a specific insult ("pooh-pooh-head") induces anger and aggression. We could then do a replication to see if the same insult produces the same result with 35-year-old adults. As Anderson and Bushman state, the findings for 5-year-olds probably wouldn't be replicated with the 35-year-olds because "'pooh-pooh-head' just doesn't pack the same 'punch' for 5- and 35-year-old people" (p. 21). However, if we wish to establish the external validity of the idea that "insults increase aggressive behavior," we can use different words that are meaningful insults for each population.

When Anderson and Bushman (1997) examined variables related to aggression at the conceptual level, they found that findings from experiments conducted in laboratory settings and findings from correlational studies in real-world settings were very similar. They concluded that "artificial" laboratory experiments do provide meaningful information about aggression because they demonstrate the same conceptual relationships that are observed in real-world aggression. Furthermore, laboratory experiments allow researchers to isolate the potential causes of aggression and to investigate boundary conditions for when aggression will or will not occur.

What about when results in the lab and the real world disagree? Anderson and Bushman (1997) argue that these discrepancies, rather than evidence for the weakness of either method, should be used to help us refine our theories about aggression. That is, the discrepancies should make us recognize that different psychological processes may be at work in each setting. When we increase our understanding of these discrepancies, we will increase our understanding of aggression.

Establishing the external validity of *each* finding in psychology by performing partial replications or conceptual replications would be virtually impossible. But if we take arguments like those of Dawes (1991) and Sue (1999) seriously, as indeed we should, it would appear that we are facing an impossible task. How, for instance, could we show that an experimental finding obtained with a group of college students will generalize to groups of older adults, working professionals, less educated individuals, and so forth? Underwood and Shaughnessy (1975) suggest one possible approach worth considering. Their notion is that we should assume that behavior is relatively continuous across time, subjects, and settings unless we have reason to assume otherwise. Ultimately, the external validity of research findings is likely to be established more by the good judgment of the scientific community than by definitive empirical evidence.

MATCHED GROUPS DESIGN

- A matched groups design may be used to create comparable groups when there are too few subjects available for random assignment to work effectively.
- Matching subjects on the dependent variable task is the best approach for creating matched groups, but performance on any matching task must correlate with the dependent variable task.
- After subjects are matched on the matching task, they should then be randomly assigned to the conditions of the independent variable.

To work effectively, the random groups design requires samples of sufficient size to ensure that individual differences among subjects will be balanced through random assignment. That is, the assumption of the random groups design is that individual differences "average out" across groups. But how many subjects are required for this averaging process to work as it should? The answer is "It depends." More subjects will be needed to average out individual differences when samples are drawn from a heterogeneous population than from a homogeneous one.

We can be relatively confident that random assignment will *not* be effective in balancing the differences among subjects when small numbers of subjects are tested from heterogeneous populations. However, this is exactly the situation researchers face in several areas of psychology. For example, some developmental psychologists study newborn infants; others study the elderly. Both newborns and the elderly certainly represent diverse populations, and developmental psychologists often have available only limited numbers of participants.

One alternative that researchers have in this situation is to administer all the conditions of the experiment to all the subjects, using a repeated measures design (to be discussed in Chapter 7). Nevertheless, some independent variables require separate groups of subjects for each level. For instance, suppose researchers wish to compare two types of postnatal care for premature infants and it is not possible to give both types of care to each infant. In this situation, and many others, researchers will need to test separate groups in the experiment.

Key Concept }

The **matched groups design** is a good alternative when neither the random groups design nor the repeated measures design can be used effectively. The logic of the matched groups design is simple and compelling. Instead of trusting random assignment to form comparable groups, the researcher makes the groups equivalent by matching subjects. Once comparable groups have been formed based on the matching, the logic of the matched groups design is the

FIGURE 6.5 Random assignment is not likely to be effective in balancing differences among subjects when small numbers of subjects from heterogeneous populations are tested (e.g., newborns). In this situation, researchers may want to consider the matched groups design.

same as that for the random groups design (see Figure 6.5). In most uses of the matched groups design, a pretest task is used to match subjects. The challenge is to select a pretest task (also called a matching task) that equates the groups on a dimension that is relevant to the outcome of the experiment. *The matched groups design is useful only when a good matching task is available.*

The most preferred matching task is one that uses the same task that will be used in the experiment itself. For example, if the dependent variable in the experiment is blood pressure, participants should be matched on blood pressure prior to the start of the experiment. The matching is accomplished by measuring the blood pressure of all participants and then forming pairs or triples or quadruples of participants (depending on the number of conditions in the experiment) who have identical or very similar blood pressures. Thus, at the start of the experiment, participants in the different groups will have, *on average,* equivalent blood pressure. Researchers can then reasonably attribute any group differences in blood pressure at the end of the study to the treatment (presuming other potential variables have been held constant or balanced).

In some experiments, the primary dependent variable cannot be used to match subjects. For example, consider an experiment that teaches participants different approaches to solving a puzzle. If a pretest were given to see how long it took individuals to solve this puzzle, the participants would likely learn the solution to the puzzle during the pretest. If so, then it would be impossible to observe differences in the speed with which different groups of participants solved the puzzle following the experimental manipulation. In this situation the next best alternative for a matching task is to use a task from the *same class or category* as the experimental task. In our problem-solving experiment, participants could be matched on their performance when solving a different puzzle from the experimental puzzle. A less preferred, but still possible, alternative for matching is to use a task that is from a *different class* than the experimental task. For our problem-solving experiment, participants could be matched on some test of general ability, such as a test of spatial ability. When using these alternatives, however, researchers must confirm that performance on the matching task correlates with the performance on the task that is used as the dependent variable. In general, as the correlation between the matching task and the dependent variable decreases, the advantage of the matched groups design, relative to the random groups design, also decreases.

Even when a good matching task is available, matching is not sufficient to form comparable groups in an experiment. For example, consider a matched groups design to compare two different methods of caring for premature infants so as to increase their body weight. Six pairs of premature infants could be matched on their initial body weight. There remain, however, potentially relevant characteristics of the participants beyond those measured by the matching task. For example, the two groups of premature infants may not be comparable in their general health or in their degree of parental attachment. It is important, therefore, to use random assignment in the matched groups design to try to balance other potential factors beyond the matching task. Specifically, after matching the infants on body weight, individuals in each pair would be randomly assigned to one of the two treatment groups. In conclusion, *the matched groups design is a better alternative than the random groups design when a good matching task is available and when only a small number of subjects is available for an experiment that requires separate groups for each condition.*

NATURAL GROUPS DESIGN

- Individual differences variables (or subject variables) are selected rather than manipulated to form natural groups designs.
- The natural groups design represents a type of correlational research in which researchers look for covariations between natural groups variables and dependent variables.
- Causal inferences cannot be made regarding the effects of natural groups variables because plausible alternative explanations for group differences exist.

Key Concept }

Researchers in many areas of psychology are interested in independent variables that are called **individual differences variables,** or *subject variables*. An individual differences variable is a characteristic or trait that varies across individuals. Religious affiliation is an example of an individual differences variable. Researchers can't manipulate this variable by randomly assigning people to Catholic, Jewish, Muslim, Protestant, or other groups. Instead, researchers "control" the religious affiliation variable by systematically selecting individuals who *naturally* belong to these groups. Individual differences variables such as gender, introversion–extraversion, race, or age are important independent variables in many areas of psychology.

It is important to differentiate experiments involving independent variables whose levels are *selected* from those involving independent variables whose levels are *manipulated.* Experiments involving independent variables whose levels are selected—like individual differences variables—are called **natural groups designs.** The natural groups design is frequently used in situations in which ethical and practical constraints prevent us from directly manipulating independent variables. For example, no matter how interested we might be in the effects of major surgery on subsequent depression, we could not ethically perform major surgery on a randomly assigned group of introductory psychology students and then compare their depression symptoms with those of another group who did not receive surgery! Similarly, if we were interested in the relationship between divorce and emotional disorders, we could not randomly assign some people to get divorced. By using the natural groups design, however, we can compare people who have had surgery with those who have not. Similarly, people who have chosen to divorce can be compared with those who have chosen to stay married.

Researchers use natural groups designs to meet the first two objectives of the scientific method: description and prediction. For example, studies have shown that people who are separated or divorced are much more likely to receive psychiatric care than are those who are married, widowed, or have remained single. On the basis of studies like these, we can describe divorced and married individuals in terms of emotional disorders, and we can predict which group is more likely to experience emotional disorders.

Serious problems can arise, though, when the results of natural groups designs are used to make causal statements. For instance, the finding that divorced persons are more likely than married persons to receive psychiatric care shows that these two factors covary. This finding could be taken to mean that divorce causes emotional disorders. But, before we conclude that divorce *causes* emotional disorders, we must assure ourselves that the time-order condition for a causal inference has been met. Does divorce precede the emotional disorder, or does the emotional disorder precede the divorce? A natural groups design does not tell us.

The natural groups design also poses problems when we try to satisfy the third condition for demonstrating causality, eliminating plausible alternative causes. The individual differences studied in the natural groups design are usually confounded—groups of individuals are likely to differ in many ways *in addition* to the variable used to classify them. For example, individuals who divorce and individuals who stay married may differ with respect to a number of characteristics other than their marital status, for example, their religious practices or financial circumstances. Any differences observed between divorced and married individuals may be due to these other characteristics, not to divorce. The manipulation done by "nature" is rarely the controlled type we have come to expect in establishing the internal validity of an experiment.

There are approaches for drawing causal inferences in the natural groups design. One effective approach requires that individual differences be studied in combination with independent variables that can be manipulated. This combination of more than one independent variable in one experiment requires the use of a complex design, which we will describe in Chapter 8. For now, recognize that drawing causal inferences based on the natural groups design can be a treacherous enterprise. Although such designs are sometimes referred to as "experiments," there are important differences between an experiment involving an individual differences variable and an experiment involving a manipulated variable.

SUMMARY

Researchers conduct experiments to test hypotheses derived from theories, but experiments can also be used to test the effectiveness of treatments or programs in applied settings. The experimental method is ideally suited to identifying cause-and-effect relationships when the control techniques of manipulation, holding conditions constant, and balancing are properly implemented.

In Chapter 6 we focused on applying these control techniques in experiments in which different groups of subjects are given different treatments representing the levels of the independent variable (see Figure 6.6). In the random groups design, the groups are formed using randomization procedures such that the groups are comparable at the start of the experiment. If the groups perform differently following the manipulation, and all other conditions were held constant, it is presumed that the independent variable is responsible for the difference. Random assignment is the most common method of forming comparable groups. By distributing subjects' characteristics equally across the conditions of the experiment, random assignment is an attempt to ensure that the differences among subjects are balanced, or averaged, across groups in the experiment. The most common technique for carrying out random assignment is block randomization.

There are several threats to the internal validity of experiments that involve testing independent groups. Testing intact groups even when the groups are randomly assigned to conditions should be avoided because the use of intact groups is highly likely to result in a confounding. Extraneous variables, such as

FIGURE 6.6   In this chapter we introduced three independent groups designs.

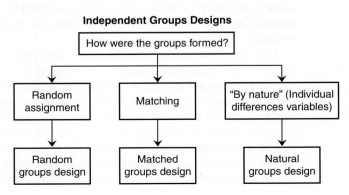

different rooms or different experimenters, must not be allowed to confound the independent variable of interest.

A more serious threat to the internal validity of the random groups design is involved when subjects fail to complete the experiment successfully. Selective subject loss occurs when subjects are lost differentially across the conditions and some characteristic of the subject that is related to the outcome of the experiment is responsible for the loss. We can help prevent selective loss by restricting subjects to those likely to complete the experiment successfully, or we can compensate for it by selectively dropping comparable subjects from the group that did not experience the loss. Demand characteristics and experimenter effects can be minimized through the use of proper experimental procedures, but they can best be controlled by using placebo control and double-blind procedures.

Data analysis and statistics provide an alternative to replication for determining whether the results of a single experiment can be used as evidence to claim that an independent variable has had an effect on behavior. Data analysis involves the use of both descriptive statistics and inferential statistics. Describing the results of an experiment typically involves the use of means, standard deviations, and measures of effect size. Meta-analysis makes use of measures of effect size to provide a quantitative summary of the results of a large number of experiments on an important research question.

Inferential statistics are important in data analysis because researchers need a way to decide whether the obtained differences in an experiment are due to chance or are due to the effect of the independent variable. Confidence intervals and null hypothesis testing are two effective statistical techniques researchers can use to analyze experiments. Statistical analysis cannot guarantee, however, that experimental findings will be meaningful or be of practical significance. Replication remains the ultimate test of the reliability of a research finding.

Researchers also strive to establish the external validity of their experimental findings. When testing psychological theories, researchers tend to emphasize internal validity over external validity. One effective approach for establishing the external validity of findings is to select representative samples of all dimensions on which you wish to generalize. By conducting field experiments, researchers can increase the external validity of their research findings to real-world settings. Partial replications and conceptual replications are two common ways that researchers use to establish external validity.

The matched groups design is an alternative to the random groups design when only a small number of subjects is available, when a good matching task is available, and when the experiment requires separate groups for each treatment. The biggest problem with the matched groups design is that the groups are equated only on the characteristic measured by the matching task. In the natural groups design, researchers select the levels of independent variables (usually individual differences, or subject, variables) and look for systematic relationships between these independent variables and other aspects of behavior. Essentially, the natural groups design involves looking for correlations between subjects' characteristics and their performance. Such correlational research designs pose problems in drawing causal inferences.

KEY CONCEPTS

internal validity   187
independent groups designs   188
random assignment   188
random groups design   188
block randomization   194
threats to internal validity   195
mechanical subject loss   197
selective subject loss   197
experimenter effects   200
placebo control group   200
double-blind procedure   201

replication   202
effect size   204
Cohen's *d*   205
meta-analysis   205
null hypothesis significance
   testing (NHST)   208
statistically significant   208
confidence interval   209
matched groups design   215
individual differences variable   217
natural groups design   218

REVIEW QUESTIONS

1 Describe two reasons why psychologists conduct experiments.

2 Describe how the control techniques of manipulation, holding conditions constant, and balancing contribute to meeting the three conditions necessary for a causal inference.

3 Explain why comparable groups are such an essential feature of the random groups design, and describe how researchers achieve comparable groups.

4 Identify what a "block" refers to in block randomization and explain what this procedure accomplishes.

5 What preventive steps could you take if you anticipated that selective subject loss could pose a problem in your experiment?

6 Explain how placebo control and double-blind techniques can be used to control demand characteristics and experimenter effects.

7 Explain why meta-analysis allows researchers to draw stronger conclusions about the principles of psychology.

8 Explain what a statistically significant outcome of an inferential statistics test tells you about the effect of the independent variable in an experiment.

9 Explain what you could conclude if the confidence intervals did not overlap when you were testing for a difference between means for two conditions in an experiment.

10 Briefly describe four ways researchers can establish the external validity of a research finding.

11 Briefly explain the logic of the matched groups design, and identify the three conditions under which the matched groups design is a better alternative than the random groups design.

12 How do individual differences variables differ from manipulated independent variables, and why does this difference make it difficult to draw causal inferences on the basis of the natural groups design?

CHALLENGE QUESTIONS

1 An experimenter is planning to do a random groups design experiment to study the effect of the rate of presenting stimuli on people's ability to recognize the stimuli. The independent variable is the presentation rate, and it will be manipulated at four levels: Very Fast, Fast, Slow, and Very Slow. The experimenter is seeking your help and advice with the following aspects of the experiment:

A The experimenter asks you to prepare a block-randomized schedule such that there will be four participants in each of the four conditions. To do this, you can use the following random numbers that were taken from the random number table in the Appendix (Table A.1).

1-5-6-6-4-1-0-4-9-3-2-0-4-9-2-3-8-3-9-1
9-1-1-3-2-2-1-9-9-9-5-9-5-1-6-8-1-6-5-2
2-7-1-9-5-4-8-2-2-3-4-6-7-5-1-2-2-9-2-3

B The experimenter is considering restricting participants to those who pass a stringent reaction time test so as to be sure that they will be able to perform the task successfully with the Very Fast presentation rate. Explain what factors the experimenter should consider in making this decision, being sure to describe clearly what risks, if any, are taken if only this restricted set of participants is tested.

C The experimenter discovers that it will be necessary to test participants in two different rooms. How should the experimenter arrange the testing of the conditions in these two rooms so as to avoid possible confounding by this extraneous variable?

2 A researcher conducted a series of experiments on the effects of external factors that might influence people's persistence in exercise programs. In one of these experiments, the researcher manipulated three types of distraction while participants walked on a treadmill. The three types of distraction were concentrating on one's own thoughts (concentration group), listening to a tape of music (music group), and watching a video of people engaging in outdoor recreation (video group). The dependent variable was how strenuous the treadmill exercise was at the time the participant decided to end the session (the incline of the treadmill was regularly increased as the person went through the session, thereby making the exercise increasingly strenuous). In an introductory psychology course, 120 students volunteered to participate in the experiment, and the researcher randomly assigned 40 students to each of the three levels of the distraction variable. The researcher expected that the mean strenuousness score would be highest in the video group, next highest in the music group, and lowest in the concentration group.

After only 2 minutes on the treadmill, each participant was given the option to stop the experiment. This brief time interval was chosen so that participants were given the option to stop before any of them could reasonably be expected to be experiencing fatigue. Data for the participants who decided to stop after only 2 minutes were not included in the analysis of the final results. Fifteen students chose to stop in the concentration group; 10 stopped in the music group; and no students stopped in the video group. The results did not support the researcher's predictions. The mean strenuousness score (on a scale from 0 to 100) for students who completed the experiment was highest for the concentration group (70), next highest for the music group (60), and lowest for the video group (50).

A Identify a possible threat to the internal validity of this experiment, and explain how this problem could account for the unexpected results of the study.

B Assume that a pretest measure was available for each of the 120 participants and that the pretest measured the degree to which each subject was likely to persist at exercise. Describe how you could use these pretest scores to confirm that the problem you identified in question 2A had occurred.

3 The newspaper headline summarizing research that had been reported in a medical journal read: "Study: Exercise Helps at Any Age." The research described in the article involved a 10-year study of nearly 10,000 men—and only men. The men were given a treadmill test between 1970 and 1989. Then they were given a second treadmill test 5 years after the first test, and their health was monitored for another 5 years. Men who were judged unfit on both treadmill tests had a death rate over the next 5 years of 122 per 10,000. Men judged fit on both treadmill tests had a 5-year death rate of only 40 per 10,000. Most interestingly, men judged unfit on the first treadmill test but fit on the second had a death rate of 68 per 10,000. The benefits of exercise were even greater when only deaths from heart attacks were examined. The benefits from exercise were present across a wide range of ages—thus, the headline.

A Why is the newspaper headline for this article potentially misleading?

B Why do you think the researchers tested only men?

C Identify two different ways of obtaining evidence that you could use to decide whether the results of this study could be applied to women. One of the ways would make use of already published research, and the other way would require doing a new study.

4 An experiment was done to test the effectiveness of a new drug that is being considered for possible use in the treatment of people who experience chronic anxiety. Fifty people who are chronically anxious are identified through a local health clinic, and all 50 people give their informed consent to participate in the experiment. Twenty-five people are randomly assigned to the experimental group, and they receive the new drug. The other 25 people are randomly assigned to the control group, and they receive the commonly used drug. The participants in both groups are monitored by a physician and a clinical psychologist during the 6-week treatment period. After the treatment period, the participants provide a self-rating on a reliable and valid 20-point scale indicating the level of anxiety they are experiencing (higher scores indicate greater anxiety). The mean self-rating in

the experimental group was 10.2 ($SD = 1.5$), and the mean rating in the control group was 13.5 ($SD = 2.0$). The .95 confidence interval for the mean self-rating in the experimental group was 9.6 to 10.8. The .95 confidence interval for the control group was 12.7 to 14.3.

A Explain why a double-blind procedure would be useful in this experiment, and describe how the double-blind procedure could be carried out in this experiment.

B Focus on the descriptive statistics for this experiment. How would you describe the effect of the drug variable on anxiety ratings using the means for each condition? What do the standard deviations tell you about the anxiety ratings in the experiment?

C The probability associated with the test for the mean difference between the two groups was $p = .01$. What claim would you make about the effect of the treatment based on this probability? What claim would you make based on the estimates of the population means for the two groups in this experiment based on a comparison of the confidence intervals?

D The effect size for the treatment variable in this experiment is $d = .37$. What information does this effect size tell you about the effectiveness of the drug beyond what you know from the test of statistical significance and from comparing the confidence intervals?

Answer to Stretching Exercise I

1 Bushman (2005) manipulated the independent variable of type of television program in his study. There were four levels of the independent variable: violent, sexually explicit, violent and sex, and neutral.

2 Bushman (2005) held several factors constant: the same advertisements were used in each condition, participants were tested in small groups in the same setting, and ads were placed at approximately the same point in each program.

3 Bushman (2005) balanced the characteristics of the participants across the four levels by randomly assigning participants to conditions. Thus, participants in each level were equivalent, on average, in their memory ability and their exposure to television programs and products. Bushman also used two random orders of the ads to balance any potential effects due to placement of the ads during the TV programs.

Answer to Stretching Exercise II

1 When one of your authors completed this exercise, she obtained a mean value of 5.65 for the experimental group and a mean of 5.35 for the control group. The two groups were approximately equivalent in terms of average memory ability (a *t*-test could be computed to determine if the mean scores differ statistically).

2 The experimental group had three "participants" with scores of 2 (and no aces). When these were dropped, the new mean for memory ability was 6.4. Compared to the control group mean of 5.35, the experimental group had, on average, greater memory ability following selective subject loss.

3   To compensate for the three subjects lost, similar "participants" were dropped from the control group (scores of 2, 1, and 1). The new mean for the control group was 6.06. This improved the initial comparability of the two groups.

4   The means for the four groups when one of the authors did this were: (1) 5.6 (2) 4.8 (3) 5.3, and (4) 6.3, indicating greater variability in the average memory ability score across the groups. The fewer the participants randomly assigned to conditions, the more difficult it is for random assignment to create, on average, equivalent groups. Now, put away the cards and get back to studying Chapter 6!

Answer to Challenge Question 1

A   The first step is to assign a number from 1 to 4 to the respective conditions: 1 = Very Fast; 2 = Fast; 3 = Slow; and 4 = Very Slow. Then, using the random numbers, select four sequences of the numbers from 1 to 4. In doing this you skip any numbers greater than 4 and any number that is a repetition of a number already selected in the sequence. For example, if the first number you select is a 1, you skip all repetitions of 1 until you have selected all the numbers for the sequence of 1 to 4. Following this procedure and working across the rows of random numbers from left to right, we obtained the following four sequences for the four blocks of the randomized block schedule. The order of the conditions for each block is also presented. The block-randomized schedule specifies the order of testing the conditions for the first 16 participants in the experiment.

Block 1: 1-4-3-2 Very Fast, Very Slow, Slow, Fast

Block 2: 4-2-3-1 Very Slow, Fast, Slow, Very Fast

Block 3: 1-3-2-4 Very Fast, Slow, Fast, Very Slow

Block 4: 2-3-4-1 Fast, Slow, Very Slow, Very Fast

B   The investigator is taking a reasonable step to avoid selective subject loss, but restricting participants to those who pass a stringent reaction time test entails the risk of decreased external validity of the obtained findings.

C   The rooms can be balanced by assigning entire blocks from the block-randomized schedule to be tested in each room. Usually, the number of blocks assigned to each room is equal, but this is not essential. For effective balancing, however, several blocks should be tested in each room.

CHAPTER SEVEN

Repeated Measures Designs

CHAPTER OUTLINE

OVERVIEW

Key Concept

Thus far we have considered experiments in which subjects participate in only one condition of the experiment. They are randomly assigned to one condition in the random groups and matched groups designs, or they are selected to be in one group in natural groups designs. These independent groups designs are powerful tools for studying the effects of a wide range of independent variables. There are times, however, when it is more effective to have each subject participate in all the conditions of an experiment. These designs are called **repeated measures designs** (or within-subjects designs). In an independent groups design, a separate group serves as a control for the group given the experimental treatment. In a repeated measures design, subjects *serve as their own controls* because they participate in both the experimental and control conditions.

We begin this chapter by exploring the reasons why researchers choose to use a repeated measures design. We then describe one of the central features of repeated measures designs. Specifically, in repeated measures designs, participants can undergo changes during the experiment as they are repeatedly tested. Participants may improve with practice, for example, because they learn more about the task or because they become more relaxed in the experimental situation. They also may get worse with practice—for example, because of fatigue or reduced motivation. These temporary changes are called *practice effects*.

We described in Chapter 6 that individual differences among participants cannot be eliminated in the random groups design, but they can be balanced by using random assignment. Similarly, the practice effects that participants experience due to repeated testing in the repeated measures designs cannot be eliminated. Like individual differences in the random groups design, however, practice effects can be balanced, or averaged, across the conditions of a repeated measures design experiment. When balanced across the conditions, practice effects are not confounded with the independent variable and the results of the experiment are interpretable.

Our primary focus in this chapter is to describe the techniques that researchers can use to balance practice effects. We also introduce data analysis procedures for repeated measures designs. We conclude the chapter with a consideration of problems that can arise in repeated measures designs.

WHY RESEARCHERS USE REPEATED MEASURES DESIGNS

- Researchers choose to use a repeated measures design in order to (1) conduct an experiment when few participants are available, (2) conduct the experiment more efficiently, (3) increase the sensitivity of the experiment, and (4) study changes in participants' behavior over time.

Researchers gain several advantages when they choose to use a repeated measures design. First, repeated measures designs require fewer participants than an independent groups design, so these designs are ideal for situations in which only a small number of participants is available. Researchers who do experiments with children, the elderly, or special populations such as individuals with brain injuries frequently have a small number of participants available.

Researchers choose to use repeated measures designs even when sufficient numbers of participants are available for an independent groups design. The repeated measures designs often are more convenient and efficient. For example, Ludwig, Jeeves, Norman, and DeWitt (1993) conducted a series of experiments studying communication between the two hemispheres of the brain. The investigators measured how long it took participants to decide whether two briefly presented letters had the same name. The letters came from the set AaBb. Participants were to press the "match" key when the letters had the same name (AA, aa, Bb, bb) and the "no match" key when the letters had different names (AB, ab, Ab, aB). There were several different ways in which the pairs of letters were presented across four experiments, but there were two major conditions in these experiments. Either both letters were presented to one hemisphere (unilateral) or one letter of the pair was presented to each hemisphere (bilateral). Across four experiments, bilateral presentation led to faster response times than did unilateral presentation. In these experiments, two hemispheres were better than one!

Each trial in the Ludwig et al. (1993) experiment required only a few seconds to complete. The researchers could have tested separate groups of participants for the unilateral and bilateral conditions, but this approach would have been horribly inefficient. It would have taken more time to instruct participants regarding the nature of the task than it would have to do the task itself! A repeated measures design in which each participant was tested on both unilateral and bilateral trials provided the experimenters with a far more convenient and efficient way to answer their question about how the brain processes information.

Key Concept }

Another important advantage of repeated measures designs is that they are generally more sensitive than an independent groups design. The **sensitivity** of an experiment refers to the ability to detect the effect of the independent variable even if the effect is a small one. Ideally, participants in a study respond similarly to an experimental manipulation. In practice, however, we know that people don't all respond the same way. This *error variation* can be due to variations in the procedure each time the experiment is conducted or to individual differences among the participants. An experiment is more sensitive when there is less variability in participants' responses within a condition of an experiment, that is, less error variation. In general, participants in a repeated measures design will vary within themselves less over the time of an experiment than participants in a random groups design will vary from other participants. Another way to say this is that there is usually more variation *between* people than there is *within* people. Thus, error variation will generally be less in a repeated measures design. The less error variation, the easier it is to detect the effect of an independent variable. The increased sensitivity of repeated measures designs is especially attractive to researchers who study independent variables that have small (hard-to-see) effects on behavior.

Researchers also choose to use a repeated measures design because some areas of psychological research require its use. When the research question involves studying changes in participants' behavior over time, such as in a learning experiment, a repeated measures design is needed. Further, whenever

---

BOX 7.1

REPEATED MEASUREMENTS AND THE REPEATED MEASURES DESIGN

It is important to distinguish among different situations in which researchers test participants repeatedly. For example, in Chapter 5 we saw that survey researchers administer surveys more than once to the same people in a longitudinal survey design in order to assess changes in respondents over time. In a repeated measures design *experiment,* researchers manipulate an independent variable to compare measures of participants' behavior in two or more conditions. The critical difference is that an independent variable is manipulated in the repeated measures design, but not in the longitudinal survey design.

Repeated testing also may be used when researchers investigate the reliability (consistency) of a measure. Researchers may obtain two (or more) measures of the same individuals in order to establish the reliability of a measure, called test–retest reliability (see Chapter 5). Repeated testing associated with the reliability of measurements differs from the repeated measures design. Only the repeated measures design involves an independent variable in which participants' responses are contrasted in different experimental conditions.

---

the experimental procedure requires that participants compare two or more stimuli relative to one another, a repeated measures design must be used. For example, a repeated measures design would have to be used if a researcher wanted to measure the minimum amount of light that must be added before participants could detect that a spot of light had become brighter. It would also be called for if a researcher wanted participants to rate the relative attractiveness of a series of photographs. Research areas such as psychophysics (illustrated by the light-detection experiment) and scaling (illustrated by the ratings of attractiveness) rely heavily on repeated measures designs. Journals such as *Perception & Psychophysics* and *Journal of Experimental Psychology: Human Perception and Performance* frequently publish results of experiments using repeated measures designs (see also Box 7.1).

The Role of Practice Effects in Repeated Measures Designs

- Repeated measures designs cannot be confounded by individual differences variables because the same individuals participate in each condition (level) of the independent variable.
- Participants' performance in repeated measures designs may change across conditions simply because of repeated testing (not because of the independent variable); these changes are called practice effects.
- Practice effects may threaten the internal validity of a repeated measures experiment when the different conditions of the independent variable are presented in the same order to all participants.
- There are two types of repeated measures designs (complete and incomplete) that differ in the specific ways in which they control for practice effects.

Defining Practice Effects

The repeated measures designs have another important advantage in addition to the ones we have already described. In a repeated measures design, the characteristics of the participants cannot confound the independent variable being manipulated in the experiment. The *same* participants are tested in all the conditions of a repeated measures design, so it is impossible to end up with brighter, healthier, or more motivated participants in one condition than in another condition. Stated more formally, *there can be no confounding by individual differences variables in repeated measures designs.* The absence of the potential for confounding by individual differences variables is a great advantage of the repeated measures designs. This does not mean, however, that there are no threats to the internal validity of experiments that are done using repeated measures designs.

One potential threat to internal validity arises because participants may change over time. The repeated testing of participants in the repeated measures design gives them practice with the experimental task. As a result of this practice, participants may get better and better at doing the task because they learn more about the task, or they may get worse at the task because of such factors as fatigue and boredom (see Figure 7.1). The changes participants undergo

FIGURE 7.1   There are both positive and negative effects of practicing a new skill. Repeating the same experience can lead to improvement, but it also can lead to fatigue, a decrease in motivation, and even boredom.

Key Concept }

Key Concept }

with repeated testing in the repeated measures designs are called **practice effects.** In general, practice effects should be balanced across the conditions in repeated measures designs so that practice effects "average out" across conditions. The key to conducting interpretable experiments using the repeated measures designs is learning to use appropriate techniques to balance practice effects. We will briefly introduce the two types of repeated measures designs before describing the use of specific balancing techniques.

The two types of repeated measures designs are the complete and the incomplete design. The specific techniques for balancing practice effects differ for the two repeated measures designs, but the general term used to refer to these balancing techniques is **counterbalancing.** In the *complete design*, practice effects are balanced for *each* participant by administering the conditions to each participant several times, using different orders each time. Each participant can thus be considered a "complete" experiment. In the *incomplete design*, each condition is administered to each participant *only once*. The order of administering the conditions is varied across participants rather than for each participant, as is the case in the complete design. Practice effects in the incomplete design average out when the results are combined for all participants. This may seem a bit confusing at this point, but hopefully it will become clearer as we describe these types of designs more fully. Just keep in mind that a major goal when using a repeated measures design is to control for practice effects.

Balancing Practice Effects in the Complete Design

- Practice effects are balanced in complete designs within each participant using block randomization or ABBA counterbalancing.
- In block randomization, all of the conditions of the experiment (a block) are randomly ordered each time they are presented.
- In ABBA counterbalancing, a random sequence of all conditions is presented, followed by the opposite of the sequence.
- Block randomization is preferred over ABBA counterbalancing when practice effects are not linear, or when participants' performance can be affected by anticipation effects.

Research has shown that participants who view photographs depicting posed facial expressions of six basic human emotions (happiness, surprise, fear, sadness, anger, and disgust) can readily and accurately identify the expressed emotion. Sackeim, Gur, and Saucy (1978) used a repeated measures design to determine whether one side of our face expresses emotion more intensely than the other. They developed a photograph of a full face and a photograph of its mirror image. They then split both photographs down the middle making two composite photographs—one from the two versions of the left side of the face and one from the two versions of the right side. Illustrative photographs are presented in Figure 7.2. In the center is a photograph of a person expressing disgust. The two composite photographs made from the center photograph are presented on either side of the original. Does one of the two composites in Figure 7.2 look more disgusted than the other?

FIGURE 7.2   (a) Left-side composite, (b) original, and (c) right-side composite of the same face. The face is expressing disgust. (From Sackeim et al., 1978.)

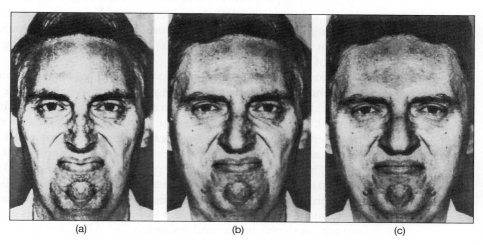

(a)   (b)   (c)

Participants were shown slides of photographs like those in Figure 7.2 and were asked to rate each slide on a 7-point scale indicating the intensity of the expressed emotion. The slides were presented individually for 10 seconds, and participants were then given 35 seconds to make their rating. The critical independent variable in the experiment was the version of the photograph depicting one of the emotions (left composite, original, or right composite). Each participant rated 54 slides: 18 left composites, 18 originals, and 18 right composites.

Participants' ratings of emotional intensity were consistently higher for the left composite than for the right composite. Does this finding match your judgment that the face in panel (a) in Figure 7.2 appears more disgusted than the face in panel (c)? Sackeim et al. interpreted these findings in terms of hemispheric specialization of the brain. In general, the left hemisphere controls the right side of the body and the right hemisphere controls the left side of the body. Thus, the left composite reflects control by the right hemisphere, and the right composite reflects control by the left hemisphere. The higher ratings of emotional intensity for the left composite photographs suggest that the right hemisphere may be more heavily involved than the left hemisphere in the production of emotional expression.

The interpretation of the differences in the ratings depends critically on the order in which the slides were presented to participants. Consider what could happen if all the original versions were presented first, followed by all the right composites, then by all the left composites. If you imagine yourself in this experiment making a rating for each of the slides in this long sequence (over 40 minutes), you will get a sense of what we mean by practice effects. Surely your attention, motivation, and experience in rating the emotionality of photographs will change as you work through the sequence of slides. If you gave higher ratings for the slides shown at the end of this long sequence, your ratings may reflect the intensity of your own emotions of boredom and fatigue rather than the intensity of the emotions actually depicted in the photographs. To avoid this possibility, Sackeim et al. used balancing techniques specifically developed for use with the complete design in repeated measures experiments. By using these balancing techniques, they ensured that each of the three versions of the photographs was equally likely to appear at any point in the long series of slides.

In the complete design, participants are given each treatment enough times to balance practice effects for each participant. When the task is simple enough and not too time consuming (such as judging the emotional intensity of photographs), it is possible to give one participant several experiences with each treatment. In fact, in some complete designs, only one or two participants are tested, and each participant experiences literally hundreds of trials. More commonly, however, researchers use procedures like those used by Sackeim et al. That is, several participants are tested, and each participant is given each treatment only a relatively small number of times. Researchers have two choices in deciding how to arrange the order in which the treatments in a complete design are administered: block randomization and ABBA counterbalancing.

Block Randomization   We introduced block randomization in Chapter 6 as an effective technique for assigning participants to conditions in the random groups design. *Block randomization* can also be used to order the conditions for each participant in a complete design. For instance, Sackeim et al. administered each of the three versions of their photographs (left composite, original, and right composite) 18 times to each participant. The sequence of trials shown in Table 7.1 illustrates how block randomization could be used to arrange the order of the three conditions in their experiment. The sequence of 54 trials is broken up into 18 blocks of 3 trials. Each block of trials contains the three conditions of the experiment in random order. In general, *the number of blocks in a block-randomized schedule is equal to the number of times each condition is administered, and the size of each block is equal to the number of conditions in the experiment.*

If a participant rated the photographs following the sequence in the block-randomized schedule shown in Table 7.1, it is unlikely that changes in the participant's attention, motivation, or experience with rating photographs would affect any one of the conditions more than any other. The practice effects can reasonably be expected to average out over the three experimental conditions. Determining the average position of each of the three conditions in the block-randomized sequence gives a rough indication of the balancing of practice effects. This can be done by summing the trial numbers on which each condition appears and dividing by 18. For instance, the original version of the photographs ("O") appeared on trials 1, 5, 8, 11, 13, 18, 21, 24, 27, 28, 33, 34, 39, 40, 44, 48, 49, and 53. The average position of the original photographs, therefore, was 27.6. The corresponding values for the left and right composite photographs are 27.7 and 27.2, respectively. That these average values are so similar tells us that any one version of the photographs was not more likely to appear at the beginning, middle, or end of the sequence of 54 trials.

Block randomization is effective in balancing practice effects, but each condition must be repeated several times before we can expect practice effects to

TABLE 7.1   BLOCK-RANDOMIZED SEQUENCE OF 54 TRIALS IN AN EXPERIMENT
WITH THREE CONDITIONS ADMINISTERED 18 TIMES EACH

Trial	Conditions		Trial	Conditions
1	O	First	28	O
2	L	Block	29	L
3	R		30	R
4	R		31	R
5	O		32	L
6	L		33	O
7	R		34	O
8	O		35	R
9	L		36	L
10	L		37	L
11	O		38	R
12	R		39	O
13	O		40	O
14	L		41	R
15	R		42	L
16	R		43	R
17	L		44	O
18	O		45	L
19	R		46	R
20	L		47	L
21	O		48	O
22	L		49	O
23	R		50	R
24	O		51	L
25	R		52	R
26	L		53	O
27	O		54	L

Note: The conditions are the three versions of the photographs used by
Sackeim et al. (1978): L = left composite, O = original, R = right composite.

average out. We should not expect practice effects to be balanced after two or
three blocks—any more than we would expect sample sizes of two or three
in the random groups design to result in comparable groups. Fortunately,
a technique is available to balance practice effects when it is not possible to
administer each condition often enough for the averaging process of block randomization to work effectively.

ABBA Counterbalancing   In its simplest form, ABBA counterbalancing can be
used to balance practice effects in the complete design with as few as two
administrations of each condition. *ABBA counterbalancing* involves presenting
the conditions in one sequence (i.e., A then B) followed by the opposite of that

TABLE 7.2   ABBA COUNTERBALANCED SEQUENCE OF TRIALS IN AN EXPERIMENT WITH THREE CONDITIONS (LEFT COMPOSITE, ORIGINAL, AND RIGHT COMPOSITE)

		Trial 1	Trial 2	Trial 3	Trial 4	Trial 5	Trial 6
	Condition:	Left	Original	Right	Right	Original	Left
Practice effect (linear)		+0	+1	+2	+3	+4	+5
Practice effect (nonlinear)		0	+6	+6	+6	+6	+6

same sequence (i.e., B then A). Its name describes the sequences when there are only two conditions (A and B) in the experiment, but ABBA counterbalancing is not limited to experiments with just two conditions. Sackeim et al. could have presented the versions of their photographs according to the ABBA sequence outlined in the top row of Table 7.2 labeled "Condition." Note that in this case it literally would be ABCCBA since there are three conditions. The order of the three conditions on the first three trials is simply reversed for trials 4 to 6.

ABBA counterbalancing is appropriately used only when practice effects are linear. If practice effects are linear, the same amount of practice effects is added to or subtracted from performance on each successive trial. The row of Table 7.2 labeled "Practice effect (linear)" illustrates how ABBA counterbalancing can balance practice effects. In this example, one "unit" of hypothetical practice effects is added to performance on each trial. Because there would be no practice effect associated with the first trial, the amount of practice added to Trial 1 in the table is zero. Trial 2 has one unit of hypothetical effects added because of participants' experience with the first trial; in Trial 3 there are two units added because of participants' experience with two trials, and so on.

We can get an idea of the influence of practice effects by adding the values for each condition. For example, the left composite condition gets the least (0) and the greatest (+5) influence from practice effects; the right composite condition gets two intermediate amounts (+2 and +3). The sum of the hypothetical practice effects is +5 for both conditions. (What would the sum of the practice effects be for the original condition?) The ABBA cycle can be applied with any number of conditions, but there must be an even number of repetitions of each condition. ABBA counterbalancing balances practice effects even more effectively with larger numbers of repetitions of the cycle. Usually, however, ABBA counterbalancing is used when the number of conditions and the number of repetitions of each condition are relatively small.

Although ABBA counterbalancing provides a simple and elegant means to balance practice effects, it is not without limitations. For example, ABBA counterbalancing is ineffective when practice effects for a task are not linear. This is illustrated in the last row of Table 7.2, labeled "Practice effect (nonlinear)." Nonlinear practice effects can occur when participants' performance changes dramatically after exposure to one or more trials. In this example, the left composite receives a total of only six hypothetical units of practice effects, and the other two conditions receive a total of 12 units each. When practice effects involve abrupt initial changes followed by little change thereafter, researchers often ignore performance on the early trials and wait until the practice effects reach a "steady state." Reaching a steady state is likely to take several repetitions of each condition, so researchers tend to use block randomization to balance practice effects in these situations.

ABBA counterbalancing is also ineffective when anticipation effects can occur. *Anticipation effects* occur when a participant develops expectations about which condition should occur next in the sequence. The participant's response to that condition may then be influenced more by this expectation than by the actual experience of the condition itself. For example, consider a time-perception experiment in which the participant's task is to estimate the length of time that has passed between a signal presented on a computer screen indicating the start of an interval and another signal indicating the end of the interval. (Of course, participants have to be prevented somehow from marking off time during the interval by counting or rhythmically tapping.) If the time intervals in such an experiment are 12, 24, and 36 seconds, then one possible ABBA sequence of conditions could be 12-24-36-36-24-12. If this cycle were repeated several times, participants probably would recognize the pattern and expect a series of increasing and then decreasing intervals. Their time estimates might soon begin to reflect this pattern rather than their perception of each independent interval. If anticipation effects are likely, block randomization should be used rather than ABBA counterbalancing.

Balancing Practice Effects in the Incomplete Design

- Practice effects are balanced *across* subjects in the incomplete design rather than for each subject, as in the complete design.
- The rule for balancing practice effects in the incomplete design is that each condition of the experiment must be presented in each ordinal position (first, second, etc.) equally often.
- The best method for balancing practice effects in the incomplete design with four or fewer conditions is to use all possible orders of the conditions.
- Two methods for selecting specific orders to use in an incomplete design are the Latin Square and random starting order with rotation.
- Whether using all possible orders or selected orders, participants should be randomly assigned to the different sequences.

In the incomplete design, each participant is given each treatment *only once*. The results for any one participant, therefore, cannot be interpreted because the levels of the independent variable for each participant are perfectly confounded with the order in which those levels were presented. For instance, the first participant in an incomplete design experiment might be tested first in the experimental condition (E) and second in the control condition (C). Any differences in the participant's performance between the experimental and control conditions could be due to the effect of the independent variable *or* to the practice effects resulting from the EC order. To break this confounding of the order of conditions and the independent variable, we can administer different orders of the conditions to different participants. For example, we could administer the conditions of our incomplete design experiment to a second participant in the CE order, testing the control condition first and the experimental condition second. In this way, we could balance the effects of order across the two conditions using two participants instead of one.

To illustrate the techniques for balancing practice effects in the incomplete design, we will use a repeated-measures experiment from the field of health psychology that investigated the effects of aerobic exercise on participants' moods (Hansen, Stevens, & Coast, 2001). The purpose of the study was to determine the time interval(s) of exercise required for mood improvements, and the researchers compared 30 minutes of quiet resting (0 exercise) to 10, 20, and 30 minutes of exercise. The exercise consisted of riding a stationary ergometric bicycle that allowed heart rate (HR) monitoring. During the exercise sessions, a warmup period was used to reach a target HR of moderate exercise intensity, then participants cycled for the required amount of time in the trial while maintaining that heart rate. Before exercise and after a cooldown period (following exercise), participants completed a mood inventory to assess their mood "at that moment." Each female participant was tested in each of the four conditions, with testing sessions on the same day of the week, one week apart for four consecutive weeks. Participants were randomly assigned to an order of the four conditions.

Before describing the technique that can be used to balance practice effects for an independent variable in the incomplete design, we will take a brief look at the results of the Hansen et al. study. The dependent variable in this study was the difference between participants' mood ratings before exercise and after exercise (and before and after resting in the 0 exercise condition). The researchers examined changes in depression, anxiety, anger, fatigue, and confusion (e.g., feeling overwhelmed), and a positive mood state of vigor. Overall, results indicated that exercise improved vigor and decreased confusion, fatigue, and total negative mood (a sum of mood scores). How much exercise was needed to see these effects? Analyses indicated that these improvements occurred with just 10 minutes of exercise! With 20 minutes of exercise participants experienced further improvements in feelings of confusion; no additional mood gains were seen when participants reached 30 minutes of exercise. Hansen et al. (2001) concluded that, in conjunction with recommendations regarding fitness (e.g., Centers for Disease Control), "to experience positive fitness and health benefits, healthy adults should participate in a total of thirty minutes of moderate physical exercise daily, accumulated in short bouts throughout the day" (p. 267).

We turn our attention now to the balancing techniques that are used in the incomplete design. In an incomplete design it is essential that practice effects be balanced by varying the order in which the conditions are presented. The general rule for balancing practice effects in the incomplete design is a simple one: *Each condition of the experiment must appear in each ordinal position (1st, 2nd, 3rd, etc.) equally often.* Several techniques are available for satisfying this general rule. These techniques differ in what additional balancing they accomplish, but so long as the techniques are properly used, the basic rule will be met and the experiment will be interpretable. That is, if appropriate balancing is carried out, then we will be in a position to determine whether the independent variable, not practice effects, influenced the participants' behavior.

All Possible Orders   The preferred technique for balancing practice effects in the incomplete design is to use all possible orders of the conditions. Each participant is randomly assigned to one of the orders. With only two conditions there are only two possible orders (AB and BA); with three conditions there are six possible orders (ABC, ACB, BAC, BCA, CAB, CBA). In general, there are $N!$ (which is read "N factorial") possible orders with N conditions, where $N!$ equals $N(N - 1)(N - 2) \ldots (N - [N - 1])$. As we just saw, there are six possible orders with three conditions, which is 3! ($3 \times 2 \times 1 = 6$). The number of required orders increases dramatically with increasing numbers of conditions. For instance, for five conditions there are 120 possible orders, and for six conditions there are 720 possible orders. Because of this, the use of all possible orders is usually limited to experiments involving four or fewer conditions.

Because there were four conditions in the Hansen et al. (2001) exercise experiment, 24 sequences would be required to obtain all possible orders of conditions. These sequences (orders of conditions) are presented in the left half of Table 7.3. Using all possible orders certainly meets the general rule of ensuring that all conditions appear in each ordinal position equally often. The first ordinal position shows this balancing most clearly: The first six sequences begin with the 0 exercise condition, and each of the next six sets of sequences begins with one of the three exercise conditions. The same pattern applies at each of the four ordinal positions. For example, the "0" condition also appears six times in the second ordinal position, six times in the third ordinal position, and six times in the fourth ordinal position. The same is true for the 10-, 20-, and 30-minute exercise conditions.

TABLE 7.3   ALTERNATIVE TECHNIQUES TO BALANCE PRACTICE EFFECTS IN AN INCOMPLETE REPEATED MEASURES DESIGN EXPERIMENT WITH FOUR CONDITIONS

| All Possible Orders | | | | All Possible Orders | | | | Selected Orders — Latin Square | | | | Selected Orders — Random Starting Order with Rotation | | | |
| Ordinal Position | | | | Ordinal Position | | | | Ordinal Position | | | | Ordinal Position | | | |
1st	2nd	3rd	4th	1st	2nd	3rd	4th	1st	2nd	3rd	4th	1st	2nd	3rd	4th
0	10	20	30	20	0	10	30	0	10	20	30	10	20	30	0
0	10	30	20	20	0	30	10	10	30	0	20	20	30	0	10
0	20	10	30	20	10	0	30	30	20	10	0	30	0	10	20
0	20	30	10	20	10	30	0	20	0	30	10	0	10	20	30
0	30	10	20	20	30	0	10								
0	30	20	10	20	30	10	0								
10	0	20	30	30	0	10	20								
10	0	30	20	30	0	20	10								
10	20	0	30	30	10	0	20								
10	20	30	0	30	10	20	0								
10	30	0	20	30	20	0	10								
10	30	20	0	30	20	10	0								

Note: The four conditions are identified using the time of exercise in the Hansen et al. (2001) experiment: 0 exercise, 10 minutes, 20 minutes, and 30 minutes.

There is one other issue that must be addressed in deciding to use all possible orders. For this technique to be effective, it is essential that at least one participant be tested with each of the possible orders of the conditions. That is, at least one participant should receive the 0-10-20-30 order, at least one should receive the 0-10-30-20 order, and so on. Therefore, the use of all possible orders requires at least as many participants as there are possible orders. Thus, if there are four conditions in the experiment, at least 24 participants are needed (or 48, or 72, or some other multiple of 24). This restriction makes it very important that a researcher has a good idea of the number of potential participants available before testing the first participant.[1]

Selected Orders   We have just described the preferred method for balancing practice effects in the incomplete design, all possible orders. There are times, however, when the use of all possible orders is not practical. For example, if we wanted to use the incomplete design to study an independent variable with seven levels, we would need to test 5,040 participants if we used all possible orders—one participant for each of the possible orders of the seven conditions (7! orders). We obviously need some alternative to using all possible orders if we are to use the incomplete design for experiments with five or more conditions.

Practice effects can be balanced by using just some of all the possible orders. The number of selected orders will always be equal to some multiple of the number of conditions in the experiment. For example, to do an experiment with one independent variable with seven levels, we need to select 7, 14, 21, 28, or some other multiple of seven orders to balance practice effects. The two basic variations of using selected orders are illustrated in Table 7.3. To allow you to compare the types of balancing more directly, we have illustrated the techniques for selected orders with the four-level independent variable from the Hansen et al. (2001) experiment that we described in the previous section.

The first type of balancing using selected orders is called the Latin Square. In a *Latin Square*, the general rule for balancing practice effects is met. That is, each condition appears at each ordinal position once. For example, just to the right of the center of Table 7.3, we can see that in the Latin Square, condition "0" appears exactly once in the first, second, third, and fourth ordinal positions. This is true for each condition. Additionally, in a Latin Square each condition precedes and follows each other condition exactly once. Examination of the Latin Square in Table 7.3 shows that the order "0–10" appears once, as does the order "10–0." The order "10–20" appears once, as does the order "20–10," and so on, for every combination of conditions. (The procedure for constructing a Latin Square is described in Box 7.2.)

The second balancing technique using selected orders requires you to begin with a random order of the conditions and to rotate this sequence systematically

---

[1]The number of participants ($N = 14$) in the Hansen et al. (2001) exercise study made it impossible for them to use all possible orders. Instead, they identified a random order of conditions for each participant. This leaves open the possibility that practice effects were not completely balanced in their design. For example, if the 10-minute exercise period was more often last in the sequence, participants' mood improvement may have been due to relief over a shorter exercise period, not the exercise itself.

BOX 7.2

HOW TO CONSTRUCT A LATIN SQUARE

A simple procedure for constructing a square *with an even number (N) of conditions* is as follows:

1   Randomly order the conditions of the experiment.
2   Number the conditions in your random order 1 through N.

   Thus, if you had $N = 4$ conditions (A, B, C, D) and the random order (from Step 1) was B, A, D, C, then B = 1, A = 2, D = 3, C = 4.

3   To generate the first row (first order of conditions), use the rule

   1, 2, N, 3, $N - 1$, 4, $N - 2$, 5, $N - 3$, 6, etc.

   In our example, this would yield 1, 2, 4, 3.

4   To generate the second row (second order of conditions), add 1 to each number in the first row but with the understanding that 1 added to $N = 1$.
   We would then have 2, 3, 1, 4.

5   The third row (third order of conditions) is generated by adding 1 to each number in the second row and again $N + 1 = 1$.

   The third row would be 3, 4, 2, 1.

6   A similar procedure is carried out for each successive row.

Can you construct the fourth row in this 4×4 square?

7   Assign the conditions to their corresponding numbers as determined in Step 2.

The Latin Square for this example would be

B A C D
A D B C
D C A B
C B D A

If there is an odd number of conditions, then two squares must be constructed. The first can be made according to the rule given above for even-numbered squares. The second square is generated by reversing the rows in the first square. For example, assume $N = 5$ and the first row of the first square is B A E C D. The first row of the second square would then be D C E A B. The two squares are joined to make an $N \times 2N$ square. In either case, even or odd, subjects should be assigned randomly to the rows of the square. Thus, you must have available at least as many subjects as there are multiples of rows. (Procedures for selecting or constructing Latin Squares are also described in Winer, Brown, and Michels [1991, pp. 674–679].)

---

with each condition moving one position to the left each time (see the example on the right in Table 7.3). Using a random starting order with rotation effectively balances practice effects because, like the Latin Square, each condition appears in each ordinal position. However, the systematic rotation of the sequences means that each condition always follows and always precedes the *same* other conditions (e.g., 30 always comes after 20 and before 0), which is not like the Latin Square technique. The simplicity of the random starting order with rotation technique and its applicability to experiments with more than four conditions are its primary advantages.

   The use of all possible orders, Latin Squares, and random starting orders with rotation are equally effective in balancing practice effects because all three techniques ensure that each condition appears in each ordinal position equally often. Regardless of which technique one uses to balance practice effects, the sequences of conditions should be fully prepared prior to testing the first participant, and participants should be randomly assigned to these sequences.

Data Analysis of Repeated Measures Designs

Describing the Results

- Data analysis for a complete design begins with computing a summary score (e.g., mean, median) for each participant.
- Descriptive statistics are used to summarize performance across all participants for each condition of the independent variable.

After checking the data for errors and outliers, the first step in analyzing a repeated measures experiment is to summarize participants' performance in each condition of the experiment. In random groups designs, this means simply listing the scores of the participants tested in each of the conditions of the experiment and then summarizing these scores with descriptive statistics such as the mean and standard deviation. In an incomplete repeated measures design, each participant provides one score in each condition, but it is still relatively straightforward to summarize the scores for each condition. In doing so, you need to be careful as you "unwind" the various orders in which the participants were tested to be sure participants' scores are listed with the correct condition. Once all the scores for each condition have been listed together, means and standard deviations can be computed to describe performance in each condition.

An additional step needs to be taken when analyzing a complete repeated measures design. You first must compute a score for each participant in each condition before you begin to summarize and describe the results. This additional step is necessary because each participant is tested in each condition more than once in a complete design. For example, five participants were tested in a time-perception experiment done as a classroom demonstration of a complete repeated measures design. The purpose of the experiment was not to test the accuracy of participants' time estimates compared with the actual interval lengths. Instead, the purpose of the experiment was to determine whether participants' estimates of time increased systematically with increasing lengths. In other words, could participants discriminate between intervals of different lengths?

Each participant in the experiment was tested six times on each of four interval lengths (12, 24, 36, and 48 seconds). Block randomization was used to determine the order in which the intervals were presented. Thus, each participant provided 24 time estimates, six estimates for each of the four interval lengths. Any one of the six estimates for a given time interval is contaminated by practice effects, so some measure that combines information across the six estimates is needed. Typically, the mean across the six estimates for each interval would be calculated for each participant to provide a single estimate of performance in each condition. As you may remember, however, extreme scores can influence the mean; it is quite possible that participants gave extreme estimates of the time intervals for at least one of the six tests of each interval. Thus, for this particular set of data, the median of the six estimates probably provides the best measure to reflect the participants' estimates of the time intervals. These median estimates (rounded to the nearest whole number) are listed in Table 7.4. (You may be used to seeing the mean and median as descriptive statistics summarizing a

TABLE 7.4   DATA MATRIX TABLE FOR A REPEATED MEASURES DESIGN EXPERIMENT

	Data Matrix			
	Interval Length			
Participant	12	24	36	48
1	13	21	30	38
2	10	15	38	35
3	12	23	31	32
4	12	15	22	32
5	16	36	69	60
Mean (*SD*)	12.6 (2.0)	22.0 (7.7)	38.0 (16.3)	39.4 (10.5)

Note: Each value in the table represents the median of the participants' six responses at each level of the interval length variable. The means in the bottom row are the averages of the medians (from six responses made by the five participants at each interval length).

group's performance; however, as this example illustrates, these summary statistics also can be used to represent one *person's* performance when that performance is an "average" across trials or tests.)

Once an individual score for each participant in each condition has been obtained, the next step is to summarize the results across participants, using appropriate descriptive statistics. The mean estimate and standard deviation (*SD*) for each of the four intervals are listed in the row labeled "Mean (*SD*)" in Table 7.4. Even though the data for only five participants are included in the table, these mean estimates indicate that participants appear to have discriminated between intervals of different lengths, at least for intervals up to 36 seconds.

As we mentioned in Chapter 6, it is a good idea to include measures of effect size when describing the results of an experiment. A typical measure of effect size for a repeated measures design is the strength of association measure called eta squared (η^2). The value of eta squared for the time-perception experiment was .80. This value indicates that a large proportion of variation in participants' time estimates can be accounted for by the independent variable of interval length. You can find more information about the calculation of effect sizes and their interpretation in Chapters 11 and 12. In Chapter 12 we illustrate how to calculate eta squared using the data found in Table 7.4.

Confirming What the Results Reveal

- The general procedures and logic for null hypothesis testing and for confidence intervals for repeated measures designs are similar to those used for random groups designs.

Data analysis for experiments using repeated measures designs involves the same general procedures we described in Chapter 6 for the analysis of random groups design experiments. Researchers use null hypothesis testing and confidence intervals to make claims about whether the independent variable produced an effect on behavior. We will use the time-perception experiment to illustrate how researchers confirm what the data reveal when they use repeated measures designs.

The focus of the analysis of the time-perception experiment was on whether the participants could discriminate intervals of different lengths. We cannot make the claim that participants were able to discriminate intervals of varying lengths until we know that the mean differences in Table 7.4 are greater than would be expected on the basis of error variation alone. That is, even though it may *appear* that participants were able to discriminate between the different intervals, we do not know if their performance was different from that which would occur by chance. Thus, we must consider using analytical tools of null hypothesis testing and the construction of confidence intervals to help us make a decision about the effectiveness of the independent variable.

One distinctive characteristic of the analysis of repeated measures designs is the way in which error variation is estimated. We described in Chapter 6 that for the random groups design, individual differences among participants within the groups provides an estimate of error variation. In repeated measures designs, however, differences among participants are not just balanced—they are actually eliminated from the analysis. The ability to eliminate systematic variation due to participants in repeated measures designs makes these designs generally more sensitive than random groups designs. The source of error variation in the repeated measures designs is the differences in the ways the conditions affect different participants.

STRETCHING EXERCISE

For this exercise you are to compute the mean for each level of the independent variable in this complete repeated measures design. You must first compute a summary score for each participant in each condition before you summarize and describe the results for the three conditions.

In a perception experiment, three participants were tested for their ability to identify complex visual patterns. On each presentation the participants briefly viewed a complex pattern (target), followed by a test with a set of four patterns (the target and three other similar patterns). Their task was to pick out the target pattern from the set. The independent variable was the delay between the target and the test, with three levels: 10s, 30s, 50s. On each of six trials, participants made 50 judgments at one level of the independent variable. The table shows the ABBA counterbalanced sequence of trials for each participant on each trial. The values in parentheses represent the number of errors (the dependent variable) made by each participant on each trial (50 max.). Use this table to describe the effect of the delay independent variable on the number of errors.

Participant	Trial 1	Trial 2	Trial 3	Trial 4	Trial 5	Trial 6
1	30s (9)	50s (6)	10s (2)	10s (6)	50s (10)	30s (3)
2	50s (10)	30s (6)	10s (2)	10s (4)	30s (8)	50s (8)
3	10s (1)	50s (6)	30s (7)	30s (3)	50s (8)	10s (3)

The fact that error variation is estimated differently in a repeated measures design than it is in an independent groups design means that the calculation of the *t*-test and *F*-test used in null hypothesis testing also differs. Similarly, there is change in the way that confidence intervals are calculated. In Chapter 12 we use the data in Table 7.4 to show how both the *F*-test and confidence intervals are used in decision making as part of a repeated measures design. The null hypothesis for an analysis of the data in Table 7.4 is that the population means, estimated by the sample means, are the same across interval-length conditions. Having carried out an analysis of variance for these data (see Chapter 12), we can tell you that the probability associated with the *F*-test for the effect of interval length was $p = .0004$. Because this obtained probability is less than the conventional level of significance (.05), the effect of the interval length variable was statistically significant. Based on this outcome, we can make the claim that participants' time estimates did differ systematically as a function of interval length. We already know from our calculation of the effect size (eta squared = .80) that it represents a large effect.

In Chapter 12 we used the same data to calculate .95 confidence intervals for the means seen in Table 7.4. The confidence intervals (in seconds) for the four conditions are (12) 5.4–19.8; (24) 14.8–29.2; (36) 30.8–45.2; (48) 32.2–46.6. As you learned in Chapter 6 (see also Box 11.5), when intervals do not overlap, we can claim that the population means estimated by the sample means are different. Does an inspection of these intervals tell you which means would be judged to be different? A convenient way to examine the relationship among confidence intervals is to plot them in a graph. For example, take a look at Figure 12.2 in Chapter 12, in which the intervals presented here are plotted around the sample means obtained in the time estimation experiment.

THE PROBLEM OF DIFFERENTIAL TRANSFER

- Differential transfer occurs when the effects of one condition persist and influence performance in subsequent conditions.
- Variables that may lead to differential transfer should be tested using a random groups design because differential transfer threatens the internal validity of repeated measures designs.
- Differential transfer can be identified by comparing the results for the same independent variable when tested in a repeated measures design and in a random groups design.

Key Concept

Researchers can overcome the potential problem of practice effects in repeated measures designs by using appropriate techniques to balance practice effects. There is a much more serious potential problem that can arise in repeated measures designs that is known as differential transfer (Poulton, 1973, 1975, 1982; Poulton & Freeman, 1966). **Differential transfer** arises when performance in one condition differs depending on the condition that precedes it.

Consider a problem-solving experiment in which two types of instructions are being compared in a repeated measures design. One set of instructions (A) is expected to enhance problem solving, whereas the other set of instructions (B) serves as the neutral control condition. It is reasonable to expect that participants tested in the order AB will be unable or unwilling to abandon the approach outlined in the A instructions when they are supposed to be following the B instructions. Giving up the "good thing" participants had under instruction A would be the counterpart of successfully following the admonition "Don't think of pink elephants!" When participants fail to give up the instruction from the first condition (A) while they are supposed to be following instruction B, any difference between the two conditions is reduced. For those participants, after all, condition B was not really tried. The experiment becomes a situation in which participants are tested in an "AA" condition, not an "AB" condition.

In general, the presence of differential transfer threatens internal validity because it becomes impossible to determine if there are true differences between the conditions. It also tends to underestimate differences between the conditions and thereby reduces the external validity of the findings. *Therefore, when differential transfer could occur, researchers should choose an independent groups design.* Differential transfer is sufficiently common with instructional variables to advise against the use of repeated measures designs for these studies (Underwood & Shaughnessy, 1975). Unfortunately, differential transfer can arise in any repeated measures design. For instance, the effect of 50 units of marijuana may be different if administered after the participant has received 200 units than if administered after the participant has received the placebo (e.g., if the participant has an increased tolerance for marijuana after receiving the 200 dose). There are ways, however, to determine whether differential transfer is likely to have occurred.

The best way to determine whether differential transfer is a problem is to do two separate experiments (Poulton, 1982). The same independent variable would be studied in both experiments, but a random groups design would be used in one experiment and a repeated measures design in the other. The random groups design cannot possibly involve differential transfer because each participant is tested in only one condition. If the experiment using a repeated measures design shows the same effect of the independent variable as that shown in the random groups design, then there has likely been no differential transfer. If the two designs show different effects for the same independent variable, however, differential transfer is likely to be responsible for producing the different outcome in the repeated measures design. When differential transfer does occur, the results of the random groups design should be used to provide the best description of the effect of the independent variable.

SUMMARY

Repeated measures designs provide an effective and efficient way to conduct an experiment by administering all the conditions in the experiment to each participant (see Figure 7.3). Repeated measures designs are useful when only very few participants are available or when an independent variable can be

FIGURE 7.3 In this chapter we introduced repeated measures designs and methods for counterbalancing.

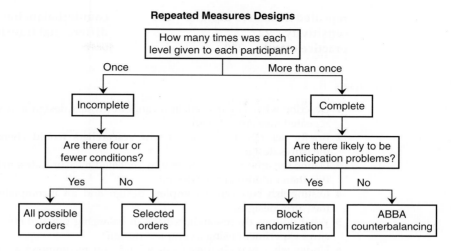

studied most efficiently by testing fewer participants several times. Repeated measures designs are generally more sensitive experiments. Finally, particular areas of psychological research (e.g., psychophysics) may require the use of repeated measures designs.

For any repeated measures design experiment to be interpretable, however, practice effects must be balanced. Practice effects are changes that participants undergo because of repeated testing. In a complete repeated measures design, practice effects are balanced for each participant. Block randomization and ABBA counterbalancing can be used to balance practice effects in a complete repeated measures design. ABBA counterbalancing should not be used, however, if practice effects are expected to be nonlinear or if anticipation effects are likely.

In an incomplete repeated measures design, each participant receives each treatment only once, and the balancing of practice effects is accomplished across participants. Techniques for balancing practice effects in an incomplete repeated measures design involve either the use of all possible orders or selected orders (the Latin Square and rotation of a random starting order).

The process of data analysis of the results of repeated measures designs is essentially the same as that for analyzing the results of random groups designs. An added step for the complete repeated measures design is that each participant's scores first must be summarized within each condition. The data are examined for errors and then summarized using descriptive statistics such as the mean, standard deviation, and measures of effect size. Null hypothesis testing and confidence intervals are used to make claims that the independent variable has produced an effect on behavior.

The most serious problem in any repeated measures design is differential transfer—when performance in one condition differs depending on which condition it follows. Procedures for detecting the presence of differential transfer are available, but there is little that can be done to salvage a study in which it occurs.

Key Concepts

repeated measures designs 226	counterbalancing 230
sensitivity 227	differential transfer 243
practice effects 230	

Review Questions

1 Describe what is balanced in a random groups design and what is balanced in a repeated measures design.
2 Briefly describe four reasons why researchers would choose to use a repeated measures design.
3 Define sensitivity and explain why repeated measures designs are often more sensitive than random groups designs.
4 Distinguish between a complete design and an incomplete design for repeated measures designs.
5 What options do researchers have in balancing practice effects in a repeated measures experiment using a complete design?
6 Under what two circumstances would you recommend against the use of ABBA counterbalancing to balance practice effects in a repeated measures experiment using a complete design?
7 State the general rule for balancing practice effects in repeated measures experiments using an incomplete design.
8 Briefly describe the techniques that researchers can use to balance practice effects in the repeated measures experiments using an incomplete design. Identify which of these techniques is preferred and explain why.
9 Explain why an additional initial step is required to summarize the data for an experiment involving a complete repeated measures design.
10 Describe how researchers can determine if differential transfer has occurred in a repeated measures experiment.

CHALLENGE QUESTIONS

1 The following problems represent different situations in the repeated measures designs in which practice effects need to be balanced.
 A Consider a repeated measures experiment using a complete design involving one independent variable. The independent variable in the experiment is task difficulty with three levels (Low, Medium, and High). You are to prepare an order for administering the conditions of this experiment so that the independent variable is balanced for practice effects. You are first to use block randomization to balance practice effects and then to use ABBA counterbalancing to balance practice effects. Each condition should appear twice in the order you prepare. (You can use the first row of the random number table (Table A.1) in the

Appendix to determine your two random orders for block randomization.)
 B Consider a repeated measures experiment using an incomplete design. The independent variable in the experiment is the font size in which a paragraph has been printed, and there are six levels (7, 8, 9, 10, 11, and 12). Present a table showing how you would determine the order of administering the conditions to the first six participants of the experiment. Be sure that practice effects are balanced for these participants.

2 The pursuit rotor is a test of perceptual-motor coordination. It involves a turntable with a disk about the size of a dime embedded in it. The participant is given a pointer and is asked to keep the pointer on the disk while the turntable is

rotating. The dependent variable is the percentage of time on each trial that the participant keeps the pointer on the disk. Learning on this task is linearly related to trials over many periods of practice, and the task generally takes a long time to master. A researcher wants to study the influence of time of day on the performance on this task with four different times (10 A.M., 2 P.M., 6 P.M., and 10 P.M.). The participants will receive a constant number of trials under each of the four conditions, and participants will be tested in one condition per day over four consecutive days.

A What design is being used for the time-of-day variable in this experiment?

B Prepare a Latin Square to balance practice effects across the conditions of this experiment.

C The researcher decides to use all possible orders to balance practice effects. The researcher assigns each participant to one of the 24 possible orders of the conditions. Which experimental design is included when you look only at the first condition to which each participant was assigned?

D How could the researcher test whether differential transfer occurred when all possible orders were used to balance practice effects?

3 The following table represents the order of administering the conditions to participants in a repeated measures experiment using an incomplete design in which the independent variable was

the loudness of a tone to be detected by the participants while they were concentrating on another task. The three tones were extremely soft (ES), very soft (VS), and soft (S). The values in parentheses represent the number of times each participant detected the tone in each condition. Use this table, when necessary, to answer questions that follow.

Participant	Order of Conditions		
1	ES (2)	VS (9)	S (9)
2	VS (3)	S (5)	ES (7)
3	S (4)	ES (3)	VS (5)
4	ES (6)	S (10)	VS (8)
5	VS (7)	ES (8)	S (6)
6	S (8)	VS (4)	ES (4)

A What method was used to balance practice effects in this experiment?

B Present the values you would use to describe the overall effect of the loudness variable. Include a verbal description of the effect along with the descriptive statistics that you use as a basis of your description.

C What claim would you make about the effect of the loudness variable if the probability associated with the *F*-test for the effect of the loudness variable was $p = .04$?

Answer to Stretching Exercise

The first step is to compute a mean for each participant for each level of the independent variable by averaging responses across the two trials for the same condition. For Participant 1 the means for the three conditions are

10s	30s	50s
$(2 + 6)/2 = 4$	$(9 + 3)/2 = 6$	$(6 + 10)/2 = 8$

For Participant 2 the means for the three conditions are 3 (10s), 7 (30s), and 9 (50s), and for Participant 3 the means are 2 (10s), 5 (30s), and 7 (50s).

The next step is to compute the means for each condition by averaging the summary scores for each participant:

$$10s: (4 + 3 + 2)/3 = 3$$

$$30s: (6 + 7 + 5)/3 = 6$$

$$50s: (8 + 9 + 7)/3 = 8$$

We can now describe the effect of the independent variable, delay between target and test, on the dependent variable, number of errors. The means indicate that the number of errors on the pattern-identification task increased as the delay between target and test increased. Inferential statistics using null hypothesis testing or confidence intervals could be done to confirm whether the delay variable produced a reliable effect.

Answer to Challenge Question 1

A Assigning the values 1, 2, and 3 to the Low, Medium, and High conditions, respectively, and using the first row of the random number table (Table A.1) in the Appendix beginning with the first number in the row, the block-randomized sequence is Low-High-Medium-Low-Medium-High. One possible ABBA counterbalanced sequence is Low-Medium-High-High-Medium-Low.

B Because there are six conditions, all possible orders are not feasible. Therefore, either a Latin Square or a random starting order with rotation is needed to balance practice effects. A possible set of sequences using rotation is

Participant	Position					
	1st	2nd	3rd	4th	5th	6th
1	8	10	11	9	7	12
2	10	11	9	7	12	8
3	11	9	7	12	8	10
4	9	7	12	8	10	11
5	7	12	8	10	11	9
6	12	8	10	11	9	7

CHAPTER EIGHT

Complex Designs

CHAPTER OUTLINE

OVERVIEW

In Chapters 6 and 7 we focused on the basic experimental designs that researchers use to study the effect of an independent variable. We described how an independent variable could be implemented with a separate group of participants in each condition (independent groups designs) or with each participant experiencing all the conditions (repeated measures designs). We limited our discussion to experiments involving only one independent variable because we wanted you to concentrate on the basics of experimental research. Experiments involving only one independent variable are not, however, the most common type of experiment in contemporary psychological research. Instead, researchers most often use **complex designs** in which two or more independent variables are studied simultaneously in one experiment.

> *Key Concept*

Complex designs can also be called *factorial designs* because they involve factorial combination of independent variables. *Factorial combination* involves pairing each level of one independent variable with each level of a second independent variable. This makes it possible to determine the effect of each independent variable alone (*main effect*) and the effect of the independent variables in combination (*interaction effect*).

Complex designs may seem a bit complicated at this point, but the concepts will become clearer as you progress through this chapter. We begin with a review of the characteristics of experimental designs that can be used to investigate independent variables in a complex design. We then describe the procedures for producing, analyzing, and interpreting main effects and interaction effects. We introduce the analysis plans that are used for complex designs. We conclude the chapter by giving special attention to the interpretation of interaction effects in complex designs.

DESCRIBING EFFECTS IN A COMPLEX DESIGN

- Researchers use complex designs to study the effects of two or more independent variables in one experiment.
- In complex designs, each independent variable can be studied with an independent groups design or with a repeated measures design.
- The simplest complex design is a 2 × 2 design—two independent variables, each with two levels.
- The number of different conditions in a complex design can be determined by multiplying the number of levels for each independent variable (e.g., 2 × 2 = 4).
- More powerful and efficient complex designs can be created by including more levels of an independent variable or by including more independent variables in the design.

An experiment with a complex design has, by definition, more than one independent variable. Each independent variable in a complex design must be implemented using either an independent groups design or a repeated measures design according to the procedures described in Chapters 6 and 7. When a complex design has both an independent groups variable and a repeated measures variable, it is called a *mixed design*.

The simplest possible experiment involves one independent variable manipulated at two levels. Similarly, the simplest possible complex design experiment involves two independent variables, each with two levels. Complex designs are identified by specifying the number of levels of each of the independent variables in the experiment. A 2×2 (which is read "2 by 2") design, then, identifies the most basic complex design. Conceptually, there is an unlimited number of complex designs because any number of independent variables can be studied and each independent variable can have any number of levels. In practice, however, it is unusual to find experiments involving more than four or five independent variables, and two or three is more typical. Regardless of the number of independent variables, the number of conditions in a complex design can be determined by multiplying the number of levels of the independent variables. For example, if there are two independent variables with each having two levels (a 2×2 design), there are four conditions. In a 3×3 design there are two independent variables with three levels each, so there are nine conditions. In a $3 \times 4 \times 2$ design there are three independent variables with three, four, and two levels, respectively, and a total of 24 conditions. The primary advantage of all complex designs is the opportunity they provide for identifying interactions between independent variables.

Understanding the 2×2 design lays a foundation for understanding complex designs. The 2×2 design barely scratches the surface, however, when it comes to tapping the potential of complex designs. Complex designs can be extended beyond the 2×2 design in one of two ways. Researchers can add levels to one or both of the independent variables in the design, yielding designs such as the 3×2, the 3×3, the 4×2, the 4×3, and so on. Researchers can also build on the 2×2 design by increasing the number of independent variables in the same experiment. The number of levels of each variable can range from 2 to some unspecified upper limit. The addition of a third or fourth independent variable yields designs such as the $2 \times 2 \times 2$, the $3 \times 3 \times 3$, the $2 \times 2 \times 4$, the $2 \times 3 \times 3 \times 2$, and so on.

First we will illustrate main effects and interaction effects in the complex design by working through an example of a 2×2 design.

An Example of a 2 × 2 Design

The nature of main effects and interaction effects is essentially the same in all complex designs, but they can be seen most easily in a 2×2 design. For an example of this design we will draw from the rich literature in the field of psychology and law. There are few areas in the legal arena that have gone untouched by social scientists. Jury selection, the nature and credibility of eyewitnesses, race of the defendant, jury decision making, and attorney arguments are only some of the many topics investigated by researchers. Recall that in Chapter 6 we discussed a research study by Ceci (1993) on children's eyewitness testimony. In the study to be discussed here the researchers looked at variables that might lead to false confessions from suspects brought in for questioning.

Kassin, Goldstein, and Savitsky (2003) used a 2×2 design to investigate whether interrogators' expectations regarding a suspect's guilt or innocence influence the interrogation tactics they use. Kassin and his colleagues have conducted many studies to identify factors that lead to false confessions by innocent people. In the present study, Kassin et al. hypothesized that one potential reason for false confessions is that interrogators have a *confirmation bias* in which their initial beliefs about a suspect's guilt cause them to interrogate more aggressively, ask questions in a manner that presumes guilt, and cause suspects to behave defensively (which is interpreted as guilt). In general, this behavioral confirmation theory has three parts: (1) the perceiver forms a belief about a target person; (2) the perceiver behaves toward the person in ways that are consistent with the belief; and (3) the target person then responds in ways that support the perceiver's belief. Ultimately, in the criminal justice context the end result of this process can be a confession of guilt by an innocent person.

Kassin and his colleagues (2003) tested the behavioral confirmation theory in a clever experiment involving college student participants. Pairs of students participated as interrogators and suspects. "Interrogators" were asked to play the role of a detective trying to solve a case in which $100 was stolen from a locked cabinet. Importantly, the researchers manipulated the interrogator's expectations regarding the suspect's guilt. Half of the student interrogators were randomly assigned to the *guilty expectation* condition, in which the experimenter said that 4 out of every 5 suspects in the experiment actually committed the crime. Thus, these research participants were led to believe their chances of interrogating a guilty suspect were high (80% likelihood). In the *innocent expectation* condition, research participants were told their chance of interrogating a guilty suspect was low because only 1 out of 5 suspects was actually guilty (20%). This independent variable, *interrogator expectation*, was manipulated to initiate a confirmation bias among interrogators.

Other students played the role of suspect. Because suspects' behavior in an actual interrogation is influenced by their true guilt or innocence, Kassin et al. manipulated students' guilt or innocence using the independent variable, *suspect status*. In the *guilty* condition, students were asked to commit a mock theft in which they were instructed to enter a room, find a key hidden behind a VCR, use the key to open a cabinet, take $100, return the key, and leave with the $100. Students in the *innocent* condition were asked to approach the same room, knock on the door, wait for an answer (which did not occur), and then meet the experimenter. Half of the student-suspects were randomly assigned to the guilty role and half were assigned to the innocent role. All suspects were instructed to convince the interrogator of their innocence and to not confess. Interrogators were given the conflicting goals of trying to obtain a confession but also to determine whether the suspect was actually guilty or innocent. The interrogations were tape recorded.

Factorial combination of the two independent variables created four conditions in this 2 × 2 complex design:

1 Actual guilt/Guilty expectation
2 Actual guilt/Innocent expectation
3 Actual innocence/Guilty expectation
4 Actual innocence/Innocent expectation

Keep in mind that each group formed by the combination of variables represents a random group of participants. The design looks like this:

	Interrogator Expectation	
Suspect Status	Guilty	Innocent
Actual guilt	1	2
Actual innocence	3	4

Kassin et al. (2003) measured several dependent variables so that they could determine if there was converging evidence in support of the behavioral confirmation theory. For example, they measured dependent variables for the interrogators and suspects, and for new, additional participants who listened to the tape-recorded interrogations (much like potential jurors might hear). We will focus on three dependent variables from their experiment to illustrate main effects and interactions. Let's see what they found.

Main Effects and Interaction Effects

- The overall effect of each independent variable in a complex design is called a main effect and represents the differences among the average performance for each level of an independent variable collapsed across the levels of the other independent variable.
- An interaction effect between independent variables occurs when the effect of one independent variable differs depending on the levels of the second independent variable.

Key Concept

In any complex factorial design it is possible to test predictions regarding the overall effect of each independent variable in the experiment while ignoring the effect of the other independent variable(s). The overall effect of an independent variable in a complex design is called a **main effect.** We will examine two main effects Kassin and his colleagues observed in their experiment for two different dependent variables.

Prior to their interrogation of the suspect, student interrogators were given information about interrogation techniques, including a list of possible questions they could ask about the theft. Twelve questions were written as pairs (but presented randomly in the list). One question of the pair was written in such a way that the suspect's guilt was presumed (e.g., "How did you find the key that was hidden behind the VCR?") and the second question in the pair was written so as not to presume guilt (e.g., "Do you know anything about the key that was hidden behind the VCR?"). Student interrogators were asked to select six questions they might later want to ask. Thus, students could select from 0 to 6 questions that presumed guilt. Based on the behavioral confirmation theory, Kassin et al. predicted that interrogators in the guilty-expectation condition would select more guilt-presumptive questions than would interrogators

TABLE 8.1   A MAIN EFFECT OF INTERROGATOR EXPECTATION ON THE
NUMBER OF GUILT-PRESUMPTIVE QUESTIONS

Suspect Status	Interrogator Expectation	
	Guilty	Innocent
Actual guilt	3.54	2.54
Actual innocence	3.70	2.66
Means for interrogator expectation	3.62	2.60

Hypothetical cell means based on Kassin et al. (2003).

in the innocent-expectation condition. Thus, they predicted a *main effect* of the interrogator-expectation independent variable.

The data for this dependent variable, number of guilt-presumptive questions selected, are presented in Table 8.1. The overall mean number of guilt-presumptive questions for participants in the guilty-expectation condition (3.62) is obtained by averaging the means of the actual-guilt and actual-innocence conditions for interrogators in the guilty-expectation condition: (3.54 + 3.70)/2 = 3.62. Similarly, the overall mean for the innocent-expectation condition is computed to be 2.60: (2.54 + 2.66)/2 = 2.60.[1] *The means for a main effect represent the overall performance at each level of a particular independent variable collapsed across (averaged over) the levels of the other independent variable.* In this case we collapsed (averaged) over the suspect status variable to obtain the means for the main effect of the interrogator expectation variable. The *main effect* of the interrogator-expectation variable is the difference between the means for the two levels of the variable (3.62 − 2.60 = 1.02). In the Kassin et al. experiment, the main effect of the interrogator-expectation variable indicates that the overall number of guilt-presumptive questions selected was greater when interrogators expected a guilty suspect (3.62) than when they expected an innocent suspect (2.60). Inferential statistics tests confirmed that the main effect of interrogator expectation was statistically significant. This supported the researchers' hypothesis based on behavioral confirmation theory.

Let's now turn to a dependent variable for which there was a statistically significant main effect of the suspect-status independent variable. The researchers also coded the tape-recorded interviews to analyze the techniques used by the interrogators to obtain a confession. Student interrogators were given brief, written instructions regarding the powerful techniques police use to break down a suspect's resistance. Researchers counted the number of interrogator statements that reflected these persuasive techniques, such as building rapport, assertions of the suspect's guilt or disbelief in the suspect's statements, appeals

[1]The simple averaging of the values within each row and column to obtain the means for the main effects is possible only when there are equal numbers of participants contributing to each mean in the table. For procedures to calculate weighted means when the cells of the table involve different sample sizes, see Keppel (1991).

TABLE 8.2 A MAIN EFFECT OF SUSPECT STATUS ON THE NUMBER OF PERSUASIVE TECHNIQUES

	Interrogator Expectation		Means for Suspect Status
Suspect Status	Guilty	Innocent	
Actual guilt	7.71	6.59	7.15
Actual innocence	11.96	10.88	11.42

Hypothetical cell means based on Kassin et al. (2003).

to the suspect's self-interest or conscience, threats of punishment, promises of leniency, and presentation of false evidence.

The data for this dependent variable, number of persuasive techniques, are presented in Table 8.2. The overall mean number of persuasive techniques interrogators used when they interviewed suspects who were actually guilty was 7.15. This mean is computed by averaging across the two levels of the interrogator-expectation variable in the actual-guilt condition: $(7.71 + 6.59)/2$. The overall mean number of persuasive techniques used when interrogators interviewed a suspect who was actually innocent was 11.42, computed by averaging across the interrogator-expectation variable in the actual-innocence condition: $(11.96 + 10.88)/2$. The difference between these means $(11.42 - 7.15 = 4.27)$ represents the main effect of the suspect-status independent variable. On average, interrogators used 4.27 more persuasive techniques when the suspect was actually *innocent* compared to guilty. Kassin and his colleagues were surprised by the finding that innocent suspects in both interrogator-expectation conditions were interrogated more aggressively than suspects who were actually guilty.

Finally, we can also examine data for which Kassin et al. observed an interaction effect between the interrogator-expectation and suspect-status independent variables. In a second phase of the experiment a new sample of students was asked to listen to the tape-recorded interrogation and to make judgments about the behavior of the interrogator and suspect. One question asked these students to rate on a 10-point scale how hard the interrogator worked to get a confession from the suspect, with higher numbers indicating greater effort. These data are presented in Table 8.3.

TABLE 8.3 AN INTERACTION EFFECT BETWEEN INTERROGATOR EXPECTATION AND SUSPECT STATUS ON EFFORT TO OBTAIN A CONFESSION

	Interrogator Expectation	
Suspect Status	Guilty	Innocent
Actual guilt	5.64	5.56
Actual innocence	7.17	5.85

Cell means provided by Dr. Saul Kassin.

Key Concept }

When two independent variables interact, we know that both variables together influence participants' performance on the dependent variable, in this case, ratings of the interrogators' effort to obtain a confession. Stated formally, an **interaction effect** occurs when the effect of one independent variable differs depending on the level of a second independent variable. To understand the interaction, examine the first row of Table 8.3. If only suspects who were actually guilty had been tested in the experiment, we would have concluded that the interrogators' expectations had *no effect* on effort ratings because the means for the guilty-expectation and innocent-expectation conditions are nearly identical. On the other hand, if only suspects who were actually innocent had been tested (second row of Table 8.3), we would have decided that interrogator expectations had a *large effect* on interrogators' efforts to obtain a confession.

An interaction effect is most easily seen when the means for the conditions are graphed. Figure 8.1 plots the four means found in Table 8.3. These results indicate that ratings of the interrogators' effort depend on whether the suspect is actually innocent or guilty *and* whether the interrogator expects the suspect to be guilty or innocent—that is, *both* independent variables are necessary to explain the effect. We describe the statistical analysis of interaction effects in complex designs in a later section, "Analysis of Complex Designs." For now, it is sufficient if you recognize that *an interaction effect occurs when the effect of one independent variable differs depending on the levels of a second independent variable.*

When one independent variable interacts with a second independent variable, the second independent variable must interact with the first one (that is, the order of the independent variables doesn't matter). For example, we described the interaction in Table 8.3 by stating that the effect of interrogators' expectations depends on the suspect's status. The reverse is also true; the effect of suspect status depends on the interrogators' expectations.

FIGURE 8.1   Graph illustrating the interaction effect between interrogator expectation and suspect status on effort to obtain a confession. (Data provided by Dr. Saul Kassin.)

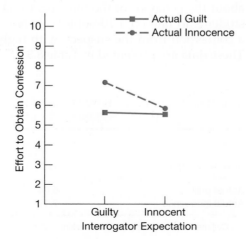

STRETCHING EXERCISE I

In this exercise you are asked to examine Tables 8.1, 8.2, and 8.3 to answer the following questions.

1 (a) In Table 8.1, what are the means for the main effect of the suspect-status independent variable?
  (b) How does the main effect of the suspect-status variable compare to the main effect of the interrogator-expectation variable for these data?
  (c) Is an interaction effect likely present in these data?

2 (a) In Table 8.2, what are the means for the main effect of the interrogator-expectation independent variable?

  (b) How does the main effect of the interrogator-expectation variable compare to the main effect of the suspect-status variable for these data?
  (c) Is an interaction effect likely present in these data?

3 (a) In Table 8.3, what are the means for the main effect of the interrogator-expectation independent variable?
  (b) What are the means for the main effect of the suspect-status independent variable?
  (c) Kassin et al. (2003) observed these main effects to be statistically significant. Using the means you computed, describe the main effects of the interrogator-expectation and suspect-status variables in Table 8.3.

We are now in a position to describe the conclusions that Kassin et al. (2003) made based on their data analyses of all their data. Using behavioral confirmation theory, they hypothesized that interrogators' expectations of guilt would cause them to conduct an interrogation that would confirm their beliefs. Their results supported this hypothesis; overall, interrogators who suspected guilt conducted more aggressive interrogations. In turn, suspects in the guilty-expectation condition became more defensive and were perceived as guilty by the neutral observers. That the interrogators in the guilty-expectation condition were even more aggressive when trying to obtain a confession for suspects who were actually innocent demonstrates the power of their expectations of guilt and the power of the behavioral confirmation process. In the criminal justice context, police interrogations that are based on a preexisting bias of the suspect's guilt can trigger a biased chain of events that may lead to tragic conclusions, including false confessions by innocent people.

Describing Interaction Effects

- Evidence for interaction effects can be identified using descriptive statistics presented in graphs (e.g., nonparallel lines) or tables (subtraction method).
- The presence of an interaction effect is confirmed using inferential statistics.

How you choose to describe the results of an interaction effect depends on which aspect of the interaction effect you want to emphasize. For example, Kassin et al. (2003) emphasized the effect of the interrogation-expectation variable on innocent and guilty suspects to test their predictions based on behavioral confirmation theory. That is, the manipulation of interrogators' expectations of a suspect's guilt or innocence allowed them to test their predictions that interrogators would seek to confirm their expectations. By adding the second independent variable, Kassin et al. accomplished two things. First, the study more

STRETCHING EXERCISE II

In this exercise you will have the opportunity to practice identifying main effects and interaction effects in 2 × 2 complex designs using only descriptive statistics.

In the spirit of practice makes perfect, let us now turn our attention to the exercise we have prepared to help you learn to identify main effects and interaction effects. Your task is to identify main effects and interaction effects in each of six complex design experiments (A through F). In each table or graph in this box, you are to determine whether the effect of each independent variable differs depending on the level of the other independent variable. In other words,

is there an interaction effect? After checking for the interaction effect, you can also check to see whether each independent variable produced an effect when collapsed across the other independent variable. That is, is there a main effect of one or both independent variables? The exercise will be most useful if you also practice translating the data presented in a table (Figure 8.2) into a graph and the data presented in graphs (Figures 8.3 and 8.4) into tables. The idea of the exercise is to become as comfortable as you can with the various ways of depicting the results of a complex design.

FIGURE 8.2   Mean number of correct responses as a function of task difficulty and anxiety level.

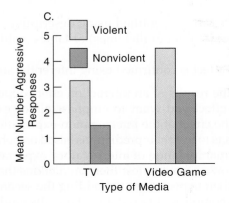

A.

		Task Difficulty	
		Easy	Hard
Anxiety Level	Low	3.3	3.3
	High	5.6	1.2

B.

		Task Difficulty	
		Easy	Hard
Anxiety Level	Low	6.2	3.1
	High	4.2	1.1

FIGURE 8.3   Mean number of aggressive responses as a function of type of media and content.

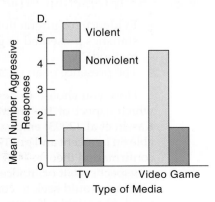

FIGURE 8.4 Mean reaction time as a function of delay and pattern complexity.

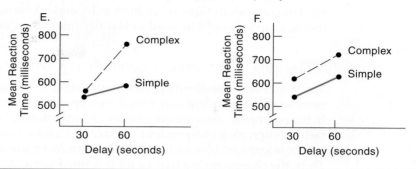

realistically conformed to real-world interrogations in which suspects are guilty or innocent; and second, they were able to demonstrate that interrogators who expect guilt work even harder to obtain a confession despite contrary evidence (e.g., the suspect's assertions of innocence). These findings also strongly indicate how the study of interaction effects in complex designs allows researchers to achieve greater understanding than is possible by doing experiments with only one independent variable.

There are three common ways to report a summary of the descriptive statistics in a complex design: tables, bar graphs, and line graphs. The procedures for preparing such tables and figures and the criteria for deciding which type of presentation to use are described in Chapter 13. In general, tables can be used for any complex design and are most useful when the exact values for each condition in the experiment need to be known. Bar graphs and line graphs, on the other hand, are especially useful for showing patterns of results without emphasizing the exact values. Line graphs are particularly useful for depicting the results of complex designs because an interaction effect can be seen so readily in a line graph. *Nonparallel lines in the graph suggest an interaction effect; parallel lines suggest no interaction effect.* See, for example, Figure 8.1.

When the results of a 2 × 2 design are summarized in a table, it is easiest to assess the presence or absence of an interaction effect by using the *subtraction method*. The subtraction method involves comparing the differences between the means in each row (or column) of the table. If the differences are different, an interaction effect is likely. In applying the subtraction method, it is essential that the differences be calculated in the same direction. For example, to use the subtraction method for the data reported in Table 8.3, you could subtract the mean ratings for the two levels of suspect status (actual guilt and actual innocence) for the guilty-expectation condition ($5.64 - 7.17 = -1.53$) and then do the same for the innocent-expectation condition ($5.56 - 5.85 = -0.29$). The sign of the obtained difference should also be carefully noted. The subtraction method shows you that these differences are different and, thus, an interaction effect between the two variables is likely. The subtraction method can be used only when one of the independent variables has two lev-els. For complex designs when both independent variables have three or more levels, graphs should be used to identify interaction effects.

Complex Designs with Three Independent Variables

The power and complexity of complex designs increase substantially when the number of independent variables in the experiment increases from two to three. In the two-factor design there can be only one interaction effect, but in the three-factor design each independent variable can interact with each of the other two independent variables and all three independent variables can interact together. Thus, the change from a two-factor to a three-factor design introduces the pos-sibility of obtaining four different interaction effects. If the three independent variables are symbolized as A, B, and C, the three-factor design allows a test of the main effects of A, B, and C; two-way interaction effects of A × B, A × C, B × C; and the three-way interaction effect of A × B × C. The efficiency of an experiment involving three independent variables is remarkable. An experiment investigating discrimination in the workplace will give you a sense of just how powerful complex designs can be.

Pingitore, Dugoni, Tindale, and Spring (1994) investigated possible discrimi-nation against moderately obese people in a mock job interview. Participants in the experiment viewed videotapes of job interviews. In one of their experi-ments they used a 2 × 2 × 2 design. The first independent variable was the weight of the applicant (normal or overweight). The role of the applicant for the job in the videotapes was played by professional actors who were of nor-mal weight. In the moderately obese conditions, the actors wore makeup and prostheses so that they appeared 20% heavier. The second independent vari-able in the experiment was the sex of the applicant (male or female). The third independent variable was participants' concern about their own body and the importance of body awareness to their self-concept (high or low). This variable was defined using a self-report measure of how participants viewed their body. A natural groups design was used to study this "body-schema variable." Partic-ipants were randomly assigned to evaluate male or female applicants who were normal weight or moderately obese (random groups designs). The dependent variable was the participants' rating on a 7-point scale of whether they would hire the applicant (1 = *definitely not hire* and 7 = *definitely hire*).

The results of the Pingitore et al. experiment for these three variables are shown in Figure 8.5. As you can see, displaying the means for a three-variable experiment requires a graph with more than one "panel." One panel of the fig-ure shows the results for two variables at one level of the third variable, and the other panel shows results for the same two variables at the second level of the third independent variable.

As you are now familiar with main effects and simple (two-way) interaction effects, let us concentrate on understanding a three-factor or three-way inter-action effect. As you can see in Figure 8.5, a two-way interaction effect of the applicant's weight and sex occurred only with participants who were high in concern about their own bodies. That is, those high on the body-schema variable

FIGURE 8.5 Illustration of an interaction effect for a 2 × 2 × 2 complex design.

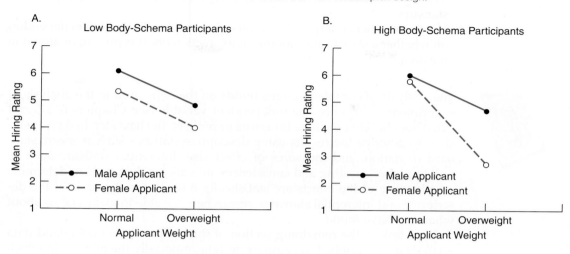

(right panel of Figure 8.5) gave overweight female applicants especially low ratings but rated normal male and female applicants the same. Participants who were low on the body-schema variable (left panel of Figure 8.5), on the other hand, gave lower ratings to overweight applicants, but the difference between their ratings for male and female applicants was the same for both levels of the applicant weight variable.

One way to summarize the Pingitore et al. (1994) findings shown in Figure 8.5 is to say that the interaction effect of the independent variables of the applicants' weight and the applicants' sex depended upon the participants' body schema. We call this type of finding a three-way (or triple) interaction effect. As you can see, when we have a three-way interaction effect, all three independent variables must be taken into account when describing the results. In general, when there are two independent variables, an interaction effect occurs when the effect of one of the independent variables differs depending on the level of the second independent variable. *When there are three independent variables in a complex design, a three-way interaction effect occurs when the interaction of two of the independent variables differs depending on the level of the third independent variable.* The results shown in Figure 8.5 illustrate this well. The pattern of results for the first two independent variables (applicants' body weight and sex) differs depending on the level of the third variable (participants' body schema). By including the third independent variable of body-schema, Pingitore et al. provided a much better understanding of discrimination based on an applicant's weight than would have been the case had they included only the independent variables of sex and weight.

ANALYSIS OF COMPLEX DESIGNS

- In a complex design with two independent variables, inferential statistics are used to test three effects: the main effects for each independent variable and the interaction effect between the two independent variables.

- Descriptive statistics are needed to interpret the results of inferential statistics.
- How researchers interpret the results of a complex design differs depending on whether a statistically significant interaction effect is present or absent in the data.

The analysis of complex designs builds on the logic used in the analysis of experiments with only one independent variable (see Chapters 6, 11, and 12). After checking the data for errors or outliers, the next step in data analysis is to describe the results using descriptive statistics such as mean, standard deviation, and measures of effect size. Inferential statistics such as null hypothesis testing and confidence intervals are then used to determine whether any of the effects are statistically reliable. On the basis of the descriptive and inferential statistics, researchers are able to make claims about what they have found.

Your task in the remaining section of this chapter is to understand data analysis as it is applied to complex designs, especially the manner in which an investigator interprets interaction effects and main effects. It may be helpful for you first to read the introduction that follows in this section, "Analysis of Complex Designs" and then to review the discussion of this topic in Chapter 12. The emphasis in both of these chapters is on the rationale and logic of these analyses, rather than on the nitty-gritty of computation. Fortunately, computers spare us the need to do the extensive calculations required of data produced in complex designs. On the other hand, computers cannot interpret the outcome of these calculations. That is where you come in. Go slowly; study this material carefully and be sure to examine the tables and figures that accompany the description in the text.

As you have come to understand, a complex design involving two variables has three potential *sources of systematic variation*. There are two potential main effects and a possible interaction effect. We describe the specific procedures for using null hypothesis testing (and the *F*-test) and confidence intervals to analyze complex designs in Chapter 12. A statistically significant effect in a complex design (as in any analysis) is an effect associated with a probability under the null hypothesis that is less than the accepted level of .05 (see Chapter 6). Inferential statistics tests are used in conjunction with descriptive statistics to determine whether an interaction effect has, in fact, occurred. After examining the data for an interaction effect, researchers may examine the data for the presence of main effects for each independent variable.

In a complex design, just as in an experiment with one independent variable, additional analyses may be needed to interpret the results. For example, a researcher might use confidence intervals to test differences between means. We illustrate such an approach in Chapter 12. The analysis plan for complex design experiments differs depending upon whether a statistically significant interaction effect is present in the experiment. Table 8.4 provides guidelines for interpreting a complex design experiment when an interaction effect does occur

TABLE 8.4 GUIDELINES FOR THE ANALYSIS OF A TWO-FACTOR EXPERIMENT

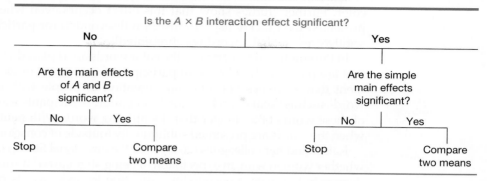

and when one does not. We will illustrate both paths in Table 8.4 by describing an experiment in which there is a statistically significant interaction effect present and then describing a study in which the interaction effect is not statistically significant.

Analysis Plan with an Interaction Effect

- If the analysis of a complex design reveals a statistically significant interaction effect, the source of the interaction effect is identified using simple main effects analyses and comparisons of two means.
- A simple main effect is the effect of one independent variable at one level of a second independent variable.

In order to understand the analysis of interaction effects within a complex design, we will examine a contemporary approach to understanding the effect of prejudice on individuals who are stigmatized. Social psychologists suggest that one effect of prejudice is that people who belong to stigmatized groups (e.g., ethnic minorities, gays and lesbians) develop belief systems about being devalued in society. With this "social-identity threat," stigmatized individuals develop expectations that cause them to be especially alert to cues in their environment that indicate they are viewed negatively (Kaiser, Vick, & Major, 2006). This attention to cues can occur at a *conscious* level, in which individuals are aware of their special attention to stigma cues. More recently, however, researchers have tested the extent to which social-identity threat causes people to be vigilant for potentially stigmatizing information without conscious awareness.

One method for examining nonconscious attention is the "emotional Stroop task." You may be familiar with the original version of the Stroop task in which participants are asked to name the color in which words are printed. The Stroop task was designed to show that reading is automatic (at least for adults). People find it impossible to ignore the printed words while naming the colors. This automatic-processing effect is demonstrated most dramatically in the condition in which color words are printed in a color other than the written word (e.g., "red" printed in blue ink). It takes participants longer to name colors in this "mismatch" condition because reading the word interferes with naming the color. Further studies show that this effect occurs even when the words are presented too quickly (e.g., 15 msec [milliseconds]) for participants to be consciously aware that a word was presented!

In the emotional Stroop task, the color words are replaced with content words that are particularly relevant to participants' concerns. For example, an experiment that examines nonconscious attention in people with phobias may use words such as "snake" and "spider." For phobic participants, identifying the color of these words takes longer than identifying words with neutral content, even when the words are presented subliminally (outside of conscious awareness).

Kaiser and her colleagues (2006) used the emotional Stroop task to investigate whether women with an expectation of being stigmatized through sexism would demonstrate greater nonconscious attention to sexist words compared to nonsexist words. They tested 35 women in a 2 × 3 complex design. The first manipulated independent variable was *social-identity* with two conditions, threat and safety, in a random groups design. Participants were led to believe that after completing the computer task, they would partner with a male participant (actually fictitious) to complete a group project. They were supplied with information about their partner so that they could get a sense of his personal characteristics. In the *identity-threat* condition, their partner held sexist views (e.g., strongly agreeing with statements such as "I could not work for a female boss because women can be overly emotional"). In the *identity-safety* condition, the partner was presented as nonsexist and strongly disagreed with sexist statements.

The second independent variable in their 2 × 3 design was *word type* with three levels: social-identity threatening, illness threatening, or nonthreatening. This variable was manipulated using a repeated measures design; thus, all participants were tested with all three word types in a completely counterbalanced order. The *social-identity threatening* words were sexist in content, such as *ho* and *hooters*. The *illness-threatening* words (e.g., *cancer, mono*) were included as a control condition to determine whether women in the identity-threat condition would pay attention to threatening words in general and not just social-identity threatening words. The *nonthreatening* words, also a control condition, described common household objects, such as *broom* and *curtains*. In one part of Kaiser et al.'s experiment, all three types of words were presented subliminally (15 msec) in different colors (red, yellow, blue, green), and participants' task was to identify the color. Tests showed that participants were unaware that words were presented. The dependent variable in this study was the response time for identifying the color (in milliseconds). This response-time measure assessed the amount of subliminal attention given to the different word types; longer response times indicate greater subliminal attention to the word and therefore a longer time to identify the color. The mean response times for each of the six conditions are presented in Table 8.5.

As Kaiser and her colleagues predicted, an interaction effect occurred between the two independent variables. Women in the identity-threat condition (first row of Table 8.5) took longest to name colors when social-identity threatening words were presented compared to illness-threatening and nonthreatening words. Longer response times to name the colors indicate that the women paid more subliminal attention to the words. Thus, women who expected to

TABLE 8.5   MEAN RESPONSE TIMES (IN MSEC) AS A FUNCTION OF SOCIAL IDENTITY
AND WORD TYPE (SUBLIMINAL PRESENTATION)

Social Identity Condition	Word Type		
	Social-Identity Threatening	Illness Threatening	Non-Threatening
Threat	598.9	577.7	583.9
Safety	603.9	615.0	614.5

Data adapted from Kaiser et al. (2006).

interact with a sexist partner paid more subliminal attention to words that threatened their social identity. In contrast, women who anticipated interacting with a nonsexist man in the identity-safety condition (second row of Table 8.5) did not differ substantially in the attention given to the three different types of words. An interaction effect is present because the effect of the word-type variable differed depending on the level of the social-identity variable (threat, safety). Inferential statistics tests of these results using null hypothesis significance testing confirmed that the interaction effect was statistically significant.

Once an interaction effect is confirmed in the data, the specific source of the interaction is located using additional statistical tests. As outlined in Table 8.4, the specific tests for tracing the source of a significant interaction are called simple main effects and comparisons of two means (see Chapter 12).

Key Concept }

A **simple main effect** is the effect of one independent variable at *one level* of a second independent variable. We can illustrate the use of simple main effects by returning to the results of the Kaiser et al. (2006) experiment. There are five simple main effects in Table 8.5: the effect of word type at each of the two levels of social identity and the effect of social identity at each of the three levels of word type. Kaiser et al. predicted that the subliminal attention effect (the difference between means for the three different word types) would occur for women in the identity-threat condition but not for women in the identity-safety condition. Therefore, they chose to test the simple main effects of word type at each level of the social-identity independent variable. They found, as predicted, that the simple main effect of word type was statistically significant in the identity-threat condition, but the simple main effect of word type was not statistically significant in the identity-safety condition.

When three or more means are tested in a simple main effect, as occurs for the word-type independent variable in Kaiser et al.'s experiment, comparisons of means tested two at a time can be done to identify the source of the simple main effect (see Chapter 12). First, no additional analyses are needed for the identity-safety condition because the simple main effect of word type was not statistically significant. The next step is to analyze the means more carefully for the identity-threat condition, where the simple main effect was statistically significant.

In their analyses of means considered two at a time, Kaiser and her colleagues noted both an expected and an unexpected effect for women in the identity-threat condition. As expected, mean response times were longer for social-identity threatening words than for illness-threatening words. Unexpectedly, mean response times did not differ when nonthreatening words were compared to either social-identity threatening words or to illness-threatening words. This raises an important question: Why did women allocate similar subliminal attention to nonthreatening words as they did to social-identity threatening words? Kaiser et al. reasoned that when women were expecting to interact with a sexist man, words describing household objects (e.g., *stove, broom, microwave*) in the nonthreatening condition may have been nonconsciously associated with sex-typed domestic tasks such as cooking and cleaning. According to Kaiser et al. (2006), "In retrospect, these nonthreatening words may not have provided the best comparison" (p. 336). Their interpretation of this unexpected finding illustrates how interpreting an experiment depends critically on how the experiment is done and how the data are analyzed.

Once an interaction effect has been thoroughly analyzed, researchers can also examine the main effects of each independent variable. However, the main effects are of much less interest when we know that an interaction effect occurred. For instance, the interaction effect in this experiment tells us that the subliminal attention given to different word types differs depending on the level of social-identity threat. Once we know this, we would not add much by learning whether, overall, women in the identity-safety condition had longer response times across all word types compared to women in the identity-threat condition. In the Kaiser et al. study, the main effects of the word-type and social-identity independent variables were not statistically significant. Nonetheless, there are experiments in which the interaction effect and the main effects are all of interest.

Analysis Plan with No Interaction Effect

- If the analysis of a complex design indicates the interaction effect between independent variables is not statistically significant, the next step in the analysis plan is to determine whether the main effects of the variables are statistically significant.
- The source of a statistically significant main effect can be specified more precisely by performing comparisons of two means or using confidence intervals to compare means two at a time.

We can use the results from a different part of the social-identity experiment conducted by Kaiser et al. (2006) to examine the analysis of a complex design when an interaction effect is *not* statistically significant. The results we just described were for words presented *subliminally*, that is, at a speed too fast (15 msec) for participants to detect the presence of the words. However, participants in this experiment also were tested with words presented at a *conscious* level. In the conscious-attention condition, women looked at the words on the screen until they responded by naming the color of the word.[2]

---

[2]The astute reader may see that the Kaiser et al. (2006) study is a 2 (social identity) × 3 (word type) × 2 (word presentation: subliminal, conscious) complex (mixed) design. The two levels of word presentation were manipulated using a repeated measures design. The 2 × 3 × 2 interaction among these independent variables was statistically significant. To further analyze the source of this three-way interaction, Kaiser et al. (2006) analyzed the 2 (social identity) × 3 (word type) interaction separately for subliminal presentation and conscious presentation. As described here, the 2 × 3 interaction was statistically significant for subliminal presentation but not for conscious presentation.

FIGURE 8.6 Results of a 2 × 3 complex design in which there was no interaction effect but there was a main effect. (Data provided by Dr. Cheryl R. Kaiser.)

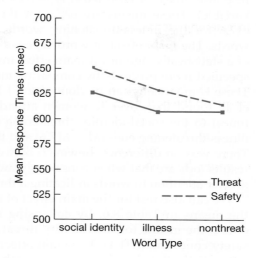

The mean response times for the three word types (social-identity threatening, illness threatening, and nonthreatening) for the two different groups of women (identity-threat, identity-safety) are presented in Figure 8.6. The interaction effect, or, more accurately, the lack of an interaction effect, can be seen in the figure. Although the two lines in the figure are not perfectly parallel, the mean response times appear to decrease in both groups at approximately the same rate. Inferential statistics tests confirmed that the interaction effect was not statistically significant. The data shown in Figure 8.6 illustrate a general principle of data analysis: *The pattern of findings as shown by the descriptive statistics is not sufficient to decide whether an interaction effect is present in an experiment. Inferential statistics tests, such as the F-test; must be done to confirm whether the effects are statistically reliable.*

When the interaction effect is not statistically significant, the next step is to examine the main effects of each independent variable (see Table 8.4). The means for the Kaiser et al. conscious-awareness experiment are presented again in Table 8.6 to make it easier to determine the main effects. By collapsing

TABLE 8.6 MEAN RESPONSE TIMES (IN MSEC) AS A FUNCTION OF SOCIAL IDENTITY AND WORD TYPE (CONSCIOUS PRESENTATION)

Social Identity Condition	Word Type			Means for Social Identity
	Social-Identity Threatening	Illness Threatening	Non-Threatening	
Threat (n = 18)	625.9	607.4	607.5	613.6
Safety (n = 16)	650.6	629.0	614.5	631.4
Means for word type	637.5*	617.6*	610.8*	

Data provided by Dr. Cheryl R. Kaiser.
*Weighted means were calculated due to unequal sample sizes for the social-identity conditions.

(averaging) across the two social-identity conditions, we obtain the mean response times for each word type (i.e., for the main effect of the word-type variable). These means are 637.5 for the social-identity threatening words, 617.6 for the illness-threatening words, and 610.8 for the nonthreatening words. The main effect of word type was statistically significant. The source of a statistically significant main effect involving three or more means can be specified more precisely by comparing means two at a time (see Chapter 12). These comparisons can be done using *t*-tests or confidence intervals. Kaiser et al. found that, overall, women attended more (i.e., had longer response times) to the social-identity threatening cues ($M = 637.5$) than to both the illness-threatening cues ($M = 617.6$) and the nonthreatening cues ($M = 610.8$). There was no difference, however, between the latter two conditions. These results indicate that when consciously aware of the word types, women paid greater attention to words indicating a threat to their social identity.

We can also test for the main effect of the social-identity variable by using the means in Table 8.6. By collapsing across the word-type variable, we obtain the means for the identity-threat condition (613.6) and the identity-safety condition (631.4). The main effect of the social-identity variable was not statistically significant, indicating that, on average, response times were similar for women in the threat and safety conditions. That the two means appear to be different reinforces the need for statistical analyses to determine whether mean differences are reliable.

The analysis of Kaiser et al.'s social-identity experiment illustrates that much can be learned from a complex design even when there is no statistically significant interaction effect.

INTERPRETING INTERACTION EFFECTS

Interaction Effects and Theory Testing

- Theories frequently predict that two or more independent variables interact to influence behavior; therefore, complex designs are needed to test theories.
- Tests of theories can sometimes produce contradictory findings. Interaction effects can be useful in resolving these contradictions.

Theories play a critical role in the scientific method. Complex designs greatly enhance researchers' ability to test theories because they can test for both main effects and interaction effects. For example, Kaiser et al. (2006) tested hypotheses about attention to prejudice cues in the environment based on social-identity theory. Prior research had demonstrated that when individuals' social identity is threatened, they are *consciously* aware of cues in their environment relating to potential prejudice. Kaiser et al. extended this research by testing the hypothesis that threatened individuals pay attention to prejudice cues *nonconsciously*, without awareness. Because they used a complex design, Kaiser et al.'s data provide evidence that women expecting to experience sexism, compared to women expecting a "safe" situation, paid greater subliminal attention to sexist words than to other words. Their data supported the social-identity theory of prejudice, in which "members of stigmatized groups develop belief systems about being devalued and that these expectations cause them to become especially alert or vigilant for signs of devaluation" (Kaiser et al., 2006, p. 332).

In addition, Kaiser et al. noted that theories of attentional processes state that attention is a limited resource. People who experience prejudice may allocate attention toward cues that threaten their social identity and therefore have less attentional resources available for other tasks. For example, students in a classroom setting who perceive possible prejudice may allocate their attention, both consciously and nonconsciously, to potential threats to their social identity, and this diverted attention could impair their classroom performance. Importantly, however, because Kaiser et al. manipulated the independent variable of social-identity threat with two levels, threat and safety, they were able to demonstrate that attentional resources are not diverted to potential threats when individuals believe they are safe from social-identity threats. This finding reinforces the importance of creating environments that are as free of prejudice as possible.

Psychological theories involving topics such as social identity and prejudice are often complex. In order to explain prejudice, for example, psychologists need to describe behavioral, cognitive, and emotional processes at individual, group, and societal levels. As you might imagine, experimental tests of complex theories can lead to contradictory findings. For example, consider a hypothetical example in which a study of prejudice shows that members of a devalued group do *not* experience heightened nonconcious attention to social-identity threats. How would this seemingly contradictory finding be incorporated into a theory of prejudice which states that stigmatized individuals attend to potential threats to their identity? As data from the Kaiser et al. experiment suggest, one interpretation of this finding might involve the independent variable of social-identity condition, threat or safety. The contradictory finding could be interpreted by suggesting that participants in the hypothetical study of prejudice felt safe from social-identity threats and therefore did not allocate attention to potential sources of devaluation.

A common approach to resolving contradictory findings is to include in the research design independent variables that address potential sources of contradictory findings (for example, by including threat and safety conditions in the design). More generally, complex designs can be extremely useful in tracking down the reasons for seemingly contradictory findings when theories are tested. The process can be a painstaking one, but it can also be very worthwhile.

Interaction Effects and External Validity

- When no interaction effect occurs in a complex design, the effects of each independent variable can be generalized across the levels of the other independent variable; thus, external validity of the independent variables increases.
- The presence of an interaction effect identifies boundaries for the external validity of a finding by specifying the conditions in which an effect of an independent variable occurs.

In Chapter 6 we discussed at some length the procedures for establishing the external validity of a research finding when an experiment involves only one independent variable. We described how partial replications could be done to establish external validity—that is, the extent to which research findings may be generalized. We also discussed how field experiments allow researchers to examine independent variables in real-world settings. We can now examine the role of complex designs in establishing the external validity of a finding. The presence or absence of an interaction effect is critical in determining the external validity of the findings in a complex design.

When no interaction effect occurs in a complex design, we know that the effects of each independent variable can be generalized across the levels of the other independent variable. For instance, consider again the findings from Kassin et al.'s (2003) study on interrogators' expectations when interrogating a suspect. They found that when interrogators expected the suspect to be guilty, they selected more guilt-presumptive questions than when interrogators expected the suspect to be innocent, regardless of whether the suspect was actually guilty or innocent. That is, there was no interaction effect between the interrogator-expectation variable and the suspect-status variable. Thus, interrogators' selection of guilt-presumptive questions when they expect guilt can be generalized across situations in which the suspect is actually guilty or innocent.

Of course, we cannot generalize our findings beyond the boundaries or conditions that were included in the experiment. For example, the absence of an interaction effect between interrogator expectations and suspect status does not allow us to conclude that the selection of guilt-presumptive questions would be similar if other groups were tested, such as law enforcement officials. Similarly, we do not know whether the same effects would occur if other manipulations of interrogators' expectations were used. We also must remember that not finding a statistically significant interaction effect does not necessarily mean that an interaction effect is not really present; we may not have performed an experiment with sufficient sensitivity to detect it.

As we have seen, the absence of an interaction effect increases the external validity of the effects of each independent variable in the experiment. Perhaps more important, the *presence* of an interaction effect identifies boundaries for the external validity of a finding. For example, Kassin et al. (2003) also found that interrogators who expected the suspect to be guilty, rather than innocent, applied greater pressure to obtain a confession on suspects who were actually innocent compared to those who were guilty. This interaction effect clearly sets limits on the external validity of the effect of interrogators' expectations on pressure to obtain a confession. Given this finding, the best way to respond to someone's query regarding the general effect of interrogators' expectations on their effort to obtain a confession is to say, "It depends." In this case, it depends on whether the suspect is actually guilty or innocent. The presence of the interaction effect sets boundaries for the external validity, but the interaction effect also specifies what those boundaries are.

The possibility of interaction effects among independent variables should lead us to be cautious about saying that an independent variable does not have an effect on behavior. Independent variables that influence behavior are called relevant independent variables. In general, a **relevant independent variable** is one that influences behavior directly (results in a main effect) or produces an interaction effect when studied in combination with a second independent variable. Distinguishing between factors that affect behavior and those that do not is essential for developing adequate theories to explain behavior and for designing effective interventions to deal with problems in applied settings such as schools, hospitals, and factories (see Chapters 9 and 10).

There are several reasons why we should be cautious about identifying an independent variable as *irrelevant*. First, if an independent variable is shown to have no effect in an experiment, we cannot assume that this variable wouldn't have an effect if different levels of the independent variable had been tested. Second, if an independent variable has no effect in a single-factor experiment, this doesn't mean that it won't interact with another independent variable when used in a complex design. Third, if an independent variable does not have an effect in an experiment, it may be that an effect could have been seen with different dependent variables. Fourth, the absence of a statistically significant effect may or may not mean that the effect is not present. Minimally, we would want to consider the sensitivity of our experiment and the power of our statistical analysis before deciding that we have identified an irrelevant variable. (See Chapter 12 for a discussion of the power of a statistical analysis.) For now, it is best if you avoid being dogmatic about identifying any independent variable as not having any effect.

Interaction Effects and Ceiling and Floor Effects

- When participants' performance reaches a maximum (ceiling) or a minimum (floor) in one or more conditions of an experiment, results for an interaction effect are uninterpretable.

Consider the results of a 3 × 2 experiment investigating the effects of increasing amounts of practice on performance during a physical-fitness test. There were six groups of participants in this plausible but hypothetical experiment. Participants were first given 10, 30, or 60 minutes to practice, doing either easy or hard exercises. Then they took a fitness test using easy or hard exercises (the same they had practiced). The dependent variable was the percentage of exercises that each participant was able to complete in a 15-minute test period. Results of the experiment are presented in Figure 8.7.

The pattern of results in Figure 8.7 looks like a classic interaction effect; the effect of amount of practice time differed for the easy and hard exercises. Increasing practice time improved test performance for the hard exercises, but performance leveled off after 30 minutes of practice with the easy exercises. If a standard analysis was applied to these data, the interaction effect would very likely be statistically significant. Unfortunately, this interaction effect would be essentially uninterpretable. For those groups given practice with the easy exercises, performance reached the maximum level after 30 minutes of practice, so no improvement beyond this point could be shown in the 60-minute group. Even if the participants given 60 minutes of practice had further benefited from the extra practice, the experimenter could not measure this improvement on the chosen dependent variable.

FIGURE 8.7   Illustration of a ceiling effect.

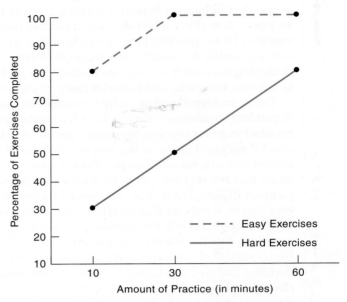

Key Concepts }

The preceding experiment illustrates the general measurement problem referred to as a ceiling effect. Whenever performance reaches a maximum in any condition of an experiment, there is danger of a **ceiling effect.** The corresponding name given to this problem when performance reaches a minimum (e.g., zero errors on a test) is a **floor effect.** Researchers can avoid ceiling and floor effects by selecting dependent variables that allow ample "room" for performance differences to be measured across conditions. For example, in the fitness experiment it would have been better to test participants with a greater number of exercises than anyone could be expected to complete in the time allotted for the test. The mean number of exercises completed in each condition could then be used to assess the effects of the two independent variables without the danger of a ceiling effect. It is important to note that ceiling effects also can pose a problem in experiments that don't involve a complex design. If the fitness experiment had included only the easy exercises, there would still be a ceiling effect in the experiment.

Interaction Effects and the Natural Groups Design

- Researchers use complex designs to make causal inferences about natural groups variables when they test a theory for why natural groups differ.
- Three steps for making a causal inference involving a natural groups variable are to state a theory for why group differences exist, manipulate an independent variable that should demonstrate the theorized process, and test whether an interaction effect occurs between the manipulated independent variable and natural groups variable.

The natural groups design, described briefly in Chapter 6, is one of the most popular research designs in psychology. Groups of people are formed by selecting individuals who differ on some characteristic such as gender, age, introversion–extraversion, or aggressiveness, to name just a few individual differences variables. Researchers then look for systematic relationships between these individual differences variables and other aspects of behavior. The natural groups design is an effective one for establishing correlations between individuals' characteristics and their performance. As we also described in Chapter 6, however, the natural groups design is perhaps the most challenging design when it comes to drawing conclusions about the causes of behavior.

The difficulty in interpreting the natural groups design arises when we try to conclude that differences in performance are *caused* by the characteristics of the people we used to define the groups. For instance, consider an experiment in which participants are selected because of their musical training. One group of participants includes people with 10 or more years of formal musical training, and one group includes people with no formal training. Both groups are tested on their ability to remember the musical notation for simple 10-note melodies. Not surprisingly, the results of these tests show that those with musical training perform far better than those without such training.

We can conclude on the basis of these results that memory for simple melodies varies with (is correlated with) amount of musical training. But we cannot conclude that musical training *causes* superior memory performance. Why not? There are probably many additional ways in which people with 10 years of musical training differ from those without such training. The groups may differ in amount and type of general education, family background, socioeconomic status, and amount and type of experience they have had listening to music. Also, those with musical training may have generally better memories than those without such training, and their superior memory for simple melodies may reflect this general memory ability. Finally, those who sought out musical training may have done so because they had a special aptitude for music. Accordingly, they might have done better on the memory task even if they had not had any musical training. In short, there are many possible causes other than individual differences in musical training for the difference in memory performance that was observed.

There is a potential solution to the problem of drawing causal inferences based on the natural groups design (Underwood & Shaughnessy, 1975). The key to this solution is to develop a theory regarding the critical individual difference variable. For example, Halpern and Bower (1982) were interested in how memory for musical notation differs between musicians and nonmusicians. Halpern and Bower developed a theory of how musical training would influence the cognitive processing of musical notation by those who had such training. Their theory was based on a memory concept called "chunking." You can get some sense of the memory advantage provided by chunking if you imagine trying to memorize the following strings of 15 letters: HBOFBICNNUSAWWW. Chunking helps memory by changing the same string of letters to a series of five more easily remembered chunks: HBO-FBI-CNN-USA-WWW.

Halpern and Bower theorized that musical training led musicians to "chunk" musical notation into meaningful musical units, thereby reducing the amount of information they needed to remember in order to reproduce the notation for a simple melody. Furthermore, if this process were responsible for the difference between the memory performance of musicians and nonmusicians, then the difference between musicians and nonmusicians should be greater for melodies with good musical structure than for melodies with poor musical structure. Halpern and Bower manipulated the independent variable of musical structure to test their theory. To do this, they used three different types of melodies to test their groups of musicians and nonmusicians. They prepared sets of simple melodies whose notations had similar visual structures but that were good, bad, or random in musical structure.

The critical test in Halpern and Bower's experiment was whether they would obtain an interaction effect between the two independent variables: musical training and type of melodies. Specifically, they expected that the difference in memory performance between musicians and nonmusicians would be largest for the melodies exhibiting good structure, next largest for the melodies exhibiting bad structure, and smallest for the random melodies. The results of Halpern and Bower's experiment conformed exactly to their predictions.

The obtained interaction effect allowed Halpern and Bower to rule out many alternative hypotheses for the difference in memory performance between musicians and nonmusicians. Such characteristics as amount and type of general education, socioeconomic status, family background, and good memory ability are not likely to explain why there is a systematic relationship between the structure of the melodies and the size of the difference in memory performance between musicians and nonmusicians. These potential alternative hypotheses cannot explain why there was little difference in the two groups' memory performance for random melodies. The interaction effect makes such simple correlational explanations much less plausible.

There are several steps that the investigator must take in carrying out the general procedure for drawing causal inferences based on the natural groups design.

Step 1: Develop a Theory   The first step is to develop a theory explaining why a difference should occur in the performance of groups that have been differentiated on the basis of an individual differences variable. For example, Halpern and Bower theorized that musicians and nonmusicians differed in musical performance because of the way that these groups cognitively organize ("chunk") melodies.

Step 2: Identify a Relevant Variable to Manipulate   The second step is to select an independent variable that can be manipulated and that is presumed to influence the likelihood that this theoretical process will occur. Halpern and Bower suggested that type of musical structure was a variable associated with ease of chunking.

Step 3: Test for an Interaction   The most critical aspect of the recommended approach is to strive to produce an interaction effect between the manipulated variable and the individual differences variable. Thus, the relevant manipulated independent variable is applied to both natural groups. Halpern and Bower sought an interaction effect between the individual differences variable (musician vs. nonmusician) and the manipulated variable (type of musical structure) in a 2 × 3 complex design. The approach can be strengthened even further by testing predictions of interaction effects of three independent variables: two manipulated independent variables and the individual differences variable (see, for example, Anderson & Revelle, 1982).

SUMMARY

A complex design is one in which two or more independent variables are studied in the same experiment. A complex design involving two independent variables allows researchers to determine the overall effect of each independent variable (the main effect of each variable). More important, complex designs can be used to reveal the interaction effect between independent variables. Interaction effects occur when the effect of each independent variable depends on the level of the other independent variable.

The simplest possible complex design is the 2 × 2 design, in which two independent variables are both studied at two levels. The number of conditions in a factorial design is equal to the product of the levels of the independent variables (e.g., 2 × 3 = 6). Complex designs beyond the 2 × 2 can be even more useful for understanding behavior. Additional levels of one or both of the independent variables can be added to yield designs such as the 3 × 2, the 3 × 3, the 4 × 2, the 4 × 3, and so on. Additional independent variables can also be included to yield designs such as the 2 × 2 × 2, the 2 × 3 × 3, and so on. Experiments involving three independent variables are remarkably efficient. They allow researchers to determine the main effects of each of the three variables, the three two-way interaction effects, and the simultaneous interaction effect of all three variables.

When two independent variables are studied in a complex design, three potential sources of systematic variation can be interpreted. Each independent variable can produce a statistically significant main effect, and the two independent variables can combine to produce a statistically significant interaction effect. Interaction effects can be initially identified by using the subtraction method when the descriptive statistics are reported in a table, or by the presence of nonparallel lines when the results appear in a line graph. If the interaction effect does prove to be statistically significant, we can analyze the results further by examining simple main effects and, if necessary, comparisons of means considered two at a time. When no interaction effect arises, we examine the main effects of each independent variable, and we can use comparisons of two means or confidence intervals when necessary.

Complex designs play a critical role in the testing of predictions derived from psychological theories. Complex designs are also essential to resolve contradictions that arise when theories are tested. When a complex design is used and no interaction effect occurs, we know that the effects of each independent variable can be generalized across the levels of the other independent variable(s). When an interaction effect does occur, however, boundaries on the external validity of a finding can be clearly specified. The possibility of interaction effects requires that we expand the definition of a relevant independent variable to include those that influence behavior directly (produce main effects) and those that produce an interaction effect when studied in combination with another independent variable. Interaction effects that may arise because of measurement problems such as ceiling or floor effects must not be confused with interaction effects that reflect the true combined effect of two independent variables. Interaction effects can also be most helpful in solving the problem of drawing causal inferences based on the natural groups design.

KEY CONCEPTS

complex designs   250
main effect   253
interaction effect   256

simple main effect   265
relevant independent variable   271
ceiling and floor effects   272

REVIEW QUESTIONS

1 Identify the number of independent variables, the number of levels for each independent variable, and the total number of conditions for each of the following examples of complex design experiments: (a) 2×3 (b) 3×3 (c) $2 \times 2 \times 3$ (d) 4×3.

2 Identify the conditions in a complex design when the following independent variables are factorially combined: (1) type of task with three levels (visual, auditory, tactile) and (2) group of children tested with two levels (normal, developmentally delayed).

3 Use the Kassin et al. results in Table 8.3 for interrogators' efforts to obtain a confession to show there are two possible ways to describe the interaction effect.

4 Describe how you would use the subtraction method to decide whether an interaction effect was present in a table showing the results of a 2×2 complex design.

5 Describe the pattern in a line graph that indicates the presence of an interaction effect in a complex design.

6 Outline the steps in the analysis plan for a complex design with two independent variables when there is an interaction effect and when there is not an interaction effect.

7 Use an example to illustrate how a complex design can be used to test predictions derived from a psychological theory.

8 How is the external validity of the findings in a complex design influenced by the presence or absence of an interaction effect?

9 Explain why researchers should be cautious about saying that an independent variable does not have an effect on behavior.

10 Describe the pattern of descriptive statistics that would indicate a ceiling (or floor) effect may be present in a data set, and describe how this pattern of data may affect the interpretation of inferential statistics (e.g., F-test) for these data.

11 Explain how interaction effects in a complex design can be used as part of the solution to the problem of drawing causal inferences on the basis of the natural groups design.

CHALLENGE QUESTIONS

1 Consider an experiment in which two independent variables have been manipulated. Variable *A* has been manipulated at three levels, and Variable *B* has been manipulated at two levels.

A Draw a graph showing a main effect of Variable *B*, no main effect of Variable *A*, and no interaction effect between the two variables.

B Draw a graph showing no main effect of Variable *A*, no main effect of Variable *B*, but an interaction effect between the two variables.

C Draw a graph showing a main effect of Variable *A*, a main effect of Variable *B*, and no interaction effect between the *A* and *B* variables.

2 A researcher has used a complex design to study the effects of training (untrained and trained) and problem difficulty (easy and hard) on participants' problem-solving ability. The researcher tested a total of 80 participants, with 20 randomly assigned to each of the four groups resulting from the factorial combination of the two independent variables. The data presented below represent the mean percentage of the problems that participants solved in each of the four conditions.

	Training	
Problem Difficulty	Untrained	Trained
Easy	90	95
Hard	30	60

A Is there evidence of a possible interaction effect in this experiment?

B What aspect of the results of this experiment would lead you to be hesitant to interpret an interaction effect if one were present in this experiment?

C How could the researcher modify the experiment so as to be able to interpret an interaction effect if it should occur?

3 A psychologist is interested in whether older people suffer a deficit with respect to their reaction time in processing complex visual patterns. Fifty 65-year-old people and 50 college-age young adults volunteer to participate in the experiment. The participants are tested using an embedded figures test. The psychologist presents a simple figure to each participant followed immediately by a complex pattern that contains the simple figure. The participant must indicate as quickly as possible the location of the simple figure in the complex pattern. Participants are timed from the onset of complex pattern until they locate the simple pattern. As the psychologist had expected, the mean reaction times for the older adults were markedly longer than those for the young adults. By any standard the results were statistically significant.

A The psychologist claims based on these results that the differences in reaction times in this experiment were caused by a deficit in the older adults' ability to process complex information. You recognize that a complex design experiment would need to be done before he could conclude that older adults suffered a deficit in their processing of *complex* visual patterns. What additional reaction-time test could the psychologist give to both groups in order to make his experiment into a complex design? Describe an outcome of the complex design experiment that would support the claim that older adults suffer a deficit in processing complex information and another outcome that would lead you to question the claim.

B Recognizing that his original study is flawed, the psychologist tries to use post hoc (after the fact) matching to try to equate his two groups. He decides to match on general health (i.e., the better your general health, the faster your reaction time). Although he cannot get an exact matching across groups, he does find that when he looks only at the 15 healthiest older adults, their reaction times are only slightly longer than the mean for the young adults. Explain how this outcome would change the psychologist's conclusion concerning the effect of age on reaction time. Could the psychologist reach the general conclusion that older adults do not suffer a deficit in reaction time in this task? Why or why not?

Answer to Stretching Exercise I

1 (a) Actual guilt: $M = 3.04$, Actual innocence: $M = 3.18$

(b) The difference between the means for the suspect-status independent variable is 0.14, which is a very small difference compared to the mean difference observed for the statistically significant effect of interrogator expectation on the number of presumptive questions ($3.62 - 2.60 = 1.02$).

(c) Using the subtraction method, the difference between the actual-guilt and actual-innocent conditions in the guilty-expectation condition is -0.16 ($3.54 - 3.70$). In the innocent-expectation condition, this difference is -0.12 ($2.54 - 2.66$). Because these differences are very similar, an interaction effect is unlikely.

2 (a) Expect guilty: $M = 9.84$, Expect innocent: $M = 8.74$

   (b) The difference between the means for the expect-guilty and expect-innocent conditions is 1.1 (i.e., approximately 1 more persuasive technique in the expect-guilty condition than in the expect-innocent condition). In contrast, for the statistically significant main effect of the suspect-status independent variable, the difference in the number of persuasive techniques used between actual-guilt and actual-innocent conditions is 4.27 ($11.42 - 7.15$).

   (c) An interaction effect is unlikely. Using the subtraction method, the difference between the actual-guilt and actual-innocent conditions in the guilty-expectation condition ($7.71 - 11.96 = -4.25$) is very similar to the computed value for the innocent-expectation condition ($6.59 - 10.88 = -4.29$).

3 (a) Expect guilty: $M = 6.40$, Expect innocent: $M = 5.70$

   (b) Actual guilt: $M = 5.60$, Actual innocence: $M = 6.51$

   (c) The statistically significant main effect of the interrogator-expectation variable indicates that effort to obtain a confession (the dependent variable) was higher in the expect-guilty condition ($M = 6.40$) than in the expect-innocent condition ($M = 5.70$).

   The statistically significant main effect of the suspect-status variable indicates that effort to obtain a confession was higher in the actual-innocence condition ($M = 6.51$) than in the actual-guilt condition ($M = 5.60$).

Answer to Stretching Exercise II

A interaction effect, main effect of the task difficulty

B no interaction effect, main effects of task difficulty and anxiety level

C no interaction effect, main effects of type of media and content

D interaction effect, main effects of type of media and content

E interaction effect, main effects of delay and pattern complexity (additional statistical analyses are needed to test these effects)

F no interaction effect, main effects of delay and pattern complexity

Answer to Challenge Question 1

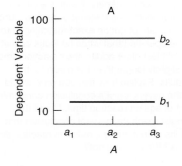
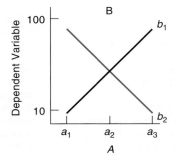
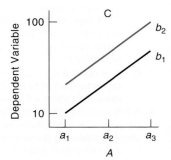

PART FOUR

Applied Research

CHAPTER NINE

Single-Case Designs and Small-*n* Research

CHAPTER OUTLINE

OVERVIEW

So far in this book we have emphasized *group methodology*—research designed to examine the average performance of one or more groups of participants. This was particularly evident in Chapters 6, 7, and 8 when we were considering experimental methods. In this chapter we introduce two alternative methodologies that emphasize the study of a single individual. We call these methodologies *single-case research designs.*

Single-case designs have been used since scientific psychology began in the 19th century. Psychophysical methods had their origin in the work of Gustav Fechner and were described in his 1860 book, *Elemente der Psychophysik*. Fechner, and countless other psychophysicists since, relied on data obtained through experiments with one or two individuals. Hermann Ebbinghaus is another major figure in the early history of psychology who used a single-case design. In fact, the single case that Ebbinghaus studied was himself. He was both the participant and the experimenter for the research he published in his monograph on memory in 1885. Over a period of many months he learned and then attempted to relearn hundreds of series of nonsense syllables. His data provided psychologists with the first systematic evidence of forgetting over time.

Single-case studies appear regularly in psychology journals, dealing with issues ranging from cognitive therapy for Vietnam veterans (Kubany, 1997) to the study of brain processes in amnesic patients (Gabrieli, Fleischman, Keane, Reminger, & Morrell, 1995) and the treatment of motor and vocal tics associated with Tourette's syndrome (Gilman, Connor, & Haney, 2005). Cognitive psychologists who study expert performance, whether it be that of a ballet dancer, chess player, or musician, rely heavily on these methods (e.g., Ericsson & Charness, 1994). For example, several researchers recently reported on their observations of "Donny, a young autistic savant who is possibly the fastest and most accurate calendar prodigy ever described" (Thioux, Stark, Klaiman, & Schultz, 2006, p. 1155). In less than a second he can tell you the day of the week when you were born! Donny had been diagnosed with autism at age 6 years and had an IQ near the borderline of mental retardation. Yet, he was accurate 98% of the time when quizzed about days of the week between March 1, 1900, and February 28, 2100. He made systematic errors outside this range due to the fact that he seemed not to recognize that century years are leap years only if they are divisible by 400. Donny was evaluated over a 1-year period utilizing a variety of testing conditions. The researchers developed a cognitive model to explain Donny's performance and speculated on the development of savant skills in autistic individuals.

In this chapter we discuss two specific single-case research methodologies, the case study method and single-subject experimental designs. The *case study method* is frequently associated with the field of clinical psychology, but investigators from fields such as anthropology, criminology, neurology, and sociology also make use of this important method. For example, neurologist Oliver Sacks (1985, 1995, 2007) captivated millions with his vivid case studies of individuals with peculiar, and rather fascinating, brain disorders. One of Sacks' popular books is *Musicophilia: Tales of Music and the Brain* (2007). Where does our interest or propensity to enjoy music ("musicophilia") come from? Is it innate? What parts of the brain govern our musical abilities and appreciation? Is music related to language? Sacks probes the answers to these and other questions through a review of case studies of individuals with unusual musical propensities. He begins this book with the clinical story of a man who survived being hit by lightning to find that he had developed an obsession with music. He had no real interest in music before this event but now found an intense craving to hear piano music. He began listening to musical recordings and discovered that music kept playing in his head. He took piano lessons and began to write his own compositions! These "clinical tales," as Sacks calls them, not only provide insights into the relationship between mind and brain, but also reveal how individuals adapt, cope, and succeed when faced with profound neurological deficits. We will review the advantages and the disadvantages of the case study method.

The emphasis in a *single-subject experimental design* typically is on manipulation of variables and interpretation for a single subject, even if a few subjects or a single "group" is observed. Single-subject experimental designs are also frequently called "$N = 1$ experimental designs" or "small-*n* research designs." These designs are characteristic of approaches called the *experimental analysis of behavior* and *applied behavior analysis*. As you will see, these approaches represent basic and applied applications, respectively, of a small-*n* approach. Single-subject designs are more systematic and controlled than are case studies. We will examine the rationale behind the use of these designs and provide specific illustrations of the more common single-subject experimental designs. These experimental designs represent a special case of the repeated measures design introduced in Chapter 7.

THE CASE STUDY METHOD

Characteristics

- Case studies, intensive descriptions and analyses of individuals, lack the degree of control found in small-*n* experimental designs.
- Case studies are a source of hypotheses and ideas about normal and abnormal behavior.

Key Concept }

A **case study** is an intensive description and analysis of a single individual. Case studies frequently make use of qualitative data, but this is not always the case (e.g., Smith, Harré, & Van Langenhove, 1995). Researchers who use the case study method obtain their data from several sources, including naturalistic observation and archival records (Chapter 4), interviews, and psychological tests (Chapter 5). A clinical case study frequently describes the application and results of a particular treatment. For example, a clinical case study may describe an individual's symptoms, the methods used to understand and treat the symptoms, and evidence for the treatment's effectiveness. Thus, case studies provide a potentially rich source of information about individuals.

Treatment variables in clinical case studies are rarely controlled systematically. Instead, several treatments may be applied simultaneously, and the psychologist may have little control over extraneous variables (e.g., home and work environments that influence the client's symptoms). Thus, *a fundamental characteristic of case studies is that they often lack a high degree of control*. Without control, it is difficult for researchers to make valid inferences about variables that influence the individual's behavior (including any treatment). Degree of control is one distinguishing feature between the case study method and single-subject experimental designs, with single-subject experimental designs having a higher degree of control (see, for example, Kazdin, 2002).

The form and content of case studies are extremely varied. Published case studies may be only a few printed pages long or may fill a book. Many aspects of the case study method make it a unique means of studying behavior. It differs from more experimental approaches in terms of its goals, the methods used, and the types of information obtained (Kazdin, 2002). For example, the case study method is often characterized as "exploratory" in nature and a source of hypotheses and ideas about behavior (Bolgar, 1965). Experimental approaches, on the other hand, are frequently viewed as opportunities to test specific hypotheses. The case study method has sometimes been viewed as antagonistic to more controlled methods of investigation. A more appropriate perspective is suggested by Kazdin (2002), who sees *the case study method as interrelated with and complementary to other research methods in psychology*.

The case study method offers both advantages and disadvantages to the research psychologist (see, for example, Bolgar, 1965; Hersen & Barlow, 1976; Kazdin, 2002). Before reviewing its advantages and disadvantages, however, we will illustrate the method with a summary of an actual case study reported by Kirsch (1978). It is important that you read this slightly abbreviated version of a case study carefully because we will review it when discussing the advantages and disadvantages of the case study method (see Box 9.1).

BOX 9.1

CAN CLIENTS BE THEIR OWN THERAPISTS? A CASE STUDY ILLUSTRATION

This article reports on the use of self-management training (SMT), a therapeutic strategy which capitalizes on the advantages of brief therapies, while at the same time reducing the danger of leaving too many tasks not fully accomplished. . . . The essence of this approach involves teaching the client how to be his or her own behavior therapist. The client is taught how to assess problems along behavioral dimensions and to develop specific tactics, based on existing treatment techniques, for overcoming problems. As this process occurs, the traditional client–therapist relationship is altered considerably. The client takes on the dual role of client and therapist, while the therapist takes on the role of supervisor.

The case of Susan

Susan, a 28-year-old married woman, entered therapy complaining that she suffered from a deficient memory, low intelligence, and lack of self-confidence. The presumed deficiencies "caused" her to be inhibited in a number of social situations. She was unable to engage in discussions about films, plays, books, or magazine

(continued)

articles "because" she could not remember them well enough. She often felt that she could not understand what was being said in a conversation and that this was due to her low intelligence. She attempted to hide her lack of comprehension by adopting a passive role in these interactions and was fearful lest she be discovered by being asked for more of a response. She did not trust her own opinions and, indeed, sometimes doubted whether she had any. She felt dependent on others to provide opinions for her to adopt.

Administering a Wechsler Adult Intelligence Scale (WAIS), I found her to have a verbal IQ of about 120, hardly a subnormal score. Her digit span indicated that at least her short-term memory was not deficient. The test confirmed what I had already surmised from talking with her: that there was nothing wrong with her level of intelligence or her memory. After discussing this conclusion, I suggested that we investigate in greater detail what kinds of things she would be able to do if she felt that her memory, intelligence, and level of self-confidence were sufficiently high. In this way, we were able to agree upon a list of behavioral goals, which included such tasks as stating an opinion, asking for clarification, admitting ignorance of certain facts, etc. During therapy sessions, I guided Susan through overt and covert rehearsals of anxiety-arousing situations . . . structured homework assignments which constituted successive approximations of her behavioral goals, and had her keep records of her progress. In addition, we discussed negative statements which she was making to herself and which were not warranted by the available data (e.g., "I'm stupid"). I suggested that whenever she noticed herself making a statement of this sort, she counter it by intentionally saying more appropriate, positive statements to herself (e.g., "I'm not stupid—there is no logical reason to think that I am").

During the fifth session of therapy, Susan reported the successful completion of a presumably difficult homework assignment. Not only had she found it easy to accomplish, but, she reported, it had not aroused any anxiety, even on the first trial. . . . It was at this point that the nature of the therapeutic relationship was altered.

During future sessions, Susan rated her progress during the week, determined what the next step should be, and devised her own homework assignments. My role became that of a supervisor of a student therapist, reinforcing her successes and drawing attention to factors which she might be overlooking.

After the ninth therapy session, direct treatment was discontinued. During the following month, I contacted Susan twice by phone. She reported feeling confident in her ability to achieve her goals. In particular, she reported feeling a new sense of control over her life. My own impressions are that she had successfully adopted a behavioral problem-solving method of assessment and had become fairly adept at devising strategies for accomplishing her goals.

Follow-up

Five months after termination of treatment, I contacted Susan and requested information on her progress. She reported that she talked more than she used to in social situations, was feeling more comfortable doing things on her own (i.e., without her husband), and that, in general, she no longer felt that she was stupid. She summarized by saying: "I feel that I'm a whole step or level above where I was."

I also asked her which, if any, of the techniques we had used in therapy she was continuing to use on her own. . . . Finally, she reported that on at least three separate occasions during the 5-month period following termination of treatment, she had told another person: "I don't understand that— will you explain it to me?" This was a response which she had previously felt she was not capable of making, as it might expose her "stupidity" to the other person.

Three months after the follow-up interview, I received an unsolicited letter from Susan (I had moved out of state during that time), in which she reminded me that "one of [her] imaginary exercises was walking into a folk dancing class and feeling comfortable; well, it finally worked."*

*Source: Kirsch, I. (1978). Teaching clients to be their own therapists: A case study illustration. *Psychotherapy: Theory, Research, and Practice, 15*, 302–305. (Reprinted by permission.)

Advantages of the Case Study Method

- Case studies provide new ideas and hypotheses, opportunities to develop new clinical techniques, and a chance to study rare phenomena.
- Scientific theories can be challenged when the behavior of a single case contradicts theoretical principles or claims, and theories can receive tentative support using evidence from case studies.
- Idiographic research (the study of individuals to identify what is unique) complements nomothetic research (the study of groups to identify what is typical).

Sources of Ideas About Behavior Case studies provide a rich source of information about individuals and insights into possible causes of people's behavior. These insights, when translated into research hypotheses, can then be tested using more controlled research methods. This aspect of the case study method was acknowledged by Kirsch (1978) when discussing the successful psychotherapy with the woman named Susan. He stated that the "conclusions [of this case study] . . . should be viewed as tentative. It is hoped that the utility of [this technique] will be established by more controlled research" (p. 305). The case study method is a natural starting point for a researcher who is entering an area of study about which relatively little is known.

Opportunity for Clinical Innovation The case study method provides an opportunity "to try out" new therapeutic techniques or to try unique applications of existing techniques. The use of self-management training (SMT) in psychotherapy represents a clinical innovation because Kirsch changed the typical client–therapist relationship. The SMT approach is based on teaching clients to be their own therapists—in other words, to identify problems and design behavioral techniques for dealing with them. The client is both client and therapist, while the therapist acts as supervisor. In a similar vein, Kubany (1997) reported the effect of a "marathon" 1-day cognitive therapy session with a Vietnam War veteran suffering from multiple sources of combat-related guilt. Therapy of this kind generally occurs over many sessions, but the fact that this intensive session appeared to be successful suggests a new way to conduct this type of clinical intervention.

Method to Study Rare Phenomena Case studies are also useful for studying rare events. Some events appear so infrequently in nature that we can describe them only through the intensive study of single cases. Many of the case studies described in books by Oliver Sacks, for example, describe individuals with rare brain disorders. The study of autistic savants and other individuals with exceptional memory abilities, which we mentioned at the beginning of this chapter, are also examples of how the case study is used to investigate rare events.

Challenge to Theoretical Assumptions A theory that all Martians have three heads would quickly collapse if a reliable observer spotted a Martian with only two heads. The case study method can often advance scientific thinking by providing a "counterinstance": a single case that violates a general proposition or universally accepted principle (Kazdin, 2002). Consider a theory suggesting that the ability to process and produce human speech is to some extent based on our ability to appreciate tonality, especially in such tonally dependent languages as Chinese. The ability to process speech intonations and inflections, as well as the "sing-song" aspect of some speech, would seem to bear a resemblance to music appreciation. How would such a theory explain normal speech perception and production by someone who cannot hear music? Are there such individuals?

Oliver Sacks (2007) relates several case studies of persons with congenital "amusia," or the inability to hear music. One individual, for example, was a woman who had never heard music, at least not in the way music is heard by most of us. She could not discriminate between melodies, nor tell if one musical note was higher or lower. When asked what music sounded like to her, she replied that it was like someone throwing pots and pans on the floor. Only in her seventies was her condition diagnosed and she was introduced to others with this unusual neurological disorder. Yet she and others with amusia show normal speech perception and production. Clearly, a theory closely linking language ability and musical appreciation would need to be modified based on these case studies.

Tentative Support for a Psychological Theory   Evidence from a case study can provide tentative support for a psychological theory. Although results of case studies are not used to provide *conclusive* evidence for a particular hypothesis, the outcome of a case study can sometimes provide important evidence in support of a psychological theory.

An illustration that case studies can provide support for a theory comes from the memory literature. In the 1960s, Atkinson and Shiffrin proposed a model of human memory that was to have considerable influence on research in this field for decades to come. The model, which was based on principles of information processing, described both a short-term memory (STM) system and a long-term memory (LTM) system. Although results of numerous experiments provided evidence for this dual nature of our memory, Atkinson and Shiffrin considered the results of several case studies as "perhaps the most convincing demonstrations of a dichotomy in the memory system" (1968, p. 97). These case studies involved patients who had been treated for epilepsy via surgical removal of parts of the brain within the temporal lobes, including a subcortical structure known as the hippocampus. Of particular importance to Atkinson and Shiffrin's theory was the case study of a patient known as H.M. (see Hilts, 1995; Scoville & Milner, 1957). Following the brain operation, H.M. was found to have a disturbing memory deficit. Although he could carry on a normal conversation and remember events for a short period of time, H.M. could not remember day-to-day events. He was able to read the same magazine over and over again without finding its contents familiar. It looked as though H.M. had an intact short-term memory system but could not get information into a long-term memory system. Subsequent testing of H.M. and patients with similar memory deficits revealed that the nature of this memory problem is more complex than originally suggested, but the case study of H.M.

BOX 9.2

A SINGLE CASE THAT CONTINUES TO SHINE LIGHT ON PSYCHOLOGY

Henry Gustav Molaison, known only as H.M. to psychology researchers for more than five decades, died on December 2, 2008. He was 82, and for most of his life he lived only in the present, unaware for more than a few minutes of the contributions he was making to the field of memory research (see text). In an obituary published in the *Los Angeles Times* (T.H. Maugh, II, December 9, 2008), Nobel laureate Eric Kandel was quoted as saying, "That single case enlightened a whole body of knowledge." Yet H.M.'s contributions to science did not stop with his death. Many years ago, in consultation with a relative, H.M. agreed to donate his brain to science (see B. Carey, *The New York Times*, December 22, 2009). Researchers at the University of California, San Diego, have now stored more than 2000 slices of H.M.'s brain that will be digitally reproduced on slides for researchers around the world to examine. Thin whole-brain slicing techniques, combined with 21st-century computer technology, have the potential to reveal the brain's architecture in a way never before possible. Thank you, H.M.

continues to be important whenever theories of human memory are discussed (for example, see Schacter, 1996, and Box 9.2).

Complement to the Nomothetic Study of Behavior   Psychology (like science in general) seeks to establish broad generalizations, "universal laws" that will apply to a wide population of organisms. As a consequence, psychological research is often characterized by studies that use the nomothetic approach. The **nomothetic approach** involves large numbers of participants, and it seeks to determine the "average" or typical performance of a group. This average may or may not represent the performance of any one individual in the group. Rather, a researcher hopes to be able to predict, on the basis of this average performance, what organisms will be like "in general."

Key Concept

Some psychologists, notably Allport (1961), argue that a nomothetic approach is inadequate—that the individual is more than what can be represented by the collection of average values on various dimensions. Allport argues that the individual is both unique and lawful; the individual operates in accordance with internally consistent principles. Allport argues further that the study of the individual, called an **idiographic approach** to research, is an important goal for psychological research (see also Smith et al., 1995).

Key Concept

Allport illustrates the need for an idiographic approach by describing the task confronting the clinical psychologist. The clinician's goal "is not to predict the aggregate, but to foretell 'what any one man [sic] will do.' In reaching this ideal, actuarial predictions may sometimes help, universal and group norms are useful, but they do not go the whole distance" (p. 21). Allport suggests that our approach to understanding human nature should be neither exclusively nomothetic nor exclusively idiographic, but should represent an "equilibrium" between the two. At the very least the idiographic approach, as represented by the case study method, permits the kind of detailed observation that has the power to reveal various nuances and subtleties of behavior that a "group"

STRETCHING EXERCISE

In this exercise you are to respond to the questions that follow this brief description.

One of your friends is taking an introductory psychology class this semester, and she is describing to you over lunch her reactions to what happened in her class that morning. The topic for the day's class was adult development, and the professor described two research studies related to marriage and divorce. The professor emphasized that both studies represented excellent research that had been done by leading experts in the field. The first study involved a large sample of married couples that had been randomly selected from a well-defined population. The results of this study indicated that slightly more than half of marriages end in divorce and that factors such as persistent conflict between spouses and a family history of divorce were reliable predictors of divorce. The professor highlighted statistical analyses that confirmed the reliability of these predictors. The second study was a lengthy narrative description of a couple's experiences in therapy with a marriage and family counselor. The case study described how the couple entered therapy seriously considering divorce, but they decided after a year in therapy to stay married. The professor described several specific techniques the

therapist used while working with the couple to help them understand and deal with issues such as conflict in their marriage and a family history of divorce that put them at risk for divorce.

The class period ended before the professor had a chance to describe how the findings of these two studies were related and what conclusions about divorce could be drawn from them. How would you respond to the questions and concerns your friend had after this class?

1 One of your friend's questions is how she can decide which study's results to believe. The first study seems to say that marital conflict and a history of divorce lead to divorce, but the second study indicates that these factors need not lead to divorce. Your friend describes that she is inclined to believe the results of the second study. She finds the personal examples the professor described from the second study more compelling than the numbers he used to support the findings of the first study. What do you think?

2 Your friend also questions whether either of these studies will have implications for her own life experience. That is, can she tell based on the results of these studies whether she will experience a divorce if she someday chooses to get married? What do you think?

approach may miss. And, as you have seen, case studies have the ability to teach us about typical or average behavior by carefully studying individuals who are atypical.

Disadvantages of the Case Study Method

- Researchers are unable to make valid causal inferences using the case study method because extraneous variables are not controlled and several "treatments" may be applied simultaneously in case studies.
- Observer bias and biases in data collection can lead to incorrect interpretations of case study outcomes.
- Whether results from a case study may be generalized depends on the variability within the population from which the case was selected; some characteristics (e.g., personality) vary more across individuals than others (e.g., visual acuity).

Difficulty of Drawing Cause-Effect Conclusions   You are well aware by now that one of the goals of science is to discover the causes of phenomena—to identify unambiguously the specific factors that produce a particular event. One disadvantage of the case study method is that cause-effect conclusions can rarely be drawn on the basis of results that are obtained from case studies. This disadvantage arises primarily because researchers are unable to control extraneous variables in case studies. Thus, the behavior changes that take place in case studies can be explained by several plausible alternative hypotheses.

Consider, for instance, the treatment of Susan through SMT reported by Kirsch (1978). Although Susan apparently benefited from the SMT therapy, can we be sure that SMT *caused* her improvement? Many illnesses and emotional disorders improve without treatment. Case study researchers must always consider the alternative hypothesis that individuals may have improved *without* treatment. In addition, several aspects of the situation may have been responsible for Susan's improvement. Her care was in the hands of a "clinical psychologist" who provided reassurance. Also, Susan may have changed her attitudes toward herself because of the insights of her therapist and the feedback she received from her test results, not because of SMT. The therapist also asked Susan, as part of her therapy, to rehearse anxiety-arousing situations covertly and overtly. This technique is similar to rehearsal desensitization, which may itself be an effective treatment (Rimm & Masters, 1979).

Because several treatments were used simultaneously, we cannot argue convincingly that SMT was the unambiguous "cause" of Susan's improvement. As we have seen, Kirsch himself was sensitive to the limitations of the case study method and suggested that the inferences he drew based on the results of his study should be considered tentative until they were investigated more rigorously.

The difficulty of drawing cause-and-effect conclusions from case studies is also illustrated by results of recent research on amusia. As we noted previously, theories attempting to link music appreciation and language development appear to be weakened when individuals are discovered who have normal speech perception and speech production, but lack the ability to "hear" music. Nevertheless, there is evidence for many forms of amusia, each, most likely, with its own neural basis. Some cases involve the perception of rhythm; others the recognition of melodies; and still others an inability to recognize discordant sounds (see Sacks, 2007). Thus, more research is needed to give us a better understanding of the relationship between music and language abilities.

Potential Sources of Bias   The outcome of a case study often depends on conclusions drawn by a researcher who is both participant and observer (Bolgar, 1965). That is, a therapist observes the client's behavior *and* participates in the therapeutic process. It is reasonable to assume that the therapist may be motivated to believe that the treatment helps the client. As a result, the therapist, even if well intentioned, may not accurately observe the client's behavior. The potential for biased interpretation is not peculiar to the case study method. We have previously considered the problems of observer bias (Chapter 4) and experimenter bias (Chapter 6).

The outcome of a case may be based mainly on the "impressions" of the observer (Hersen & Barlow, 1976). For example, Kirsch (1978) described the client

Susan's "feelings" about her ability to achieve her goals and told how she reported a "sense of control" over her life. He stated that his "impressions are that she successfully adopted a behavioral problem-solving method of assessment and had become fairly adept at devising strategies for accomplishing her goals" (p. 304). A serious weakness of the case study method is that interpretation of the outcome is often based solely on the subjective impressions of the observer.

Bias can also occur in case studies when information is obtained from sources such as personal documents, session notes, and psychological tests. Archival records, as we described in Chapter 4, are open to several sources of bias. Further, when individuals provide information about themselves (self-reports), they may distort or falsify the information in order to "look good." This possibility existed in Susan's treatment. We have no way of knowing whether she exaggerated her self-reports of improvement. Another potential source of bias occurs when reports are based on individuals' memory. Cognitive psychologists have demonstrated repeatedly that memory can be inaccurate, particularly for events that happened long ago.

Problem of Generalizing from a Single Individual   One of the most serious limitations of the case study method concerns the external validity of case study findings. To what extent can we generalize the findings for one individual to a larger population? Our initial response might be that the findings for one person cannot be generalized at all. Our ability to generalize from a single case, however, depends on the degree of variability in the population from which the case was selected. For example, psychologists who study visual perception are often able to generalize their findings based on the study of one individual. Vision researchers assume that visual systems in all humans are very similar. Therefore, only one or several cases may be used to understand how the visual system works. In contrast, other psychological processes are much more variable across individuals, such as learning, memory, emotions, personality, and mental health. When studying processes that vary greatly in the population, it is impossible to claim that what is observed in one individual will hold for all individuals.

Thus, even if we accept Kirsch's (1978) conclusion regarding the effectiveness of the SMT technique of psychotherapy, we do not know whether this particular treatment would be as successful for other individuals who might differ from the client Susan in any of numerous ways, including intelligence, age, family background, and gender. As with findings from group methodologies, the important next step is to *replicate* the findings across a variety of individuals.

Thinking Critically About Testimonials Based on a Case Study

- Being mindful of the limitations of the case study method can be helpful when evaluating individuals' testimonials about the effectiveness of a particular treatment.

Case studies sometimes offer dramatic demonstrations of "new" findings or provide evidence for the "success" of a particular treatment. Consider advertisements for products you see in the media (e.g., infomercials). How many people who worry about their weight can resist the example of a formerly overweight individual who is shown to have lost considerable weight by using Product X? Evidence from case studies can be very persuasive. This is both an advantage and a disadvantage for the scientific community. Case studies demonstrating new or unusual findings may lead scientists to reconsider their theories or may lead them to new and fruitful avenues of research. Case studies, then, can help advance science.

The disadvantage of case studies, however, is that their findings are often accepted uncritically. Individuals eager to lose weight or be cured of an illness may not consider the limitations of case study evidence. Instead, the evidence offers a ray of hope for a cure. For people who have (or think they have) few alternatives, this grasping at straws may not be totally unreasonable. Too often, however, people do not consider (perhaps they do not want to consider) the reasons a particular treatment would *not* work for them.

SINGLE-SUBJECT (SMALL-*n*) EXPERIMENTAL DESIGNS

- In applied behavioral analysis, the methods developed within the experimental analysis of behavior are applied to socially relevant problems.

In the remainder of this chapter we will describe single-subject experimental (small-*n*) designs. These experimental designs have their roots in an approach to the study of behavior that was developed by B. F. Skinner in the 1930s. The approach is called an *experimental analysis of behavior*. It presents a unique behavioral view of human nature that not only contains prescriptions for the way psychologists should do research but also has implications for the way society should be organized. Several of Skinner's books, including *Walden Two* and *Beyond Freedom and Dignity,* describe how the principles derived from an experimental analysis of behavior can be put to work to improve society.

In the experimental analysis of behavior (unlike the group methodologies discussed in previous chapters), it is often the case that the sample is a single subject or a small number of subjects (small-*n*). Experimental control is demonstrated by arranging experimental conditions such that the individual's behavior changes systematically with the manipulation of an independent variable (see Figure 9.1). As Skinner (1966) commented,

> Instead of studying a thousand rats for one hour each, or a hundred rats for ten hours each, the investigator is likely to study one rat for a thousand hours. The procedure is not only appropriate to an enterprise which recognizes individuality; it is at least equally efficient in its use of equipment and of the investigator's time and energy. The ultimate test of uniformity or reproducibility is not to be found in the methods used but in the degree of control achieved, a test which the experimental analysis of behavior usually passes easily. (p. 21)

FIGURE 9.1   Applied behavior analysis is an extension of B. F. Skinner's basic research on animal behavior.

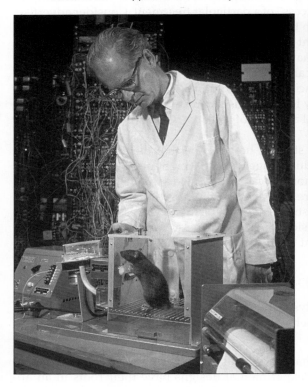

Often there is a minimum of statistical analysis associated with single-subject experimental designs. Conclusions regarding the effects of an experimental variable (treatment) typically are made by visually inspecting the behavioral record in order to observe whether behavior changes systematically with the introduction and withdrawal of the experimental treatment. Therefore, there is considerable emphasis on appropriately *defining, observing,* and *recording* behavior. Has the behavior been defined clearly and objectively so that it can be reliably observed and recorded? Will a continuous (cumulative) record of behavior be kept or will observations be made at regular intervals? Although frequency of responding is a common measure of behavior, duration of behavior or other characteristics are sometimes measured. Moreover, as you will see later in this chapter, statistical issues sometimes do arise, such as excessive variability in the behavioral record, and must be dealt with. A discussion of other statistical issues associated with single-subject research designs would necessarily go beyond our brief introduction (see, for example, Kratochwill & Levin, 1992; Parker & Brossart, 2003).

In *applied behavior analysis,* the methods that are developed within an experimental analysis of behavior are applied to socially relevant problems. These applications are frequently referred to as *behavior modification,* but when applied to clinical populations the term *behavior therapy* is preferred (Wilson, 1978). Behavior therapy is seen by many psychologists as a more effective approach to clinical treatment than that based on a psychodynamic model of therapy. Instead of seeking insight into the unconscious roots of problems, behavior therapy focuses on observable behavior. For example, self-stimulatory behaviors (e.g., prolonged body rocking, gazing at lights, or spinning) that often characterize autistic children may be conceptualized as behaviors under the control of reinforcement contingencies. In this way, clinicians and teachers may be able to control their frequency of occurrence by using behavior modification techniques (see Lovaas, Newsom, & Hickman, 1987). Numerous studies have been published showing how behavior modification and behavior therapy can be employed successfully to change the behavior of stutterers, normal and mentally impaired children and adults, psychiatric patients, and many others (see Figure 9.2). Approaches based

FIGURE 9.2   Applied behavior analysis is used to investigate methods of controlling maladaptive behavior of children and adults.

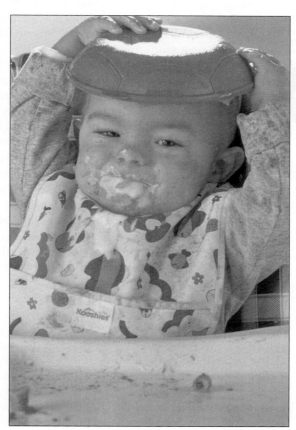

on applied behavior analysis have also been successfully used by school psychologists in educational settings (see Kratochwill & Martens, 1994). A primary source for these published studies is the *Journal of Applied Behavior Analysis*.

Characteristics of Single-Subject Experiments

- Researchers manipulate an independent variable in single-subject experiments; therefore, these designs allow more rigorous control than case studies.
- In single-subject experiments, baseline observations are first recorded to describe what an individual's behavior is like (and predicted to be like in the future) without treatment.
- Baseline behavior and behavior following the intervention (treatment) are compared using visual inspection of recorded observations.

Key Concept }

The **single-subject experiment,** as its name suggests, typically focuses on an examination of behavior change in one individual or, at most, a few individuals. However, as we will see later in this chapter, the behavior of a single "group" of individuals also may be the focus. In a single-subject experiment the researcher contrasts treatment conditions for one individual whose behavior is being continuously monitored. That is, the independent variable of interest (usually a treatment) is manipulated systematically for one individual. Single-subject experimental designs are an important alternative to the relatively uncontrolled case study method (Kazdin, 1982). Single-subject experiments also have advantages over multiple-group experiments as described in Box 9.3.

Key Concept }

The first stage of a single-subject experiment is usually an observation stage, or **baseline stage.** During this stage researchers record the subject's behavior prior to any treatment. Clinical researchers typically measure the frequency of the target behavior within a unit of time, such as a day or an hour. For example, a researcher might record the number of times during a 10-minute interview that an excessively shy child makes eye contact, the number of headaches reported each week by a migraine sufferer, or the number of verbal pauses per minute made by a chronic stutterer. Using the baseline record, researchers are able to *describe* behavior before they provide treatment. Most importantly, the baseline allows researchers to *predict* what behavior will be like in the future without treatment (Kazdin, 2002). Of course, unless behavior is actually monitored, researchers don't know for sure what future behavior will be like, but baseline measures allow them to predict what the future holds if no treatment is provided.

Once researchers observe that the individual's behavior is relatively stable—that is, it exhibits little fluctuation between recording intervals—they introduce an intervention (treatment). The next step is to record the individual's behavior with the same measures used during the baseline stage. By comparing the behavior observed immediately following an intervention with the baseline performance, researchers are able to determine the effect of the treatment. The effect of the treatment is seen most easily using a graph of the behavioral record. How did behavior change, in other words, following the experimental treatment? By visually inspecting the difference between behavior following

---

BOX 9.3

ADVANTAGES OF SINGLE-SUBJECT DESIGNS OVER GROUP DESIGNS: LESS CAN BE MORE

Single-subject experimental designs may be more appropriate than multiple-group designs for certain kinds of applied research (see Hersen & Barlow, 1976). One such situation is when research is directed toward changing the behavior of a specific individual. For example, the outcome of a group experiment may lead to recommendations about what treatments are effective "in general" in modifying behavior. It is not possible to say, however, what the effect of that treatment would be on any particular individual based on a group average. Kazdin (1982) summarizes this characteristic of single-subject experiments well: "Perhaps the most obvious advantage [of single-case experimental designs] is that the methodology allows investigation of the individual client and experimental evaluation of treatment for the client" (p. 482).

Another advantage of single-subject experiments over multiple-group experiments involves the ethical problem of withholding treatment that can arise in clinical research. In a multiple-group design, a potentially beneficial treatment must be withheld from individuals in order to provide a control group that satisfies the requirements of internal validity. Because single-subject experimental designs contrast conditions of "no-treatment" and "treatment" within the same individual, the problem of withholding treatment can be avoided. Moreover, investigators doing clinical research often have difficulty gaining access to enough clients to do a multiple-group experiment. For instance, a clinician may be able to identify only a few clients experiencing claustrophobia (excessive fear of enclosed spaces). The single-subject experiment provides a practical solution to the problem of investigating cause-effect conclusions when only a few participants are available.

---

treatment and what was predicted would occur without treatment, we can infer whether the treatment effectively changed the individual's behavior. Traditionally, the analysis of single-subject experiments has not involved the use of tests of statistical significance, but there has been some controversy about this (Kratochwill & Brody, 1978). Later in this chapter we will discuss some of the problems that can arise when visual inspection is used to determine whether a treatment was effective (see also Kazdin, 2002).

Although researchers have many design possibilities available (Hersen & Barlow, 1976; Kazdin, 1980), the most common single-subject designs are the ABAB design and multiple-baseline designs (Kazdin, 2002).

Specific Experimental Designs

- In the ABAB design, baseline (A) and treatment (B) stages are alternated to determine the effect of treatment on behavior.
- Researchers conclude that treatment causes behavior change when behavior changes systematically with the introduction and withdrawal of treatment.
- Interpreting the causal effect of the treatment is difficult in the ABAB design if behavior does not reverse to baseline levels when treatment is withdrawn.

- Ethical considerations may prevent psychologists from using the ABAB design.
- In multiple-baseline designs, a treatment effect is shown when behaviors in more than one baseline change only following the introduction of a treatment.
- Multiple baselines may be observed across individuals, behaviors, or situations.
- Interpreting the causal effect of treatment is difficult in multiple-baseline designs when changes are seen in a baseline before an experimental intervention; this can occur when treatment effects generalize.

Key Concepts }

The ABAB Design   Researchers use the **ABAB design** to demonstrate that behavior changes systematically when they alternate "no-treatment" and "treatment" conditions. An initial baseline stage (A) is followed by a treatment stage (B), next by a return to baseline (A), and then by another treatment stage (B). Because treatment is removed during the second A stage, and any improvement in behavior is likely to be reversed at this point, this design is also called a **reversal design.** The researcher using the ABAB design observes whether behavior changes immediately upon introduction of a treatment variable (first B), whether behavior reverses when treatment is withdrawn (second A), and whether behavior improves again when treatment is reintroduced (second B). If behavior changes following the introduction and withdrawal of treatment, the researcher gains considerable evidence that the treatment caused the behavior change.

Horton (1987) used an ABAB design to assess the effects of facial screening on the maladaptive behavior of a severely mentally impaired 8-year-old girl. Facial screening is a mildly aversive technique involving the application of a face cover (e.g., a soft cloth) when an undesirable behavior occurs. Previous research had shown this technique to be effective in reducing the frequency of self-injurious behaviors such as face slapping. Horton sought to determine whether it would reduce the frequency of spoon banging by the young child at mealtime. The spoon banging prevented the girl from dining with her classmates at the school for exceptional children that she attended. The banging was disruptive not only because of the noise but also because it often led her to fling food on the floor or resulted in her dropping the spoon on the floor.

A clear definition of spoon banging was made to distinguish it from normal scooping motions. Then, a paraprofessional was trained to make observations and to administer the treatment. A frequency count was used to assess the magnitude of spoon banging within each 15-minute eating session. During the initial, or baseline, period the paraprofessional recorded frequency and, with each occurrence of the response, said "no bang," gently grasped the girl's wrist, and returned her hand to her dish. The procedure was videotaped, and an independent observer viewed the films and recorded frequency as a reliability check. Interobserver reliability was approximately 96%. The baseline stage was conducted for 16 days.

The first treatment period began on Day 17 and lasted for 16 days. Each time spoon banging was observed, the paraprofessional continued to give the

FIGURE 9.3   Frequency of spoon-banging responses across baseline, treatment, and follow-up phases of study. (Adapted from Horton, 1987.)

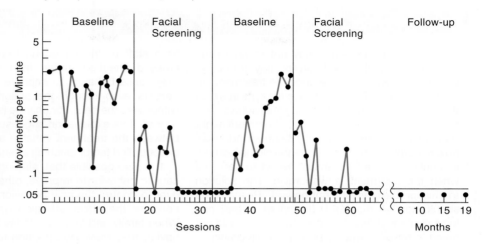

corrective feedback of "no bang" and returned the girl's hand to her dish. However, the paraprofessional now also pulled a terry-cloth bib over the girl's entire face for 5 seconds. Release from facial screening was contingent on the participant's not banging for 5 seconds. The first treatment phase was followed by a second baseline period and another treatment phase. Posttreatment observations were also made at 6, 10, 15, and 19 months.

Figure 9.3 shows changes in the frequency of the girl's spoon-banging behavior as a function of alternating baseline and treatment phases. Facial screening was not only effective in reducing this behavior during treatment phases; follow-up observations revealed that the spoon banging was still absent months later. Following the final treatment phase, the girl no longer required direct supervision during mealtime at either school or home and was permitted to eat with her peers. There was clear evidence that the application of the facial screening was responsible for eliminating the spoon banging. The facial screening was the only treatment that was administered, and visual inspection of Figure 9.3 shows that behavior changed systematically with the introduction and withdrawal of treatment. The facial-screening technique was a successful procedure for controlling the maladaptive behavior of the young child when other, less intrusive procedures had failed.

Methodological Issues Associated with ABAB Designs   A major methodological problem that sometimes arises in the context of an ABAB procedure can be illustrated by looking again at the results of the Horton (1987) study shown in Figure 9.3. In the second baseline stage, when application of the facial screening was withdrawn, spoon banging increased. That is, the improvement observed under the preceding treatment stage was reversed. What if the spoon-banging behavior had remained low even when the treatment was withdrawn? What can the researcher conclude about the effectiveness of the treatment when behavior in a second baseline stage does not revert to what it was during the

WHY REVERSAL MAY NOT OCCUR IN THE REVERSAL DESIGN

One reason the behavior may not revert to the baseline level is that the behavior may not be expected logically to change once the treatment led to improvement. This occurs in situations in which the treatment involves teaching individuals new skills. For example, a researcher's treatment might be teaching a developmentally disabled individual how to commute to work. Once the skill is learned, it is unlikely to be "unlearned" (revert to baseline) when the treatment is withdrawn. The solution to this problem is straightforward. Researchers should not use the ABAB design when they can logically expect that the target behavior would not revert to baseline when treatment is withdrawn.

What other reasons are there for behavior not to return to baseline in the second stage? One possibility is that a variable *other than* the treatment variable caused behavior to change in the first shift from baseline to treatment stages. For example, the individual may receive increased attention from staff or friends during treatment. This increased attention—rather than the treatment—may cause behavior to improve. If the attention persists even though the specific treatment is withdrawn, the behavior change is likely to persist as well. This explanation suggests a confounding between the treatment variable and some other, uncontrolled factor (such as attention).

It is also possible that, although the treatment caused behavior to improve, other variables took over to control the new behavior. Again, we can consider the effect attention has on behavior. When family and friends witness a change in behavior, they may pay attention to the individual. Think of the praise people get when they have lost weight or quit smoking. Positive reinforcement in the form of attention may maintain the behavior change that was initiated by the treatment and so we would not expect behavior to return to baseline levels when the treatment was withdrawn.

initial baseline period? In Box 9.4 we describe reasons why behavior might not revert to the baseline level when the treatment is withdrawn.

If for whatever reason behavior does not revert to baseline levels when treatment is withdrawn, researchers cannot safely conclude that the treatment caused the initial behavior change (Kazdin, 1980, 2002). The researcher must examine the situation carefully with the hope of identifying variables that might be confounding the treatment variable or replicate the procedure with different subjects (Hersen & Barlow, 1976).

Researchers can also face an ethical problem when using the ABAB design. Suppose the treatment seems to improve the individual's behavior relative to the baseline. Is it ethical to remove what appears to be a beneficial treatment to determine if the treatment actually caused the improvement? As you might imagine, withdrawing a beneficial treatment may not be justified in all cases. Some behaviors might be life-threatening or exceptionally debilitating, and it would not be ethical to remove treatment once a positive effect is observed. For example, some autistic children exhibit self-injurious behaviors such as head banging. If a clinical researcher succeeds in reducing the frequency of this behavior, it would be unethical to withdraw treatment to meet the requirements of the ABAB design. Fortunately, there is a single-case experimental design that does not involve withdrawal of treatment and that may be appropriate in such situations—the multiple-baseline design.

The Multiple-Baseline Design   The multiple-baseline design also makes use of baseline and treatment stages, but not by withdrawing a treatment as in the ABAB design. As the name suggests, researchers establish several baselines when using a multiple-baseline design. The multiple-baseline design demonstrates the effect of a treatment by showing that behaviors in more than one baseline change following the introduction of a treatment.

One example of the multiple-baseline design is to treat one person's behavior in different situations. In this case, the first step in the multiple-baseline design is to record behavior (such as the aggressiveness of a child) as it normally occurs in several situations (such as at home, in the classroom, and at an after-school daycare facility). The researcher establishes the baseline frequency of the behavior in each situation (i.e., multiple baselines). Next the treatment is introduced in one of the situations (e.g., at home), *but not* in the other situations. The researcher continues to monitor behavior in all of the situations. A critical feature of the multiple-baseline design is that treatment is applied to only one baseline at a time. The behavior in the treated situation should improve; the behavior in the baseline situations should not improve. The next step is to apply the treatment in a second situation (treatment may continue in the first situation as well) but leave the third situation as a continuing baseline. Behavior should change only in the treated situation, not in the baseline situation. The final step is to administer the treatment in the third situation; again, the behavior should change when the treatment is administered in the third situation. The key evidence for the effectiveness of a treatment in the multiple-baseline design is the demonstration that behavior changes only when the treatment is introduced.

There are several variations on the multiple-baseline design, depending on whether multiple baselines are established for different individuals, for different behaviors in the same individual, or for the same individual in different situations. Although they sound complex, multiple-baseline designs are frequently used and easily understood. We will describe each type of multiple-baseline design using an applied research example.

Key Concept } In the **multiple-baseline design across individuals,** baselines are first established for different individuals. When the behavior of each individual has stabilized, an intervention is introduced for one individual, then for another individual, later for another, and so on. As in all multiple-baseline designs, the treatment is introduced at a different time for each baseline (in this case, for each individual). If the treatment is effective, then a change in behavior will occur immediately following the application of the treatment in each individual.

An example of the use of a multiple-baseline design across individuals comes from the field of sports psychology. Allison and Ayllon (1980) were interested in evaluating the effectiveness of a coaching method that involved several behavioral techniques on the acquisition of specific football, tennis, and gymnastic skills. Although they found that the method was effective for each sport, we will describe their test of the effectiveness of behavioral coaching for the acquisition of a football skill. The participants in this experiment were second-string members of a citywide football program chosen because they "completely lacked fundamental football skills" (p. 299).

The skill to be acquired in the Allison and Ayllon (1980) study was blocking. Blocking skill was defined operationally in terms of eight elements, ranging from the body's first being behind the line of scrimmage to maintaining body contact until the whistle was blown. Behavioral coaching involved specific procedures implemented by the team coach, including systematic verbal feedback, positive and negative reinforcement, and several other behavioral techniques. The experimenter first established baselines for several different members of the football team under "standard coaching" conditions. In the standard procedure, the coach used verbal instructions, provided occasional modeling or verbal approval, and, when execution was incorrect, "loudly informed the player and, at times, commented on the player's stupidity, lack of courage, awareness, or even worse" (p. 300). In short, it was an all-too-typical example of negative coaching behavior.

The experimenter and a second observer recorded the frequency of correct blocks made in sets of 10 trials. Behavioral coaching was begun, in accordance with the multiple-baseline design, at different times for each of four football players. Results of this intervention are shown in Figure 9.4. Across four individuals, behavioral coaching was shown to be effective in increasing the frequency of correctly executed blocks. The agreement between the two observers on blocking performance ranged from 84% to 94%, indicating that the observation of behavior was reliable. The skill execution changed for each player at the point at which the behavioral coaching was introduced. Thus, there is evidence in this multiple-baseline design that the coaching method caused the change in each player's performance.

Key Concept }

A second type of multiple-baseline design involves establishing two or more baselines by observing different behaviors in the same individual, a **multiple-baseline design across behaviors.** A treatment is directed first at one behavior, then at another, and so on. Evidence for a causal relationship between treatment and behavior is obtained if performance changes for each behavior immediately after the treatment is introduced. For example, Gena, Krantz, McClannahan, and Poulson (1996) attempted to teach several different socially appropriate affective behaviors to youths with autism. As the researchers noted, children with autism often show inappropriate affective behaviors, which limit their opportunities to communicate effectively with others and to develop interpersonal relationships. Treatment included verbal praise and tokens (exchangeable for rewards) that were delivered contingent on appropriate affective responses in three or four different behavior categories. Target behaviors were selected from among the following: showing appreciation, talking about favorite things, laughing about absurdities, showing sympathy, and indicating dislike. Visual inspection of the behavioral records showed evidence for the effectiveness of the treatment for each individual. As required in the multiple-baseline design, the different affective behaviors changed immediately after introduction of the intervention for that behavior.

Key Concept }

The third major variation on the multiple-baseline design involves establishing two or more baselines for an individual's behavior across different situations, a **multiple-baseline design across situations.** For example, as we described when we introduced the multiple-baseline design, a researcher might

FIGURE 9.4 Multiple baselines showing percentage of football blocks executed correctly by four players as a function of standard coaching and behavioral coaching. (From Allison & Ayllon, 1980.)

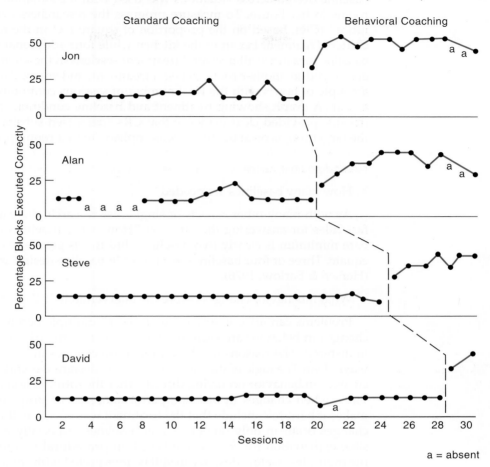

establish baselines showing the frequency of a child's aggressive behavior at home, in the classroom, and at an after-school daycare facility. As with other variations of this design, the treatment is applied at different times and the behavioral records are examined to determine whether behavior changes systematically with the introduction of treatment.

Hartl and Frost (1999) successfully treated a 53-year-old woman for compulsive hoarding. The clutter in her house took up approximately 70% of the living space such that rooms could not be used for their intended purpose. In the TV room, for example, newspapers, paid and unpaid bills, letters, and other items were piled 3 feet high on the couch and spilled onto the floor, burying a coffee table. In other rooms and hallways there were numerous gifts that the client had bought with no particular recipient in mind, the piles at time reaching the ceiling. Treatment consisted of "training in decision-making and categorization, exposure and habituation to discarding, and cognitive restructuring . . . each woven into the context of weekly excavation sessions" (p. 454). A multiple-baseline design across situations was used with the situations being different rooms in her house. To measure progress the researchers computed "clutter ratios" (CRs) based on the proportion of square feet in the room covered by clutter. Treatment began in the kitchen while four additional rooms provided baseline measures; after several treatment sessions in the kitchen, the researchers moved to another room to begin treatment, and so on. Each session lasted a couple of hours with the total number of sessions continuing for more than a year. A graph showing treatment and baseline conditions across situations (rooms) provided clear evidence that CRs "decreased substantially in each of the target rooms once treatment was applied" to that room (p. 456).

Methodological Issues Associated with Multiple-Baseline Designs

- How many baselines are needed?

As with many other aspects of single-case research, there are no hard-and-fast rules for answering the question "How many baselines do I need?" The bare minimum is clearly two baselines, but this is generally considered inadequate. Three or four baselines in a multiple-baseline design are recommended (Hersen & Barlow, 1976).

- What if behavior changes before the intervention?

Problems can arise in any of the types of multiple-baseline designs when changes in behavior are seen in a baseline before the treatment has been administered. The reasons for these premature changes in a baseline are not always clear. The logic of the multiple-baseline designs depends critically on the changes in behavior occurring directly after the introduction of the treatment. Thus, when changes in baseline performance occur prior to treatment, this makes it hard to conclude that the treatment was effective. If the pretreatment changes occur in only one of several baselines (especially if there is a plausible explanation for the change based on procedural or situational factors), the multiple-baseline design can still be interpreted with some confidence. For instance, Kazdin and Erickson (1975) used a multiple-baseline design across individuals to help severely mentally impaired individuals respond to instructions. Participants who followed instructions were reinforced with candy-coated cereal and praise, and this intervention was introduced in each of four small groups at different points in time. Performance changed directly with the application of the positive reinforcement procedure in three groups, but not in the fourth. In this group, which had the longest baseline, behavior gradually improved prior to the intervention. The researchers reasonably suggested that this occurred because individuals in this group saw other participants comply with instructions and then imitated the treated participants' behavior.

- What if the treatment generalizes to other behaviors or situations?

A problem sometimes seen in multiple-baseline designs occurs when changes in one behavior *generalize* to other behaviors or situations. When Hartl and Frost (1999) successfully treated a woman for excessive hoarding, one might speculate that treatment in one room of her house would lead her to decrease clutter in other rooms. No such decrease was observed, however, and clutter even increased slightly in the bedroom that served as a control room with no intervention.

In dealing with possible problems of generalization, researchers need to keep in mind the maxim "An ounce of prevention is worth a pound of cure." If altering the behavior of one individual is likely to affect the behaviors of others, if behavior in one situation is likely to influence behavior in another situation, or if changing one type of behavior is likely to affect other behaviors, then multiple-baseline designs may need to be modified or perhaps abandoned (Kazdin, 2002). Unfortunately, anticipating when changes will occur simultaneously in more than one baseline is not always easy, but these problems appear to be relatively infrequent exceptions to the effects usually seen in a multiple-baseline design (Kazdin, 2002). What is clear, however, is that concluding a treatment is effective using a multiple-baseline design requires that behavior changes directly follow the introduction of the treatment in each baseline.

Problems and Limitations Common to All Single-Subject Designs

- Interpreting the effect of a treatment can be difficult if the baseline stage shows excessive variability or increasing or decreasing trends in behavior.
- The problem of low external validity with single-subject experiments can be reduced by testing small groups of individuals.

Problems with Baseline Records   An ideal baseline record and response to an intervention are shown in panel A of Figure 9.5. Behavior during the baseline stage is very stable, and behavior changes immediately following the introduction of treatment. If this were the outcome of the first stages of either an ABAB or a multiple-baseline design, we would be headed in the direction of showing that our treatment is effective in modifying behavior. However, consider the baseline and treatment stages shown in panel B of Figure 9.5. Although the desired behavior appears to increase in frequency following an intervention, the baseline shows a great deal of variability. It is difficult to know whether the treatment produced the change or behavior just happened to be on the upswing. In general, it is hard to decide whether an intervention was effective when there is excessive variability in the baseline.

There are several ways to deal with the problem of excessive baseline variability. One way is to look for factors in the situation that might be producing the variability and remove them. The presence of a particular staff member, for instance, might be causing changes in the behavior of a psychiatric patient. Another approach is to "wait it out"—to continue taking baseline measures until behavior stabilizes. It is, of course, not possible to predict when and if this might occur. Introducing the intervention before behavior has stabilized, however, would jeopardize a clear interpretation of the outcome. A final way to deal with excessive variability is to average data points. By charting a behavioral record using averages of several points, researchers can sometimes reduce the "appearance" of variability (Kazdin, 1978).

FIGURE 9.5   Examples of behavioral records showing possible relationships between baseline and intervention phases of a behavior modification program. The arrow indicates the start of an intervention.

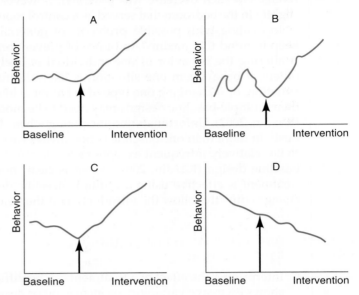

Panel C of Figure 9.5 illustrates another potential problem that can arise when baselines show an increasing or decreasing trend. If the goal of the intervention was to increase frequency of behavior, the decreasing trend shown in panel C poses no problem of interpretation. An intervention that reversed the decreasing trend can be taken as evidence that the treatment was effective. If the goal of the intervention was to reduce the frequency of a behavior, however, the problem would be more serious. This situation is illustrated in panel D. Here we see a decreasing trend in the baseline stage and continued reduction of frequency in the treatment stage. It would be difficult to know whether the treatment had an effect because the decrease following the intervention could be due to the intervention or to a continuation of the baseline trend. When an intervention is expected to have an effect in the same direction as a baseline trend, the change following the intervention must be much more marked than that shown in panel D to support a conclusion that the treatment had been effective (Kazdin, 1978). This problem becomes even more troubling because a treatment effect in a single-subject design is usually judged by visually inspecting the behavioral record. It is often difficult to say what constitutes a "marked" change in the behavioral record (see, for example, Parsonson & Baer, 1992). It is an especially good idea in these circumstances to complement the observations of the target behavior with other means of evaluation such as making comparisons with "normal" individuals or asking for subjective evaluations from others familiar with the individual.

Questions of External Validity   A frequent criticism of single-subject research designs is that the findings have limited external validity. In other words, the single-subject experiment appears to have the same limitation as the case study method. Because each person is unique, it can be argued that there is no way of knowing whether the effect of a particular intervention will generalize to other individuals. There are several reasons, however, why the external validity of findings from single-subject experiments may not be as limited as it seems.

First, the types of intervention used in single-subject experiments are often potent ones and frequently produce dramatic and sizable changes in behavior (Kazdin, 1978). Consequently, these types of treatments are often found to generalize to other individuals. Other evidence for the generality of effects based on single-subject experiments comes from the use of multiple-baseline designs. A multiple-baseline design across individuals, for example, is often able to show that a particular intervention was successful in modifying the behavior of several individuals. Similarly, multiple baselines across situations and behaviors can attest to the external validity of a treatment effect.

Perhaps the best way to establish the external validity of a treatment effect in a single-subject experiment is to test a "single group" of subjects. The procedures associated with single-subject designs are sometimes used with small groups of individuals (i.e., small-*n*). For example, Kazdin and Erickson (1975) found that positive reinforcement improved responsiveness to instructions in small groups of mentally impaired individuals. The researchers were able to demonstrate that a treatment was, on average, effective for a small group of participants as well as for individuals in the group. In a sense, the treatment effect was replicated several times across members of a group. Single-subject experiments like these offer impressive evidence for both internal and external validity.

SUMMARY

Two important single-case research designs are the case study and the single-subject experiment, or small-*n* design. The case study method can be an important source of hypotheses about behavior, can provide an opportunity for clinical innovation (e.g., trying out new approaches to therapy), can permit the intensive study of rare phenomena, can challenge theoretical assumptions, and can provide tentative support for a psychological theory. The intensive study of individuals that is the hallmark of the case study method is called idiographic research, and it can be viewed as complementary to the nomothetic approach (seeking general laws or principles) that is also characteristic of psychology. Problems arise when the case study method is used to draw cause-effect conclusions, or when biases in the collection of, or interpretation of, data are not identified. The case study method also involves potential problems of generalizing findings based on the study of a single individual. Moreover, the "dramatic" results obtained from some case studies, though they may give scientific investigators important insights, are frequently accepted as valid by people who are not aware of the limitations of this method.

B. F. Skinner developed the experimental analysis of behavior. Applied behavior analysis seeks to apply principles derived from an experimental analysis of behavior to socially relevant problems. The major methodology of these approaches is the single-subject experiment, or small-*n* research. Although there are many kinds of single-subject designs, the most common are the ABAB design and the multiple-baseline design.

An ABAB design, or reversal design, allows a researcher to confirm a treatment effect by showing that behavior changes systematically with conditions of no treatment (baseline) and treatment. Methodological problems arise in this design when behavior that changed during the first treatment (B) stage does not reverse when treatment is withdrawn during the second baseline (A) stage. When this occurs, it is difficult to establish that the treatment, rather than some other factor, was responsible for the initial change. One may encounter ethical problems when using the ABAB design if a treatment that has been shown to be beneficial is withdrawn during the second baseline stage.

A multiple-baseline design demonstrates the effectiveness of a treatment by showing that behaviors across more than one baseline change as a consequence of the introduction of a treatment. Baselines are first established across different individuals, or across behaviors or across situations in the same individual. Methodological problems arise when behavior does not change immediately with the introduction of a treatment or when a treatment effect generalizes to other individuals, other behaviors, or other situations.

Problems of excessive baseline variability as well as of increasing or decreasing baselines sometimes make it difficult to interpret the outcome of single-subject designs. The problem of excessive baseline variability can be approached by seeking out and removing sources of variability, by extending the time during which baseline observations are made, or by averaging data points to remove the "appearance" of variability. Increasing or decreasing baselines may require the researcher to obtain other kinds of evidence for the effectiveness of a treatment. Finally, the single-subject design is often criticized for its lack of external validity. However, because treatments typically produce substantial changes in behavior, these changes can often be easily replicated in different individuals. The use of single "groups" of subjects (small-*n* research) can also provide immediate evidence of generality across subjects.

KEY CONCEPTS

case study 282	multiple-baseline design across
nomothetic approach 287	individuals 299
idiographic approach 287	multiple-baseline design across
single-subject experiment 294	behaviors 300
baseline stage 294	multiple-baseline design across
ABAB design (reversal design) 296	situations 300

REVIEW QUESTIONS

1 Identify and give an example of each of the advantages of the case study method.
2 Distinguish between a nomothetic and an idiographic approach to research.
3 Identify and give an example of each of the disadvantages of the case study method.

4 What is the major limitation of the case study method in drawing cause-effect conclusions?

5 Under what conditions might a single-subject design be more appropriate than a multiple-group design?

6 Distinguish between baseline and intervention stages of a single-subject experimental design.

7 Why is an ABAB design also called a reversal design?

8 What methodological problems are specifically associated with an ABAB design?

9 Outline the general procedures and logic that are common to all the major forms of multiple-baseline designs.

10 What methodological problems are specifically associated with multiple-baseline designs?

11 What methodological problems must be addressed in all single-subject designs?

12 What evidence supports the external validity of single-subject designs?

CHALLENGE QUESTIONS

1 A case study showing how "mud therapy" was successful in treating an individual exhibiting excessive anxiety was reported in a popular magazine. The patient's symptoms included trouble sleeping, loss of appetite, extreme nervousness when in groups of people, and general feelings of arousal that led the individual always to feel "on edge" and fearful. The California therapist who administered the mud therapy was known for this treatment, having appeared on several TV talk shows. He first taught the patient a deep relaxation technique and a "secret word" to repeat over and over in order to block out all disturbing thoughts. Then the patient was asked to lie submerged for 2 hours each day in a special wooden "calm tub" filled with mud. During this time the patient was to practice the relaxation exercises and to concentrate on repeating the secret word whenever the least bit of anxiety was experienced. The therapy was very costly, but after 6 weeks the patient reported to the therapist that he no longer had the same feelings of anxiety that he reported previously. The therapist pronounced him cured and attributed the success of the treatment to immersion in the calming mud. The conclusion drawn by the author of the magazine article describing this therapy was that "it is a treatment that many people could benefit from." On the basis of your knowledge of the limitations of the case study method, answer the following questions:

   A What possible sources of bias were there in the study?

   B What alternative explanations can you suggest for the successful treatment?

   C What potential problem arises from studying only one individual?

2 A 5-year-old child frequently gets skin rashes, and the mother has been told by her family doctor that the problem is due to "something" the child eats. The doctor suggests that she "watch carefully" what the child eats. The mother decides to approach this problem by recording each day whether the child has a rash and what the child ate the day before. She hopes to find some relationship between eating a particular food and the presence or absence of the rash. Although this approach might help discover a relationship between eating certain foods and the appearance of the rash, a better approach might be one based on the logic and procedures associated with single-subject designs. Explain how the mother might use such an alternative approach. Be specific and point to possible problems that may arise in this application of behavioral methodology.

3 During the summer months, you find employment in a camp for mildly mentally impaired children. As a counselor you are asked to supervise a small group of children, as well as to look for ways to improve their attention to various camp activities that take place indoors (e.g., craft-making and sewing). You decide to explore the possibility of using a system of rewards (M&M candies) for "time on task." You realize that the camp director will want evidence of the effectiveness of your intervention strategy as well as some assurance that it will work with other children in the camp. Therefore you are to

   A Plan an intervention strategy based on reinforcement principles that has as its goal an increase in the time children spend on a camp activity.

(continued)

B Explain what behavioral records you will need to keep and how you will determine whether your intervention has produced a change in the children's behavior. You will need, for example, to specify exactly when and how you will measure behavior, as well as to justify your use of a particular design to carry out your "experiment."

C Describe the argument you will use to convince the director that your intervention strategy (assuming that it works) will work with other, similar children.

4 A teacher asks your help in planning a behavioral intervention that will help manage the behavior of a problem child in his classroom. The child does not stay at her desk when asked to do so, does not remain quiet during "quiet times," and exhibits other behaviors that disrupt the teaching environment. Explain specifically how a positive reinforcer, such as candy or small toys, might be used as part of a multiple-baseline across behaviors design to improve the child's behavior.

Answer to Stretching Exercise

1 You may be inclined to agree with your friend. Personal examples are often more compelling than quantitative evidence. In evaluating these two studies, however, it is important to recognize that they represent two different approaches to doing research. The first study represents the nomothetic approach, which relies on the study of large groups and tends to use quantitative measures to describe the groups. The second study represents the idiographic approach, which involves the intensive study of individual cases and qualitative description. After recognizing these differences in the two approaches, careful examination of the findings indicates there is no need to choose between the two studies. The first study does indicate that slightly more than half of marriages end in divorce, but this means that slightly less than half of all marriages do not end in divorce. The second study indicates that even marriages that are at risk for divorce because of such factors as conflict and a family history of divorce do not necessarily end in divorce. The second study suggests that it may take additional effort to overcome these risk factors. For example, the couple considering divorce when they entered therapy was willing to spend a year in therapy to work on their marriage. The findings of these two studies illustrate the general idea that nomothetic and idiographic research can complement rather than compete with each other.

2 Your friend's second question is an example of a general question that students of psychology often ask (and should ask): What does all this research evidence have to do with me? The findings of these two studies provide potentially useful information for your friend as she considers her future. The first study tells us that divorce does occur frequently and that certain factors have been identified as indicators of when divorce is more likely to occur. The second study tells us that marriages can succeed even when these risk factors are present. This information can be useful because it provides evidence from systematic and controlled study that complements what we can learn from our own experience. Your friend will not be able to determine based on these findings whether she will, in fact, divorce should she choose to marry. More generally, the findings of psychological research cannot yet tell us the answer to Gordon Allport's question of what any one person will do.

Answer to Challenge Question 1

A One source of bias in this case study was that the same individual served as therapist and as researcher with the commensurate problems of observer bias. A second source of bias is that the therapist based his conclusion solely on the self-reports of the patient.

B The successful treatment may have resulted from the relaxation technique alone; the use of the "secret word" in the face of anxiety; attention the patient received from the therapist; or even the high cost of the treatment.

C The major problem that arises from studying one individual is a potential lack of external validity.

CHAPTER TEN

Quasi-Experimental Designs and Program Evaluation

CHAPTER OUTLINE

OVERVIEW

In the most general sense, an experiment is a test; it is a procedure we use to find out something that we don't yet know. In this sense we experiment when we add new ingredients to a chili recipe in order to see whether they improve its taste. We experiment with new ways to catch fish by changing the lures we use. We experiment when we take a different route to our job in order to find a faster way to commute. As you no doubt recognize, however, these kinds of informal "experiments" are much different from the experiments that are typically carried out in psychological research. Experimental methods, unlike other research techniques such as observation and surveys, are viewed as the most efficient way to determine causation. But determining causation is not always easy, and in the last few chapters you were introduced to the complexity of the task facing researchers who seek to understand a phenomenon by discovering what caused it.

In this chapter we continue our discussion of experimental methods, but we focus on experiments as they are conducted in natural settings such as hospitals, schools, and businesses. You will see that the task of drawing cause-effect conclusions in these settings often becomes even more difficult, and that new problems arise when an investigator leaves the confines of the laboratory to do experiments in natural settings.

There are many reasons why researchers do experiments in natural settings. One reason for these "field experiments" is to test the external validity of a laboratory finding (see Chapter 6). That is, we seek to find out if a treatment effect observed in the laboratory works in a similar way in another setting. Other reasons for experimenting in natural settings are more practical. Research in natural settings is likely to be associated with attempts to improve conditions under which people live and work. The government may experiment with a new tax system or a new method of job training for the economically disadvantaged. Schools may experiment by changing lunch programs, after-school care, or curricula. A business may experiment with new product designs, methods of delivering employee benefits, or flexible work hours. In these cases, as is true in the laboratory, it is important to determine whether the "treatment" caused a change. Did a change in the way patients are admitted to a hospital emergency room cause patients to be treated more quickly and efficiently? Did a college energy conservation program cause a decrease in energy consumption? Knowing whether a treatment was effective permits us to make important decisions about continuing the treatment, about spending additional money, about investing more time and effort, or about changing the present situation on the basis of our knowledge of the results. Research that seeks to determine the effectiveness of changes made by institutions, government agencies, and other organizations is one goal of *program evaluation.*

In this chapter we describe obstacles to doing experiments in natural settings, and we discuss ways of overcoming these obstacles so that true experiments are done whenever possible. Nevertheless, true experiments are sometimes not feasible outside the laboratory. In these cases, experimental procedures that only approximate the conditions of laboratory experiments must be considered. We discuss several of these *quasi-experimental* techniques. We conclude by providing a brief introduction to the logic, procedures, and limitations of program evaluation.

TRUE EXPERIMENTS

Characteristics of True Experiments

- In true experiments, researchers manipulate an independent variable with treatment and comparison condition(s) and exercise a high degree of control (especially through random assignment to conditions).

As we have noted, although many everyday activities (such as altering the ingredients of a recipe) might be called experiments, we would not consider them "true" experiments in the sense in which experimentation has been discussed in this textbook. Analogously, many "social experiments" carried out by the government and those that are conducted by company officials or educational administrators are also not true experiments. *A true experiment is one that leads to an unambiguous outcome regarding what caused an event.*

True experiments exhibit three important characteristics:

1 In a true experiment some type of intervention or treatment is implemented.

2 True experiments are marked by the high degree of control that an experimenter has over the arrangement of experimental conditions, assignment of participants, systematic manipulation of independent variables, and choice of dependent variables. The ability to assign participants randomly to experimental conditions is often seen as the most critical defining characteristic of the true experiment (Judd, Smith, & Kidder, 1991).

3 Finally, true experiments are characterized by an appropriate comparison. Indeed, the experimenter exerts control over a situation to establish a proper comparison to evaluate the effectiveness of a treatment. In the simplest of experimental situations, this comparison is one between two comparable groups that are treated exactly alike except for the variable of interest.

When the conditions of a true experiment are met, any differences in a dependent variable that arise can logically be attributed to the differences between levels of the independent variable. There are differences, however, between true experiments done in natural settings and experiments done in a laboratory. A few of the most important differences are described in Box 10.1.

Obstacles to Conducting True Experiments in Natural Settings

- Researchers may experience difficulty obtaining permission to conduct true experiments in natural settings and gaining access to participants.
- Although random assignment is perceived by some as unfair because it may deprive individuals of a new treatment, it is still the best way and fairest way to determine if a new treatment is effective.

BOX 10.1

DIFFERENCES BETWEEN EXPERIMENTS IN THE LAB AND IN NATURAL SETTINGS

Experiments that are conducted outside the laboratory are likely to differ in a number of significant ways from those done in the laboratory. Not every experiment in a natural setting differs from laboratory experiments in all of these ways, of course. But if you are thinking of doing research in a natural setting, we urge you to consider the following critical issues.

Control

More than anything else, the scientist is concerned with control. Only by controlling those factors that are assumed to influence a phenomenon can we make a decision about what caused it. For instance, random assignment of participants to conditions of an experiment is a method of control used to balance individual differences across conditions. Or, researchers can hold other factors constant that are likely to influence a phenomenon. In a natural setting, a researcher may not always have the same degree of control over assignment of participants or over the conditions of an experiment that she or he would have in a laboratory. A researcher may even be asked to evaluate whether an intervention was effective without having been involved in the planning or conduct of the "experiment." This kind of "after-the-fact" evaluation is especially difficult because those conducting the study may not have considered important factors in the planning and execution of the intervention.

External validity

The high degree of control in the "artificial" environment of the laboratory that increases the internal validity of research often decreases the external validity of the findings. Experiments in natural settings may therefore need to be done in order to establish the external validity of a laboratory finding. When an experiment is done primarily to test a specific psychological theory, however, the external validity of a laboratory finding may not be all that important (e.g., Mook, 1983). In contrast, the external validity of research done in natural settings is often very important. This is especially true

when social experimentation serves as the basis for large-scale social changes, such as trying out new ways to curb drunk driving or new procedures for registering voters. Will the results of a program that is judged to be beneficial for curbing drunk driving in a midwestern state generalize to states in other areas of the country? These are, of course, questions about the external validity of research findings.

Goals

Experimentation in natural settings often has different goals from those of laboratory research (see Chapter 2). Laboratory research frequently represents *basic research* with the single goal of understanding a phenomenon—of determining how "nature" works. It may be done to gain knowledge merely for knowledge's sake. *Applied research* is also directed toward discovering the reasons for a phenomenon, but it is likely to be done only when knowing the reasons for an event will lead to changes that will improve the present situation. Experimentation in natural settings, therefore, is more likely than laboratory research to have practical goals.

Consequences

Sometimes experiments are conducted that have far-reaching impact on communities and society, affecting large numbers of people. The Head Start program for disadvantaged children and the *Sesame Street* television show were social experiments designed to improve the education of hundreds of thousands of children across the nation (see Figure 10.1). Social experiments are also carried out on a smaller scale in natural settings such as in local schools or businesses. Clearly, society's "experiments" are likely to have consequences of greater immediate impact than those of laboratory research. By contrast, the immediate consequences of a laboratory experiment can be substantial, but they are much more likely to be minimal. They may directly affect only the lives of a few researchers and of those relatively few participants recruited to participate.

FIGURE 10.1 As a social experiment, *Sesame Street* was designed to improve the education of hundreds of thousands of children.

Experimental research is an effective tool for solving problems and answering practical questions. Nevertheless, two major obstacles often arise when we try to carry out experiments in natural settings. The first problem is obtaining permission to do the research from individuals in positions of authority. Unless they believe that the research will be useful, school board presidents and government and business leaders are unlikely to support research financially or otherwise. The second, and often more pressing, obstacle to doing experiments in natural settings is the problem of access to participants. This problem can prove especially troublesome if participants are to be randomly assigned to either a treatment group or a comparison group.

Random assignment to conditions appears unfair at first—after all, random assignment requires that a potentially beneficial treatment be withheld from some participants. Suppose that a new approach to the teaching of foreign languages was to be tested at your college or university. Suppose further that, when you went to register for your next semester's classes, you were told that you would be randomly assigned to one of two sections taught at the time you selected—one section involving the old method and one involving the new method. How would you react? Your knowledge of research methods tells you that the two methods must be administered to comparable groups of students and that random assignment is the best way to ensure such comparability. Nonetheless, you might be tempted to feel that random assignment is not fair, especially if you are assigned to the section using the old (old-fashioned?) method. Let's take a closer look at the fairness of random assignment.

If those responsible for selecting the method of foreign language instruction already knew that the new method was more effective than the old method at schools such as yours, there would be little justification for testing the method again. Under such circumstances we would agree that withholding the new method from students in the control group would be unjust. If we do not know whether the new method is better, however, any approach other than conducting a true experiment will leave us in doubt about the new method's effectiveness. Random assignment to treatments—call it a "lottery" if you prefer—may be the fairest procedure for assigning students to sections. The old method of instruction, after all, was considered effective before the development of the new method. If the new method proves less effective, random assignment will have actually "protected" the control participants from receiving an ineffective treatment.

There are ways to offer a potentially effective treatment to all participants while still maintaining comparable groups. One way is to alternate treatments. For example, Atkinson (1968) randomly assigned students to receive computer-assigned instruction (the treatment) in either English or math and then tested both groups in English and math. Each group served as a control for the other on the test for which its members had not received computer-assisted instruction. After completing the experiment, both groups could then be given computer-assisted instruction in the subject matter to which they had not been previously exposed. Thus, all participants received all potentially beneficial treatments.

Establishing a proper control group is also possible if there is more demand for a service than an agency can meet. People who are waiting to receive the service can become a *waiting-list control group.* It is essential, however, that people be assigned to the waiting list randomly. People who are first in line are no doubt different on important dimensions from those who arrive last (e.g., more eager for treatment). Random assignment is necessary to distribute these characteristics in an unbiased way between treatment and comparison groups.

There will always be circumstances in which random assignment simply cannot be used. For example, in clinical trials involving tests of new medical treatments, it may be extremely difficult to get patients to agree to be randomly assigned to either the treatment group or the control (no treatment) group. As you will see, *quasi-experimental designs* can be used in these situations. The logic and procedures for these quasi-experimental designs will be described later in this chapter.

Threats to Internal Validity Controlled by True Experiments

- Threats to internal validity are confounds that serve as plausible alternative explanations for a research finding.
- Major classes of threats to internal validity include history, maturation, testing, instrumentation, regression, subject attrition, selection, and additive effects with selection.

Prior to doing an experiment, we want to consider what major classes of possible explanations can be ruled out by our experimental procedure. Only by controlling all possible alternative explanations can we arrive at a definite causal inference. In previous chapters, we referred to various uncontrolled factors that threaten the internal validity of an experiment as confounding factors (they are also called confounds). Several types of confounds were identified in earlier chapters (see especially Chapter 6). Campbell and Stanley (1966; Cook & Campbell, 1979; see also Shadish, Cook, & Campbell, 2002; West, 2010) have identified eight classes of confounds that they call **threats to internal validity.** You have already been introduced to some of these; others will be new. After reviewing these major threats to internal validity, we will be able to judge the extent to which various experimental procedures control for these kinds of alternative explanations of a treatment effect.

Key Concept

History   The occurrence of an event other than the treatment can threaten internal validity if it produces changes in the research participants' behavior. A true experiment requires that participants in the experimental group and in the control group be treated the same (have the same history of experiences while in the experiment) except for the treatment. In the laboratory, this is usually accomplished by balancing or holding conditions constant. When doing experiments in natural settings, however, the researcher may not be able to maintain a high degree of control, so confounding due to history can threaten internal validity. For example, suppose that you set out to test whether a college-level critical thinking course does, in fact, change students' thinking. And suppose further that you simply examined students' performance on a critical thinking test at the beginning of the course and then again at the end of the course. Without an appropriate comparison group, **history** would be a threat to internal validity if events other than the treatment (i.e., the critical thinking course) occurred that might improve students' critical thinking abilities. For instance, suppose many students in the course also accessed a website designed to teach critical thinking that wasn't required for the course. The students' history, now including the website experience, would confound the treatment and therefore pose a threat to the internal validity of the study.

Key Concept

Maturation   Participants in an experiment necessarily change as a function of time. They grow older, become more experienced, and so forth. Change associated with the passage of time per se is called maturation. For example, suppose a researcher is interested in evaluating children's learning over a school year using a new teaching technique. Without a proper comparison, a researcher might attribute the changes in children's performance between the beginning and the end of the school year to the effect of the teaching intervention when, in reality, the changes were simply due to a **maturation** threat to validity. That is, the children's learning may have improved simply because their cognitive abilities increased as they aged.

Key Concept

Testing   Taking a test generally has an effect on subsequent testing. Consider, for example, the fact that many students often improve from the initial test in a course to the second test. During the first test the students gain familiarity with the testing procedure and with the instructor's expectations. This familiarity then affects their performance on the second test. Likewise, in the context of a psychology experiment in which more than one test is given (e.g., in a pretest-posttest design), **testing** is a threat to internal validity if the effect of a treatment cannot be separated from the effect of testing.

Key Concept }

Instrumentation　Changes over time can take place not only in the participants of an experiment (e.g., maturation or increased familiarity with testing), but also in the instruments used to measure participants' performance. This is most clearly a possibility when human observers are used to assess behavior. For instance, observer bias can result from fatigue, expectations, and other characteristics of observers. Unless controlled for, these changes in the observers represent an **instrumentation** threat to internal validity by providing alternative explanations for differences in behavior between one observation period and another. Mechanical instruments also may change with repeated use. A researcher known to the authors once found that a machine used to present material in a learning experiment was not working the same at the end of the experiment as it was at the beginning. Measures made near the end of the experiment differed from those made at the beginning of the experiment. Thus, what looked like a learning effect was really just a change in the instrument used to measure learning.

Key Concept }

Key Concept }

Regression　Statistical **regression** is always a problem when individuals have been selected to participate in an experiment because of their "extreme" scores. Extreme scores on one test are not likely to be as extreme on a second test. In other words, a very, very bad performance, or a very, very good performance (both of which we have all experienced), is likely to be followed by a performance that is not quite so bad, or not quite so good, respectively. Consider, for instance, your best ever performance on a classroom examination. What did it take to "nail" this test? It took, no doubt, a lot of hard work. But it is also likely that some luck was involved. Everything has to work just right to produce an extremely good performance. If we are talking about an exam, then it is likely that the material tested was that which you just happened to study the hardest, or the test format was one you particularly like, or it came at a time when you were feeling particularly confident, or all of these and more. Particularly good performances are "extreme" because they are inflated (over our usual or typical performance) by chance. Similarly, an especially bad test performance is likely to have occurred because of some bad luck. When tested again (following either a very good or a very bad performance), it is simply not likely that chance factors will "gang up" the same way to give us that super score or that very poor score. We will likely see a performance closer to the average of our overall scores. This phenomenon frequently is called *regression to the mean*. Statistical regression is more likely when a test or measure is unreliable. When an unreliable test is used, we can expect scores to be inconsistent over time.

　　Now, consider an attempt to raise the academic performance of a group of college students who performed very poorly during their first semester of college (the "pretest"). Participants are selected because of their extreme performance (in this case, extremely poor performance). Let us assume that a treatment (e.g., a 10-hour study skills workshop) is then applied. Statistical regression is a threat to internal validity because we would expect these students to perform slightly better after the second semester (the "posttest") *without any treatment* simply due to statistical regression. An unknowing researcher may mistakenly confuse this "regression effect" with a "treatment effect."

Subject Attrition   As discussed in Chapter 6, a threat to internal validity occurs when participants are lost from an experiment, for example, when participants drop out of the research project. The **subject attrition** threat to internal validity rests on the assumption that the loss of participants changes the nature of the group that was established prior to the treatment—for example, by destroying the equivalence of groups established through random assignment. This might occur, for instance, if an experimental task is very difficult and causes some experimental participants to become frustrated and to drop out of the experiment. Participants who are left in the experimental group will differ from those who dropped out (and possibly from those in a control group) if for no other reason than that they were able to do the task (or at least stuck it out).

Selection   When, from the outset of a study, differences exist between the kinds of individuals in one group and those in another group in the experiment, there is a threat to internal validity due to **selection.** That is, the people who are in the treatment group may differ from people in the comparison group in many ways other than their group assignment. In the laboratory, this threat to internal validity is generally handled by balancing participant characteristics through random assignment. When one is doing experiments in natural settings, there are often many obstacles to randomly assigning participants to treatment and comparison conditions. These obstacles prevent doing a true experiment and hence present a possible threat to internal validity due to selection.

Additive Effects with Selection   Individual threats to internal validity such as history and maturation can be a source of additional concern because they can combine with the selection threat to internal validity. Specifically, when comparable groups are not formed by random assignment, there are possible problems due to additive effects of (1) selection and maturation, (2) selection and history, and (3) selection and instrumentation. For example, *additive effects of selection and maturation* could occur if first-year students in college who served as an experimental group were compared with sophomores who served as a control group. Changes in students that occur during their first year (as students gain familiarity with the college environment) might be presumed to be greater than the changes that occur during the sophomore year. These differences in maturation rates might explain any observed differences between the experimental and control groups, rather than the differences being due to the experimental intervention.

An *additive effect of selection and history* results when events occurring in time have a different effect on one group of participants than on another. This is particularly a problem when intact groups are compared. Perhaps due to events that are peculiar to one group's situation, an event may have more of an impact on that group than on another. Consider, for example, research involving an investigation of the effectiveness of an AIDS awareness campaign involving two college campuses (one treatment and one control). Nationwide media attention to AIDS might reasonably be assumed to affect students on both campuses equally. However, if a student with AIDS died at one college during the study and the story was featured in the college newspaper, we would assume that research participants at this student's college would be affected differently compared to those at the other. In terms of assessing the effect of an AIDS awareness campaign, this situation would represent an additive effect of selection and history.

Finally, an *additive effect of selection and instrumentation* might occur if a test instrument is relatively more sensitive to changes in one group's performance than to changes in another's. This occurs, for instance, when ceiling or floor effects are present. Such is the case when a group scores initially so low on an instrument (floor effect), that any further drop in scores cannot be reliably measured, or so high (ceiling effect) that any more gain cannot be assessed. As you can imagine, a threat to internal validity would be present if an experimental group showed relatively no change (due to floor or ceiling effects), while a control group changed reliably because its mean performance was initially near the middle of the measurement scale.

One of the great advantages of true experiments is that they *control* for all these threats to internal validity. As Campbell (1969) emphasizes, true experiments should be conducted when possible, but if they are not feasible, quasi-experiments should be conducted. "We must do the best we can with what is available to us" (p. 411). Quasi-experiments represent the best available compromise between the general aim of gaining valid knowledge regarding the effectiveness of a treatment and the realization that true experiments are not always possible.

Problems That Even True Experiments May Not Control

- Threats to internal validity that can occur in any study include contamination, experimenter expectancy effects, and novelty effects.
- Contamination occurs when information about the experiment is communicated between groups of participants, which may lead to resentment, rivalry, or diffusion of treatment.
- Novelty effects occur when people's behavior changes simply because an innovation (e.g., a treatment) produces excitement, energy, and enthusiasm.
- Threats to external validity occur when treatment effects may not be generalized beyond the particular people, setting, treatment, and outcome of the experiment.

Before considering specific quasi-experimental procedures, we should point out that even true experiments may not control for all possible threats to the interpretation of an experimental outcome. Although major threats to internal validity are eliminated by the true experiment, there are some additional threats that the investigator who is working in natural settings must guard against. We

BOX 10.2

EXPERIMENTAL CONTAMINATION

There are several possible effects resulting from communication between groups of experimental participants. These include (1) *resentment* on the part of individuals receiving less desirable treatments, (2) *rivalry* among groups receiving different treatments, and (3) a general *diffusion of treatments* across the groups (see Cook & Campbell, 1979; Shadish et al., 2002).

- *Resentment*   Consider a situation in which individuals have been randomly assigned to a control group. Further, assume that control group participants learn that "other" participants are receiving a beneficial treatment. What do you think might be the reaction of the control participants? One possibility is that the control participants will feel resentful and demoralized. As Cook and Campbell explain, in an industrial setting the person receiving the less desirable treatment may retaliate by lowering productivity. In an educational setting, teachers or students might "lose heart" or become angry. This effect of "leaked" information about a treatment may make a treatment look better than it ordinarily would because of the lowered performance of the control group that responds with resentment.

- *Rivalry*   Another possible effect that may occur when a control group learns about another group's good fortune is a spirit of competition or rivalry. That is, a control group might become motivated to reduce the expected difference between itself and the treatment group. As Cook and Campbell point out, this may be likely when intact groups (such as departments, work crews, branch offices, and the like) are assigned to various conditions. Realizing that another group will look better depending on how much it distinguishes itself from the control group, participants comprising the control group may be motivated to "try harder" so as not to look bad by comparison.

- *Diffusion of treatments*   Yet another possible effect of contamination is diffusion of treatments. According to Cook and Campbell, this occurs when participants in a control group use information given to others to help them change their own behavior. For example, control participants may use the information given to participants in the treatment group to imitate the behavior of individuals who were given the treatment. Of course, this reduces the differences between the treated and untreated groups and affects the internal validity of the experiment.

Key Concept }

will use the term *contamination* to describe one general class of threats to internal validity. **Contamination** occurs when there is communication of information about the experiment between groups of participants. Box 10.2 describes the several unwanted effects that can occur with contamination.

True experiments can also be affected by threats due to *experimenter expectancy effects* that occur when an experimenter unintentionally influences the results. Observer bias occurs when researchers' biases and expectancies lead to systematic errors in observing, identifying, recording, and interpreting behavior. (Various ways to control observer or experimenter effects were outlined in Chapter 4 and Chapter 6, e.g., using a double-blind procedure.)

Key Concept }

Novelty effects can occur when an innovation, such as an experimental treatment, is introduced (Shadish et al., 2002). For example, if little in the way of change or innovation has occurred for some time at a work site, employees may become excited or energized by the novelty (or newness) of their work environment when an intervention is introduced. Employees' newfound enthusiasm, rather than the intervention itself, may account for the "success" of the intervention. The opposite of a novelty effect can occur as a *disruption effect*, in which an innovation, perhaps with new work procedures, disrupts employees' work to such an extent that they cannot maintain their typical effectiveness.

One specific novelty effect has been labeled the *Hawthorne effect*. This refers to changes in people's behavior brought about by the interest that "significant others" show in them. The effect was named after events occurring at the Hawthorne plant of the Western Electric Company in Cicero, Illinois, near Chicago, between 1924 and 1932 (Roethlisberger, 1977). Studies were conducted to examine the relationship between productivity and conditions of the workplace. In one experiment, the amount of lighting in the plant was varied and worker performance was examined. Results revealed that *both* experimental and control groups increased their productivity during the study. Although there is some controversy surrounding the exact factors responsible for this effect (e.g., Parsons, 1974), a Hawthorne effect generally refers to a change in behavior that results from participants' awareness that someone is interested in them.

As one example of the Hawthorne effect, consider a study in which prisoners are chosen to participate in research examining the relationship between changes in prison-cell conditions and attitudes toward prison life (see Figure 10.2). If positive changes in prisoners' attitudes are obtained, the results could be due to the actual changes in cell conditions that were made, or they could be due to an increase in morale because prisoners saw the prison administration as expressing concern for them. Researchers working in natural settings must be conscious of the fact that changes in participants' behavior may be partially due to their awareness that others are interested in them. Thus, you can see that a Hawthorne effect represents a specific kind of reactivity (i.e., an awareness that one is being observed), which we discussed in previous chapters (especially Chapter 4).

FIGURE 10.2   Research investigating methods for improving prison life may be subject to Hawthorne effects.

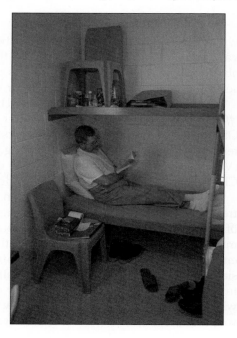

In addition to problems resulting from threats to internal validity, true experiments can be weakened by *threats to external validity*. External validity depends mainly on how representative our sample is of the persons, settings, and times to which we want to generalize. Representativeness is normally achieved through random sampling. Because random sampling is used so infrequently (see Shadish et al., 2002), however, we can rarely say that our sample of participants, or the situation in which we are making observations, or the times during which we test individuals are representative samples of all persons, settings, treatments, or outcomes. Therefore, the investigator must be aware of possible interactions between the independent variable of an experiment and, for example, the type of individual or the nature of the setting that is involved in the experiment. Is a difference, for instance, between an experimental group and a control group that is observed with volunteers from an inner-city school in the winter also likely to be found when nonvolunteers are tested in a suburban school in the spring of the year?

Cook and Campbell describe several approaches to evaluating threats to external validity; the most important is attempting to determine the representativeness of the sample. They point out, however, that *the best test of external validity is replication*. Thus, the question of external validity is best answered by repeating the experiment with different types of participants, in different settings, with different treatments, and at different times. Occasionally partial replications can be "built into" an experiment—for example, by selecting more than one group to participate. Testing schoolchildren from a lower socioeconomic group and a higher socioeconomic group in an experiment designed to determine the effectiveness of a new educational program would provide evidence of the generality of the treatment's effectiveness across these two socioeconomic groups.

QUASI-EXPERIMENTS

- Quasi-experiments provide an important alternative when true experiments are not possible.
- Quasi-experiments lack the degree of control found in true experiments; most notably, quasi-experiments typically lack random assignment.
- Researchers must seek additional evidence to eliminate threats to internal validity when they do quasi-experiments rather than true experiments.
- The one-group pretest-posttest design is called a pre-experimental design or a bad experiment because it has so little internal validity.

Key Concept

A dictionary will tell you that one definition of the prefix *quasi-* is "resembling." Quasi-experiments involve procedures that *resemble* those of true experiments. Generally speaking, **quasi-experiments** include some type of intervention or treatment and they provide a comparison, but they lack the degree of control found in true experiments. Just as randomization is the hallmark of true experiments, so *lack of randomization* is the hallmark of quasi-experiments. As Campbell and Stanley (1966) explain, quasi-experiments arise when researchers lack the control necessary to perform a true experiment.

Quasi-experiments are recommended when true experiments are not feasible. Some knowledge about the effectiveness of a treatment is more desirable than none. The list of possible threats to internal validity that we reviewed earlier can be used as a checklist in deciding just how good that knowledge is. Moreover, the investigator must be prepared to look for additional kinds of evidence that might rule out a threat to internal validity that is not specifically controlled in a quasi-experiment. For example, suppose that a quasi-experiment does not control for history threats that would be eliminated by a true experiment. The investigator may be able to show that the history threat is implausible based on a logical analysis of the situation or based on evidence provided by a supplementary analysis. If the investigator can show that the history threat is implausible, then a stronger argument can be made for the internal validity of the quasi-experiment. Researchers must recognize the specific shortcomings of quasi-experimental procedures, and they must work like detectives to provide whatever evidence they can to overcome these shortcomings. As we begin to consider the appropriate uses of quasi-experiments, we need to acknowledge that there is a great difference between the power of the true experiment and that of the quasi-experiment. *Before facing the problems of interpretation that result from quasi-experimental procedures, the researcher should make every effort possible to approximate the conditions of a true experiment.*

Perhaps the most serious limitation researchers face in doing experiments in natural settings is that they are frequently unable to assign participants randomly to conditions. This occurs, for instance, when an intact group is singled out for treatment and when administrative decisions or practical considerations prevent randomly assigning participants. For example, children in one classroom or school and workers at a particular plant represent intact groups that might receive a treatment or intervention without the possibility of randomly assigning individuals to conditions. If we assume that behavior of a group is measured both before and after treatment, such an "experiment" can be described as follows:

$$O_1 \quad X \quad O_2$$

where O_1 refers to the first observation of a group, or pretest, X indicates a treatment, and O_2 refers to the second observation, or posttest.

This *one-group pretest-posttest* design represents a pre-experimental design or, more simply, may be called a bad experiment. Any obtained difference between the pretest and posttest scores could be due to the treatment *or* to any of several threats to internal validity, including history, maturation, testing, and instrumentation threats (as well as experimenter expectancy effects and novelty effects). The results of a bad experiment are inconclusive with respect to the effectiveness of a treatment. Fortunately, there are quasi-experiments that improve upon this pre-experimental design.

The Nonequivalent Control Group Design

- In the nonequivalent control group design, a treatment group and a comparison group are compared using pretest and posttest measures.

STRETCHING EXERCISE

In this exercise we ask you to consider possible threats to internal validity in this brief description of a one-group pretest-posttest design.

A psychologist interested in the effect of a new therapy for depression recruited a sample of 20 individuals who sought relief from their depression. At the beginning of the study he asked all participants to complete a questionnaire about their symptoms of depression. The mean depression score for the sample was 42.0 (the highest possible score is 63.0), indicating severe depressive symptoms. (Individuals who are not depressed typically score in the 0 to 10 range on this measure.) During the next 16 weeks the psychologist treated participants in the study with the new treatment. At the end of the treatment the participants completed the depression questionnaire again. The mean score for the posttest was 12.0, indicating that, on average,

participants' depression symptoms were dramatically reduced and indicated only mild depression. The psychologist concluded that the treatment was effective; that is, the treatment caused their depressive symptoms to improve.

Cause-and-effect statements, such as the one made by this psychologist, are essentially impossible to make when the one-group pretest-posttest design is used. To understand why this is true, we ask you to think of potential threats to internal validity in this study.

1 How might a *history* effect threaten the internal validity of this study?
2 Explain how *maturation* likely plays a role in this study.
3 Are *testing* and *instrumentation* threats likely in this study?
4 Explain how *statistical regression* might influence the interpretation of these findings.

- If the two groups are similar in their pretest scores prior to treatment but differ in their posttest scores following treatment, researchers can more confidently make a claim about the effect of treatment.
- Threats to internal validity due to history, maturation, testing, instrumentation, and regression can be controlled in a nonequivalent control group design.

The one-group pretest-posttest design can be modified to create a quasi-experimental design with greatly superior internal validity if two conditions are met: (1) there exists a group "like" the treatment group that can serve as a comparison group, and (2) there is an opportunity to obtain pretest and posttest measures from individuals in both the treatment and the comparison groups. Campbell and Stanley (1966) call a quasi-experimental procedure that meets these two conditions a **nonequivalent control group design.** Because a comparison group is selected on bases other than random assignment, we cannot assume that individuals in the treatment and control groups are equivalent on all important characteristics (i.e., a selection threat arises). Therefore, it is essential that a pretest be given to both groups to assess their similarity on the dependent measure. A nonequivalent control group design can be outlined as follows:

Key Concept

$$O_1 \ X \ O_2$$
$$- - - - - -$$
$$O_1 \qquad O_2$$

The dashed line indicates that the treatment and comparison groups were not formed by assigning participants randomly to conditions.

By adding a comparison group, researchers can control threats to internal validity due to history, maturation, testing, instrumentation, and regression. A brief review of the logic of experimental design will help show why this occurs. We wish to begin an experiment with two similar groups; then one group receives the treatment and the other does not. If the two groups' posttest scores differ following treatment, we first must rule out alternative explanations before we can claim that treatment caused the difference. If the groups are truly comparable, and both groups have similar experiences (except for the treatment), then we can assume that history, maturation, testing, instrumentation, and regression effects occur to both groups equally. Thus, we may assume that both groups change naturally at the same rate (maturation), experience the same effect of multiple testing, or are exposed to the same external events (history). If these effects are experienced in the *same* way by both groups, they cannot possibly be used to account for group *differences* on posttest measures. Therefore, they no longer are threats to internal validity. Thus, researchers gain a tremendous advantage in their ability to make causal claims simply by adding a comparison group. These causal claims, however, depend critically on forming comparable groups at the start of the study, and ensuring that the groups then have comparable experiences, except for the treatment. Because this is difficult to realize in practice, as we'll see, threats to internal validity due to additive effects with selection typically are not eliminated in this design.

As you approach the end of a course on research methods in psychology, you might appreciate learning about the results of a nonequivalent control group design that examined the effect of taking a research methods course on reasoning about real-life events (VanderStoep & Shaughnessy, 1997). Students enrolled in two sections of a research methods course (and who happened to be using an edition of this textbook) were compared with students in two sections of a developmental psychology course on their performance on a test emphasizing methodological reasoning about everyday events. Students in both kinds of classes were administered tests at the beginning and at the end of the semester. Results revealed that research methods students showed greater improvement than did students in the control group. Taking a research methods course improved students' ability to think critically about real-life events.

With that bit of encouraging news in mind, let us now examine in detail another study using a nonequivalent control group design. This will give us the opportunity to review both the specific strengths and limitations of this quasi-experimental procedure.

Nonequivalent Control Group Design: The Langer and Rodin Study

- Quasi-experiments often assess the overall effectiveness of a treatment that has many components; follow-up research may then determine which components are critical for achieving the treatment effect.

Langer and Rodin (1976) hypothesized that environmental changes associated with old age contribute, in part, to feelings of loss, inadequacy, and low self-esteem among the elderly. Of particular importance is the change that occurs when elderly persons move into a nursing home. Although they usually care for the elderly quite adequately in physical terms, nursing homes often provide what Langer and Rodin call a "virtually decision-free" environment. The elderly are no longer called on to make even the simplest decisions, such as what time to get up, whom to visit, what movie to watch, and the like. In a nursing home, many or most of these everyday decisions are made for the elderly, leaving them with little personal responsibility and choice.

To test the hypothesis that the lack of opportunity to make personal decisions contributes to the psychological and even the physical debilitation sometimes seen in the elderly, Langer and Rodin carried out a quasi-experiment in a Connecticut nursing home. The independent variable was the type of responsibility given to two groups of nursing home residents. One group was informed of the many decisions they needed to make regarding how their rooms were arranged, visiting, care of plants, movie selection, and so forth. These residents were also given a small plant as a gift (if they decided to accept it) and told to take care of it as they wished. This was the responsibility-induced condition. The second group of residents, the comparison group, was also called together for a meeting, but instructions for this group stressed the staff's responsibility for them. These residents also received a plant as a gift (whether they chose to have one or not) and were told the nurses would water and care for the plants for them.

Residents of the nursing home had been assigned to a particular floor and room on the basis of availability, and some residents had been there for a long time. As a consequence, randomly assigning residents to the two responsibility groups was impractical—and probably undesirable from the administration's point of view. Therefore, the two sets of responsibility instructions were given to residents on two different floors of the nursing home. These floors were chosen, in the words of the authors, "because of similarity in the residents' physical and psychological health and prior socioeconomic status, as determined from evaluations made by the home's director, head nurses, and social worker" (Langer & Rodin, 1976, p. 193). The floors were randomly assigned to one of the two treatments. In addition, questionnaires were given to residents 1 week before and 3 weeks after the responsibility instructions. The questionnaires contained items that related to "how much control they felt over general events in their lives and how happy and active they felt" (p. 194). Furthermore, staff members on each floor were asked to rate the residents, before and after the experimental manipulation, on such traits as alertness, sociability, and activity. The investigators also included a clever posttest measure of social interest by holding a competition that asked participants to guess the number of jelly beans in a large jar. Residents entered the contest if they wished by simply filling out a piece of paper giving their estimate and name. Thus, there were a number of dependent variables to assess the residents' perceptions of control, happiness, activity, interest level, and so forth.

The Langer and Rodin study nicely illustrates the procedures of a nonequivalent control group design (see Figure 10.3). Moreover, differences between

FIGURE 10.3   Langer and Rodin (1976) used a nonequivalent control group design to study the effect of two different types of responsibility instructions on the behavior of nursing home residents. Because a "true experiment" was not conducted, the researchers examined features of the study to determine if any threats to internal validity were present.

pretest and posttest measures showed that the residents in the responsibility-induced group were generally happier, more active, and more alert following the treatment than were residents in the comparison group. Behavioral measures such as frequency of movie attendance also favored the responsibility-induced group, and, although 10 residents from this group entered the jelly bean contest, only 1 resident from the comparison group participated! The investigators point to possible practical implications of these findings. Specifically, they suggest that some of the negative consequences of aging can be reduced or reversed by giving the elderly the opportunity to make personal decisions and to feel competent.

Before turning to the specific limitations associated with this design, let us call your attention to another feature of the Langer and Rodin study, one that characterizes many experiments in natural settings. The treatment in the Langer and Rodin study actually had several components. For example, residents in the treatment group were encouraged by the staff to make decisions about a number of different things (e.g., movies, rooms, etc.), and they were offered a plant to take care of. The experiment evaluated, however, the treatment "package." That is, the effectiveness of the overall treatment, not individual components of the treatment, was assessed. We only know (or at least we assume based on the evidence) that the treatment with all its components worked; we don't necessarily know whether the treatment would work with fewer components or whether one component is more critical than others.

Research in natural settings is often characterized by treatments with many components. Moreover, the initial goal of such research is often to assess the overall effect of the treatment "package." Finding evidence for an overall treatment effect, therefore, may be only the first stage in a research program if we want to identify the critical elements of a treatment. There may be practical as well as theoretical benefits to such identification. On practical grounds, should research reveal that only some of the treatment's features are critical to produce the effect, then perhaps the less critical features could be dropped. This may make the treatment more cost-effective and more likely to be adopted and carried out. From a theoretical standpoint, it is important to determine whether components of the treatment specified by a theory as being critical are, indeed, the critical components. When you hear about research showing an overall treatment effect you might think about how additional research could reveal what specific components are critical to the treatment's effect.

Sources of Invalidity in the Nonequivalent Control Group Design

- To interpret the findings in quasi-experimental designs, researchers examine the study to determine if any threats to internal validity are present.
- The threats to internal validity that must be considered when using the nonequivalent control group design include additive effects with selection, differential regression, observer bias, contamination, and novelty effects.
- Although groups may be comparable on a pretest measure, this does not ensure that the groups are comparable in all possible ways that are relevant to the outcome of the study.

According to Cook and Campbell (1979), the nonequivalent control group design generally controls for all major classes of potential threats to internal validity except those due to additive effects of (1) selection and maturation, (2) selection and history, (3) selection and instrumentation, and (4) those due to differential statistical regression. We will explore how each of these potential sources of invalidity might pose problems for Langer and Rodin's interpretation of their findings. We will then explain how Langer and Rodin offered both logical argument and empirical evidence to refute the possible threats to the internal validity of their study. We will also examine how experimenter bias and problems of contamination were controlled. Finally, we will comment briefly on challenges of establishing external validity that are inherent in the nonequivalent control group design.

An important initial finding in Langer and Rodin's study was that the residents in the two groups did not differ significantly on the pretest measures. It would not have been surprising to find a difference between the two groups before the treatment was introduced because the residents were not randomly assigned to conditions. Even when pretest scores show no difference between groups, however, we cannot assume that the groups are "equivalent" (Campbell & Stanley, 1966). We will explain why we cannot conclude that the groups are equivalent in the discussion that follows.

Selection-Maturation Effect   An additive effect of selection and maturation occurs when individuals in one group grow more experienced, more tired, or more bored at a faster rate than individuals in another group (Shadish et al., 2002). A selection-maturation effect is more likely to be a threat to internal validity when the treatment group is self-selected (the members deliberately sought out exposure to the treatment) and when the comparison group is from a different population from the treatment group (Campbell & Stanley, 1966). Langer and Rodin selected their groups (but not individuals) randomly from the same population of individuals. Consequently, their design more closely approaches a true experiment than it would if individuals in the two groups had come from different populations (Campbell & Stanley, 1966). A selection-maturation effect would have been more likely, for example, if residents in a nursing home were compared with those attending a sheltered workshop program for the elderly, or if residents on different floors of a nursing facility require different levels of care.

The possibility of a selection-maturation effect is one reason we cannot conclude the groups are equivalent (comparable) even when pretest scores are the same on average for the treatment and control groups. The natural growth rate of two groups from different populations might be different, but the pretest may have been taken at a time when both groups happened to be about the same. This problem is illustrated in Figure 10.4. The normal rate of change is greater in Group A than in Group B, but the pretest is likely to show that the groups do not differ. Because of the differential growth rate, however, the groups would probably show a difference at the posttest that could be mistaken for a treatment effect. There is a second, and more general,

FIGURE 10.4   Possible differential growth rates for two groups (A and B) in the absence of treatment.

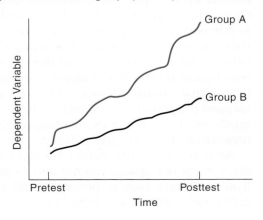

reason why we cannot conclude that groups are comparable based only on the absence of a difference between the groups on the pretest. The pretest is likely to measure respondents on only one measure, or at best on a few measures. The mere fact that individuals do not differ on one measure does not mean they don't differ on other measures that are relevant to their behavior in this situation.

Is there any reason to suspect a selection-maturation effect in the Langer and Rodin study? That is, would it be reasonable to expect that residents on the treatment floor would change naturally at a faster rate than would patients on the no-treatment floor? Several kinds of evidence suggest that this would not be the case. First, the procedure the nursing home used to assign residents to the two floors was basically random, and the floors were assigned randomly to the treatment and no-treatment conditions. Langer and Rodin also reported that the residents of the two floors were, on the average, equivalent on measures such as socioeconomic status and length of time at the nursing home. Finally, although it is not sufficient evidence in itself, residents on the two floors did not differ on the pretest measures. Thus, the evidence strongly indicates that there was not a threat to the internal validity of the Langer and Rodin study due to the additive effects of selection and maturation.

Selection-History Effect   Another threat to internal validity that is not controlled in the nonequivalent control group design is the additive effect of selection and history. Cook and Campbell (1979) refer to this problem as *local history effects*. This problem arises when an event other than the treatment affects one group and not the other. Local history, for example, could be a problem in the Langer and Rodin study if an event affecting the residents' happiness and alertness occurred on one floor of the nursing home but not on the other. You can probably imagine a number of possibilities. A change in nursing staff on one floor, for instance, might bring about either an increase or a decrease in residents' morale, depending on the nature of the change and any differences between the behavior of a new nurse and that of the previous one. Problems of local history become more problematic the more the settings of the individuals in the treatment and comparison groups differ. Langer and Rodin do not specifically address the problem of local history effects.

Selection-Instrumentation Effect   A threat due to the combination of selection and instrumentation occurs when changes in a measuring instrument are more likely to be detected in one group than they are in another. Floor or ceiling effects, for instance, could make it difficult to detect changes in behavior from pretest to posttest. If this is more of a problem in one group than in another, a selection-instrumentation effect is present. Shadish et al. (2002) point out that this threat to internal validity is more likely to be a problem the greater the nonequivalence of the groups and the closer the group scores are to the end of the scale. Because Langer and Rodin's groups did not differ on the pretest, and because performance of the groups did not suggest floor or ceiling effects on the measurement scales that were used, this threat to internal validity seems implausible in their study.

Differential Statistical Regression   The final threat to internal validity that is not controlled in the nonequivalent control group design is differential statistical regression (Shadish et al., 2002). As we described earlier, regression toward the mean is to be expected when individuals are selected on the basis of extreme scores (e.g., the poorest readers, the workers with the lowest productivity, the patients with the most severe problems). *Differential regression* can occur when regression is more likely in one group than in another. For example, consider a nonequivalent control group design in which the participants with the most serious problems are placed in the treatment group. It is possible, even likely, that regression would occur for this group. The changes from pretest to posttest may be mistakenly interpreted as a treatment effect if regression is more likely in the treatment group than in the control group. Because the groups in the Langer and Rodin study came from the same population and there is no evidence that one group's pretest scores were more extreme than another's, a threat to internal validity due to differential statistical regression is not plausible in their study.

Expectancy Effects, Contamination, and Novelty Effects   Langer and Rodin's study could also have been influenced by three additional threats to internal validity that can even affect true experiments—expectancy effects, contamination, and novelty effects. If observers in their study had been aware of the research hypothesis, it is possible that they inadvertently might have rated residents as being better after the responsibility instructions than before. This observer bias, or expectancy effect, appears to have been controlled, however, because all the observers were kept unaware of the research hypothesis. Langer and Rodin were also aware of possible contamination effects. Residents in the control group might have become demoralized if they learned that residents on another floor were given more opportunity to make decisions. In this case, the use of different floors of the nursing home was advantageous; Langer and Rodin (1976) indicate that "there was not a great deal of communication between floors" (p. 193). Thus, contamination effects do not seem to be present, at least on a scale that would destroy the internal validity of the study.

Novelty effects would be present in the Langer and Rodin study if residents on the treatment floor gained enthusiasm and energy as a result of the innovative responsibility-inducing treatment. Thus, this new enthusiasm, rather than treatment residents' increased responsibility, may explain any treatment effects. In addition, the special attention given the treatment group may have produced a Hawthorne effect in which residents on the treated floor felt better about themselves. It is difficult to rule out completely novelty effects or a Hawthorne effect in this study. According to the authors, however, "There was no difference in the amount of attention paid to the two groups" (p. 194). In fact, communications to both groups stressed that the staff cared for them and wanted them "to be happy." Thus, without additional evidence to the contrary, we can conclude that the changes in behavior Langer and Rodin observed were due to the effect of the independent variable, not to the effect of an extraneous variable that the investigators failed to control.

For investigators to decide whether an independent variable "worked" in the context of a particular experiment, they must systematically collect and carefully weigh evidence for and against the interpretation that the treatment caused behavior to change. As Cook and Campbell (1979) explain:

> Estimating the internal validity of a relationship is a deductive process in which the investigator has to systematically think through how each of the internal validity threats may have influenced the data. Then, the investigator has to examine the data to test which relevant threats can be ruled out. In all of this process, the researcher has to be his or her own best critic, trenchantly examining all of the threats he or she can imagine. When all of the threats can plausibly be eliminated, it is possible to make confident conclusions about whether a relationship is probably causal. When all of them cannot, perhaps because the appropriate data are not available or because the data indicate that a particular threat may indeed have operated, then the investigator has to conclude that a demonstrated relationship between two variables may or may not be causal. (pp. 55–56)

The Issue of External Validity

- Similar to internal validity, the external validity of research findings must be critically examined.
- The best evidence for the external validity of research findings is replication with different populations, settings, and times.

We must make the same systematic inquiry into the external validity of a quasi-experiment that we did into its internal validity. What evidence is there that the particular pattern of results is restricted to a particular group of participants, setting, or time? For example, although Langer and Rodin suggest that certain changes be made in the way the elderly are cared for, we might question whether the effectiveness of the responsibility-inducing treatment would hold for all elderly residents, for all types of nursing facilities, and at different times. That the particular nursing home selected by Langer and Rodin (1976) was described as "rated by the state of Connecticut as being among the finest care units" (p. 193) suggests that the residents, facilities, and staff might be different from those found in other facilities. For instance, if residents at this particular nursing home were relatively more independent before coming to the home than residents at other homes (perhaps because of differences in socioeconomic status), then the changes experienced upon moving into a home might have had greater impact on them. Consequently, the opportunity to be more independent of staff might be more important to these residents relative to residents in other homes. Similarly, if staff members at this home were more competent than those at other homes, they might be more effective in communicating with the residents than would the staff members at other homes.

In the last analysis, the investigator must be ready to *replicate* an experimental finding with different populations, settings, and times in order to establish external validity. The deductive process applied to questions of internal validity must also be used to examine a study's external validity. Moreover, *we must be ready to live with the fact that one study is not likely to answer all questions about a research hypothesis.*

Interrupted Time-Series Designs

- In a simple interrupted time-series design, researchers examine a series of observations both before and after a treatment.
- Evidence for treatment effects occurs when there are abrupt changes (discontinuities) in the time-series data at the time treatment was implemented.
- The major threats to internal validity in the simple interrupted time-series design are history effects and changes in measurement (instrumentation) that occur at the same time as the treatment.

Key Concept

A second quasi-experiment, a **simple interrupted time-series design,** is possible when researchers can observe changes in a dependent variable for some time before and after a treatment is introduced (Shadish et al., 2002). The essence of this design is the availability of periodic measures before and after a treatment has been introduced. The simple interrupted time-series design can be outlined in the following way:

$$O_1 \ O_2 \ O_3 \ O_4 \ O_5 \ X \ O_6 \ O_7 \ O_8 \ O_9 \ O_{10}$$

The simple interrupted time-series design can be used to assess the effect of a treatment in situations such as when a new product has been introduced, a new social reform instituted, or a special advertising campaign begun. Campbell (1969) investigated the effect of a social policy change in Connecticut in the mid-1950s. The governor had ordered a crackdown on speeding, and Campbell made use of an interrupted time-series design to determine the effect of this order on traffic fatalities. Campbell was able to obtain a wealth of archival data to use as pretreatment and posttreatment measures because statistics related to traffic accidents are regularly kept by state agencies. Besides number of fatalities, Campbell looked at number of speeding violations, number of drivers having their licenses suspended, and other measures related to driving behavior. Figure 10.5 shows the percentage of suspensions of licenses for speeding (as a percentage of all license suspensions) before and after the crackdown. There is a clear discontinuity in the graph that coincides with the onset of the treatment. This discontinuity provides evidence for an effect of the treatment. Indeed, *a discontinuity in the time series is the major evidence of an effect of treatment.*

As Campbell points out, only abrupt changes in the time-series graph can be interpreted because gradual changes are indistinguishable from normal fluctuations over time. Unfortunately, changes often are not nearly so dramatic as those seen in Figure 10.5. In fact, Campbell's analysis of traffic fatalities over the same time period did reveal evidence for an effect of the crackdown, but the change in traffic fatalities was not as abrupt as that associated with suspension of drivers' licenses (see Campbell, 1969, Figure 2).

A variation of the interrupted time-series design was used to assess the effect of avoiding the "dread risk of flying" following the terrorist attacks on the United States on September 11, 2001 (Gigerenzer, 2004). The rationale for this study was as follows. People tend to fear "dread risks," which are defined

FIGURE 10.5 Suspensions of licenses for speeding, as a percentage of all suspensions. (From Campbell, 1969.)

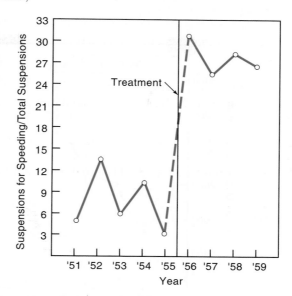

as "low-probability, high-consequence events, such as the terrorist attacks on September 11, 2001" (Gigerenzer, 2004, p. 286). If Americans, in order to avoid the dread risk of flying, instead drove to their destinations, then an increase in traffic fatalities would be expected. To test this hypothesis, Gigerenzer (2004) examined data from the U.S. Department of Transportation for the 3 months following September 11, 2001. Data also were analyzed for the 5 years prior to that date. The mean number of fatalities in these preceding years was compared with the numbers after September 11, 2001. The results of this analysis are seen in Figure 10.6.

The graph shows fatal traffic accidents for all 12 months of the year for both the preceding 5 years (circles depict the means in the graphed line) and for the year 2001 (depicted by squares). In addition, the highest and lowest values for each month in the preceding 5 years are shown (the bars around each mean). The data for fatalities during October, November, and December reveal that in the year 2001, the number of fatal traffic accidents was as high as or higher than the highest value for the preceding 5 years. On the basis of these data (and statistical analyses), Gigerenzer (2004) was able to conclude that traffic fatalities increased by 353 people in October, November, and December 2001. He attributed this increase to Americans' dread fear of flying following the events of 9/11. Gigerenzer compared this increase of 353 deaths to the 266 passengers and crew who were killed in the four plane crashes (and of course many more on the ground). The researcher suggested that "if the public were better informed about psychological reactions to catastrophic events, and the potential risk of avoiding risk," perhaps this "psychologically motivated toll" could be prevented (p. 287).

FIGURE 10.6   Number of fatal traffic accidents in the United States in 1996 through 2000, versus 2001. The graphed line represents the means for the years 1996–2000; the bars around the means indicate the lowest and highest values for those years. The squares indicate the numbers of fatal traffic accidents for each month in 2001. (From Gigerenzer, 2004.)

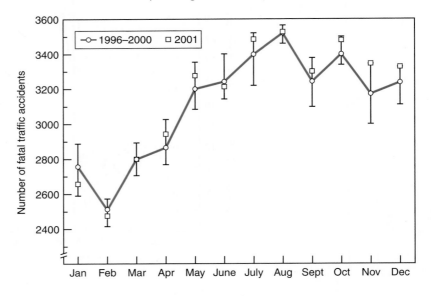

Although results of the interrupted time-series design and other quasi-experimental designs are sometimes able to be interpreted on the basis of visual inspection (see, for example, Figure 10.5), statistical analyses are often needed. Gigerenzer (2004), for example, used a chi-square test of statistical significance to demonstrate that there was a statistically significant increase in the frequency of traffic fatalities following September 11, 2001, compared to the preceding 5 years. We previously mentioned the chi-square test in Chapter 5. In other situations, more sophisticated analyses may need to be conducted (e.g., Michielutte, Shelton, Paskett, Tatum, & Velez, 2000). For more information, refer to Shadish et al.'s (2002) text, *Experimental and Quasi-Experimental Designs for Generalized Causal Inference.*

Campbell and Stanley (1966) summarize the problem facing researchers using the simple interrupted time-series design: "The problem of internal validity boils down to the question of plausible competing hypotheses that offer likely alternate explanations of the shift in the time series other than the effect of X" (p. 39). An effect of history is the main threat to internal validity in this type of design (Shadish et al., 2002). For instance, is it possible that some factor other than avoiding "dread risk" was responsible for the increase in fatal traffic accidents in the last months of 2001 (see Figure 10.6)?

Particularly threatening to the internal validity of the time-series design are influences of a cyclical nature, including seasonal variation (Cook & Campbell,

1979). For instance, when analyzing the effect of the Connecticut governor's crackdown on speeding, Campbell (1969) gathered data from neighboring states to rule out possible regional trends due to weather in order to strengthen his case for the effect of this particular social policy change.

Instrumentation must also be considered a threat to internal validity in the simple interrupted time-series design (Shadish et al., 2002). When new programs or new social policies are instituted, for example, there are often accompanying changes in the way records are kept or in the procedures used to collect information. A program intended to reduce crime may lead authorities to modify their definitions of particular crimes or to become more careful when observing and reporting criminal activities. Nevertheless, for an instrumentation threat to be plausible, the changes in instrumentation must be shown to have occurred at *exactly* the time as the intervention (Campbell & Stanley, 1966). Threats to internal validity due to maturation, testing, and regression are controlled in the simple interrupted time-series design. None of these threats can be ruled out when only a single pretest and posttest measure is available. These threats are nearly eliminated, however, by the presence of multiple observations both before and after treatment. For example, an effect of maturation would not normally be expected to show a sharp discontinuity in the time series, although this might be possible in some situations (Campbell & Stanley, 1966).

Threats to external validity in the simple interrupted time-series design must be examined carefully. When pretreatment observations of behavior are based on multiple tests, then it is very likely that an effect of the treatment may be restricted to those individuals who have had these multiple test experiences. Moreover, the interrupted time-series design generally involves testing only a single group that has not been randomly selected. This aspect of the design leaves open the possibility that the results are limited to people with characteristics similar to those who took part in the study.

Time Series with Nonequivalent Control Group

- In a time series with nonequivalent control group design, researchers make a series of observations before and after treatment for both a treatment group and a comparable comparison group.

Key Concept }

The internal validity of the interrupted time-series design can be enhanced greatly by including a control group following the procedures we described earlier for the nonequivalent control group design. For the **time series with nonequivalent control group design** the researcher must find a group that is comparable to the treatment group and that allows a similar opportunity for multiple observations before and after the time that the treatment is administered to the experimental group. This design is outlined as follows:

$$O_1\ O_2\ O_3\ O_4\ O_5\ \ X\ \ O_6\ O_7\ O_8\ O_9\ O_{10}$$

$$O_1\ O_2\ O_3\ O_4\ O_5\ \ \ \ \ \ O_6\ O_7\ O_8\ O_9\ O_{10}$$

As before, a dashed line is used to indicate that the control group and the experimental group were not randomly assigned. The interrupted time series with nonequivalent control group design permits researchers to rule out many threats due to history. As was mentioned earlier, Campbell (1969) used traffic-fatality data obtained from neighboring states to provide a comparison with traffic-fatality data following the crackdown on speeding in Connecticut. Although traffic fatalities in Connecticut showed a decline immediately following the crackdown, data from comparable states did not exhibit any such decline. This finding tends to rule out claims that the decrease in traffic fatalities in Connecticut were due to factors such as favorable weather conditions, improved automobile design, or any other factors that were likely shared by Connecticut and the neighboring states.

PROGRAM EVALUATION

- Program evaluation is used to assess the effectiveness of human service organizations and provide feedback to administrators about their services.
- Program evaluators assess needs, process, outcome, and efficiency of social services.
- The relationship between basic research and applied research is reciprocal.
- Despite society's reluctance to use experiments, true experiments and quasi-experiments can provide excellent approaches for evaluating social reforms.

Organizations that produce goods have a ready-made index of success. If a company is set up to make microprocessors, its success is ultimately determined by its profits from the sale of microprocessors. At least theoretically, the efficiency and effectiveness of the organization can be easily assessed by examining the company's financial ledgers. Increasingly, however, organizations of a different sort play a critical role in our society. Because these organizations typically provide services rather than goods, Posavac (2011) refers to them as human service organizations. For example, hospitals, schools, police departments, and government agencies provide a variety of services ranging from emergency room care to fire prevention inspections. Because profit-making is not their goal, some other method must be found to distinguish between effective and ineffective agencies. One useful approach to assessing the effectiveness of human service organizations is program evaluation.

Key Concept

According to Posavac (2011), **program evaluation** is

> a methodology to learn the depth and extent of need for a human service and whether the service is likely to be used, whether the service is sufficiently intensive to meet the unmet needs identified, and the degree to which the service is offered as planned and actually does help people in need at a reasonable cost without unacceptable side effects. (p. 1)

The definition of program evaluation includes several components; we will take up each of these components in turn. Posavac emphasizes, however, that the overarching goal of program evaluation is *to provide feedback regarding human service activities.* Program evaluations are designed to provide feedback to the administrators of human service organizations to help them decide what services to provide to whom and how to provide them most effectively and efficiently. Program evaluation is an integrative discipline that draws on political science, sociology, economics, education, and psychology. We are discussing program evaluation at the end of this chapter on research in natural settings because it represents perhaps the largest-scale application of the principles and methods we have been describing throughout this book.

Posavac (2011) identifies four questions that are asked by program evaluators. These questions are about needs, process, outcome, and efficiency. An assessment of *needs* seeks to determine the unmet needs of the people for whom an agency might provide a service. Consider, for example, a city government that has received a proposal to institute a program of recreational activities for senior citizens in the community. The city would first want to determine whether senior citizens actually need or want such a program. If the senior citizens do want such a program, the city would further want to know what kind of program would be most attractive to them. The methods of survey research are used extensively in studies designed to assess needs. Administrators can use the information obtained from an assessment of needs to help them plan what programs to offer.

Once a program has been set up, program evaluators may ask questions about the *process* that has been established. Observational methods are often useful in assessing the processes of a program. Programs are not always implemented the way they were planned, and it is essential to know what actually is being done when a program is implemented. If the planned activities were not being used by the senior citizens in a recreational program designed specifically for them, it might suggest that the program was inadequately implemented. An evaluation that provides answers to questions about process, that is, about how a program is actually being carried out, permits administrators to make adjustments in the delivery of services in order to strengthen the existing program (Posavac, 2011).

The next set of questions a program evaluator is likely to ask involves the *outcome*. Has the program been effective in meeting its stated goals? For example, do senior citizens now have access to more recreational activities, and are they pleased with these activities? Do they prefer these particular activities over other activities? The outcome of a neighborhood-watch program designed to curb neighborhood crime might be evaluated by assessing whether there were actual decreases in burglaries and assaults following the implementation of the program. It is possible to use archival data like those described in Chapter 4 to carry out evaluations of outcome. For example, examining police records in order to document the frequency of various crimes is one way to assess the effectiveness of a neighborhood-watch program. Evaluations of outcome may also involve both experimental and quasi-experimental methods for research in natural settings. An evaluator may, for example, use a nonequivalent control group design to assess the effectiveness of a school reform program by comparing students' performance in two different school districts, one with the reform program and one without.

The final questions evaluators might ask are about the *efficiency* of the program. Most often, questions about efficiency relate to the cost of the program. Choices often have to be made among possible services that a government or other institution is capable of delivering. Information about how successful a program is (outcome evaluation) and information about the program's cost (efficiency evaluation) are necessary if we want to make informed decisions about continuing the program, how to improve it, whether to try an alternative program, or whether to cut back on the program's services.

Earlier in this chapter and in Chapter 2 we described differences between *basic and applied research.* Program evaluation is perhaps the extreme case of applied research. The purpose of program evaluation is practical, not theoretical. Nevertheless, even in the context of blatantly practical goals, a case can be made for a reciprocal relationship between basic and applied research (see Box 10.1). One such model of this relationship is illustrated in Figure 10.7. The idea is that each domain of research serves the other in an ongoing circular way. Specifically, basic research provides us with certain abstractions (e.g., scientifically based principles) that express certain regularities in nature. When these principles are examined in the complex and "dirty" world where they supposedly apply, new complexities are recognized and new hypotheses are called for. These new complexities are then tested and evaluated in the lab before being tried out again in the real world.

The work of Ellen Langer serves as a concrete example of this circular relationship (see Salomon, 1987). She identified a decline in elderly people's health once they entered nursing homes (see Langer, 1989; Langer & Rodin, 1976, described in this chapter). These naturalistic observations led her to develop a theory of mindfulness, which she has tested under controlled experimental conditions and which has implications for more general theories of cognitive development and of education (see, for example, Langer, 1989, 1997; Langer & Piper, 1987). The theory provides a guide for her applied work—designing new models of nursing homes. Tests of the practical effects of changes in the care

FIGURE 10.7   Model illustrating reciprocal relationship between basic and applied research. (From Salomon, 1987, p. 444.)

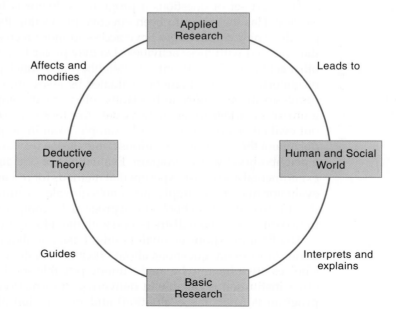

given by nursing homes on the residents' health and well-being will undoubtedly lead to modifications of her theory of mindfulness.

According to Campbell (1969), it is important for public officials involved with social experiments to emphasize the importance of the problem rather than the importance of the solution. Instead of pushing for one certain cure-all (which, in most cases, has little opportunity for success), officials must be ready to execute reform in a manner that permits the clearest evaluation and must be prepared to try different solutions if the first one fails. Public officials must, in other words, be ready to use the experimental method to identify society's problems and to determine effective solutions.

Campbell's (1969) idea that social reforms and experimental methods be routinely brought together has had some impact on social policymakers, but it is still underutilized (see Berk et al., 1987, and Box 10.3). The reasons are some of the same ones initially identified by Campbell. Nevertheless, without

---

BOX 10.3

REMOVING THE "CLOAK OF IGNORANCE" FROM SOCIETY'S EXPERIMENTS

Perhaps the greatest difference between basic research and program evaluation lies in the political and social realities surrounding program evaluation. Governments at both local and national levels regularly propose, plan, and execute various types of social reforms. Tax relief programs, work incentive programs, educational reforms, police reforms, and medical care for senior citizens are just a few of the types of social reform programs that a government might initiate. Unfortunately, as the late Donald Campbell (1969), a past president of the American Psychological Association, pointed out, the outcome of these social reforms often cannot be meaningfully evaluated. Did a change in police techniques lead to less crime? Are more elderly people gaining access to public transportation after a reduction in fares? Does a work incentive program take more people off the unemployment rolls? The answers to such questions often cannot be found, said Campbell, because most social reforms are instituted in a political climate that is not ready for hardheaded evaluation. What public official, for instance, wants to be associated with a program that failed? As Campbell suggested, there is "safety under the cloak of ignorance" (pp. 409–410). Furthermore, many social reforms are begun under the assumption that they are

certain to be successful. Otherwise, why spend all that tax money? For many public administrators it is advantageous to leave that assumption in people's minds rather than face the truth about what happened.

Campbell put forth the argument that

the United States and other modern nations should be ready for an experimental approach to social reform, an approach in which we try out new programs, in which we learn whether or not these programs are effective, and in which we retain, imitate, modify, or discard them on the basis of apparent effectiveness on the multiple imperfect criteria available. (p. 409)

Social scientists need to convince administrators to use true experiments, if at all possible, or quasi-experiments at the very least, when instituting new social programs. For example, a randomization procedure, perhaps based on public lottery, could be used to decide which group receives a pilot program or gains access to scarce resources. Groups not receiving the program or the available resources would become comparison groups. The effect of a social "treatment" could then be meaningfully evaluated. At present, decisions regarding who gets what are often influenced by particular interest groups—as the result of intense lobbying, for example—or made on the basis of political favoritism.

social experimentation, especially that which makes use whenever possible of randomized field experiments, policymakers and the community at large may believe a treatment works when it doesn't or vice versa. Such incorrect decisions lead us to allocate money and resources to ineffective programs.

Not too many years ago, a show called "Scared Straight" was aired on national television. It described a juvenile education program implemented at Rahway State Prison in New Jersey. The program involved taking youthful offenders into a prison to meet with selected convicts from the inmate population. The goal was to inform juveniles about the reality of prison life and, thereby, the program leaders hoped, dissuade them from further illegal activity. Unsubstantiated claims were made for the effectiveness of the program, including some suggesting a success rate as high as 80% to 90% (see Locke, Johnson, Kirigin-Ramp, Atwater, & Gerrard, 1986). The Rahway program is just one of several similar programs around the country. But do these programs really work?

Several evaluation studies of the exposure-to-prison programs produced mixed results, including positive findings, findings of no difference between control and experimental participants, as well as results suggesting that the program may actually increase juvenile crime among some types of delinquents. There is a possibility that less hardened juvenile offenders may increase their criminal activity after meeting the prisoners. It has been suggested that, because these less hardened offenders have recently begun a lifestyle wherein they are being recognized and reinforced by their peers for their toughness, this image is also reinforced by the tough image often projected by the prisoners. On the other hand, hardened juvenile offenders, who have achieved a level of status among their peers for some period of time, may be more threatened by the prospects of prison life because it would mean loss of that status (see Locke et al., 1986).

Attempts to evaluate the effectiveness of this significant social program provide good examples of the difficulties inherent in evaluation research: the difficulty of randomly assigning participants, of getting administrators to cooperate with experimental procedures, and of dealing with loss of participants during the evaluation. Nevertheless, program evaluation based on sound experimental methodology offers policymakers at all levels (institution, community, city, state, federal) the information that can help them make informed choices among possible treatments for social problems. Because resources inevitably are in short supply, it is critical that resources be put to the best possible use. *Our hope is that your knowledge of research methods will allow you to participate knowledgeably and perhaps contribute constructively to the ongoing debate concerning the role of experimentation in society.*

SUMMARY

Experimentation in natural settings differs in many ways from experimentation in psychology laboratories. The reasons for doing experiments in natural settings include testing the external validity of laboratory findings and assessing the effects of "treatments" aimed at improving conditions under which people work and live.

Many social scientists have argued that society must be willing to take an experimental approach to social reform—one that will allow the clearest evaluation of the effectiveness of new programs. In many situations (for instance, when available resources are scarce), true experiments involving randomization of individuals to treatment and no-treatment conditions are recommended. However, if a true experiment is not feasible, quasi-experimental procedures are the next best approach. Quasi-experiments differ from true experiments in that fewer plausible rival hypotheses for an experimental outcome are controlled. When specific threats to the internal validity of an experiment are not controlled, then the experimenter, by logically examining the situation and by collecting additional evidence, must seek to rule out these threats to internal validity.

A particularly strong quasi-experimental procedure is the nonequivalent control group design. This procedure generally controls for all major threats to internal validity except those associated with additive effects of (1) selection and history, (2) selection and maturation, (3) selection and instrumentation, and (4) threats due to differential statistical regression. In addition to the major threats to internal validity, an experimenter must be sensitive to possible contamination resulting from communication between groups of participants. Problems of experimenter expectancy effects (observer bias); questions of external validity; and novelty effects, including the Hawthorne effect, are potential problems in all experiments, whether conducted in the laboratory or in the field.

When it is possible to observe changes in a dependent measure before and after a treatment is administered, one can carry out a simple interrupted time-series design. The researcher using this design looks for an abrupt change (discontinuity) in the time series that coincides with the introduction of the treatment. The major threat to internal validity in this design is history—some event other than the treatment may have been responsible for the change in the time series. Instrumentation also can be a problem, especially when the treatment represents a type of social reform that may lead to changes in the way records are kept or data collected. By including a control group that is as similar as possible to the experimental group, one can strengthen the internal validity of a simple time-series design. A time series with nonequivalent control group, for example, controls for many possible history threats.

A particularly important goal of research in natural settings is program evaluation. Professionals other than psychologists (such as educators, political scientists, and sociologists) are often involved in this process. Types of program evaluation include assessment of needs, process, outcome, and efficiency. Perhaps the most serious constraints on program evaluation are the political and social realities that surround it. The reluctance of public officials to seek an evaluation of social reforms is often an obstacle to be overcome. Nevertheless, social scientists have called on program evaluators to make themselves available to human services organizations. By answering this call, we may help change society in a way that will bring the most effective services to those most in need.

KEY CONCEPTS

REVIEW QUESTIONS

1 Identify two reasons why it might be especially important to carry out experiments in natural settings.

2 Explain how laboratory experiments and those in natural settings differ in control, external validity, goals, and consequences.

3 Describe the three distinguishing characteristics of true experiments, and identify how the independent variable can be defined in terms of these characteristics.

4 What obstacles do researchers have to overcome when they try to carry out experiments in natural settings?

5 Identify two procedures that permit researchers to assign participants randomly to conditions while still giving all participants access to the experimental treatment.

6 Describe and explain the consequences of the three ways in which participants in a control group might respond when contamination occurs.

7 Explain how novelty effects, including the Hawthorne effect, may influence a researcher's interpretation of the effectiveness of an experimental treatment.

8 What do Cook and Campbell (1979) consider the best test of external validity?

9 Explain why it is essential to use a pretest in the nonequivalent control group design.

10 Explain how one threat to internal validity is controlled in the nonequivalent control group design, and describe a threat to internal validity that is not controlled in this design.

11 Identify two reasons why we cannot conclude that the treatment and control groups in a nonequivalent control group design are equivalent even when the pretest scores are the same for both groups.

12 Explain the difference between a history threat to internal validity and what is called a "local history effect" in the nonequivalent control group design.

13 What is the major evidence for an effect of the treatment in a simple interrupted time-series design, and what are the major threats to internal validity in this design?

14 Explain how the addition of a nonequivalent control group to a simple interrupted time-series design reduces the threat to the internal validity of the design.

15 Describe what type of information is being sought when evaluators ask each of the four questions typically addressed in program evaluation.

CHALLENGE QUESTIONS

1 A quasi-experiment was used to determine whether multimedia instruction is effective. Two sections of introductory psychology were taught by the same instructor, both in the early afternoon. In one section (the treatment group), the instructor used multimedia instruction. In the other section, the instructor covered the same material but did not use multimedia instruction. Students did not know when they registered for the course whether multimedia instruction would be used, but the students were not randomly assigned to sections. Students' knowledge of the course material was assessed using two forms of a comprehensive introductory psychology test. The comprehensive test can be considered a reliable and valid test that can be used to compare the effectiveness of the instruction in the two sections. The students in both sections were tested on the second day of class (the pretest) and at the final (the posttest). Different forms of the test were used at the pretest and at the posttest.

   A What quasi-experimental design is used in the study?

   B The instructor initially considered doing a true experiment rather than a quasi-experiment. Comment critically on the fairness of random assignment if you were arguing in favor of doing a true experiment to test the effectiveness of multimedia instruction.

   C Explain why the quasi-experimental design used by the instructor is more effective than if the instructor had tested only students who had received multimedia instruction. Identify one threat to internal validity that was controlled in this study that would not have been controlled if only students who received multimedia instruction had been tested.

2 A psychologist published a book describing the effects of divorce on men, women, and children. She was interested in the effects of divorce that occurred 10 years after the divorce. She found that even 10 years after a divorce half of the women and one third of the men were still intensely angry. Although half the men and women described themselves as happy, 25% of the women and 20% of the men remained unable to "get their lives back on track." In only 10% of the divorced families did both the former husbands and wives have happy, satisfying lives a decade later. Finally, more than half of the children of divorce entered adulthood as underachieving and self-deprecating

men and women. These findings were based on a 15-year study of 60 divorced couples and their 131 children living in Marin County, California (an affluent suburban area including mostly well-educated people). Explain how the use of a quasi-experimental design would have been helpful in order to specify which of the reported results are due to the effects of divorce.

3 The police force of a large city had to decide between two different approaches to keeping the officers on the force informed about the changes in laws. An enlightened administrator of this force decided to put the two approaches to test in a research study. She decided to do a true experiment and assigned 30 officers randomly to each of the two programs for a period of 6 months. At the end of this time, all the officers who successfully completed the training under the two approaches were given a final test on their knowledge of the law. The 20 officers who completed Program A showed a reliably higher mean score on this test than did the 28 officers who completed Program B. The administrator wisely chose not to accept these results as decisive evidence of the effectiveness of the two programs. Using only the data reported in this problem, explain why she made this decision. Next, explain how her decision would have been different if only 20 officers completed both programs (from the original 30 assigned to each) and there was still a sizable difference favoring Program A. Be sure to mention any limitations on the conclusions she could reach concerning the overall effectiveness of these programs.

4 A small undergraduate college with a new physical-fitness center decided to introduce a health enhancement program for faculty and staff. The program is designed to take one semester to complete with three 1-hour sessions per week. Comment critically on each of the following questions regarding the evaluation of this program.

   A How might an assessment of needs have played a role in planning the program?

   B What questions about the process of the program would be useful once the program was under way to help ensure that the evaluation of the outcome of the program could be interpreted appropriately?

   C Explain how you would test the effectiveness of the proposed program if it were not possible to do a true experiment.

Answer to Stretching Exercise

1 History is a threat when an event other than the treatment can explain the participants' improvement. For example, participants may have read self-help books, tried herbal supplements, talked to friends or pastors, or experienced any number of potentially beneficial "treatments." Any of these other events may have caused the depression to improve, rather than the psychologist's treatment.

2 Maturation occurs when participants naturally change over time. One of the things we know about depression is that it tends to improve with time. Therefore, the participants' improvement may reflect natural decreases in depression over time, rather than the effect of the treatment.

3 A testing threat occurs when a first administration of a test influences subsequent testing. In this study, participants may have remembered their earlier responses on the depression measure and, perhaps in an effort to demonstrate they improved, chose responses that indicated less depression at posttest (even if they didn't feel less depressed). An instrumentation threat occurs when the measure used to assess thoughts, feelings, and behavior changes over time. Because the same questionnaire was used for both the pretest and posttest, this threat is less likely.

4 Statistical regression is possible when participants are selected because they are extreme on a pretest measure. In this study, participants were selected because they were depressed—they scored high on a measure of depression. It's possible that the lower scores at posttest indicated improvement because of statistical regression to the mean, not because of the effects of treatment.

Answer to Challenge Question 1

A The nonequivalent control group design was used in this study.

B Students may perceive random assignment to the two sections as unfair because they would not have a choice about which section they would take. If we do not know whether multimedia instruction is effective, then random assignment is the best and fairest method to determine whether multimedia instruction is effective.

C If only the students who had received multimedia instruction had been tested, the design of the study would have been a single group pretest-posttest design. There are several threats to the internal validity of a pretest-posttest single group design. That is why it is referred to as a pre-experimental design or a bad experiment. One possible threat in this study is due to testing; that is, students often improve from an initial test in a course to the second test because they gain familiarity with the testing procedure and the instructor's expectations. This improvement would be expected to occur even if multimedia instruction had not been used. The nonequivalent control group design in this study controls for this threat because any increase in test scores due to testing effects would likely be the same for both groups. A *greater* increase from the pretest to the posttest for the group given multimedia instruction, relative to the control group, can be interpreted as an effect of the instruction.

PART FIVE

Analyzing and Reporting Research

CHAPTER ELEVEN

Data Analysis and Interpretation: Part I. Describing Data, Confidence Intervals, Correlation

CHAPTER OUTLINE

OVERVIEW

The primary goal of data analysis is to determine whether our observations support a claim about behavior (Abelson, 1995). The claim may be that children of drug-addicted mothers exhibit more learning difficulties than those born to drug-free mothers, or that a program intended to prevent depression has worked. Whatever the claim, our case must be prepared with careful attention given to the quality of the evidence and to the way it is presented. When a quantitative research study is conducted, the evidence is primarily the numerical data we collected. To prepare a convincing argument, we need to know what to look for in these data, how to summarize that information, and how best to evaluate the information.

Data, of course, do not come out of thin air; we can assume results were obtained using a particular research method (e.g., observation, survey, experiment). If serious errors were made in the data collection stage, then there may be nothing we can do to "save" the data and it may be best to start again. Thus, we need to ensure that the data for the analysis were gathered after giving careful consideration to the statement of the research hypothesis (i.e., our tentative claim about behavior), the choice of a proper research design to test that hypothesis, selection of appropriate response measures, and assessment of statistical power. And, of course, we want to make sure that the data were collected in a manner that minimizes the contribution of demand characteristics, experimenter biases, confoundings, or other artifacts of the research situation. In short, we seek data from a "good" research study, one that is internally and externally valid, sensitive, and reliable.

Key Concept }

Trusting we have obtained data based on a sound research study, what should we do next? There are three distinct, but related **stages of data analysis: getting to know the data, summarizing the data,** and **confirming what the data reveal** (see Box 11.1). Whether conducting an observational study (see Chapter 4) or an experiment (see Chapters 6–8) based on quantitative data, the first two stages of data analysis, *getting to know the data* and *summarizing the data*, proceed in much the same way. When conducting a survey (see Chapter 5) or other research study in which evidence for covariation between two variables is sought, data summary proceeds somewhat differently. We will use several research examples to illustrate the stages of data analysis, including those that focus on mean performance of one or more groups as well as those that emphasize the correlation between variables.

There are different, but complementary, approaches to the third stage of analysis, *confirming what the data tell us*. One approach makes use of confidence intervals to provide evidence for the range and precision of estimation of population parameters. Another relies on null hypothesis significance testing (NHST). Both of these approaches were briefly introduced in Chapter 6, and, as we said, these approaches are related; however, there are important differences and we will introduce them first separately and then show how information from both approaches might be combined in the final analysis story. In this chapter we discuss confidence intervals and in Chapter 12, NHST. In Chapter 12 we also discuss the important concept of statistical power and its relationship to confidence intervals and NHST.

BOX 11.1

THREE STAGES OF DATA ANALYSIS

The three major stages of data analysis can be described as follows:

I Getting to Know the Data   In the first stage we want to become familiar with the data. This is an exploratory or investigative stage (Tukey, 1977). We inspect the data carefully, get a feel for it, and even, as some experts have said, "make friends" with it (Hoaglin, Mosteller, & Tukey, 1991, p. 42). Questions we ask include, What is going on in this number set? Are there errors in the data? Do the data make sense or are there reasons for "suspecting fishiness" (Abelson, 1995, p. 78)? Visual displays of distributions of numbers are important at this stage. What do the data look like? Only when we have become familiar with the general features of the data, have checked for errors, and have assured ourselves that the data make sense, should we proceed to the second stage.

II Summarizing the Data   In the second stage we seek to summarize the data in a meaningful way. The use of descriptive statistics and creation of graphical displays are important at this stage. How should the data be organized? Which ways of describing and summarizing the data are most informative? What happened in this study as a function of the factors of interest? What trends and patterns do we see? Which graphical display best reveals these trends and patterns? When the data are appropriately summarized, we are ready to move to the confirmation stage.

III Confirming What the Data Reveal   In the third stage we decide what the data tell us about behavior. Do the data confirm our tentative claim (research

hypothesis) made at the beginning of the study? What can we claim based on the evidence? Sometimes we look for a categorical, yes-no judgment, and act as judge and jury to render a verdict. Do we have evidence to convict? Yes or no: Is the effect real? At this stage we may use various statistical techniques to counter arguments that our results are simply "due to chance." Null hypothesis testing, when appropriate, is performed at this stage of analysis. Our evaluation of the data, however, need not always lead us to a categorical judgment about the data (e.g., Schmidt, 1996). We don't, in other words, have to attempt a definitive statement about the "truth" of the results. Our claim about behavior may be based on an evaluation of the probable range of effect sizes for the variable of interest. What, in other words, is likely to happen when this variable is present? Confidence intervals are particularly recommended for this kind of evaluation (e.g., Cohen, 1995; Hunter, 1997; Loftus, 1996).

The confirmation process actually begins at the first or exploratory stage of data analysis, when we first get a feel for what our data are like. As we examine the general features of the data, we start to appreciate what we found. In the summary stage we learn more about trends and patterns among the observations. This provides feedback that helps to confirm our hypotheses. The final step in data analysis is called the confirmation stage to emphasize that it is typically at this point when we come to a decision about what the data mean. Information obtained at each stage of data analysis, however, contributes to this confirmatory process (e.g., Tukey, 1977).

The Analysis Story

- When data analysis is completed, we must construct a coherent narrative that explains our findings, counters opposing interpretations, and justifies our conclusions.

Making a convincing argument for a claim about behavior requires more than simply analyzing the data. A good argument requires a good story. A trial attorney, in order to win a case, not only must call a jury's attention to the facts of a case, but also must be able to weave those facts into a coherent and logical story. If the evidence points to the butler, then we want to know "why" the butler (not the cook) might have done it. Abelson (1995) makes a similar point regarding a research argument:

> High-quality evidence, embodying sizeable, well-articulated and general effects, is necessary for a statistical argument to have maximal persuasive impact, but it is not sufficient. Also vital are the attributes of the research story embodying the argument. (p. 13)

Consequently, when data analysis is completed, we must construct a coherent narrative that explains our findings, counters opposing interpretations, and justifies our conclusions. In Chapters 12 and 13 we'll return to the analysis story when we introduce guidelines to help you develop an appropriate narrative for your research study.

COMPUTER-ASSISTED DATA ANALYSIS

- Researchers typically use computers to carry out the statistical analysis of data.
- Carrying out statistical analyses using computer software requires that the researcher must have a good knowledge of research design and statistics.

Most researchers have ready access to computers that include appropriate software to carry out the statistical analysis of data sets. The ability to set up and carry out an analysis using a statistical software package and the ability to interpret the output are essential skills that must be learned by researchers. Some of the more popular software packages are known by abbreviations like BMDP, SAS, SPSS, and STATA. You likely have access to one or more of these programs on the computers in your psychology department or at your campus computer center, or perhaps even on your laptop.

Carrying out statistical analyses using computer software requires that the researcher have a good knowledge of research design and statistics. In Chapters 6, 7, and 8 we introduced various experimental designs. This knowledge is essential if you wish to use computer-assisted analysis. A computer is not able to determine what research design you used or the rationale behind the use of that design (although some of the user-friendly programs provide prompts to guide your thinking). To carry out computer-assisted data analysis, you must enter information such as the type of design that was used (e.g., random groups or repeated measures); the number of independent variables (e.g., single factor or multifactor); the number of levels of each independent variable; and the number of dependent variables and the level of measurement employed for each. You must also be able to articulate your research hypotheses and to plan appropriate statistical tests of your research hypotheses. A computer will quickly and efficiently perform the computations necessary for obtaining descriptive and inferential statistics. To use the computer effectively as a research tool, however, you must give it specific directions regarding which statistical test you want it to perform and which data are to be used in computing the test. Finally, when the computer has carried out the computations, you must be able to interpret correctly the output showing the results of the analysis.

ILLUSTRATION: DATA ANALYSIS FOR AN EXPERIMENT COMPARING MEANS

How many words do you know? That is, what is the size of your vocabulary? You may have asked yourself this question as you prepared for college entrance exams such as the SAT or ACT, or perhaps it crossed your mind as you thought about preparing for professional school exams such as the LSAT or GRE, as all of these exams emphasize vocabulary knowledge. Surprisingly, estimating a person's vocabulary size is a complex task (e.g., Anglin, 1993; Miller & Wakefield, 1993). Problems immediately arise, for instance, when we begin to think about what we mean by a "word." Is "play, played, playing" one word or three? Are we interested in highly technical or scientific words, including six-syllable names of chemical compounds? What about made-up words, or the name of your dog, or the word you use to call your significant other? One rather straightforward approach is to ask how many words a person knows in a dictionary of the English language. But even here we run into difficulties because dictionaries vary in size and scope, and thus results will vary depending on the specific dictionary that was used to select a word sample. And, of course, estimates of vocabulary knowledge will vary depending on how knowledge is tested. Multiple-choice tests will reveal more knowledge than will tests requiring written definitions of words.

One of the authors of your textbook was interested in the question of vocabulary size and conducted a study examining the vocabulary size of college students and older adults (see Zechmeister, Chronis, Cull, D'Anna, & Healy, 1995). A stratified (by letter of the alphabet) random sample of 191 words was selected from a modest-sized dictionary of the English language. Then a multiple-choice test with five alternatives was prepared. The correct meaning of the word appeared along with four lures or distractors chosen to make discrimination of the correct meaning difficult. For example, respondents were asked to identify the meaning of the word "chivalry" among the following alternatives: a. warfare, b. herb, c. bravery, d. lewdness, e. courtesy. The random sample of dictionary words was presented in booklets to 26 college-age students (mean age 18.5) and 26 older adults (mean age 76). On the basis of previous studies, the older adult group was expected to perform better than the younger group on the test of vocabulary knowledge.

We'll use data from this study of vocabulary size to illustrate the three stages of data analysis.

Stage 1: Getting to Know the Data

- We begin data analysis by examining the general features of the data and edit or "clean" the data as necessary.
- It is important to check carefully for errors such as missing or impossible values (e.g., numbers outside the range of a given scale), as well as outliers.
- A stem-and-leaf display is particularly useful for visualizing the general features of a data set and for detecting outliers.
- Data can be effectively summarized numerically, pictorially, or verbally; good descriptions of data frequently use all three modes.

Cleaning the Data   We want to begin by examining the general features of the data and edit or "clean" the data as necessary (Mosteller & Hoaglin, 1991). We check carefully for errors such as missing or impossible values (e.g., numbers outside the range of a given scale). Errors can arise because participants misuse a scale (e.g., by reversing the order of importance) or because someone entering data into a computer skips a number or transposes a digit. When typing a manuscript, most of us rely on a "spell checker" to catch our many typos and misspellings. Unfortunately, there is no such device for detecting numerical errors that are entered into a computer (however, see Kaschak & Moore, 2000, for suggestions to reduce errors). It is up to the researcher to make sure that data are clean prior to moving ahead.

Of particular importance is the detection of anomalies and errors. As we have seen, an anomaly sometimes signals an error in data recording, such as would be the case if the number 8 appears among data based on respondents' use of a 7-point scale, or if an IQ score of 10 was recorded in a sample of college student participants. Other anomalies are outliers. An *outlier* is an extreme number in an array; it just doesn't seem to "go with" the main body of data even though it may be within the realm of possible values. When doing a reaction-time study, for instance, where we expect most responses to be less than 1,500 msec, we might be surprised to see a reaction time of 4,000 msec. If nearly all of the other values in a large data set are less than 1,500, a value of 4,000 in the same data set certainly could be viewed as an outlier. Yet such values are possible in reaction-time studies when participants sneeze, absent-mindedly look away from a display, or mistakenly think that data collection has halted and start to leave. A respondent completing a questionnaire may misread a question and submit a response that is far more extreme than any other response in the data set. Unfortunately, researchers do not rely on a single definition of an outlier, and several "rules of thumb" are used (see, for example, Zechmeister & Posavac, 2003).

When anomalies appear in a data set, we must decide whether they should be excluded from additional analyses. Those anomalies that clearly can be judged to be errors should be corrected or dropped from the data set, but, when doing so, a researcher must report their removal from the data analysis and explain, if possible, why the anomaly occurred.

In the first stage of data analysis we also want to look for ways to describe the distribution of scores meaningfully. What is the dispersion (variability) like? Are the data skewed or relatively normally distributed? One of the goals of this first stage of analysis is to determine whether the data require transformation prior to proceeding. Transforming data is a process of "re-expression" (Hoaglin, Mosteller, & Tukey, 1983). Examples of relatively simple transformations include those that express inches as feet, degrees Fahrenheit as Celsius, or number correct as percent correct. More sophisticated statistical transformations are also sometimes useful.

The best way to get a feel for a set of data is to construct a picture of it. An advantage of computer-aided data analysis is that we can quickly and easily plot data using various display options (e.g., frequency polygons, histograms) and just as easily incorporate changes of scale (e.g., inches to feet) to see how the data picture is altered. Minimally, by experimenting with different ways to visualize our data set, we become more familiar with it. Which visual representation reveals the most about our data? What do we learn about our data when we compare plots with the axes defined differently? Is a polygon or histogram more informative? A picture not only is worth a proverbial 1,000 words, but also it can quickly summarize 1,000 numbers. As we become more familiar with different pictures of our data, we learn that some pictures are better than others.

The data from our example vocabulary study represented the number of correct meanings identified out of a possible 191. Because participants without knowledge of the correct answer can be correct by chance on multiple-choice tests, a standard correction for guessing was applied to individual responses. However, two typographical errors appeared in the booklets given to the older adult group, so these items were deleted from further analysis. Also, examination of the test booklets revealed that several of the older participants omitted a page when working through the test booklet. Thus, the number of possible words was reduced for these individuals. Because of these problems, the data were transformed to percent correct to account for differences in the total number of possible responses among participants.

After cleaning the data set, the researchers obtained the following data in the first stage of the analysis. These data are expressed in terms of percent correct multiple-choice performance for college students and older adults.

College ($n = 26$): 59, 31, 47, 43, 54, 42, 38, 44, 48, 57, 42, 48, 30, 41, 59, 23, 62, 27, 53, 51, 39, 38, 50, 58, 56, 45.

Older adults ($n = 26$): 70, 59, 68, 68, 57, 66, 78, 78, 64, 43, 53, 83, 74, 69, 59, 44, 73, 65, 32, 60, 54, 64, 82, 62, 62, 78.

Key Concept }

Stem-and-Leaf Displays   A **stem-and-leaf display** is particularly useful for visualizing the general features of a data set and for detecting outliers (Tukey, 1977). A stem-and-leaf display obtains its name through the convention of using leading digits in a numerical array as "stems" and trailing digits as "leaves."

The following is a stem-and-leaf display for the college student data from our example vocabulary study:

2*	3
2	7
3*	01
3	889
4*	12234
4	5788
5*	0134
5	67899
6*	2

The leading digits are the first or tens' digits (e.g., 2-, 3-, 4-,) and the trailing digits are just that, those that trail the leading or most significant digits; in this example the trailing digits are the units' or ones' digits (e.g., -5, -6, -8). The display is made by arranging the leading digits in a vertical array beginning with the smallest at the top. A leading digit is followed, in ascending order, by as many trailing digits as appear in the distribution. Each line in the display is a stem followed by its leaves (Tukey, 1977). For example, the stem 3 in the above display has three leaves, 8,8,9, indicating that the numbers 38, 38, and 39 appear in the distribution. By convention, when many numbers are displayed, or when the entire data set contains only a few leading digits, a leading digit followed by an asterisk(*) is frequently used to indicate the first half of an interval (see Tukey, 1977). For example, 5* would be the stem for leaves 0,1,2,3, and 4 (i.e., numbers 50–54); the leading digit 5 (without the *) would be the stem for leaves 5,6,7,8,9 (i.e., numbers 55–59). In the above display, for instance, the stem 2* has one leaf, 3, and the stem 2 has one leaf, 7, corresponding to the numbers 23 and 27, respectively.

There also may be more than one leading digit. For example, if scores varied between 50 and 150, single leading digits would be used for numbers less than 100 (8-, 9-, etc.), and two leading digits for numbers equal to or greater than 100 (10-, 11-, 12-, etc.).

As you might see, a stem-and-leaf display is something of a histogram on its side. It has an advantage over a histogram, however, in that each value is displayed; thus, specific item information is not lost, as occurs when a histogram is formed using class intervals (Howell, 2002). The most important advantage of a stem-and-leaf display is that it can clearly reveal the shape of the distribution and the presence, if any, of outliers.

Look carefully at the stem-and-leaf display for the vocabulary data of the 26 college students. What do you see? Is the general shape of the distribution "normal" (i.e., symmetrical and bell-shaped) or skewed (i.e., asymmetrical with scores trailing off in one direction)? Is there a lot of dispersion, or do the numbers tend to center around a particular value? Are anomalous values present? We suggest that the stem-and-leaf display for these data reveals that the data are concentrated around the 40 and 50 percentages with the distribution somewhat negatively skewed (note how the "tail" trails off toward the low, or negative, end of the distribution). Outliers do not seem to be present (e.g., there are no single-digit percentages or percentages beyond the 60s).

It can be particularly revealing to display two stem-and-leaf displays side-by-side when comparing two groups of data. Consider the display pictured on the next page. The same stems are used with trailing digits in one distribution increasing from right to left (e.g., 997 5) and leaves in the other distribution ascending (on the same line) from left to right (e.g., 5 67899). This indicates that the first distribution had scores of 57, 59, and 59, and the second distribution had scores of 56, 57, 58, 59, and 59. Side-by-side stem-and-leaf displays might be meaningfully used, for instance, to compare responses to a questionnaire item when a researcher is comparing two groups that differ in socioeconomic status, age, gender, or in some other meaningful way.

A side-by-side stem-and-leaf display for the two conditions of the vocabulary study looks like this:

Older Adults		College Students
	2*	3
	2	7
2	3*	01
	3	889
43	4*	12234
	4	5788
43	5*	0134
997	5	67899
44220	6*	2
98865	6	
430	7*	
888	7	
32	8*	

Look at the display on the left, the one for the older participants. How would you characterize it? The data seem to be somewhat normally distributed, although an extreme score, an outlier, appears to be present. The "32" doesn't seem to belong with the rest of the data. (There are ways to operationalize outliers in terms of their distance from the middle of the distribution, and some computer programs will do this automatically.) Without additional information about the nature of the respondent (e.g., amount of medication taken that day, or possible reading problems), the experimenters could find no reason to exclude this score from the study. The presence of this possible outlier necessarily increases the amount of variability present in this group relative to what it would be without this score. Nevertheless, we must acknowledge that some data sets are naturally going to be more variable than others. For example, the older adults in this study simply may represent a more heterogeneous group of individuals than those in the college student sample. (There is a moral here: Obtain as much relevant information about your participants as is conveniently possible at the time you collect data. An extreme score should be treated as a true score unless you know the score is extreme due to error or to circumstances unrelated to the study.)

Now look at what the side-by-side stem-and-leaf display reveals about both distributions. You should immediately see that scores in the groups overlap to some degree, but there are many more scores above 60 in the older group than in the college group. This "picture" of the data begins to confirm the idea that the older adults performed better overall than the college students on this test of vocabulary size.

Conclusion   In the first stage of data analysis—the process of getting to know our data—we should identify

(a) the nature and frequency of any errors in the data set and, if errors are present, whether corrections could be made or data need to be dropped;

   (b) anomalous values, including outliers, and, if they are present, what reasons there might be for the presence of these values and what should be done about them (retained or dropped);

   (c) the general features and shape of the distribution of numbers; and

   (d) alternative ways to more meaningfully express the data.

Stage 2: Summarizing the Data

- Measures of central tendency include the mean, median, and mode.
- Important measures of dispersion or variability are the range and standard deviation.
- The standard error of the mean is the standard deviation of the theoretical sampling distribution of means and is a measure of how well we have estimated the population mean.
- Effect size measures are important because they provide information about the strength of the relationship between the independent variable and the dependent variable that is independent of sample size.
- An important effect size measure when comparing two means is Cohen's *d*.

Data can be effectively summarized numerically, pictorially, or verbally. Good descriptions of data frequently use all three modes. In this chapter we will focus mainly on ways to summarize data numerically, that is, using descriptive statistics, although we do present some graphs. Information about drawing graphs to summarize data is also found in Chapter 13. Verbal description of data also is a major topic of Chapter 13 (see especially guidelines for writing the Results section of a research report).

The data from the vocabulary study will be summarized using measures of central tendency, dispersion, standard error of the mean, and effect size.

Key Concepts

Central Tendency   Measures of central tendency include the mean, median, and mode. These **measures of central tendency** do just what their name implies: They indicate the score that the data tend to center around. The **mode** is the crudest measure of central tendency: It simply indicates the score in the frequency distribution that occurs most often. If two scores in the distribution occur with higher frequency than do other scores in the distribution, and if these two scores occur at different locations in the frequency distribution, this distribution is said to be bimodal (i.e., to have two modes).

Key Concept

   The **median** is defined as the middle point in the frequency distribution. It is calculated by ranking all the scores from lowest to highest and identifying the value that splits the distribution into two halves, each half having the same number of values. Consider this data set: 4, 5, 6, 7, 8, 8. For these data the median would be 6.5. When there are an even number of values, the median is defined as the average of the two middle numbers [in this case, $(6 + 7)/2 = 6.5$]. When there are an odd number of values, the median is, by convention, the middle value when numbers are arranged in ascending or descending order. For the number set 4, 5, 6, 17, 18, the median is 6. Note that the median would still be 6 if the highest value were 180, not 18. *The median is the best measure of central tendency* *when the distribution includes extreme scores because it is less influenced by the extreme scores than is the mean.*

Key Concept

The **mean** is the most commonly reported measure of central tendency and is determined by dividing the sum of the scores by the number of scores contributing to that sum. The mean of a population is symbolized as μ (Greek letter mu); the mean of a sample is indicated by M when reported in text, for example, in a Results section. (The symbol $\overline{X}$ [read "X bar"] is typically used in statistical formulas.) The mean should always be reported as a measure of central tendency unless there are extreme scores in the distribution. When people speak of an "average" score, they usually are referring to the arithmetic mean. Measures of central tendency for the two groups in the vocabulary study are

	College	Older Adult
Mean (*M*)	45.58	64.04
Median	46.00	64.50
Mode	38,42,48,59	78

As you can see, the mean performance of the college group is much lower than the mean or average performance of the older adults. This confirms what we saw in the side-by-side stem-and-leaf display: The older group performed better overall on the average than did the college group. Note that the mean and median within each group are similar; thus, even though we identified an extreme score in the older sample when looking at the stem-and-leaf display, the presence of this score does not seem to have "thrown off" the mean as a measure of central tendency. There is more than one mode in the college data, each appearing twice; the most frequent score in the older group is 78, and it appeared only three times. As you can see, the mode is not particularly helpful in summarizing these small data sets.

Dispersion or Variability   Whenever you report a measure of central tendency, it should always be accompanied by an appropriate **measure of dispersion (variability).** Measures of central tendency indicate the value in a frequency distribution on which scores tend to "center"; measures of dispersion indicate the breadth, or variability, of the distribution.

Key Concepts

The crudest measure of dispersion (the counterpart of the mode) is the **range.** The range is determined by subtracting the lowest score in the distribution from the highest score. For example, in a small distribution made up of the scores 1, 3, 5, 7 the range would be equal to $7 - 1$, or 6.

The most commonly used measure of dispersion (the counterpart of the mean) is the **standard deviation.** The standard deviation tells you approximately how far on the average a score is from the mean. It is equal to the square root of the average squared deviations of scores in the distribution about the mean.

For reasons that need not concern us here, the average of the squared deviations about the mean involves division by $N - 1$ rather than N so as to provide an unbiased estimate of the population standard deviation based on the sample. The standard deviation of a population is symbolized as σ (Greek letter sigma); the standard deviation of a sample of scores is indicated as *SD* when appearing in text, but it is often symbolized as *s* in statistical formulas. The variance, a measure of dispersion that is important in the calculation of various inferential statistics, is the square of the standard deviation, that is, s^2.

Measures of variability for the two vocabulary groups are

	College	Older Adult
Range	23–62	32–83
Variance (s^2)	109.45	150.44
Standard deviation (*SD* or *s*)	10.46	12.27

Note that the stem-and-leaf display showed greater dispersion among the older adults; with the *SD* we have a number to reflect that characteristic of the distribution.

Standard Error of the Mean   In doing inferential statistics, we use the sample mean as a point estimate of the population mean. That is, we use a single value ($\overline{X}$) to estimate (infer) the population mean (μ). It is often helpful to be able to determine how much error there is in estimating μ on the basis of $\overline{X}$. The central limit theorem in mathematics tells us that if we draw an infinite number of samples of the same size and we compute $\overline{X}$ for each of these samples, the mean of these samples means ($\mu_{\overline{X}}$) will be equal to the population mean (μ), and the standard deviation of the sample means will be equal to the population standard deviation (σ) divided by the square root of the sample size (N). The standard deviation of this theoretical sampling distribution of the mean is called the **standard error of the mean** ($\sigma_{\overline{X}}$) and is defined as

Key Concept

$$\sigma_{\overline{X}} = \frac{\sigma}{\sqrt{N}}$$

Typically, we do not know the standard deviation of the population, so we estimate it using the sample standard deviation (s). Then we may obtain an **estimated standard error of the mean** using the formula

Key Concept

$$s_{\overline{X}} = \frac{s}{\sqrt{N}}$$

Small values of $s_{\overline{X}}$ suggest that we have a good estimate of the population mean, and large values of $s_{\overline{X}}$ suggest that we have only a rough estimate of the population mean. The formula for the standard error of the mean indicates that our ability to estimate the population mean on the basis of a sample depends on the size of the sample (large samples lead to better estimates) and on the variability in the population from which the sample was drawn, as estimated by the sample standard deviation (the less variable the scores in a population, the better our estimate of the population mean will be). As we will show later, the standard error of the mean plays an important role in the construction of confidence intervals and is frequently displayed along with sample means in a figure summarizing results of a research study.

Measures of Effect Size   When we do an experiment, we are interested in determining whether the independent variable had an effect and, if it did, how much of an effect there was. The concept of effect size was introduced in Chapter 6. Measures of *effect size* or what are more generally called measures of "effect magnitude" (see Kirk, 1996) are important because they provide information about the strength of the relationship between the independent variable and the dependent variable that is independent of sample size (see, especially, Grissom & Kim, 2005).

One commonly used measure of effect size in experimental research when comparisons are made between two means is called Cohen's *d*. It is a ratio that measures the difference between the means for the levels of the independent variable divided by the within-group standard deviation. Remember that the standard deviation tells us approximately how far, on the average, scores vary from a group mean. It is a measure of the "dispersal" of scores around a mean and, in the case of the within-group standard deviation, tells us about the degree of "error" due to individual differences (i.e., how individuals vary in their responses). The standard deviation serves as a useful metric to assess a difference between means. That is, the "size" of the effect of the independent variable (the difference between group means for the independent variable) is always in terms of the average amount of dispersal of scores occurring in an experiment.

The effect size measure, *d*, defined as the difference between sample means divided by the common population standard deviation, is called Cohen's *d* after the late statistician Jacob Cohen (see Cohen, 1988, for more information about *d*).

$$\text{Cohen's } d = \frac{\overline{X}_1 - \overline{X}_2}{\sigma}$$

The population standard deviation (σ) is obtained by pooling the within-group variability across groups and dividing by the total number (N) of scores in both groups. A formula for the common population standard deviation using sample variances is

$$\sigma = \sqrt{\frac{(n_1 - 1)s_1^2 + (n_2 - 1)s_2^2}{N}}$$

where

n_1 = sample size of Group 1

n_2 = sample size of Group 2

s_1^2 = variance of Group 1

s_2^2 = variance of Group 2

$N = n_1 + n_2$

If there is a lot of within-group variability (i.e., the within-group standard deviation is large), the denominator for *d* is large. To be able to observe the effect of the independent variable, given this large within-group variability, the difference between two group means must be large. When the within-group variability is small (the denominator for *d* is small), the same difference between means will reflect a larger effect size. Because effect sizes are presented in standard deviation units, they can be used to make meaningful comparisons of effect sizes across experiments using different dependent variables. For example, an effect size from a study of vocabulary knowledge that compared college students and older adults on tests emphasizing discrimination of word meanings (i.e., multiple-choice tests) and an effect size from a study contrasting performance of two similar groups using recall of word definitions could be directly compared. Such comparisons form the bases of *meta-analyses,* which seek to summarize the effect of a particular independent variable across many different studies (see Chapter 6).

There are some guidelines to help us interpret *d* ratios. J. Cohen (1992) provided a useful classification of effect sizes with three values—small, medium, and large. He describes the rationale for his classification of effect size (ES) as follows:

> My intent was that medium ES represent an effect likely to be visible to the naked eye of a careful observer. (It has since been noted in effect-size surveys that it approximates the average size of observed effects in various fields.) I set small ES to be noticeably smaller than medium but not so small as to be trivial, and I set large ES to be the same distance above medium as small was below it. Although the definitions were made subjectively, with some minor adjustments, these conventions . . . have come into general use. (p. 156)

Each of the classes of effect size can be expressed in quantitative terms; for example, a medium effect for a two-group experiment is a *d* of .50; a small and large effect are *d*s of .20 and .80, respectively. These expressions of effect magnitude are especially useful when comparing results from similar studies.

It is important to note that researchers define the standardized difference between means in slightly different ways (see, for example, Cohen, 1988; Kirk, 1996; Rosenthal, 1991). Which measure of effect size to use is a decision left up to the investigator. But, given the differences in measures appearing in the psychology literature, *it is very important to identify in a research report precisely how a measure of effect size was calculated.*

An effect size for the vocabulary study using Cohen's *d* is

$$d = \frac{\overline{X}_1 - \overline{X}_2}{\sigma} = \frac{64.04 - 45.58}{\sqrt{\dfrac{(26 - 1)(150.04) + (26 - 1)(109.45)}{52}}} = 1.65$$

To interpret the value of 1.65, we can use J. Cohen's (1992) classification of effect sizes of $d = .20$ for a small effect size, $d = .50$ for a medium effect size, and $d = .80$ for a large effect size. Because our value is larger than .80, we can conclude that "age" had a large effect on vocabulary knowledge.

Conclusion   In the second, summary stage of data analysis, we should identify

  (a) the central tendency (e.g., mean) of each condition or group in the study;
  (b) measures of dispersion (variability), such as the range and standard deviation, for each condition of the study;

(c) the effect size for each of the major independent variables; and

(d) how to best present pictorial summaries of the data (e.g., figure showing mean performance across conditions).

Note: Although a graph showing mean performance in the two groups of the vocabulary study could be drawn, a figure usually is not needed when only two group means are involved. Pictorial summaries become more important when summarizing the results of studies with more than two groups.

Stage 3: Using Confidence Intervals to Confirm What the Data Reveal

• An important approach to confirming what the data are telling us is to construct confidence intervals for the population parameter, such as a mean or difference between two means.

Key Concept

In the third stage of data analysis we seek to confirm impressions of the evidence obtained as we familiarized ourselves with the data and obtained summary measures. A major approach in this third stage is the calculation of a **confidence interval for a population parameter.** A confidence interval (*CI*) may be calculated for a single population mean or population mean difference. We first review the use of confidence intervals for one population mean. Then we introduce confidence intervals for the difference between two population means and discuss the interpretation of intervals when there are three or more means.

Confidence intervals may already be familiar to you under a different name. Have you not heard reports in the media of survey results based on a sample of respondents? And with these reports have you sometimes heard a "margin of error" presented? In Box 11.2 we review the concept of margin of error and its relation to a confidence interval.

Confidence Intervals for a Single Mean   The mean of a random sample from a population is a point estimate of the population mean. However, we can expect variability among sample means from one situation to another due to random variation. The estimated standard error of the mean ($s_{\overline{X}}$) provides information about the "normal" range of sampling error. In computing a confidence interval we specify a range of values that we state with a certain degree of confidence includes the population mean. As you may suspect, the larger the interval we specify, the greater our confidence that the mean will be included; but larger intervals give us less specific information about the exact value of the population mean. As a compromise, researchers have agreed that the 95% confidence interval and the 99% confidence interval are the best intervals to use when an interval estimate of the population mean is desired.

The confidence interval is centered about our point estimate ($\overline{X}$) of the population mean, and the boundaries of the 95% confidence interval can be calculated using the following formulas:

$$\text{Upper limit of 95\% confidence interval: } \overline{X} + [t_{.05}][s_{\overline{X}}]$$

$$\text{Lower limit of 95\% confidence interval: } \overline{X} - [t_{.05}][s_{\overline{X}}]$$

BOX 11.2

THE MARGIN OF ERROR IN SURVEY RESULTS

As you learned in Chapter 5, survey research relies heavily on sampling. Survey research is conducted when we would like to know the characteristics of a population (e.g., preferences, attitudes, demographics), but often it is impractical to survey the entire population. Responses from a sample are used to describe the larger population. Well-selected samples will provide good descriptions of the population, but it is unlikely that the results for a sample will describe the population exactly. For example, if the average age in a classroom of 33 college students is 26.4, it is unlikely that the mean age for a sample of 10 students from the class will be exactly 26.4. Similarly, if it were true that 65% of a city's population favor the present mayor and 35% favor a new mayor, we wouldn't necessarily expect an exact 65:35 split in a sample of 100 voters randomly selected from the city population. We expect some "slippage" due to sampling, some "error" between the actual population values and the estimates from our sample. At issue, then, is how accurately the responses from the sample represent the larger population.

It is possible to estimate the margin of error between the sample results and the true population values. Rather than providing a precise estimate of a population value (e.g., "65% of the population prefer the present mayor"), the margin of error presents a range of values that are likely to contain the true population value (e.g., "between 60% and 70% of the population prefer the present mayor"). What specifically is this range?

The margin of error provides an estimate of the difference between the sample results and the population values due simply to chance or random factors. The margin of error gives us the range of values we can expect due to sampling error—remember that we expect some error; we don't expect to describe the population exactly. Let us assume that a poll of many voters is taken and a media spokesperson gives the following report: "Results indicate that 63% of those sampled favor the incumbent, and we can say

with 95% confidence that the poll has a margin of error of 5%." The reported margin of error with the specified level of confidence (usually 95%) indicates that the percentage of the actual population who favor the incumbent is estimated to be found in the interval between 58% and 68% (5% is subtracted from and added to the sample value of 63%). It's important to remember, however, that we usually don't know the true population value. The information we get from the sample and the margin of error is the following: 63% of the sample favor the incumbent, and we are 95% confident that if the entire population were sampled, between 58% and 68% of the population would favor the incumbent. This can be represented on a graph by plotting the value obtained for the sample (63%), with error bars representing the margin of error. Figure 11.1 displays error bars around the sample estimate.

Margins of error are routinely included in media reports of national surveys. The goal of these surveys is to tell you with a "margin of error" what the true population value is. Similarly, the goal of many scientific studies is to tell you the margin of error, now usually called a confidence interval, for an estimate of a population value.

FIGURE 11.1 Error bars are used to represent the margin of error for the estimate of the population value.

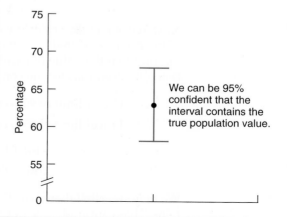

We can be 95% confident that the interval contains the true population value.

We have already described procedures for computing the sample mean ($\overline{X}$) and the estimated standard error of the mean ($s_{\overline{X}}$). The unfamiliar symbols in the two equations for the limits of the 95% confidence interval are t and .05.

We briefly discussed the alpha (α) level of .05 in Chapter 6. It is typically associated with inferential tests of statistical significance (i.e., NHST), and we will have much more to say about alpha levels in Chapter 12. In the case of confidence intervals, $\alpha = (1 -$ level of confidence) is expressed as a proportion. So, for the 95% confidence interval, $\alpha = (1 - .95) = .05$ and for the 99% confidence interval, $\alpha = (1 - .99) = .01$.

The t statistic included in the equation is defined by the number of degrees of freedom, and the statistical significance of t can be determined by looking in Appendix Table A.2. For a single sample mean, the degrees of freedom are $N - 1$. You will learn more about the t statistic in Chapter 12 when we discuss NHST. At this point let us simply concentrate on the calculation and proper interpretation of a confidence interval using the above formulas.

An example will illustrate how we obtain a confidence interval for a single mean. Suppose you obtained a random sample of students at your university and measured their intelligence using a brief but valid and reliable measure of this construct. Assume 30 students ($N = 30$) were tested and the mean intelligence score was 115 with a sample standard deviation of 14. The population of students is represented by the thousands of students attending your university. And while the sample mean is a good point estimate of the population mean (i.e., our best guess of the population mean), we must acknowledge that if another random sample of 30 students were selected and tested the sample mean would not likely be exactly 115. There will be some slippage, or "error," due to this random process. Recall that the standard error of the mean is one measure of the error in estimation.

Rather than rely simply on a point estimate of the population mean, we can obtain an interval estimate by finding the 95% confidence interval for the population mean using the formulas presented earlier. We first calculate the estimated standard error of the mean:

$$s_{\overline{X}} = \frac{s}{\sqrt{N}} = \frac{14}{\sqrt{30}} = \frac{14}{5.48} = 2.55$$

Next, we obtain the critical t value. Because there were 30 students, the degrees of freedom associated with the t statistic are $30 - 1$ or 29. Using Table A.2 we can find that the value of t with alpha of .05 and 29 degrees of freedom is 2.04. Using the formulas for the confidence interval, we have

Upper limit of 95% confidence interval = 115 + [2.04][2.55]

Lower limit of 95% confidence interval = 115 − [2.04][2.55]

Upper limit = 115 + 5.20 = 120.20

Lower limit = 115 − 5.20 = 109.80

We may state that there is a .95 probability that the interval 109.80 to 120.20 contains ("has captured") the population mean (see Box 11.3).

BOX 11.3

INTERPRETING CONFIDENCE INTERVALS FOR A SINGLE MEAN: RINGS AND STAKES

Having calculated the .95 confidence interval for a population mean we may state that

> the odds are 95/100 that the obtained confidence interval contains the true population mean.

The confidence interval either does or does not contain the true mean (e.g., Mulaik, Raju, & Harshman, 1997). A .95 probability associated with the confidence interval for a mean refers to the probability of capturing the true population mean if we were to construct many confidence intervals based on different random samples of the same size. That is, confidence intervals around the sample mean tell us what happens if we were to repeat this study under the same conditions (e.g., Estes, 1997). In 95 of 100 replications we would expect to capture the true mean with our confidence intervals.

Having calculated the 95% confidence interval for a population mean we should NOT state that

> the odds are 95/100 that the true mean falls in this interval.

This statement may seem to be identical to the statement above. It isn't. Keep in mind that the value in which we are interested is fixed, a constant; it is a population characteristic or parameter. Intervals are not fixed; they are characteristics of sample data. Intervals are constructed from sample means and measures of dispersion that are going to vary from study to study and, consequently, so do confidence intervals.

Howell (2002) provides a nice analogy to help understand how these facts relate to our interpretation of confidence intervals. He suggests we think of the parameter (e.g., the population mean) as a stake and confidence intervals as rings. From the sample data the researcher constructs rings of a specified width that are tossed at the stake. When the 95% confidence interval is used, the rings will encircle the stake 95% of the time and will miss it 5% of the time. "The confidence statement is a statement of the probability that the ring has been on target; it is not a statement of the probability that the target (parameter) landed in the ring" (Howell, 2002, p. 208).

The narrower the interval, the better is our interval estimate of the population mean. You can see by examining the formulas for the upper and lower limits that the width of the interval depends on both the t statistic and the standard error of the mean. Both of these values are related to sample size such that each decreases as sample size increases; however, increases in sample size have the most effect on the standard error. Consider that doubling the sample size in the above example would produce a standard error of 1.81 ($14/\sqrt{60}$) and consequently a much narrower confidence interval. *The bottom line: Increasing sample size will improve the interval estimate of the mean.*

Confidence Intervals for a Comparison Between Two Independent Group Means
The procedure and logic for constructing confidence intervals for a difference between means is similar to that for setting confidence intervals for a single mean. Because our interest is now in the difference between the population means (i.e., "the effect" of our independent variable) we substitute $\overline{X}_1 - \overline{X}_2$

for $\overline{X}$ and use the estimated standard error of the difference between means. The 95% confidence interval for the difference between two population means is defined as

$$CI(95\%) = (\overline{X}_1 - \overline{X}_2) \pm (t_{0.5})(s_{\overline{X}_1 - \overline{X}_2})$$

where t is found in Table A.2 with degrees of freedom equal to $[(n_1 + n_2) - 2]$ at alpha = .05.

The estimated standard error of the difference between means is defined as

$$s_{\overline{X}_1 - \overline{X}_2} = \sqrt{\left[\frac{(n_1 - 1)s_1^2 + (n_2 - 1)s_2^2}{n_1 + n_2 - 2}\right]\left[\frac{1}{n_1} + \frac{1}{n_2}\right]}$$

As an illustration, let us calculate the confidence limits for the difference between the two means in our example vocabulary research study. The critical t value for alpha set at .05 is found in Table A.2 with degrees of freedom equal to $26 + 26 - 2$, or 50. This value is 2.009. We can obtain the estimated standard error of the difference between two means by

$$s_{\overline{X}_1 - \overline{X}_2} = \sqrt{\left[\frac{(26 - 1)109.45 + (26 - 1)150.44}{26 + 26 - 2}\right]\left[\frac{1}{26} + \frac{1}{26}\right]} = 3.16$$

Therefore, the 95% confidence interval for the population mean difference is

$$CI(95\%) = 18.46 \pm (2.009)(3.16)$$
$$= 18.46 \pm 6.35$$

Thus, the upper limit is $18.46 + 6.35 = 24.81$, and the lower limit is $18.46 - 6.35 = 12.11$. Thus, we have .95 confidence that the interval 12.11 to 24.81 contains the true population difference for percentage correct on the vocabulary test when comparing older adults and college students. Note that the value of zero (0.0) is not within the interval. This is important when interpreting confidence intervals for the difference between two means (see Box 11.4). If the value of zero is within the inteval, then zero is a "plausible" value for the true difference between two means (Cumming & Finch, 2005). In Chapter 13 we show you how to report an analysis based on confidence intervals in the Results section of your research report.

Confidence Intervals for a Comparison Between Two Means in a Repeated Measures Design   Thus far we have considered experiments involving two independent groups of subjects. As you are aware, experiments also can be carried out by having each subject participate in each condition of the experiment or by "matching" subjects on some measure related to the dependent variable (e.g., IQ scores, weight). Such experiments are called matched groups designs, within-subjects designs, or repeated measures designs (see Chapter 7). For example, suppose a cognitive psychologist wants to compare people's performance on

---

BOX 11.4

INTERPRETING CONFIDENCE INTERVALS FOR A DIFFERENCE BETWEEN TWO MEANS: LOOKING FOR ZERO

Having calculated a 95% confidence interval for the difference between two means, we can state that

> the odds are 95/100 that the obtained confidence interval contains the true population mean difference or absolute effect size.

The width of the confidence interval provides information about effect size. By using confidence intervals we obtain information about the probable effect size of our independent variable. Obtained effect sizes vary from study to study as characteristics of samples and procedures differ (see, for example, Grissom & Kim, 2005). The confidence interval "specifies a probable range of magnitude for the effect size" (Abelson, 1997, p. 130). It indicates that the effect size likely could be as small as the value of the lower boundary and as large as the value of the upper boundary. Researchers are sometimes amazed to see just how large an interval is needed to specify an

effect size with a high degree of confidence (e.g., Cohen, 1995). Thus, the narrower the width of the confidence interval, the better job we have done at estimating the true effect size of our independent variable. Of course, the size (width) of the confidence interval is directly related to sample size. By increasing sample size we get a better idea of exactly what our effect looks like.

It is important to determine if the confidence interval for a mean difference includes the value of zero. *When zero is included in the confidence interval, we must accept the possibility that the two population means do not differ.* Thus, we cannot conclude that an effect of the independent variable is present. Remember, confidence intervals give us a probable range for our effect. If zero is among the probable values, then we should admit our uncertainty regarding the presence of an effect (e.g., Abelson, 1997). You will see in Chapter 12 that this situation is similar to that when a nonsignificant result is found using NHST.

---

two different puzzles. Rather than asking two different groups of people to work on each puzzle, she might ask just one group of people to work on both puzzles. (Procedures for presenting materials in a repeated measures design were described in Chapter 7.) All the participants would then provide a score on both puzzles. As you will see, the difference between their scores serves as the measure of interest in a repeated measures design.

Procedures for assessing effect size in a matched groups or repeated measures design are somewhat more complex than those we reviewed for an independent groups design (see Cohen, 1988; and Rosenthal & Rosnow, 1991, for information pertaining to the calculation of d in these cases). One suggestion is to calculate an effect size measure as if the study were an independent groups design and apply Cohen's guidelines (i.e., .20, .50, .80) as before (e.g., Zechmeister & Posavac, 2003).

Confidence intervals, too, can be constructed for the population mean difference in a repeated measures design involving two conditions. However, the underlying calculations change for this situation. Specifically, when each subject is in both conditions of the experiment, t is based on difference scores (see Chapter 12). A difference score is obtained by subtracting the two scores provided by each subject. The mean of the difference scores ("D bar") is defined as

$$\overline{D} = \Sigma D/N$$

where D = a difference score and N is the number of difference scores (i.e., number of pairs of scores). Note that $\overline{D} = \overline{X}_1 - \overline{X}_2$.

The estimated standard error of the difference scores ($s_{\overline{D}}$) is defined as

$$s_{\overline{D}} = \frac{s_D}{\sqrt{N}} \quad \text{where } s_D \text{ is the standard deviation of difference scores}$$

Critical values of t are obtained by consulting Appendix Table A.2 with degrees of freedom equal to $N - 1$. Note that in this case N refers to the number of participants or pairs of scores in the experiment.

The confidence interval for the difference between two means in a repeated measures design can be defined as

$$CI = \overline{D} \pm (t_{0.5})(s_{\overline{D}})$$

Confidence Intervals for a Comparison Among Several Independent Group Means To illustrate the use of confidence intervals to analyze and interpret results when there are more than two means, we consider a study on how infants "grasp the nature of pictures" (DeLoache, Pierroutsakos, Uttal, Rosengren, & Gottlieb, 1998). Have you ever wondered whether infants understand that a picture of an object is not the same thing as the object itself? DeLoache and her colleagues were intrigued by research demonstrating that infants as young as 5 months seem to recognize the similarity between objects and their pictures, but also seem to recognize they're not the same. However, these research findings do not correspond well to anecdotes of infants' behavior toward pictures in which infants and young children try to grasp or pick up the objects represented in pictures, and even try to step into a picture of a shoe! These anecdotal reports suggest that infants and children treat pictured objects as if they are real objects, despite the two-dimensional representation in the picture. In four studies, DeLoache et al. examined "to what extent infants would treat depicted objects as if they were real objects" (p. 205).

We will focus on the results of the fourth study carried out by DeLoache et al. (1998). In the first three studies the researchers found that

- a large majority of 9-month-old infants, when exploring a picture book with "eight highly realistic color photographs of individual objects (common plastic toys)," tried to grasp a pictured object at least once (the average was 3.7 attempts) (Study 1);
- infants' grasping at pictures was not because the infants could not discriminate between two- and three-dimensional objects (Study 2); and
- "Beng infants from severely impoverished and largely nonliterate families living in a rural village in the West African nation of Côte d'Ivoire (Ivory

FIGURE 11.2   Infants' understanding of the nature of pictures was examined by observing how they investigate and point to pictured objects. (Research conducted by Dr. Alma Gottlieb among Beng infants in Ivory Coast from DeLoache, et al., 1998)

Coast)" manually explored and grasped at the pictures (including pictures of objects common in the Beng community) in the same way as American infants (Study 3). (See Figure 11.2.)

The purpose of the fourth study was to determine how children's behavior toward pictures changes with age.

Three age groups were tested: 9-month-olds, 15-month-olds, and 19-month-olds. Each group had 16 children, 8 girls and 8 boys. In addition to observing children's behaviors of investigating the pictures with their hands (grasping and other investigative behaviors), the researchers coded instances of pointing at pictured objects. Their results for infants' investigative behaviors are shown in Figure 11.3.

The independent variable, age of the children, is a natural groups design with three levels: 9 months, 15 months, and 19 months. This variable appears on the horizontal axis (x-axis). The dependent variable was number of investigative behaviors, and the mean number of these behaviors appears on the vertical axis (y-axis). As you can see in Figure 11.3, the mean number of investigative behaviors is highest for 9-month-olds, and much lower for 15-month-olds and 19-month-olds. The other important piece of information in the figure is the "bars" that surround each mean. We can use these bars to make decisions about whether there was an effect of the independent variable, age.

The bars around each mean in Figure 11.3 represent confidence intervals. As you have learned, confidence intervals tell us about the range of values we can expect for a population value. We cannot estimate the population value precisely because of sampling error, but we can estimate a range of probable values. The smaller the range of values expressed in our confidence interval, the better is our

FIGURE 11.3   Mean number of investigative behaviors with 95% confidence intervals for 9-month-olds, 15-month-olds, and 19-month-olds. (From DeLoache et al., 1998; used with permission.)

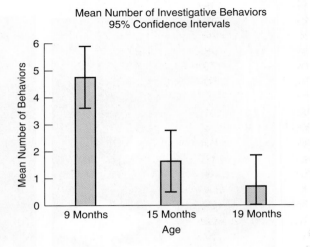

estimate of the population value. Each of the bars in Figure 11.3 represents a 95% confidence interval. However, the calculation of this interval in a multigroup study differs slightly from that when only one mean is present. Specifically, when calculating the estimated standard error of the mean, we may make use of the pooled variance from all the groups in the study. Let us illustrate.

The formula for the 95% confidence interval is the same as it was when there was only one mean:

$$\text{Upper limit of 95\% confidence interval: } \overline{X} + [t_{0.5}][s_{\overline{X}}]$$

$$\text{Lower limit of 95\% confidence interval: } \overline{X} - [t_{0.5}][s_{\overline{X}}]$$

However, the calculation of $s_{\overline{X}}$ differs from that with one mean; so, too, does the calculation of the degrees of freedom for the critical value of t. To estimate the standard error of the mean, we may pool the variances from the various groups to obtain one measure of variability. In this case we pool the information from as many groups as we have in the study. When the comparison involves two or more means from independent groups, the estimated standard error of the mean is calculated as follows. First, we find the standard deviation based on the pooled variance:[1]

$$s_{\text{pooled}} = \sqrt{\frac{(n_1 - 1)s_1^2 + (n_2 - 1)s_2^2 + (n_3 - 1)s_3^2 + \ldots}{(n_1 - 1) + (n_2 - 1) + (n_3 - 1) + \ldots}}$$

[1]The pooled estimate of the population standard deviation is equivalent to the square root of the mean square error in a between-groups analysis of variance (ANOVA). That is, $s_{\text{pooled}} = \sqrt{MS\text{error}}$. See Chapter 12 for discussion of ANOVA.

When sample sizes are equal, the estimated standard error is then defined as

$$s_{\overline{X}} = \frac{s_{\text{pooled}}}{\sqrt{n}} \quad \text{where } n = \text{sample size for each group}$$

Degrees of freedom are then calculated as $k(n - 1)$, where k is equal to the number of independent groups.

Looking again at Figure 11.3, we can see that for 9-month-olds, the mean number of investigative behaviors for the sample was 4.75. The expression $[t_{.05}][s_{\overline{X}}]$ in the equation for the 95% confidence interval in this analysis is 1.14. We can be 95% confident that the interval between 3.61 and 5.89 (4.75 ± 1.14) contains the population mean for 9-month-olds. Thus, the sample of 16 nine-month-old infants in this study is used to estimate the average number of investigative behaviors that would be demonstrated if the larger population of 9-month-olds were tested in this situation. For 15-month-olds, the mean number of investigative behaviors was 1.63, and we can be 95% confident that the interval between .49 and 2.77 (1.63 ± 1.14) contains the population mean. The sample mean for 19-month-olds was .69, and the 95% confidence interval has a lower bound of 0.0 (restricted by the range of permissible values) and an upper bound of 1.83 (.69 ± 1.14).

Box 11.5 provides information about how to interpret confidence intervals when there are three or more means.

BOX 11.5

INTERPRETING CONFIDENCE INTERVALS WHEN THERE ARE THREE OR MORE MEANS: DO INTERVALS OVERLAP?

In many research situations, we are not really interested in estimating the specific value of the population mean. For example, we aren't really interested in knowing the average number of times 9-month-olds can be expected to grasp at pictures. Instead, we are interested in the pattern of population means and comparing the relationships among population means (Loftus & Masson, 1994). That is, we wish to be able to compare the behavior of different groups. This, too, can be accomplished using confidence intervals. Consider once again the data from DeLoache et al.'s study.

We can use our estimates of the population means to ask: Do infants in the different age groups demonstrate different amounts of investigative behaviors? To answer this question we can examine the overlap of the 95% confidence intervals in Figure 11.3. Remember, the confidence interval is associated with a probability (e.g., .95) that the interval contains the population mean; the width of the interval tells us how precise is our estimate. We want to keep in mind that confidence intervals are intended to provide information about how well we have estimated a population value, usually a mean. Confidence intervals are not statistical tests like the *t*-test or *F*-test, where the emphasis is on comparing directly two or more means to see if the differences are "statistically significant." Nevertheless, as we stated previously, researchers often are interested in the pattern of population means, and we can use confidence intervals to help us detect these patterns.

When the intervals do not overlap, we can be confident that the population means differ. Nonoverlapping intervals tell us that the population means estimated by the sample means are probably not the same. For example, the 95% confidence interval for 9-month-olds does not overlap with the interval for 15-month-olds. From this

(continued)

we can conclude that infants who are 9 months old differ from those who are 15 months old in the number of investigative behaviors made when looking at pictures. (Examination of the sample means shows that the 9-month-olds investigate pictures more than the 15-month-olds.) A similar conclusion can be made when comparing intervals for 9-month-olds and 19-month-olds. A different conclusion must be made when comparing the intervals for 15-month-olds and 19-month-olds. Figure 11.3 demonstrates that the intervals for these two groups overlap. What should we now conclude? *If intervals overlap slightly, then we must acknowledge our uncertainty about the true mean difference and postpone judgment. If the intervals overlap such that the sample mean of one group lies within the interval of another group, we may conclude that the population means do not differ* (see Zechmeister & Posavac, 2003). Cumming and Finch (2005) provide a more precise analysis of the interpretation given to overlapping intervals based on *proportion overlap*.

Given these guidelines, what might we conclude about the difference between 15-month-olds and 19-month-olds observed in Figure 11.3? As can be seen in the figure, the 95% intervals overlap such that the confidence interval for the 15-month-olds contains the sample mean for the 19-month-olds. Thus, we can suggest that the population means do not differ. Even though the sample means differ (1.63 and .69, respectively), we cannot conclude that the population means differ (and in psychological research we are more interested in describing the population than the sample). For example, given the overlap of intervals seen in Figure 11.3, it is possible that the true population mean for the children who are 15 months old is really .69 (which is the sample mean of those who are 19 months old). Based on the means and confidence intervals presented in Figure 11.3, we may conclude that 9-month-old infants investigate pictures with their

hands more than 15-month-olds and 19-month-olds, and that these two older groups do not differ in the amount of investigative behavior they demonstrate. Note that we do not say that there is no possibility of a difference between the two older groups (populations). *Given these data,* we cannot say that a difference is present; however, the data also do not tell us with certainty that no difference is present. We must wait until more research is done, perhaps using larger sample sizes in order to obtain more precise estimates of the population means.

DeLoache et al.'s data for infants' *pointing* at pictures are presented in Figure 11.4. What conclusions can you draw based on the means and confidence intervals presented in this figure? Do 15-month-old infants differ from 9-month-old infants in their pointing behavior? Why or why not? Do 19-month-old infants differ from 15-month-old infants? Why or why not?

FIGURE 11.4 Mean number of pointing behaviors with 95% confidence intervals for 9-month-olds, 15-month-olds, and 19-month-olds. (From DeLoache et al., 1998; used with permission.)

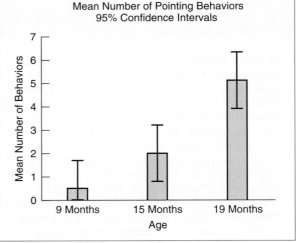

A final word of caution is necessary when examining "bars" drawn in graphs of research results. Bars presented in graphs of data in journal articles sometimes represent confidence intervals, but may also represent the standard error of the mean or standard deviations (Cumming & Finch, 2005). (A quick technique for approximating 95% confidence intervals is to multiply the standard error of the mean by 2.) To complicate matters further, authors sometimes fail to inform readers what is presented. When bars are presented, it is important to inform readers what they represent and how they were calculated (Estes, 1997).

ILLUSTRATION: DATA ANALYSIS FOR A CORRELATIONAL STUDY

- A correlation exists when two different measures of the same people, events, or things vary together—that is, when scores on one variable covary with scores on another variable.

Prediction, as you saw in Chapter 2, is an important goal of the scientific method. Correlational research frequently provides the basis for this prediction. A *correlation* exists when two different measures of the same people, events, or things vary together—that is, when scores on one variable covary with scores on another variable. For example, a widely known relationship exists between smoking and lung disease. The more individuals smoke (e.g., measured by duration of smoking), the greater their likelihood of contracting lung disease. Thus, smoking and lung disease covary, or go together. This correlation also can be expressed in these terms: the less people smoke, the lower their chances for contracting lung disease. Based on this correlation we can make predictions about lung disease. For example, if we know how long an individual has smoked, we can predict (to some degree) his or her likelihood of developing lung disease. The nature of our predictions and the confidence we have in making them depend on the direction and the strength of the correlation.

Correlational analyses are frequently associated with survey research (see Chapter 5). Respondents complete questionnaires asking about demographic variables (e.g., age, income), as well as their attitudes, opinions,

---

STRETCHING EXERCISE
A TEST OF YOUR UNDERSTANDING OF CONFIDENCE INTERVALS

Although the reporting of confidence intervals when analyzing data is strongly recommended, their use is only beginning to be seen in many psychology journals. Confidence intervals do share some of the problems of interpretation frequently associated with tests of statistical significance, specifically, with null hypothesis significance testing (NHST). Nevertheless, confidence intervals can and should be incorporated in your data analysis. To make sure you use them correctly, we have provided the following test of your understanding of this analysis technique.

Assume that an independent groups design was used to examine the effect on behavior of an independent variable with three levels (A, B, C). There were 15 participants randomly assigned to each condition, and measures of central tendency and variability were determined for each condition. The investigator also constructed 95% confidence intervals for each of the means. True or false? The researcher may reasonably conclude on the basis of this outcome that

1. The width of the confidence interval indicates how precise is the estimation of the population means.
2. If two intervals overlap, we know for sure that the population means are the same.
3. The odds are 95% that the true population mean falls in each interval.
4. If two intervals do not overlap, there is a 95% probability that the population means differ.
5. If two intervals do not overlap, we have good evidence that the population means differ.

and psychological well-being. A researcher then seeks to show how various responses are related, that is, how they are correlated. Do people who claim to have low self-esteem also report having difficulty dating? Is length of time children spend in day care related to measures of their attachment to their mothers? Do SAT scores predict success after college?

In what follows we examine how researchers analyze and interpret a correlational study.

Stage 1: Getting to Know the Data

Because there are always two sets of scores in a correlational study and because the relationship between these scores is of primary interest, the stages of data analysis proceed somewhat differently than when a comparison between means is the focus of the study. For purposes of illustration, assume that a researcher is interested in correlating two measures of psychological well-being obtained from self-reports of college students (see Chapter 5 for a discussion of self-report data). Both measures are in the form of 10-point rating scales. One measure is based on the question "How much do you worry about grades?" (1 = *not at all*, 10 = *very much*). The second measure is based on the question "How much difficulty do you experience concentrating during class exams?" (1 = *not at all*, 10 = *very much*).

Cleaning the Data   Each respondent provides two scores, and both sets of scores should be checked carefully for errors such as impossible values (e.g., numbers outside the range of the scale), as well as outliers. A stem-and-leaf display may be used to examine the data in each set. When possible responses are limited, as they typically are when scales are used, outliers are less likely to be present than when there is no limit on a response (e.g., reporting annual income).

Conclusion   Only when the investigator is assured that the data contain no errors or values that are likely to distort the findings should the analysis proceed.

Stage 2: Summarizing the Data

- The major descriptive techniques for correlational data are the construction of a scatterplot and the calculation of a correlation coefficient.
- The magnitude or degree of correlation is seen in a scatterplot by determining how well the points correspond to a straight line; stronger correlations more clearly resemble a straight line (linear trend) of points.
- The magnitude of a correlation coefficient ranges from −1.0 (a perfect negative relationship) to +1.0 (a perfect positive relationship); a correlation coefficient of 0.0 indicates no relationship.

Data summary begins by examining descriptive statistics for each set of scores. Then the degree of relationship between these sets of scores is summarized both graphically and numerically.

Central Tendency and Variability Measures of central tendency and variability should be calculated for both sets of scores. The means and standard deviations for the two sets of responses in our hypothetical study are

	Worry	Concentration difficulty
M	5.45	5.30
SD	1.93	1.98

Key Concept

In a correlational study our primary interest is not in the difference between the means but in the relationship between the sets of scores. The major descriptive techniques for correlational data are the construction of a *scatterplot* and the calculation of a *correlation coefficient*. A **scatterplot** describes the relationship between the two sets of scores. The correlation coefficient provides a quantitative summary of the relationship observed in the scatterplot. It is important to examine carefully the scatterplot before attempting to interpret a correlation coefficient. We first illustrate the construction of scatterplots and then show how a correlation coefficient is obtained and interpreted.

Drawing a Scatterplot The nature of a correlation can be represented graphically using a scatterplot. Scores for the two variables are represented on the *x*-axis and *y*-axis. Each individual has a value (or score) for each variable (e.g., ratings of worry and concentration difficulty). A scatterplot shows the intersecting points for each pair of scores. The magnitude or degree of correlation is seen in a scatterplot by determining how well the points correspond to a straight line; stronger correlations more clearly resemble a straight line of points. Figure 11.5 shows three different scatterplots. The correlation is stronger in the first (*a*) and third (*c*) panels than in the second (*b*) panel because the points in (*a*) and (*c*) more closely approximate a straight line.

FIGURE 11.5 Three scatterplots illustrating a positive (*a*), zero (*b*), and negative (*c*) correlation between scores on two variables: X and Y.

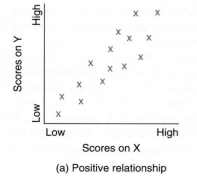

(a) Positive relationship

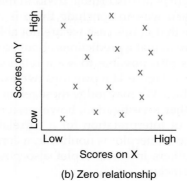

(b) Zero relationship

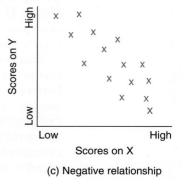

(c) Negative relationship

The direction of a correlation can be seen in the scatterplot by noting how the points are arranged. When the pattern of points seems to move from the lower left corner to the upper right [panel (*a*)], the correlation is positive (low scores on the *x*-axis go with low scores on the *y*-axis and high scores on the *x*-axis go with high scores on the *y*-axis). When the pattern of points is from the upper left to the lower right [panel (*c*)], the correlation is negative (low scores on the *x*-axis go with high scores on the *y*-axis and high scores on the *x*-axis go with low scores on the *y*-axis).

Assume that 20 college students provided responses to the two questions we described above. Assume further that the data were carefully inspected for errors and any anomalies and that the data were judged to be clean.

We wish to find out whether scores on one measure are related to (i.e., "go with") scores on the second measure. Is reported worry about grades related to self-reported difficulty concentrating on exams? To find out we can construct a scatterplot showing the relationship between the scores. A scatterplot is constructed by drawing a graph showing the intersection of the two measures from each respondent. The axes on the graph represent the two measures of interest. By convention, the measure of the behavior that "comes first" or that is used to predict the second behavior is placed on the horizontal or *x*-axis. The second behavior or that which is predicted by the first is placed on the vertical or *y*-axis. In many situations such a decision is easy. If you were correlating volunteers' blood alcohol levels and a measure of their performance on a driving simulator, we would easily see that alcohol was first consumed and then simulated driving performance was measured. Blood alcohol levels would be used to predict performance on a driving simulator. In other situations the decision is not as easy. Does worry about grades come before difficulty concentrating on exams? Or does difficulty concentrating on exams lead to worry about grades? We believe a case could be made for either.

Key Concept }

We want to examine the scatterplot for possible trends. More specifically, we look to see if there is evidence of a **linear trend** in the scatterplot. Simply, a linear trend is one that may be summarized by a straight line. As you have seen, scatterplots (*a*) and (*c*) in Figure 11.5 show evidence of a linear trend. It is also possible to see no trend in the scatterplot. In this case, scores on one measure are just as likely to go with low, middle, or high scores on the second measure. If there is no discernible trend in the graph, as in the middle panel of Figure 11.5, then we can conclude there is no relationship between the sets of scores. Note that in this case we are not able to use our knowledge of scores on one measure to make predictions about scores on the second measure.

Finally, it is also possible to see a relationship in the scatterplot, but one that is not linear. Figure 11.6 provides two examples of nonlinear relationships between variables. We may judge these relationships to be interesting and even worthy of further investigation; however, a nonlinear relationship poses serious problems of interpretation for a correlation coefficient. Consequently, if the trend in the scatterplot is nonlinear, a correlation coefficient should not be calculated. Outliers in a scatterplot also pose problems when interpreting a correlation coefficient.

FIGURE 11.6   Two examples of nonlinear relationships between two variables: X and Y.

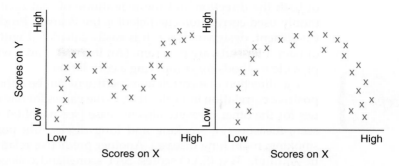

Figure 11.7 shows a scatterplot describing the relationship between scores on the worry (X) and concentration difficulty (Y) measures from our hypothetical survey. Since we really don't know in this case which factor "comes first," we have arbitrarily put the measure of worry on the *x*-axis and the measure of concentration difficulty on the *y*-axis in the scatterplot found in Figure 11.7. That is, we are using the measure of worry to predict the measure of concentration. Can you see a trend in the scatterplot? If so, is it generally linear?

Calculating a Correlation Coefficient   The direction and strength of a correlation are determined by computing a *correlation coefficient.* The correlation coefficient is a quantitative index of how well we are able to predict one set of scores (e.g., concentration ratings) using another set of scores (e.g., worry ratings). A

FIGURE 11.7   Scatterplot showing relationship between scores on self-report measure of degree of worry about grades (X) and self-report measure of difficulty concentrating during an exam (Y). Each point in the graph is the intersection of the two measures for each respondent.

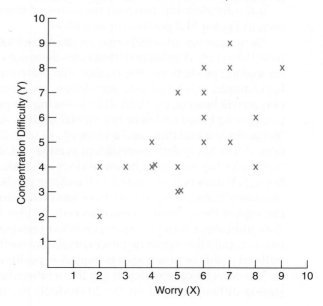

correlation coefficient expresses the relationship between two variables in terms of both the direction and the magnitude of that relationship. The most commonly used correlation coefficient is the Pearson Product-Moment Correlation Coefficient, designated as *r*. It is easily calculated with an electronic calculator or computer software program. (An Internet search will identify web sites that provide methods for computing a correlation.)

Key Concept

The direction of a correlation coefficient can be either positive or negative. A **positive correlation** indicates that, as the values for one measure increase, the values for the other measure also increase [see panel (*a*) in Figure 11.5]. As we've seen, measures of smoking and lung disease are positively correlated (more smoking, more lung disease). Another predictive relationship concerns Scholastic Aptitude Test (SAT) scores: SAT scores and college students' first-semester GPAs are positively correlated. Thus, we can predict that students with higher SAT scores should have higher first-semester GPAs, and students with lower SAT scores should have lower first-semester GPAs. With correlations, the "reverse" prediction can be made too. If we know only the first-semester GPAs of students, we can "predict" what their SAT scores were prior to entering college. Students with higher GPAs would be more likely to have higher SAT scores, and students with lower GPAs would be likely to have lower SAT scores.

Key Concept

In a **negative correlation,** as the value of one measure increases, the value of the other measure decreases [see panel (*c*) in Figure 11.5]. A national survey of high school seniors showed a negative correlation between the amount of time spent watching TV and the number of correct answers on an academic achievement test (Keith, Reimers, Fehrmann, Pottebaum, & Aubrey, 1986). Students who spent more time watching TV answered fewer questions correctly on an achievement test. What about the reverse prediction? Based on this finding, if you knew that a student scored very high on the achievement test, would you predict that the student had spent "a lot" of time or "a little" time watching TV?

Is the relationship between measures of worry and concentration difficulty seen in Figure 11.7 positive or negative?

The magnitude (degree) of a correlation coefficient can range in absolute values from 0.0 to 1.00. A value of 0.0 indicates there is no correlation and there is no basis for making predictions. The relationship between intelligence and mental illness, for example, exhibits a zero correlation; we cannot predict the likelihood that a person will become mentally ill by knowing the person's IQ (nor can we predict a person's IQ based on his or her mental health). A value of +1.00 indicates a perfect positive correlation, and a value of −1.00 indicates a perfect negative correlation. When a correlation coefficient is either +1.00 or −1.00, all the points in the scatterplot fall on a straight line and we can make predictions with absolute confidence. Values between 0 and 1.00 indicate predictive relationships of intermediate strength and, therefore, we have less ability to predict confidently. Remember, the sign of the correlation signifies only its direction; a correlation coefficient of −.46 indicates a stronger (more predictive) relationship than one of +.20. (*Note:* In practice, only the sign of negative correlation coefficients is indicated; a coefficient without a plus or minus sign is treated as positive, that is, +.20 = .20.)

The correlation coefficient for the relationship between worry and concentration difficulty based on the 20 students in our hypothetical study is .62. As indicated in the scatterplot in Figure 11.7, low scores on the worry measures tend to go with low scores on the concentration measure, and high scores with high scores. We may state that the two variables are positively related. More specifically, we can say that the more students worry, the more likely they are to have difficulty concentrating during exams. But can we say that worrying *causes* students to have difficulty concentrating?

Correlation and Causality   As you may recall from our discussion of correlations in Chapters 4 and 5, "correlation does not imply causation." Knowing that two variables are correlated does not allow us to infer that one causes the other (even if one precedes the other in time). It may be that worry about grades causes concentration difficulty during exams, or that the experience of difficulty while concentrating during exams causes worry about grades. In addition, a *spurious relationship* exists when a third variable can account for the positive correlation between worry about grades and concentration difficulty during exams. For example, number of hours employed might serve as a third variable that can account for this relationship. As number of hours employed increases, students might experience greater concern about grades and greater difficulty concentrating during exams.

Conclusion   A Pearson Product-Moment Correlation Coefficient may be used to summarize the relationship between two variables. It is important, however, to inspect the scatterplot of the two variables prior to calculating a Pearson r to make sure that the relationship is best summarized with a straight line, that is, that there is a linear trend. As the correlation coefficient approaches 1.00, the relationship between the two variables observed in the scatterplot approaches a straight line, and our ability to predict one variable based on knowledge of another increases.

Stage 3: Constructing a Confidence Interval for a Correlation

- We can obtain a confidence interval estimate of the population correlation, ρ, just as we did for the population mean, μ.

A Pearson r calculated from a sample is an estimate of the correlation in the population just as a sample mean is an estimate of a population mean (μ). The population correlation is symbolized with the Greek letter rho (ρ). Moreover, just as a sample mean is subject to sampling error or variation from sample to sample, so, too, is a correlation coefficient. Thus, in some situations we may wish to obtain an interval estimate of the population value, ρ, just as we did for the population value, μ. In other words, we can calculate a confidence interval for ρ. We will leave this topic, however, for books providing more comprehensive treatment of statistical procedures (e.g., Zechmeister & Posavac, 2003).

SUMMARY

There are three distinct, but related stages of data analysis: getting to know the data, summarizing the data, and confirming what the data reveal. In the first stage we want to become familiar with the data, inspecting them carefully, checking for errors and anomalous values. We want to be particularly sensitive to the presence of outliers, extreme values that just don't seem to go with the other values. Creating a stem-and-leaf display is a good way to visualize the distribution of numbers in a data set and to detect outliers. In the second stage we want to summarize the data set using descriptive statistics and graphical displays. Measures of central tendency (mean, median, mode) and measures of dispersion or variability (range and standard deviation) are particularly useful at this point. When a study involves the effect of an independent variable on a dependent variable, it is important to describe "how much of an effect" the independent variable had on the dependent variable. Measures of effect size are important when conducting meta-analyses, which summarize the effect of a particular variable across many different studies. An important effect size measure when two means are compared is Cohen's *d*.

In the third stage of data analysis, confirming what the data reveal, we determine what we may reasonably claim based on the evidence obtained in our study. There are two complementary approaches to this stage of analysis: null hypothesis significance testing (NHST) and the construction of confidence intervals. Both approaches rely on estimates of sampling variability to help a researcher make decisions about the true values of population parameters. Although the mean of a random sample is a good point estimate of the population mean, there will be variation ("error") in this estimate from sample to sample due to random or chance factors. The estimated standard error of the mean assesses how well a sample mean estimates the population mean. NHST focuses the researcher on the probability that the obtained results are "due to chance." A confidence interval specifies a range of values that have a certain probability (usually 95%) of containing a population value (e.g., the population mean). Confidence intervals are directly analogous to the "margin of error" that you may have heard in media reports of survey results. The narrower the interval, the better is our estimate of the population value; increasing sample size will improve the interval estimate.

Confidence intervals for the difference between two means provide evidence for the difference between the population means represented by the two sample means in a study. The width of the interval yields information concerning the probable effect size of an independent variable. When constructing confidence intervals for a difference between two means, if the interval includes the value of zero, then we do not want to say that an effect is present. In other words, if zero is within the interval, we should admit our uncertainty regarding the effect of the variable. Confidence intervals can be constructed for both independent groups and repeated measures designs.

When there are three or more means, confidence intervals are constructed for each mean. Conclusions about differences between means in a multigroup study are made by examining whether intervals overlap. When intervals do not overlap, we can be confident that the population means estimated by these sample means do in fact differ. However, when intervals overlap, we do NOT say that there is no difference between population means; rather, we must admit uncertainty about the true difference and wait until more research is done.

A correlational study is frequently carried out when the researcher's goal is that of prediction, for example, when predicting test performance from a paper-and-pencil measure of test anxiety. A correlation exists when two different measures of the same people, events, or things vary together. Just as we do when a study involves a comparison between means, we should carefully inspect and summarize the data from a correlational study. A scatterplot describes the relationship between two sets of scores; a correlation coefficient produces a quantitative summary of the relationship observed in the scatterplot. More specifically, the correlation coefficient describes how well the data in the scatterplot fit a straight line. The value of a correlation coefficient may vary from −1.00 to +1.00. The sign of the correlation coefficient (− or +) indicates the direction of the relationship; the absolute value of the coefficient (0.0 to 1.00) indicates the magnitude of the relationship. The closer the correlation coefficient approaches 1.00 (positive or negative), the more the points in the scatterplot fall on a straight line, and the stronger is the relationship.

A positive correlation exists when values for one measure increase as values on a second measure increase. In a negative correlation, as values of one measure increase, values on a second measure decrease. Knowing that there is a relationship (correlation) between two measures permits a researcher to predict scores on one measure based on knowledge of scores on a second measure. The closer the correlation coefficient is to 1.00, the better is the ability to predict. It is important to keep in mind that correlation alone is not evidence for a causal relationship between variables: Correlation does not imply causality.

KEY CONCEPTS

stages of data analysis 347	range 356
getting to know the data 347	standard deviation 356
summarizing the data 347	standard error of the mean 357
confirming what the data	estimated standard error of
reveal 347	the mean 357
stem-and-leaf display 352	confidence interval for a
measures of central tendency 355	population parameter 360
mode 355	scatterplot 373
median 355	linear trend 374
mean 356	positive correlation 376
measures of dispersion	negative correlation 376
(variability) 356	

REVIEW QUESTIONS

1 Identify the three major stages of data analysis and indicate what specific things a researcher typically will look to do at each stage.

2 What does a researcher attempt to do when constructing an "analysis story" to go with the results of a study?

3 Why must a researcher have a good knowledge of research methodology and statistical procedures to be able to use computer software to analyze results of a study?

4 Construct a stem-and-leaf display for the following set of numbers; then, report what you have learned by examining the data in this way. 36,42,25,26,26,21,22,43,40,69,21, 21,23,31,32,32,34,37,37,38,43,20,21,24,23,42,24,21,27,29,34,30,41,25,28.

5 Calculate the mean, median, and mode for the following data set: 7,7,2,4,2,4,5,6,4,5. Describe the advantages and disadvantages of the three measures of central tendency: mean, median, mode.

6 Calculate the standard deviation for the data set in Question 5. What does the standard deviation as a measure of variability tell you?

7 What does the estimated standard error of the mean tell you about a sample mean?

8 A study was done to investigate a newly created drug to increase memory performance. The study was done with rats. The dependent measure was number of errors made while learning a maze after being injected with the memory drug or a saline solution (control). Rats were randomly assigned to either the memory-enhancing drug or the control. A total of 30 rats was tested; there were 15 in each group. The mean (and standard deviation) for the drug group was 11.7 (4.7); that of the control group was 15.1 (5.1). (Lower numbers mean better performance.) What is the effect size for this study?

9 Why is a confidence interval also called a "margin of error"?

10 A random sample of 25 students was asked their opinion of the food service in the college dining hall. Students used a 7-point scale (1 = *horrible*, 7 = *great*) to indicate their opinion. The mean rating for the 25 students was 4.7 with a standard deviation (*s*) of 1.2.
A What is the 95% confidence interval for the population mean?
B Describe in words what the confidence interval tells you about the population mean.

11 What is the 95% confidence interval for the difference between the two means reported in Question 8? What is the correct interpretation of this interval?

12 How do you use confidence intervals to reach a conclusion about differences among means in a study with three or more means?

13 When inspecting data depicted in a scatterplot, why is it important to look for a linear trend in the data?

14 A researcher investigates whether there is a relationship between vocabulary size and performance on a reading comprehension test. Each of 15 sixth-grade students is given both a vocabulary test and a reading comprehension test (both tests are scored in terms of percentage correct). The results for the 15 schoolchildren are (with vocabulary scores given first): 44,67; 24,33; 67,45; 75,54; 34,45; 88,79; 57,67; 44,32; 87,95; 77,67; 87,78; 54,67; 90,78; 36,55; 79,91. Draw a scatterplot and calculate a correlation coefficient for these data.

15 Explain whether you could use the correlation you computed in Question 14 to support the claim that increasing vocabulary size causes increases in reading comprehension.

CHALLENGE QUESTIONS

1 A cognitive psychologist investigates the effect of four presentation conditions on the retention of a lengthy passage describing the Battle of Gettysburg. Let us simply denote the presentation conditions as A, B, C, and D. Sixty-four (N = 64) college students are randomly assigned in equal numbers to the four conditions (n = 16). Memory is tested after students hear the passage read aloud one time. The dependent variable is number of idea units recalled in the immediate written recall of the passage. The mean recall and standard deviation for each of the four presentation conditions are

	A	B	C	D
M	16.4	29.9	24.6	19.5
SD	4.6	7.1	5.9	6.3

A Calculate the 95% confidence intervals for the population means estimated by the four sample means.
B Interpret the pattern of confidence intervals by stating what we may conclude about the differences between the various population means.

2 A developmental psychologist investigates the effect of mothers' carrying behavior on infant sleep patterns. Specifically, the investigator solicits help from 40 mothers of newborns. The psychologist trains 20 mothers in a carrying method that presses the newborn's head against the mother's breast; the other 20 mothers are not instructed in a particular carrying method. All mothers are trained to record the number of hours their newborn sleeps each 24-hour period. Records are kept for 3 months in both groups. The mean 24-hour sleep period for infants in the instructed group was 12.6 ($SD = 5.1$); in the uninstructed group the mean was 10.1 ($SD = 6.3$).

  A Calculate the 95% confidence interval for the difference between the two means.

  B What may be said about the effect of training based on an examination of the confidence interval for this experiment?

  C What is the effect size for this experiment? Interpret the effect size measure based on Cohen's guidelines for small, medium, and large effects.

3 A researcher asks college students to play a demanding video game while listening to classical music and while listening to hard rock. All of the 10 students in the experiment play the video game for 15 minutes under each of the music conditions. Half of the students play while listening first to classical music and then to hard rock music; the other half perform with the types of music in the reverse order (see Chapter 7 for information on counterbalancing in a repeated measures design). The dependent variable is the number of correct "hits" in the game over the 15-minute period. The scores for the 10 students are

Student	Classical	Hard rock
1	46	76
2	67	69
3	55	51
4	63	78
5	49	66
6	76	67
7	58	63
8	75	75
9	69	78
10	77	85

  A Calculate the means for each condition. What trend do you see in the comparison of means?

  B Calculate the estimated standard error of the difference scores.

  C Find the 95% confidence interval for the difference between the two means in this repeated measures design.

  D State a conclusion regarding the effect of type of music on performance given the analysis of these results.

4 A social psychologist seeks to determine the relationship between a paper-and-pencil measure of prejudice and people's attitudes toward racial profiling as a crime deterrent. At the beginning of the semester, students in a general psychology class are asked to complete six different questionnaires. Among the questionnaires is a measure of prejudice. Later in the semester, students are invited to take part in an experiment examining attitudes about criminal behavior and law enforcement tactics. As part of the experiment, students complete a questionnaire asking about attitudes toward racial profiling as a crime deterrent. The researcher wishes to find out if scores on the prejudice measure obtained earlier will predict people's attitudes about racial profiling. Higher scores on the prejudice measure indicate greater prejudice, and higher scores on the profiling scale indicate greater support for racial profiling. Scores on both measures are obtained for 22 students as follows:

Student	1	2	3	4	5	6	7	8	9	10	11
Prejudice	19	15	22	12	9	19	16	21	24	13	10
Profiling	7	6	9	6	4	7	8	9	5	5	7

Student	12	13	14	15	16	17	18	19	20	21	22
Prejudice	12	17	23	19	23	18	11	10	19	24	22
Profiling	4	8	9	10	10	5	6	4	8	8	7

  A Draw a scatterplot showing the relationship between these two measures.

  B Inspect the scatterplot and comment on the presence or absence of a linear trend in the data.

  C Calculate a correlation coefficient for these data and comment on the direction and strength of the relationship.

  D On the basis of the correlational analysis, the researcher concludes that prejudicial thinking causes people to support racial profiling by law enforcement agencies. Comment on this conclusion based on what you know about the nature of correlational evidence.

Answer to Stretching Exercise

Statements 1 and 5 are True; 2, 3, and 4 are False.

Answer to Challenge Question 1

A   Begin by calculating s_{pooled} for the four groups, being sure to note that the problem provides the standard deviation for each group and the formula for s_{pooled} makes use of the variances. Thus, each standard deviation must be squared before multiplying by $n - 1$. The value of s_{pooled} is 6.04. The estimated standard error of the mean ($s_{\bar{X}}$) is, therefore, $6.04/\sqrt{n}$, or 1.51. The critical value of t at the .05 level is 2.00 (60 *df*) from Table A.2. The confidence intervals for the means are

A $16.4 \pm (2.00)(1.51) = 13.38$ to 19.42
B $29.9 \pm (2.00)(1.51) = 26.88$ to 32.92
C $24.6 \pm (2.00)(1.51) = 21.58$ to 27.62
D $19.5 \pm (2.00)(1.51) = 16.48$ to 22.52

B   (*Hint:* It may be helpful to draw a figure with columns representing the mean performance in each group and bars around the means corresponding to the confidence intervals. You may also want to review the information found in Box 11.5.) It can be seen that the A interval overlaps only the D interval. The C and D intervals overlap. Although the observed pattern of group means is our best estimate of the locations of the population values, the confidence intervals also provide information about the precision of our estimates. On the basis of these data, we may conclude that the population mean estimated by sample mean A differs from the population means represented by B and C. We will want to withhold judgment about the difference between A and D. We may also conclude that population means B and D differ, but admit we are uncertain about the true difference between B and C.

CHAPTER TWELVE

Data Analysis and Interpretation: Part II. Tests of Statistical Significance and the Analysis Story

CHAPTER OUTLINE

OVERVIEW

In Chapter 11 we introduced the three major stages of data analysis: *getting to know the data, summarizing the data, and confirming what the data tell us.* In the final stage of data analysis we evaluate whether we have sufficient evidence to make a claim about behavior. What, given these data, can we say about behavior? This stage is sometimes called *confirmatory data analysis* (e.g., Tukey, 1977). At this point we seek confirmation for what the data are telling us. In Chapter 11 we emphasized the use of confidence intervals to confirm what the data tell us. In this chapter we continue our discussion of confirmatory data analysis by focusing on tests of statistical significance, or what is more formally known as *null hypothesis significance testing* (NHST).

NHST is the most common approach to performing confirmatory data analysis. Nevertheless, tests of statistical significance have received persistent criticism (e.g., Cohen, 1995; Hunter, 1997; Loftus, 1991, 1996; Meehl, 1967; Schmidt, 1996), and for good reason. Researchers have been misusing (and misinterpreting) them for decades, all the time ignoring warnings that they were doing so (e.g., Finch, Thomason, & Cumming, 2002). There are critics who suggest we discard NHST altogether (e.g., Hunter, 1997; Schmidt, 1996). For example, an alternative approach focuses not on significance testing but on the probability of replicating an effect. This statistic, noted as p_{rep}, can be computed whenever an effect size can be calculated (see Killeen, 2005). However, the majority of experts suggest that we continue to use NHST but be cautious about its use (e.g., Abelson, 1995, 1997; Chow, 1988; Estes, 1997; Greenwald, Gonzalez, Harris, & Guthrie, 1996; Hagen, 1997; Krueger, 2001; Mulaik, Raju, & Harshman, 1997). Whatever the outcome of this debate within the psychology community, there is nearly universal agreement on the need (a) to understand exactly what it is that NHST can and cannot do, and (b) to increase our use of alternative methods of data analysis, especially the use of confidence intervals and the reporting of effect sizes. Sometimes these alternative techniques will supplant NHST, at other times they will complement NHST.

In what immediately follows we first provide an overview of NHST. Next we discuss the important concepts of experimental sensitivity and statistical power. Then we illustrate the NHST approach to data analysis using the same data we used in Chapter 11 to construct confidence intervals for the difference between two means. By using the same data, we can contrast the information obtained from NHST with that provided by confidence intervals. We point out what we can and cannot say based on NHST and suggest that information obtained from NHST can complement information obtained with confidence intervals. Finally, we provide some recommendations for you to follow when evaluating evidence for a claim about behavior involving two means and illustrate how to create an analysis story for your study.

The most common technique of confirmatory data analysis associated with studies involving more than two groups is a form of NHST called *analysis of variance (ANOVA)*. The rationale for using an ANOVA, the computational procedures associated with ANOVA, and the interpretation of ANOVA results are discussed in the second half of this chapter.

Null Hypothesis Significance Testing (NHST)

- Null hypothesis testing is used to determine whether mean differences among groups in an experiment are greater than the differences that are expected simply because of error variation.
- The first step in null hypothesis testing is to assume that the groups do not differ—that is, that the independent variable did not have an effect (the null hypothesis).
- Probability theory is used to estimate the likelihood of the experiment's observed outcome, assuming the null hypothesis is true.
- A statistically significant outcome is one that has a small likelihood of occurring if the null hypothesis were true.
- Because decisions about the outcome of an experiment are based on probabilities, Type I (rejecting a true null hypothesis) or Type II (failing to reject a false null hypothesis) errors may occur.

Statistical inference is both inductive and indirect. It is inductive because we draw general conclusions about populations on the basis of the specific samples we test in our experiments, as we do when constructing confidence intervals. However, unlike the approach using confidence intervals, this form of statistical inference is also indirect because it begins by assuming the null hypothesis. The **null hypothesis (H_0)** is the assumption that the independent variable has had no effect. Once we make this assumption, we can use probability theory to determine the likelihood of obtaining this difference (or a larger difference) observed in our experiment *IF* the null hypothesis were true. If this likelihood is small, we reject the null hypothesis and conclude that the independent variable did have an effect on the dependent variable. Outcomes that lead us to reject the null hypothesis are said to be *statistically significant*. A statistically significant outcome means only that the difference we obtained in our experiment is larger than would be expected if error variation alone (i.e., chance) were responsible for the outcome (see Box 12.1).

A statistically significant outcome is one that has only a small likelihood of occurring if the null hypothesis were true. But just how small is small enough? Although there is no definitive answer to this important question, the consensus among members of the scientific community is that outcomes associated with probabilities of less than 5 times out of 100 (or .05) if the null hypothesis were true are judged to be statistically significant. The probability we elect to use to indicate an outcome is statistically significant is called the **level of significance.** The level of significance is indicated by the Greek letter alpha (α). Thus, we speak of the .05 level of significance, which we report as $\alpha = .05$.

Just what do our results tell us when they are statistically significant? The most useful information we gain is that we know that something interesting has happened. More specifically, we know that the smaller the exact probability of the observed outcome, the greater is the probability that an exact replication will produce a statistically significant finding. But we must be careful what we mean by this statement. Researchers sometimes mistakenly say that when a result occurs with $p < .05$, "This outcome will be obtained 95/100 times if the study is repeated." This is simply not true. Simply achieving statistical

Key Concept

Key Concept

Perhaps you can appreciate the process of statistical inference by considering the following dilemma. A friend, with a sly smile, offers to toss a coin with you to see who pays for the meal you just enjoyed at a restaurant. Your friend just happens to have a coin ready to toss. Now it would be convenient if you could directly test whether your friend's coin is biased (by asking to look at it). Not willing to appear untrusting, however, the best you can do is test your friend's coin indirectly by assuming it is not biased and seeing if you consistently get outcomes that differ from the expected 50:50 split of heads and tails. If the coin does not exhibit the ordinary 50:50 split (after many trials of flipping the coin), you might surmise that your friend is trying, by slightly underhanded means, to get you to pay for the meal. Similarly, we would like to make a direct test of statistical significance for

an obtained outcome in our experiments. The best we can do, however, is to compare our obtained outcome with the expected outcome of no difference between frequencies of heads and tails. *The key to understanding null hypothesis testing is to recognize that we can use the laws of probability to estimate the likelihood of an outcome only when we assume that chance factors are the sole cause of that outcome.* This is not different from flipping your friend's coin a number of times to make your conclusion. You know that, based on chance alone, 50% of the time the coin should come up heads, and 50% of the time it should be tails. After many coin tosses, anything different from this probable outcome would lead you to conclude that something other than chance is working—that is, your friend's coin is biased.

significance (i.e., $p < .05$) does not tell us about the probability of replicating the results. For example, a result just below .05 probability (and thus statistically significant) has only about a 50:50 chance of being statistically significant (i.e., $p < .05$) if replicated exactly (Greenwald et al., 1996). On the other hand, knowing the exact probability of the results does convey information about what will happen if a replication were done. The smaller the exact probability of an initial finding, the greater the probability that an exact replication will produce a statistically significant ($p < .05$) finding (e.g., Posavac, 2002). Consequently, and as recommended by the American Psychological Association (APA), *always report the exact probability of results when carrying out NHST.*

Strictly speaking, there are only two conclusions possible when you do an inferential statistics test: Either you *reject* the null hypothesis or you *fail to reject* the null hypothesis. Note that we did *not* say that one alternative is to accept the null hypothesis. Let us explain.

When we conduct an experiment and observe the effect of the independent variable is not statistically significant, we do not reject the null hypothesis. However, neither do we necessarily accept the null hypothesis of no difference. There may have been some factor in our experiment that prevented us from observing an effect of the independent variable (e.g., ambiguous instructions to subjects, poor operationalization of the independent variable). As we will show later, too small a sample often is a major reason why a null hypothesis is not rejected. Although we recognize the logical impossibility of proving that a null hypothesis is true, we also must have some method of deciding which

TABLE 12.1   POSSIBLE OUTCOMES OF DECISION MAKING WITH INFERENTIAL STATISTICS

	States of the World	
	Null Hypothesis Is False.	Null Hypothesis Is True.
Reject null hypothesis	Correct decision	Type I error
Fail to reject null hypothesis	Type II error	Correct decision

independent variables are not worth pursuing. NHST can help with that decision. A result that is not statistically significant suggests we should be cautious about concluding that the independent variable influenced behavior in more than a trivial way. At this point you will want to seek more information, for example, by noting the size of the sample and the effect size (see the next section, "Experimental Sensitivity and Statistical Power").

There is a troublesome aspect to the process of statistical inference and our reliance on probabilities for making decisions. No matter what decision you reach, and no matter how carefully you reach it, there is always some chance you are making an error. The two possible "states of the world" and the two possible decisions an experimenter can reach are listed in Table 12.1. The two "states of the world" are that the independent variable either does or does not have an effect on behavior. The two possible correct decisions the researcher can make are represented by the upper-left and lower-right cells of the table. If the independent variable does have an effect, the researcher should reject the null hypothesis; if it does not, the researcher should fail to reject the null hypothesis.

The two potential errors (Type I error and Type II error) are represented by the other two cells of Table 12.1. These errors arise because of the probabilistic nature of statistical inference. When we decide an outcome is statistically significant because the outcome's probability of occurring under the null hypothesis is less than .05, we acknowledge that in 5 out of every 100 tests, the outcome could occur even if the null hypothesis were true. The level of significance, therefore, represents the probability of making a **Type I error:** rejecting the null hypothesis when it is true. The probability of making a Type I error can be reduced simply by making the level of significance more stringent, perhaps .01. The problem with this approach is that it increases the likelihood of making a **Type II error:** failing to reject the null hypothesis when it is false.

Key Concepts }

The problem of Type I errors and Type II errors should not immobilize us, but it should help us understand why researchers rarely use the word "prove" when they describe the results of an experiment that involved tests of statistical significance. Instead, they describe the results as "consistent with the hypothesis," or "confirming the hypothesis," or "supporting the hypothesis." These tentative statements are a way of indirectly acknowledging that the possibility of making a Type I error or a Type II error always exists. The .05 level of significance represents a compromise position that allows us to strike a balance and avoid making too many of either type of error. The problem of Type I errors and Type II errors also reminds us that *statistical inference can never replace replication as the best test of the reliability of an experimental outcome.*

EXPERIMENTAL SENSITIVITY AND STATISTICAL POWER

- Sensitivity refers to the likelihood that an experiment will detect the effect of an independent variable when, in fact, the independent variable truly has an effect.
- Power refers to the likelihood that a statistical test will allow researchers to reject correctly the null hypothesis of no group differences.
- The power of statistical tests is influenced by the level of statistical significance, the size of the treatment effect, and the sample size.
- The primary way for researchers to increase statistical power is to increase sample size.
- Repeated measures designs are likely to be more sensitive and to have more statistical power than independent groups designs because estimates of error variation are likely to be smaller in repeated measures designs.
- Type II errors are more common in psychological research using NHST than are Type I errors.
- When results are not statistically significant (i.e., $p > .05$), it is incorrect to conclude that the null hypothesis is true.

Key Concept

The *sensitivity of an experiment* is the likelihood that it will detect an effect of the independent variable if the independent variable does, indeed, have an effect (see Chapter 7). An experiment is said to have sensitivity; a statistical test is said to have **power.** The power of a statistical test is the probability that the null hypothesis will be rejected when it is false. The null hypothesis is the hypothesis of "no difference" and, thus, is false and should be rejected when the independent variable has made a difference. Recall that we defined a Type II error as the probability of failing to reject the null hypothesis when it is false. Power can also be defined as 1 minus the probability of a Type II error.

Power tells us how likely we are to "see" an effect that is there and is an estimate of the study's replicability. Because power tells us the probability of rejecting a false null hypothesis, we know how likely we are to miss a real effect. For instance, if a result is not significant and power is only .30, we know that a study with these characteristics detects an effect equal to the size we observed only 3 out of 10 times. Therefore, 7 of 10 times we do this study we will miss seeing the effect. In this case we may want to suspend judgment until the study can be redone with greater power.

The power of a statistical test is determined by the interplay of three factors: the level of statistical significance, the size of the treatment effect, and the sample size (Keppel, 1991). For all practical purposes, however, *sample size is the primary factor that researchers use to control power.* The differences in sample size that are needed to detect effects of different sizes can be dramatic. For example, Cohen (1988) reports the sample sizes needed for an independent groups design experiment with one independent variable manipulated at three levels. It takes a sample size of 30 to detect a large treatment effect; it takes a sample size of 76 to detect a medium treatment effect; and it takes a sample size of 464 to detect a small treatment effect. It thus takes over 15 times more participants to detect a small effect than it does to detect a large effect!

Using repeated measures experiments can also affect the power of the statistical analyses researchers use. As described in Chapter 7, repeated measures experiments are generally more sensitive than are independent groups experiments. This is because the estimates of error variation are generally smaller in repeated measures experiments. The smaller error variation leads to an increased ability to detect small treatment effects in an experiment. And that is just what the power of a statistical analysis is—the ability to detect small treatment effects when they are present.

When introducing NHST we suggested that making a so-called Type I error is equivalent to alpha (.05 in this case). Logically, to make this kind of error, the null hypothesis must be capable of being false. Yet, critics argue that the null hypothesis defined as zero difference is "always false" (e.g., Cohen, 1995, p. 1000) or, somewhat more conservatively, is "rarely true" (Hunter, 1997, p. 5). If an effect is always, or nearly always, present (i.e., there is more than a zero difference between means), then we can't possibly (or at least hardly ever) make a mistake by claiming that an effect is there when it is not. Following this line of reasoning, the only error we are capable of making is a Type II error (see Hunter, 1997; Schmidt & Hunter, 1997), that is, saying a real effect is not there. This type of error, largely due to low statistical power in many psychological studies, typically is much greater than .05 (e.g., Cohen, 1990; Hunter, 1997; Schmidt & Hunter, 1997). Let us suggest that Type I errors do occur if the null hypothesis is taken literally, that is, if there really is a literally zero difference between the population means or if we believe that in some situations it is worth testing an effect against a hypothesis of no difference (see Abelson, 1997; Mulaik et al., 1997). As researchers we must be alert to the fact that in some situations it may be important not to conclude an effect is present when it is not, at least not to more than a trivial degree (see Box 12.2).

BOX 12.2

DO WE EVER ACCEPT THE NULL HYPOTHESIS?

Despite what we have said thus far, there may be some instances in which researchers will choose to accept the null hypothesis (rather than simply fail to reject it). Yeaton and Sechrest (1986, pp. 836–837) argue persuasively that findings of no difference are especially critical in applied research. Consider some questions they cite to illustrate their point: Are children who are placed in daycare centers as intellectually, socially, and emotionally advanced as children who remain in the home? Is a new, cheaper drug with fewer side effects as effective as the existing standard in preventing heart attacks?

These important questions clearly illustrate situations in which accepting the null hypothesis (no effect) involves more than a theoretical issue—life and death consequences rest on making the correct decision. Frick (1995) argues that never accepting the null hypothesis is neither desirable nor practical for psychology. There may be occasions when we want to be able to state with confidence that there is no (meaningful) difference (see also Shadish, Cook, & Campbell, 2002).

Type II errors are likely when power is low, and low power has characterized many studies in the literature: *The most common error in psychological research using NHST is a Type II error.* Just because we did not obtain statistical significance does not mean that an effect is not present (e.g., Schmidt, 1996). In fact, one important reason for obtaining a measure of effect size is that we can compare the obtained effect with that found in other studies, whether or not the effect was statistically significant. This is the goal of meta-analysis (see Chapter 6). Although a nonsignificant finding does not tell us that an effect is absent, assuming that our study was conducted with sufficient power, a nonsignificant finding may indicate that an effect is so small that it isn't worth worrying about.

To determine the power of your study *before* it is conducted, you must first estimate the effect size anticipated in your experiment. An examination of the effect sizes obtained in previous studies for the independent variable of interest should guide your estimate. Once an effect size is estimated, you must then turn to "power tables" to obtain information about the sample size you should use in order to "see" the effect. These steps for conducting a power analysis are described more fully in various statistics textbooks (e.g., Zechmeister & Posavac, 2003), and power tables can be found on the Web. *When you have a good estimate of the effect size you are testing, it is strongly recommended that you perform a power analysis before doing a research study.*

Power tables are also used after the fact. When a study is completed and the finding is not statistically significant, the APA *Publication Manual* (2010) recommends that the power of your study be reported. In this way you communicate to other researchers the likelihood of detecting an effect that was there. If that likelihood was low, then the research community may wish to suspend judgment regarding the meaning of your findings until a more powerful replication of your study is carried out. On the other hand, a statistically nonsignificant result from a study with sufficient power may suggest to the research community that this is an effect not worth pursuing.

NHST: Comparing Two Means

- The appropriate inferential test when comparing two means obtained from different groups of subjects is a *t*-test for independent groups.
- A measure of effect size should always be reported when NHST is used.
- The appropriate inferential test when comparing two means obtained from the same subjects (or matched groups) is a repeated measures (within-subjects) *t*-test.

We now illustrate the use of NHST when comparing the difference between two means. First, we consider a research study involving two independent means. The data for this study are from our example vocabulary study, which we described in Chapter 11. Then we consider a situation where there are two dependent means, that is, when a repeated measures design was used.

Independent Groups

Key Concept

Recall that a study was conducted in which the vocabulary size of college students and older adults was assessed. The appropriate inferential test for this situation is a **t-test for independent groups.** We may use this test to evaluate the difference between the mean percent multiple-choice performance of the college and older adult samples. Statistical software programs typically provide the actual probability of an obtained t as part of the output. In fact, the APA *Publication Manual* (2010) advises that the exact probability be reported. When the exact probability is less than .001 (e.g., $p = .0004$), statistical software programs frequently report the exact probability as .000. (This was the case for the analysis reported above.) Of course, the exact probability is not .000 but something less than .001.

Therefore, for the vocabulary study we have been discussing, the result of the inferential statistics test can be summarized as

$$t(50) = 5.84, p < .001$$

In Chapter 11 we showed how an effect size, d, can be calculated for a comparison between two means. *A measure of effect size should always be reported when NHST is used.* You may recall that in Chapter 11 we calculated d for the vocabulary study as 1.65. Cohen's d also can be calculated from the outcome of the independent groups t-test according to the following formula:

$$d = \frac{2t}{\sqrt{df}} \quad \text{(see Rosenthal \& Rosnow, 1991)}$$

That is,

$$d = \frac{2(5.84)}{\sqrt{50}} = \frac{11.68}{7.07} = 1.65$$

Repeated Measures Designs

Thus far we have considered experiments involving two independent groups of subjects. As you are aware, experiments can also be carried out by having each subject participate in each condition of the experiment or by "matching" subjects on some measure related to the dependent variable (e.g., IQ scores, weight). Such experiments are called matched groups (see Chapter 6), within-subjects designs, or repeated measures designs (see Chapter 7). The logic of NHST is the same in a repeated measures design as it is in an independent groups design. However, the t-test comparing two means takes on a different form in a repeated measures design. The t-test in this situation is typically

Key Concept

called a direct-difference t or **repeated measures (within-subjects) t-test.** When carrying out a computer-assisted analysis when subjects are in both conditions of the experiment you will find that the data are entered differently than when independent groups of subjects are tested.

The numerator of the repeated measures t is the mean of the difference scores ($\overline{D}$) and is algebraically equivalent to the difference between the sample means (i.e., $\overline{X}_1 - \overline{X}_2$). The denominator is the estimated standard error of the difference scores (see Chapter 11). Statistical significance is determined by comparing the obtained t with critical values of t with df equal to $N - 1$. In this case, N refers to the number of participants or pairs of scores in the experiment. You interpret the obtained t as you would the t obtained in an independent groups design.

As noted in Chapter 11, assessing effect size in a matched groups or repeated measures design is somewhat more complex than for an independent groups design (see Cohen, 1988, and Rosenthal & Rosnow, 1991, for information pertaining to the calculation of d in these cases).

STATISTICAL SIGNIFICANCE AND SCIENTIFIC OR PRACTICAL SIGNIFICANCE

- We must recognize the fact that statistical significance is not the same as scientific significance.
- We also must acknowledge that statistical significance is not the same as practical or clinical significance.

Tests of statistical significance are an important tool in the analysis of research findings. We must be careful, however, to interpret statistically significant findings correctly (see Box 12.3). We must also be careful not to confuse a statistically significant finding with a scientifically significant finding. Whether the results of a study are important to the scientific community will depend on the nature of the variable under study (the effects of some variables are simply more important than those of others), how sound the study is (statistically significant findings can be produced with poorly done studies), and other criteria such as effect size (see, for example, Abelson, 1995).

Similarly, the practical or clinical significance of a treatment effect depends on factors other than statistical significance. These include the external validity associated with the study, the size of the effect, and various practical considerations (including financial ones) associated with a treatment's implementation. Even a statistically significant outcome showing a large effect size is not a guarantee of its practical or clinical significance. A very large effect size might be obtained as a part of a study that does not generalize well from the laboratory to the real world (i.e., has low external validity); thus, the results may be of little value to the applied psychologist. Moreover, a relatively large treatment effect that does generalize well to real-world settings may never be applied because it is too costly, too difficult to implement, too controversial, or too similar in its effects to existing treatments.

It is also possible that, given enough power, a small effect size will be statistically significant. Small effect sizes may not be practically important outside the laboratory. As we described in Chapter 6, external validity is an empirical question. It is important to conduct a study under conditions similar to those in which the treatment will be used in order to see whether a finding is practically

---

BOX 12.3

WHAT WE SHOULD NOT SAY WHEN A RESULT IS STATISTICALLY SIGNIFICANT ($p < .05$)

- We cannot specify the exact probability for the real difference between the means. For example, it is wrong to say that the probability is .95 that the observed difference between the means reflects a real (true) mean difference in the populations.

  The outcome of NHST reveals the probability of a difference this great by chance (given these data) assuming the null hypothesis is true. It does not tell us about probabilities in the real world (e.g., Mulaik et al., 1997). If results occur with a probability less than our chosen alpha level (e.g., .05), then all we can conclude is that the outcome is not likely to be a chance event in this situation.

- Statistically significant results do not demonstrate that the research hypothesis is correct. (For example, the data from the vocabulary study do not prove that older adults have greater vocabulary knowledge than do younger adults.)

  NHST (as well as confidence intervals) cannot prove that a research hypothesis is correct. A statistically significant result is (reasonably) sometimes said to "provide support for" or to "give evidence for" a hypothesis, but it alone cannot prove that the research hypothesis is correct. There are a couple of important reasons why. First, NHST is a game of probabilities; it provides answers in the form of likelihoods that are never 1.00 (e.g., p greater or less than .05).

There is always the possibility of error. If there is "proof," it is only "circumstantial" proof. As we have seen, the research hypothesis can only be tested indirectly by referring to the probability of these data assuming the null hypothesis is true. If the probability that our results occurred by chance is very low (assuming a true null hypothesis), we may reason that the null hypothesis is really not true; this does not, however, mean our research hypothesis is true. As Schmidt and Hunter (1997, p. 59) remind us, researchers doing NHST "are focusing not on the actual scientific hypothesis of interest." Second, evidence for the effect of an independent variable is only as good as the methodology that produced the effect. The data used in NHST may or may not be from a study that is free of confounds or experimenter errors. It is possible that another factor was responsible for the observed effect. (For example, suppose that the older adults in the vocabulary study, but not the college students, had been recruited from a group of expert crossword puzzle players.) As we have mentioned, a large effect size can easily be produced by a bad experiment. Evidence for a research hypothesis must be sought by examining the methodology of a study as well as considering the effect produced on the dependent variable. *Neither NHST, confidence intervals, nor effect sizes tell us about the soundness of a study's methodology.*

---

significant. We are not likely to carry out such an empirical test, however, if the effect size is small (although see Rosenthal, 1990, for important exceptions).

RECOMMENDATIONS FOR COMPARING TWO MEANS

We offer the following recommendations when evaluating the data from a study looking at the difference between two means. First, keep in mind the final goal of data analysis: to make a case based on our observations for a claim about behavior. In order to make the best case possible, you will want to explore various alternatives for data analysis. Don't fall into the trap of thinking that there is one and only one way to provide evidence for a claim about behavior. When there is a choice (and there almost always is), as recommended by the APA's

Task Force on Statistical Inference (Wilkinson et al., 1999), use the simplest possible analysis. Second, when using NHST be sure to understand its limitations and what the outcome of NHST allows you to say. Always consider reporting a measure of effect magnitude when using NHST, and also a measure of power, especially when a nonsignificant result is found. Although there will be some situations when effect size information is not warranted—for example, when testing a theoretical prediction of direction only (e.g., Chow, 1988), these situations are relatively rare. In many research situations, and in nearly all applied situations, effect size information is an important, even necessary, complement to NHST. Finally, researchers must "break the habit" of relying solely on NHST and consider reporting confidence intervals for effect sizes in addition to, or even rather than, *p* values associated with results of inferential tests. The APA *Publication Manual* (2010, p. 33) strongly recommends the use of confidence intervals.

REPORTING RESULTS WHEN COMPARING TWO MEANS

We are now in a position to model a statement of results that takes into account the information gained from all three stages of data analysis, the complementary evidence obtained by using confidence intervals (Chapter 11) and NHST, and the recommendations of the APA *Publication Manual* (2010) regarding reporting results (see especially pp. 32–35 of the *Manual*). Additional help on reporting results using both NHST and a confidence interval (abbreviated *CI* in a Results section) is found in Chapter 13.

Reporting Results of the Vocabulary Study   We may report the results as follows:

> The mean performance on the multiple-choice vocabulary test for college students was 45.58 (*SD* = 10.46); the mean of the older group was 64.04 (*SD* = 12.27). This difference was statistically significant, $t(50) = 5.84$, $p < .001$, $d = 1.65$, 95% CI [12.11, 24.81]. Older participants in this study had a greater vocabulary size than did the younger participants.

Commentary   Descriptive statistics in the forms of means and standard deviations summarize "what happened" in the experiment as a function of the independent variable (age). Because the exact probability was less than .001, results are reported at $p < .001$, but note that exact probabilities are to be reported when .001 or greater. The exact probability conveys information about the probability of an exact replication (Posavac, 2002). That is, we know that the results are "more reliable" than if a larger exact *p* value had been obtained. This information is not learned when only confidence intervals are reported. The sentence beginning "Older participants in this study . . ." summarizes in words what the statistical analysis revealed. It is always important to tell your reader directly what the analysis shows. This becomes increasingly important as the number and complexity of analyses performed and reported in a research study increase. An effect size (i.e., *d*) is also reported as recommended by the APA *Publication Manual*. This information is valuable to researchers doing meta-analyses and who wish to compare results of studies using similar variables. On the other hand, confidence intervals provide a range of possible effect sizes in terms of actual mean differences and not a single value such as Cohen's *d*. Because zero is not within the interval, we know that the outcome would be statistically significant at the .05 level (see Chapter 11). However, as the APA *Manual* emphasizes, confidence intervals provide information about precision of estimation and location of an effect that is not given by NHST alone. Recall from Chapter 11 that the smaller the confidence interval, the more precise is our estimate.

Power Analysis   When we know the effect size, we can determine the statistical power of an analysis. Power, as you will recall, is the probability that a statistically significant effect will be obtained. Suppose that a previous study of vocabulary size contrasting younger and older adults produced an effect size of .50, a medium effect according to Cohen's (1988) rule of thumb. We can use power tables created by Cohen to determine the number of participants needed in a test of mean differences to "see" an effect of size .50 with alpha .05. A power table identifies the power associated with various effect sizes as a function of sample size. It turns out that the sample size (in each group) of a two-group study would have to be about 64 to achieve power of .80 (for a two-tailed test). Looking for a medium effect size, we would need a total of 128 (64 × 2) participants to obtain statistical significance in 8 of 10 tries. Had the researchers been looking for a medium effect, their vocabulary study would have been underpowered. As it turns out, anticipating a large effect size, a sample size of 26 was appropriate to obtain power of .80.

If the result is not statistically significant, then an estimate of power should be reported. If, for example, using an independent groups design the outcome had been $t(28) = 1.96$, $p > .05$, with an effect size of .50, we can determine the power of the study after the fact. Assuming equal-size groups in the study, we know that there were 15 subjects in each group ($df = n_1 + n_2 - 2$, or $28 = 15 + 15 - 2$). A power analysis will reveal that power for this study is .26. A statistically significant outcome would be obtained in only about 1 of 4 attempts with this sample size and when a medium (.50) effect must be found. In this case, researchers

STRETCHING EXERCISE
A TEST OF (YOUR UNDERSTANDING OF) THE NULL HYPOTHESIS TEST

As should be apparent by now, understanding, applying, and interpreting results of NHST is no easy task. Even seasoned researchers occasionally make mistakes. To help you avoid mistakes, we provide a true-false test based on the information presented thus far about NHST.

Assume that an independent groups design was used to assess performance of participants in an experimental and control group. There were 12 participants in each condition, and results of NHST with alpha set at .05 revealed

$t(22) = 4.52$, $p = .006$. True or false? The researcher may reasonably conclude on the basis of this outcome that

1 The null hypothesis should be rejected.
2 The research hypothesis has been shown to be true.
3 The results are of scientific importance.
4 The probability that the null hypothesis is true is only .006.
5 The probability of finding statistical significance at the .05 level if the study were replicated is greater than if the exact probability had been .02.

would need to decide if practical or theoretical decisions should be made on the basis of this result or if "more research is needed." Should you pursue advanced study in psychology, you will want to explore more about power analysis.

DATA ANALYSIS INVOLVING MORE THAN TWO CONDITIONS

Thus far we have discussed the stages of data analysis in the context of an experiment with two conditions, that is, two levels of one independent variable. What happens when we have more than two levels (conditions) or, as is often the case in psychology, more than two independent variables? The most frequently used statistical procedure for analyzing results of psychology experiments in these situations is the analysis of variance (ANOVA).

We illustrate how ANOVA is used to test null hypotheses in four specific research situations: single-factor analysis of independent groups designs; single-factor analysis for repeated measures designs; two-factor analysis for independent groups designs; and two-factor analysis for mixed designs. We recommend that, before proceeding, you review the information presented in Chapters 6, 7, and 8 that describes these research designs.

ANOVA FOR SINGLE-FACTOR INDEPENDENT GROUPS DESIGN

- Analysis of variance (ANOVA) is an inferential statistics test used to determine whether an independent variable has had a statistically significant effect on a dependent variable.
- The logic of analysis of variance is based on identifying sources of error variation and systematic variation in the data.
- The F-test is a statistic that represents the ratio of between-group variation to within-group variation in the data.
- The results of the initial overall analysis of an omnibus F-test are presented in an analysis of variance summary table; comparisons of two means can then be used to identify specific sources of systematic variation in an experiment.
- Although analysis of variance can be used to decide whether an independent variable has had a statistically significant effect, researchers examine the descriptive statistics to interpret the meaning of the experiment's outcome.
- Effect size measures for independent groups designs include eta squared (η^2) and Cohen's f.
- A power analysis for independent groups designs should be conducted prior to implementing the study in order to determine the probability of finding a statistically significant effect, and power should be reported whenever nonsignificant results based on NHST are found.
- Comparisons of two means may be carried out to identify specific sources of systematic variation contributing to a statistically significant omnibus F-test.

Key Concept }

Overview   Statistical inference requires a test to determine whether or not the outcome of an experiment was statistically significant. The most commonly used inferential statistics test in the analysis of psychology experiments is the **ANOVA.** As its name implies, the analysis of variance is based on analyzing different sources of variation in an experiment. In this section we briefly introduce how the analysis of variance is used to analyze experiments that involve independent groups with one independent variable, or what is called a **single-factor independent groups design.** Although ANOVA is used to analyze the results of either random groups or natural groups designs, the assumptions underlying ANOVA strictly apply only to the random groups design.

There are two sources of variation in any random groups experiment. First, variation within each group can be expected because of individual differences among subjects who have been randomly assigned to a group. The variation due to individual differences cannot be eliminated, but this variation is presumed to be balanced across groups when random assignment is used. In a properly conducted experiment, the differences among subjects within each group should be the only source of error variation. Participants in each group should be given instructions in the same way, and the level of the independent variable to which they've been assigned should be implemented in the same way for each member of the group (see Chapter 6).

The second source of variation in the random groups design is variation between the groups. If the null hypothesis is true (no differences among groups), any observed differences among the means of the groups can be attributed to error variation (e.g., the different characteristics of the participants in the groups). As we've seen previously, however, we don't expect sample means to be exactly identical. Fluctuations produced by sampling error make it likely that the means will vary somewhat—this is error variation. Thus, the variation among the different group means, when the null hypothesis is assumed to be true, provides a second estimate of error variation in an experiment. If the null hypothesis is true, this estimate of error variation *between* groups should be similar to the estimate of error variation *within* groups. Thus, the random groups design provides two independent estimates of error variation, one within the groups and one between the groups.

Now suppose that the null hypothesis is false. That is, suppose the independent variable has had an effect in your experiment. If the independent variable has had an effect, the means for the different groups should be different. An independent variable that has an effect on behavior should produce systematic differences in the means across the different groups of the experiment. That is, the independent variable should introduce a source of variation among the groups of the experiment—it should cause the groups to vary. This systematic variation will be added to the differences in the group means that are already present due to error variation. That is, between-group variation will increase.

The *F*-Test We are now in a position to develop a statistic that will allow us to tell whether the variation due to our independent variable is larger than would be expected on the basis of error variation alone. This statistic is called *F*; it is named after Ronald Fisher, the statistician who developed the test. The conceptual definition of the ***F*-test** is

$$F = \frac{\text{Variation between groups}}{\text{Variation within groups}} = \frac{\text{Error variation} + \text{systematic variation}}{\text{Error variation}}$$

If the null hypothesis is true, there is no systematic variation between groups (no effect of the independent variable) and the resulting F-test has an expected value of 1.00 (since error variation divided by error variation would equal 1.00). As the amount of systematic variation increases, however, the expected value from the F-test becomes greater than 1.00.

The analysis of experiments would be easier if we could isolate the systematic variation produced by the independent variable. Unfortunately, the systematic variation between groups comes in a "package" along with error variation. Consequently, the value of the F-test may sometimes be larger than 1.00 simply because our estimate of error variation between groups happens to be larger than our estimate of error variation within groups (i.e., the two estimates should be similar but can differ due to chance factors). How much greater than 1.00 does the F statistic have to be before we can be relatively sure that it reflects true systematic variation due to the independent variable? Our earlier discussion of statistical significance provides an answer to this question. To be statistically significant, the F value needs to be large enough so that its probability of occurring if the null hypothesis were true is less than our chosen level of significance, usually .05.

We are now ready to apply the principles of NHST and the procedures of ANOVA to analyze a specific experiment.

Analysis of Single-Factor Independent Groups Design   The first step in doing an inferential statistics test like the F-test is to state the research question the analysis is intended to answer. Typically, this takes the form of "Did the independent variable have any overall effect on performance?" Once the research question is clear, the next step is to develop a null hypothesis for the analysis. The experiment we will discuss as an example examines the effect on memory retention of several kinds of memory training. There are four levels (conditions) of this independent variable and, consequently, four groups of participants. Each sample or group represents a population. The initial overall analysis of the experiment is called an **omnibus F-test.** The null hypothesis for such omnibus tests is that all the population means are equal. Remember that the null hypothesis assumes no effect of the independent variable. The formal statement of a null hypothesis (H_0) is always made in terms of population characteristics. These population characteristics are indicated by Greek letters, and the population mean is symbolized as μ ("mu"). We can use a subscript for each mean to represent the levels of the independent variable. Our null hypothesis then becomes

Key Concept

$$H_0\text{: } \mu_1 = \mu_2 = \mu_3 = \mu_4$$

The alternative to the null hypothesis is that one or more of the means of the populations are not equal. In other words, the alternative hypothesis (H_1) states that H_0 is wrong; there is a difference somewhere. The alternative hypothesis becomes

$$H_1\text{: NOT } H_0$$

TABLE 12.2   NUMBER OF WORDS RECALLED IN A MEMORY EXPERIMENT

| | Instruction (A) | | | | | | |
Subject	Control (a_1)	Subject	Story (a_2)	Subject	Imagery (a_3)	Subject	Rhymes (a_4)
1	12	6	15	11	16	16	14
2	10	7	14	12	16	17	14
3	9	8	13	13	13	18	15
4	11	9	12	14	12	19	12
5	8	10	12	15	15	20	12
Mean	10.0		13.2		14.4		13.4
Standard deviation	1.6		1.3		1.8		1.3
Range	8–12		12–15		12–16		12–15

If the type of memory training does have an effect on retention (i.e., if the independent variable produces systematic variation), then we will want to reject the null hypothesis.

The data in Table 12.2 represent the number of words correctly recalled (out of a possible 20) on a retention test in an experiment investigating memory training techniques. Five participants were randomly assigned to each of four groups (defined by the method of study that individuals were instructed to use to learn the words in preparation for the memory test). The control method involved no specific instructions, but in the three experimental groups participants were instructed to study by making up a story using the to-be-remembered words (story method), to use visual imagery (imagery method), or to use rhymes to remember the words (rhyme method). The independent variable being manipulated is "instruction," and it can be symbolized by the letter "A." The levels of this independent variable can be differentiated by using the symbols a_1, a_2, a_3, and a_4 for the four respective groups. The number of participants within each group is referred to as n; in this case, $n = 5$. The total number of individuals in the experiment is symbolized as N; in this case, $N = 20$.

An important step in the analysis of any experiment is to set up a data matrix like the one in Table 12.2. The number of correct responses is listed for each person in each of the four groups with each participant identified with a unique subject number. In order to understand the results of an experiment, it is essential to summarize the data prior to examining the outcome of the ANOVA. Below the data matrix the mean, range (minimum and maximum scores), and standard deviation are provided for each group.

Before examining the "significance" of any inferential test, try to get an impression of what the summary statistics are telling you. Look to see if there is a visible "effect" of the independent variable; that is, see if there is substantial variation among the means. By examining the ranges and standard deviations, get a sense of the variability in each group. (Remember, the less scores vary around their sample means, the better the chance of seeing an effect that is present.) The range, or difference between the minimum and maximum values,

TABLE 12.3   ANALYSIS OF VARIANCE SUMMARY TABLE FOR MEMORY EXPERIMENT

Source	Sum of Squares	df	Mean Square	F-Ratio	p
Group	54.55	3	18.18	7.80	0.002
Error	37.20	16	2.33		
Total	91.75	19			

is useful in identifying floor and ceiling effects. Is the variability among the groups similar? We want the variation to be relatively homogeneous as wide discrepancies in within-group variability can create interpretation problems when using ANOVA.

Our examination of the summary statistics reveals that there appears to be systematic variation among the means; the largest difference is seen between the Control (10.0) and the Imagery Group (14.4). All the experimental means are larger than the Control mean. Note that the range is similar for all the groups; the standard deviations, too, are fairly similar. This attests to the homogeneity (similarity) of variance among the groups. (Many computer programs provide a test of "homogeneity of variance" along with the ANOVA output.) Moreover, an inspection of the highest scores in each group shows that ceiling effects are not a problem in this data set (as total possible was 20).

The next step in an analysis of variance is to do the computations to obtain the estimates of variation that make up the numerator and denominator of the F-test. Calculations for F-tests are best done using a computer. We will focus, therefore, on interpreting the results of the computations. The results of an analysis of variance are presented in *Analysis of Variance Summary Table* (see Table 12.3).

Interpreting the ANOVA Summary Table   The summary table for the omnibus F-test for the independent groups design used to investigate the effect of memory training is found in Table 12.3. Remember that there were four groups of size $n = 5$ and, thus, overall $N = 20$. It is critically important you know what the ANOVA summary table contains. Thus, we examine the components of the summary table before looking at the outcome of the F-test for the experiment.

The left column of the summary table lists the two sources of variation described earlier. In this case the independent variable of the training group ("Group") is a source of variation between the groups, and the within-groups differences provide an estimate of error variation. The total variation in the experiment is the sum of the variation between and within groups. The third column is the degrees of freedom (df). In general, the statistical concept of degrees of freedom is defined as the number of entries of interest minus 1. Since there are 4 levels of the training independent variable, there are 3 df between groups. There are 5 participants within each group, so there are 4 df or $(n - 1)$ within each of the 4 groups. Because all 4 groups are the same size, we can determine the within-groups df by multiplying the df within each group by the number of groups (4×4) for 16 df. The total df is the number of subjects minus 1 ($N - 1$), or the sum of df between groups plus df within groups ($3 + 16 = 19$).

The sums of squares (*SS*) and the mean square (*MS*) are computational steps in obtaining the *F* statistic. The *MS* between groups (row 1) is an estimate of systematic variation plus error variation and is calculated by dividing the *SS* between groups by the *df* between groups (54.55/3 = 18.18). The *MS* within groups (row 2) is an estimate of error variation only and is computed by dividing the *SS* within groups by the *df* within groups (37.20/16 = 2.33). The *F*-test is calculated by dividing the *MS* between groups by the *MS* within groups (18.18/2.33 = 7.80).

We are now ready to use the information in the summary table to test for the statistical significance of the outcome in the memory training experiment. You may anticipate the conclusion already, knowing that when the null hypothesis is assumed to be true (i.e., no effect of the independent variable), the estimate of systematic variation plus error variation (numerator of the *F*-test) should be approximately equal to the estimate of error variation only (denominator of the *F*-test). As we see here, the estimate of systematic variation plus error variation (18.18) is quite a bit larger than the estimate of error variation alone (2.33).

The obtained *F* value in this analysis (7.80) appears in the second to last column of the summary table. The probability of obtaining an *F* as large as 7.80 if the null hypothesis were true is shown in the last column of the summary table (0.002). The obtained probability of .002 is less than the level of significance (α = .05), so we reject the null hypothesis and conclude that the overall effect of memory training is statistically significant. The results of NHST using ANOVA would be summarized in your research report as

$$F(3, 16) = 7.80, p = .002$$

An *F* statistic is identified by its degrees of freedom. In this case there are 3 *df* between groups and 16 *df* within groups (i.e., 3, 16). Note that the exact probability (i.e., .002) is reported because it gives us information about the probability of replication.

Just what have we learned when we find a statistically significant outcome in an analysis of variance testing an omnibus null hypothesis? In one sense, we have learned something very important. We are now in a position to state that manipulating the independent variable produced a change in performance (i.e., participants' memory for the to-be-remembered words). In another sense, merely knowing our outcome is statistically significant tells us little about the nature of the effect of the independent variable. The descriptive statistics (in our example, the mean number of words recalled as reported in Table 12.2) allow us to describe the nature of the effect. Note that only by examining the pattern of group means do we begin to learn what happened in our experiment as a function of the independent variable. *Never try to interpret a statistically significant outcome without referring to the corresponding descriptive statistics.*

Although we know that the omnibus *F*-test was statistically significant, we do not know the degree of relationship between the independent and dependent variables, and thus we should consider calculating an effect size for our independent variable. Based on the omnibus test alone we also are unable to state which of the group means differed significantly. Fortunately, there are analysis techniques that allow us to locate more specifically the sources of systematic variation in our experiments. One approach that is highly recommended is the use of confidence intervals (see Chapter 11). Confidence intervals can provide evidence for the pattern of population means estimated by our samples (see especially Box 11.5). Another technique is that of comparing two means. We first discuss an effect size measure for the independent groups ANOVA, as well as power analysis for this design, and then turn our attention to comparisons of two means.

Calculating Effect Size for Designs with Three or More Independent Groups

We mentioned earlier that the psychology literature contains many different measures of effect magnitude, which depend on the particular research design, test statistic, and other peculiarities of the research situation (e.g., Cohen, 1992; Kirk, 1996; Rosenthal & Rosnow, 1991). When we know one measure of effect magnitude, we usually can translate it to another, comparable measure without much difficulty. An important class of effect magnitude measures that applies to experiments with more than two groups is based on measures of "strength of association" (Kirk, 1996). What these measures have in common is that they allow estimates of the proportion of total variance accounted for by the effect of the independent variable on the dependent variable. A popular strength of association measure is **eta squared**, or η^2. It is easily calculated based on information found in the ANOVA Summary Table (Table 12.3) for the omnibus F-test (although many computer programs automatically provide eta squared as a measure of effect size). Eta squared is defined as

Key Concept

$$\frac{\text{Sum of squares between groups}}{\text{Total sum of squares}}$$

In our example (see Table 12.3),

$$\text{eta squared } (\eta^2) = \frac{54.55}{[(54.55) + (37.20)]} = .59$$

Eta squared can also be computed directly from the F-ratio for the between-groups effect when the ANOVA table is not available (see Rosenthal & Rosnow, 1991, p. 441):

$$\text{eta squared } (\eta^2) = \frac{(F)(df \text{ effect})}{[(F)(df \text{ effect})] + (df \text{ error})}$$

or, in our example,

$$\text{eta squared } (\eta^2) = \frac{(7.80)(3)}{[(7.80)(3)] + 16} = .59$$

Another measure, designed by J. Cohen, for designs with three or more independent groups is f (see Cohen, 1988). It is a standardized measure of effect size similar to d, which we saw was useful for assessing effect sizes in a two-group experiment. However, unlike d, which defines an effect in terms of the difference between two means, **Cohen's f** defines an effect in terms of a measure of dispersal among group means. Both d and f express the effect relative to (i.e., "standardized" on) the within-population standard deviation. Cohen has provided guidelines for interpreting f. Specifically, he suggests that small, medium, and large effects sizes correspond to f values of .10, .25, and .40. The calculation of f is not easily accomplished using the information found in the ANOVA Summary Table (Table 12.3), but it can be obtained without much difficulty once eta squared is known (see Cohen, 1988), as

$$f = \sqrt{\frac{\eta^2}{1 - \eta^2}}$$

or, in our example,

$$f = \sqrt{\frac{.59}{1 - .59}} = 1.20$$

We can thus conclude that memory training accounted for .59 of the total variance in the dependent variable and produced a standardized effect size, f, of 1.20. Based on Cohen's guidelines for interpreting f (.10, .25, .40), it is apparent that memory training had a large effect on recall scores.

Assessing Power for Independent Groups Designs

Once the effect size is known, we can obtain an estimate of power for a specific sample size and degrees of freedom associated with the numerator (between-groups effect) of the F-ratio. In our example, we set alpha at .05; the experiment was done with $n = 5$ and $df = 3$ for the between-groups effect (number of groups minus 1). The effect size, f, associated with our data set is very large (1.20), and there is no good reason to conduct a power analysis for this large effect which was statistically significant.

However, assume that the ANOVA in our example yielded a nonsignificant F and effect size was $f = .40$, still a large effect according to Cohen's guidelines. An important question to answer is "What was the power of our experiment?" How likely were we to see an effect of this size given an alpha of .05, a sample size of $n = 5$, and $df = 3$ for our effect? A power analysis reveals that under these conditions power was .26. In other words, the probability of obtaining statistical significance in this situation was only .26. In only approximately one-fourth of the attempts under these conditions would we obtain a significant result. The experiment would be considered underpowered, and it is unreasonable to make much of the fact that NHST did not reveal a significant result. To do so would ignore the very important fact that the effect of our independent variable was, in fact, large.

Although learning about power after the fact can be important, particularly when we obtain a nonsignificant outcome based on NHST, ideally power analysis should be conducted prior to an experiment in order to reveal the *a priori* (from the beginning) probability of finding a statistically significant effect. An experimenter who begins an experiment knowing that power is only

.26 would appear to be wasting time and resources given that the odds of *not* finding a significant effect are .74. Let us assume, therefore, that the experiment has not yet been conducted and that the investigator examined the literature on memory training and found that a large effect was often obtained by previous researchers in this area. Let us further assume that the researcher wants power to be .80 in the experiment. Because power is typically increased by increasing sample size, the researcher will want to find out what the sample size should be in order to find a large effect with power .80. Power analysis can do that and the researcher should take this information into consideration before doing the experiment.

Comparing Means in Multiple-Group Experiments

As we noted, knowing that "something happened" in a one-factor, multiple-group experiment is often not very interesting. We generally do research, or at least we should, with more specific hypotheses in mind than "this variable will have an effect" on the dependent variable. Neither the results of the omnibus *F*, nor a measure of overall effect size, tell us which means are significantly different from which other means. We cannot, for instance, look at the four means in our memory experiment and judge that the "imagery" mean is significantly different from the "story" mean. The results of the omnibus *F* simply tell us there is variation present among all the groups that is larger than would be expected by chance in this situation.

We can suggest two complementary ways to learn more about what happened in a multiple-group, single-factor experiment. One approach is to examine the probable pattern of population means by calculating 95% confidence intervals for the mean estimates in our experiment. This approach was illustrated in Chapter 11 when we showed how confidence intervals could be used to compare means in a multiple-group experiment. Confidence intervals can be used to make decisions about the probable differences among population means that are estimated by the means of our experimental groups. These decisions are made by examining whether confidence intervals overlap, and if they do, to what degree they overlap (see especially Box 11.5). Remember that the width of the confidence intervals provides information about the precision of our estimates.

The construction of confidence intervals for the memory experiment follows the procedure outlined in Chapter 12. Because the square root of the MS_{error} from the ANOVA summary table is equivalent to s_{pooled}, we can define the 95% confidence interval as

$$95\% \ CI = \overline{X} \pm \left[\sqrt{(MS_{error}/n)}\right](t_{crit})$$

where t_{crit} is the value for t with degrees of freedom associated with the MS_{error}.

In our example, the degrees of freedom for MS_{error} are 16 (see ANOVA Summary Table) and t_{crit} at the .05 level (two-tailed test) is 2.12. Therefore,

$$95\% \ CI = \overline{X} \pm \left[\sqrt{(2.33/5)}\right](2.12) = \overline{X} \pm (\sqrt{.466})(2.12) = \overline{X} \pm (.683)(2.12)$$
$$= \overline{X} \pm 1.45$$

FIGURE 12.1   Means and 95% confidence intervals for the memory-training experiment.

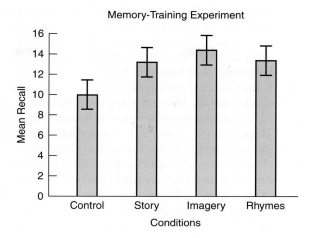

Results based on the construction of confidence intervals for the memory ex-periment are shown in Figure 12.1. You should be able by now to interpret these results, but see Box 11.5 in Chapter 11 if you need a refresher.

Key Concept }

A second approach makes use of NHST and focuses on a small set of two-group comparisons in order to specify the source of the overall effect of our independent variable. A **comparison of two means** allows the researcher to focus on a particular difference of interest. These comparisons can be quite sophisticated, for example, comparing the average of two or more groups in an experiment with the mean of another group or the average of two or more other groups. However, most of the time we will be interested in the differ-ence between just two means that are represented by individual groups. These two-mean comparisons are usually made after we have determined that our omnibus *F*-test is statistically significant.

One approach for carrying out comparisons of two means is to use a *t*-test; however, there is a slight modification in the way that *t* is calculated when comparing means in a multiple-group experiment. Specifically, we want to use a *pooled variance* estimate based on the within-group variation estimate (MS_{error}) found in our omnibus *F*-test. That is, our variance estimate uses information obtained from *all* the groups in our experiment, not just the two groups of inter-est. Therefore, the formula for this *t*-test is

$$t = \frac{\overline{X}_1 - \overline{X}_2}{\sqrt{[MS_{error}]\left[\frac{1}{n_1} + \frac{1}{n_2}\right]}}$$

The value for the MS_{error} is obtained from the ANOVA Summary Table of our omnibus *F*-test, and the degrees of freedom for our comparison *t*-test are those associated with the MS_{error} [or $k(n-1)$, where k = number of groups]. For ex-ample, the *MS* within groups (error) for the analysis reported in Table 12.3 is 2.33 with 16 degrees of freedom [$4(5-1) = 16$].

One comparison of two means we could make for the memory experiment is to compare the mean performance for the memory-training groups (combined) and the control group. The mean retention for the three memory training groups is 13.67 ($n = 15$), and the mean for the control group is 10.00 ($n = 5$). We can ask, does memory training, regardless of type (i.e., story, imagery, rhymes), lead to better memory retention than no memory training (control)? The null hypothesis is that the two population means do not differ (and the sample means differ by chance alone). When the appropriate values are substituted into the formula for t given above, we observe a statistically significant effect, $t(16) = 4.66, p = .0003$. Thus, memory training in this experiment, regardless of type, resulted in better memory retention for the words compared to no training. You can see that this statement is more specific than the statement we could make based on the omnibus F test, in which we could say only that the variation across the four conditions of the experiment was larger than that expected based on chance alone.

Cohen's d may be calculated for comparisons of two means using the results of the t-test. The formula for Cohen's d in this situation is

$$d = \frac{2(t)}{\sqrt{df_{\text{error}}}}$$

For the comparison between the three memory-training groups and the control group, substituting the value of 4.66 into the formula and with 16 df_{error}, the effect size, d, is 2.33. According to Cohen's criteria for effect sizes, this can be interpreted as a large effect of memory instruction relative to no instruction.

When using a t-test we are seeking to make a decision about rejecting or not rejecting the null hypothesis with a specific probability (e.g., $p = .05$). As noted previously, the exact probability associated with the outcome of NHST can be important when interpreting results (e.g., Posavac, 2002). The lower the exact probability, the greater is the likelihood that an exact replication would permit rejecting the null hypothesis at $p < .05$ (see Zechmeister & Posavac, 2003). Minimally, we want to report the lowest probability for statistical significance for which we have information. (Computers automatically give the exact probability of our test result.)

The results of the t comparison also permit us to contrast results with previous studies in two ways. First, we can note whether our experiment's findings for statistical significance are similar to those observed in a previous experiment. That is, did we *replicate* a statistically significant finding? Second, we can calculate an effect size (e.g., Cohen's d) for this two-mean comparison that may be compared with effects obtained in previous experiments, perhaps as part of a meta-analysis. Neither of these contrasts is easy to do using confidence intervals. That is, unlike NHST, confidence intervals do not provide an exact probability associated with a difference seen in our experiment and the calculation of an effect size is more directly carried out following a t-test (see Chapter 11).

In summary, we encourage you to look at your data and differences between means using more than one statistical technique, seeking evidence for "what happened" from different approaches to data analysis.

It will be necessary, of course, to prepare a written report of the results of your experiment. In Chapter 13 we provide you with help doing just that and model a typical results statement based on the recommendations of the APA *Publication Manual* (2010).

REPEATED MEASURES ANALYSIS OF VARIANCE

- The general procedures and logic for null hypothesis testing using repeated measures analysis of variance are similar to those used for independent groups analysis of variance.
- Before beginning the analysis of variance for a complete repeated measures design, a summary score (e.g., mean, median) for each participant must be computed for each condition.
- Descriptive data are calculated to summarize performance for each condition of the independent variable across all participants.
- The primary way that analysis of variance for repeated measures differs is in the estimation of error variation, or residual variation; residual variation is the variation that remains when systematic variation due to the independent variable and subjects is removed from the estimate of total variation.

The analysis of experiments using repeated measures designs involves the same general procedures used in the analysis of independent groups design experiments. The principles of NHST are applied to determine whether the differences obtained in the experiment are larger than would be expected on the basis of error variation alone. The analysis begins with an omnibus analysis of variance to determine whether the independent variable has produced any systematic variation among the levels of the independent variable. Should this omnibus analysis prove statistically significant, confidence intervals and comparisons of two means can be made to find the specific source of the systematic variation—that is, to determine which specific levels differed from each other. We have already described the logic and procedures for this general analysis plan for experiments that involve independent groups designs. We will focus in this section on the analysis characteristics specific to repeated measures designs and describe an example ANOVA summary table. The data used to illustrate this analysis are based on the time-perception experiment described in Chapter 7 and you may wish to review that discussion before proceeding.

Summarizing the Data   Recall that in a repeated measures design, each participant experiences every condition of the experiment. In a complete design, each participant experiences every condition more than once; in an incomplete design, each participant experiences every condition exactly once. In Chapter 7 we described an experiment in which participants estimated the duration of four time intervals (12, 24, 36, and 48 seconds) in a complete repeated measures design. For example, on a single trial, participants experienced a randomly determined time interval (e.g., 36 seconds) and then were asked to estimate the duration of the interval.

TABLE 12.4   DATA MATRIX AND ANALYSIS OF VARIANCE SUMMARY TABLE FOR A REPEATED
MEASURES DESIGN EXPERIMENT

Data Matrix

	Interval Length			
Participant	12	24	36	48
1	13	21	30	38
2	10	15	38	35
3	12	23	31	32
4	12	15	22	32
5	16	36	69	60
Mean (SD)	12.6 (2.0)	22.0 (7.7)	38.0 (16.3)	39.4 (10.5)

Note: Each value in the table represents the median of the participants' six responses at each level of the interval-length variable.

Source of Variation	df	SS	MS	F	p
Subjects	4	1553.5	—	—	—
Interval length	3	2515.6	838.5	15.6	.000
Residual (error variation)	12	646.9	53.9		
Total	19	4716.0			

The first step is to calculate a score to summarize each individual's performance in each condition. In the time-perception experiment, participants experienced each condition six times; thus, with four conditions in the experiment, each participant made 24 estimates. A median was used to summarize each participant's performance in each of the four conditions. The next step in summarizing the data is to calculate descriptive statistics across the participants for each of the conditions. The means and standard deviations (in parentheses) for each condition appear in Table 12.4. (See also Table 7.4).

The focus of the analysis was on whether the participants could discriminate intervals of different lengths. The null hypothesis for an omnibus analysis of variance for the data in Table 12.4 is that the population means estimated for each interval are the same. To perform an *F*-test of this null hypothesis, we need an estimate of error variation plus systematic variation (the numerator of an *F*-test). The variation among the mean estimates across participants for the four intervals provides the information we need for the numerator. We know, that if the different interval lengths did systematically affect the participants' judgments, then the mean estimates for the intervals would reflect this systematic variation. To complete the *F*-test, we also need an estimate of error variation alone (the denominator of the *F*-test). The source of variation in the repeated design is the differences in the ways the conditions affect different participants. This variance estimate is called *residual variation.* See Box 12.4.

Interpreting the ANOVA Summary Table   The analysis of variance summary table for this analysis is presented in the lower portion of Table 12.4. The computations

---

BOX 12.4

ESTIMATING ERROR AND SENSITIVITY IN A REPEATED MEASURES DESIGN

One distinctive characteristic of the analysis of repeated measures designs is the way in which error variation is estimated. We described earlier that for the random groups design, individual differences among participants that are balanced across groups provide the estimate of error variation, which becomes the denominator of the *F*-test. Because individuals participate in only one condition in these designs, differences among participants cannot be eliminated—they can only be balanced. In repeated measures designs, on the other hand, there is systematic variation among participants. Some participants consistently perform better across conditions, and some participants consistently perform worse. Because

each individual participates in each condition of repeated measures designs, however, differences among participants contribute equally to the mean performance in each condition. Accordingly, any differences among the means for each condition in repeated measures designs cannot be the result of systematic differences among participants. In repeated measures designs, however, differences among participants are not just balanced—they are actually eliminated from the analysis. *The ability to eliminate systematic variation due to participants in repeated measures designs makes these designs generally more sensitive than random groups designs.*

---

of a repeated measures analysis of variance would be done using a statistical software package on a computer. Our focus now is on interpreting the values in the summary table and not on how these values are computed. Table 12.4 lists the four sources of variation in the analysis of a repeated measures design with one manipulated independent variable. Reading from the bottom of the summary table up, these sources are (1) total variation, (2) residual variation, (3) variation due to interval length (the independent variable), and (4) variation due to subjects.

As in any summary table, the most critical pieces of information are the *F*-test for the effect of the independent variable of interest and the probability associated with that *F*-test assuming the null hypothesis is true. The important *F*-test in Table 12.4 is the one for interval length. The numerator for this *F*-test is the mean square (*MS*) for interval length; the denominator is the residual *MS*. There are four interval lengths, so there are 3 degrees of freedom (*df*) for the numerator. There are 12 *df* for the residual variation. We can obtain the *df* for the residual variation by subtracting the *df* for subjects and for interval length from the total *df*($19 - 4 - 3 = 12$). The obtained *F* of 15.6 has a probability under the null hypothesis of .0004, which is less than the .05 level of significance we have chosen as our criterion for statistical significance. So we reject the null hypothesis and conclude that the interval length was a source of systematic variation. This means that we can conclude that the participants' estimates did differ systematically as a function of interval length.

Figure 12.2 shows 95% confidence intervals around the means in the time-perception experiment. The procedure for constructing these intervals is the same as that for the independent groups experiment. Intervals were constructed using the MS_{error} (residual) in the omnibus ANOVA (as recommended by Loftus & Masson, 1994). That is,

$$95\% \; CI = \overline{X} \pm \left[\sqrt{(MS_{error}/n)} \right](t_{crit})$$

FIGURE 12.2 Means and 95% confidence intervals for the time-perception experiment.

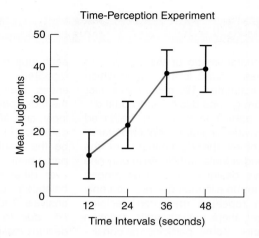

where t_{crit} is the value of t with the degrees of freedom associated with the MS_{error} (residual). The interpretation of confidence intervals in the repeated measures design is the same as that of the independent groups design (see Chapter 11).

Effect Size Measures As we mentioned previously, it is a good idea to include measures of effect size for your analyses. A typical measure of effect size for a repeated measures design is the strength of association measure called eta squared (η^2). It may be calculated by dividing the sum of squares for the within-subjects effect by the combined sums of squares for the within-subjects effect and residual or error. For our sample study,

$$\text{eta squared } (\eta^2) = \frac{SS_{effect}}{SS_{effect} + SS_{error}} = \frac{2515.6}{2515.6 + 646.9} = .795$$

This indicates the proportion of variance accounted for by the independent variable. In some cases, the omnibus analysis of variance would be followed by comparisons of two means as we saw in the independent groups design.

Two-Factor Analysis of Variance for Independent Groups Designs

The two-factor analysis of variance for independent groups designs is used for the analysis of experiments in which each of two independent variables was manipulated at two or more levels. The logic of complex designs with two independent variables and the conceptual basis for the analysis of these experiments are described in Chapter 8. In Chapter 8 you also learned to describe both main effects and interaction effects. We will focus in this chapter on the computer-assisted analysis of a factorial design that involves F-tests for the main effect of A, the main effect of B, and the interaction effect, A $\times$ B. The two-factor analysis for independent groups is applicable to experiments in which both independent variables are manipulated using a random groups design, in which both independent variables represent the natural groups design, or in which one independent variable represents the natural groups design and the other represents the random groups design. As we noted in Chapter 8, the analysis of a complex design proceeds somewhat differently depending on whether the omnibus F-test does or does not reveal an interaction effect. We first consider the analysis plan when an interaction effect is detected.

Analysis of a Complex Design with an Interaction Effect

- If the omnibus analysis of variance reveals a statistically significant interaction effect, the source of the interaction effect is identified using simple main effects analyses and comparisons of two means.
- A simple main effect is the effect of one independent variable at one level of a second independent variable.
- If an independent variable has three or more levels, comparisons of two means can be used to examine the source of a simple main effect by comparing means two at a time.
- Confidence intervals may be drawn around group means to provide information regarding the precision of estimation of population means.

Consider a hypothetical complex design involving two independent variables (A $\times$ B), each involving independent groups (random groups or natural groups). Variable A has two levels and Variable B has three levels. Thus, the design is a 2 $\times$ 3 independent groups design. The details of the experiment need not concern us, although let us assume there are five participants in each group ($n = 5$; $N = 30$). Table 12.5 shows mean performance for the six groups in this example. By now we trust that you know first to examine the summary statistics to see what trends are present in the data. How would you describe the results seen in Table 12.5? One way would be to state that there was very little difference among means across three levels of B for the first level of A, that is, for level a_1. On the other hand, means changed quite a bit across the same three levels of B for level a_2. Yet another way to describe these results is to use the subtraction method we discussed in Chapter 8 when complex designs

TABLE 12.5   MEAN PERFORMANCE OF GROUPS IN HYPOTHETICAL 2 $\times$ 3 DESIGN

		Variable B		
		b_1	b_2	b_3
Variable A	a_1	19.0	19.0	20.0
	a_2	10.6	15.8	18.2

were first introduced. Using this method will help determine whether there is an interaction effect. Examining the differences between the two means for a_1 and a_2 at each level of B (b_1, b_2, b_3) will show that the three differences (8.4, 3.2, 1.8) are different. This suggests that an interaction effect is present. As you learned in Chapter 8, graphing the means also will help you see the nature of this interaction effect. Let us assume that an omnibus F-test has confirmed that the interaction effect was statistically significant ($p < .05$).

Once we have confirmed that there is an interaction of two independent variables, we must locate more precisely the source of that interaction effect. There are statistical tests specifically designed for tracing the source of a significant interaction effect. Theses tests are called simple main effects and comparisons of two means (see Keppel, 1991) and were discussed briefly in Chapter 8. Comparisons between two means were also described earlier in this chapter.

Recall that a *simple main effect* is the effect of one independent variable at one level of a second independent variable. In fact, one definition of an interaction effect is that the simple main effects across levels are different. In a 2×3 design there are actually five simple main effects. Three of the simple main effects are represented by the effect of Variable A at each level of Variable B. The other two simple main effects are represented by the effect of Variable B at each level of Variable A. Which set of simple main effects are chosen for analysis will depend on the rationale behind the experiment. That is, it may be more important for interpreting the results to highlight one set of simple main effects more than another. Of course, finding that simple main effects are different for levels of either variable indicates an interaction effect.

How do we compute a simple main effect? Statistical software packages do not always permit simple main effects analyses to be computed and, when they do, can vary in the specific computational procedures that are followed. There are relatively simple ways to do these analyses with a calculator (e.g., Zechmeister & Posavac, 2003). However, let us suggest the following procedure that is easily done using an ANOVA software package.

Consider our example above. Suppose we wish to analyze the simple main effect for the first level of variable A, that is, for a_1. There are three "groups" (a_1b_1, a_1b_2, a_1b_3) in this analysis. One approach is to perform a simple (one-way) independent groups ANOVA for these data. In other words, assume that there are three random groups of participants assigned to three levels of an independent variable. Carry out this analysis and identify in the ANOVA Summary Table the mean square (MS) between groups (i.e., the MS for the effect of your variable). It is the sum of squares between groups divided by its df, which is the number of groups minus 1, or, in this case, $3 - 1$, and $df = 2$. To obtain an F-ratio you want to divide the MS between groups from this analysis by the MS_{error} (within groups) based on the overall F-test that you originally performed when examining effects in the 2×3 complex design. In our example, with 30 participants the df for the MS_{error} in the 2×3 design will be 24, so the critical F is that associated with 2 and 24 degrees of freedom.

Two of the simple main effects in our hypothetical experiment involve three means (i.e., levels a_1 and a_2 across three levels of B). If a statistical analysis reveals a significant simple main effect at one of these levels, then one can conclude that there is a difference among the means (i.e., among the three means at that level of variable A). If that is the case, then the next step is to conduct comparisons of two means to analyze the simple main effect more fully. Comparisons of two means will help determine the nature of the differences among the levels. The statistical analysis for comparison between two means makes use of the *t*-test as described earlier in this chapter. The MS_{error} from the omnibus 2 × 3 ANOVA Summary Table is used in the *t* formula and the *df* associated with that term (24 in our example) are used to find the critical *t* value at the .05 level.

If you are carrying out a simple main effects analysis for just two levels of an independent variable, such as comparing mean performance at a_1 and a_2 for the three levels of B, then you may use a *t*-test as you would for a two-mean comparison. Note that the sample sizes for your two-group *t*-test are based on the number of participants in each of the two cells that you are contrasting. In our hypothetical experiment $n = 5$ for each group. Finally, as we did with the two-mean comparisons discussed above, you may again use the MS_{error} from the 2 × 3 ANOVA as the error term for your *t*-test. Degrees of freedom for this two-group *t*-test will be that associated with the MS_{error} for your omnibus ANOVA. With two levels, a simple main effect compares the difference between two means and no additional comparisons are necessary.

Once an interaction effect has been thoroughly analyzed, researchers can also examine the main effect of each independent variable. In general, however, main effects are less interesting when an interaction effect is statistically significant.

Analysis with No Interaction Effect

- If an omnibus analysis of variance indicates the interaction effect between independent variables is not statistically significant, the next step is to determine whether the main effects of the variables are statistically significant.
- The source of a statistically significant main effect can be specified more precisely by performing comparisons that compare means two at a time and by constructing confidence intervals.

When the interaction effect is not statistically significant, the next step is to examine the main effects of each independent variable. If the overall main effect for an independent variable is not statistically significant, then there is nothing more to do. However, if a main effect is statistically significant, there are several approaches a researcher may take. For example, if there are three or more levels of the independent variable, the source of a statistically significant main effect can be specified more precisely by performing comparisons of two means using *t*-tests. Once again another approach is to construct confidence intervals around the group means as we illustrated in Chapter 11 when analyzing a single-factor independent groups design. The difference for the complex design is that the data for one independent variable are collapsed across the levels of other independent variables.

Effect Sizes for Two-Factor Design with Independent Groups

A common measure of effect size for a complex design using ANOVA is eta squared (η^2), or proportion of variance accounted for, which was discussed earlier in the context of single-factor designs. In calculating eta squared, it is recommended that we focus only on the effect of interest (see Rosenthal & Rosnow, 1991). Specifically, eta squared can be defined as

$$\eta^2 = \frac{SS_{\text{effect of interest}}}{SS_{\text{effect of interest}} + SS_{\text{within}}} \quad \text{(see Rosenthal \& Rosnow, 1991, p. 352)}$$

Thus, eta squared may be obtained for each of the three effects in an A $\times$ B design.

As noted above (and see Rosenthal & Rosnow, 1991), when the sums of squares for the effects are not available, eta squared can be computed using the *F* ratio (and *df*) for each effect of interest.

ROLE OF CONFIDENCE INTERVALS IN THE ANALYSIS OF COMPLEX DESIGNS

The analysis of a complex design can be aided by the construction of confidence intervals for the means of interest. For example, each mean in a 2 $\times$ 3 design can be bracketed with a confidence interval following the procedures outlined in Chapter 11 and earlier in this chapter. Recall that the formula is

$$\text{Upper limit of 95\% confidence interval: } \overline{X} + [t_{.05}][s_{\overline{X}}]$$

$$\text{Lower limit of 95\% confidence interval: } \overline{X} - [t_{.05}][s_{\overline{X}}]$$

When sample sizes are equal, the estimated standard error is defined as

$$s_{\overline{X}} = \frac{s_{\text{pooled}}}{\sqrt{n}} \quad \text{where } n = \text{sample size for each group}$$

Because the square root of the MS_{error} from the ANOVA Summary Table is equivalent to s_{pooled}, we can define the 95% confidence interval as

$$95\% \; CI = \overline{X} \pm (t_{.05})\left[\sqrt{(MS_{\text{error}}/\sqrt{n})}\right]$$

where $t_{.05}$ is defined by the degrees of freedom associated with the MS_{error}.

Figure 12.3 shows the confidence intervals around the six means in the hypothetical experiment we introduced above. An examination of the *CIs* tells us about the precision of our estimates. We want to examine the interval width and the probable pattern of *population* means by looking to see if the intervals around the sample means overlap and, if so, to what degree they overlap. Recall that a rule of thumb for interpreting confidence intervals suggests that if the intervals around means do not overlap, then the two means would likely be statistically significant if tested using NHST (see Box 11.5 in Chapter 11).

TWO-FACTOR ANALYSIS OF VARIANCE FOR A MIXED DESIGN

The two-factor analysis of variance for a mixed design is appropriate when one independent variable represents either the random groups or natural groups design and the second independent variable represents the repeated measures

FIGURE 12.3 Mean responses as a function of Variable A (a_1, a_2) and Variable B (b_1, b_2, b_3). The 95% confidence interval is shown around each mean.

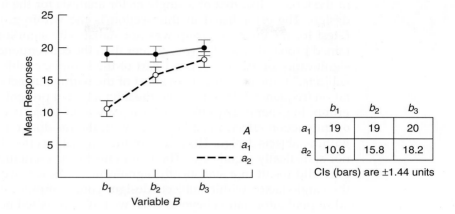

	b_1	b_2	b_3
a_1	19	19	20
a_2	10.6	15.8	18.2

CIs (bars) are ±1.44 units

design. The first independent variable is called the between-subjects factor (here symbolized as A). The second independent variable is called the within-subjects factor (symbolized as B). The two-factor analysis for a mixed design is somewhat of a hybrid of the single-factor analysis for independent groups and the single-factor analysis for the repeated measures designs. This particular complex design was discussed in Chapter 8 when we reported the results of a study by Kaiser et al. (2006) using the emotional Stroop test.

As you should now be aware, it is important to review the appropriate summary statistics and to appreciate the trends in the data before looking at the ANOVA Summary Table. An outline of a typical computer output for a two-factor analysis of variance for a mixed design is presented below. The details of the experiment providing the data for this analysis need not concern us. Be aware that some computer programs separate the output of a mixed design, showing first the output for the between-groups analysis and then the output for the within-subjects analysis (which includes the interaction effect). You may find that you have to scroll the computer screen to get all of the information.

	Between Subjects				
Source	SS	df	MS	F	p
Group	0.225	1	0.225	1.718	0.226
Error	1.049	8	0.131		
	Within Subjects				
Present	15.149	2	7.574	58.640	0.000
Present × Group	0.045	2	0.022	0.173	0.843
Error	2.067	16	0.129		

The summary table is divided into two parts. The "Between subjects" section includes the *F*-ratio for the main effect of groups. The form of this part of the table is like that of a single-factor analysis for the independent groups design. The error listed in this section is the within-groups variation. The *F*-test for the effect of group was not statistically significant because the obtained probability of .226 was greater than the conventional level of statistical significance of .05. The second part of the summary table is headed "Within subjects." It includes the main effect of the within-subjects variable of presentation frequency ("Present") and the interaction of presentation frequency and group. In general, any effect including a within-subjects variable (main effect or interaction effect) must be tested with the residual error term used in the within-subjects design. The *F*-test for the interaction effect is less than 1, so was not statistically significant. The main effect of presentation frequency, however, did result in a statistically significant *F*. (As was true in the analysis of the single-factor within-subjects design, your computer output may include additional information beyond what we have presented here.)

Interpreting the results of a two-factor analysis for a mixed design follows the logic for any complex design. Care must be taken, however, when analyzing a mixed design to use the appropriate error term for analyses beyond those listed in the summary table (i.e., simple main effects, comparisons of two means). For example, if a significant interaction effect is obtained, it is recommended that simple main effects be analyzed by treating each simple effect as a single-factor ANOVA at that level of the second independent variable. If, for instance, we had obtained a significant interaction effect between group and presentation frequency in our sample experiment, a simple main effect for a treatment group would involve carrying out a repeated measures ANOVA for only that group (see Keppel, 1991, for more information on these comparisons).

Effect size estimates in a mixed design also frequently make use of eta squared, that is, an estimate of proportion of variance accounted for by the independent variable. As you have seen, eta squared is defined as the *SS* effect divided by the *SS* effect plus the *SS* error for that effect.

REPORTING RESULTS OF A COMPLEX DESIGN

Reporting results of a complex design follows the general form of a report for a single-factor ANOVA but gives special attention to the nature of an interaction effect when it is present. The following are important elements of a report of the results of a complex design:

—description of variables and definition of levels (conditions) of each;
—summary statistics for cells of the design matrix in text, table, or figure, including when appropriate, confidence intervals for group means;
—report of *F*-tests for main effects and interaction effect with exact probabilities;
—effect size measure for each effect;
—statement of power for nonsignificant effects;
—simple main effects analysis when interaction effect is statistically significant;

—verbal description of statistically significant interaction effect (when present), referring reader to differences between cell means across levels of the independent variables;

—verbal description of statistically significant main effect (when present), referring reader to differences among cell means collapsed across levels of the independent variables;

—comparisons of two means, when appropriate, to clarify sources of systematic variation among means contributing to main effect;

—conclusion that you wish reader to make from the results of this analysis.

Additional tips for writing a Results section according to APA style requirements can be found in Chapter 13.

SUMMARY

Statistical tests based on null hypothesis significance testing (NHST) are commonly used to perform confirmatory data analysis in psychology. NHST is used to determine whether differences produced by independent variables in an experiment are greater than what would be expected solely on the basis of error variation (chance). The null hypothesis is that the independent variable did not have an effect. A statistically significant outcome is one that has a small probability of occurring if the null hypothesis were true. Two types of errors may arise when doing NHST. A Type I error occurs when a researcher rejects the null hypothesis when it is true. The probability of a Type I error is equivalent to alpha or the level of significance, usually .05. A Type II error occurs when a false null hypothesis is not rejected. Type II errors can occur when a study does not have enough power to correctly reject a null hypothesis. The primary way researchers increase power is by increasing sample size. By using power tables researchers may estimate, before a study is conducted, the power needed to reject a false null hypothesis and, after a study is completed, the likelihood of detecting the effect that was found. The exact probability associated with the result of a statistical test should be reported.

The appropriate statistical test for comparing two means is the *t*-test. When the difference between two means is tested, an effect size measure, such as Cohen's *d*, should also be reported. The APA *Publication Manual* strongly recommends that confidence intervals be reported as well as the results of NHST. When reporting the results of NHST, it is important to keep in mind that statistical significance (or nonoverlapping confidence intervals) is not the same as scientific or practical significance. Moreover, neither NHST, confidence intervals, nor effect sizes tell us about the soundness of a study's methodology. That is, none of these measures alone may be used to state that the alternative hypothesis (that the independent variable did have an effect) is correct. Only after we have examined carefully the methodology used to obtain the data for an analysis will we want to venture a claim about what influenced behavior.

Analysis of variance (ANOVA) is the appropriate statistical test when comparing three or more means. The logic of ANOVA is based on identifying both error variation and sources of systematic variation in the data. An *F*-test is constructed that represents error variation and systematic variation (if any) divided by error variation alone. Results of the overall analysis, called an omnibus *F*-test, are reported in an ANOVA Summary Table. A large *F*-ratio provides evidence that the independent variable had an effect. Effect size measures for a single-factor independent groups design include Cohen's *f* and eta squared (η^2). Comparisons of two means may be conducted following results of an omnibus *F*-test in order to more clearly specify the sources of systematic variation contributing to a significant omnibus *F*-test. Confidence intervals, too, may be meaningfully used to complement an ANOVA conducted with data from a multiple-group study and should be reported when the results of NHST are summarized.

A two-factor ANOVA is appropriate when a researcher examines simultaneously the effect on behavior of two or more independent variables in a complex design. When one independent variable represents an independent groups variable (random or natural groups) and another is a repeated measures within-subjects variable, we speak of a mixed design. An omnibus *F*-test is carried out to assess both main effects and the interaction effect of variables. When a statistically significant interaction effect is found, the source of the interaction effect may be pursued by conducting simple main effects. A simple main effect is the effect of an independent variable at only one level of a second independent variable. Confidence intervals, too, may be used to help understand the effect of an independent variable in a complex design. A commonly used measure of effect size in a complex design is eta squared.

KEY CONCEPTS

null hypothesis (H_0)   385
level of significance   385
Type I error   387
Type II error   387
power   388
t-test for independent groups   391
repeated measures
   (within-subjects) *t*-test   391
ANOVA   396

single-factor independent
   groups design   397
F-test   397
omnibus *F*-test   398
eta squared (η^2)   402
Cohen's *f*   403
comparison of two means   405

REVIEW QUESTIONS

1 What does it mean to say that the results of a statistical test are "statistically significant"?
2 Differentiate between Type I and Type II errors as they occur when carrying out NHST.
3 What three factors determine the power of a statistical test? Which factor is the primary one that researchers can use to control power?
4 Why is a repeated measures design likely to be more sensitive than a random groups design?
5 Describe one advantage and one limitation of using measures of effect size.
6 Why may a statistically significant result be neither scientifically nor practically significant?

7 Outline briefly the logic of the F-test.
8 Distinguish between the information you gain from an omnibus F-test and from comparisons of two means.
9 What is the primary way that a repeated measures ANOVA differs from that of an ANOVA for independent groups?
10 How does a simple main effect differ from an overall main effect?

CHALLENGE QUESTIONS

1 A researcher conducts an experiment comparing two methods of teaching young children to read. An older method is compared with a newer one, and the mean performance of the new method was found to be greater than that of the older method. The results are reported as $t(120) = 2.10$, $p = .04$ ($d = .34$).
   A Is the result statistically significant?
   B How many participants were in this study?
   C Based on the effect size measure, d, what may we say about the size of the effect found in this study?
   D The researcher states that on the basis of this result the newer method is clearly of practical significance when teaching children to read and should be implemented right away. How would you respond to this statement?
   E What would the construction of confidence intervals add to our understanding of these results?

2 A social psychologist compares three kinds of propaganda messages on college students' attitudes toward the war on terrorism. Ninety ($N = 90$) students are randomly assigned in equal numbers to the three different communication conditions. A paper-and-pencil attitude measure is used to assess students' attitudes toward the war after they are exposed to the propaganda statements. An ANOVA is carried out to determine the effect of the three messages on student attitudes. Here is the ANOVA Summary Table:

Source	Sum of Squares	df	Mean Square	F	p
Commun-ication	180.10	2	90.05	17.87	0.000
Error	438.50	87	5.04		

A Is the result statistically significant? Why or why not?
B What effect size measure can be easily calculated from these results? What is the value of that measure?
C How could doing comparisons of two means contribute to the interpretation of these results?
D Although the group means are not provided, it is possible from these data to calculate the width of the confidence interval for the means based on the pooled variance estimate. What is the width of the confidence interval for the means in this study?

3 A developmental psychologist gives 4th-, 6th-, and 8th-grade children two types of critical thinking tests. There are 28 children tested at each grade level; 14 received one form (A or B) of the test. The dependent measure is the percentage correct on the tests. The mean percentage correct for the children at each grade level and for the two tests is as follows:

Test	4th	6th	8th
Form A	38.14	63.64	80.21
Form B	52.29	68.64	80.93

Here is the ANOVA Summary Table for this experiment:

Source	Sum of Squares	df	Mean Square	F	p
Grade	17698.95	2	8849.48	96.72	.000
Test	920.05	1	920.05	10.06	.002
Grade × Test	658.67	2	329.33	3.60	.032
Error	7136.29	78	91.49		

(continued)

A Draw a graph showing the mean results for this experiment. Based on your examination of the graph, would you suspect a statistically significant interaction effect between the variables? Explain why or why not.

B Which effects were statistically significant? Describe verbally each of the statistically significant effects.

C What are the eta-squared values for the main effects of grade and test?

D What further analyses could you do to determine the source of the interaction effect?

E What is the simple main effect of Test for each level of Grade?

F Calculate confidence intervals for the six means in the experiment, and draw them around the means in your graph of these results

Answer to Stretching Exercise

Statements 1 and 5 are True; 2, 3, and 4 are False.

Answer to Challenge Question 1

A Yes. The obtained probability of this result assuming the null hypothesis is true is less than .05, the conventional level of significance.

B The degrees of freedom (*df*) are reported to be 120. For an independent groups *t*-test, $df = n_1 + n_2 - 2$. Thus, there must have been 122 participants.

C Cohen's guidelines suggest that an effect size of .20 is a small effect, .50 a medium or average effect, and .80 a large effect. An effect size of .34 is between a small and medium effect.

D The results of NHST do not speak directly to practical significance. If the newer method is much more expensive, too time-consuming to implement, or requires resources (e.g., new reading materials) that are not immediately available, then the practical significance of this finding (at least in the short run) is likely to be small. This may be especially the case because the effect size is not large. Also, the fact that $p = .04$ suggests that the probability of replicating this statistically significant finding at the .05 level is not that high. Finally, we would want to examine carefully the methodology of the study to determine that the study was sound, free of confounds and experimenter errors.

E Constructing a confidence interval for the difference between the two population means would provide evidence of the size of the difference between these methods and indicate (based on examining the width of the interval) the precision of the estimation of the difference between two population means.

CHAPTER THIRTEEN

Communication in Psychology

CHAPTER OUTLINE

INTRODUCTION

Scientific research is a public activity. A clever hypothesis, an elegant research design, meticulous data collection procedures, reliable results, and an insightful theoretical interpretation of the findings are not useful to the scientific community unless they are made public. As one writer suggests most emphatically, "Until its results have gone through the painful process of publication, preferably in a refereed journal of high standards, scientific research is just play. Publication is an indispensable part of science" (Bartholomew, 1982, p. 233). Bartholomew expresses a preference for a "refereed" journal because refereed journals involve the process of *peer review*. Submitted manuscripts are reviewed by other researchers ("peers") who are experts in the specific field of research addressed in the paper under review. These peer reviewers decide whether the research is methodologically sound and whether it makes a substantive contribution to the discipline of psychology. These reviews are then submitted to a senior researcher who serves as editor of the journal. It is the editor's job to decide which papers warrant publication. Peer review is the primary method of quality control for published psychological research.

There are dozens of psychology journals in which researchers can publish their findings. *Psychological Science, Memory & Cognition, Child Development, Journal of Personality and Social Psychology, Psychological Science in the Public Interest,* and *Journal of Clinical and Consulting Psychology* are but a few. As we mentioned, editors of these journals make the final decisions about which manuscripts will be published. Their decisions are based on (a) the quality of the research and (b) the effectiveness of its presentation in the written manuscript, as assessed by the editor and the peer reviewers. Thus, both content and style are important. Editors seek the best research, clearly described, and set rigorous standards for acceptance. *Typically, only about one of every three manuscripts submitted to the more than two dozen APA journals is accepted for publication* (e.g., American Psychological Association, 2006).

In addition to judging a manuscript on its style and content, a journal editor first will decide if what was submitted is appropriate for this journal. Experimental memory studies with animal subjects typically do not get published in a journal emphasizing research on child development. Many sources are available for publication besides those sponsored by APA and APS. However, to begin to get a feel for what is out there, you may want to review descriptions of journals published by these major organizations: www.apa.org/pubs/journals/ and www.psychologicalscience.org/journals/.

Editorial review and the publication process can take a long time. Up to a year (and sometimes longer) may elapse between when a paper is submitted and when it finally appears in the journal. The review of the manuscript can take several months before a decision whether to accept the paper is made. Several months are also required for the publication process between the time the paper is accepted and when it is actually published in the journal. To provide a more timely means of reporting research findings, professional societies such as the American Psychological Association, the Association for Psychological Science, the Psychonomic Society, the Society for Research in Child Development, and regional societies such as the Eastern, Midwestern, Southeastern, and Western Psychological Associations sponsor conferences at which researchers give brief oral presentations or present posters describing their recent work. Such conferences provide an opportunity for timely discussion and debate among investigators interested in the same research questions. Research that is "in press" (i.e., waiting completion of the publication process) may be discussed, thus giving conference attendees a preview of important, but yet-to-be-published, research findings.

Researchers often must obtain financial support in the form of a grant from a government or private agency in order to carry out their research. Grants are awarded on the basis of a competitive review of research proposals. Research proposals also typically are required of graduate students when preparing a master's thesis or dissertation. A faculty committee then reviews the proposal before the thesis or dissertation research is begun. So, too, undergraduate students often are required to prepare a research proposal as part of a research methods or laboratory class in psychology. Finally, researchers at all levels will find that research proposals are required by Institutional Review Boards in order to assess the ethical nature of proposed research at an institution (see Chapter 3). Research proposals require a slightly different style and format from a journal article that reports results of a completed study. We provide suggestions for preparing a research proposal later in this chapter.

Tips on Manuscript Preparation   The primary resource for scientific writing in psychology is the *Publication Manual of the American Psychological Association* (APA, 2010), now in its sixth edition. Journal editors and authors use this manual to ensure a consistent style across the many different journals in psychology. The manual is an invaluable source for almost any question pertaining to the style and format of a manuscript intended for publication in a psychological journal. It contains information on the appropriate content and organization of a manuscript; the expression of ideas and reducing bias in language; displaying results in tables and figures; reference list format including referencing electronic media; and policies regarding manuscript acceptance and production, including guidelines for electronic submission of manuscripts. The manual also discusses ethical issues in scientific writing (see our discussion of this in Chapter 3). However, APA also acknowledges that neither editorial style nor the technology of publishing is static. Anyone seeking to prepare a manuscript under the APA guidelines should also consult the APA website, which provides updates to the *Publication Manual* and latest changes in APA style and in APA policies and procedures: www.apastyle.org.

The APA website provides a free tutorial on APA basic style, including presentation of a sample manuscript, and a frequently asked questions and answers section.

What do journal articles, oral presentations, and research proposals have to do with you? If you attend graduate school in psychology, you will likely have to describe your research using all three of these types of scientific communication. Even if you do not pursue a professional career in psychology, the principles of good written and oral research reports are applicable to a wide variety of employment situations. For example, a memo to your department manager describing the outcome of a recent sales event may have much the same format as a short journal article. Of more immediate concern, you may have to prepare a research proposal and write or deliver a research report in your research methods course. This chapter will help you do these things well.

This chapter is intended primarily to help you get started with manuscript preparation and it is not a substitute for the *Publication Manual of the American Psychological Association* (2010). What follows is an interpretation of the *Manual* by the authors and publisher (McGraw-Hill), and we recommend you consult the latest edition of the *APA Manual* and the APA website for the most up-to-date, definitive APA style.

THE INTERNET AND RESEARCH

Access to the Internet has already become an indispensable tool for research psychologists, especially for communication via electronic mail (e-mail). For many researchers, *e-mail* is their primary means of communication with colleagues, journal editors, research collaborators, directors of granting agencies, and other professionals. Have a question about an article you just read? Ask the author by sending an e-mail message. E-mailing is simple, efficient, and convenient. The first author of your textbook, for example, can be reached by sending an e-mail message to John J. Shaughnessy (Hope College) at shaughnessy@hope.edu.

There is also a home page on the Web dedicated to this textbook, which can be accessed for student resources (e.g., practice tests) and information about the authors, changes in editions, additional resources for doing psychological research, and errors or omissions in the current edition, publisher's address, ordering information, and so on. Visit our page: www.mhhe.com/shaughnessy9.

The Internet also serves students and professional psychologists in many other important ways, including discussion groups, databases, electronic journals, and original research.

Discussion groups, called "Listservs," allow interested individuals to discuss psychological issues in which they share an interest. The group consists of a "list" of "subscribers" who wish to contribute to an ongoing discussion. List members are immediately "served" any message posted by a subscriber. There are hundreds of Listservs on the Internet that link researchers around the world discussing a wide variety of topics, including addiction, religion, and women's studies. Some Listservs are open to anyone who wishes to take part in the discussion, including those who want to participate only passively ("lurk"). Other Listservs are open only to individuals with certain credentials (e.g., members of a particular APA division). APA and APS also sponsor discussion groups for students that can be accessed through www.apa.org/apags/ and www.psychologicalscience.org/apssc/.

Databases on the Internet are just that: electronic data files that are stored on the Internet and that can be accessed electronically. Databases related to medicine, alcoholism, and opinion polls are available, to mention but a few. Databases are particularly useful when doing archival research (see Chapter 4) and time-series analyses (Chapter 10). Large databases, in which data for hundreds of variables and large numbers of participants are available, have become important to many researchers who seek to answer research questions in psychology (e.g., in clinical, social, and developmental psychology). Electronic access to databases frees researchers from the expense and time needed to collect data that may already be available, thereby eliminating wasteful duplication of researchers' and participants' efforts.

Electronic journals are becoming common, and electronic submission of manuscripts is now the norm for journals and for conferences. The wide availability of Internet access and e-mail has facilitated the review process, such that the manuscript submission, peer reviews, and editorial feedback to authors can be completed using the Internet. In addition, some journals are offered exclusively in electronic form. Subscribers receive articles in their electronic mailboxes, and readers can electronically submit their comments on the articles. *Current Research in Social Psychology* and *Prevention and Treatment* are examples of electronic journals. Whether submitting manuscripts to electronic or printed journals, authors seeking publication in respected journals should expect peer review of their research.

Original research, as you saw in earlier chapters, can also be done electronically (see, for example, Azar, 1994a, 1994b; Birnbaum, 2000; Kardas & Milford, 1996; Kelley-Milburn & Milburn, 1995). To repeat a comment made in Chapter 1: The Web allows practically any type of psychological research that uses computers as equipment and humans as participants (Krantz & Dalal, 2000; see especially Kraut et al., 2004, for helpful information about doing online research). How useful you will find the Internet in planning and conducting research will depend both on your specific needs and on your ability to use the Internet. If you are just beginning, we recommend Fraley's guide, *How to Conduct Behavioral Research over the Internet* (2004; New York: Guilford Press).

GUIDELINES FOR EFFECTIVE WRITING

Learning to write well is like learning to swim, drive a car, or play the piano. Improvement is unlikely to result solely from reading about how the activity is to be done. Heeding expert advice, though, can help a person get off to a good start. Thus, one key to writing well is getting critical feedback from writing "coaches"—teachers, friends, editors, and even yourself. Lee Cronbach (1992), author of several of the most widely cited articles in the *Psychological Bulletin*, summarizes these ideas well.

> My advice must be like the legendary recipe for jugged hare, which begins, "First catch your hare." First, have a message worth delivering. Beyond that, it is care in writing that counts. . . . Rework any sentence that lacks flow or cadence, any sentence in which first-glance reading misplaces the emphasis, and any sentence in which comprehension comes less than instantly to that most knowledgeable of readers, the writer of the sentence. At best, technical writing can aspire to literary virtues—a change of pace from abstract thesis to memorable example, from brisk to easeful, from matter-of-fact to poetic. (p. 391)

Good writing, like good driving, is best done defensively. Assume that whatever can be misunderstood, will be! To avoid these writing accidents, we offer the following tips to consider *before* you begin writing.

- **KNOW YOUR AUDIENCE.**   If you assume your readers know more than they actually do, you will leave them confused. If you underestimate your readers, you risk boring them with unnecessary details. Either risk increases the likelihood that what you have written will not be read. But if you must err, it is better to underestimate your readers. For example, when you prepare a research report in a psychology class, you might reasonably assume that your intended audience is your instructor. Writing for your instructor might lead you to leave a lot out of your paper because, after all, you assume your instructor knows all that anyway. It would probably be better to consider students in another section of your research methods course as your audience. This might result in your including more detail than necessary, but it will be easier for your instructor to help you learn to "edit out" the nonessential material than to "edit in" essential material that you have omitted. Whatever audience you choose, be sure to make the selection before you begin to write, and keep your audience in mind every step of the way.

- **IDENTIFY YOUR PURPOSE.**   Journal articles fall within the general category of expository writing. *Webster's Dictionary* defines exposition as "discourse designed to convey information or explain what is difficult to understand." The principal purposes of a journal article are to describe and to convince. You want first to describe what you have done and what you have found and, second, to convince the reader that your interpretation of these results is an appropriate one.

- **WRITE CLEARLY.**   The foundation of good expository writing is clarity of thought and expression. As Cronbach (1992) commented, "It is care in writing that counts." You will need to work and rework sentences in order to achieve a smooth and logical flow of your ideas. As the *Publication Manual* notes (p. 65), "The prime objective of scientific reporting is clear communication."

- **BE CONCISE.**   If you say only what needs to be said, you will achieve economy of expression. Short words and short sentences are easier for readers to understand. The best way to eliminate wordiness is by editing your own writing across successive drafts and asking others to edit drafts of your paper.

- **BE PRECISE.**   Precision in using language means choosing the right word for what you want to say. It requires choosing words that mean exactly what you intend them to mean. For example, in scientific psychology, *belief* is not the same as *attitude*; nor are *sensations* the same as *feelings*.

- **FOLLOW GRAMMATICAL RULES.**   Adherence to grammatical rules is absolutely necessary for good writing because failure to do so distracts the reader and can introduce ambiguity. It also makes you, the writer, look bad and, as a consequence, can serve to weaken your credibility (and your argument) with your reader.

- **WRITE FAIRLY.** As a writer you should also strive to choose words and use constructions that acknowledge people fairly and without bias. The American Psychological Association has outlined its policy regarding bias in the language authors use (*Publication Manual*, 2010, pp. 71–77):

> Scientific writing must be free of implied or irrelevant evaluation of the group or groups being studied. As an organization, APA is committed both to science and to the fair treatment of individuals and groups, and this policy requires that authors who write for APA publications avoid perpetuating demeaning attitudes and biased assumptions about people in their writing. Constructions that might imply bias of gender, sexual orientation, racial or ethnic group, disability, or age are unacceptable. (pp. 70–71)

The *Publication Manual* (2010, pp. 71–77) provides important information to help you achieve unbiased communication. The following is only the briefest introduction based on the guidelines found in the *Manual* (see also www.apastyle.org):

(a) Describe people at the appropriate level of specificity. For example, the phrase *men and women* is more accurate than the generic term *man* when referring to human adults. "Chinese Americans" or "Mexican Americans" would be a more specific reference for research participants than would be Asian Americans or Hispanic Americans.

(b) Be sensitive to labels when referring to people, for example, when using terms to refer to people's racial or ethnic identity. The best way to follow this guideline is to avoid labeling people whenever possible and use wording that preserves participants' individuality. For example, rather than talk about *the amnesiacs* or *the demented,* a better option is to refer to "amnesic patients" or "those in a dementia group." A label that is perceived by the labeled group as pejorative should never be used. In trying to follow this guideline, it is important to remember that preferences for labeling groups of individuals change with time and that people within a group may disagree about what label is preferred. For example, although some persons indigenous to North America may prefer to be called "Native North Americans," others may prefer "Indians," and still others might wish to be called by their specific group name, for example, Navajo, or even more appropriately using their native language, *Diné* instead of Navajo, for instance.

(c) Write about people in a way that clearly identifies your study's participants. One way to accomplish this is to describe participants using more descriptive terms such as *college students* or *children* rather than the more impersonal term, *subjects*. Active voice is better than passive voice in acknowledging participation. For example, "the students completed the survey" is preferred over "the survey was administered to the students."

- **WRITE AN INTERESTING REPORT.**　Scientific writing need not be dull! Clearly, scientific writers do not have the license given a novelist or essayist, nor is this the place to show off what you have learned in a "creative writing" course. Nevertheless, an effort should be made to write in a way that will interest your reader in what you did, what was found, and what you concluded. As Cronbach said, "Technical writing can aspire to literary virtues." One way to try to achieve an appropriate tone in writing your research reports is to strive to tell a good story about your research. Good research makes for good stories, and well-told stories are good for advancing research.

As you make preparations for writing a research report, we urge you to read journal articles reporting research in an area of psychology that interests you. Ultimately, however, you will develop the skills for writing research reports only by actually writing them.

STRUCTURE OF A RESEARCH REPORT

The structure of a research report serves complementary purposes for the author and for the reader. The structure provides an organization that the author can use to present a clear description of the research and a convincing interpretation of the findings. The reader of a research report can expect to find certain information in each section. If you want to know how an experiment was done, you would look in the Method section; if you want information about the analysis of the data in the study, you would refer to the Results section. A research report consists of the following sections:

Title Page (with Author Note)
Abstract
Introduction　⎫
Method　　　⎪　**Main Body**
Results　　　⎬　**of Report**
Discussion　⎭
References
Footnotes (if any)
Tables and Figures
Appendices (if any)

> Tips on Manuscript Format　You will need to go to www.apastyle.org or use the *Publication Manual* to learn about preferred typeface, spacing, margins, paragraph construction, page numbering, proper use of headings, and other aspects of manuscript format. See also the "sample paper" in both these sources for a look at how the structure of your completed manuscript should appear.

Title Page

The first page of a research report is the title page. It indicates what the research is about (i.e., the title), who did the research (i.e., the authors), where the research was done (i.e., authors' affiliation), a brief heading to indicate to readers what the article is about (the "running head"), and an author note. The author note identifies the author's professional affiliation and contact information, as well as listing any acknowledgments.

The title is perhaps the most critical aspect of your paper because it is the part that is most likely to be read! By identifying key variables or theoretical issues, the title should clearly indicate the central topic of your paper. Avoid needless words such as "A Laboratory Study of . . . " or "An Investigation of . . . ."

> **Tips on Writing a Title**   A common format for the title of a research report is "[The Dependent Variable(s)] as a Function of [the Independent Variable(s)]." For example, "Anagram Solution Time as a Function of Problem Difficulty" would be a good title. The title must not only be informative, but it should also be brief. Most important, be sure your title describes as specifically as possible the content of your research.

Under the title appears the name(s) of the author(s) and the institution with which each author is affiliated. We discussed the criteria for authorship in Chapter 3; only those who meet these criteria should be listed as authors of a research report. Others who contributed to the research are acknowledged in an author note.

Abstract

The abstract is a concise one-paragraph summary of the content and purpose of the research report. Rules regarding word limits for an abstract differ among scientific journals. Consult the *Publication Manual* for these guidelines. The abstract of an empirical study typically will identify the following:

(a) the problem under investigation;
(b) the method, including tests and apparatus that were used, data-gathering procedures, and pertinent characteristics of participants;
(c) the major findings; and
(d) the conclusions and implications of the findings.

The abstract, in other words, should highlight the critical points made in the Introduction, Method, Results, and Discussion sections of the research report. A well-written abstract can have a big influence on whether the rest of a journal article will be read. Abstracts are used by information services to index and retrieve articles, and thus an author should include keywords related to the study. The *Publication Manual* describes more fully the critical elements of an abstract for empirical studies and also how abstracts should differ for literature reviews, meta-analyses, theory papers, methodological papers, and case studies.

Tips on Writing an Abstract   Writing a good abstract is challenging. The best way to meet this challenge is to write it last. By writing the abstract after you have written the rest of the report, you will be able to *abstract*, or paraphrase, your own words more easily.

Introduction

Objectives for the Introduction   The Introduction serves three primary objectives:

1 to introduce the problem being studied and to indicate why the problem is an important one to study;
2 to summarize briefly the relevant background literature related to the study and to describe the theoretical implications of the study; and
3 to describe the purpose, rationale, and design of the present study with a logical development of the predictions or hypotheses guiding the research.

The order in which you address these objectives in your paper may vary, but the order we describe here is a common one.

As mentioned, the Introduction includes a summary of related research studies. This review is not intended to provide an exhaustive literature review. Instead, you should carefully select those studies that are most directly related to your research. In summarizing these selected studies, you should emphasize whatever details of the earlier work will best help the reader understand what you have done and why. You must acknowledge the contributions of other researchers to your understanding of the problem. Of course, if you quote directly from another person's work, you must use quotation marks (see Chapter 3 for advice about citing others' work).

Reference is usually made to the work of other researchers in one of two ways. Either you refer to the authors of the article you are citing by their last names, with the year in which the paper was published appearing in parentheses immediately after the names, or you make a general reference to their work and follow it with both the names and the year of publication in parentheses. For example, if you were citing a study by Lorna Hernandez Jarvis and Patricia V. Roehling that was published in 2007, you would write either "Jarvis and Roehling (2007) found . . ." or "Recent research (Jarvis & Roehling, 2007) showed that. . . ." Complete bibliographical information on the Jarvis and Roehling paper, including the journal title, volume number, and specific pages, would appear in the References section. Footnotes are not used to cite references in a research report in psychology. We suggest that you review in Chapter 3 the discussion of ethical issues related to citing references for your work (see Reporting of Psychological Research subsection).

In summary, the problem under investigation, related research findings, and the rationale and design of your study should be introduced in a clear, interesting manner.

Tips on Writing the Introduction In order to write an effective introduction, *before* beginning to write, be sure that you have articulated for yourself exactly what you did and why. One of the best ways to "test" yourself is to attempt to describe orally to someone unfamiliar with your work the purpose of your study, its relation to other studies in this area (e.g., how your study differs from what is already known), the theoretical implications, and what you hoped to achieve. You will likely find that your listener has questions, and by answering them you will perhaps recognize what needs to be made clear when actually writing your introduction.

Searching the Psychological Literature Whatever your topic or research question, there undoubtedly will come a time when you need to search the psychological literature. For example, although you may have an idea for an experiment, you will want to determine whether the experiment has already been done. Or you may have read an article describing a study on which you would like to base an experiment; thus, to write an introduction it will be important to learn about other, related studies. As you learn more about this area of investigation, you may find that your initial idea for a study may need to be modified. An important source for additional reading is the References section of articles related to your topic.

The primary online database for searching the psychological literature is PsycINFO. PsycINFO can be accessed through online databases such as *First-Search* and *InfoTrac*. Check with your local library staff to find out what online services are available to you. An electronic database makes it possible to scan the titles and abstracts of articles in the database and to identify all those that contain particular keywords. The most effective approach to this type of search is to have intersecting keywords, both of which need to be present before the computer will "flag" an article. For example, a student was interested in conducting a survey to determine the incidence of rapes and other sexual assaults on dates (i.e., date rapes). The student used the keyword RAPE and the letter string DAT to guide her search. She chose the letter string DAT in order to catch such variants as DATE, DATES, and DATING.

After searching such vast databases multiple times with different keywords, we may become unduly confident that we have identified "all that there is on the subject." However, it is possible that *pertinent information can be missed in any given search of an electronic database.* Keywords can also prove tricky. The string DAT identified all studies using the word DATA, so a number of the student's references provided data about rape—but not solely in the context of dating. When electronic databases are used properly, the advantages of searching the psychological literature using PsycINFO far outweigh their disadvantages.

Method

The second major section of the body of a research report is the Method section. Writing a good Method section can be difficult. It sounds easy because all you have to do is describe exactly what you have done. But if you want to get a sense of how challenging this can be, just try to write a clear and interesting paragraph describing how to tie your shoelaces.

Tips on Writing the Method Section   The key to writing a good Method section is organization. Fortunately, the structure of this section is so consistent across research reports that a few basic subsections provide the pattern of organization you need for most research reports. However, we should address the question that students writing their first research report ask most frequently: "How much detail should I include?" The quality of your paper will be adversely affected if you include either too much or too little detail. That you used a "No. 2 pencil" to record the results is clearly too much detail! A good rule of thumb is: Include enough information so that an interested investigator can replicate your study. Reading the Method sections of journal articles will help you with this writing task. See also the *Publication Manual*, especially pages 29–32, for help in writing a Method section.

In the Method section you will be describing the number and nature of the participants (subjects) that took part in your study, the particular materials, instrumentation, or apparatus that was used, as well as exactly how you carried out the study (i.e., your "procedure"). These kinds of information typically are presented in different subsections (e.g., Participants, Materials, Procedure) and it is important that you review APA guidelines for the content of these subsections. It is also a good idea to read the Method sections of published journal articles to get a feel for what goes into these subsections.

Results

In many ways this is the most exciting part of a research report because the Results section contains the climax of the research report—the actual findings of the study. For many students, though, the excitement of describing the climax is blunted by concern about the necessity of reporting statistical information in the Results section. The best way to alleviate this concern, of course, is to develop the same command of statistical concepts that you have of other concepts. A helpful first step is to adopt a simple organizational structure to guide your writing of the Results section (see Table 13.1).

You should use the Results section to answer the questions you raised in your Introduction. However, the guiding principle in the Results section is to "stick to the facts, just the facts." You will have the opportunity to move beyond just the facts when you get to the Discussion section.

Reporting Statistics   The raw data of your study (e.g., individual scores) should not be included in the Results section. Rather, you will want to use summary statistics (e.g., means, standard deviations) and report results of all inferential statistical tests related to your hypotheses (both favorable and unfavorable!). For complex studies, the use of tables and figures is often important. The Results section lays the groundwork for the conclusions you report in the Discussion section. It is in the Discussion section, not the Results section, that the implications of your study should be mentioned. As we said: In the Results section, stick to the facts and only the facts!

TABLE 13.1   STRUCTURE OF A TYPICAL PARAGRAPH IN THE RESULTS SECTION

1. State the purpose of the analysis.
2. Identify the descriptive statistic to be used to summarize results.
3. Present a summary of this descriptive statistic across conditions in the text itself, in a table, or in a figure.
4. If a table or figure is used, point out the major findings on which the reader should focus.
5. Present the reasons for, and the results of, confidence intervals, effect sizes, and inferential statistical tests.
6. State the conclusion that follows from each test, but do not discuss implications. These belong in the Discussion section.

Sample paragraph

To examine retention as a function of instructions given at the time of study, the number of words recalled by each participant in each instruction condition was determined. Words were scored as correct only if they matched a word that had appeared on the target list. Misspelled words were accepted if the spelling was similar to a target item. Mean numbers of words recalled (with the corresponding standard deviations) were: 15.6 (1.44), 15.2 (1.15), and 10.1 (1.00) in the bizarre imagery condition, the standard imagery condition, and the control condition, respectively. The 95% CIs were: bizarre imagery [13.18, 18.02], standard imagery [12.78, 17.62], control [7.68, 12.52]. Overall, the mean differences were statistically significant, $F(2, 72) = 162.84$, $p < .001$, $MSE = 1.47$, $\eta^2 = .82$. Comparisons of the confidence intervals revealed that both of the imagery conditions differed from the control condition, but that the two imagery conditions did not differ. In conclusion, retention by participants instructed to use imagery was higher than that by participants given no specific study instructions, but retention did not differ for the two types of imagery instructions.

Tips on Writing a Good Results Section   We suggest you follow these steps when writing your Results section.

- *Step 1*. A Results section paragraph begins by stating the purpose of the analysis. The reason(s) for doing an analysis should be stated succinctly; often, no more than a phrase is necessary. In the sample paragraph, for example, the purpose of the analysis is "to examine retention as a function of the instructions given at the time of study."
- *Step 2*. The second step in writing a Results section paragraph is to identify the descriptive statistic (e.g., mean, median, total frequency) that will be used to summarize the results for a given dependent variable. For example, in the sample paragraph the researchers used mean numbers of words recalled when summarizing results.
- *Step 3*. The third step is to present a summary of this descriptive statistic across conditions. Measures of central tendency should be accompanied by corresponding measures of variability such as reporting a standard deviation along with each mean. A measure of effect size is also strongly recommended. If there are only two or three conditions in your experiment, this summary can be presented in the text itself. If you have more data to summarize, you will need to present your findings in either a table or a figure (graph). We will describe the procedures for constructing tables and figures later in this section.

- *Step 4.* A table or figure should not be considered self-sufficient. Your reader will need help to gain as much information as possible from a table or figure. You are in the best position to offer this help because you are the person most familiar with your results. You should direct your readers' attention to the highlights of the data in the table or figure, focusing especially on those aspects of the results that are consistent (or discrepant) with the hypotheses you proposed in the introduction. Usually the same data are not reported in both a table and a figure. Whichever you choose, be sure to highlight in the text itself the critical results that the table or figure reveals.

- *Step 5.* The fifth step in writing a paragraph of the Results section is to present the results of inferential statistical tests. The following information should always be reported with any inferential statistical test: the name of the test (usually indicated by a symbol such as t, r, or F); the degrees of freedom for the test (presented in parentheses after the test is identified); the value of the test statistic that you obtained; the exact probability of the test outcome (unless p value is less than .001, as in the sample paragraph); and measures of effect size. You should also include the mean square error (MSE) as illustrated in Table 13.1 (see sample paragraph). The MSE (the denominator of the F ratio) permits interested readers to calculate additional statistics from your results and facilitates subsequent meta-analyses. As we discussed in Chapters 11 and 12, reporting confidence intervals is strongly recommended. Again, refer to the sample paragraph for examples of how this information is incorporated into the Results section.

- *Concluding Step.* The final step in writing a paragraph in the Results section is to state a brief conclusion that follows from each test you report. For example, consider a study in which the mean number correct in the experimental group is 10 and that in the control group is 5 and the confidence intervals for these two means do not overlap. An appropriate concluding statement would be "The control group did worse than the experimental group." In this simple example the conclusion may seem obvious, but appropriate concluding statements are essential, especially for complex analyses.

Each paragraph of the Results section follows the structure outlined in Table 13.1. The idea is not to overload your reader with statistics. The challenge is to select those findings that are most critical, being sure to report all the data pertinent to the questions raised in your introduction. Before concluding our discussion of the Results section, we will briefly describe the basic procedures for constructing tables and figures.

Presenting Data in Tables   Tables are an effective and efficient means for presenting large amounts of data in concise form. The table should supplement and not duplicate information in the text of the paper, but it should be well integrated into the text. The tables in a research report are numbered consecutively. Numbering the tables makes it easy to refer to them in the text by their numbers. Each table should also have a brief explanatory title, and the columns and rows of the table should be labeled clearly. The data entries in the table should all be reported to the same degree of precision (i.e., all values should have the same number of decimal places), and the values should be consistently aligned with the corresponding row and column headings. You will want to refer to the *Publication Manual* in order to see the various ways tables are constructed according to APA stylistic requirements (see especially Chapter 5 of the *Manual*).

Presenting Data in Figures   Figures, like tables, are a concise way to present large amounts of information. A figure has two principal axes: the horizontal axis, or *x*-axis, and the vertical axis, or *y*-axis. Typically, the levels of the independent variable are plotted on the *x*-axis, and those of the dependent variable are plotted on the *y*-axis. When there are two or more independent variables, the levels of the second and succeeding independent variables serve as labels for the data within the figure or are indicated in a figure legend. In Figure 13.1 the values of the dependent variable (mean number recalled) are plotted on the *y*-axis, and the levels of one independent variable (serial position) are indicated on the *x*-axis. The levels of the second independent variable (cued [C] or noncued [NC]) label the data within the figures, and the levels of the third independent variable (instructions) serve as the headings for each of the two separate panels of the figure.

Two general types of figures are commonly used in psychology: line graphs and bar graphs. The most common type of figure is the line graph like the one

FIGURE 13.1   Mean number of words recalled (of a possible 10) as a function of serial position within blocks, cuing (C = Cued; NC = Noncued), and instructional condition.

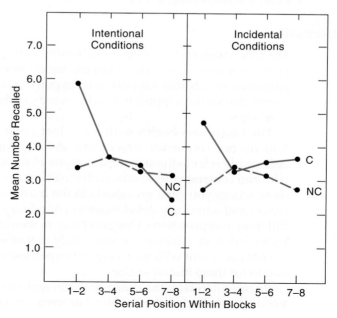

FIGURE 13.2   Proportion recognition errors made by two groups of college students after rating verbal items for either familiarity or meaning. The items were nonwords (NW) and words appearing less than 1 time, 1 through 10 times, and more than 40 times per million in the Thorndike-Lorge count.

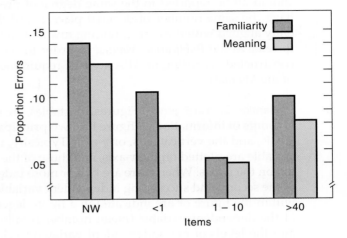

shown in Figure 13.1. When the independent variable plotted on the *x*-axis is a nominal-scale variable, however, a bar graph is often used. For example, if you were plotting the mean GPA (dependent variable) of students enrolled in different academic majors (independent variable), you could use a bar graph. An illustration of a bar graph is presented in Figure 13.2. There are alternative ways to construct useful graphic presentations and you should consult the *Publication Manual* (Chapter 5) to see various options. All figures must be drawn clearly and labeled appropriately so that readers can understand exactly what is represented.

Discussion

The Discussion section, unlike the Results section, contains "more than just the facts." It is now time to draw out the implications of your research, emphasize particular results that support your hypothesis and comment critically on any results that do not support it. In other words, make a final summation to the jury of readers.

The Discussion begins with a succinct statement of the essential findings. You do not repeat the descriptive statistics in this summary, nor do you necessarily refer to the statistical analyses of the findings. You will want to compare and contrast your results with the findings of others in this area, especially those whom you cited previously in the introduction. Be "up front" with your reader and admit any deficiencies in your design or analysis that could lead to different interpretations. One good way to identify limitations or problems is to try to anticipate criticisms of your study that others might make. If your results are not consistent with your original hypotheses, you should suggest an explanation for these discrepancies.

Be careful to keep the statements you make in the discussion consistent with the data reported in the Results. For instance, you should not report that one group did better than another if the difference between the means for these groups was not reliable—at least not without some qualification of what you mean by "better."

If appropriate, conclude the Discussion by proposing additional research that should be done on the problem you are investigating. Strive to be specific about what research should be done and why it needs to be done. That is, be sure to explain what the new research should reveal that we do not already know. The reader will not learn much if you say, "It would be interesting to do this experiment with younger participants." The reader can learn much more if you explain how you would expect the results to differ with younger participants and what you would conclude if the results of the proposed experiment were to turn out as expected.

Tips on Writing the Discussion Section An outline for the Discussion section might be something like this:

- A brief review of the problem and your hypotheses (expectations).
- A summary of the major results supporting (or not supporting) your hypothesis.
- Comparison with findings from other researchers in this area.
- Comments on the limitations of your study (and there are always some!).
- Suggestions for future research (be specific!).
- Comments on the importance of the findings and, if appropriate, possible practical implications.

References

Four types of references typically are found in the majority of research reports: journal articles, books, chapters in edited books, and Internet sources. Table 13.2 illustrates how these references would be cited in the References section of a manuscript. The specific formatting rules when reporting these references and many other types according to APA style are best reviewed by consulting the *Publication Manual*. The free tutorial found at www.apastyle.org also can help you with formatting references.

The rapid spread of electronic publishing has led to the need for electronic "identifiers" for information retrieved from the Internet. For example, anyone using the Internet will be familiar with URLs (uniform resource locators). They typically begin with "http://" and are followed by a host name (often preceded by www.), path, and title of document. For example, the URL for a very helpful online source to help you find relevant research on psychological topics ("Library Research in Psychology") is: http://www.apa.org/education/undergrad/library-research.aspx. Should you cite information retrieved using the Internet, it is important that you provide specific information required to locate the source.

A more recent form of electronic identifier is a digital object identifier (DOI). The DOI is an alphanumeric string that identifies the content and electronic location of an article or other information source found on the Internet. The DOI is usually found on the title page of a published article. APA stylistic

TABLE 13.2   ILLUSTRATION OF FORMAT OF REFERENCE CITATIONS

Journal Article without DOI

Loftus, E. F., & Burns, T. E. (1982). Mental shock can produce retrograde amnesia. *Memory & Cognition, 10*, 318–323.

Journal Article with DOI

Hyde, J. S. (2005). The gender similarities hypothesis. *American Psychologist, 60*, 581–592. doi:10.1037/0003-066X.60.6.581

Book

Posavac, E. J. (2011). *Program evaluation* (8th ed.). Englewood Cliffs, NJ: Prentice Hall.

Chapter in an Edited Book

Weiss, J. M. (1977). Psychological and behavioral influences on gastrointestinal lesions in animal models. In J. D. Maser & M. E. P. Seligman (Eds.), *Psychopathology: Experimental models* (pp. 232–269). San Francisco, CA: W. H. Freeman.

Technical or Research Report Retrieved Online

Lenhart, A., Madden, M., & Hitlin, P. (2005). *Teens and technology: Youth are leading the transition to a fully wired and mobile nation*. Retrieved from http://www.pewinternet.org/pdfs/PIP_Teens_Tech_July2005web.pdf

guidelines indicate that whenever a DOI is available you should include it as part of your citation in the References section. An easy way to use the DOI is to add it after http://dx.doi.org/ when searching. Thus, the article in Table 13.2 with the identifier 10.1037/0003-066X.60.6.581 can be found by using http://dx.doi.org/10.1037/0003-066X.60.6.581 with your search engine. Try using this DOI and see if you find the Hyde (2005) reference. Once again, we refer you to the *Publication Manual* for a more complete discussion of electronic sources and recommended reference formats.

You can save your readers much aggravation if you follow the reference formats closely and proofread your reference list carefully. The references are listed in alphabetical order by the last name of the first author of each article.

Footnotes

Footnotes are rare in journal articles and even more rare in students' research reports. When they do appear, they should be numbered consecutively in the text and placed on a separate page following the References section.

Appendices

Appendices are rare in published research articles, but they are a bit more common in students' research reports. When they are intended for a published article, each appendix begins on a separate manuscript page, and they appear at the end of the paper following the references. (*Note:* Instructors may require you to submit an appendix including your raw data, the worksheets for a statistical analysis, or the computer printout of the analyses. The appendix can also be used to provide a verbatim copy of the instructions to participants or a list of the specific materials used in an experiment.) Each appendix is identified by letter (A, B, C, and so on), and any reference to the appendix in the body of the text is made using this letter. For instance, you might write, "The complete instructions can be found in Appendix A."

Tips on Submitting Your Manuscript to a Journal Editor   The *Publication Manual* provides important information on the publication process, including descriptions of editorial policies, author responsibilities, a manuscript checklist, a sample cover letter to a journal editor, and the APA Compliance with Ethical Principles Form that may be required when submitting manuscripts to APA journals. (Tables 1, 2, and 3 in the Appendix to the *Manual* contain extensive information recommended for inclusion in manuscripts reporting original data collection. A review of these critical elements will help even experienced researchers identify what may be missing from their research report.)

ORAL PRESENTATIONS

Research psychologists regularly attend professional conventions at which they present brief oral descriptions of their research. Similarly, students may give oral presentations of their research either in class or at a department research symposium involving students from a number of different classes or at undergraduate research conferences. All of these settings share one characteristic—the time allowed for the presentation is usually no more than 10 to 15 minutes. In this length of time it is impossible to provide the detailed description that is included in a journal article.

A good oral presentation provides a succinct overview of the problem, the methodology, major results, and conclusions. It is in many ways like an expanded abstract of your study. Researchers frequently make available written copies of their study that contain more details than can be given in the oral presentation. This frees the presenter to go over the highlights of a study and not get bogged down in the fine details of the method or the analyses. Resist reporting specific statistical outcomes ("the *F* value from the ANOVA was 4.67"). Simply report that a "significant difference was obtained" or that "conditions differed reliably." Listeners can look up the specifics in your written handout.

Tips on Giving an Effective Oral Presentation   Because it is an "oral" presentation does not mean that you should omit preparing a complete written version. Be careful, however, to write as you would speak and not, for example, as you would write a journal article. Use simple sentences and mark places where you might want to pause or refer to a visual aid. Most of us speak faster when nervous, so pause marks on your pages will remind you to speak at a moderate pace and pause occasionally. The written version you use for speaking need not (and perhaps should not) be the same as a written handout distributed to your audience. It is up to you whether to memorize your presentation before giving it, perhaps with helpful cues from PowerPoint visuals, or to read it. If you are not comfortable with public speaking, do not be embarrassed to read it. Given very restricted time limits, your presentation must hit only the highlights of your study. Once you are satisfied with your written presentation, the next step is to rehearse it aloud to yourself so that you become familiar with what you will be saying and can stay within your time limit. Then, you will want to practice your talk before a critical (but friendly) audience. Ask members of your practice audience what they didn't understand or would like clarified. Could they follow what you reported doing and what you found? Did you speak loudly enough? Were your visuals (if any) clear and effective? Can they repeat back your main points? Were you within your allowed time limit? Finally, when delivering your presentation before a "real" audience, be sure to leave time for questions.

RESEARCH PROPOSALS

In the last section of this chapter we discuss writing again—but this time the writing of research proposals. As we mentioned at the beginning of this chapter, researchers must often seek financial support for their research by submitting grant proposals to private or government agencies. Students in research methods classes are also sometimes required to submit proposals describing research they might do. Even if a written proposal is not required, only a foolhardy researcher would tackle a research project without careful prior consideration of related literature, possible practical problems, workable statistical analyses of the data, and eventual interpretation of the expected results. This careful prior consideration will help you develop a research project that is feasible and one that can be analyzed and interpreted appropriately.

The purpose of a research proposal is to ensure a workable research design that, when implemented, will result in an interpretable empirical finding of significant scientific merit. No research proposal, no matter how carefully prepared, can guarantee important results. Researchers learn early in their careers about Murphy's Law. In essence, Murphy's Law states, "Anything that can go wrong will go wrong." Nonetheless, it is worthwhile to develop a research proposal, if only to avoid the research problems that are avoidable.

A written research proposal follows the general format of a journal article, but the headings of the various sections are slightly different. The proposal should include the following main sections:

Introduction
Method
Expected Results and Proposed Data Analysis Plan
Conclusions
References
Appendix
Information for Institutional Review Board

An abstract is not included in a research proposal. The introduction of a research proposal is likely to include a more extensive review of the relevant literature than is required for a journal article. The statement of the research problem and the logical development of hypotheses in a research proposal are the same as required in a journal article. Similarly, the Method section in the proposal should be as close as possible to the one that will accompany the finished research.

The section of the proposal titled "Expected Results and Proposed Data Analysis Plan" should include a brief discussion of the anticipated results of the research. In most cases the exact nature of the results will not be known. Nevertheless, you will always have some idea (in the form of a hypothesis or prediction) of the outcome of the research. The Expected Results section may include tables or figures of the results as you expect (hope) that they will come out. The expected results that are most important to the project should be highlighted. A proposed data analysis plan for the expected results should be in this section. For example, if you are proposing a complex design, you would need to indicate which effects you will be testing and what statistical tests you will use. Reasonable alternatives to the expected results should also be mentioned, as well as possible problems of interpretation that will arise if the results deviate from the research hypothesis. The body of a research proposal ends with a Conclusions section that provides a brief statement of the conclusions and implications based on the expected results.

The References section should be in exactly the same form as the one you would submit with the final report. An appendix should complete the research proposal and should include a list of all materials that will be used in doing the study. For example, if you are conducting an experiment involving students' memory for lists of words, the following must be included in the appendix: actual word lists with randomizations made, type of apparatus used for presentation, instructions to participants for all conditions, and randomizations of conditions.

Finally, a research proposal should include material to be submitted to an Institutional Review Board (IRB) or similar committee designed to review the ethics of the proposed research (see Chapter 3). Your institution no doubt has standard forms that are to be submitted with your proposal.

Appendix

Statistical Tables

APPENDIX OUTLINE

TABLE A.1   TABLE OF RANDOM NUMBERS*

Col. Line	(1)	(2)	(3)	(4)	(5)	(6)	(7)	(8)	(9)	(10)	(11)	(12)	(13)	(14)
1	10480	15011	01536	02011	81647	91646	69179	14194	62590	36207	20969	99570	91291	90700
2	22368	46573	25595	85393	30995	89198	27982	53402	93965	34095	52666	19174	39615	99505
3	24130	48360	22527	97265	76393	64809	15179	24830	49340	32081	30680	19655	63348	58629
4	42167	93093	06243	61680	07856	16376	39440	53537	71341	57004	00849	74917	97758	16379
5	37570	39975	81837	16656	06121	91782	60468	81305	49684	60672	14110	06927	01263	54613
6	77921	06907	11008	42751	27756	53498	18602	70659	90655	15053	21916	81825	44394	42880
7	99562	72905	56420	69994	98872	31016	71194	18738	44013	48840	63213	21069	10634	12952
8	96301	91977	65463	07972	18876	20922	94595	56869	69014	60045	18425	84903	42508	32307
9	89579	14342	63661	10281	17453	18103	57740	84378	25331	12566	58678	44947	05585	56941
10	85475	36857	53342	53988	53060	59533	38867	62300	08158	17983	16439	11458	18593	64952
11	28918	69578	88231	33276	70997	79936	56865	05859	90106	31595	01547	85590	91610	78188
12	63553	40961	48235	03427	49626	69445	18663	72695	52180	20847	12234	90511	33703	90322
13	09429	93969	52636	92737	88974	33488	36320	17617	30015	08272	84115	27156	30613	74952
14	10365	61129	87529	85689	48237	52267	67689	93394	01511	26358	85104	20285	29975	89868
15	07119	97336	71048	08178	77233	13916	47564	81506	97735	85977	29372	74461	28551	90707
16	51085	12765	51821	51259	77452	16308	60756	92144	49442	53900	70960	63990	75601	40719
17	02368	21382	52404	60268	89368	19885	55322	44819	01188	65255	64835	44919	05944	55157
18	01011	54092	33362	94904	31273	04146	18594	29852	71585	85030	51132	01915	92747	64951
19	52162	53916	46369	58586	23216	14513	83149	98736	23495	64350	94738	17752	35156	35749
20	07056	97628	33787	09998	42698	06691	76988	13602	51851	46104	88916	19509	25625	58104
21	48663	91245	85828	14346	09172	30168	90229	04734	59193	22178	30421	61666	99904	32812
22	54164	58492	22421	74103	47070	25306	76468	26384	58151	06646	21524	15227	96909	44592
23	32639	32363	05597	24200	13363	38005	94342	28728	35806	06912	17012	64161	18296	22851
24	29334	27001	87637	87308	58731	00256	45834	15298	46557	41135	10367	07684	36188	18510
25	02488	33062	28834	07351	19731	92420	60952	61280	50001	67658	32586	86679	50720	94953
26	81525	72295	04839	96423	24878	82651	66566	14778	76797	14780	13300	87074	79666	95725
27	29676	20591	68086	26432	46901	20849	89768	81536	86645	12659	92259	57102	80428	25280
28	00742	57392	39064	66432	84673	40027	32832	61362	98947	96067	64760	64584	96096	98253
29	05366	04213	25669	26422	44407	44048	37937	63904	45766	66134	75470	66520	34693	90449
30	91921	26418	64117	94305	26766	25940	39972	22209	71500	64568	91402	42416	07844	69618
31	00582	04711	87917	77341	42206	35126	74087	99547	81817	42607	43808	76655	62028	76630
32	00725	69884	62797	56170	86324	88072	76222	36086	84637	93161	76038	65855	77919	88006
33	69011	65795	95876	55293	18988	27354	26575	08625	40801	59920	29841	80150	12777	48501
34	25976	57948	29888	88604	67917	48708	18912	82271	65424	69774	33611	54262	85963	03547
35	09763	83473	93577	12908	30883	18317	28290	35797	05998	41688	34952	37888	38917	88050
36	91567	42595	27958	30134	04024	86385	29880	99730	55536	84855	29080	09250	79656	73211
37	17955	56349	90999	49127	20044	59931	06115	20542	18059	02008	73708	83517	36103	42791
38	46503	18584	18845	49618	02304	51038	20655	58727	28168	15475	56942	53389	20562	87338
39	92157	89634	94824	78171	84610	82834	09922	25417	44137	48413	25555	21246	35509	20468
40	14577	62765	35605	81263	39667	47358	56873	56307	61607	49518	89696	20103	77490	18062
41	98427	07523	33362	64270	01638	92477	66969	98420	04880	45585	46565	04102	46880	45709
42	34914	63976	88720	82765	34476	17032	87589	40836	32427	70002	70663	88863	77775	69348
43	70060	28277	39475	46473	23219	53416	94970	25832	69975	94884	19661	72828	00102	66794
44	53976	54914	06990	67245	68350	82948	11398	42878	80287	88267	47363	46634	06541	97809
45	76072	29515	40980	07391	58745	25774	22987	80059	39911	96189	41151	14222	60697	59583
46	90725	52210	83974	29992	65831	38857	50490	83765	55657	14361	31720	57375	56228	41546
47	64364	67412	33339	31926	14883	24413	59744	92351	97473	89286	35931	04110	23726	51900
48	08962	00358	31662	25388	61642	34072	81249	35648	56891	69352	48373	45578	78547	81788
49	95012	68379	93526	70765	10592	04542	76463	54328	02349	17247	28865	14777	62730	92277
50	15664	10493	20492	38391	91132	21999	59516	81652	27195	48223	46751	22923	32261	85653

Source: Table of 105,000 Random Decimal Digits, Statement no. 4914, File no. 261-A-1, Interstate Commerce Commission, Washington, D.C. May 1949.

TABLE A.2   SELECTED VALUES FROM THE *t* DISTRIBUTION*

Instructions for use: To find a value of *t*, locate the row in the left-hand column of the table corresponding to the number of degrees of freedom (*df*) associated with the standard error of the mean, and select the value of *t* listed for your choice of α (nondirectional). The value given in the column labeled $\alpha = .05$ is used in the calculation of the 95% confidence interval, and the value given in the column labeled $\alpha = .01$ is used to calculate the 99% confidence interval.

df	$\alpha = .05$	$\alpha = .01$	df	$\alpha = .05$	$\alpha = .01$
1	12.71	63.66	18	2.10	2.88
2	4.30	9.92	19	2.09	2.86
3	3.18	5.84	20	2.09	2.84
4	2.78	4.60	21	2.08	2.83
5	2.57	4.03	22	2.07	2.82
6	2.45	3.71	23	2.07	2.81
7	2.36	3.50	24	2.06	2.80
8	2.31	3.36	25	2.06	2.79
9	2.26	3.25	26	2.06	2.78
10	2.23	3.17	27	2.05	2.77
11	2.20	3.11	28	2.05	2.76
12	2.18	3.06	29	2.04	2.76
13	2.16	3.01	30	2.04	2.75
14	2.14	2.98	40	2.02	2.70
15	2.13	2.95	60	2.00	2.66
16	2.12	2.92	120	1.98	2.62
17	2.11	2.90	Infinity	1.96	2.58

*This table is adapted from Table 12 in *Biometrika Tables for Statisticians,* vol. 1 (3d ed.), New York: Cambridge University Press, 1970, edited by E. S. Pearson and H. O. Hartley, by permission of the *Biometrika* Trustees.

TABLE A.3   CRITICAL VALUES OF THE *F*-DISTRIBUTION*

Instructions for use: To find the critical value of *F*, locate the cell in the table formed by the intersection of the row containing the degrees of freedom associated with the denominator of the *F*-ratio and the column containing the degrees of freedom associated with the numerator of the *F*-ratio. The numbers listed in boldface type are the critical values of *F* at α = .05; the numbers listed in Roman type are the critical values of *F* at α = .01. As an example, suppose we have adopted the 5% level of significance and wish to evaluate the significance of an *F* with df_{num} = 2 and df_{denom} = 12. From the table we find that the critical value of $F(2, 12)$ = 3.89 at α = .05. If the obtained value of *F* equals or exceeds this critical value, we will reject the null hypothesis; if the obtained value of *F* is smaller than this critical value, we will not reject the null hypothesis.

Degrees of Freedom for Numerator

		1	2	3	4	5	6	7	8	9	10	12	15	20	24	30	40	60	Infinity
1		**161**	**200**	**216**	**225**	**230**	**234**	**237**	**239**	**241**	**242**	**244**	**246**	**248**	**249**	**250**	**251**	**252**	**254**
		4052	4999	5403	5625	5764	5859	5928	5981	6022	6056	6106	6157	6209	6325	6261	6287	6313	6366
2		**18.5**	**19.0**	**19.2**	**19.2**	**19.3**	**19.3**	**19.4**	**19.4**	**19.4**	**19.4**	**19.4**	**19.4**	**19.4**	**19.4**	**19.5**	**19.5**	**19.5**	**19.5**
		98.5	99.0	99.2	99.2	99.3	99.3	99.4	99.4	99.4	99.4	99.4	99.4	99.4	99.5	99.5	99.5	99.5	99.5
3		**10.1**	**9.55**	**9.28**	**9.12**	**9.01**	**8.94**	**8.89**	**8.85**	**8.81**	**8.79**	**8.74**	**8.70**	**8.66**	**8.64**	**8.62**	**8.59**	**8.57**	**8.53**
		34.1	30.8	29.5	28.7	28.2	27.9	27.7	27.5	27.4	27.2	27.0	26.9	26.7	26.6	26.5	26.4	26.3	26.1
4		**7.71**	**6.94**	**6.59**	**6.39**	**6.26**	**6.16**	**6.09**	**6.04**	**6.00**	**5.96**	**5.91**	**5.86**	**5.80**	**5.77**	**5.75**	**5.72**	**5.69**	**5.63**
		21.2	18.0	16.7	16.0	15.5	15.2	15.0	14.8	14.7	14.6	14.4	14.2	14.0	13.9	13.8	13.8	13.6	13.5
5		**6.61**	**5.79**	**5.41**	**5.19**	**5.05**	**4.95**	**4.88**	**4.82**	**4.77**	**4.74**	**4.68**	**4.62**	**4.56**	**4.53**	**4.50**	**4.46**	**4.43**	**4.26**
		16.3	13.3	12.1	11.4	11.0	10.7	10.5	10.3	10.2	10.0	9.89	9.72	9.55	9.47	9.38	9.29	9.20	9.02
6		**5.99**	**5.14**	**4.76**	**4.53**	**4.39**	**4.28**	**4.21**	**4.15**	**4.10**	**4.06**	**4.00**	**3.94**	**3.87**	**3.84**	**3.81**	**3.77**	**3.74**	**3.67**
		13.8	10.9	9.78	9.15	8.75	8.47	8.26	8.10	7.98	7.87	7.72	7.56	7.40	7.31	7.23	7.14	7.06	6.88
7		**5.59**	**4.74**	**4.35**	**4.12**	**3.97**	**3.87**	**3.79**	**3.73**	**3.68**	**3.64**	**3.57**	**3.51**	**3.44**	**3.41**	**3.38**	**3.34**	**3.30**	**3.23**
		12.2	9.55	8.45	7.85	7.46	7.19	6.99	6.84	6.72	6.62	6.47	6.31	6.16	6.07	5.99	5.91	5.82	5.65
8		**5.32**	**4.46**	**4.07**	**3.84**	**3.69**	**3.58**	**3.50**	**3.44**	**3.39**	**3.35**	**3.28**	**3.22**	**3.15**	**3.12**	**3.08**	**3.04**	**3.01**	**2.93**
		11.3	8.65	7.59	7.01	6.63	6.37	6.18	6.03	5.91	5.81	5.67	5.52	5.36	5.28	5.20	5.12	5.03	4.86
9		**5.12**	**4.26**	**3.86**	**3.63**	**3.48**	**3.37**	**3.29**	**3.23**	**3.18**	**3.14**	**3.07**	**3.01**	**2.94**	**2.90**	**2.86**	**2.83**	**2.79**	**2.71**
		10.6	8.02	6.99	6.42	6.06	5.80	5.61	5.47	5.35	5.26	5.11	4.96	4.81	4.73	4.65	4.57	4.48	4.31
10		**4.96**	**4.10**	**3.71**	**3.48**	**3.33**	**3.22**	**3.14**	**3.07**	**3.02**	**2.98**	**2.91**	**2.85**	**2.77**	**2.74**	**2.70**	**2.66**	**2.62**	**2.54**
		10.0	7.56	6.55	5.99	5.64	5.39	5.20	5.06	4.94	4.85	4.71	4.56	4.41	4.33	4.25	4.17	4.08	3.91
11		**4.84**	**3.98**	**3.59**	**3.36**	**3.20**	**3.09**	**3.01**	**2.95**	**2.90**	**2.85**	**2.79**	**2.72**	**2.65**	**2.61**	**2.57**	**2.53**	**2.49**	**2.40**
		9.65	7.21	6.22	5.67	5.32	5.07	4.89	4.74	4.63	4.54	4.40	4.25	4.10	4.02	3.94	3.86	3.78	3.60
12		**4.75**	**3.89**	**3.49**	**3.26**	**3.11**	**3.00**	**2.91**	**2.85**	**2.80**	**2.75**	**2.69**	**2.62**	**2.54**	**2.51**	**2.47**	**2.43**	**2.38**	**2.30**
		9.33	6.93	5.95	5.41	5.06	4.82	4.64	4.50	4.39	4.30	4.16	4.01	3.86	3.78	3.70	3.62	3.54	3.36
13		**4.67**	**3.81**	**3.41**	**3.18**	**3.03**	**2.92**	**2.83**	**2.77**	**2.71**	**2.67**	**2.60**	**2.53**	**2.46**	**2.42**	**2.38**	**2.34**	**2.30**	**2.21**
		9.07	6.70	5.74	5.21	4.86	4.62	4.44	4.30	4.19	4.10	3.96	3.82	3.66	3.59	3.51	3.43	3.34	3.17
14		**4.60**	**3.74**	**3.34**	**3.11**	**2.96**	**2.85**	**2.76**	**2.70**	**2.65**	**2.60**	**2.53**	**2.46**	**2.39**	**2.35**	**2.31**	**2.27**	**2.22**	**2.13**
		8.86	6.51	5.56	5.04	4.69	4.46	4.28	4.14	4.03	3.94	3.80	3.66	3.51	3.43	3.35	3.27	3.18	3.00
15		**4.54**	**3.68**	**3.29**	**3.06**	**2.90**	**2.79**	**2.71**	**2.64**	**2.59**	**2.54**	**2.48**	**2.40**	**2.33**	**2.29**	**2.25**	**2.20**	**2.16**	**2.07**
		8.68	6.36	5.42	4.89	4.56	4.32	4.14	4.00	3.89	3.80	3.67	3.52	3.37	3.29	3.21	3.13	3.05	2.87
16		**4.49**	**3.63**	**3.24**	**3.01**	**2.85**	**2.74**	**2.66**	**2.59**	**2.54**	**2.49**	**2.42**	**2.35**	**2.28**	**2.24**	**2.19**	**2.15**	**2.11**	**2.01**
		8.53	6.23	5.29	4.77	4.44	4.20	4.03	3.89	3.78	3.69	3.55	3.41	3.26	3.18	3.10	3.02	2.93	2.75
17		**4.45**	**3.59**	**3.20**	**2.96**	**2.81**	**2.70**	**2.61**	**2.55**	**2.49**	**2.45**	**2.38**	**2.31**	**2.23**	**2.19**	**2.15**	**2.10**	**2.06**	**1.96**
		8.40	6.11	5.18	4.67	4.34	4.10	3.93	3.79	3.68	3.59	3.46	3.31	3.16	3.08	3.00	2.92	2.83	2.65
18		**4.41**	**3.55**	**3.16**	**2.93**	**2.77**	**2.66**	**2.58**	**2.51**	**2.46**	**2.41**	**2.34**	**2.27**	**2.19**	**2.15**	**2.11**	**2.06**	**2.02**	**1.92**
		8.29	6.01	5.09	4.58	4.25	4.01	3.84	3.71	3.60	3.51	3.37	3.23	3.08	3.00	2.92	2.84	2.75	2.57

(continued)

TABLE A.3   CRITICAL VALUES OF THE *F*-DISTRIBUTION* (*Concluded*)

		Degrees of Freedom for Numerator																
		1	2	3	4	5	6	7	8	9	10	12	15	20	24	30	40	60	Infinity
Degrees of Freedom for Denominator	19	4.38	3.52	3.13	2.90	2.74	2.63	2.54	2.48	2.42	2.38	2.31	2.23	2.16	2.11	2.07	2.03	1.98	1.88
		8.18	5.93	5.01	4.50	4.17	3.94	3.77	3.63	3.52	3.43	3.30	3.15	3.00	2.92	2.84	2.76	2.67	2.49
	20	4.35	3.49	3.10	2.87	2.71	2.60	2.51	2.45	2.39	2.35	2.28	2.20	2.12	2.08	2.04	1.99	1.95	1.84
		8.10	5.85	4.94	4.43	4.10	3.87	3.70	3.56	3.46	3.37	3.23	3.09	2.94	2.86	2.78	2.69	2.61	2.42
	22	4.30	3.44	3.05	2.82	2.66	2.55	2.46	2.40	2.34	2.30	2.23	2.15	2.07	2.03	1.98	1.94	1.89	1.78
		7.95	5.72	4.82	4.31	3.99	3.76	3.59	3.45	3.35	3.26	3.12	2.98	2.83	2.75	2.67	2.58	2.50	2.31
	24	4.26	3.40	3.01	2.78	2.62	2.51	2.42	2.36	2.30	2.25	2.18	2.11	2.03	1.98	1.94	1.89	1.84	1.73
		7.82	5.61	4.72	4.22	3.90	3.67	3.50	3.36	3.26	3.17	3.03	2.89	2.74	2.66	2.58	2.49	2.40	2.21
	26	4.23	3.37	2.98	2.74	2.59	2.47	2.39	2.32	2.27	2.22	2.15	2.07	1.99	1.95	1.90	1.85	1.80	1.69
		7.72	5.53	4.64	4.14	3.82	3.59	3.42	3.29	3.18	3.09	2.96	2.81	2.66	2.58	2.50	2.42	2.33	2.13
	28	4.20	3.34	2.95	2.71	2.56	2.45	2.36	2.29	2.24	2.19	2.12	2.04	1.96	1.91	1.87	1.82	1.77	1.65
		7.64	5.45	4.57	4.07	3.75	3.53	3.36	3.23	3.12	3.03	2.90	2.75	2.60	2.52	2.44	2.35	2.26	2.06
	30	4.17	3.32	2.92	2.69	2.53	2.42	2.33	2.27	2.21	2.16	2.09	2.01	1.93	1.89	1.84	1.79	1.74	1.62
		7.56	5.39	4.51	4.02	3.70	3.47	3.30	3.17	3.07	2.98	2.84	2.70	2.55	2.47	2.39	2.30	2.21	2.01
	40	4.08	3.23	2.84	2.61	2.45	2.34	2.25	2.18	2.12	2.08	2.00	1.92	1.84	1.79	1.74	1.69	1.64	1.51
		7.31	5.18	4.31	3.83	3.51	3.29	3.12	2.99	2.89	2.80	2.66	2.52	2.37	2.29	2.20	2.11	2.02	1.80
	60	4.00	3.15	2.76	2.53	2.37	2.25	2.17	2.10	2.04	1.99	1.92	1.84	1.75	1.7	1.65	1.59	1.53	1.39
		7.06	4.98	4.13	3.65	3.34	3.12	2.95	2.82	2.72	2.63	2.50	2.35	2.20	2.12	2.03	1.94	1.84	1.60
	120	3.92	3.07	2.68	2.45	2.29	2.17	2.09	2.02	1.96	1.91	1.83	1.75	1.66	1.61	1.55	1.50	1.43	1.25
		6.85	4.79	3.95	3.48	3.17	2.96	2.79	2.66	2.56	2.47	2.34	2.19	2.03	1.95	1.86	1.76	1.66	1.38
	INFINITY	3.84	3.00	2.60	2.37	2.21	2.10	2.01	1.94	1.88	1.83	1.75	1.67	1.57	1.52	1.46	1.39	1.32	1.00
		6.63	4.61	3.78	3.32	3.02	2.80	2.64	2.51	2.41	2.32	2.18	2.04	1.88	1.79	1.70	1.59	1.47	1.00

*This table is abridged from Table 18 in *Biometrika Tables for Statisticians,* vol. 1 (3d ed.), New York: Cambridge University Press, 1970, edited by E. S. Pearson and H. O. Hartley, by permission of the *Biometrika* Trustees.

Glossary

ABAB design (reversal design)   A single-subject experimental design in which an initial baseline stage (A) is followed by a treatment stage (B), a return to baseline (A), and then another treatment stage (B); the researcher observes whether behavior changes on introduction of the treatment, reverses when the treatment is withdrawn, and improves again when the treatment is reintroduced.

alpha   See **level of significance.**

ANOVA   The analysis of variance, or ANOVA, is the most commonly used inferential test for examining a null hypothesis when comparing more than two means in a single-factor study, or in studies with more than one factor (i.e., independent variable). The ANOVA test is based on analyzing different sources of variation in an experiment.

applied research   Research that seeks knowledge that will improve a situation. See also **basic research.**

archival records   Source of evidence based on records or documents relating the activities of individuals, institutions, governments, and other groups; used as an alternative to or in conjunction with other research methods.

attrition   See **subject attrition.**

baseline stage   First stage of a single-subject experiment in which a record is made of the individual's behavior prior to any intervention.

basic research   Research that seeks knowledge to increase understanding of behavior and mental processes and to test theories. See also **applied research.**

block randomization   The most common technique for carrying out random assignment in the random groups design; each block includes a random order of the conditions, and there are as many blocks as there are subjects in each condition of the experiment.

case study   An intensive description and analysis of a single individual.

causal inference   Identification of the cause or causes of a phenomenon, by establishing covariation of cause and effect, a time-order relationship with cause preceding effect, and the elimination of plausible alternative causes.

ceiling (and floor) effect   Measurement problem whereby the researcher cannot measure the effects of an independent variable or a possible interaction effect because performance has reached a maximum (minimum) in any condition of the experiment.

central tendency   See **measures of central tendency.**

coding   The initial step in data reduction, especially with narrative records, in which units of behavior or particular events are identified and classified according to specific criteria.

Cohen's *d*   A frequently used measure of effect size in which the difference in means for two conditions is divided by the average variability of participants' scores (within-group standard deviation). Based on Cohen's guidelines, *d* values of .20, .50, and .80 represent small, medium, and large effects, respectively, of an independent variable.

Cohen's *f*   A measure of effect size when there are more than two means that defines an effect relative to the degree of dispersion among group means. Based on Cohen's guidelines, an *f* value of .10, .25, and .40 defines a small, medium, and large effect size, respectively.

comparison of two means   A statistical technique that can be applied (usually after obtaining a statistically significant omnibus *F*-test) to locate the specific source of systematic variation in an experiment by comparing means two at a time.

complex design   Experiment in which two or more independent variables are studied simultaneously.

confidence interval   Indicates the range of values which we can expect to contain a population value with a specified degree of confidence (e.g., 95%).

confidence interval for a population parameter   A range of values around a sample statistic (e.g., sample mean) with specified probability (e.g., .95) that the population parameter (e.g., population mean) has been captured within that interval.

confirming what the data reveal   In the third stage of data analysis the researcher determines what the data tell us about behavior. Statistical techniques are used to counter arguments that the results are simply "due to chance."

confounding   Occurs when the independent variable of interest systematically covaries with a second, unintended independent variable.

construct   A concept or idea used in psychological theories to explain behavior or mental processes; examples include aggression, depression, intelligence, memory, and personality.

contamination   Occurs when there is communication of information about the experiment between groups of participants.

content analysis   Any of a variety of techniques for making inferences by objectively identifying specific characteristics of messages, usually written communications but may be any form of message; used extensively in the analysis of archival data.

control   Key component of the scientific method whereby the effects of various factors possibly responsible for a phenomenon are isolated; three basic types of control are manipulation, holding conditions constant, and balancing.

correlation   Exists when two different measures of the same people, events, or things vary together; the presence of a correlation makes it possible to predict values on one variable by knowing the values on the second variable.

correlation coefficient   Statistic indicating how well two measures vary together; absolute size ranges from 0.0 (no correlation) to 1.00 (perfect correlation); direction of covariation is indicated by the sign of the coefficient, a plus (+) indicating that both measures covary in the same direction and a minus (−) indicating that the variables vary in opposite directions.

correlational research   Research to identify predictive relationships among naturally occurring variables.

counterbalancing   A control technique for distributing (balancing) practice effects across the conditions of a repeated measures design. How counterbalancing is accomplished depends on whether a complete or an incomplete repeated measures design is used.

cross-sectional design   Survey research design in which one or more samples of the population are selected and information is collected from the samples at one time.

data reduction   Process in the analysis of behavioral data whereby results are meaningfully organized and statements summarizing important findings are prepared.

debriefing   Process following a research session through which participants are informed about the rationale for the research in which they participated, about the need for any deception, and about their specific contribution to the research. Important goals of debriefing are to clear up any misconceptions and to leave participants with a positive feeling toward psychological research.

deception   Intentionally withholding information from a participant about significant aspects of a research project or presenting misinformation about the research to participants.

demand characteristics   Cues and other information used by participants to guide their behavior in a psychological study, often leading participants to do what they believe the observer (experimenter) expects them to do.

dependent variable   Measure of behavior used by the researcher to assess the effect (if any) of the independent variable.

differential transfer   Potential problem in repeated measures designs when performance in one condition differs depending on the condition preceding it.

double-blind procedure   Both the participant and the observer are kept unaware (blind) of what treatment is being administered.

effect size   Index of the strength of the relationship between the independent variable and dependent variable that is independent of sample size.

empirical approach   Approach to acquiring knowledge that emphasizes direct observation and experimentation as a way of answering questions.

estimated standard error of the mean   An estimate of the true standard error obtained by dividing the sample standard deviation by the square root of the sample size.

eta squared (η^2)   A measure of the strength of association (or effect size) based on the proportion of variance accounted for by the effect of the independent variable on the dependent variable.

ethnocentrism   An attempt to understand the behavior of individuals in different cultures based solely on experiences in one's own culture.

experiment   A controlled research situation in which scientists manipulate one or more factors and observe the effects of this manipulation on behavior.

experimenter effects   Experimenters' expectations that may lead them to treat subjects differently in different groups or to record data in a biased manner.

external validity   The extent to which the results of a research study can be generalized to different populations, settings, and conditions.

factorial design   See **complex design.**

field experiment   Procedure in which one or more independent variables is manipulated by an observer in a natural setting to determine the effect on behavior.

floor effect   See **ceiling effect.**

F-test   In the analysis of variance, or ANOVA, the ratio of between-group variation and within-group or error variation.

getting to know the data   In this first stage of data analysis the researcher inspects the data for errors and outliers and generally becomes familiar with the general features of the data.

Hawthorne effect   See **novelty effects.**

history   The occurrence of an event other than the treatment that can threaten internal validity if it produces changes in the research participants' behavior.

hypothesis   A tentative explanation for a phenomenon.

idiographic approach   Intensive study of an individual, with an emphasis on both individual uniqueness and lawfulness.

independent groups design   Each separate group of subjects in the experiment represents a different condition as defined by the level of the independent variable.

independent variable   Factor for which the researcher manipulates at least two levels in order to determine its effect on behavior.

individual differences variable   A characteristic or trait that varies consistently across individuals, such as level of depression, age, intelligence, gender. Because this variable is formed from preexisting groups (i.e., it occurs "naturally") an individual differences variable is sometimes called a natural groups variable. Another term sometimes used synonymously with individual differences variable is subject variable.

informed consent   Explicitly expressed willingness to participate in a research project based on clear understanding of the nature of the research, of the consequences of not participating, and of all factors that might be expected to influence willingness to participate.

instrumentation   Changes over time can take place not only in the participants of an experiment, but also in the instruments used to measure the participants' performance. These changes due to instrumentation can threaten internal validity if they cannot be separated from the effect of the treatment.

interaction effect   When the effect of one independent variable differs depending on the level of a second independent variable.

internal validity   Degree to which differences in performance can be attributed unambiguously to an effect of an independent variable, as opposed to an effect of some other (uncontrolled) variable; an internally valid study is free of confounds.

interobserver reliability   Degree to which two independent observers are in agreement.

interrupted time-series design   See **simple interrupted time-series design** and **time series with nonequivalent control group design.**

interviewer bias   Occurs when the interviewer tries to adjust the wording of a question to fit the respondent or records only selected portions of the respondent's answers.

level of significance   The probability when testing the null hypothesis that is used to indicate whether an outcome is statistically significant. Level of significance, or alpha, is equal to the probability of a Type I error.

linear trend   A trend in the data that is appropriately summarized by a straight line.

longitudinal design   Research design in which the same sample of respondents is interviewed (surveyed) more than once.

main effect   Overall effect of an independent variable in a complex design.

matched groups design   Type of independent groups design in which the researcher forms comparable groups by matching subjects on a pretest task and then randomly assigns the members of these matched sets of subjects to the conditions of the experiment.

maturation   Change associated with the passage of time *per se* is called maturation. Changes participants undergo in an experiment that are due to maturation and not due to the treatment can threaten internal validity.

mean   The arithmetic mean, or average, is determined by dividing the sum of the scores by the number of scores contributing to that sum. The mean is the most commonly used measure of central tendency.

measurement scale   One of four levels of physical and psychological measurement: nominal (categorizing), ordinal (ranking), interval (specifying distance between stimuli), and ratio (having an absolute zero point).

measures of central tendency   Measures such as the mean, median, and mode that identify a score that the data tend to center around.

measures of dispersion (variability)   Measures such as the range and standard deviation that describe the degree of dispersion of numbers in a distribution.

mechanical subject loss   Occurs when a subject fails to complete the experiment because of equipment failure or because of experimenter error.

median   The middle point in a distribution, above which half the scores fall and below which half fall.

meta-analysis   Analysis of results of several (often, very many) independent experiments investigating the same research area; the measure used in a meta-analysis is typically effect size.

minimal risk   A research participant is said to experience minimal risk when probability and magnitude of harm or discomfort anticipated in the research is not greater than that ordinarily encountered in daily life or during the performance of routine tests.

mode   The score that appears most frequently in the distribution.

multimethod approach   Approach to hypothesis testing that seeks evidence by collecting data using several different research procedures and measures of behavior; a recognition of the fact that any single observation of behavior is susceptible to error in the measuring process.

multiple-baseline design (across individuals, across behaviors, across situations)   A single-subject experimental design in which the effect of a treatment is demonstrated by showing that behaviors in more than one baseline change as a consequence of the introduction of a treatment; multiple baselines are established for different individuals, for different behaviors in the same individual, or for the same individual in different situations.

$N = 1$ **designs**   See **single-subject experiment.**

narrative record   Record intended to provide a more or less faithful reproduction of behavior as it originally occurred.

natural groups design   Type of independent groups design in which the conditions represent the selected levels of a naturally occurring independent variable, for example, the individual differences variable age.

naturalistic observation   Observation of behavior in a more or less natural setting without any attempt by the observer to intervene.

negative correlation   A relationship between two variables in which values for one measure increase as the values of the other measure decrease.

nomothetic approach   Approach to research that seeks to establish broad generalizations or laws that apply to large groups (populations) of individuals; the average or typical performance of a group is emphasized.

nonequivalent control group design   Quasi-experimental procedure in which a comparison is made between control and treatment groups that have been established on some basis other than through random assignment of participants to groups.

nonprobability sampling   A sampling procedure in which there is no way to estimate the probability of each element's being included in the sample; a common type is convenience sampling.

novelty effects   Threats to internal validity of a study that occur when people's behavior changes simply because an innovation (e.g., a treatment) produces excitement, energy, and enthusiasm; a Hawthorne effect is a special case of novelty effects.

null hypothesis (H_0)   Assumption used as the first step in statistical inference whereby the independent variable is said to have had no effect.

null hypothesis significance testing (NHST)   A procedure for statistical inference used to decide whether a variable has produced an effect in a study. NHST begins with the assumption that the variable has no effect (see **null hypothesis**), and probability theory is used to determine the probability that the effect (e.g., a mean difference between conditions) observed in a study would occur simply by error variation ("chance"). If the likelihood of the observed effect is small (see **level of significance**), assuming the null hypothesis is true, we infer the variable produced a reliable effect (see **statistically significant**).

observer bias   Systematic errors in observation often resulting from the observer's expectancies regarding the outcome of a study (i.e., expectancy effects).

omnibus *F*-test   The initial overall analysis based on ANOVA.

operational definition   Procedure whereby a concept is defined solely in terms of the observable procedures used to produce and measure it.

participant observation   Observation of behavior by someone who also has an active and significant role in the situation or context in which behavior is recorded.

physical traces   Source of evidence that is based on the remnants, fragments, and products of past behavior; used as an alternative to or in conjunction with other research methods.

placebo control group   Procedure by which a substance that resembles a drug or other active substance but that is actually an inert, or inactive, substance is given to participants.

plagiarism   Presentation of another's ideas or work without clearly identifying the source.

population   Set of all the cases of interest.

positive correlation   A relationship between two variables in which values for one measure increase as the values of the other measure also increase.

power   Probability in a statistical test that a false null hypothesis will be rejected; power is related to the level of significance selected, the size of the treatment effect, and the sample size.

practice effects   Changes that participants undergo with repeated testing. Practice effects are the summation of both positive (e.g., familiarity with a task) and negative (e.g., boredom) factors associated with repeated measurement.

privacy   Right of individuals to decide how information about them is to be communicated to others.

probability sampling   Sampling procedure in which the probability that each element of the population will be included in the sample can be specified.

program evaluation   Research that seeks to determine whether a change proposed by an institution, government agency, or other unit of society is needed and likely to have an effect as planned, and, when implemented, to have the desired effect at a reasonable cost.

quasi-experiments   Procedures that resemble characteristics of true experiments, for example, that some type of intervention or treatment is used and a comparison is provided, but are lacking in the degree of control that is found in true experiments.

questionnaire   A set of predetermined questions for all respondents that serves as the primary research instrument in survey research.

random assignment   Most common technique for forming groups as part of an independent groups design; the goal is to establish equivalent groups by balancing individual differences.

random groups design   Most common type of independent groups design in which subjects are randomly assigned to each group such that groups are considered comparable at the start of the experiment.

random sampling   See **simple random sampling.**

range   The difference between the highest and lowest number in a distribution.

reactivity   Influence that an observer has on the behavior under observation; behavior influenced by an observer may not be representative of behavior that occurs when an observer is not present.

regression (to the mean)   Statistical regression can occur when individuals have been selected to participate in an experiment because of their "extreme" scores. Statistical regression is a threat to internal validity because individuals selected from extreme groups would be expected to have less extreme scores on a second test (the "posttest") *without any treatment* simply due to statistical regression.

relevant independent variable   Independent variable that has been shown to influence behavior, either directly, by producing a main effect, or indirectly, by resulting in an interaction effect in combination with a second independent variable.

reliability   A measurement is reliable when it is consistent.

repeated measures designs   Research designs in which each subject participates in all conditions of the experiment (i.e., measurement is repeated on the same subject).

repeated measures (within-subjects) *t*-test   An inferential test for comparing two means from the same group of subjects or from two groups of subjects "matched" on some measure related to the dependent variable.

replication   Repeating the exact procedures used in an experiment to determine whether the same results are obtained.

representativeness   A sample is representative to the extent that it has the same distribution of characteristics as the population from which it was selected; our ability to generalize from sample to population is critically dependent on representativeness.

response rate bias   Threat to the representativeness of a sample that occurs when some participants selected to respond to a survey systematically fail to complete the survey (e.g., due to failure to complete a lengthy questionnaire or to comply with a request to participate in a phone survey).

reversal design   See **ABAB design.**

risk/benefit ratio   Subjective evaluation of the risk to a research participant relative to the benefit both to the individual and to society of the results of the proposed research.

sample   Something less than all the cases of interest; in survey research, a subset of the population actually drawn from the sampling frame.

scatterplot   A graph showing the relationship between two variables by indicating the intersection of two measures obtained from the same person, thing, or event.

scientific method   Approach to knowledge that emphasizes empirical rather than intuitive processes, testable hypotheses, systematic and controlled observation of operationally defined phenomena, data collection using accurate and precise instrumentation, valid and reliable measures, and objective reporting of results; scientists tend to be critical and, most important, skeptical.

selection   Selection is a threat to internal validity when, from the outset of a study, differences exist between the kinds of individuals in one group and those in another group in the experiment.

selection bias   Threat to the representativeness of a sample that occurs when the procedures used to select a sample result in the over- or underrepresentation of a significant segment of the population.

selective deposit   Bias that results from the way physical traces are laid down and the way archival sources are produced, edited, or altered, as they are established; when present, the bias severely limits generality of research findings.

selective subject loss   Occurs when subjects are lost differentially across the conditions of the experiment as the result of some characteristic of each subject that is related to the outcome of the study.

selective survival   Bias that results from the way physical traces and archives survive over time; when present, the bias severely limits the external validity of research findings.

sensitivity   Refers to the likelihood in an experiment that the effect of an independent variable will be detected when that variable does, indeed, have an effect; sensitivity is increased to the extent that error variation is reduced (e.g., by holding variables constant rather than balancing them).

simple interrupted time-series design   Quasi-experimental procedure in which changes in a dependent variable are observed for some period of time both before and after a treatment is introduced.

simple main effect   Effect of one independent variable at one level of a second independent variable in a complex design.

simple random sampling (random selection)   Type of probability sampling in which each possible sample of a specified size in the population has an equal chance of being selected.

single-factor independent groups design   An experiment that involves independent groups with one independent variable.

single-subject experiment   A procedure that focuses on behavior change in one individual by systematically contrasting conditions within that individual while continuously monitoring behavior.

situation sampling   Random or systematic selection of situations in which observations are made with the goal of representativeness across circumstances, locations, and conditions.

small-*n* research   See **single-subject experiment.**

social desirability   Pressures on survey respondents to answer as they think they should respond in accordance with what is most socially acceptable, and not in accordance with what they actually believe.

spurious relationship   What exists when evidence falsely indicates that two or more variables are associated.

stages of data analysis   Three stages of data analysis are getting to know the data, summarizing the data, and confirming what the data reveal.

standard deviation   The most commonly used measure of dispersion that indicates approximately how far on the average scores differ from the mean.

standard error of the mean   The standard deviation of the sampling distribution of means.

statistically significant   When the probability of an obtained difference in an experiment is smaller than would be expected if error variation alone were assumed to be responsible for the difference, the difference is statistically significant.

stem-and-leaf display   A technique for visualizing both the general features of a data set and specific item information by creating leading digits as "stems" and trailing digits as "leaves."

stratified random sampling   Type of probability sampling in which the population is divided into subpopulations called strata and random samples are drawn from each of these strata.

structured observation   Variety of observational methods using intervention in which the degree of control is often less than in field experiments; frequently used by clinical and developmental psychologists when making behavioral assessments.

subject attrition   A threat to internal validity occurs when participants are lost from an experiment, for example, when participants drop out of the research project. The loss of participants changes the nature of a group from that established prior to the introduction of the treatment—for example, by destroying the equivalence of groups that had been established through random assignment.

successive independent samples design   Survey research design in which a series of cross-sectional surveys is done and the same questions are asked of each succeeding sample of respondents.

summarizing the data   In this second stage of data analysis the researcher uses descriptive statistics and graphical displays to summarize the information in a data set. Trends and patterns in the data set are described.

testing   Taking a test generally has an effect on subsequent testing. Testing can threaten internal validity if the effect of a treatment cannot be separated from the effect of testing.

theory Logically organized set of propositions that serves to define events, describe relationships among events, and explain the occurrence of these events; scientific theories guide research and organize empirical knowledge.

threats to internal validity Possible causes of a phenomenon that must be controlled so a clear cause-effect inference can be made.

time sampling Selection of observation intervals either systematically or randomly with the goal of obtaining a representative sample of behavior.

time series with nonequivalent control group design (See also **simple interrupted time-series design**.) Quasi-experimental procedure that improves on the validity of a simple time-series design by including a nonequivalent control group; both treatment and comparison groups are observed for a period of time both before and after the treatment.

t-**test for independent groups** An inferential test for comparing two means from different groups of subjects.

Type I error The probability of rejecting the null hypothesis when it is true, equal to the level of significance, or alpha.

Type II error The probability of failing to reject the null hypothesis when it is false.

unobtrusive (nonreactive) measures Measures of behavior that eliminate the problem of reactivity because observations are made in such a way that the presence of the observer is not detected by those being observed.

validity The "truthfulness" of a measure; a valid measure is one that measures what it claims to measure.

variability See **measures of dispersion.**

References

Abelson, R. P. (1995). *Statistics as principled argument.* Hillsdale, NJ: Erlbaum.

Abelson, R. P. (1997). On the surprising longevity of flogged horses: Why there is a case for the significance test. *Psychological Science, 8,* 12–15.

Adler, T. (1991, December). Outright fraud rare, but not poor science. *APA Monitor,* 11.

Allison, M. G., & Ayllon, T. (1980). Behavioral coaching in the development of skills in football, gymnastics, and tennis. *Journal of Applied Behavior Analysis, 13,* 297–314.

Allport, G. W. (1961). *Pattern in growth and personality.* New York: Holt, Rinehart and Winston.

Altmann, J. (1974). Observational study of behavior: Sampling methods. *Behavior, 48,* 1–41.

Ambady, N., & Rosenthal, R. (1993). Half a minute: Predicting teacher evaluations from thin slices of nonverbal behavior and physical attractiveness. *Journal of Personality and Social Psychology, 64,* 431–441.

American Psychiatric Association. (2000). *Diagnostic and statistical manual of mental disorders* (4th ed., Text Revision). Washington, DC: Author.

American Psychological Association. (2002). Ethical principles of psychologists and code of conduct. *American Psychologist, 57,* 1060–1073.

American Psychological Association. (2006). Summary report of journal operations, 2005. *American Psychologist, 61,* 559–560.

American Psychological Association. (2010). *Publication manual* (6th ed). Washington, DC: Author.

Anderson, C. A., Berkowitz, L., Donnerstein, E., Huesmann, L. R., Johnson, J. D., Linz, D., Malamuth, N. M., & Wartella, E. (2003). The influence of media violence on youth. *Psychological Science in the Public Interest, 4,* 81–110.

Anderson, C. A., & Bushman, B. J. (1997). External validity of "trivial" experiments: The case of laboratory aggression. *Review of General Psychology, 1,* 19–41.

Anderson, C. R. (1976). Coping behaviors as intervening mechanisms in the inverted-U stress-performance relationship. *Journal of Applied Psychology, 61,* 30–34.

Anderson, J. R. (1990). *The adaptive character of thought.* Hillsdale, NJ: Erlbaum.

Anderson, J. R. (1993*). Rules of the mind.* Hillsdale, NJ: Erlbaum.

Anderson, J. R., & Milson, J. R. (1989). Human memory: An adaptive perspective. *Psychological Review, 96,* 703–719.

Anderson, K. J., & Revelle, W. (1982). Impulsivity, caffeine, and proofreading: A test of the Easterbrook hypothesis. *Journal of Experimental Psychology: Human Perception and Performance, 8,* 614–624.

Anglin, J. M. (1993). Vocabulary development: A morphological analysis. *Monographs of the Society for Research in Child Development, 58* (10, Serial No. 238).

Arnett, J. J. (2008). The neglected 95%: Why American psychology needs to become less American. *American Psychologist, 63,* 602–614. doi: 10.1037/0003-066x.63.7.602

Atkinson, R. C. (1968). Computerized instruction and the learning process. *American Psychologist, 23,* 225–239.

Atkinson, R. C., & Shiffrin, R. M. (1968). Human memory: A proposed system and its control processes. In K. W. Spence & J. T. Spence (Eds.), *The psychology of learning and motivation* (Vol. 2, pp. 89–195). New York: Academic Press.

Azar, B. (1994a, August). Computers create global research lab. *APA Monitor, 1,* 16.

Azar, B. (1994b, August). Research made easier by computer networks. *APA Monitor,* 16.

Bagemihl, B. (2000). *Biological exuberance: Animal homosexuality and natural diversity.* New York, New York: St. Martin's Press.

Baker, T. B., McFall, R. M., & Shoham, V. (2009). Current status and future prospects of clinical psychology: Toward a scientifically principled approach to mental and behavioral health care. *Psychological Science in the Public Interest, 9,* 67–103. doi: 10.1111/j.1539-6053.2009.01036.x

Banaji, M. R., & Crowder, R. G. (1989). The bankruptcy of everyday memory. *American Psychologist, 44,* 1185–1193.

Bard, K. A., Myowa-Yamakoshi, M., Tomonaga, M., Tanaka, M., Costall, A., & Matsuzawa, T. (2005). Group differences in the mutual gaze of chimpanzees (*Pan Troglodytes*). *Developmental Psychology, 41,* 616–624.

Barker, R. G., Wright, H. F., Schoggen, M. F., & Barker, L. S. (1978). Day in the life of Mary Ennis. In R. G. Barker et al. (Eds.), *Habitats, environments, and human behavior* (pp. 51–98). San Francisco: Jossey-Bass.

Baron, R. M., & Kenny, D. A. (1986). The moderator-mediator variable distinction in social psychological research: Conceptual, strategic, and statistical considerations. *Journal of Personality and Social Psychology, 51,* 1173–1182.

Bartholomew, G. A. (1982). Scientific innovation and creativity: A zoologist's point of view. *American Zoologist, 22,* 227–335.

Bartlett, M. Y., & DeSteno, D. (2006). Gratitude and prosocial behavior: Helping when it costs you. *Psychological Science, 17,* 319–325.

Baumeister, R. F., Vohs, K. D., & Funder, D. C. (2007). Psychology as the science of self-reports and finger movements: Whatever happened to actual behavior? *Perspectives on Psychological Science, 2,* 396–403. doi: 10.1111/j.1745-6916.2007.00051.x

Baumrind, D. (1985). Research using intentional deception: Ethical issues revisited. *American Psychologist, 40,* 165–174.

Becker-Blease, K. A., & Freyd, J. J. (2006). Research participants telling the truth about their lives: The ethics of asking and not asking about abuse. *American Psychologist, 61,* 218–226.

Behnke, S. (2003). Academic and clinical training under APA's new ethics code. *Monitor on Psychology, 34,* 64.

Berdahl, J. L., & Moore, C. (2006). Workplace harassment: Double jeopardy for minority women. *Journal of Applied Psychology, 91,* 426–436.

Berk, R. A., Boruch, R. F., Chambers, D. L., Rossi, P. H., & Witte, A. D. (1987). Social policy experimentation: A position paper. In D. S. Cordray & M. W. Lipsey (Eds.), *Evaluation Studies Review Annual* (Vol. 11, pp. 630–672). Newbury Park, CA: Sage.

Bickman, L. (1976). Observational methods. In C. Selltiz, L. S. Wrightsman, & S. W. Cook (Eds.), *Research methods in social relations* (pp. 251–290). New York: Holt, Rinehart and Winston.

Birnbaum, M. H. (2000). Decision making in the lab and on the Web. In M. H. Birnbaum (Ed.), *Psychological experiments on the Internet* (pp. 3–34). San Diego, CA: Academic Press.

Blanchard, F. A., Crandall, C. S., Brigham, J. C., & Vaughn, L. A. (1994). Condemning and condoning racism: A social context approach to interracial settings. *Journal of Applied Psychology, 79,* 993–997.

Blanck, P. D., Bellack, A. S., Rosnow, R. L., Rotheram-Borus, M. J., & Schooler, N. R. (1992). Scientific rewards and conflicts of ethical choices in human subjects research. *American Psychologist, 47,* 959–965.

Bolgar, H. (1965). The case study method. In B. B. Wolman (Ed.), *Handbook of clinical psychology* (pp. 28–39). New York: McGraw-Hill.

Boring, E. G. (1954). The nature and history of experimental control. *American Journal of Psychology, 67,* 573–589.

Brandt, R. M. (1972). *Studying behavior in natural settings.* New York: Holt, Rinehart and Winston: University Press of America, 1981.

Bröder, A. (1998). Deception can be acceptable. *American Psychologist, 53,* 805–806.

Brown, R., & Kulik, J. (1977). Flashbulb memories. *Cognition, 5,* 73–99.

Bryant, A. N., & Astin, H. A. (2006). *The spiritual struggles of college students.* Manuscript under editorial review.

Buchanan, T. (2000). Potential of the Internet for personality research. In M. H. Birnbaum (Ed.), *Psychological experiments on the Internet* (pp. 121–139). San Diego, CA: Academic Press.

Burger, J. M. (2009). Replicating Milgram: Would people still obey today? *American Psychologist, 64,* 1–11. doi: 10.1037/a0010932

Bushman, B. J. (2005). Violence and sex in television programs do not sell products in advertisements. *Psychological Science, 16,* 702–708.

Bushman, B. J., & Cantor, J. (2003). Media ratings for violence and sex: Implications for policymakers and parents. *American Psychologist, 58,* 130–141.

Campbell, D. T. (1969). Reforms as experiments. *American Psychologist, 24,* 409–429.

Campbell, D. T., & Stanley, J. C. (1966). *Experimental and quasi-experimental designs for research.* Chicago: Rand McNally.

Candland, D. K. (1993). *Feral children and clever animals.* New York: Oxford University Press.

Carnagey, N. L., & Anderson, C. A. (2005). The effects of reward and punishment in violent video games on aggressive affect, cognition, and behavior. *Psychological Science, 16,* 882–889.

Ceci, S. J. (1993). Cognitive and social factors in children's testimony. Master lecture presented at the American Psychological Association Convention.

Chastain, G., & Landrum, R. E. (1999). *Protecting human subjects: Departmental subject pools and institutional review boards.* Washington, DC: American Psychological Association.

Chernoff, N. N. (2002, December). Nobel Prize winner pushes economic theory despite hurdles. *APS Observer, 15,* 9–10.

Chow, S. L. (1988). Significance test or effect size? *Psychological Bulletin, 103,* 105–110.

Christensen, L. (1988). Deception in psychological research: When is its use justified? *Personality and Social Psychology Bulletin, 14,* 664–675.

Clark, H. H., & Schober, M. F. (1992). Asking questions and influencing answers. In J. M. Tanur (Ed.), *Questions about questions: Inquiries into the cognitive bases of surveys.* New York: Russell Sage Foundation.

Cohen, J. (1988*). Statistical power analysis for the behavioral sciences* (2nd ed.). Hillsdale, NJ: Erlbaum.

Cohen, J. (1990). Things I have learned (so far). *American Psychologist, 45,* 1304–1312.

Cohen, J. (1992). A power primer. *Psychological Bulletin, 112,* 155–159.

Cohen, J. (1995). The earth is round ($p < .05$). *American Psychologist, 49,* 997–1003.

Cook, T. D., & Campbell, D. T. (1979). *Quasi-experimentation: Design and analysis issues for field settings.* Chicago: Rand McNally.

Coon, D. J. (1992). Testing the limits of sense and science: American experimental psychologists combat spiritualism, 1880–1920. *American Psychologist, 47,* 143–151.

Cordaro, L., & Ison, J. R. (1963). Psychology of the scientist: X. Observer bias in classical conditioning of the planarian. *Psychological Reports, 13,* 787–789.

Cronbach, L. J. (1992). Four *Psychological Bulletin* articles in perspective. *Psychological Bulletin, 12,* 389–392.

Crossen, C. (1994). *Tainted truth: The manipulation of fact in America.* New York: Simon & Schuster.

Cumming, G., Fidler, F., Leonard, M., Kalinowski, P., Christiansen, A., Kleinig, A., Lo, J., McMenamin, N., & Wilson, S. (2007). Statistical reform in psychology: Is anything changing? *Psychological Science, 18,* 230–232.

Cumming, G., & Finch, S. (2005). Inference by eye: Confidence intervals and how to read pictures of data. *American Psychologist, 60,* 170–180.

Curtiss, S. R. (1977). *Genie: A psycholinguistic study of a modern-day "wild child."* New York: Academic Press.

Dallam, S. J., Gleaves, D. H., Cepeda-Benito, A., Silberg, J. L., Kraemer, H. C., & Spiegel, D. (2001). The effects of child sexual abuse: Comment on Rind, Tromovitch, and Bauserman (1998). *Psychological Bulletin, 127,* 715–733.

Dawes, R. M. (1991, June). *Problems with a psychology of college sophomores.* Paper presented at the Third Annual Convention of the American Psychological Society, Washington, DC.

DeLoache, J. S., Pierroutsakos, S. L., Uttal, D. H., Rosengren, K. S., & Gottlieb, A. (1998). Grasping the nature of pictures. *Psychological Science, 9,* 205–210.

Dickie, J. R. (1987). Interrelationships within the mother-father-infant triad. In P. W. Berman & F. A. Pedersen (Eds.), *Men's transitions to parenthood: Longitudinal studies of early family experience* (pp. 113–143). Hillsdale, NJ: Erlbaum.

Diener, E. (2009). Introduction to special issue on the next big questions in psychology. *Perspectives on Psychological Science, 4,* 325. doi: 10.1111/j.1745-6924.2009.0133.x

Diener, E., & Crandall, R. (1978). *Ethics in social and behavioral research.* Chicago: The University of Chicago Press.

Dittmar, H., Halliwell, E., & Ive, S. (2006). Does Barbie make girls want to be thin? The effect of experimental exposure to images of dolls on the body image of 5- to 8-year-old girls. *Developmental Psychology, 42,* 283–292.

Dolan, C. A., Sherwood, A., & Light, K. C. (1992). Cognitive coping strategies and blood pressure responses to real-life stress in healthy young men. *Health Psychology, 11,* 233–240.

Eberhardt, J. L., Davies, P. G., Purdie-Vaughns, V. J., & Johnson, S. L. (2006). Looking death-worthy: Perceived stereotypicality of Black defendants predicted capital-sentencing outcomes. *Psychological Science, 17,* 383–386.

Eibl-Eibesfeldt, I. (1975). *Ethology: The biology of behavior.* New York: Holt, Rinehart and Winston.

Ekman, P. (1994). Strong evidence for universals in facial expressions: A reply to Russell's mistaken critique. *Psychological Bulletin, 115,* 268–287.

Endersby, J. W., & Towle, M. J. (1996). Tailgate partisanship: Political and social expression through bumper stickers. *The Social Science Journal, 33,* 307–319.

Entwisle, D. R., & Astone, N. M. (1994). Some practical guidelines for measuring youth's race/ethnicity and socioeconomic status. *Child Development, 65,* 1521–1540.

Epley, N., & Huff, C. (1998). Suspicion, affective response, and educational benefit as a result of deception in psychology research. *Personality and Social Psychology Bulletin, 24,* 759–768.

Epstein, S. (1979). The stability of behavior: On predicting most of the people much of the time. *Journal of Personality and Social Psychology, 37,* 1097–1126.

Ericsson, K. A., & Charness, N. (1994). Expert performance: Its structure and acquisition. *American Psychologist, 49,* 725–747.

Estes, W. K. (1997). On the communication of information by displays of standard errors and confidence intervals. *Psychonomic Bulletin & Review, 4,* 330–341.

Evans, G. W., Gonnella, C., Marcynyszyn, L. A., Gentile, L., & Salpekar, N. (2005). The role of chaos in poverty and children's socioemotional adjustment. *Psychological Science, 16,* 560–565.

Evans, R., & Donnerstein, E. (1974). Some implications for psychological research of early versus late term participation by college students. *Journal of Research in Personality, 8,* 102–109.

Feeney, D. M. (1987). Human rights and animal welfare. *American Psychologist, 42,* 593–599.

Festinger, L., Riecken, H., & Schachter, S. (1956). *When prophecy fails.* Minneapolis: University of Minnesota Press.

Fidler, F., Thomason, N., Cumming, G., Finch, S., & Leeman, J. (2004). Editors can lead researchers to confidence intervals, but can't make them think. *Psychological Science, 15,* 119–126.

Finch, S., Thomason, N., & Cumming, G. (2002). Past and future American Psychological Association guidelines for statistical practice. *Theory & Psychology, 12,* 825–853.

Fine, M. A., & Kurdek, L. A. (1993). Reflections on determining authorship credit and authorship order on faculty-student collaborations. *American Psychologist, 48,* 1141–1147.

Fisher, C. B., & Fryberg, D. (1994). Participant partners: College students weigh the costs and benefits of deceptive research. *American Psychologist, 49,* 417–427.

Fossey, D. (1981). Imperiled giants of the forest. *National Geographic, 159,* 501–523.

Fossey, D. (1983). *Gorillas in the mist.* Boston: Houghton-Mifflin.

Fowler, R. D. (1992). Report of the chief executive officer: A year of building for the future. *American Psychologist, 47,* 876–883.

Fraley, R. C. (2004). *How to conduct behavioral research over the Internet.* New York: Guilford Press.

Frick, R. W. (1995). Accepting the null hypothesis. *Memory & Cognition, 23,* 132–138.

Friedman, H. S., Tucker, J. S., Schwartz, J. E., Tomlinson-Keasy, C., Martin, L. R., Wingard, D. L., & Criqui, M. H. (1995). Psychosocial and behavioral predictors of longevity: The aging and death of the "Termites." *American Psychologist, 50,* 69–78.

Friedman, M. P., & Wilson, R. W. (1975). Application of unobtrusive measures to the study of textbook usage by college students. *Journal of Applied Psychology, 60,* 659–662.

Gabrieli, J. D. E., Fleischman, D. A., Keane, M. M., Reminger, S. L., & Morrell, F. (1995). Double dissociation between memory systems underlying explicit and implicit memory in the human brain. *Psychological Science, 6,* 76–82.

Gena, A., Krantz, P. J., McClannahan, L. E., & Poulson, C. L. (1996). Training and generalization of affective behavior displayed by youth with autism. *Journal of Applied Behavioral Analysis, 29,* 291–304.

Gigerenzer, G. (2004). Dread risk, September 11, and fatal traffic accidents. *Psychological Science, 15,* 286–287.

Gigerenzer, G., Krauss, S., & Vitouch, O. (2004). The null ritual: What you always wanted to know about significance testing but were afraid to ask. In D. Kaplan (Ed.), *The Sage handbook of quantitative methodology for the social sciences* (pp. 391–408). Thousand Oaks, CA: Sage.

Gilman, R., Connor, N., & Haney, M. (2005). A school-based application of modified habit reversal for Tourette syndrome via a translator: A case study. *Behavior Modification, 29,* 823–838.

Glaser, J., Dixit, J., & Green, D. P. (2002). Studying hate crime with the Internet: What makes racists advocate racial violence? *Journal of Social Issues, 58,* 177–193.

Goodall, J. (1987). A plea for the chimpanzees. *American Scientist, 75,* 574–577.

Gordon, R. T., Schatz, C. B., Myers, L. J., Kosty, M., Gonczy, C., Kroener, J., . . . Zaayer, J. (2008). The use of canines in the detection of human cancers. *Journal of Alternative Complementary Medicine, 14,* 61–67. doi: 10.1089/acm.2006.6408

Gosling, S. D., Vazire, S., Srivastava, S., & John, O. P. (2004). Should we trust Web-based studies? A comparative analysis of six preconceptions about Internet questionnaires. *American Psychologist, 59,* 93–104.

Greenwald, A. G., Gonzalez, R., Harris, R. J., & Guthrie, D. (1996). Effect sizes and *p* values: What should be reported and what should be replicated? *Psychophysiology, 33,* 175–183.

Griskevicius, V., Tybur, J. M., & Van den Bergh, B. (2010). Going green to be seen: Status, reputation, and conspicuous conservation. *Journal of Personality and Social Psychology, 98,* 392–404. doi: 10.1037/a0017346

Grissom, R. J., & Kim, J. J. (2005). *Effect sizes for research: A broad practical approach.* Mahwah, NJ: Erlbaum.

Hagen, R. L. (1997). In praise of the null hypothesis statistical test. *American Psychologist, 52,* 15–24.

Haggbloom, S. J., Warnick, R., Warnick, J. E., Jones, V. K., Yarbrough, G. L., Russell, T. M., et al. (2002). The 100 most eminent psychologists of the 20th century. *Review of General Psychology, 6,* 139–152.

Halpern, A. R., & Bower, G. H. (1982). Musical expertise and melodic structure in memory for musical notation. *American Journal of Psychology, 95,* 31–50.

Hansen, C. J., Stevens, L. C., & Coast, J. R. (2001). Exercise duration and mood state: How much is enough to feel better? *Health Psychology, 20,* 267–275. doi: 10.1037/0278-6133.20.4.267

Harlow, H. F., & Harlow, M. K. (1966). Learning to love. *American Scientist, 54,* 244–272.

Hartl, T. L., & Frost, R. O. (1999). Cognitive-behavioral treatment of compulsive hoarding: A multiple-baseline experimental case study. *Behaviour Research and Therapy, 37,* 451–461.

Hartup, W. W. (1974). Aggression in childhood: Development perspectives. *American Psychologist, 29,* 336–341.

Heatherton, T. F., Mahamedi, F., Striepe, M., Field, A. E., & Keel, P. (1997). A 10-year longitudinal study of body weight, dieting, and eating disorder symptoms. *Journal of Abnormal Psychology, 106,* 117–125.

Heatherton, T. F., Nichols, P., Mahamedi, F., & Keel, P. K. (1995). Body weight, dieting, and eating disorder symptoms among college students 1982 to 1992. *American Journal of Psychiatry, 152,* 1623–1629.

Heatherton, T. F., & Sargent, J. D. (2009). Does watching smoking in movies promote teenage smoking? *Current Directions in Psychological Science, 18,* 63–67. doi: 10.1111/j.1467-8721.2009.01610.x

Hersen, M., & Barlow, D. H. (1976). *Single-case experimental designs: Strategies for studying behavior change.* New York: Pergamon Press.

Hertzog, C., Kramer, A. F., Wilson, R. S., & Lindenberger, U. (2008). Enrichment effects on adult cognitive development: Can the functional capacity of older adults be preserved and enhanced? *Psychological Science in the Public Interest, 9,* 1–65. doi: 10.1111/j.1539-6053.2009.01034.x

Hilts, P. J. (1995). Memory's ghost: The nature of memory and the strange tale of Mr. M. New York: Simon & Schuster.

Hippler, H. J., & Schwarz, N. (1987). Response effects in surveys. In H. J. Hippler, N. Schwarz, & S. Sudman (Eds.), *Social information processing and survey methodology* (pp. 102–122). New York: Springer-Verlag.

Hoaglin, D. C., Mosteller, F., & Tukey, J. W. (Eds.). (1983). *Understanding robust and exploratory data analysis.* New York: Wiley.

Hoaglin, D. C., Mosteller, F., & Tukey, J. W. (Eds.). (1991). *Fundamentals of exploratory analysis of variance.* New York: Wiley.

Holden, C. (1987). Animal regulations: So far, so good. *Science, 238,* 880–882.

Holmbeck, G. N. (1997). Toward terminological, conceptual, and statistical clarity in the study of mediators and moderators: Examples from the child-clinical and pediatric psychology literatures. *Journal of Consulting and Clinical Psychology, 65,* 599–610.

Holsti, O. R. (1969). *Content analysis for the social sciences.* Reading, MA: Addison-Wesley.

Horton, S. V. (1987). Reduction of disruptive mealtime behavior by facial screening. *Behavior Modification, 11,* 53–64.

Howell, D. C. (2002). *Statistical methods for psychology* (5th ed.). Belmont, CA: Wadsworth.

Hunt, M. (1997). *How science takes stock: The story of meta-analysis.* New York: Russell Sage Foundation.

Hunter, J. E. (1997). Needed: A ban on the significance test. *Psychological Science, 8,* 3–7.

Hyman, I. E., Boss, S. M., Wise, B. M., McKenzie, K. E., & Caggiano, J. M. (2009). Did you see the unicycling clown? Inattentional blindness while walking and talking on a cell phone. *Applied Cognitive Psychology,* published online in Wiley InterScience (www.interscience.wiley.com). doi: l0.l002/acp.1638

Johnson, D. (1990). Animal rights and human lives: Time for scientists to right the balance. *Psychological Science, 1,* 213–214.

Judd, C. M., Smith, E. R., & Kidder, L. H. (1991). *Research methods in social relations* (6th ed.). Fort Worth, TX: Holt, Rinehart and Winston.

Kahneman, D. (2003). A perspective on judgment and choice: Mapping bounded rationality. *American Psychologist, 58,* 697–720.

Kahneman, D., & Tversky, A. (1973). On the psychology of prediction. *Psychological Review, 80,* 237–251.

Kaiser, C. R., Vick, S. B., & Major, B. (2006). Prejudice expectations moderate preconscious attention to cues that are threatening to social identity. *Psychological Science, 17,* 332–338.

Kardas, E. P., & Milford, T. M. (1996). *Using the Internet for social science research and practice.* Belmont, CA: Wadsworth.

Kaschak, M. P., & Moore, C. F. (2000). On the documentation of statistical analyses in the "Clicky-Box" era. *American Psychologist, 55,* 1511–1512.

Kassin, S. M., Goldstein, C. C., & Savitsky, K. (2003). Behavioral confirmation in the interrogation room: On the dangers of presuming guilt. *Law and Human Behavior, 27,* 187–203.

Kassin, S. M., & Kiechel, K. L. (1996). The social psychology of false confessions: Compliance, internalization, and confabulation. *Psychological Science, 7,* 125–128.

Kazdin, A. E. (1978). Methodological and interpretive problems of single-case experimental designs. *Journal of Consulting and Clinical Psychology, 46,* 629–642.

Kazdin, A. E. (1980). *Behavior modification in applied settings* (rev. ed.). Homewood, IL: Dorsey Press.

Kazdin, A. E. (1982). Single-case experimental designs. In P. C. Kendall & J. N. Butcher (Eds.), *Handbook of research methods in clinical psychology* (pp. 416–490). New York: Wiley.

Kazdin, A. E. (2002). *Research designs in clinical psychology* (4th ed.). Boston: Allyn and Bacon.

Kazdin, A. E., & Erickson, L. M. (1975). Developing responsiveness to instructions in severely and profoundly retarded residents. *Journal of Behavior Therapy and Experimental Psychiatry, 6,* 17–21.

Keel, P. K., Baxter, M. G., Heatherton, T. F., & Joiner, T. E., Jr. (2007). A 20-year longitudinal study of body weight, dieting, and eating disorder symptoms. *Journal of Abnormal Psychology, 116,* 422–432. doi: 10.1037/0021-843X.116.2.422

Keith, T. Z., Reimers, T. M., Fehrmann, P. G., Pottebaum, S. M., & Aubrey, L. W. (1986). Parental involvement, homework, and TV time: Direct and indirect effects on high school achievement. *Journal of Educational Psychology, 78,* 373–380.

Keller, F. S. (1937). *The definition of psychology.* New York: Appleton-Century-Crofts.

Kelley-Milburn, D., & Milburn, M. A. (1995). Cyberpsych: Resources for psychologists on the Internet. *Psychological Science, 6,* 203–211.

Kelman, H. C. (1967). Human use of human subjects: The problem of deception in social psychological experiments. *Psychological Bulletin, 67,* 1–11.

Kelman, H. C. (1972). The rights of the subject in social research: An analysis in terms of relative power and legitimacy. *American Psychologist, 27,* 989–1016.

Kenny, D. A. (1979). *Correlation and causality.* New York: Wiley.

Keppel, G. (1991). *Design and analysis: A researcher's handbook* (3rd ed.). Englewood Cliffs, NJ: Prentice-Hall.

Kidd, S. A. (2002). The role of qualitative research in psychological journals. *Psychological Methods, 7,* 126–138.

Kidd, S. A., & Kral, M. J. (2002). Suicide and prostitution among street youth: A qualitative analysis. *Adolescence, 37,* 411–430.

Killeen, P. R. (2005). An alternative to null-hypothesis significance tests. *Psychological Science, 16,* 345–353.

Kimble, G. A. (1989). Psychology from the standpoint of a generalist. *American Psychologist, 44,* 491–499.

Kimmel, A. J. (1996). *Ethical issues in behavioral research: A survey.* Cambridge, MA: Blackwell.

Kimmel, A. J. (1998). In defense of deception. *American Psychologist, 53,* 803–805.

Kirk, R. E. (1996). Practical significance: A concept whose time has come. *Educational and Psychological Measurement, 56,* 746–759.

Kirkham, G. L. (1975). Doc cop. *Human Behavior, 4,* 16–23.

Kirsch, I. (1978). Teaching clients to be their own therapists: A case-study illustration. *Psychotherapy: Theory, Research and Practice, 15,* 302–305.

Kirsch, I., & Sapirstein, G. (1998). Listening to Prozac but hearing placebo: A meta-analysis of antidepressant medication. *Prevention & Treatment, 1(2).* doi: 10.1037/ 1522-3736.1.1.12a, prevention/volume1/pre0010002a.html.

Klinesmith, J., Kasser, T., & McAndrew, F. T. (2006). Guns, testosterone, and aggression: An experimental test of a meditational hypothesis. *Psychological Science, 17,* 568–571.

Kohlberg, L. (Ed.). (1981). *The philosophy of moral development: Essays on moral development* (Vol. I). San Francisco: Harper & Row.

Kohlberg, L. (Ed.). (1984). *The philosophy of moral development: Essays on moral development* (Vol. II). San Francisco: Harper & Row.

Krantz, J. H., & Dalal, R. (2000). Validity of Web-based psychological research. In M. H. Birnbaum (Ed.), *Psychological experiments on the Internet* (pp. 35–60). San Diego, CA: Academic Press.

Kratochwill, T. R., & Brody, G. H. (1978). Single subject designs: A perspective on the controversy over employing statistical inference and implications for research and training in behavior modification. *Behavior Modification, 2,* 291–307.

Kratochwill, T. R., & Levin, J. R. (Eds.). (1992). *Single-case research designs and analysis: New directions for psychology and education.* Mahwah, NJ: Erlbaum.

Kratochwill, T. R., & Martens, B. K. (1994). Applied behavior analysis and school psychology. *Journal of Applied Behavior Analysis, 27,* 3–5.

Kraut, R., Olson, J., Banaji, M. R., Bruckman, A., Cohen, J., & Couper, M. (2004). Psychological research online: Report of Board of Scientific Affairs' Advisory Group on the conduct of research on the Internet. *American Psychologist, 59,* 105–117.

Krueger, J. (2001). Null hypothesis significance testing: On the survival of a flawed method. *American Psychologist, 56,* 16–26.

Kruglanski, A. W., Crenshaw, M., Post, J. M., & Victoroff, J. (2007). What should this fight be called? Metaphors of counterterrorism and their implications. *Psychological Science in the Public Interest, 8,* 97–133. doi: 10.1111/j.1539-6053.2008.00035.x

Kubany, E. S. (1997). Application of cognitive therapy for trauma-related guilt (CT-TRG) with a Vietnam veteran troubled by multiple sources of guilt. *Cognitive and Behavioral Practice, 4,* 213–244.

LaFrance, M., & Mayo, C. (1976). Racial differences in gaze behavior during conversations: Two systematic observational studies. *Journal of Personality and Social Psychology, 33,* 547–552.

Lakatos, I. (1978). *The methodology of scientific research.* London: Cambridge University Press.

Lambert, N. M., Clark, M. S., Durtschi, J., Fincham, F. D., & Graham, S. M. (2010). Benefits of expressing gratitude: Expressing gratitudes to a partner changes one's view of the relationship. *Psychological Science, 21,* 574–580. doi: 10.1177/09567976103644003

Langer, E. J. (1989). *Mindfulness.* Reading, MA: Addison-Wesley.

Langer, E. J. (1997). *The power of mindful learning.* Reading, MA: Addison-Wesley.

Langer, E. J., & Piper, A. I. (1987). The prevention of mindlessness. *Journal of Personality and Social Psychology, 53,* 280–287.

Langer, E. J., & Rodin, J. (1976). The effects of choice and enhanced personal responsibility for the aged: A field experiment in an institutional setting. *Journal of Personality and Social Psychology, 34,* 191–198.

Larson, R. (1989). Beeping children and adolescents: A method for studying time use and daily experience. *Journal of Youth and Adolescence, 18,* 511–530.

Larson, R. W., Richards, M. H., Moneta, G., Holmbeck, G., & Duckett, E. (1996). Changes in adolescents' daily interactions with their families from ages 10 to 18: Disengagement and transformation. *Developmental Psychology, 32,* 744–754.

Latané, B., & Darley, J. M. (1970). *The unresponsive bystander: Why doesn't he help?* New York: Appleton-Century-Crofts.

LeBlanc, P. (2001, September). "And mice." (Or tips for dealing with the animal subjects review board). *APS Observer, 14,* 21–22.

Lee, S. W. S., Schwarz, N., Taubman, D., & Hou, M. (2010). Sneezing in times of a flu pandemic: Public sneezing increases perception of unrelated risks and shifts preferences for federal spending. *Psychological Science, 21,* 375–377. doi: 10.1177/0956797609359876

Lenhart, A., Madden, M., & Hitlin, P. (2005). *Teens and technology: Youth are leading the transition to a fully wired and mobile nation.* Retrieved from http://www.pewinternet.org/pdfs/PIP_Teens_Tech_July2005web.pdf.

Levine, R. V. (1990). The pace of life. *American Scientist, 78,* 450–459.

Levitt, S. D., & Dubner, S. J. (2005). *Freakonomics: A rogue economist explores the hidden side of everything.* New York: HarperCollins.

Levitt, S. D., & Dubner, S. J. (2009). *SuperFreakonomics: Global cooling, patriotic prostitutes, and why suicide bombers should buy life insurance.* New York: HarperCollins.

Li, M., Vietri, J., Galvani, A. P., & Chapman, G. B. (2010). How do people value life? *Psychological Science, 21,* 163–167. doi: 10.1177/0956797609357707

Locke, T. P., Johnson, G. M., Kirigin-Ramp, K., Atwater, J. D., & Gerrard, M. (1986). An evaluation of a juvenile education program in a state penitentiary. *Evaluation Review, 10,* 281–298.

Loftus, E. F. (2003, August). Loftus: The need to defend scientific freedom. *APS Observer, 16,* 1, 32.

Loftus, G. R. (1991). On the tyranny of hypothesis testing in the social sciences. *Contemporary Psychology, 36,* 102–105.

Loftus, G. R. (1996). Psychology will be a much better science when we change the way we analyze data. *Current Directions in Psychological Science, 5,* 161–171.

Loftus, G. R., & Masson, M. E. J. (1994). Using confidence intervals in within-subject designs. *Psychonomic Bulletin & Review, 1,* 476–490.

Lovaas, O. I., Newsom, C., & Hickman, C. (1987). Self-stimulatory behavior and perceptual reinforcement. *Journal of Applied Behavior Analysis, 20,* 45–68.

Lucas, R. E. (2005). Time does not heal all wounds: A longitudinal study of reaction and adaptation to divorce. *Psychological Science, 16,* 945–950.

Lucas, R. E., Diener, E., & Suh, E. (1996). Discriminant validity of well-being measures. *Journal of Personality and Social Psychology, 71,* 616–628.

Ludwig, T. E., Jeeves, M. A., Norman, W. D., & DeWitt, R. (1993). The bilateral field advantage on a letter-matching task. *Cortex, 29,* 691–713.

MacCoun, R. (2002, December). Why a psychologist won the Nobel Prize in economics. *APS Observer, 15,* 1, 8.

Madigan, C. M. (1995, March 19). Hearing it right: Small turnout spoke. *Chicago Tribune,* pp. 1–2.

Maestripieri, D., & Carroll, K. A. (1998). Child abuse and neglect: Usefulness of the animal data. *Psychological Bulletin, 123,* 211–223.

Marx, M. H. (1963). The general nature of theory construction. In M. H. Marx (Ed.), *Theories in contemporary psychology* (pp. 4–46). New York: Macmillan.

Matsumoto, D., & Willingham, B. (2006). The thrill of victory and the agony of defeat: Spontaneous expressions of medal winners of the 2004 Athens Olympic Games. *Journal of Personality and Social Psychology, 91,* 568–581.

McCallum, D. M. (2001, May/June). "Of men . . ." (Or how to obtain approval from the human subjects review board). *APS Observer, 14,* 28–29, 35.

McCarthy, D. E., Piasecki, T., M., Fiore, M. C., & Baker, T. B. (2006). Life before and after quitting smoking: An electronic diary study. *Journal of Abnormal Psychology, 115,* 454–466.

McCulloch, M., Jezierski, T., Broffman, M., Hubbard A., Turner, K., & Janecki, T. (2006). Diagnostic accuracy of canine scent detection in early- and late-stage lung and breast cancers. *Integrative Cancer Therapies, 5,* 30–39. doi: l0.1177/1534735405285096

McGrew, W. C. (1972). *An ethological study of children's behavior.* New York: Academic Press.

McGuire, W. J. (1997). Creative hypothesis generating in psychology: Some useful heuristics. *Annual Review of Psychology, 48,* 1–30.

Medvec, V. H., Madey, S. F., & Gilovich, T. (1995). When less is more: Counterfactual thinking and satisfaction among Olympic medalists. *Journal of Personality and Social Psychology, 69,* 603–610.

Meehl, P. E. (1967). Theory-testing in psychology and physics: A methodological paradox. *Philosophy of Science, 34,* 103–115.

Meehl, P. E. (1978). Theoretical risks and tabular asterisks: Sir Karl, Sir Ronald, and the slow progress of soft psychology. *Journal of Consulting and Clinical Psychology, 46,* 806–834.

Meehl, P. E. (1990a). Appraising and amending theories: The strategy of Lakatosian defense and two principles that warrant it. *Psychological Inquiry, 1,* 108–141.

Meehl, P. E. (1990b). Why summaries of research on psychological theories are often uninterpretable. *Psychological Reports, 66,* 195–244 (Monograph Supplement 1-V66).

Michielutte, R., Shelton, B., Paskett, E. D., Tatum, C. M., & Velez, R. (2000). Use of an interrupted time-series design to evaluate a cancer screening program. *Health Education Research, 15,* 615–623.

Miles, M. B., & Huberman, A. M. (1994). *Qualitative data analysis* (2nd ed.). Thousand Oaks, CA: Sage.

Milgram, S. (1974). *Obedience to authority*. New York: Harper & Row.

Milgram, S. (1977, October). Subject reaction: The neglected factor in the ethics of experimentation. *Hastings Center Report*.

Milgram, S., Liberty, H. J., Toledo, R., & Wackenhut, J. (1986). Response to intrusion into waiting lines. *Journal of Personality and Social Psychology, 51,* 683–689.

Miller, G. A., & Wakefield, P. C. (1993). On Anglin's analysis of vocabulary growth. *Monographs of the Society for Research in Child Development, 58* (10, Serial No. 238).

Miller, J. D. (1986, May). *Some new measures of scientific illiteracy.* Paper presented at the meeting of the American Association for the Advancement of Science, Philadelphia.

Miller, N. E. (1985). The value of behavioral research on animals. *American Psychologist, 40,* 423–440.

Mooallem, J. (2010, April 4). The love that dare not squawk its name: Inside the science of same-sex animal pairings. *The New York Times Magazine,* pp. 26–35, 44, 46.

Mook, D. G. (1983). In defense of external invalidity. *American Psychologist, 38,* 379–387.

Mosteller, F., & Hoaglin, D. C. (1991). Preliminary examination of data. In D. C. Hoaglin, F. Mosteller, & J. W. Tukey (Eds.), *Fundamentals of exploratory analysis of variance* (pp. 40–49). New York: Wiley.

Mulaik, S. A., Raju, N. S., & Harshman, R. A. (1997). There is a time and place for significance testing. In L. L. Harlow, S. A. Mulaik, & J. H. Steiger (Eds.), *What if there were no significance tests?* (pp. 65–115). Mahwah, NJ: Erlbaum.

Musch, J., & Reips, U. (2000). A brief history of Web experimenting. In M. H. Birnbaum (Ed.), *Psychological experiments on the Internet* (pp. 61–87). San Diego, CA: Academic Press.

Myers, D. G., & Diener, E. (1995). Who is happy? *Psychological Science, 6,* 10–19.

National Research Council. (1996). *Guide for the care and use of laboratory animals.* A report of the Institute of Laboratory Animal Resources committee. Washington, DC: National Academy Press.

Neisser, U. (1967). *Cognitive psychology.* New York: Appleton-Century-Crofts.

Neisser, U., & Harsch, N. (1992). Phantom flashbulbs: False recollections of hearing the news about *Challenger.* In E. Winograd & U. Neisser (Eds.), *Affect and accuracy in recall: Studies of "flashbulb memories"* (pp. 9–31). New York: Cambridge University Press.

Newburger, E. C. (2001, September, U.S. Census Bureau). *Home computers and Internet use in the United States: August 2000.* Retrieved June 1, 2004, from http://www.census.gov/prod/2001pubs/p23-207.pdf

Newhagen, J. E., & Ancell, M. (1995). The expression of emotion and social status in the language of bumper stickers. *Journal of Language and Social Psychology, 14,* 312–323.

Nosek, B. A., Banaji, M. R., & Greenwald, A. G. (2002). E-Research: Ethics, security, design, and control in psychological research on the Internet. *Journal of Social Issues, 58,* 161–176.

Novak, M. A. (1991, July). "Psychologists care deeply" about animals. *APA Monitor,* 4.

Ondersma, S. J., Chaffin, M., Berliner, L., Cordon, I., Goodman, G. S., & Barnett, D. (2001). Sex with children is abuse: Comment on Rind, Tromovitch, and Bauserman (1998). *Psychological Bulletin, 127,* 707–714.

Orne, M. T. (1962). On the social psychology of the psychological experiment: With particular reference to demand characteristics and their implications. *American Psychologist, 17,* 776–783.

Ortmann, A., & Hertwig, R. (1997). Is deception necessary? *American Psychologist, 52,* 746–747.

Ortmann, A., & Hertwig, R. (1998). The question remains: Is deception acceptable? *American Psychologist, 53,* 806–807.

Park, C. L., Armeli, S., & Tennen, H. (2004). Appraisal-coping goodness of fit: A daily Internet study. *Personality and Social Psychology Bulletin, 30,* 558–569.

Parker, R. I., & Brossart, D. F. (2003). Evaluating single-case research data: A comparison of seven statistical methods. *Behavior Therapy, 34,* 189–211. doi: 10.1016/S0005-7893(03)80013-8

Parry, H. J., & Crossley, H. M. (1950). Validity of responses to survey questions. *Public Opinion Quarterly, 14,* 61–80.

Parsons, H. M. (1974). What happened at Hawthorne? *Science, 183,* 922–932.

Parsonson, B. S., & Baer, D. M. (1992). The visual analysis of data, and current research into the stimuli controlling it. In T. R. Kratochwill & J. R. Levin (Eds.), *Single-case research design and analysis* (pp. 15–40). Hillsdale, NJ: Erlbaum.

Pashler, H., McDaniel, M., Rohrer, D., & Bjork, R. (2008). Learning styles: Concepts and evidence. *Psychological Science in the Public Interest, 9,* 105–109. doi: 10.1111/j.1539-6053.2009.01038.x

Pease, A., & Pease, B. (2004). *The definitive book of body language.* New York: Bantam Dell.

Pennebaker, J. W. (1989). Confession, inhibition, and disease. In L. Berkowitz (Ed.), *Advances in experimental social psychology* (Vol. 22, pp. 211–244). New York: Academic Press.

Pennebaker, J. W., & Francis, M. E. (1996). Cognitive, emotional, and language processes in disclosure. *Cognition and Emotion, 10,* 601–626.

Piaget, J. (1965). *The child's conception of number.* New York: Norton.

Pickren, W. E. (2003). An elusive honor: Psychology, behavior, and the Nobel Prize. *American Psychologist, 58,* 721–722.

Pingitore, R., Dugoni, B. L., Tindale, R. S., & Spring, B. (1994). Bias against overweight job applicants in a simulated employment interview. *Journal of Applied Psychology, 79,* 909–917.

Popper, K. R. (1959). *The logic of scientific discovery.* New York: Basic Books.

Popper, K. R. (1976). *Unended quest.* Glasgow: Fontana/Collins.

Posavac, E. J. (2002). Using *p* values to estimate the probability of a statistically significant replication. *Understanding Statistics, 1,* 101–112.

Posavac, E. J. (2011). *Program evaluation* (8th ed.). Englewood Cliffs, NJ: Prentice-Hall.

Poulton, E. C. (1973). Unwanted range effects from using within-subject experimental designs. *Psychological Bulletin, 80,* 113–121.

Poulton, E. C. (1975). Range effects in experiments on people. *American Journal of Psychology, 88,* 3–32.

Poulton, E. C. (1982). Influential companions. Effects of one strategy on another in the within-subjects designs of cognitive psychology. *Psychological Bulletin, 91,* 673–690.

Poulton, E. C., & Freeman, P. R. (1966). Unwanted asymmetrical transfer effects with balanced experimental designs. *Psychological Bulletin, 66,* 1–8.

Pryor, J. H., Hurtado, S., DeAngelo, L., Patuki Blake, L., & Tran, S. (2009). *The American freshman: National norms fall 2009.* Los Angeles: Higher Education Research Institute, UCLA.

Rachels, J. (1986). *The elements of moral philosophy.* New York: McGraw-Hill.

Rasinski, K. A., Willis, G. B., Baldwin, A. K., Yeh, W., & Lee, L. (1999). Methods of data collection, perceptions of risks and losses, and motivation to give truthful answers to sensitive survey questions. *Applied Cognitive Psychology, 13,* 465–484.

Rauscher, F. H., Shaw, G. L., & Ky, K. N. (1993). Music and spatial task performance. *Nature, 365,* 611.

Richardson, D. R., Pegalis, L., & Britton, B. (1992). A technique for enhancing the value of research participation. *Contemporary Social Psychology, 16,* 11–13.

Richardson, J. & Parnell, P. (2005). *And Tango makes three.* Simon Schuster.

Rimm, D. C., & Masters, J. C. (1979). *Behavior therapy: Techniques and empirical findings* (2nd ed.). New York: Academic Press.

Rind, B., & Tromovitch, P. (2007). National samples, sexual abuse in childhood, and adjustment in adulthood: A commentary on Najman, Dunne, Purdie, Boyle, and Coxeter (2005). *Archives of Sexual Behavior, 36*, 101–106, doi: 10.1007/s10508-006-9058-y

Rind, B., Tromovitch, P., & Bauserman, R. (1998). A meta-analytic examination of assumed properties of child sexual abuse using college samples. *Psychological Bulletin, 124*, 22–53.

Rind, B., Tromovitch, P., & Bauserman, R. (2001). The validity and appropriateness of methods, analyses, and conclusions in Rind et al. (1998): A rebuttal of victimological critique from Ondersma et al. (2001) and Dallam et al. (2001). *Psychological Bulletin, 127*, 734–758.

Robins, R. W., Gosling, S. D., & Craik, K. H. (1999). An empirical analysis of trends in psychology. *American Psychologist, 54*, 117–128.

Roethlisberger, F. J. (1977). *The elusive phenomena: An autobiographical account of my work in the field of organized behavior at the Harvard Business School.* Cambridge, MA: Division of Research, Graduate School of Business Administration (distributed by Harvard University Press).

Rogers, A. (1999). *Barbie culture.* Thousand Oaks, CA: Sage.

Rosenfeld, A. (1981). Animal rights vs. human health. *Science, 81*, 18, 22.

Rosenhan, D. L. (1973). On being sane in insane places. *Science, 179*, 250–258.

Rosenthal, R. (1963). On the social psychology of the psychological experiment: The experimenter's hypothesis as unintended determinant of experimental results. *American Scientist, 51*, 268–283.

Rosenthal, R. (1966). *Experimenter effects in behavioral research.* New York: Appleton-Century-Crofts.

Rosenthal, R. (1976). *Experimenter effects in behavioral research.* (Enlarged ed.). New York: Irvington.

Rosenthal, R. (1990). How are we doing in soft psychology? *American Psychologist, 45*, 775–777.

Rosenthal, R. (1991). *Meta-analytic procedures for social research* (Rev. ed.). Newbury Park, CA: Sage.

Rosenthal, R. (1994a). Interpersonal expectancy effects: A 30-year perspective. *Current Directions in Psychological Science, 3*, 176–179.

Rosenthal, R. (1994b). Science and ethics in conducting, analyzing, and reporting psychological research. *Psychological Science, 5*, 127–134.

Rosenthal, R., & Rosnow, R. L. (1991). *Essentials of behavioral research: Methods and data analysis* (2nd ed.). New York: McGraw-Hill.

Rozin, P., Kabnick, K., Pete, E., Fischler, C., & Shields, C. (2003). The ecology of eating: Smaller portion sizes in France than in the United States help explain the French paradox. *Psychological Science, 14*, 450–454.

Sackeim, H. A., Gur, R. C., & Saucy, M. C. (1978). Emotions are expressed more intensely on the left side of the face. *Science, 202*, 434–436.

Sacks, O. (1985). *The man who mistook his wife for a hat and other clinical tales.* New York: Harper & Row.

Sacks, O. (1995). *An anthropologist on Mars.* New York: Knopf.

Sacks, O. (2007). *Musicophilia: Tales of music and the brain.* New york: A. A. Knopf.

Salomon, G. (1987). Basic and applied research in psychology: Reciprocity between two worlds. *International Journal of Psychology, 22*, 441–446.

Sax, L. J., Astin, A. W., Lindholm, J. A., Korn, W. S., Saenz, V. B., & Mahoney, K. M. (2003). *The American freshman: National norms for fall 2003.* Los Angeles: Higher Education Research Institute, UCLA.

Schacter, D. L. (1996). *Searching for memory.* New York: Basic Books.

Schmidt, F. L. (1996). Statistical significance testing and cumulative knowledge in psychology: Implications for training of researchers. *Psychological Methods, 1,* 115–129.

Schmidt, F. L., & Hunter, J. E. (1997). Eight common but false objections to the discontinuation of significance testing in the analysis of research data. In L. L. Harlow, S. A. Mulaik, & J. H. Steiger (Eds.), *What if there were no significance tests?* (pp. 37–64). Mahwah, NJ: Erlbaum.

Schmidt, W. C. (1997). World-Wide-Web survey research: Benefits, potential problems, and solutions. *Behavior Research Methods, Instruments, & Computers, 29,* 274–279.

Schoeneman, T. J., & Rubanowitz, D. E. (1985). Attributions in the advice columns: Actors and observers, causes and reasons. *Personality and Social Psychology Bulletin, 11,* 315–325.

Schuman, H., Presser, S., & Ludwig, J. (1981). Context effects of survey responses to questions about abortion. *Public Opinion Quarterly, 45,* 216–223.

Schwartz, P. (2010, January/February). Love, American style. *The AARP Magazine.*

Scoville, W. B., & Milner, B. (1957). Loss of recent memory after bilateral hippocampal lesions. *Journal of Neurology, Neurosurgery, and Psychiatry, 20,* 11–19.

Seale, C. (Ed.). (1999). *The quality of qualitative research.* London: Sage.

Seligman, M. E. P., Steen, T. A., Park, N., & Peterson, C. (2005). Positive psychology progress: Empirical validation of interventions. *American Psychologist, 60,* 410–421.

Shadish, W. R., Cook, T. D., & Campbell, D. T. (2002). *Experimental and quasi-experimental designs for generalized causal inference.* Boston: Houghton Mifflin.

Shapiro, K. J. (1998). *Animal models of human psychology: Critique of science, ethics, and policy.* Seattle, WA: Hogrefe & Huber.

Sharpe, D., Adair, J. G., & Roese, N. J. (1992). Twenty years of deception research: A decline in subjects' trust? *Personality and Social Psychology Bulletin, 18,* 585–590.

Shiffman, S., & Paty, J. (2006). Smoking patterns and dependence: Contrasting chippers and heavy smokers. *Journal of Abnormal Psychology, 115,* 509–523.

Sieber, J. E., Iannuzzo, R., & Rodriguez, B. (1995). Deception methods in psychology: Have they changed in 23 years? *Ethics & Behavior, 5,* 67–85.

Simmons, R. A., Gordon, P. C., & Chambless, D. L. (2005). Pronouns in marital interaction: What do "you" and "I" say about marital health? *Psychological Science, 16,* 932–936.

Simon, H. A. (1992). What is an "explanation" of behavior? *Psychological Science, 3,* 150–161.

Singer, P. (1990). The significance of animal suffering. *Behavioral and Brain Sciences, 13,* 9–12.

Skinner, B. F. (1966). Operant behavior. In W. K. Honig (Ed.), *Operant behavior: Areas of research and application* (pp. 12–32). New York: Appleton-Century-Crofts.

Skitka, L. J., & Sargis, E. G. (2005). Social psychological research and the Internet: The promise and the perils of a new methodological frontier. In Y. Amichai-Hamburger (Ed.), *The social net: The social psychology of the Internet.* New York: Oxford University Press.

Smith, J. A., Harré, R., & Van Langenhove, L. (1995). Idiography and the case study. In J. A. Smith, R. Harré, & L. Van Langenhove (Eds.), *Rethinking psychology* (pp. 59–69). Thousand Oaks, CA: Sage.

Smith, T. W. (1981). Qualifications to generalized absolutes: "Approval of hitting" questions on the GSS. *Public Opinion Quarterly, 45,* 224–230.

Sokal, M. M. (1992). Origins and early years of the American Psychological Association, 1890–1906. *American Psychologist, 47,* 111–122.

Spitz, R. A. (1965). *The first year of life.* New York: International Universities Press.

Spitzer, R. L. (1976). More on pseudoscience in science and the case for psychiatric diagnosis. *Archives of General Psychiatry, 33,* 459–470.

Sternberg, R. J. (1986). A triangular theory of love. *Psychological Review, 93,* 119–135.

Sternberg, R. J. (1997, September). What do students still most need to learn about research in psychology? *APS Observer,* 14, 19.

Sternberg, R. J., & Williams, W. M. (1997). Does the Graduate Record Examination predict meaningful success in the graduate training of psychologists? A case study. *American Psychologist, 52,* 630–641.

Strauss, A., & Corbin, J. (1990). *Basics of qualitative research.* Newbury Park, CA: Sage.

Sue, S. (1999). Science, ethnicity and bias. *American Psychologist, 54,* 1070–1077.

Surwit, R. S., & Williams, P. G. (1996). Animal models provide insight into psychosomatic factors in diabetes. *Psychosomatic Medicine, 58,* 582–589.

Susskind, J. E. (2003). Children's perception of gender-based illusory correlations: Enhancing preexisting relationships between gender and behavior. *Sex Roles, 48,* 483–494.

Talarico, J. M., & Rubin, D. C. (2003). Confidence, not consistency, characterizes flashbulb memories. *Psychological Science, 14,* 455–461.

Tassinary, L. G., & Hansen, K. A. (1998). A critical test of the waist-to-hip-ratio hypothesis of female physical attractiveness. *Psychological Science, 9,* 150–155.

Taylor, K. M., & Shepperd, J. A. (1996). Probing suspicion among participants in deception research. *American Psychologist, 51,* 886.

Thioux, M., Stark, D. E., Klaiman, C., & Schultz, R. T. (2006). The day of the week when you were born in 700 ms: Calendar computation in an autistic savant. *Journal of Experimental Psychology: Human Perception and Performance, 32,* 1155–1168.

Thomas, L. (1992). *The fragile species.* New York: Charles Scribner's Sons.

Thompson, T. L. (1982). Gaze toward and avoidance of the handicapped: A field experiment. *Journal of Nonverbal Behavior, 6,* 188–196.

Tucker, J. S., Friedman, H. S., Schwartz, J. E., Criqui, M. H., Tomlinson-Keasey, C., Wingrad, D. L., & Martin, L. R. (1997). Parental divorce: Effects on individual behavior and longevity. *Journal of Personality and Social Psychology, 73,* 381–391.

Tukey, J. W. (1977). *Exploratory data analysis.* Reading, MA: Addison-Wesley.

Tversky, A., & Kahneman, D. (1974). Judgment under uncertainty: Heuristics and biases. *Science, 185,* 1124–1131.

Ulrich, R. E. (1991). Animal rights, animal wrongs and the question of balance. *Psychological Science, 2,* 197–201.

Ulrich, R. E. (1992). Animal research: A reflective analysis. *Psychological Science, 3,* 384–386.

Underwood, B. J., & Shaughnessy, J. J. (1975). *Experimentation in psychology.* New York: Wiley: Robert E. Krieger, 1983.

U.S. Census Bureau. (2000). DP-4. Profile of selected housing characteristics: 2000. Retrieved August 5, 2004, from http://factfinder.census.gov/

Valentino, K., Cicchetti, D., Toth, S. L., & Rogosch, F. A. (2006). Mother-child play and emerging social behaviors among infants from maltreating families. *Developmental Psychology, 42,* 474–485.

van Baaren, R. B., Holland, R. W., Kawakami, K., & van Knippenberg, A. (2004). Mimicry and prosocial behavior. *Psychological Science, 15,* 71–74.

VanderStoep, S. W., & Shaughnessy, J. J. (1997). Taking a course in research methods improves reasoning about real-life events. *Teaching of Psychology, 24,* 122–124.

Watson, J. B. [1914] (1967). *Behavior: An introduction to comparative psychology.* New York: Holt, Rinehart and Winston.

Webb, E. J., Campbell, D. T., Schwartz, R. D., Sechrest, L., & Grove, J. B. (1981). *Nonreactive measures in the social sciences* (2nd ed.). Boston: Houghton-Mifflin.

Weiner, B. (1975). "On being sane in insane places": A process (attributional) analysis and critique. *Journal of Abnormal Psychology, 84,* 433–441.

Weisz, J. R., Jensen-Doss, A., & Hawley, K. M. (2006). Evidence-based youth psychotherapies versus usual clinical care. *American Psychologist, 61,* 671–689.

West, S. G. (2010). Alternatives to randomized experiments. *Current Directions in Psychological Science, 18,* 299–304. doi: 10.1111/j.1467-8721.2009.01656.x

Whitlock, J. L., Powers, J. L., & Eckenrode, J. (2006). The virtual cutting edge: The Internet and adolescent self-jury. *Developmental Psychology, 42,* 407–417.

Wilkinson, L., & Task Force on Statistical Inference. (1999). Statistical methods in psychology journals. *American Psychologist, 54,* 598–604.

Willis, C. M., Church, S. M., Guest, C. M., Cook, W. A., McCarthy, N., Bransbury, A. J., et al. (2004). Olfactory detection of human bladder cancer by dogs: Proof of principle study. *British Medical Journal, 329,* 712–716.

Wilson, G. T. (1978). On the much discussed nature of the term "behavior therapy." *Behavior Therapy, 9,* 89–98.

Winer, B. J., Brown, D. R., & Michels, K. M. (1991). *Statistical principles in experimental design* (3rd ed.). New York: McGraw-Hill.

Yeaton, W. H., & Sechrest, L. (1986). Use and misuse of no-difference findings in eliminating threats to validity. *Evaluation Review, 10,* 836–852.

Zechmeister, E. B., Chronis, A. M., Cull, W. L., D'Anna, C. A., & Healy, N. A. (1995). Growth of a functionally important lexicon. *Journal of Reading Behavior, 27,* 201–212.

Zechmeister, E. B., & Posavac, E. J. (2003). *Data analysis and interpretation in the behavioral sciences.* Belmont, CA: Wadsworth.

Zechmeister, J. S., Zechmeister, E. B., & Shaughnessy, J. J. (2001). *Essentials of research methods in psychology,* New York: McGraw-Hill.

Zimbardo, P. G. (2004). Does psychology make a significant difference in our lives? *American Psychologist, 59,* 339–351.

Zuk, M. (2003). *Sexual selections: What we can and can't learn about sex from animals.* Berkeley, CA: University of California Press.

Credits

Chapter 1

Figure 1.1a: © Imagery Majestic/Cutcaster RF; 1.1b: © Bananastock RF; Box 1.1: © Courtesy of Princeton University; Figure 1.2a: © Bettmann/Corbis; 1.2b: Courtesy of the National Library of Medicine; 1.2c: © Historicus, Inc. RF; Figure 1.3a: © Kim Steele/Getty RF; 1.3b & c: © Corbis RF.

Chapter 2

Figure 2.1 (top & bottom): Courtesy of Thomas A. Sebeok, Distinguished Professor Emeritus, Indiana University, Bloomington; Box 2.1: © J. S. Zechmeister; Figure 2.2: © PhotoLink/Getty RF; Figure 2.3a: The Museum of Questionable Medical Devices, www.museumofquackery.com; 2.3b: © Corbis RF; Figure 2.4: © David Buffington/Getty RF; Figure 2.5: From Figure 3, p. 453, of Levine, R. V. (1990). The pace of life. *American Scientist, 78,* 450–459. © 1990 by Sigma Xi, The Scientific Research Society, Inc. Illustration by Michael Szpir. Used with permission of publisher and author.

Chapter 3

Figure 3.1a: © E. B. Zechmeister; 3.1b: © Dynamic Graphics/Jupiter Images RF; 3.1c: © E. B. Zechmeister; 3.1d: © Corbis RF; Figure 3.2: © Corbis RF; Figure 3.3: Greg Gibson/AP/Wide World Photos; Figure 3.4: © Digital Vision RF; Figure 3.5: Photo of Eugene & Jeanne Zechmeister by a friendly passerby; Figure 3.6: © 1968 by Stanley Milgram, © renewed 1993 by Alexandra Milgram. From the film *Obedience* distributed by Pennsylvania State Media Sales; Figure 3.7: Ryan McVay/Getty RF; Figure 3.8a © E. B. Zechmeister; 3.8b: © J. J. Shaughnessy.

Chapter 4

Figure 4.2: © Brand X/Getty RF; Figure 4.3: © Ira E. Hyman, Jr., Western Washington University. Used with permission of author; Figure 4.4: © Farrell Grehan/Corbis; Figure 4.5: © Brand X Pictures/Punchstock RF; Table 4.3: From Dickie, J. R., & Gerber, S. C. (1980). Training in social competence: The effect on mothers, fathers, and infants. *Child Development, 51,* 1248–1251. Materials provided by Jane Dickie, Psychology Department, Hope College, Holland, MI 49423; Table 4.4: From Table 2, p. 550, of LaFrance, M., & Mayo, C. (1976). Racial differences in gaze behavior during conversations: Two systematic observational studies. *Journal of Personality and Social Psychology, 33,* 547–552, © 1976 by the American Psychological Association, reprinted by permission of publisher and author; Figure 4.6: © Jim Sugar/Corbis.

Chapter 5

Figure 5.2: © BananaStock RF; Figure 5.3: From Figure 7, p. 7, of Sax, L. J., Austin, A. W., Lindholm, J. A., Korn, W. S., Saenz, V. B., & Mahoney, K. M. (2003). *The American freshman: National norms for fall 2003.* Los Angeles: Higher Education Research Institute, UCLA. © UC Requests, used with permission of publisher; Figure 5.4: © Duncan Smith/Getty RF; Figure 5.5: © Ryan McVay/Getty RF; Table 5.1: Adapted from Table 3, p. 621, of Lucas, R. E., Diener, E., & Suh, E. (1996). Discriminant validity of well-being measures. *Journal of Personality and Social Psychology, 71,* 616–628. © 1996 by the American Psychological Association, adapted with permission of publisher and author; Figure 5.6: © Ingram Publishing/AGE Fotostock.

Chapter 6

Figure 6.1: © Indiapicture/Alamy Images; Figure 6.2: © Henny Ray Abrams/AFP/Getty Images; Figure 6.3: © Corbis RF; Table 6.1: Adapted from Table 2, p. 885, of Carnagey, N. L., & Anderson, C. A. (2005). The effects of reward and punishment in violent video games on aggressive affect, cognition, and behavior, *Psychological Science, 16,* 882–889. © 2005 by the American Psychological Society, adapted with permission of Sage Publications and author; Figure 6.4: © Brand X Pictures RF; Figure 6.5: © Photodisc/Getty RF.

Chapter 7

Figure 7.1: © Ryna McVay/Getty RF; Figure 7.2: From Figure 1, p. 434, of Sackeim, H. A., Gur, R. C., & Saucy, M. C. (1978). Emotions are expressed more intensely on the left side of the face. *Science, 202,* 434–436. © American Association for the Advancement of Science, reprinted with permission of publisher and author.

Chapter 8

Figure 8.5: Adapted from Table 2, p. 913, of Pingitore, R., Dugoni, B. L., Tindale, R. S., & Spring, B. (1994). Bias against overweight job applicants in a simulated employment interview. *Journal of Applied Psychology, 79,* 909–917. © 1994 by the American Psychological Association, adapted with permission of publisher and author; Table 9.5: Adapted from data presented on p. 336 of Kaiser, C. R., Vick, S. B., & Major, B. (2006). Prejudice expectations moderate preconscious attention to cues that are threatening to social identity. *Psychological Science, 17,* 332–338. © 2006 by the Association for Psychological Science, adapted with permission of Sage Publications and author.

Chapter 9

Case study illustration © 1978 by Division of Psychotherapy (29), American Psychological Association, adapted with permission of publisher and author, the official citation that should be used in referencing this material is Kirsch, I. (1978). Teaching clients to be their own therapists: A case study illustration. *Psychotherapy: Theory, Research & Practice, 15,* 302–305. The use of this information does not imply endorsement by the publisher; Figure 9.1a: © Nina Leen/Getty;

9.1b: © Bettmann/Corbis; Figure 9.2: © LWA-Dann Tardif/Corbis; Figure 9.3: Adapted from Figure 1, p. 60, of Horton, S. V. (1987). Reduction of disruptive mealtime behavior by facial screenings. *Behavior Modification, 11,* 53–64. © 1987 Sage Publications, Inc., adapted with permission of publisher and author; Figure 9.4: From Figure 1, p. 301, of Allison, M. G., & Allyon, T. (1980). Behavioral coaching for the development of skills in football, gymnastics, and tennis. *Journal of Applied Behavioral Analysis, 13,* 297–304. © 1980 by the Experimental Analysis of Behavior, Inc., reprinted with permission of publisher and author.

Chapter 10

Figure 10.1: © Children's Television Workshop/Hulton Archives/Getty Images; Figure 10.2: © Mikael Karlsson/Arresting Images RF; Figure 10.3: © Ryan McVay/ Getty RF; Figure 10.5: From Figure 5, p. 416, of Campbell, D. T. (1969). Reforms as experiments. *American Psychologist, 24,* 409–429. © 1969 by the American Psychological Association, reprinted with permission of publisher and author; Figure 10.6: Adapted from Figure 1, p. 287, in Gigerenzer, G. (2004). Dread risk, September 11, and fatal traffic accidents. *Psychological Science, 15,* 286–287, and data supplied by the author, © 2004 by the American Psychological Society, adapted with permission of Sage Publications and the author; Figure 10.7: Based on Figure 2, p. 444, of Salomon, G. (1987). Basic and applied research in psychology: Reciprocity between two worlds. *International Journal of Psychology, 22,* 441–446. Reprinted with permission of the International Union of Psychological Science and Psychology Press (http://www.psypress.co.UK/journals.asp) and author.

Chapter 11

Figure 11.2a & b: © Photo by Alma Gottlieb from Figure 2 of DeLoache, J. S., Pierroutsakos, S. J., Uttal, D. H., Rosengren, K. S., & Gottlieb, A. (1998). Grasping the nature of pictures. *Psychological Science, 9,* 205–210. Photo courtesy of Judy DeLoache; Figures 11.3 and 11.4: Based on data provided by Judy DeLoache and adapted from Figure 3, in DeLoache et al. (1998), *Psychological Science, 9,* 205–210, © 1998 by the American Psychological Society, adapted with permission of Sage Publications and author.

Chapter 13

Quotations from p. 65 ("Writing Style"), pp. 70–71 ("Reducing Bias in Language"), paraphrased text or content based on pp. 71–77 ("General Guidelines for Reducing Bias") and Chapter 2 ("Manuscript Structure and Content") sections (Abstract, Introduction, Method, Results, and Discussion), and pp. 25–36 from the *Publication Manual of the American Psychological Association, 6th Edition* (2010), Washington, DC. Copyright © 2010 by the American Psychological Association. Reproduced and adapted with permission. The official citation that should be used in referencing this material is:

American Psychological Association (2010). *Publication manual* (6th ed.). Washington, DC: Author.

Name Index

Abelson, R. P., 202, 347–349, 365, 384, 389, 392
Adair, J. G., 73
Adler, T., 13
Allison, M. G., 299–301
Allport, G. W., 43, 287
Altmann, J., 132
Ambady, N., 45–46
American Psychiatric Association, 40–42
American Psychological Association (APA), xii–xiv, 9–10, 12–14, 58, 75, 80–82, 84–86, 386, 390–391, 393–395, 407, 417, 422–424, 427, 435, 437, 439
Ancell, M., 109
Anderson, C. A., 3–4, 202–204, 214
Anderson, C. R., 65
Anderson, J. R., 50
Anderson, K. J., 275
Anglin, J. M., 350
Aristotle, 6
Armeli, S., 119
Arnett, J. J., 12
Association for Psychological Science (APS), 9–11, 16, 58, 153, 422, 424
Astin, A. W., 155–157
Astin, H. A., 167
Astone, N. M., 162–163
Atkinson, R. C., 286, 314
Atwater, J. D., 340
Aubrey, L. W., 376
Ayllon, T., 299–301
Azar, B., 425

Baer, D. M., 304
Bagemihl, B., 98
Baker, T. B., xiii, 16, 119
Baldwin, A. K., 150
Banaji, M. R., 59, 63, 65–66, 69, 78, 98, 130, 152–153, 214, 425
Bard, K. A., 96
Barker, L. S., 119
Barker, R. G., 119
Barlow, D. H., 283, 289, 295, 298, 302
Barnett, D., 11
Baron, R. M., 176
Bartholomew, G. A., 422
Bartlett, M. Y., 35
Baumeister, R. F., 93
Baumrind, D., 73–74
Bauserman, R., 10–11
Baxter, M. G., 158–161

Becker-Blease, K. A., 64
Begley, S., xi
Behnke, S., 83
Bellack, A. S., 66, 76, 78
Bentham, J., 81
Berdahl, J. L., 149
Berk, R. A., 339
Berkowitz, L., 3–4
Berliner, L., 11
Bickman, L., 97
Birnbaum, M. H., 11, 153, 425
Bjork, R., 3
Blanchard, F. A., 130
Blanck, P. D., 66, 76, 78
Bolgar, H., 283, 289
Boring, E. G., 30
Boruch, R. F., 339
Boss, S. M., 103–104, 115, 117
Bower, G. H., 273–275
Brandt, R. M., 114, 117
Bransbury, A. J., 32
Brigham, J. C., 130
Britton, B., 77
Bröder, A., 74
Brody, G. H., 295
Broffman, M., 32
Brossart, D. F., 292
Brown, D. R., 239
Brown, R., 50
Bruckman, A., 59, 63, 65–66, 69, 78, 98, 130, 152–153, 425
Bryant, A. N., 167
Buchanan, T., 152
Burger, J. M., 73
Bushman, B. J., 29, 193, 214

Caggiano, J. M., 103–104, 115, 117
Campbell, D. T., 53, 107, 109–111, 128, 315, 318–323, 327–336, 339, 342, 389
Candland, D. K., 99
Cantor, J., 29
Carey, B., 287
Carnagey, N. L., 202–204
Carroll, K. A., 79
Ceci, S. J., 212, 251
Centers for Disease Control, 236
Cepeda-Benito, A., 11
Chaffin, M., 11
Chambers, D. L., 339
Chambless, D. L., 121
Chapman, G. B., 169
Charness, N., 281
Chastain, G., 61
Chernoff, N. N., 8

Chow, S. L., 384, 394
Christensen, L., 74–75
Christiansen, A., xiv
Chronis, A. M., 350
Church, S. M., 32
Cicchetti, D., 104, 113, 132
Clark, H. H., 169
Clark, M. S., 139
Coast, J. R., 236–237
Cohen, J., 59, 63, 65–66, 69, 78, 98, 130, 152–153, 205–206, 348, 358–359, 365, 384, 388–389, 391–392, 395–396, 402–403, 406, 425
Connor, N., 281
Cook, T. D., 53, 315, 319–321, 327–332, 334–335, 342, 389
Cook, W. A., 32
Coon, D. J., 6
Corbin, J., 44, 120
Cordaro, L., 131
Cordon, I., 11
Costall, A., 96
Couper, M., 59, 63, 65–66, 69, 78, 98, 130, 152–153
Craik, K. H., 7
Crandall, C. S., 130
Crandall, R., 58, 70, 86, 129
Crenshaw, M., 3
Criqui, M. H., 111, 121
Cronbach, L. J., 425–426
Crossen, C., 139, 145
Crossley, A. M., 174
Crowder, R. G., 214
Cull, W. L., 350
Cumming, G., xiv, 364, 370, 384
Curtiss, S. R., 99

Dalal, R., 11, 153, 425
Dallam, S. J., 11
D'Anna, C. A., 350
Darley, J. M., 106, 174
Darwin, 7
Davies, P. G., 121
Dawes, R. M., 212, 214
DeAngelo, L., 155, 157
DeLoache, J. S., 366–370
Descartes, 6
DeSteno, D., 35
DeWitt, R., 227
Dickie, J. R., 117–118
Diener, E., 19, 58, 70, 86, 129, 139, 166, 175
Dittmar, H., 25, 188–193
Dixit, J., 101, 129

Subject Index